70°N
40°E
50°E
60°E
70°E
N
RUSSIA
Lake Ladoga
St. Petersburg
Volga R.
Moscow
Astana
50°N
KAZAKHSTAN
Volga R.
Minsk
LARUS
Aral Sea
UZBEKISTAN
Kiev
Kharkov
Dnieper R.
Don R.
KRAINE
Donetsk
Dnepropetrovsk
40°N
MOLDOVA
Chisinau
Odessa
Caspian Sea
TURKMENISTAN
IA
Ashgabat
Bucharest
GEORGIA
Tbilisi
Baku
Black Sea
AZERBAIJAN
ARMENIA
Yerevan
BULGARIA
AZER.
Istanbul
Ankara
Tehran
IRAN
TURKEY
ens
SYRIA
Nicosia
Baghdad
30°N
CYPRUS
Beirut
IRAQ
LEBANON
Damascus

WADSWORTH
CENGAGE Learning™

Why Maps?

HISTORICAL EVENTS DO NOT JUST "HAPPEN" — they happen in a specific place. Since events are often dictated by a location's specifics it is important to learn all you can about that place, and a good map can help you do this. Your textbook may include different types of maps:

Demographic or Population Maps show which groups inhabited which regions and how that distribution changed over time.

Geographic-Political Maps show territories occupied by particular nations and empires and the borders between them.

Topographic Maps show natural physical features such as oceans, rivers, elevations, forests, and deserts and manmade features such as dams and canals.

Expedition Maps show the routes followed by explorers, migrants, invaders, and military forces.

Battle Maps show the encounters and maneuvers of contending armies and navies.

Here are some basic tips to help you to get the most out of a map:

- Always look at the scale, which allows you to determine the distance in miles or kilometers between locations on the map.
- Examine the legend carefully. It explains the colors and/or symbols used on the map.
- Note the locations of mountains, rivers, oceans, and other geographic features, and consider how these would affect such human activities as agriculture, commerce, travel, and warfare.
- Read the map caption thoroughly. It provides important information sometimes not covered in the text itself. The caption may also inform you of additional resources, such as interactive maps, which may be available online.

HISTORY 121

Western Civilization

Volume 1

Jackson J. Spielvogel

CENGAGE Learning™

Australia • Brazil • Japan • Korea • Mexico • Singapore • Spain • United Kingdom • United States

CENGAGE Learning™

HISTORY 121; Western Civilization; Volume 1

Executive Editors:
Maureen Staudt
Michael Stranz

Senior Project Development Manager:
Linda deStefano

Marketing Specialist:
Courtney Sheldon

Senior Production/Manufacturing Manager:
Donna M. Brown

PreMedia Manager:
Joel Brennecke

Sr. Rights Acquisition Account Manager:
Todd Osborne

Cover Image:
Getty Images*

*Unless otherwise noted, all cover images used by Custom Solutions, a part of Cengage Learning, have been supplied courtesy of Getty Images with the exception of the Earthview cover image, which has been supplied by the National Aeronautics and Space Administration (NASA).

Western Civilization; Jackson J. Spielvogel

For product information and technology assistance, contact us at
Cengage Learning Customer & Sales Support, 1-800-354-9706
For permission to use material from this text or product,
submit all requests online at **cengage.com/permissions**
Further permissions questions can be emailed to
permissionrequest@cengage.com

This book contains select works from existing Cengage Learning resources and was produced by Cengage Learning Custom Solutions for collegiate use. As such, those adopting and/or contributing to this work are responsible for editorial content accuracy, continuity and completeness.

ISBN-13: 978-1-133-15434-1

ISBN-10: 1-133-15434-4

Cengage Learning
5191 Natorp Boulevard
Mason, Ohio 45040
USA

Cengage Learning is a leading provider of customized learning solutions with office locations around the globe, including Singapore, the United Kingdom, Australia, Mexico, Brazil, and Japan. Locate your local office at: **international.cengage.com/region.**

Cengage Learning products are represented in Canada by Nelson Education, Ltd.
For your lifelong learning solutions, visit **www.cengage.com/custom.**
Visit our corporate website at **www.cengage.com.**

Printed in the United States of America

BRIEF CONTENTS

DETAILED CONTENTS

4 THE HELLENISTIC WORLD 89

5 THE ROMAN REPUBLIC 113

6 THE ROMAN EMPIRE 147

CHAPTER 1

Excavation of Warka showing the ruins of Uruk

The Ancient Near East: The First Civilizations

CHAPTER OUTLINE AND FOCUS QUESTIONS

The First Humans

Q How did the Paleolithic and Neolithic Ages differ, and how did the Neolithic Revolution affect the lives of men and women?

The Emergence of Civilization

Q What are the characteristics of civilization, and what are some explanations for why early civilizations emerged?

Civilization in Mesopotamia

Q How are the chief characteristics of civilization evident in ancient Mesopotamia?

Egyptian Civilization: "The Gift of the Nile"

Q What are the basic features of the three major periods of Egyptian history? What elements of continuity are there in the three periods? What are their major differences?

On the Fringes of Civilization

Q What is the significance of the Indo-European-speaking peoples?

CRITICAL THINKING

Q In what ways were the civilizations of Mesopotamia and Egypt alike? In what ways were they different?

IN 1849, A DARING YOUNG Englishman made a hazardous journey into the deserts and swamps of southern Iraq. Moving south down the banks of the Euphrates River while braving high winds and temperatures that reached 120 degrees Fahrenheit, William Loftus led a small expedition in search of the roots of civilization. As he said, "From our childhood we have been led to regard this place as the cradle of the human race."

Guided by native Arabs into the southernmost reaches of Iraq, Loftus and his small group of explorers were soon overwhelmed by what they saw. He wrote, "I know of nothing more exciting or impressive than the first sight of one of these great piles, looming in solitary grandeur from the surrounding plains and marshes." One of these piles, known to the natives as the mound of Warka, contained the ruins of Uruk, one of the first cities in the world and part of the world's first civilization.

Southern Iraq in Southwest Asia was one area in the world where civilization began. Although Western civilization did not yet exist, its origins can be traced back to the ancient Near East, where people in Southwest Asia and Egypt developed organized societies, invented writing, and created the ideas and institutions that we associate with civilization. The Greeks and Romans, who later played such a crucial role in the development of Western civilization, were themselves nourished and influenced by these older societies. It is appropriate, therefore, to begin our story of Western civilization with the early civilizations of Southwest Asia and Egypt. Before considering them, however, we must briefly examine humankind's prehistory and observe how human beings made the shift from hunting and gathering to agricultural communities and ultimately to cities and civilization.

The First Humans

Focus Question: How did the Paleolithic and Neolithic Ages differ, and how did the Neolithic Revolution affect the lives of men and women?

Historians rely primarily on documents to create their pictures of the past, but no written records exist for the prehistory of humankind. In their absence, the story of early humanity depends on archaeological and, more recently, biological information, which anthropologists and archaeologists use to formulate theories about our early past. Although modern science has given us more precise methods for examining prehistory, much of our understanding of early humans still relies on conjecture.

The earliest humanlike creatures—known as hominids—existed in Africa as long as 3 to 4 million years ago. Known as Australopithecines (aw-stray-loh-PITH-uh-synz), they flourished in East and South Africa and were the first hominids to make simple stone tools.

Another stage in early human development occurred around 1.5 million years ago when *Homo erectus* ("upright human being") emerged. *Homo erectus* made use of larger and more varied tools and was the first hominid to leave Africa and move into both Europe and Asia.

Around 250,000 years ago, a crucial stage in human development began with the emergence of *Homo sapiens* (HOH-moh SAY-pee-unz) ("wise human being"). The first anatomically modern humans, known as *Homo sapiens sapiens* ("wise, wise human being"), appeared in Africa between 200,000 and 150,000 years ago. Recent evidence indicates that they began to spread outside Africa around 70,000 years ago. Map 1.1 shows probable dates for different movements, although many of these are still controversial.

These modern humans, who were our direct ancestors, soon encountered other hominids, such as the Neanderthals, whose remains were first found in the Neander valley in Germany. Neanderthal remains have since been found in both Europe and the western part of Asia and have been dated to between 200,000 and 30,000 B.C.E.

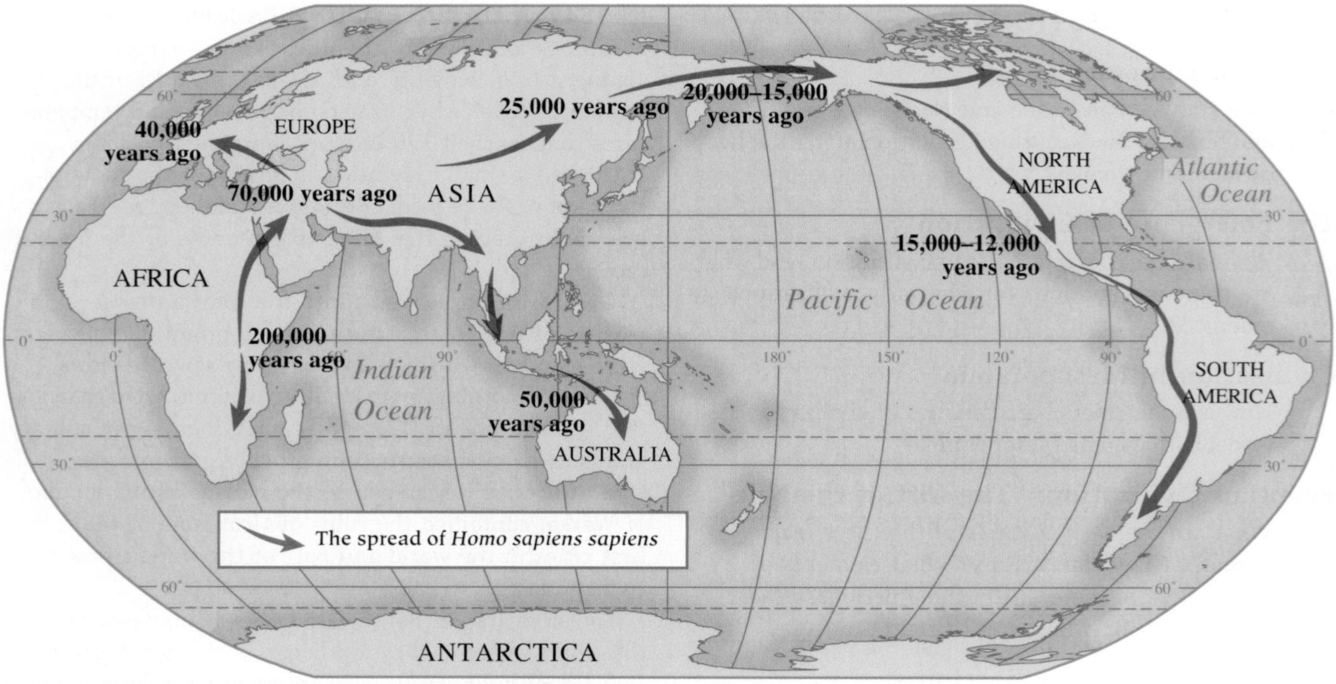

MAP 1.1 The Spread of *Homo sapiens sapiens*. *Homo sapiens sapiens* spread from Africa beginning about 70,000 years ago. Living and traveling in small groups, these anatomically modern humans were hunter-gatherers. Although groups of people advanced beyond their old hunting grounds at a rate of only 2 or 3 miles per generation, this was enough to populate the world in some tens of thousands of years.

Given that some diffusion of humans occurred during ice ages, how would such climate change affect humans and their movements, especially from Asia to Australia and Asia to North America?

View an animated version of this map or related maps on the CourseMate website.

CHRONOLOGY The First Humans

Australopithecines	Flourished c. 2–4 million years ago
Homo erectus	Flourished c. 100,000–1.5 million years ago
Neanderthals	Flourished c. 200,000–30,000 B.C.E.
Homo sapiens sapiens	Emerged c. 200,000 B.C.E.

Neanderthals relied on a variety of stone tools and were the first early people to bury their dead. By 30,000 B.C.E., *Homo sapiens sapiens* had replaced the Neanderthals, who had largely become extinct, and by 10,000 B.C.E., members of the *Homo sapiens sapiens* species could be found throughout the world. By that time, it was the only human species left. All humans today, whether they are Europeans, Australian Aborigines, or Africans, belong to the same subspecies of human being.

The Hunter-Gatherers of the Old Stone Age

One of the basic distinguishing features of the human species is the ability to make tools. The earliest tools were made of stone, and the term **Paleolithic** (Greek for "old stone") **Age** is used to designate this early period of human history (c. 2,500,000–10,000 B.C.E.).

For hundreds of thousands of years, humans relied on hunting and gathering for their daily food. Paleolithic peoples had a close relationship with the world around them, and over a period of time, they came to know which animals to hunt and which plants to eat. They did not know how to grow crops or raise animals, however. They gathered wild nuts, berries, fruits, and a variety of wild grains and green plants. Around the world, they hunted and consumed various animals, including buffalo, horses, bison, wild goats, and reindeer. In coastal areas, fish were a rich source of nourishment.

The hunting of animals and the gathering of wild plants no doubt led to certain patterns of living. Archaeologists and anthropologists have speculated that Paleolithic people lived in small bands of twenty or thirty people. They were nomadic (they moved from place to place) since they had no choice but to follow animal migrations and vegetation cycles. Hunting depended on careful observation of animal behavior patterns and required a group effort to achieve success. Over the years, tools became more refined and more useful. The invention of the spear, and later the bow and arrow, made hunting considerably easier. Harpoons and fishhooks made of bone increased the catch of fish.

Both men and women were responsible for finding food—the chief work of Paleolithic people. Since women bore and raised the children, they generally stayed close to the camps, but they played an important role in acquiring food by gathering berries, nuts, and grains. Men hunted the wild animals, an activity that often took them far from camp. Because both men and women played important roles in providing for the band's survival, scientists have argued that a rough equality existed between men and women. Indeed, some speculate that both men and women made the decisions that affected the activities of the Paleolithic band.

Some groups of Paleolithic people, especially those who lived in cold climates, found shelter in caves. Over time, they created new types of shelter as well. Perhaps the most common was a simple structure of wood poles or sticks covered with animal hides. Where wood was scarce, Paleolithic hunter-gatherers might use the bones of mammoths to build frames that were then covered with animal hides. The systematic use of fire, which archaeologists believe began around 500,000 years ago, made it possible for the caves and human-made structures to have a source of light and heat. Fire also enabled early humans to cook their food, making it taste better, last longer, and, in the case of some plants, such as wild grain, easier to chew and digest.

The making of tools and the use of fire—two important technological innovations of Paleolithic peoples—remind us how crucial the ability to adapt was to human survival. But Paleolithic peoples did more than just survive. The cave paintings of large animals found in southwestern France and northern Spain bear witness to the cultural activity of Paleolithic peoples. A cave discovered in

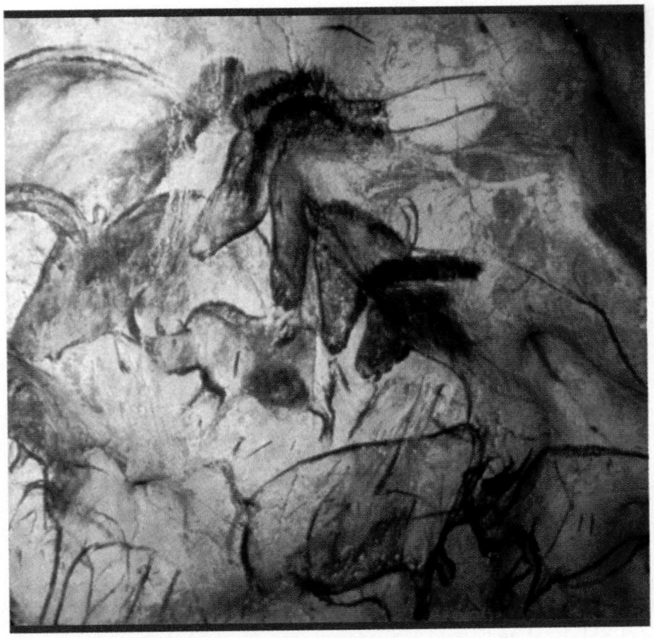

AP Images/Jean Clottes

Paleolithic Cave Painting: The Chauvet Cave. Cave paintings of large animals reveal the cultural creativity of Paleolithic peoples. This scene is part of a mural in a large underground chamber at Vallon-Pont-d'Arc, France, discovered in December 1994. It dates from around 30,000 to 28,000 B.C.E. and depicts aurochs (long-horned wild oxen), horses, and rhinoceroses. To make their paintings, Paleolithic artists used stone lamps in which they burned animal fat to illuminate the cave walls and mixed powdered mineral ores with animal fat to create red, yellow, and black pigments. Some artists even made brushes out of animal hairs with which to apply the paints.

southern France in 1994 (known as the Chauvet cave after the leader of the expedition that found it) contains more than three hundred paintings of lions, oxen, owls, bears, and other animals. Most of these are animals that Paleolithic people did not hunt, which suggests to some scholars that the paintings were made for religious or even decorative purposes. The discoverers were overwhelmed by what they saw: "There was a moment of ecstasy.... They overflowed with joy and emotion in their turn.... These were moments of indescribable madness."[1]

The Neolithic Revolution (c. 10,000–4000 B.C.E.)

The end of the last ice age around 10,000 B.C.E. was followed by what is called the **Neolithic Revolution,** a significant change in living patterns that occurred in the New Stone Age (the word *neolithic* is Greek for "new stone"). The name New Stone Age is misleading, however. Although Neolithic peoples made a new type of polished stone ax, this was not the major change that occurred after 10,000 B.C.E.

AN AGRICULTURAL REVOLUTION The biggest change was the shift from hunting animals and gathering plants for sustenance (food gathering) to producing food by systematic agriculture (food production). The planting of grains and vegetables provided a regular supply of food, while the domestication of animals, such as goats, cattle, pigs, and sheep, added a steady source of meat, milk, and fibers such as wool for clothing. Larger animals could also be used as beasts of burden. The growing of crops and the taming of food-producing animals created a new relationship between humans and nature. Historians like to speak of this as an agricultural revolution. Revolutionary change is dramatic and requires great effort, but the ability to acquire food on a regular basis gave humans greater control over their environment. It also allowed them to give up their nomadic way of life and begin to live in settled communities.

Systematic agriculture probably developed independently between 9000 and 7000 B.C.E. in four different areas of the world. In each of these areas, different plants were cultivated: wheat, barley, and lentils in the Near East, rice and millet in southern Asia, millet and yams in western Africa, and beans, potatoes, and corn (maize) in the Americas. In the Near East as elsewhere, the Neolithic agricultural revolution needed a favorable environment. The upland areas above the Fertile Crescent (present-day northern Iraq and southern Turkey) were initially more conducive to systematic farming than the river valleys. This region received the necessary rainfall and was the home of two wild plant (barley, wheat) and four wild animal (pigs, cows, goats, sheep) species that humans eventually domesticated for their use.

NEOLITHIC FARMING VILLAGES The growing of crops on a regular basis gave rise to more permanent settlements, which historians refer to as Neolithic farming villages or towns. One of the oldest known agricultural villages was Jericho, in Canaan near the Dead Sea. Jericho existed by 8000 B.C.E. and covered several acres by 7000 B.C.E. It had a wall several feet thick that enclosed houses made of sundried bricks.

Çatal Hüyük (chaht-ul hoo-YOOK), located in modern-day Turkey, was an even larger community. Its walls enclosed 32 acres, and its population probably reached six thousand inhabitants during its high point from 6700 to 5700 B.C.E. People lived in simple mudbrick houses that were built so close to one another that there were few streets. To get to their homes, people had to walk along the rooftops and then enter the house through a hole in the roof.

Archaeologists have discovered twelve cultivated products in Çatal Hüyük, including fruits, nuts, and three

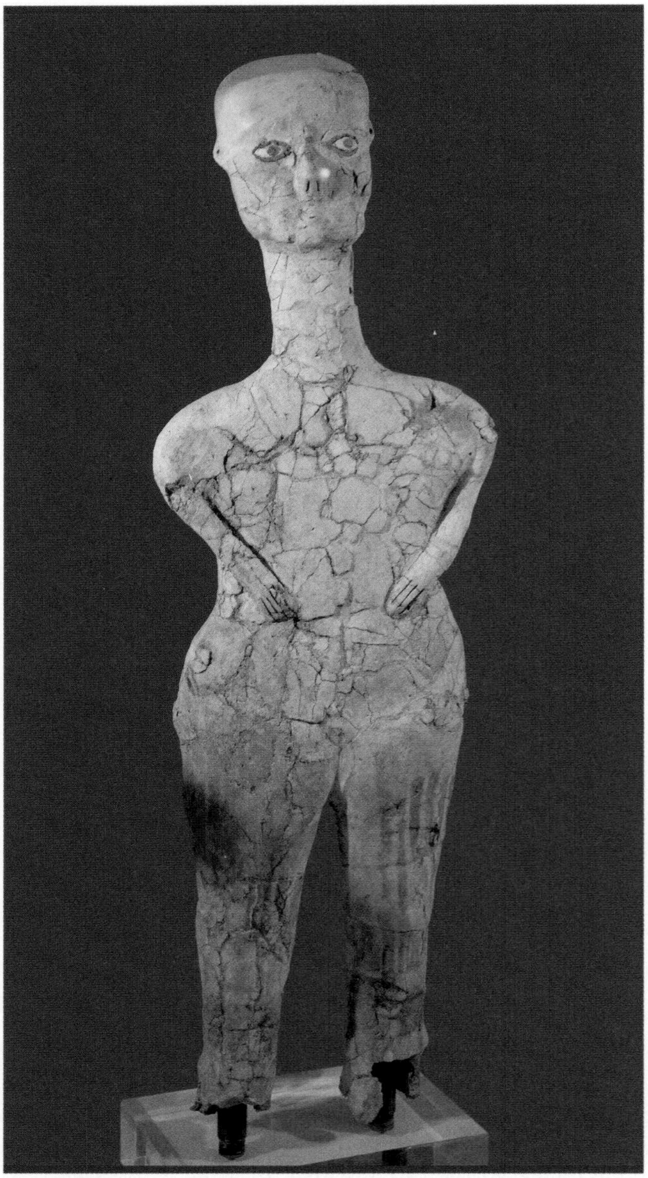

Archaeological Museum, Amman//© Erich Lessing/Art Resource, NY

Statue from Ain Ghazal. This life-size statue made of plaster, sand, and crushed chalk was discovered in 1984 in Ain Ghazal, an archaeological site near Amman, Jordan. Dating from 6500 B.C.E., it is among the oldest known statues of the human figure. Although it appears lifelike, its features are considered generic rather than a portrait of an individual face. The purpose and meaning of this sculpture may never be known.

kinds of wheat. People grew their own food and stored it in storerooms in their homes. Domesticated animals, especially cattle, yielded meat, milk, and hides. Food surpluses also made it possible for people to do things other than farming. Some people became artisans and made weapons and jewelry that were traded with neighboring peoples.

Religious shrines housing figures of gods and goddesses have been found at Çatal Hüyük, as have a number of female statuettes. Molded with noticeably large breasts and buttocks, these "earth mothers" perhaps symbolically represented the fertility of both "our mother" earth and human mothers. Both the shrines and the statues point to the growing role of religion in the lives of these Neolithic people.

CONSEQUENCES OF THE NEOLITHIC REVOLUTION The Neolithic agricultural revolution had far-reaching consequences. Once people settled in villages or towns, they built houses for protection and other structures for the storage of goods. As organized communities stored food and accumulated material goods, they engaged in far greater trade than nomadic peoples did. People also began to specialize in certain crafts, and a division of labor developed. Pottery was made from clay and baked in a fire to make it hard. The pots were used for cooking and to store grains. Woven baskets were also used for storage. Stone tools became refined as flint blades were developed to make sickles and hoes for use in the fields. Obsidian—a volcanic glass that was easily flaked—was also used to create very sharp tools. In the course of the Neolithic Age, many of the food plants still in use today began to be cultivated. Moreover, vegetable fibers from such plants as flax were used to make thread that was woven into cloth.

The change to systematic agriculture in the Neolithic Age also had consequences for the relationship between men and women. Men assumed the primary responsibility for working in the fields and herding animals, jobs that kept them away from the home. Although women also worked in the fields, many remained behind, caring for the children and weaving clothes, making cheese from milk, and performing other tasks that required considerable labor in one place. In time, as work outside the home was increasingly perceived as more important than work done at home, men came to play the more dominant role in society, a basic pattern that would persist until our own times.

Other patterns set in the Neolithic Age also proved to be enduring elements of human history. Fixed dwellings, domesticated animals, regular farming, a division of labor, men holding power—all of these are part of the human story. For all our scientific and technological progress, human survival still depends on the growing and storing of food, an accomplishment of people in the Neolithic Age. The Neolithic Revolution was truly a turning point in human history.

Between 4000 and 3000 B.C.E., significant technical developments began to transform the Neolithic towns. The invention of writing enabled records to be kept, and the use of metals marked a new level of human control over the environment and its resources. Already before 4000 B.C.E., craftspeople had discovered that metal-bearing rocks could be heated to liquefy metals, which could then be cast in molds to produce tools and weapons that were more useful than stone instruments. Although copper was the first metal to be used in producing tools, after 4000 B.C.E. craftspeople in western Asia discovered that a combination of copper and tin produced bronze, a much harder and more durable metal than copper. Its widespread use has led historians to call the period from around 3000 to 1200 B.C.E. the Bronze Age; thereafter, bronze was increasingly replaced by iron.

At first, Neolithic settlements were hardly more than villages. But as their inhabitants mastered the art of farming, more complex human societies emerged. As wealth increased, these societies began to develop armies and to build walled cities. By the beginning of the Bronze Age, the concentration of larger numbers of people in the river valleys of Southwest Asia and Egypt was leading to a whole new pattern for human life.

The Emergence of Civilization

Focus Question: What are the characteristics of civilization, and what are some explanations for why early civilizations emerged?

As we have seen, early human beings formed small groups that developed a simple culture that enabled them to survive. As human societies grew and developed greater complexity, a new form of human existence—called civilization—came into being. A **civilization** is a complex culture in which large numbers of human beings share a variety of common elements. Historians have identified a number of basic characteristics of civilization. These include (1) an urban focus: cities became the centers of political, economic, social, cultural, and religious development; (2) a distinct religious structure: the gods were deemed crucial to the community's success, and professional priestly classes, as stewards of the gods' property, regulated relations with the gods; (3) new political and military structures: an organized government bureaucracy arose to meet the administrative demands of the growing population, and armies were organized to gain land and power and for defense; (4) a new social structure based on economic power: while kings and an upper class of priests, political leaders, and warriors dominated, there also existed a large group of free people (farmers, artisans, craftspeople) and at the very bottom, socially, a class of slaves; (5) the development of writing: kings, priests, merchants, and artisans used writing to keep records; and (6) new forms of significant artistic and intellectual activity: for example, monumental architectural structures, usually religious, occupied a prominent place in urban environments.

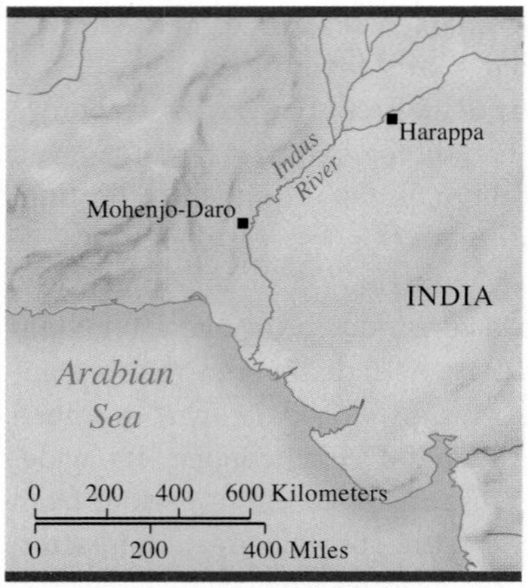

Harappa and Mohenjo-Daro

The civilizations that developed in Southwest Asia and Egypt, the forerunners of Western civilization, will be examined in detail in this chapter. But civilizations also developed independently in other parts of the world. Between 3000 and 1500 B.C.E., the valleys of the Indus River in India supported a flourishing civilization that extended hundreds of miles from the Himalayas to the coast of the Arabian Sea. Two major cities—Harappa and Mohenjo-Daro—were at the heart of this civilization in India. Many written records of this Indus valley civilization exist, but their language has not yet been deciphered. This Indus valley civilization carried on extensive trade with city-states in Southwest Asia.

Another river valley civilization emerged along the Yellow River in northern China about 4,000 years ago. Under the Shang dynasty of kings, which ruled from 1750 to 1122 B.C.E., this civilization contained impressive cities with huge outer walls, royal palaces, and large royal tombs. A system of irrigation enabled early Chinese civilization to maintain a prosperous farming society ruled by an aristocratic class whose major concern was war.

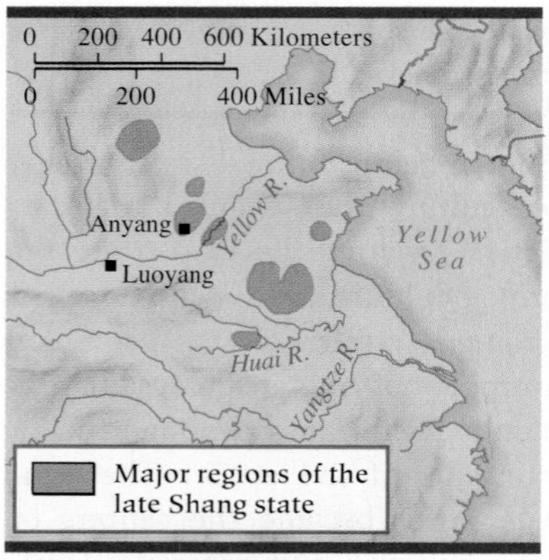

The Yellow River, China

Scholars have believed for a long time that civilization emerged only in four areas, in the fertile river valleys of the Tigris and Euphrates, the Nile, the Indus, and the Yellow River—that is, in Southwest Asia, Egypt, India, and China. Recently, however, archaeologists have discovered two other early civilizations. One of these flourished in Central Asia (in what are now the republics of Turkmenistan and Uzbekistan) around 4,000 years ago. People in this civilization built mudbrick buildings, raised sheep and goats, had bronze tools, used a system of irrigation to grow wheat and barley, and had a writing system.

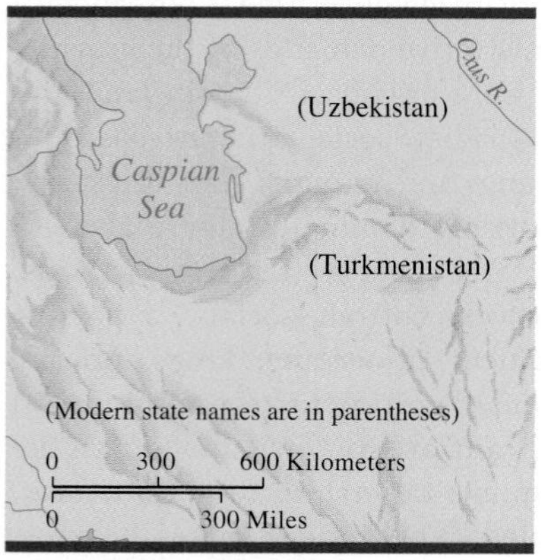

Central Asia Civilization

CHRONOLOGY The Birth of Early Civilizations

Egypt	c. 3100 B.C.E.
Mesopotamia	c. 3000 B.C.E.
India	c. 3000 B.C.E.
Peru	c. 2600 B.C.E.
China	c. 2000 B.C.E.
Central Asia	c. 2000 B.C.E.

Another early civilization was discovered in the Supe River valley of Peru. At the center of this civilization was the city of Caral, which flourished around 2600 B.C.E. It contained buildings for officials, apartment houses, and grand residences, all built of stone. The inhabitants of Caral also developed a system of irrigation by diverting a river more than a mile upstream into their fields.

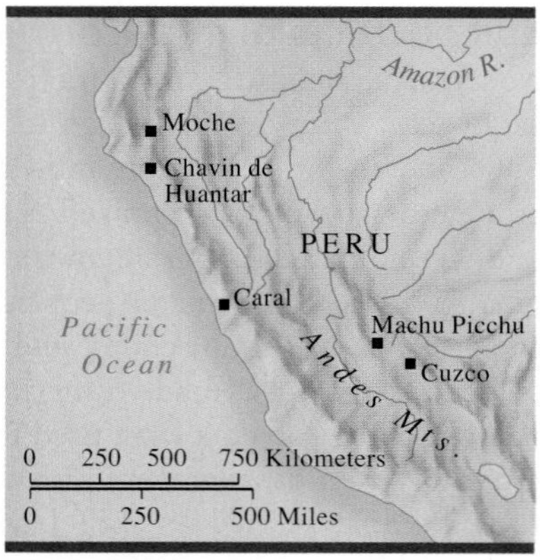

Caral, Peru

Why early civilizations developed remains difficult to explain. Since civilizations developed independently in different parts of the world, can general causes be identified that would explain why all of these civilizations emerged? A number of possible explanations of the beginning of civilization have been suggested. A theory of challenge and response maintains that challenges forced human beings to make efforts that resulted in the rise of civilization. Some scholars have adhered to a material explanation. Material forces, such as the growth of food surpluses, made possible the specialization of labor and development of large communities with bureaucratic organization. But the area of the Fertile Crescent, in which civilization emerged in Southwest Asia (see Map 1.2), was not naturally conducive to agriculture. Abundant food could be produced only with a massive human effort to carefully manage the water, an effort that created the need for organization and bureaucratic control and led to civilized cities. Some historians have argued that nonmaterial forces, primarily religious, provided the sense of unity and purpose that made such organized activities possible. Finally, some scholars doubt that we are capable of ever discovering the actual causes of early civilization.

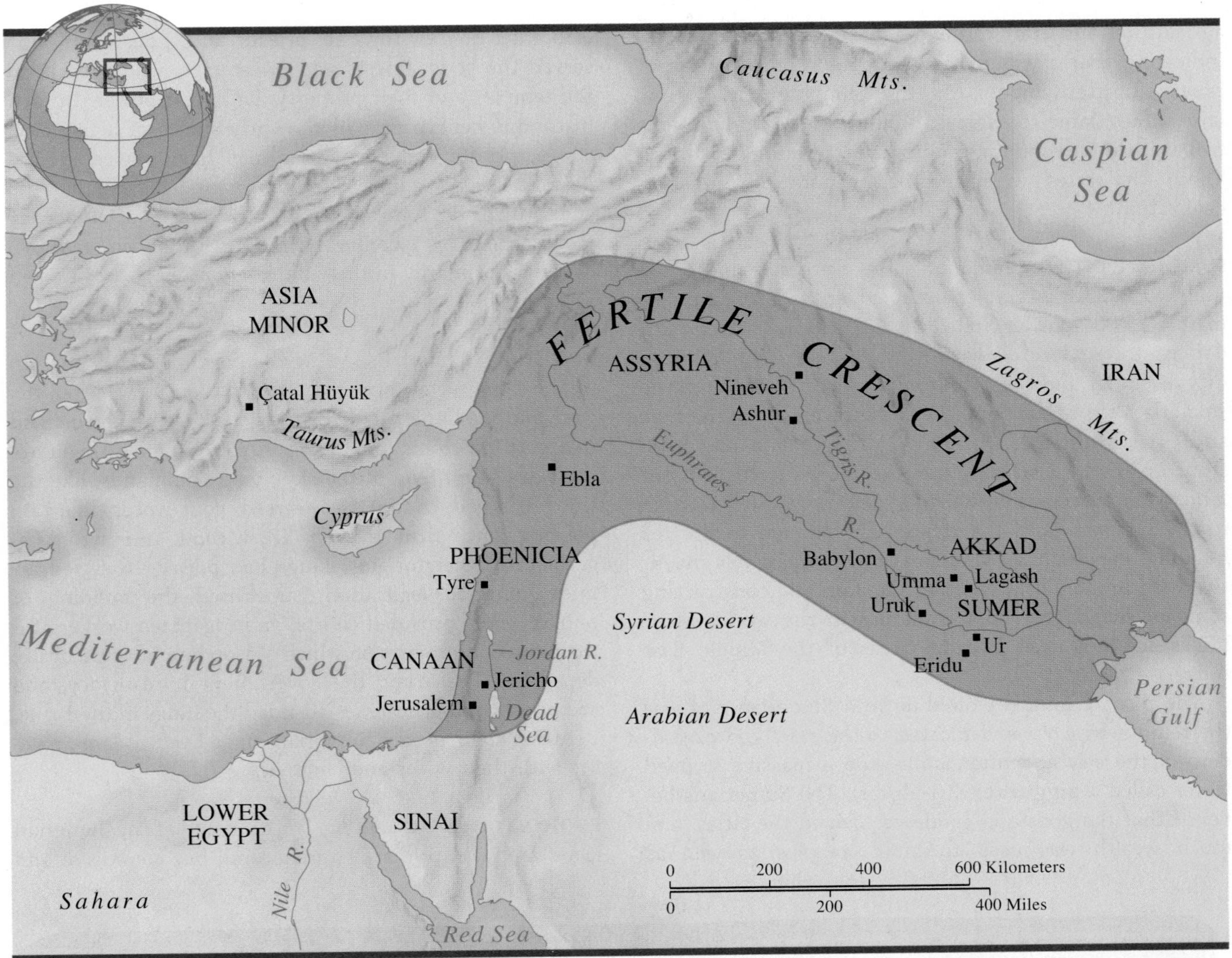

MAP 1.2 The Ancient Near East. The Fertile Crescent encompassed land with access to water. Employing flood management and irrigation systems, the peoples of the region established civilizations based on agriculture. These civilizations developed writing, law codes, and economic specialization.

What geographic aspects of the Mesopotamian city-states made conflict between them likely?

View an animated version of this map or related maps on the CourseMate website.

Civilization in Mesopotamia

Focus Question: How are the chief characteristics of civilization evident in ancient Mesopotamia?

The Greeks spoke of the valley between the Tigris and Euphrates rivers in Southwest Asia as **Mesopotamia** (mess-uh-puh-TAY-mee-uh), the land "between the rivers." The region receives little rain, but the soil of the plain of southern Mesopotamia was enlarged and enriched over the years by layers of silt deposited by the two rivers. In late spring, the Tigris and Euphrates overflow their banks and deposit their fertile silt, but since this flooding depends on the melting of snows in the upland mountains where the rivers begin, it is unpredictable and sometimes catastrophic. In such circumstances, farming could be done only when people built irrigation and drainage ditches. A complex system was required to control the flow of the rivers and produce the crops. Large-scale irrigation made possible the expansion of agriculture in this region, and the abundant food provided the material base for the emergence of civilization in Mesopotamia.

The City-States of Ancient Mesopotamia

The creators of Mesopotamian civilization were the Sumerians (soo-MER-ee-unz *or* soo-MEER-ee-unz), a people whose origins remain unclear. By 3000 B.C.E., they had established a number of independent cities in southern Mesopotamia, including Eridu, Ur, Uruk, Umma, and Lagash. There is evidence that the Sumerians were not the first people in the region. A number of Sumerian agricultural and craft terms are not Sumerian in origin, indicating that the Sumerians adopted some aspects of preexisting settlements. As the Sumerian cities grew larger, they came to exercise political and economic control over the surrounding countryside, forming city-states. These city-states were the basic units of Sumerian civilization.

SUMERIAN CITIES Sumerian cities were surrounded by walls. Uruk, for example, occupied an area of approximately 1,000 acres encircled by a wall 6 miles long with defense towers located every 30 to 35 feet along the wall. City dwellings, built of sun-dried bricks, included both the small flats of peasants and the larger dwellings of the civic and priestly officials. Although Mesopotamia had little stone or wood for building purposes, it did have plenty of mud. Mudbricks, easily shaped by hand, were left to bake in the hot sun until they were hard enough to use for building. People in Mesopotamia were remarkably inventive with mudbricks, inventing the arch and constructing some of the largest brick buildings in the world. Mudbricks are still used in rural areas of the Middle East today.

The most prominent building in a Sumerian city was the temple, which was dedicated to the chief god or goddess of the city and often built atop a massive stepped tower called a **ziggurat** (ZIG-uh-rat). The Sumerians believed that the gods and goddesses owned the cities, and much wealth was used to build temples as well as elaborate houses for the priests and priestesses who served the gods. Priests and priestesses, who supervised the temples and their property, had great power. In fact, historians believe that in the early stages of a few city-states, priests and priestesses may have played an important role in ruling. The Sumerians believed that the gods ruled the cities, making the state a **theocracy** (government by a divine authority). Ruling power, however, was primarily in the hands of worldly figures known as kings.

KINGSHIP Sumerians viewed kingship as divine in origin—kings, they believed, derived their power from the gods and were the agents of the gods. As one person said in a petition to his king: "You in your judgment, you are the son of Anu [god of the sky]; your commands, like the word of a god, cannot be reversed; your words, like rain pouring down from heaven, are without number."[2] Regardless of their origins, kings had power—they led armies, initiated legislation, supervised the building of public works, provided courts, and organized workers for the irrigation projects on which Mesopotamian agriculture depended. The army, the government bureaucracy, and the priests and priestesses all aided the kings in their rule. Befitting their power, Sumerian kings lived in large palaces with their wives and children.

ECONOMY AND SOCIETY The economy of the Sumerian city-states was primarily agricultural, but commerce and

The "Royal Standard" of Ur. This detail is from the "Royal Standard" of Ur, a box dating from around 2700 B.C.E. that was discovered in a stone tomb from the royal cemetery of the Sumerian city-state of Ur. The scenes on one side of the box depict the activities of the king and his military forces. Shown in the bottom panel are four Sumerian battle chariots. Each chariot held two men, one who held the reins and the other armed with a spear for combat. A special compartment in the chariot held a number of spears. The charging chariots are seen defeating the enemy. In the middle band, the Sumerian soldiers round up the captured enemies. In the top band, the captives are presented to the king, who has alighted from his chariot and is shown standing above all the others in the center of the panel.

industry became important as well. The people of Mesopotamia produced woolen textiles, pottery, and metalwork. Foreign trade, which was primarily a royal monopoly, could be extensive. Royal officials imported luxury items, such as copper and tin, aromatic woods, and fruit trees, in exchange for dried fish, wool, barley, wheat, and the goods produced by Mesopotamian metalworkers. Traders traveled by land to the eastern Mediterranean in the west and by sea to India in the east. The invention of the wheel around 3000 B.C.E. led to the development of carts with wheels that made the transport of goods easier.

Sumerian city-states probably contained four major social groups: elites, dependent commoners, free commoners, and slaves. Elites included royal and priestly officials and their families. Dependent commoners included the elites' clients who worked on the palace and temple estates. Free commoners worked as farmers, merchants, fishers, scribes, and craftspeople. Probably 90 percent or more of the population were farmers. They could exchange their crops for the goods of the artisans in free town markets. Slaves belonged to palace officials, who used them mostly in building projects; temple officials, who used mostly female slaves to weave cloth and grind grain; and rich landowners, who used them for farming and domestic work.

Empires in Ancient Mesopotamia

As the number of Sumerian city-states grew and the states expanded, new conflicts arose as city-state fought city-state for control of land and water. During the Early Dynastic Age (3000–2340 B.C.E.), the fortunes of various cities rose and fell over the centuries. The constant wars, with their burning and sacking of cities, left many Sumerians in deep despair, as is evident in this Sumerian poem from the city of Ur: "Ur is destroyed, bitter is its lament. The country's blood now fills its holes like hot bronze in a mold. Bodies dissolve like fat in the sun. Our temple is destroyed, the gods have abandoned us, like migrating birds. Smoke lies on our city like a shroud."[3]

THE AKKADIAN EMPIRE Located on the flat, open land of Mesopotamia, the Sumerian city-states were also vulnerable to invasion. To the north of the Sumerian city-states were the Akkadians (uh-KAY-dee-unz). We call them a Semitic people because of the language they spoke (see Table 1.1). Around 2340 B.C.E., Sargon, leader of the Akkadians, overran the Sumerian city-states and established a dynastic empire. Sargon used the former rulers of the conquered city-states as his governors. His power was based on the military, namely, his army of 5,400 men. Sargon's empire, including all of Mesopotamia as well as lands westward to the Mediterranean, inspired generations of Near Eastern leaders to emulate his accomplishment. Even in the first millennium B.C.E. Sargon was still remembered in chronicles as a king of Akkad who "had no rival or equal, spread his splendor over all the lands, and crossed the sea in the east. In his eleventh year, he conquered the western land to its furthest point, and brought it under his sole authority."[4]

TABLE 1.1 Some Semitic Languages

Akkadian	*Canaanitic*
Arabic	Hebrew
Aramaic	*Phoenician*
Assyrian	*Syriac*
Babylonian	

NOTE: Languages in italic type are no longer spoken.

One of Sargon's successors, his grandson Naram-Sin (c. 2260–2223 B.C.E.), continued the greatness of the Akkadian empire. Like his grandfather, Naram-Sin waged numerous military campaigns, which led him to an extreme level of self-glorification. He called himself "King of the Four Corners (of the Universe)" and took the extraordinary step of declaring himself a god. An inscription found in northern Iraq reads: "Naram-Sin, the strong one, king of Akkad, when the four corners (of the universe) together were hostile to him, he remained victorious in nine battles in a single year.... Because he had been able to preserve his city in the time of crisis, (the inhabitants of) his city asked . . . that he be the god of their city Akkad, and built a temple for him in the midst of Akkad."[5] By the end of his reign, however, Naram-Sin was battling hill peoples known as the Gutians, who finally caused the fall of the Akkadian empire by 2150 B.C.E.

THE THIRD DYNASTY OF UR The end of the Akkadian empire brought a return to independent city-states in Mesopotamia. Much confusion ensued, as is evident in the recorded Sumerian king list, which stated bluntly, "Who was king? Who was not king?" The confusion ended when Ur-Nammu established a new dynasty that reunified much of Mesopotamia with its capital at Ur. This Third Dynasty of Ur (c. 2112–2000 B.C.E.) witnessed a final flowering of Sumerian culture. The economy flourished, and new temples and canals were built. Each province was required to contribute goods to the central government.

Around 2000 B.C.E., however, invading peoples from Iran, known as the Elamites, destroyed Ur and brought an end to the Third Dynasty. Even earlier, the Amorites, a large group of Semitic-speaking seminomads, described by Sumerian scribes as dressed in sheepskins, living in tents, and eating raw meat, had entered the region and done battle with kings of the Third Dynasty. The Amorites or Old Babylonians gradually settled down and over the next two hundred years established their influence throughout much of Mesopotamia. One of their kings, Hammurabi (ham-uh-RAH-bee), managed to establish power and create a new empire.

HAMMURABI'S EMPIRE Hammurabi (1792–1750 B.C.E.) had a well-disciplined army of foot soldiers who carried axes, spears, and copper or bronze daggers. He learned to divide his opponents and subdue them one by one. Using such methods, he gained control of Sumer and Akkad and

CHRONOLOGY Chief Events in Mesopotamian History

Sumerian city-states: Early Dynastic Age	c. 3000–2340 B.C.E.
Sargon	c. 2340–2279 B.C.E.
Naram-Sin	c. 2260–2223 B.C.E.
Third Dynasty of Ur	c. 2112–2000 B.C.E.
Hammurabi's reign	1792–1750 B.C.E.
Invasion by Kassites	c. 1550 B.C.E.

reunified Mesopotamia almost to the old borders established by Sargon. After his conquests, Hammurabi called himself "the sun of Babylon, the king who made the four quarters of the world obedient," and established his capital at Babylon.

Hammurabi, the man of war, was also a man of peace. He followed in the footsteps of previous conquerors by assimilating Mesopotamian culture with the result that Sumerian ways continued to exist despite the end of the Sumerians as a political entity. A collection of his letters, found by archaeologists, reveals that the king took a strong interest in state affairs. He built temples, defensive walls, and irrigation canals; encouraged trade; and brought about an economic revival. Indeed, Hammurabi saw himself as a shepherd to his people: "I am indeed the shepherd who brings peace, whose scepter is just. My benevolent shade was spread over my city. I held the people of the lands of Sumer and Akkad safely on my lap."[6] Hammurabi left his dynasty strong enough that it survived until the 1550s B.C.E., when the Kassites from the northeast took over.

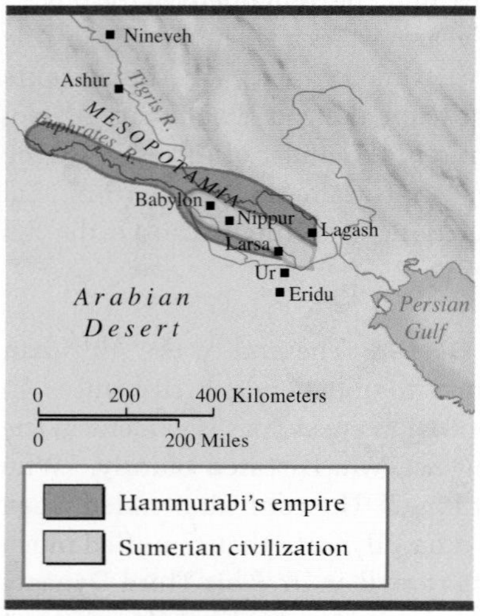

Hammurabi's Empire

Louvre, Paris//© Réunion des Musées Nationaux/Art Resource, NY

Stele of Hammurabi (Code of Hammurabi, King of Babylonia). Although the Sumerians compiled earlier law codes, Hammurabi's code was the most famous in early Mesopotamian history. The upper part of the stele depicts Hammurabi standing in front of the seated sun god Shamash. The king raises his hand in deference to the god, who gives Hammurabi the power to rule and orders the king to record the law. The lower portion of the stele contains the actual code.

The Code of Hammurabi

Code of Hammurabi

Hammurabi is best remembered for his law code, a collection of 282 laws. For centuries, laws had regulated people's relationships with one another in the lands of Mesopotamia, but only fragments of these earlier codes survive. Although many scholars today view Hammurabi's collection less as a code of laws and more as an attempt by Hammurabi to portray himself as the source of justice to his people, the code still gives us a glimpse of the Babylonian society of his time (see the box on p. 11).

The Code of Hammurabi reveals a society with a system of strict justice. Penalties for criminal offenses were severe and varied according to the social class of the victim. A crime against a member of the upper class (a noble) was punished more severely than the same offense against a member of the lower class. Moreover, the principle of "an eye for an eye, a tooth for a tooth" was fundamental to this system of justice. This meant that punishments should fit the crime: "If a freeman has destroyed the eye of a member of the aristocracy, they shall destroy his eye." Hammurabi's code also had an impact on legal ideas in Southwest Asia for hundreds of years, as the following verse from the Hebrew Bible (Leviticus 24:19–20) demonstrates: "If anyone injures his neighbor, whatever he has done must be done to him: fracture for fracture, eye for eye, tooth for tooth. As he has injured the other, so he is to be injured."

Hammurabi's code took the responsibilities of public officials very seriously. The governor of an area and city officials were expected to catch burglars. If they failed to do so, officials in the district where the crime was

The Code of Hammurabi

Hammurabi's code is the most complete Mesopotamian law code, although not the earliest. It was inscribed on a stone stele topped by a bas-relief picturing Hammurabi receiving the inspiration for the law code from the sun god Shamash, who was also the god of justice. The law code emphasizes the principle of "an eye for an eye" and punishments that vary according to social status. The following examples illustrate these concerns.

The Code of Hammurabi

25. If fire broke out in a freeman's house and a freeman, who went to extinguish it, cast his eye on the goods of the owner of the house and has appropriated the goods of the owner of the house, that freeman shall be thrown into that fire.

129. If the wife of a freeman has been caught while lying with another man, they shall bind them and throw them into the water. If the husband of the woman wishes to spare his wife, then the king in turn may spare his subject.

131. If a freeman's wife was accused by her husband, but she was not caught while lying with another man, she shall make affirmation by god and return to her house.

196. If a freeman has destroyed the eye of a member of the aristocracy, they shall destroy his eye.

198. If he has destroyed the eye of a commoner or broken the bone of a commoner, he shall pay one mina of silver.

199. If he has destroyed the eye of a freeman's slave or broken the bone of a freeman's slave, he shall pay one-half his value.

209. If a freeman struck another freeman's daughter and has caused her to have a miscarriage, he shall pay ten shekels of silver for her fetus.

210. If that woman has died, they shall put his daughter to death.

211. If by a blow he has caused a commoner's daughter to have a miscarriage, he shall pay five shekels of silver.

212. If that woman has died, he shall pay one-half mina of silver.

213. If he struck a freeman's female slave and has caused her to have a miscarriage, he shall pay two shekels of silver.

214. If that female slave has died, he shall pay one-third mina of silver.

Q What do these laws from the Code of Hammurabi reveal about Mesopotamian society?

committed had to replace the lost property. If murderers were not found, the officials had to pay a fine to the relatives of the murdered person. Soldiers were likewise expected to fulfill their duties and responsibilities for the order and maintenance of the state. If a soldier hired a substitute to fight for him, he was put to death, and the substitute was given control of his estate.

The law code also furthered the proper performance of work with what virtually amounted to consumer protection laws. Builders were held responsible for the buildings they constructed. If a house collapsed and caused the death of the owner, the builder was put to death. If the collapse caused the death of the son of the owner, the son of the builder was put to death. If goods were destroyed by the collapse, they had to be replaced and the house itself reconstructed at the builder's expense.

The number of laws in Hammurabi's code dedicated to land tenure and commerce reveal the importance of agriculture and trade in the Mesopotamian economy. Laws concerning land use and irrigation were especially strict, an indication of the danger of declining crop yields if the land was used incompetently. If landowners and tenants failed to keep dikes in good repair or to control water flow properly and thus caused damage to others' crops, they were required to pay for the grain that was destroyed.

Commercial activity was carefully regulated. Rates of interest on loans were watched closely. If the lender raised the interest rate after a loan was made, he lost the entire amount of the loan. The Code of Hammurabi even specified the precise wages of laborers and artisans, such as brickmakers and jewelers.

The largest number of laws in the code focused on marriage and the family. Parents arranged marriages for their children. After marriage, the parties involved signed a marriage contract; without it, no one was considered legally married. While the husband provided a bridal payment, the woman's parents were responsible for a dowry to the new husband.

As in many patriarchal societies, women possessed far fewer privileges and rights in the married relationship than men. A woman's place was in the home, and failure to fulfill her expected duties was grounds for divorce. If she was not able to bear children, her husband could divorce her, but he did have to return the dowry to her family. If his wife tried to leave home to engage in business, thus neglecting her house, her husband could divorce her and did not have to repay the dowry. Furthermore, if his wife was a "gadabout, . . . neglecting her house [and] humiliating her husband," she could be drowned. We do know that in practice not all women remained at home. Some worked in the fields and others in business, where they were especially prominent in running taverns.

Women were guaranteed some rights, however. If a woman was divorced without good reason, she received the dowry back. A woman could seek a divorce and get her dowry back if her husband was unable to show that she had done anything wrong. In theory, a wife was guaranteed the use of her husband's legal property in the event of his death. A mother could also decide which of her sons would receive an inheritance.

Sexual relations were strictly regulated as well. Husbands, but not wives, were permitted sexual activity outside marriage. A wife and her lover caught committing adultery were pitched into the river, although if the husband pardoned his wife, the king could pardon the guilty man. Incest was strictly forbidden. If a father had incestuous relations with his daughter, he would be banished. Incest between a son and his mother resulted in both being burned.

Fathers ruled their children as well as their wives. Obedience was duly expected: "If a son has struck his father, they shall cut off his hand." If a son committed a serious enough offense, his father could disinherit him.

The Culture of Mesopotamia

A spiritual worldview was of fundamental importance to Mesopotamian culture. To the peoples of Mesopotamia, the gods were living realities who affected all aspects of life. It was crucial, therefore, that the correct hierarchies be observed. Leaders could prepare armies for war, but success really depended on a favorable relationship with the gods. This helps explain the importance of the priestly class and is the reason why even the kings took great care to dedicate offerings and monuments to the gods. The records of these dedications are among our earliest historical documents.

THE IMPORTANCE OF RELIGION One of the most famous accounts of the creation of the universe from the ancient Near East was the Babylonian creation epic known as the *Enuma elish.* The name comes from the first three words of the first two lines of the poem:

> *When on high the heavens were not yet named,*
> *And below, the earth was not called by a name.*

The *Enuma elish* tells how the god Marduk was endowed with absolute power by the other gods to do battle with Tiamat, a primordial goddess who personified the forces of watery chaos. Marduk defeats Tiamat in battle and proceeds to create the universe by dividing Tiamat in two, one part becoming the heavens and the other the earth with her breasts as mountains. From her eyes came the Tigris and Euphrates rivers. The *Enuma elish* was recited during the New Year Festival celebrated in honor of Marduk in the city of Babylon, which the all-powerful god founded as an earthly residence for the gods after his creation of the universe.

Enuma elish

The Mesopotamians viewed their city-states as earthly copies of a divine model and order. Each city-state was sacred because it was linked to a god or goddess. Hence, Nippur, the earliest center of Sumerian religion, was dedicated to Enlil (EN-lil), the god of wind. Moreover, located at the heart of each major city-state was a temple complex. Occupying several acres, this sacred area consisted of a ziggurat with a temple at the top dedicated to the god or goddess who owned the city. The temple complex was the true center of the community. The main god or goddess dwelt there symbolically in the form of a statue, and the ceremony of dedication included a ritual that linked the statue to the god or goddess and thus supposedly harnessed the power of the deity for the city's benefit. Considerable wealth was poured into the construction of temples and other buildings used for the residences of priests and priestesses who served the gods. Although the gods literally owned the city, the temple complex used only part of the land and rented out the remainder. The temples dominated individual and commercial life, an indication of the close relationship between Mesopotamian religion and culture.

The physical environment had an obvious impact on the Mesopotamian view of the universe. Ferocious floods, heavy downpours, scorching winds, and oppressive humidity were all part of the Mesopotamian climate. These conditions and resulting famines easily convinced Mesopotamians that this world was controlled by supernatural forces and that the days of human beings

Ziggurat at Ur. This ziggurat, located at Ur, is rectangular, not square like later ones. Built around 2100 B.C.E., the ziggurat had a mudbrick base 50 feet high. Shown here is the northeastern facade, with steps that have been restored. Three stairways of one hundred steps each led to a gateway flanked by two towers. From the gateway, a central staircase led to a temple at the top, which no longer exists. This temple was dedicated to the god who was believed to own the city.

"are numbered; whatever he may do, he is but wind," as *The Epic of Gilgamesh* laments (see "Mesopotamian Literature" later in this chapter). In the presence of nature, Mesopotamians could easily feel helpless, as this poem relates:

> *The rampant flood which no man can oppose,*
> *shakes the heavens and causes earth to tremble,*
> *In an appalling blanket folds mother and child,*
> *Beats down the canebrake's full luxuriant greenery,*
> *And drowns the harvest in its time of ripeness.*
> *Rising waters, grievous to eyes of man,*
> *All-powerful flood, which forces the embankments*
> *And mows down mighty trees,*
> *Frenzied storm, tearing all things in massed confusion*
> *With it in hurtling speed.*[7]

The Mesopotamians discerned cosmic rhythms in the universe and accepted its order but perceived that it was not completely safe because of the presence of willful, powerful cosmic forces that they identified with gods and goddesses.

With its numerous gods and goddesses animating all aspects of the universe, Mesopotamian religion was **polytheistic.** The four most important deities were An, Enlil, Enki (EN-kee), and Ninhursaga (nin-HUR-sah-guh). An was the god of the sky and hence the most important force in the universe. Since his basic essence was authority, he was also viewed as the source or active principle of all authority, including the earthly power of rulers and fathers alike. In one myth, the gods address him thus:

> *What you have ordered comes true!*
> *The utterance of prince and lord is but what you have ordered, do agree with.*
> *O An! your great command takes precedence, who could gainsay it?*
> *O father of the gods, your command, the very foundations of heaven and earth, what god could spurn it?*[8]

Enlil, god of wind, was considered the second greatest power of the visible universe. In charge of the wind and thus an expression of the legitimate use of force, Enlil became the symbol of the proper use of force on earth as well. Enki was the god of the earth. Since the earth was the source of life-giving waters, Enki was also the god of rivers, wells, and canals. More generally, he represented the waters of creativity and was responsible for inventions and crafts. Ninhursaga began as a goddess associated with soil, mountains, and vegetation. Eventually, however, she was worshiped as a mother goddess, a "mother of all children," who manifested her power by giving birth to kings and conferring the royal insignia on them.

Human beings' relationship with their gods was based on subservience since, according to Sumerian myth, human beings were created to do the manual labor the gods were unwilling to do for themselves (see the box on p. 15). Moreover, humans were insecure because they could never be sure what the gods would do. But humans did make attempts to circumvent or relieve their anxiety by discovering the intentions of the gods and by trying to influence them as well; these efforts gave rise to the development of the arts of **divination.**

Divination took a variety of forms. A common form, at least for kings and priests who could afford it, involved killing animals, such as sheep or goats, and examining their livers or other organs. Supposedly, features seen in the organs of the sacrificed animals foretold events to come. Thus, one handbook states that if the animal organ has shape *x*, the outcome of the military campaign will be *y*. Private individuals relied on cheaper divinatory techniques. These included interpreting shapes in the smoke from burning incense or the pattern formed when oil was poured into water. The Mesopotamian arts of divination arose out of the desire to discover the purposes of the gods and goddesses. If people could decipher the signs that foretold events, the events would be predictable and humans could act wisely.

WRITING The realization of writing's great potential was another aspect of Mesopotamian culture. The oldest Mesopotamian texts date to around 3000 B.C.E. and were written by the Sumerians, who used a **cuneiform** ("wedge-shaped") system of writing. Using a reed stylus, they made wedge-shaped impressions on clay tablets, which were then baked or dried in the sun. Once dried, these tablets were virtually indestructible, and the several hundred thousand that have been found so far have provided a valuable source of information for modern scholars. Sumerian writing evolved from pictures of concrete objects to simplified and stylized signs, leading eventually to a phonetic system that made possible the written expression of abstract ideas.

Sumerian was the chief spoken and written language of Mesopotamia in the third millennium B.C.E., but it was replaced in the second millennium by Akkadian. After 2500 B.C.E., Sumerian cuneiform was adapted by Semitic-speaking peoples (as seen in Old Akkadian) for their own written languages. Eventually, two dialects of Old Akkadian were used in Mesopotamia, Assyrian in the north and Babylonian in the south.

Mesopotamian peoples used writing primarily for record keeping. The most common cuneiform tablets record transactions of daily life: tallies of cattle kept by cowherds for their owners, production figures, lists of taxes and wage payments, accounts, contracts, and court decisions dealing with business matters. There are also monumental texts, documents that were intended to last forever, such as inscriptions etched in stone on statues and royal buildings.

Still another category of cuneiform inscriptions includes a large body of basic texts produced for teaching purposes (see the box on p. 16). Schools for scribes were in operation by 2500 B.C.E. They were necessary because considerable time was needed to master the cuneiform system of writing. The primary goal of scribal education was to produce professionally trained scribes for careers in the temples and palaces, the military, and government service. Pupils were male and primarily from wealthy families. Gradually, the schools became important centers for culture because Mesopotamian literature was used for instructional purposes. Moreover, new literary productions came out of the scribal schools.

MESOPOTAMIAN LITERATURE Writing was important because it enabled a society to keep records and maintain knowledge of previous practices and events. Writing also made it possible for people to communicate ideas in new ways, which is especially evident in Mesopotamian literary works. The most famous piece of Mesopotamian literature was *The Epic of Gilgamesh.* This epic poem, Sumerian in origin but preserved in Akkadian, records the exploits of a legendary king of Uruk. Gilgamesh (GILL-guh-mesh), wise, strong, and perfect in body, part man, part god, abused the citizens of Uruk:

> "Gilgamesh sounds the tocsin for his amusement," the people complained, "his arrogance has no bounds by day or night. No son is left with his father, for Gilgamesh takes them all, even the children. . . . His lust leaves no virgin to her lover, neither the warrior's daughter nor the wife of the noble."[9]

The citizens asked the gods to send a competitor to oppose Gilgamesh and keep him busy. The gods comply and send a hairy, barbaric beast named Enkidu whom Gilgamesh tries to weaken by sending a prostitute to seduce him. When Enkidu finally comes to Uruk, he and Gilgamesh engage in a fierce struggle that neither can win. The two become fast friends and set off in pursuit of heroic deeds. Ishtar (Sumerian Inanna), the goddess of love, attempts to seduce Gilgamesh, but he refuses her advances. In anger, she convinces her father Anu (Sumerian An) to send the Bull of Heaven to kill Gilgamesh and Enkidu. They manage to kill the bull instead, and the gods decide that in return one of them must die. Enlil, the god of wind, rules for Enkidu, and he falls ill and dies, much to the prolonged grief of Gilgamesh. Gilgamesh experiences the pain of mortality and enters upon a search for the secret of immortality. He finds the man who had been granted "everlasting life" by the gods, Utnapishtim. The latter tells him the story of how he

Epic of Gilgamesh, Tablets I–VIII (c. 2000 B.C.E.)

Louvre, Paris/© Réunion des Musées Nationaux/Art Resource, NY

The Development of Cuneiform. Pictured here is the cone of Uruinimgina, an example of cuneiform script from an early Sumerian dynasty. The inscription announces reductions in taxes. The table shows the evolution of writing from pictographic signs to cuneiform script.

Pictographic sign, c. 3100 B.C.E.									
Interpretation	star	?sun over horizon	?stream	ear of barley	bull's head	bowl	head + bowl	lower leg	?shrouded body
Cuneiform sign, c. 2400 B.C.E.									
Cuneiform sign c. 700 B.C.E. (turned through 90°)									
Phonetic value*	dingir, an	u_4, ud	a	še	gu_4	nig_2, ninda	ku_2	du, gin, gub	lu_2
Meaning	god, sky	day, sun	water, seed, son	barley	ox	food, bread	to eat	to walk, to stand	man

*Some signs have more than one phonetic value and some sounds are represented by more than one sign; for example, u_4 means the fourth sign with the phonetic value *u*.

From the *Cultural Atlas of Mesopotamia & the Ancient Near East* by Michael Roaf/Courtesy of Andromeda Oxford Limited, Oxford

A Creation Myth: "Let Man Carry the Labor-Basket of the Gods"

This selection is taken from *Atrahasis*, a Mesopotamian poem probably composed early in the second millennium B.C.E. It is a myth that tells of the creation, destruction, and regeneration of the human race. In this excerpt, the gods create human beings to do the physical labor—digging canals—that they have grown to detest.

Atrahasis

When the gods, like man,
bore the work, carried the labor-basket—
the labor-basket of the great gods—
the work was heavy, much was the distress. . . .
Forty more years
they bore the labor night and day.
They wearied, complained,
grumbled in the workpits.
"Let us confront the throne-bearer
that he may remove from us our heavy labor.
Come on, let us confuse him in his dwelling,
Enlil, the counselor of the gods, the hero,
come on, let us confuse him in his dwelling. . . ."

[After the lesser gods who are digging the canals rebel against Enlil, who rules the surface of the earth, he agrees to create human beings to do the physical labor for the lesser gods.]

"While [Nintu the birth-goddess] is present,
let the birth-goddess create the offspring,
let man bear the labor-basket of the gods."
They called the goddess and asked her,
the midwife of the gods, wise Mami:
"You are the birth-goddess, creatress of man.
Create lullu-man, let him bear the yoke.
Let him bear the yoke, the work of Enlil;
let man carry the labor-basket of the gods. . . ."
At the new moon, the seventh day, and the full moon,
he set up a purifying bath.
We-ila, who had rationality,
they slaughtered in their assembly.
With his flesh and blood
Nintu mixed the clay.
Till the end of days they hear the drum [heartbeat].
From the flesh of the god there was spirit.
She proclaimed "alive" as its sign.
For the sake of not-forgetting there was a spirit.
After she had mixed the clay,
she called the Anunnaki, the great gods.
The Igigi, the great gods,
cast their spittle on the clay.
Mami opened her mouth
and said to the great gods,
"You commanded me a task—
I have completed it.
You slaughtered a god together with his rationality.
I have removed your heavy labor,
have placed your labor-basket on man.
You raised a cry for mankind;
I have loosened your yoke, have established
freedom."

Q What impression of the Mesopotamian gods do you get from this creation myth?

survived the Great Flood sent by the gods to destroy humankind (see the box on p. 17). Regretting what they had done, the gods bestowed immortality on Utnapishtim, who now instructs Gilgamesh to dive to the bottom of a river and find a certain plant that gives the power to grow younger. Although Gilgamesh finds the plant, a snake snatches it away before he can eat it. Gilgamesh remains mortal. The desire for immortality, one of humankind's great searches, ends in frustration. "Everlasting life," as this Mesopotamian epic makes clear, is only for the gods.

MATHEMATICS AND ASTRONOMY People in Mesopotamia made outstanding achievements in mathematics and astronomy. In math, the Sumerians devised a number system based on 60, using combinations of 6 and 10 for practical solutions. They used the processes of multiplication and division and compiled tables for the computation of interest. Geometry was used for practical purposes, such as measuring fields and building projects. In astronomy, the Sumerians made use of units of 60 and charted the chief heavenly constellations. Their calendar was based on twelve lunar months and was brought into harmony with the solar year by adding an extra month from time to time.

Egyptian Civilization: "The Gift of the Nile"

Q **FOCUS QUESTIONS**: What are the basic features of the three major periods of Egyptian history? What elements of continuity are there in the three periods? What are their major differences?

Although contemporaneous with Mesopotamia, civilization in Egypt evolved along somewhat different lines. Of central importance to the development of Egyptian civilization was the Nile River. That the Egyptian people recognized its significance is apparent in this *Hymn to the*

A Sumerian Schoolboy

This Sumerian essay, written by a teacher as a copying exercise for pupils, narrates the daily activities of a schoolboy. The boy experiences numerous trials and tribulations, including being beaten ("caned") for improper behavior. Scribal schools came into being in Sumer around 2500 B.C.E.

A Sumerian Essay for Schoolboys

"Schoolboy, where did you go from earliest day?"
"I went to school."
"What did you do in school?"
"I read my tablet, wrote it, finished it; then my prepared lines were prepared for me and in the afternoon, my hand copies were prepared for me." Upon the school's dismissal, I went home, entered the house, there was my father sitting. I spoke to my father of my hand copies, then read the tablet to him, and my father was pleased; truly I found favor with my father.
"I am thirsty, give me drink, I am hungry, give me bread, wash my feet, set up the bed, I want to go to sleep; wake me early in the morning, I must not be late, or my teacher will cane me."
When I awoke early in the morning, I faced my mother, and said to her: "Give me my lunch, I want to go to school. . . . "
My mother gave me two "rolls," I went to school.
In the tablet-house, the monitor said to me: "Why are you late?" I was afraid, my heart beat fast. I entered before my teacher, took my place.
My "school-father" read my tablet to me, said "The . . . is cut off," caned me. . . .
Who was in charge of drawing said "Why when I was not here did you stand up?" caned me.
Who was in charge of the gate said "Why when I was not here did you go out?" caned me. . . .
My teacher said "Your hand is not good," caned me.

[At this point, the student decides he needs help and suggests to his father that he invite his teacher home for dinner. The father does so, thanks the teacher, and treats him to a feast and gifts. The teacher now responds to the student.]

Young man, because you did not neglect my work, did not forsake it,
May you reach the pinnacle of the scribal art, achieve it completely
Because you gave me that which you were by no means obliged to give,
You presented me with a gift over and above my earnings, have shown me great honor, may Nidaba, the queen of the guardian deities, be your guardian deity.
May she show favor to your fashioned reed,
May she take all evil from your hand copies.
Of your brothers, may you be their leader,
Of your companions, may you be their chief,
May you rank the highest of all the schoolboys.

Q What do the activities of this schoolboy reveal about the nature of Sumerian society?

Nile (see the box on p. 18): "The bringer of food, rich in provisions, creator of all good, lord of majesty, sweet of fragrance. . . . He who . . . fills the magazines, makes the granaries wide, and gives things to the poor. He who makes every beloved tree to grow."[10] Egypt, like Mesopotamia, was a river valley civilization.

The Impact of Geography

The Nile is a unique river, beginning in the heart of Africa and coursing northward for thousands of miles. It is the longest river in the world. Thanks to the Nile, an area several miles wide on both banks of the river was capable of producing abundant harvests. The "miracle" of the Nile was its annual flooding. The river rose in the summer from rains in Central Africa and the Ethiopian highlands, crested in Egypt in September and October, and left a deposit of silt that enriched the soil. The Egyptians called this fertile land, dark from the silt and the lush crops that grew on it, the "Black Land." Beyond these narrow strips of fertile fields lay the deserts (the "Red Land").

Unlike the floods of Mesopotamia's rivers, the flooding of the Nile was gradual and usually predictable, and the river itself was seen as life-enhancing, not life-threatening. Although a system of organized irrigation was still necessary, the small villages along the Nile could make the effort without the massive state intervention that was required in Mesopotamia. Egyptian civilization consequently tended to remain more rural, with many small population centers congregated along a narrow band on both sides of the Nile. About 100 miles before it empties into the Mediterranean, the river splits into two major branches, forming the delta, a triangular-shaped territory called Lower Egypt to distinguish it from Upper Egypt, the land upstream to the south (see Map 1.3 on p. 19). Egypt's important cities developed at the tip of the delta. Even today, most of Egypt's people are crowded along the banks of the Nile River.

The surpluses of food that Egyptian farmers grew in the fertile Nile valley made Egypt prosperous. But the Nile also served as a unifying factor in Egyptian history. In ancient times, the Nile was the fastest way to travel through the land, making both transportation and communication easier.

The Great Flood

The great epic poem of Mesopotamian literature, *The Epic of Gilgamesh,* includes an account by Utnapishtim (a Mesopotamian version of the later biblical Noah), who had built a ship and survived the flood unleashed by the gods to destroy humankind. This selection recounts how the god Ea advised Utnapishtim to build a boat and how he came to land his boat at the end of the flood. In this section, Utnapishtim is telling his story to Gilgamesh.

The Epic of Gilgamesh

"In those days the world teemed, the people multiplied, the world bellowed like a wild bull, and the great god was aroused by the clamor. Enlil heard the clamor and he said to the gods in council, 'The uproar of mankind is intolerable and sleep is no longer possible by reason of the babel.' So the gods agreed to exterminate mankind. Enlil did this, but Ea [Sumerian Enki, god of the waters] because of his oath warned me in a dream . . . 'tear down your house and build a boat, abandon possessions and look for life, despise worldly goods and save your soul alive. Tear down your house, I say, and build a boat. . . . Then take up into the boat the seed of all living creatures. . . .' [Utnapishtim did as he was told, and then the destruction came.]

"For six days and six nights the winds blew, torrent and tempest and flood overwhelmed the world, tempest and flood raged together like warring hosts. When the seventh day dawned the storm from the south subsided, the sea grew calm, the flood was stifled; I looked at the face of the world and there was silence, all mankind was turned to clay. The surface of the sea stretched as flat as a rooftop; I opened a hatch and the light fell on my face. Then I bowed low, I sat down and I wept, the tears streamed down my face, for on every side was the waste of water. I looked for land in vain, but fourteen leagues distant there appeared a mountain, and there the boat grounded; on the mountain of Nisir the boat held fast, she held fast and did not budge.

". . . When the seventh day dawned I loosed a dove and let her go. She flew away, but finding no resting-place she returned. Then I loosed a swallow, and she flew away but finding no resting-place she returned. I loosed a raven, she saw that the waters had retreated, she ate, she flew around, she cawed, and she did not come back. Then I threw everything open to the four winds, I made a sacrifice and poured out a libation on the mountain top."

Q What does this selection from *The Epic of Gilgamesh* tell you about the relationship between the Mesopotamians and their gods? How might you explain the differences between this account and the biblical flood story in Genesis?

Winds from the north pushed sailboats south, and the current of the Nile carried them north. Often when they headed downstream (north), people used long poles or paddles to propel their boats forward.

Unlike Mesopotamia, which was subject to constant invasion, Egypt was blessed by natural barriers that protected it from invasion and gave it a sense of security. These barriers included the deserts to the west and east; the cataracts (rapids) on the southern part of the Nile, which made defense relatively easy; and the Mediterranean Sea to the north. These barriers, however, were effective only when they were combined with Egyptian fortifications at strategic locations. Nor did these barriers prevent the development of trade. Indeed, there is evidence of very early trade between Egypt and Mesopotamia.

In essence, Egyptian geography and topography played important roles in the early history of the country. The regularity of the Nile floods and the relative isolation of the Egyptians created a sense of security that was accompanied by a feeling of changelessness. To the ancient Egyptians, when the Nile flooded each year, "the fields laugh and people's faces light up." Unlike people in Mesopotamia, Egyptians faced life with a spirit of confidence in the stability of things. Egyptian civilization was characterized by a remarkable degree of continuity over thousands of years.

The Old and Middle Kingdoms

The basic framework for the study of Egyptian history was provided by Manetho (MAN-uh-thoh), an Egyptian priest and historian who lived in the early third century B.C.E. He divided Egyptian history into thirty-one dynasties of kings. On the basis of Manetho's and other king lists, modern historians have divided Egyptian history into three major periods known as the Old Kingdom, the Middle Kingdom, and the New Kingdom. These were periods of long-term stability characterized by strong monarchical authority, competent bureaucracy, freedom from invasion, much construction of temples and pyramids, and considerable intellectual and cultural activity. But between the periods of stability were ages known as the Intermediate Periods, which were characterized by weak political structures and rivalry for leadership, invasions, a decline in building activity, and a restructuring of society.

THE OLD KINGDOM According to the Egyptians' own tradition, their land consisted initially of numerous populated areas ruled by tribal chieftains. Around 3100 B.C.E., during the Early Dynastic Period, the first Egyptian royal dynasty, under a king called Menes, united both Upper

Significance of the Nile River and the Pharaoh

Two of the most important sources of life for the ancient Egyptians were the Nile River and the pharaoh. Egyptians perceived that the Nile River made possible the abundant food that was a major source of their well-being. This *Hymn to the Nile*, probably from the nineteenth and twentieth dynasties in the New Kingdom, expresses the gratitude Egyptians felt for the Nile.

Hymn to the Nile

Hail to you, O Nile, that issues from the earth and comes to keep Egypt alive! . . .
He that waters the meadows which Re created, in order to keep every kid alive.
He that makes to drink the desert and the place distant from water: that is his dew coming down from heaven. . . .
The lord of fishes, he who makes the marsh-birds to go upstream. . . .
He who makes barley and brings emmer [wheat] into being, that he may make the temples festive.
If he is sluggish, then nostrils are stopped up, and everybody is poor. . . .
When he rises, then the land is in jubilation, then every belly is in joy, every backbone takes on laughter, and every tooth is exposed.
The bringer of food, rich in provisions, creator of all good, lord of majesty, sweet of fragrance. . . .
He who makes every beloved tree to grow, without lack of them.

The Egyptian king, or pharaoh, was viewed as a god and the absolute ruler of Egypt. His significance and the gratitude of the Egyptian people for his existence are evident in this hymn from the reign of Sesotris III (c. 1880–1840 B.C.E.).

Hymn to the Pharaoh

He has come unto us that he may carry away Upper Egypt; the double diadem [crown of Upper and Lower Egypt] has rested on his head.
He has come unto us and has united the Two Lands; he has mingled the reed with the bee [symbols of Lower and Upper Egypt].
He has come unto us and has brought the Black Land under his sway; he has apportioned to himself the Red Land.
He has come unto us and has taken the Two Lands under his protection; he has given peace to the Two Riverbanks.
He has come unto us and has made Egypt to live; he has banished its suffering.
He has come unto us and has made the people to live; he has caused the throat of the subjects to breathe. . . .
He has come unto us and has done battle for his boundaries; he has delivered them that were robbed.

Q How do these two hymns underscore the importance of the Nile River and the institution of the pharaoh to Egyptian civilization?

and Lower Egypt into a single kingdom. Henceforth, the king would be called "King of Upper and Lower Egypt," and one of the royal crowns would be the Double Crown, combining the White Crown of Upper Egypt and the Red Crown of Lower Egypt. Just as the Nile served to unite Upper and Lower Egypt physically, kingship served to unite the two areas politically.

The Old Kingdom encompassed the third through sixth dynasties of Egyptian kings, lasting from around 2686 to 2181 B.C.E. It was an age of prosperity and splendor, made visible in the construction of the greatest and largest pyramids in Egypt's history. The capital of the Old Kingdom was located at Memphis, south of the delta.

Kingship was a divine institution in ancient Egypt and formed part of a universal cosmic scheme (see the box above): "What is the king of Upper and Lower Egypt? He is a god by whose dealings one lives, the father and mother of all men, alone by himself, without an equal."[11] In obeying their king, subjects helped maintain the cosmic order. A breakdown in royal power could only mean that citizens were offending divinity and weakening the universal structure. Among the various titles of Egyptian kings, that of pharaoh (originally meaning "great house" or "palace") eventually came to be the most common.

Although they possessed absolute power, Egyptian kings were supposed to rule not arbitrarily but according to set principles. The chief principle was called *Ma'at*, a spiritual precept that conveyed the idea of truth and justice, especially right order and harmony. To ancient Egyptians, this fundamental order and harmony had existed throughout the universe since the beginning of time. Pharaohs were the divine instruments who maintained it and were themselves subject to it.

Although theoretically absolute in their power, in practice Egyptian kings did not rule alone. Initially, members of the king's family performed administrative tasks, but by the fourth dynasty, a bureaucracy with regular procedures had developed. Especially important was

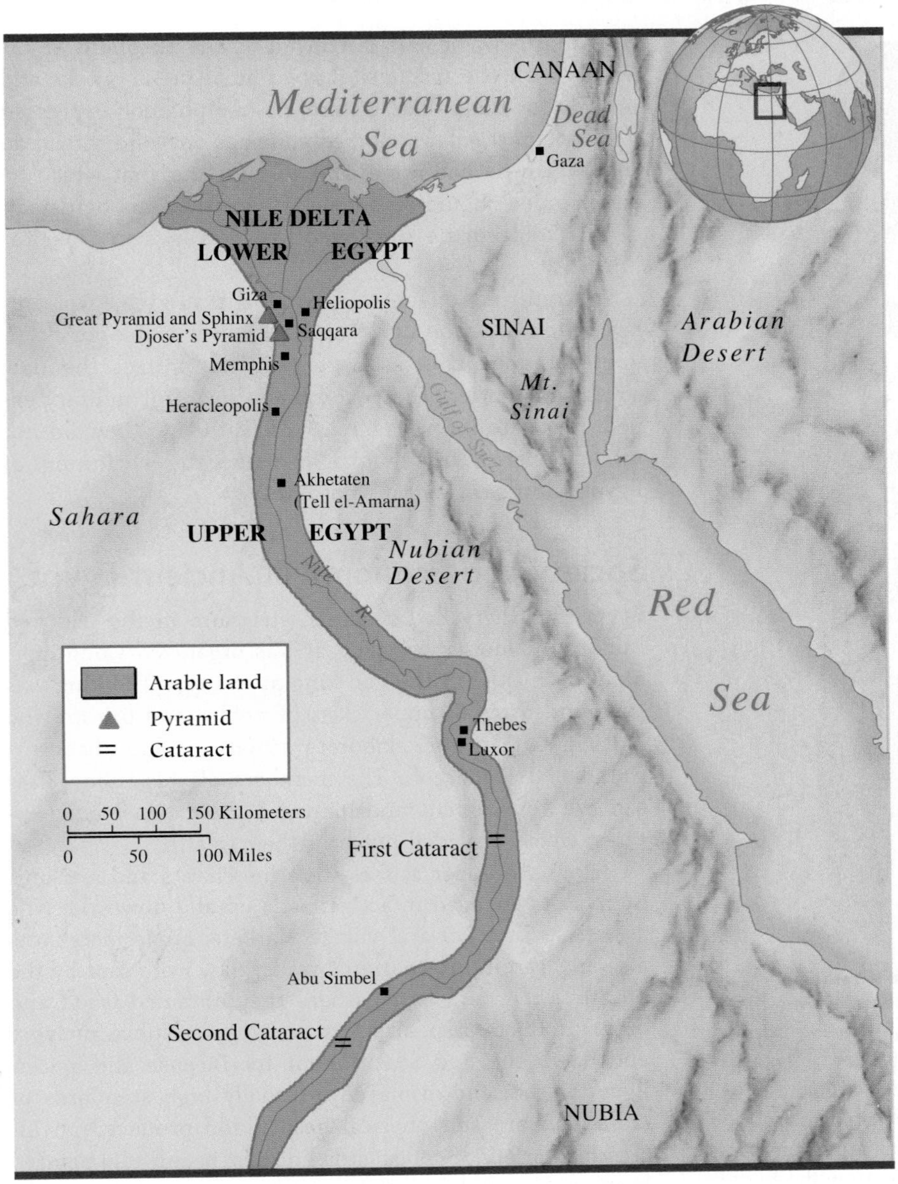

MAP 1.3 Ancient Egypt. Egyptian civilization centered on the life-giving water and flood silts of the Nile River, with most of the population living in Lower Egypt, where the river splits to form the Nile delta. Most of the pyramids, built during the Old Kingdom, are clustered at the entrance to the delta.

Q ***How did the lands to the east and west of the river help to protect Egypt from invasion?***

the office of vizier, "steward of the whole land." Directly responsible to the king, the vizier was in charge of the bureaucracy, with its numerous departments, including police, justice, river transport, and public works. Agriculture and the treasury were the most important departments. Agriculture was, of course, the backbone of Egyptian prosperity, and the treasury collected the taxes, which were paid in kind. A careful assessment of land and tenants was undertaken to establish the tax base.

For administrative purposes, Egypt was divided into provinces or nomes, as they were later called by the Greeks—twenty-two in Upper and twenty in Lower Egypt. A governor, called by the Greeks a nomarch, was head of each nome and was responsible to the king and vizier. Nomarchs, however, tended to build up large holdings of land and power within their nomes, creating a potential rivalry with the pharaohs.

THE MIDDLE KINGDOM A decline in centralized authority, a drought caused by low levels of the Nile and a decline in rainfall, and economic troubles brought about the collapse of the Old Kingdom, ushering in the First Intermediate Period (c. 2180–2055 B.C.E.). A so-called prophet named Nefer-Rohu (Neferti) described the scene:

> This land is so damaged that there is no one who is concerned with it, no one who speaks, no one who weeps.... The sun disk is covered over. It will not shine so that people may see.... The rivers of Egypt are empty, so that the water is crossed on foot. Men seek for water for the ships to sail on it.... This land is helter-skelter, and no one knows the result that will come about, which is hidden from speech, sight, or hearing.[12]

During the First Intermediate Period, new centers of power established rival dynasties, such as those at Heracleopolis near Lower Egypt and Thebes in Upper Egypt. Finally, the king of Thebes, Mentuhotep, defeated the ruler of Heracleopolis and achieved the reunification of all Egypt, thus beginning the Middle Kingdom, a new period of stability lasting from around 2055 to 1650 B.C.E.

© Hansel Mieth//Time Life Pictures/Getty Images

Pair Statue of King Menkaure and His Queen. During the Old Kingdom, kings (eventually called pharaohs) were regarded as gods, divine instruments who maintained the fundamental order and harmony of the universe and wielded absolute power. Seated and standing statues of kings were commonly placed in Egyptian royal tombs. Seen here are the standing portraits of King Menkaure and his queen, Khamerernebty, from the fourth dynasty. By artistic convention, kings and their queens were shown in a rigid pose, reflecting their timeless nature. Husband and wife show no emotion but are seen looking out into space.

Much of the Middle Kingdom's history centered around the twelfth dynasty founded by Amenemhet I, a vizier who established himself and his successors as pharaohs. Egyptians later portrayed the Middle Kingdom as a golden age, a clear indication of its stability. Several factors contributed to its vitality. The nome structure was reorganized. The boundaries of each nome were now settled precisely, and the obligations of the nomes to the state were clearly delineated. Nomarchs were confirmed as hereditary officeholders but with the understanding that their duties must be performed faithfully. These included the collection of taxes for the state and the recruitment of labor forces for royal projects, such as stone quarrying.

The Middle Kingdom was characterized by a new concern on the part of the pharaohs for the people. In the Old Kingdom, the pharaoh had been viewed as an inaccessible god-king. Now he was portrayed as the shepherd of his people with the responsibility to build public works and provide for the public welfare. As one pharaoh expressed it: "He [a particular god] created me as one who should do that which he had done, and to carry out that which he commanded should be done. He appointed me herdsman of this land, for he knew who would keep it in order for him."[13]

As confirmation of its newfound strength, Egypt embarked on a period of expansion. Lower Nubia was conquered, and fortresses were built to protect the new southern frontier. The government also sent military expeditions into Palestine and Syria. Although they did not remain there, this campaign marks the beginning of Egyptian imperialism in those areas.

Society and Economy in Ancient Egypt

Egyptian society had a simple structure in the Old and Middle Kingdoms; basically, it was organized along hierarchical lines with the god-king at the top. The king was surrounded by an upper class of nobles and priests who participated in the elaborate rituals of life that surrounded the pharaoh. The members of this ruling class ran the government and managed their own landed estates, which provided much of their wealth.

Below the upper classes were merchants and artisans. Merchants engaged in active trade up and down the Nile as well as in town and village markets. Some merchants also engaged in international trade; they were sent by the king to Crete and Syria, where they obtained wood and other products. Expeditions traveled into Nubia for ivory and down the Red Sea to Punt for incense and spices. Egyptian artisans displayed unusually high standards of craftsmanship and physical beauty and produced an incredible variety of goods: stone dishes; beautifully painted boxes made of clay; wooden furniture, especially of Lebanon cedar; gold, silver, and copper tools and containers; paper and rope made of papyrus; and linen clothes.

The great majority of people in Egypt simply worked the land. In theory, the king owned all the land but granted portions of it to his subjects. Large sections were in the possession of nobles and the temple complexes. Most of the lower classes were serfs, common people who were bound to the land and cultivated the estates. They paid taxes in the form of crops to the king, nobles, and priests; lived in small villages or towns; and provided military service and labor for building projects.

The Culture of Egypt

Egypt produced a culture that dazzled and awed its later conquerors. The Egyptians' technical achievements alone, especially visible in the construction of the pyramids, demonstrated a measure of skill unique to the world of that time. To the Egyptians, all of these achievements were part of a cosmic order suffused with the presence of the divine.

SPIRITUAL LIFE IN EGYPTIAN SOCIETY The Egyptians had no word for religion because it was an inseparable element of the world order to which Egyptian society belonged. Egypt was part of the universal cosmic scheme, and the pharaoh was the divine being whose function was to maintain its stability within that cosmic order.

The Egyptians possessed a remarkable number of gods associated with heavenly bodies and natural forces, hardly unusual in view of the importance to Egypt's well-being of the sun, the river, and the fertile land along its banks. The sun was the source of life and hence worthy of worship. A sun cult developed, especially at Heliopolis, now a suburb of modern Cairo. The sun god took on different forms and names, depending on his specific function. He was worshiped as Atum in human form and as Re, who had a human body but the head of a falcon. The pharaoh took the title "Son of Re" because he was regarded as the earthly embodiment of Re.

River and land deities included Osiris (oh-SY-russ) and Isis (Y-sis) with their child Horus, who was related to the Nile and to the sun as well. Osiris became especially important as a symbol of resurrection. A famous Egyptian myth told of the struggle between Osiris, who brought civilization to Egypt, and his evil brother Seth, who killed him, cut his body into fourteen parts, and tossed them into the Nile. Isis, the faithful wife of Osiris, found the pieces and, with help from other gods, restored Osiris to life. As a symbol of resurrection and as judge of the dead, Osiris took on an important role for the Egyptians. By identifying with Osiris, one could hope to gain new life, just as Osiris had done. The dead, embalmed and mummified, were placed in tombs (in the case of kings, in pyramidal tombs), given the name of Osiris, and by a process of magical identification became Osiris. Like Osiris, they could then be reborn. The flood of the Nile and the new life it brought to Egypt were symbolized by Isis gathering all of the parts of Osiris together and were celebrated each spring in the festival of the new land.

Later Egyptian spiritual practice began to emphasize morality by stressing the role of Osiris as judge of the dead. The dead were asked to give an account of their earthly deeds to show whether they deserved a reward. Other means were also employed to gain immortality. As seen in the *Book of the Dead* from the period of the New Kingdom, magical incantations were used to ensure a favorable journey to a happy afterlife. Specific instructions explained what to do when confronted by the judge of the dead. These instructions had two aspects. The negative confession gave a detailed list of what one had not done:

Papyrus of Ani (Egyptian *Book of the Dead*) (c. 1240 B.C.E.)

> What is said on reaching the Broad-Hall of the Two Justices [the place of the next-world judgment], absolving X [the name and title of the deceased] of every sin which he had committed, . . .
> I have not committed evil against men.

Osiris as Judge of the Dead. According to the *Book of the Dead,* after making a denial of offenses (the "negative confession"), the deceased experienced the "weighing of the heart." Shown here is a judgment scene from the *Book of the Dead* of Hunefer, a royal scribe who died around 1285 B.C.E. Hunefer's heart is placed on one side of a balance scale; on the other side is the feather of Ma'at, the goddess of truth. For Hunefer, heart and feather are of equal weight, so the god Anubis ushers him into the presence of Osiris, seated on his throne at the right. A "Swallowing Monster," a hybrid creature combining crocodile, lion, and hippopotamus, stood ready at the scale to devour the deceased if he failed the test.

I have not mistreated cattle. . . .
I have not blasphemed a god. . . .
I have not done violence to a poor man. . . .
I have not defamed a slave to his superior.
I have not made anyone sick.
I have not made anyone weep.
I have not killed. . . .
I have not caused anyone suffering. . . .
I have not had sexual relations with a boy.
I have not defiled myself. . . .
I have not driven cattle away from their pasturage.[14]

Later the supplicant made a speech listing his good actions: "I have done that which men said and that with which gods are content. . . . I have given bread to the hungry, water to the thirsty, clothing to the naked, and a ferry-boat to him who was marooned. I have provided divine offerings for the gods and mortuary offerings for the dead."[15]

At first the Osiris cult was reserved for the very wealthy, who could afford to take expensive measures to preserve the body after death. During the Middle Kingdom, however, the cult became "democratized" and was extended to all Egyptians who aspired to an afterlife.

THE PYRAMIDS One of the great achievements of Egyptian civilization, the building of pyramids, occurred in the time of the Old Kingdom. Pyramids were not built in isolation but as part of a larger complex dedicated to the dead—in effect, a city of the dead. The area included a large pyramid for the king's burial, smaller pyramids for his family, and mastabas, rectangular structures with flat roofs, as tombs for the pharaoh's noble officials. The tombs were well prepared for their residents. The rooms were furnished and stocked with numerous supplies, including chairs, boats, chests, weapons, games, dishes, and a variety of foods. The Egyptians believed that human beings had two bodies, a physical one and a spiritual one, which they called the *ka*. If the physical body was properly preserved (that is, mummified) and the tomb furnished with all the various objects of regular life, the *ka* could return and continue its life despite the death of the physical body.

To preserve the physical body after death, the Egyptians practiced mummification, a process of slowly drying a dead body to prevent it from rotting. Special workshops, run by priests, performed this procedure, primarily for the wealthy families who could afford it. According to Herodotus, an ancient Greek historian (see Chapter 3) who visited Egypt around 450 B.C.E., "The most refined method is as follows: first of all they draw out the brain through the nostrils with an iron hook. . . . Then they make an incision in the flank with a sharp Ethiopian stone through which they extract all the internal organs."[16] The liver, lungs, stomach, and intestines were then placed in four special jars that were put in the tomb with the mummy. The priests then covered the corpse with a natural salt that absorbed the body's water. Later, they filled the body with spices and wrapped it with layers of linen soaked in resin. At the end of the process, which took about seventy days, a lifelike mask was placed over the head and shoulders of the mummy, which was then sealed in a case and placed in its tomb.

Herodotus, Description of Mummification

Pyramids were tombs for the mummified bodies of pharaohs. The first pyramid was built in the third dynasty during the reign of King Djoser (ZHOH-sur). The architect Imhotep, a priest of Heliopolis, the center dedicated to the sun cult, was responsible for the step pyramid at Saqqara. Beginning with Djoser, wives and immediate families of the kings were buried in pyramids, nobles and officials in mastabas.

The first real pyramid, with each side filled in to make an even surface, was constructed in the fourth dynasty around 2600 B.C.E. by King Snefru, who built three pyramids. But the largest and most magnificent of

The Pyramids at Giza. The three pyramids at Giza, across the Nile River from Cairo, are the most famous in Egypt. At the rear is the largest of the three pyramids—the Great Pyramid of Khufu. Next to it is the pyramid of Khafre. In the foreground is the smaller pyramid of Menkaure standing behind the even smaller pyramids for the pharaohs' wives. Covering almost 13 acres, the Great Pyramid of Khufu is immense. It is estimated that the Great Pyramid contains 2.3 million stone blocks, each weighing about 2.5 tons.

all was built under Snefru's son Khufu. Constructed at Giza around 2540 B.C.E., the famous Great Pyramid covers 13 acres, measures 756 feet at each side of its base, and stands 481 feet high. Its four sides are almost precisely oriented to the four points of the compass.

The building of the Great Pyramid was an enormous construction project that used limestone blocks as well as granite from Upper Egypt. Herodotus reported that it took 100,000 Egyptians twenty years to build the Great Pyramid. But Herodotus wrote two thousand years after the event, and considerable controversy and speculation still surround the construction of the Great Pyramid, especially in view of the precision with which it was built. The stone slabs on the outside of the pyramid, for example, fit so closely side by side that a hair cannot be pushed into the joints between them. The Great Pyramid still stands as a symbol of the power of Egyptian kings of the Old Kingdom. No later pyramid ever matched its size or splendor. But an Egyptian pyramid was not just the king's tomb; it was also an important symbol of royal power. It could be seen for miles away as a visible reminder of the glory and might of the ruler, a living god on earth.

ART AND WRITING Commissioned by kings or nobles for use in temples and tombs, Egyptian art was largely functional. Wall paintings and statues of gods and kings in temples served a strictly spiritual purpose. They were an integral part of the performance of ritual, which was thought necessary to preserve the cosmic order and hence the well-being of Egypt. Likewise, the mural scenes and sculptured figures found in the tombs had a specific function. They were supposed to aid the journey of the deceased into the afterworld.

Egyptian art was also formulaic. Artists and sculptors were expected to observe a strict canon of proportions that determined both form and presentation. This canon gave Egyptian art a distinctive appearance for thousands of years. Especially characteristic was the convention of combining the profile, semiprofile, and frontal views of the human body in relief work and painting in order to represent each part of the body accurately. This fashion created an art that was highly stylized yet still allowed distinctive features to be portrayed.

Writing emerged in Egypt during the first two dynasties. It was the Greeks who later labeled Egyptian writing **hieroglyphics,** meaning "priest-carvings" or "sacred writings." Hieroglyphs (HY-uh-roh-glifs) were signs that depicted objects and had a sacred value at the same time. Although hieroglyphs were later simplified for writing purposes into two scripts, they never developed into an alphabet. Egyptian hieroglyphs were initially carved in stone, but later the two simplified scripts were written on papyrus, a paper made from the papyrus reed that grew along the Nile. Most of the ancient Egyptian literature that has come down to us was written on papyrus rolls and wooden tablets.

Disorder and a New Order: The New Kingdom

The Middle Kingdom came to an end in the midst of another period of instability. An incursion into the delta region by a people known as the Hyksos initiated this second age of disorder. The Hyksos, a Semitic-speaking people, infiltrated Egypt in the seventeenth century B.C.E. and came to dominate much of Egypt during the Second Intermediate Period. The presence of the Hyksos was not entirely negative for Egypt, however. They taught the Egyptians how to make use of bronze in new agricultural tools and weapons. More significantly, the Hyksos brought new aspects of warfare to Egypt, including the horse-drawn war chariot, a heavier sword, and the compound bow. Eventually, the Egyptians made use of their new weapons to throw off Hyksos domination.

THE EGYPTIAN EMPIRE It was the pharaoh Ahmose I who managed to defeat and expel the Hyksos from Egypt. He reunited Egypt, founded the eighteenth dynasty, established the New Kingdom (c. 1550–1070 B.C.E.), and launched the Egyptians along a new militaristic and imperialistic path. A more professional army was developed. Viziers, who were in charge of the state bureaucracy, were now chosen only from the ranks of military commanders.

During the period of the New Kingdom, Egypt became the most powerful state in the ancient Near East (see Map 1.4). Thutmosis (thoot-MOH-suss) I (c. 1524–1518 B.C.E.) expanded Egypt's border to the south by conquering the African kingdom of Nubia. Thutmosis III (c. 1480–c. 1450 B.C.E.) led seventeen military campaigns into Canaan and Phoenicia. The Egyptians occupied these lands but permitted local native princes to rule. Egypt, no longer content to remain in isolation, now pursued an active political and diplomatic policy.

The new Egyptian imperial state reached its height during the reign of Amenhotep (ah-mun-HOH-tep) III (c. 1412–1375 B.C.E.), the great-grandson of Thutmosis III. The achievements of the empire were made visible in the construction of magnificent new buildings and temples. Especially famous were the temple centers at Karnak and Luxor and the 70-foot-high statues of Amenhotep III in front of the mortuary temples along the Nile.

By the end of his reign, Amenhotep III faced a growing military challenge from a people known as the Hittites (see "The Hittite Empire" later in this chapter). His son, Amenhotep IV (c. 1364–1347 B.C.E.), proved even less able to deal with this threat, a failure that was due in large part to a religious upheaval that he had initiated in Egypt.

AKHENATEN AND RELIGIOUS CHANGE Amenhotep IV introduced the worship of Aten, god of the sun disk, as the chief god (see the box on p. 25) and pursued his worship with great enthusiasm. Changing his own name to Akhenaten (ah-kuh-NAH-tun) ("Servant of Aten"), the pharaoh closed the temples of other gods and especially endeavored to lessen the power of the priesthood dedicated to

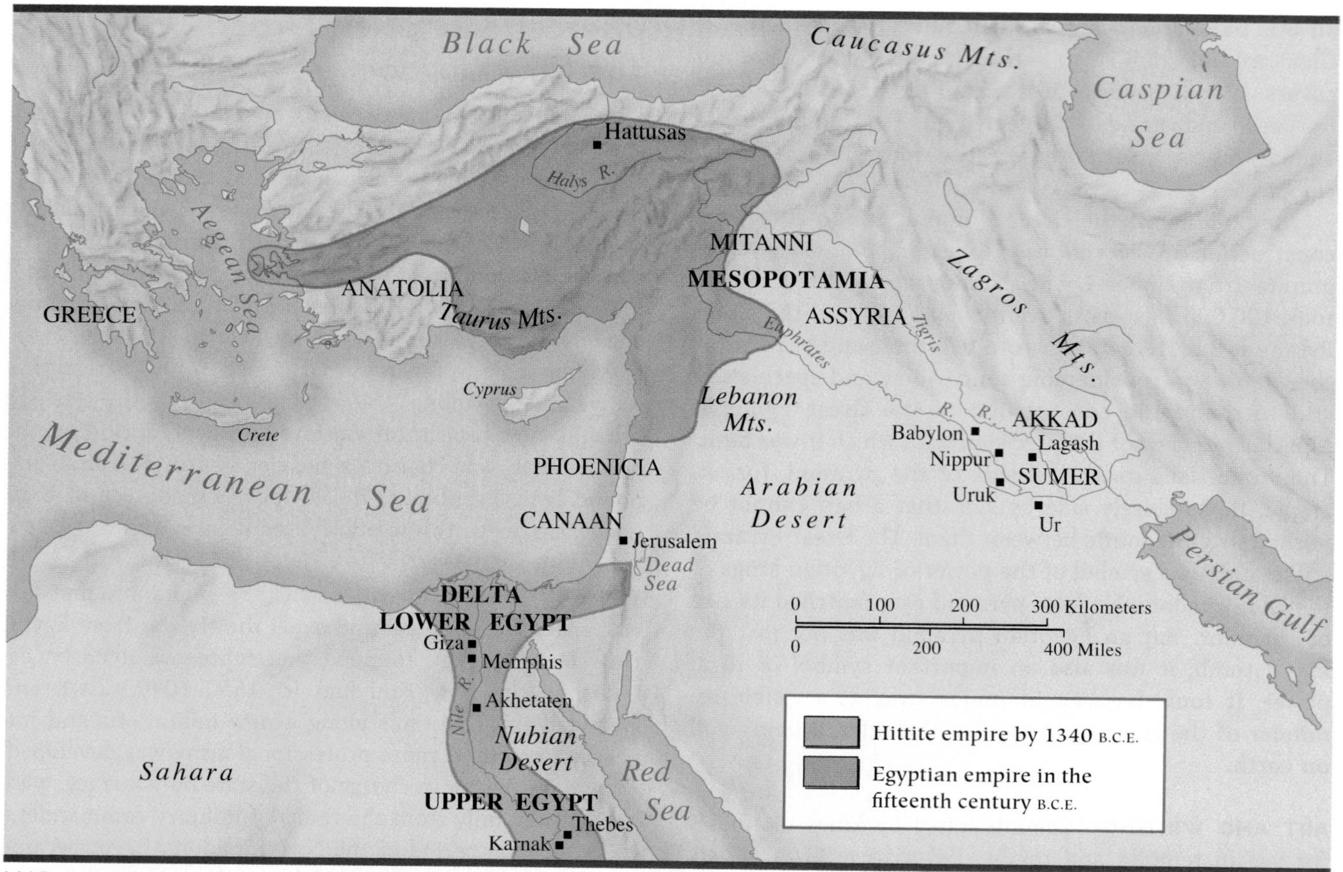

MAP 1.4 The Egyptian and Hittite Empires. The Hittite empire was the dominant power north of Egypt for roughly two centuries (see p. 30). The Hittites assimilated important linguistic, political, and religious aspects of the peoples they conquered and thus helped transmit Mesopotamian culture to the eastern Mediterranean.

Q ***What made both the Hittite and Egyptian empires vulnerable to invasion?***

the god Amon-Re at Thebes, which had become the chief landowner in Egypt. Akhenaten strove to reduce the priests' influence by replacing Thebes as the capital of Egypt with Akhetaten ("Horizon of Aten"), a new city located at modern Tell el-Amarna, 200 miles north of Thebes.

Akhenaten's attempt at religious change failed. It was too much to ask Egyptians to ignore their traditional ways and beliefs, especially since they saw the destruction of the old gods as subversive of the very cosmic order on which Egypt's survival and continuing prosperity depended. Moreover, the priests at Thebes were unalterably

Louvre, Paris//© Erich Lessing/Art Resource, NY

Nubians in Egypt. During the New Kingdom, Egypt expanded to the north, into Canaan and Syria, and to the south, into the African kingdom of Nubia. Nubia had first emerged as an African kingdom around 2300 B.C.E. Shown here in a fourteenth-century B.C.E. painting from an Egyptian official's tomb in Nubia are Nubians arriving in Egypt with bags and rings of gold. Nubia was a rich source of gold for the Egyptians.

Opposing VIEWPOINTS

Akhenaten's *Hymn to Aten* and Psalm 104 of the Hebrew Bible

Amenhotep IV, more commonly known as Akhenaten, created a religious upheaval in Egypt by introducing the worship of Aten, god of the sun disk, as the chief god. Akhenaten's reverence for Aten is evident in this hymn. Some authorities have noted a similarity in spirit and wording to the 104th Psalm of the Old Testament. In fact, some scholars have argued that there might be a connection between the two.

Hymn to Aten

Your rays suckle every meadow.
When you rise, they live, they grow for you.
You make the seasons in order to rear all that you have made,
The winter to cool them,
And the heat that they may taste you.
You have made the distant sky in order to rise therein,
In order to see all that you do make.
While you were alone,
Rising in your form as the living Aten,
Appearing, shining, withdrawing or approaching,
You made millions of forms of yourself alone.

Cities, towns, fields, road, and river—
Every eye beholds you over against them,
For you are the Aten of the day over the earth. . . .
The world came into being by your hand,
According as you have made them.
When you have risen they live,
When you set they die.
You are lifetime your own self,
For one lives only through you.
Eyes are fixed on beauty until you set.
All work is laid aside when you set in the west.
But when you rise again,
Everything is made to flourish for the king . . .
Since you did found the earth
And raise them up for your son,
Who came forth from your body: the King of Upper and Lower Egypt, . . . Akh-en-Aten, . . . and the
Chief Wife of the King . . . Nefert-iti, living and youthful forever and ever.

Psalm 104:19–25, 27–30

The moon marks off the seasons,
and the sun knows when to go down.

You bring darkness, it becomes night,
and all the beasts of the forest prowl.

The lions roar for their prey
and seek their food from God.

The sun rises, and they steal away;
they return and lie down in their dens.

Then man goes out to his work,
to his labor until evening.

How many are your works, O Lord!
In wisdom you made them all;
the earth is full of your creatures.

There is the sea, vast and spacious,
teeming with creatures beyond number—
living things both large and small. . . .

These all look to you
to give them their food at the proper time.

When you give it to them,
they gather it up;
when you open your hand,
they are satisfied with good things.

When you hide your face,
they are terrified;
when you take away their breath,
they die and return to the dust.

When you send your Spirit,
they are created,
and you renew the face of the earth.

Q What similarities do you see between Akhenaten's *Hymn to Aten* and Psalm 104 of the Hebrew Bible? How do you explain the similarities? What significant differences do you find between the two, and what do they tell you about the differences between the religion of the Egyptians and the religion of ancient Israel?

opposed to the changes, which diminished their influence and power. At the same time, Akhenaten's preoccupation with religion caused him to ignore foreign affairs and led to the loss of both Syria and Canaan. Akhenaten's changes were soon undone after his death by those who influenced his successor, the boy-pharaoh Tutankhamun (toot-ahng-KAH-muhn) (1347–1338 B.C.E.). Tutankhamun returned the government to Thebes and restored the old gods. The Aten experiment had failed to take hold, and the eighteenth dynasty itself came to an end with the rise to

CHRONOLOGY The Egyptians

Early Dynastic Period (dynasties 1–2)	c. 3100–2686 B.C.E.
Old Kingdom (dynasties 3–6)	c. 2686–2181 B.C.E.
First Intermediate Period (dynasties 7–10)	c. 2180–2055 B.C.E.
Middle Kingdom (dynasties 11–12)	c. 2055–1650 B.C.E.
Second Intermediate Period (dynasties 13–17)	c. 1650–1550 B.C.E.
New Kingdom (dynasties 18–20)	c. 1550–1070 B.C.E.
Postempire Egypt (dynasties 21–31)	1070–30 B.C.E.

power of a military officer and vizier, Horemhab, who assumed the kingship in 1333 B.C.E.

THE END OF THE EMPIRE The nineteenth dynasty managed to restore Egyptian power one more time. Under Ramesses (RAM-uh-seez) II (c. 1279–1213 B.C.E.), the Egyptians regained control of Canaan but were unable to reestablish the borders of their earlier empire. New invasions in the thirteenth century by the "Sea Peoples," as the Egyptians called them, destroyed Egyptian power in Canaan and drove the Egyptians back within their old frontiers. The days of Egyptian empire were ended, and the New Kingdom itself expired with the twentieth dynasty in 1070 B.C.E. For the next thousand years, despite periodic revivals of strength, Egypt was dominated by Libyans, Nubians, Assyrians, Persians, and finally Macedonians after the conquest of Alexander the Great (see Chapter 4). In the first century B.C.E., Egypt became a province in Rome's mighty empire.

Daily Life in Ancient Egypt

Ancient Egyptians had a very positive attitude toward daily life on earth and followed the advice of the wisdom literature, which suggested that people marry young and establish a home and family. Monogamy was the general rule, although a husband was allowed to keep additional wives if his first wife was childless. Pharaohs were entitled to harems; the queen was acknowledged, however, as the Great Wife, with a status higher than that of the other wives. The husband was master in the house, but wives were very much respected and in charge of the household and education of the children (see the box on p. 27). From a book of wise sayings (which the Egyptians called "instructions") came this advice:

> If you are a man of standing, you should found your household and love your wife at home as is fitting. Fill her belly; clothe her back. Ointment is the prescription for her body. Make her heart glad as long as you live. She is a profitable field for her lord. You should not contend with her at law, and keep her far from gaining control.... Let her heart be soothed through what may accrue to you; it means keeping her long in your house.[17]

Women's property and inheritances remained in their hands, even in marriage. Although most careers and public offices were closed to women, some women did operate businesses. Peasant women worked long hours in the fields and at numerous domestic tasks, especially weaving cloth. Upper-class women could function as priestesses, and a few queens even became pharaohs in their own right. Most famous was Hatshepsut (hat-SHEP-soot) in the New Kingdom. She initially served as regent for her stepson Thutmosis III but assumed the throne for herself and remained in power until her death.

Hatshepsut's reign was a prosperous one, as is especially evident in her building activity. She is most famous for the temple dedicated to herself at Deir el Bahri on the west bank of the Nile at Thebes. As pharaoh, Hatshepsut sent out military expeditions, encouraged mining, fostered agriculture, and sent a trading expedition up the Nile. Hatshepsut's official statues sometimes show her clothed and bearded like a king. She was addressed as "His Majesty." That Hatshepsut was aware of her unusual position is evident from

Statue of Hatshepsut. Wife of Thutmosis II, Hatshepsut served as regent for her stepson Thutmosis III after her husband's death. In 1473 B.C.E., however, she proclaimed herself pharaoh: "I myself am a god. That which happens is meant. Nothing I say is erroneous." Numerous statues of her were constructed at the temple dedicated to her at Deir el Bahri. Many of them were shattered after her death by her stepson. This red granite statue of Hatshepsut, pieced together from fragments, shows her as a man, dressed in the royal male headdress and bearded like a king. She is seen kneeling, making an offering to the sun god.

Respect for Women

Because of the high infant and child mortality rate, women were considered important for their role as childbearers and hence due respect. Any, a scribe at the court of Nefertari, one of the wives of Ramesses II, provided this advice concerning women to a young man around 1270 B.C.E.

Any, *Advice to a Young Man Concerning Women*

Beware of the woman who is a stranger, who is not known in her town. Do not stare at her as she passes by and do not have intercourse with her. A woman who is away from her husband is a deep water whose course is unknown.

Take a wife while you're young,
That she make a son for you;
She should bear for you while you're youthful.
It is proper to make people.
Happy the man whose people are many.
He is saluted on account of his progeny.

Do not control your wife in her house,
When you know she is efficient;
Don't say to her: "Where is it?" "Get it!"
When she has put it in the right place.
Let your eye observe her in silence,
Then you will recognize her skill;
It is a joy when your hand is with her,
There are many who don't know this.

Q What does this advice to a young man reveal about the circumstances of upper-class Egyptian women?

an inscription she had placed on one of her temples. It read: "Now my heart turns to and fro, in thinking what will the people say, they who shall see my monument in after years, and shall speak of what I have done."

Marriages were arranged by parents. The primary concerns were family and property, and the chief purpose of marriage was to produce children, especially sons (see the box on p. 28). Daughters were not slighted, however. Numerous tomb paintings show the close and affectionate relationship parents had with both sons and daughters. Although marriages were arranged, some of the surviving love poems from ancient Egypt would indicate an element of romance in some marriages. Here is the lament of a lovesick boy for his "sister" (lovers referred to each other as "brother" and "sister," although the practice of brother-sister marriage was probably limited to the Egyptian royal family):

Seven days to yesterday I have not seen the sister,
And a sickness has invaded me;
My body has become heavy,
And I am forgetful of my own self.
If the chief physicians come to me,
My heart is not content with their remedies. . . .
What will revive me is to say to me: "Here she is!"
Her name is what will lift me up. . . .
My health is her coming in from outside:
When I see her, then I am well.[18]

Marriages could and did end in divorce, which was allowed, apparently with compensation for the wife. Adultery, however, was strictly prohibited, and punishments were severe, especially for women, who could have their noses cut off or be burned at the stake.

Under normal circumstances, Egypt was blessed by a material abundance that not only kept its entire population fed but also enabled its upper classes to lead a life of gracious leisure. These wealthy families had attractive homes located on walled estates. Much energy was devoted to the garden, which contained fruit trees and vegetables, as well as tree-lined paths and pools for the family's leisure time.

Tomb paintings indicate that the upper classes participated in numerous banquets where guests were lavishly fed and entertained (see Images of Everyday Life on p. 29). Although some people obviously got drunk, a collection of "instructions" advises more circumspect behavior:

> If you are one of those sitting at the table of one greater than yourself, take what he may give, when it is set before your nose. You should gaze at what is before you. . . . Let your face be cast down until he addresses you, and you should speak only when he addresses you. Laugh after he laughs, and it will be very pleasing to his heart and what you may do will be pleasing to the heart.[19]

The same collection of "instructions" warns that when one has been invited to a party, "beware of approaching the women. It does not go well with the place where that is done."[20]

Entertainment, especially music, was a regular feature of parties. The Egyptians used an astonishing variety of instruments: drums, tambourines, flutes, trumpets, and stringed instruments that were plucked rather than played with a bow. Singers, accompanying themselves on lute or harp, presented songs in praise of the host's generosity and of enjoying life.

Judging from the paintings in their tombs, the upper classes found a myriad of ways to entertain themselves as well. Fowling in the stands of papyrus reeds that grew along the riverbanks was a favorite pastime. Using a reed skiff, the huntsman used a boomerang to bring down his prey, much to the delight of his family, who accompanied him. Once the waterfowl was downed, Egyptian families used trained retriever cats to swim out into the water and bring back the birds. The hunting of animals was only for the men. The hunters rode in chariots and used dogs to

A Father's Advice

Upper-class Egyptians enjoyed compiling collections of wise sayings to provide guidance for leading an upright and successful life. This excerpt is taken from *The Instruction of the Vizier Ptah-hotep* and dates from around 2450 B.C.E. The vizier was the pharaoh's chief official. In this selection, Ptah-hotep advises his son on how to be a successful official.

The Instruction of the Vizier Ptah-hotep

Then he said to his son:

Let not your heart be puffed-up because of your knowledge; be not confident because you are a wise man. Take counsel with the ignorant as well as the wise. The full limits of skill cannot be attained, and there is no skilled man equipped to his full advantage. Good speech is more hidden than the emerald, but it may be found with maidservants at the grindstones....

If you are a leader commanding the affairs of the multitude, seek out for yourself every beneficial deed, until it may be that your own affairs are without wrong. Justice is great, and its appropriateness is lasting; it has been disturbed since the time of him who made it, whereas there is punishment for him who passes over its laws. It is the right path before him who knows nothing. Wrongdoing has never brought its undertaking into port. It may be that it is fraud that gains riches, but the strength of justice is that it lasts....

If you are a man of intimacy, whom one great man sends to another, be thoroughly reliable when he sends you. Carry out the errand for him as he has spoken. Do not be reserved about what is said to you, and beware of any act of forgetfulness. Grasp hold of truth, and do not exceed it. Mere gratification is by no means to be repeated. Struggle against making words worse, thus making one great man hostile to another through vulgar speech....

If you are a man of standing and found a household and produce a son who is pleasing to god, if he is correct and inclines toward your ways and listens to your instruction, while his manners in your house are fitting, and if he takes care of your property as it should be, seek out for him every useful action. He is your son,... you should not cut your heart off from him.

But a man's seed often creates enmity. If he goes astray and transgresses your plans and does not carry out your instruction, so that his manners in your household are wretched, and he rebels against all that you say, while his mouth runs on in the most wretched talk, quite apart from his experience, while he possesses nothing, you should cast him off: he is not your son at all. He was not really born to you. Thus, you enslave him entirely according to his own speech. He is one whom god has condemned in the very womb.

Q According to this document, what social and political skills were prized by members of the Egyptian governing elite? What does the passage reveal about Egyptian bureaucrats?

pursue antelope, gazelles, and other creatures who were shot with bows and arrows. Indoor activities included board games among other things. The earliest known board games in the world have been found in Egyptian tombs. Many are made of wood decorated with ivory or ebony. The games played on them involved moving pieces on the boards according to the roll of the dice.

On the Fringes of Civilization

Q **Focus Question**: What is the significance of the Indo-European-speaking peoples?

Our story of the beginnings of Western civilization has been dominated so far by Mesopotamia and Egypt. But significant developments were also taking place on the fringes of these civilizations. Farming had spread into the Balkan peninsula of Europe by 6500 B.C.E., and by 4000 B.C.E. it was well established in southern France, central Europe, and the coastal regions of the Mediterranean. Although migrating farmers from the Near East may have brought some farming techniques into Europe, historians now believe that the Neolithic peoples of Europe domesticated animals and began to farm largely on their own.

One outstanding feature of late Neolithic Europe was the building of megalithic structures. *Megalith* is Greek for "large stone." Radiocarbon dating, a technique that allows scientists to determine the age of objects, shows that the first megalithic structures were built around 4000 B.C.E., more than a thousand years before the great pyramids were built in Egypt. Between 3200 and 1500 B.C.E., standing stones placed in circles or lined up in rows were erected throughout the British Isles and

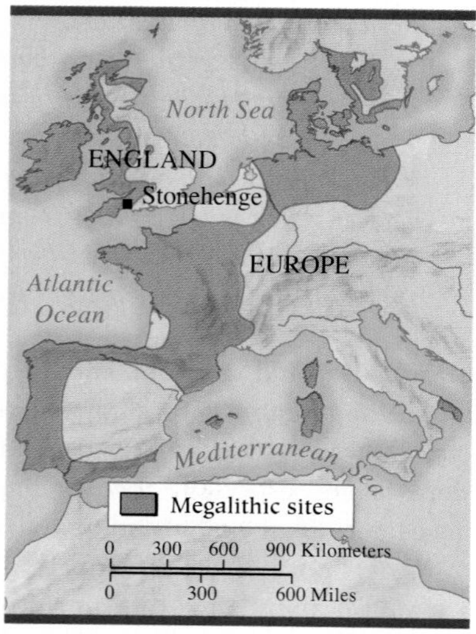

Stonehenge and Other Megalithic Sites in Europe

The Egyptian Diet

The diets of the upper and lower classes in ancient Egypt differed considerably. Various types of meat and fowl, including beef, goat, pork, goose, and pigeon, were on the tables of the rich. Fish was also an important part of the upper-class Egyptian diet. Although done for sport as well as food, hunting waterfowl in the stands of papyrus reeds that grew along the river's banks was a favorite pastime of the Egyptian upper classes. Shown on the left below is a hunting scene from the eighteenth-dynasty tomb of Nebamun in Thebes. Nebamun, a nobleman, is seen standing in his boat using his throwstick to hunt birds. He holds three birds in his right hand while a cat retrieves two in its claws and holds the wings of another in its teeth.

The basic diet of the poor consisted chiefly of bread, beer made from barley, and onions. The baking of bread was an important task in all households. The tomb painting on the lower right from the eighteenth-dynasty tomb of Mennah shows two men carrying grain while slave girls fight over leftovers in the background.

Vegetables and fruits were also part of the Egyptian diet. Among the vegetables were lettuce, radishes, squash, and cucumbers. Fruits included figs, dates, and grapes, which were mainly used by the upper classes for making wine. The third illustration shows peasants harvesting grapes from grapevines that have been attached to a trellis. Both sweet and dry wines were produced from a variety of dark and pale grapes.

Tombs of the Nobles, Thebes//© Erich Lessing/Art Resource, NY

British Museum, London//© Werner Forman/Art Resource, NY

Tombs of the Nobles, Thebes//© Erich Lessing/Art Resource, NY

northwestern France. Other megalithic constructions have been found as far north as Scandinavia and as far south as the islands of Corsica, Sardinia, and Malta. Some archaeologists have demonstrated that the stone circles were used as observatories to detect not only such simple astronomical phenomena as the midwinter and midsummer sunrises but also such sophisticated observations as the major and minor standstills of the moon.

By far the most famous of these megalithic constructions is Stonehenge in England. Stonehenge consists of a series of concentric rings of standing stones. Its construction sometime between 2100 and 1900 B.C.E. was no small accomplishment. The eighty bluestones used at Stonehenge weigh 4 tons each and were transported to the site from their original source 135 miles away. Like other megalithic structures, Stonehenge indicates a remarkable awareness of astronomy on the part of its builders, as well as an impressive coordination of workers.

The Impact of the Indo-Europeans

For many historians, both the details of construction and the purpose of the megalithic structures of Europe remain a mystery. Also puzzling is the role of the Indo-European people. The term *Indo-European* refers to people who used a language derived from a single parent tongue. Indo-European languages include Greek, Latin, Persian, Sanskrit, and the Germanic languages (see Table 1.2). It has been suggested that the original Indo-European-speaking peoples were based somewhere in the steppe region north of the Black Sea or in southwestern Asia, in modern Iran or Afghanistan. Although there had been earlier migrations, around 2000 B.C.E. they began major nomadic movements into Europe (including present-day Italy and Greece), India, and the Near East. The Indo-Europeans who moved into Asia Minor and Anatolia (modern Turkey) coalesced with the native peoples to form the first Hittite kingdom, known as the Old Kingdom (c. 1700–1400 B.C.E.), with its capital at Hattusas (Bogazkoy in modern Turkey).

The Hittite Empire

The Hittites began to spread outward around 1600 B.C.E., but it was not until around two hundred years later that a new line of kings created the Hittite New Kingdom or Hittite empire. Especially notable was Suppiluliumas (suh-PIL-oo-LEE-uh-muss) I (c. 1370–1330 B.C.E.), one of the strongest rulers of the era, who established Hittite control from western Turkey to northern Syria. He destroyed the power of the Mitanni kingdom, which had been established in the sixteenth century B.C.E. by a people known as the Hurrians from the mountainous northern border of Mesopotamia. Suppiluliumas formed an alliance with the Egyptians and then conquered Syria. The Hittites were the first of the Indo-European peoples to make use of iron, enabling them to construct weapons that were stronger and cheaper to make because of the widespread availability of iron ore.

© Adam Woolfitt/CORBIS

Stonehenge. The Bronze Age in northwestern Europe is known for its megaliths, large standing stones. Between 3200 and 1500 B.C.E., standing stones that were placed in circles or lined up in rows were erected throughout the British Isles and northwestern France. By far the most famous of these megalithic constructions is Stonehenge in England.

TABLE 1.2 Some Indo-European Languages

SUBFAMILY	LANGUAGES
Indo-Iranian	*Sanskrit,* Persian
Balto-Slavic	Russian, Serbo-Croatian, Czech, Polish, Lithuanian
Hellenic	Greek
Italic	*Latin,* Romance languages (French, Italian, Spanish, Portuguese, Romanian)
Celtic	Irish, Gaelic
Germanic	Swedish, Danish, Norwegian, German, Dutch, English

NOTE: Languages in italic type are no longer spoken.

For the next hundred years, the Hittites were in conflict with Egypt until the Egyptian pharaoh Ramesses II made a remarkable nonaggression treaty that stabilized relations between Egypt and the Hittites. The end of Hittite power came in part from internal problems but also as a result of attacks by the Sea Peoples from the west around 1200 B.C.E. and by a group of aggressive tribespeople known as the Gasga, who raided Hittite cities. By 1190 B.C.E., Hittite power had come to an end.

During its heyday, however, the Hittite empire was one of the great powers in western Asia. The Hittite ruler, known as the "Great King," controlled the core areas of the kingdom, but in western and southern Anatolia and Syria, he allowed local rulers to swear allegiance to him as his vassals. Constant squabbling over succession to the throne, however, tended to weaken the royal authority at times.

During its height, the Hittite empire also demonstrated an interesting ability to assimilate other cultures into its own. In language, literature, art, law, and religion, the Hittites borrowed much from Mesopotamia as well as from the native peoples they had subdued. Their law code, for example, though less harsh, reflected the influence of Mesopotamia. Hittite religion combined Indo-European deities and Mesopotamian gods, such as An and Ishtar. Recent scholarship has stressed the important role of the Hittites in transmitting Mesopotamian culture, as they transformed it, to later Western civilizations in the Mediterranean area, especially to the Mycenaean Greeks (see Chapter 3).

CHAPTER SUMMARY

Humanlike creatures first emerged in Africa more than 3 to 4 million years ago. Over a long period of time, Paleolithic people learned how to create more sophisticated tools, to use fire, and to adapt to and even change their physical environment. Paleolithic people were primarily nomads, who hunted animals and gathered wild plants for survival. Nevertheless, they created a culture that included sophisticated cave paintings.

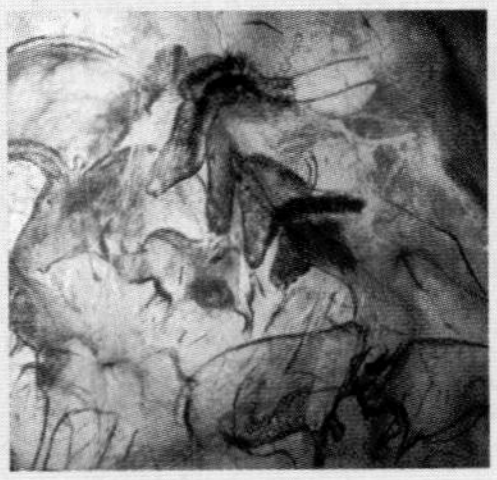

The agricultural revolution of the Neolithic Age, which began around 10,000 B.C.E., dramatically changed human patterns of living. The growing of food on a regular basis and the taming of animals made it possible for humans to stop their nomadic ways and settle in more permanent settlements. These organized communities gradually gave rise to more complex human societies.

These more complex human societies, which we call the first civilizations, emerged around 3000 B.C.E. in the river valleys of Mesopotamia, Egypt, India, and China. An increase in food production in these regions led to a significant growth in human population and the rise of cities. Efforts to control the flow of water for farming also led to organized governments in these new urban civilizations.

The peoples of Southwest Asia and Egypt laid the foundations of Western civilization. They developed cities and struggled with the problems of organized states as they moved from individual communities to larger territorial units and eventually to empires. They invented writing to keep records and created literature. They constructed monumental buildings to please their gods, give witness to their power, and preserve their culture. They developed new political, military, social, and religious structures to deal with the basic problems of human existence and organization. These first civilizations left detailed records that allow us to view how they grappled with three of the fundamental problems that humans have pondered: the nature of human relationships, the nature of the universe, and the role of divine forces in that cosmos. Although later people would provide different answers from those of the Mesopotamians and Egyptians, it was they who first posed the questions, gave answers, and wrote them down.

By the middle of the second millennium B.C.E., much of the creative impulse of the Mesopotamian and Egyptian civilizations was beginning to wane. As we shall see in Chapter 2, by 1200 B.C.E. a whole new pattern of petty states and new kingdoms would lead to the largest empires the ancient Near East had seen.

CHAPTER TIMELINE

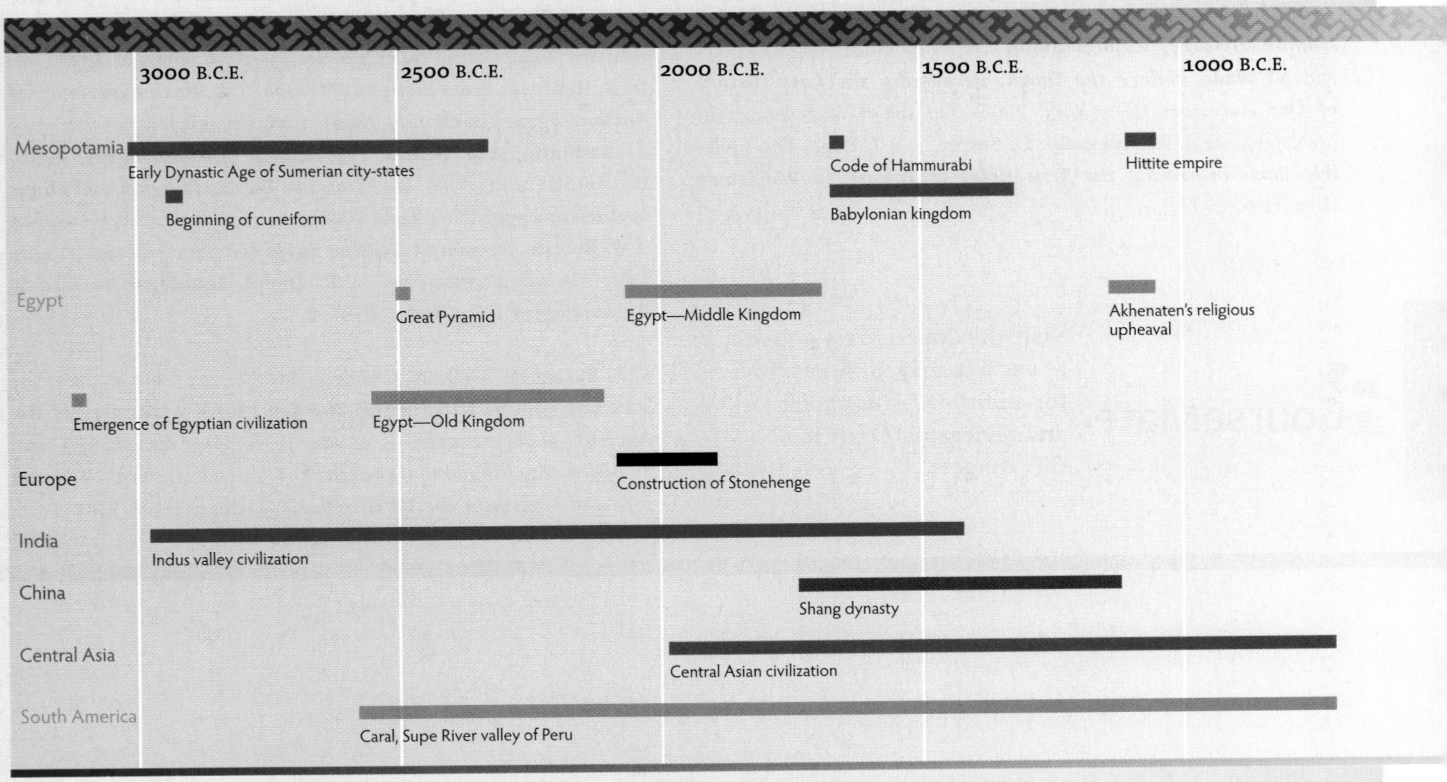

Upon Reflection

Q What achievements did early humans make during the Paleolithic and Neolithic Ages, and how did those achievements eventually make possible the emergence of civilization?

Q What roles did geography, environmental conditions, religion, politics, economics, and women and families play in the civilizations of Southwest Asia and Egypt?

Q What do you think Western civilization has derived from the civilizations of the ancient Near East?

Key Terms

Paleolithic Age (p. 3)
Neolithic Revolution (p. 4)
civilization (p. 5)
Mesopotamia (p. 7)
ziggurat (p. 8)
theocracy (p. 8)
polytheistic (p. 13)
divination (p. 13)
cuneiform (p. 13)
hieroglyphics (p. 23)

Suggestions for Further Reading

THE PREHISTORIC WORLD For a brief but sound survey, see **I. Tattersall, *The World from Beginnings to 4000 B.C.E.*** (Oxford, 2008). The following works are also of considerable value in examining the prehistory of humankind: **B. Fagan, *People of the Earth: An Introduction to World Prehistory,*** 12th ed. (New York, 2006); **S. Mithen, *After the Ice: A Global Human History, 20,000–5000 B.C.*** (Cambridge, Mass., 2006); and **N. Wade, *Before the Dawn: Recovering the Lost History of Our Ancestors*** (New York, 2006). On the role of women in prehistory, see **J. M. Adovasio, O. Soffer,** and **J. Page, *The Invisible Sex: Uncovering the True Roles of Women in Prehistory*** (New York, 2007).

Visit the CourseMate website at www.cengagebrain.com for additional study tools and review materials for this chapter.

THE ANCIENT NEAR EAST An excellent reference tool on the ancient Near East can be found in **P. Bienkowski** and **A. Milward, eds., *Dictionary of the Ancient Near East*** (Philadelphia, 2000). For a detailed survey, see **A. Kuhrt, *The Ancient Near East, c. 3000–330 B.C.,*** 2 vols. (London, 1995). A brief recent survey can be found in **M. van de Mieroop, *A History of the Ancient Near East, ca. 3000–323 B.C.,*** 2nd ed. (Oxford, 2006). **H. W. F. Saggs, *Babylonians*** (Norman, Okla., 1995), and **G. Leick, *The Babylonians*** (London, 2003), provide an overview of the peoples of ancient Mesopotamia. On the economic and social history of the ancient Near East, see **D. C. Snell, *Life in the Ancient Near East*** (New Haven, Conn., 1997).

ANCIENT MESOPOTAMIA A beautifully illustrated survey of ancient Mesopotamia can be found in **M. Roaf, *Cultural Atlas of Mesopotamia and the Ancient Near East*** (New York, 1996). The world of the Sumerians is examined in **H. Crawford, *Sumer and the Sumerians,*** 2nd ed. (Cambridge, 2004). On the spiritual perspective of ancient Mesopotamia, see **J. Bottéro, *Religion in Ancient Mesopotamia*** (Chicago, 2001). For works on daily life, see **S. Bertman, *Handbook to Life in Ancient Mesopotamia*** (New York, 2003), and **J. Bottéro, *Everyday Life in Ancient Mesopotamia*** (Baltimore, 2001).

ANCIENT EGYPT For a good introduction to ancient Egypt, see the beautifully illustrated works by **D. P. Silverman, ed., *Ancient Egypt*** (New York, 1997); **T. G. H. James, *Ancient Egypt*** (Ann Arbor, Mich., 2005); and **M. Millman, *Imagining Egypt*** (New York, 2007). Other general surveys include **I. Shaw, ed., *The Oxford History of Ancient Egypt*** (New York, 2000); **N. Grant, *The Egyptians*** (New York, 1996); and **D. J. Brewer, *Ancient Egypt: Foundations of a Civilization*** (New York, 2005), on Egypt before the period of the Old Kingdom. On the interaction of the Egyptians with the Nubians and other peoples in Africa south of Egypt, see **D. B. Redford, *From Slave to Pharaoh: The Black Experience of Ancient Egypt*** (Baltimore, 2004). Egyptian religion is covered in **J. Assmann, *The Search for God in Ancient Egypt,*** trans. **D. Lorton** (Ithaca, N.Y., 2001), and **R. David, *Religion and Magic in Ancient Egypt*** (New York, 2002). An important study on women is **G. Robins, *Women in Ancient Egypt*** (Cambridge, Mass., 1993). Daily life can be examined in **R. David, *Handbook to Life in Ancient Egypt*** (New York, 1998).

SEA PEOPLES AND HITTITES On the Sea Peoples, see the standard work by **N. Sandars, *The Sea Peoples: Warriors of the Ancient Mediterranean*** (London, 1978). On the Hittites, see **T. Bryce, *The Kingdom of the Hittites,*** 2nd ed. (Oxford, 2006) and ***Life and Society in the Hittite World*** (Oxford, 2002).

CHAPTER 2

Vatican Palace, Vatican State//© Scala/Art Resource, NY

The judgment of Solomon as painted by Raphael in the sixteenth century

The Ancient Near East: Peoples and Empires

CHAPTER OUTLINE AND FOCUS QUESTIONS

The Hebrews: "The Children of Israel"

Q How did the Israelites establish a united state, and what become of it? In what ways was the Jewish faith unique in the ancient Near East, and how did it evolve over time?

The Neighbors of the Israelites

Q Who were the neighbors of the Israelites, and what was their significance?

The Assyrian Empire

Q What methods and institutions did the Assyrians use to amass and maintain their empire?

The Neo-Babylonian Empire

Q What was the significance of the Neo-Babylonian Empire?

The Persian Empire

Q What methods and institutions did the Persians use to amass and maintain their empire, and how did these methods and institutions differ from those of the Assyrians?

CRITICAL THINKING

Q What is the relationship between the political history of the Israelites and the evolution of their religious beliefs?

AROUND 970 B.C.E., Solomon came to the throne of Israel, a small state in western Asia. He was lacking in military prowess but excelled in many other ways. Through trade and a series of foreign alliances, he created a strong, flourishing state. But he was especially famed for another of his qualities. When confronted with two women who each claimed that the child before them was her natural child, Solomon ordered his servant to cut the child in half and give half to each woman. The first woman cried out, "Please, my lord, give her the living baby! Don't kill him!" The second woman replied, "Neither I nor you shall have him. Cut him in two!" Then Solomon rendered his judgment: "Give the living baby to the first woman. Do not kill him; she is his mother." According to the biblical account, "when all Israel heard the verdict the king had given, they held the king in awe, because they saw that he had wisdom from God to administer justice." After Solomon's death, Israel began to disintegrate. But how had such a small nation been able to survive for as long as it did in a Near East dominated by mighty empires?

The destruction of the Hittite kingdom and the weakening of Egypt around 1200 B.C.E. temporarily left a power vacuum in the Near East, allowing a patchwork of petty kingdoms and city-states to emerge, especially in Syria and Canaan. One of these small states, the nation of Israel, has played a role in Western civilization completely disproportionate to its size. The Israelites were a minor factor in the politics of the ancient Near East, but their spiritual heritage—the Judeo-Christian values—is one of the basic pillars of Western civilization.

The small states did not last, however. Ever since the first city-states had arisen in the Near East around 3000 B.C.E., there had been a movement toward the creation of larger territorial states with more sophisticated systems of control. This process reached a high point in the first millennium B.C.E. with the appearance of empires that embraced the entire Near East. Between 1000 and 500 B.C.E., the Assyrians, Chaldeans, and Persians all created empires that encompassed most or all of the ancient Near East. Each had impressive and grandiose capital cities that emphasized the power and wealth of its rulers. Each brought peace and order for a period of time by employing new administrative techniques. Each eventually fell to other conquerors. In the long run, these large empires had less impact on Western civilization than the Hebrew people of Israel did. In human history, the power of ideas is often more significant than the power of empires.

The Hebrews: "The Children of Israel"

Focus Questions: How did the Israelites establish a united state, and what became of it? In what ways was the Jewish faith unique in the ancient Near East, and how did it evolve over time?

The Hebrews were a Semitic-speaking people who had a tradition concerning their origins and history that was eventually written down as part of the Hebrew Bible, known to Christians as the Old Testament. Describing themselves originally as nomads organized into clans, the Hebrews' tradition states that they were descendants of the patriarch Abraham, who had migrated from Mesopotamia to the land of Canaan, where they became identified as the "Children of Israel." Again according to tradition, a drought in Canaan caused many Hebrews to migrate to Egypt, where they lived peacefully until they were enslaved by pharaohs who used them as laborers on building projects. They remained in bondage until Moses led his people out of Egypt in the well-known Exodus, which some historians have estimated would have occurred in the first half of the thirteenth century B.C.E. According to the biblical account, the Hebrews then wandered for many years in the desert until they entered Canaan. Organized into twelve tribes, they became embroiled in conflict with the Philistines, a people who had settled in the coastal area of Canaan but were beginning to move into the inland areas.

Many scholars today doubt that the early books of the Hebrew Bible reflect the true history of the early Israelites. They argue that the early books of the Bible, written centuries after the events described, preserve only what the Israelites came to believe about themselves and that recent archaeological evidence often contradicts the details of the biblical account. Some of these scholars have even argued that the Israelites were not nomadic invaders but indigenous peoples in the Canaanite hill country. What is generally agreed, however, is that between 1200 and 1000 B.C.E., the Israelites emerged as a distinct group of people, possibly organized into tribes or a league of tribes, who established a united kingdom known as Israel.

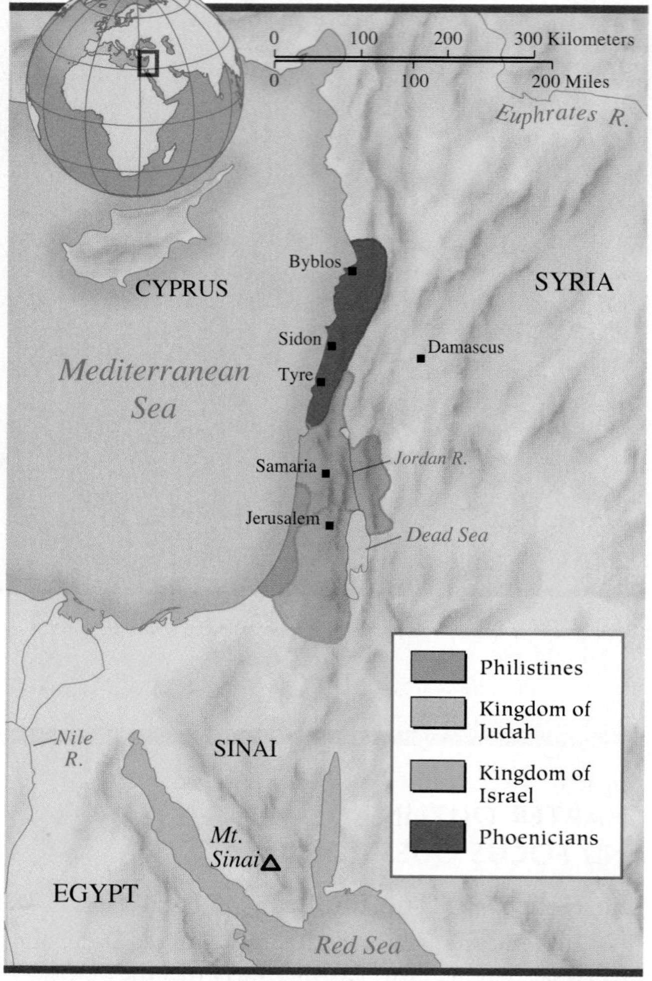

MAP 2.1 The Israelites and Their Neighbors in the First Millennium B.C.E. United under Saul, David, and Solomon, greater Israel split into two states—Israel and Judah—after the death of Solomon. With power divided, the Israelites could not resist invasions that dispersed many Jews from Canaan. Some, such as the "ten lost tribes," never returned. Others were sent to Babylon but were later allowed to return under the rule of the Persians.

Why was Israel more vulnerable to the Assyrian Empire than Judah was?

The United Kingdom

The first king of the Israelites was Saul (c. 1020–1000 B.C.E.), who initially achieved some success in the ongoing struggle with the Philistines. But after his death in a disastrous battle with this enemy, a brief period of anarchy ensued until one of Saul's lieutenants, David (c. 1000–970 B.C.E.), reunited the Israelites, defeated the Philistines, and established control over Canaan (see Map 2.1). According to the biblical account, some of his conquests led to harsh treatment for the conquered people: "David also defeated the Moabites. He made them lie down on the ground and measured them off with a length of cord. Every two lengths of them were put to death, and the third length was allowed to live. So the Moabites became subject to David and brought tribute."[1] Among David's conquests was the city of Jerusalem, which he made the capital of a united kingdom. David centralized Israel's political organization and accelerated the integration of the Israelites into a settled community based on farming and urban life.

SOLOMON David's son Solomon (c. 970–930 B.C.E.) did even more to strengthen royal power. He expanded the political and military establishments and was especially active in extending the trading activities of the Israelites. Solomon is best known for his building projects, of which the most famous was the Temple in Jerusalem. The Israelites viewed the Temple as the symbolic center of their religion and hence of the kingdom of Israel itself. The Temple now housed the Ark of the Covenant, a holy chest containing the sacred relics of the Hebrew religion and, symbolically, the throne of the invisible God of Israel. Under Solomon, ancient Israel was at the height of its power, but his efforts to extend royal power throughout his kingdom led to dissatisfaction among some of his subjects.

British Museum, London//© AAAC/The Bridgeman Art Library

The King of Israel Pays Tribute to the King of Assyria. By the end of the ninth century B.C.E., the kingdom of Israel had been forced to pay tribute to the Assyrian Empire. The Assyrians overran the kingdom in 722 or 721 B.C.E. and destroyed the capital city of Samaria. In this scene from a black obelisk, Jehu, king of Israel, is shown paying tribute to Shalmaneser III, the king of Assyria.

The Divided Kingdom

After Solomon's death, tensions between the northern and southern tribes in Israel led to the establishment of two separate kingdoms—the kingdom of Israel, composed of the ten northern tribes, with its capital eventually at Samaria, and the southern kingdom of Judah, consisting of two tribes, with its capital at Jerusalem. The northern kingdom of Israel, especially under King Ahab (869–850 B.C.E.), joined with some small Syrian states to temporarily stop the onslaught of the Assyrians (uh-SEER-ee-unz), who had consolidated their kingdom to the northeast (see "The Assyrian Empire" later in this chapter). But the power of Israel declined after Ahab, and by the end of the ninth century, the kingdom of Israel was forced to pay tribute to Assyria. In the next century, Israel itself was destroyed. The Assyrians overran the kingdom, destroyed the capital of Samaria in 722 or 721 B.C.E., and deported many Israelites to other parts of the Assyrian Empire. These dispersed Israelites (the "ten lost tribes") merged with neighboring peoples and gradually lost their identity.

British Museum, London//© Erich Lessing/Art Resource, NY

Exiles from Judah. The Assyrians overran the kingdom of Israel in 722 or 721 B.C.E., destroyed the capital city of Samaria, and then began an assault on the kingdom of Judah. In this eighth-century B.C.E. relief from the palace of Sennacherib at Nineveh, captives with baggage are shown on their way into exile, escorted by an Assyrian soldier (third figure from the left), after the Assyrian conquest of the fortified town of Lachish in Judah in 701 B.C.E. The Assyrians failed to take Jerusalem, however, and Judah remained independent, although it was forced to pay tribute to the Assyrians.

CHRONOLOGY The Israelites

Saul—first king	c. 1020–1000 B.C.E.
King David	c. 1000–970 B.C.E.
King Solomon	c. 970–930 B.C.E.
Northern kingdom of Israel destroyed by Assyria	722 or 721 B.C.E.
Southern kingdom of Judah falls to Chaldeans; destruction of Jerusalem	586 B.C.E.
Return of exiles to Jerusalem	538 B.C.E.

The southern kingdom of Judah was also forced to pay tribute to Assyria but managed to survive as an independent state as Assyrian power declined. A new enemy, however, appeared on the horizon. The Chaldeans (kal-DEE-unz) first demolished Assyria and then, under King Nebuchadnezzar (neb-uh-kud-NEZZ-ur) II, conquered Judah and completely destroyed Jerusalem in 586 B.C.E. Many upper-class people from Judah were deported to Babylonia. The memory of their exile is still evoked in the stirring words of Psalm 137:

> *By the rivers of Babylon, we sat and wept when we remembered Zion. . . .*
> *How can we sing the songs of the Lord while in a foreign land?*
> *If I forgot you, O Jerusalem, may my right hand forget its skill*
> *May my tongue cling to the roof of my mouth if I do not remember you, if I do not consider Jerusalem my highest joy.*[2]

But the Babylonian captivity of the people of Judah did not last. Upon the destruction of the Chaldean kingdom by a new set of conquerors, the Persians, the people of Judah were allowed to return to Jerusalem and rebuild their city and the Temple, although Judah remained under Persian control until the conquests of Alexander the Great in the fourth century B.C.E. The people of Judah survived, eventually becoming known as the Jews and giving their name to Judaism, the religion of Yahweh (YAH-way), the Israelite God.

The Spiritual Dimensions of Israel

The spiritual perspective of the Israelites evolved over time. Early Israelites probably worshiped many gods, including nature spirits dwelling in trees and rocks. For some Israelites, Yahweh was the chief god of Israel, but many, including kings of Israel and Judah, worshiped other gods as well. It was among the Babylonian exiles in the sixth century B.C.E. that Yahweh—the God of Israel—came to be seen as the *only* God. After the return of these exiles to Judah, their point of view eventually became dominant, and pure **monotheism,** or the belief that there is only one God for all peoples, came to be the major tenet of Judaism.

"I AM THE LORD YOUR GOD": RULER OF THE WORLD

According to the Jewish conception, there is but one God, whom the Jews called Yahweh. God is the creator of the world and everything in it. To the Jews, the gods of all other peoples were merely idols. The Jewish God ruled the world; he was subject to nothing. All peoples were his servants, whether they knew it or not. This God was also transcendent. He had created nature but was not in nature. The stars, moon, rivers, wind, and other natural phenomena were not divinities or suffused with divinity, as other peoples of the ancient Near East believed, but were God's handiwork. All of God's creations could be admired for their awesome beauty but not worshiped as gods.

This omnipotent creator of the universe was not removed from the life he had created, however, but was a just and good God who expected goodness from his people. If they did not obey his will, they would be punished. But he was also a God of mercy and love: "The Lord is gracious and compassionate, slow to anger and rich in love. The Lord is good to all; he has compassion on all he has made."[3] Despite the powerful dimensions of God as creator and sustainer of the universe, the Jewish message also emphasized that each person could have a personal relationship with this powerful being. As the psalmist sang: "My help comes from the Lord, the Maker of heaven and earth. He will not let your foot slip—he who watches over you will not slumber."[4]

The chief source of information about Israel's spiritual conceptions is the Hebrew Bible, which is the Old Testament of the Christian Bible. Its purpose was to teach the essential beliefs about the God of Israel after the Babylonian captivity of the Jews and their dispersal. During and after the Babylonian exile, the Jews recorded many of their traditions in order to preserve their identity. These writings became the core of the Hebrew Bible. The first five books, known as the **Pentateuch** (PEN-tuh-took), which cover the time from the beginning of the world until the Israelites' arrival in Canaan, constitute the **Torah** (TOR-uh), or law code, governing the lives of worshipers and their relations to one another and to the non-Jewish population. The Hebrew Bible focuses on one basic theme: the necessity for the Jews to obey their God.

"YOU ONLY HAVE I CHOSEN": COVENANT AND LAW

Three aspects of the Jewish religious tradition had special significance: the covenant, the law, and the prophets. The Israelites believed that during the Exodus from Egypt, when Moses supposedly led his people out of bondage into a land of plenty promised to them by Yahweh, a special event occurred that determined the Jewish experience for all time. According to tradition, God entered into a covenant or contract with the tribes of Israel, who believed that Yahweh had spoken to them through Moses (see the box on p. 37). The Israelites promised to

The Covenant and the Law: The Book of Exodus

According to the biblical account, it was during the Exodus from Egypt that the Israelites supposedly made their covenant with Yahweh. They agreed to obey their God and follow his law. In return, Yahweh promised to take special care of his chosen people. These selections from the Book of Exodus describe the making of the covenant and God's commandments to the Israelites.

Exodus 19:1–8

In the third month after the Israelites left Egypt—on the very day—they came to the Desert of Sinai. After they set out from Rephidim, they entered the Desert of Sinai, and Israel camped there in the desert in front of the mountain. Then Moses went up to God, and the Lord called to him from the mountain, and said, "This is what you are to say to the house of Jacob and what you are to tell the people of Israel: 'You yourselves have seen what I did to Egypt, and how I carried you on eagles' wings and brought you to myself. Now if you obey me fully and keep my covenant, then out of all nations you will be my treasured possession. Although the whole earth is mine, you will be for me a kingdom of priests and a holy nation.' These are the words you are to speak to the Israelites." So Moses went back and summoned the elders of the people and set before them all the words the Lord had commanded him to speak. The people all responded together, "We will do everything the Lord has said." So Moses brought their answer back to the Lord.

Exodus 20:1–17

And God spoke all these words, "I am the Lord your God, who brought you out of Egypt, out of the land of slavery. You shall have no other gods before me. You shall not make for yourself an idol in the form of anything in heaven above or on the earth beneath or in the waters below. You shall not bow down to them or worship them; for I, the Lord your God, am a jealous God, punishing the children for the sin of the fathers to the third and fourth generation of those who hate me, but showing love to a thousand generations of those who love me and keep my commandments. You shall not misuse the name of the Lord your God, for the Lord will not hold anyone guiltless who misuses his name. Remember the Sabbath day by keeping it holy. Six days you shall labor and do all your work, but the seventh day is a Sabbath to the Lord your God. On it you shall not do any work, neither you, nor your son or daughter, nor your manservant or maidservant, nor your animals, nor the alien within your gates. For in six days the Lord made the heavens and the earth, the sea, and all that is in them, but he rested on the seventh day. Therefore the Lord blessed the Sabbath day and made it holy. Honor your father and your mother, so that you may live long in the land the Lord your God is giving you. You shall not murder. You shall not commit adultery. You shall not steal. You shall not give false testimony against your neighbor. You shall not covet your neighbor's house. You shall not covet your neighbor's wife, or his manservant or maidservant, his ox or donkey, or anything that belongs to your neighbor."

Q What was the nature of the covenant between Yahweh and the Israelites? What was its moral significance for the Israelites? How does it differ from Hammurabi's code, and how might you explain those differences?

obey Yahweh and follow his law. In return, Yahweh promised to take special care of his people, "a peculiar treasure unto me above all people."

This covenant between Yahweh and his chosen people could be fulfilled, however, only by obedience to the law of God. Law became a crucial element of the Jewish world and had a number of different dimensions. In some instances, it set forth specific requirements, such as payments for offenses. Most important, since the major characteristic of God was his goodness, ethical concerns stood at the center of the law. Sometimes these took the form of specific standards of moral behavior: "You shall not murder. You shall not commit adultery. You shall not steal."[5] But these concerns were also expressed in decrees that regulated the economic, social, religious, and political life of the community, for God's laws of morality applied to all areas of life. These laws made no class distinctions and emphasized the protection of the poor, widows, orphans, and slaves.

THE PROPHETS The Israelites believed that certain religious leaders or holy men, called prophets, were sent by God to serve as his voice to his people. In the ninth century B.C.E., the prophets were particularly vociferous about the tendency of the Israelites to accept other gods, chiefly the fertility and earth gods of other peoples in Canaan. They warned of the terrible retribution that Yahweh would exact from the Israelites if they did not keep the covenant to remain faithful to him alone and just in their dealings with one another (see the box on p. 38).

The golden age of prophecy began in the mid-eighth century and continued during the time when the people of Israel and Judah were threatened by Assyrian and Chaldean conquerors. These "men of God" went through the land warning the Israelites that they had failed to keep God's commandments and would be punished for breaking the covenant: "I will punish you for all your iniquities." Amos prophesied the fall of the northern kingdom

The Hebrew Prophets: Micah, Isaiah, and Amos

The Hebrew prophets warned the Israelites that they must obey God's commandments or face punishment for breaking their covenant with God. These selections from the prophets Micah, Isaiah, and Amos make clear that God would punish the Israelites for their sins. Even the Assyrians, as Isaiah indicated, would be used as God's instrument to punish them.

Micah 6:9–16

Listen! The Lord is calling to the city—and to fear your name is wisdom—"Heed the rod and the One who appointed it. Am I still to forget, O wicked house, your ill-gotten treasures . . . ? Shall I acquit a man with dishonest scales, with a bag of false weights? Her rich men are violent; her people are liars and their tongues speak deceitfully. Therefore, I have begun to destroy you, to ruin you because of your sins. You will eat but not be satisfied; your stomach will still be empty. You will store up but save nothing, because what you save I will give to the sword. You will plant but not harvest; you will press olives but not use the oil on yourselves, you will crush grapes but not drink the wine. . . . Therefore I will give you over to ruin and your people to derision; you will bear the scorn of the nations."

Isaiah 10:1–6

Woe to those who make unjust laws, to those who issue oppressive decrees, to deprive the poor of their rights and withhold justice from the oppressed of my people, making widows their prey and robbing the fatherless. What will you do on the day of reckoning, when disaster comes from afar? To whom will you run for help? Where will you leave your riches? Nothing will remain but to cringe among the captives or fall among the slain. Yet for all this, his anger is not turned away, his hand is still upraised. "Woe to the Assyrian, the rod of my anger, in whose hand is the club of my wrath! I send him against a godless nation, I dispatch him against a people who anger me, to seize loot and snatch plunder, and to trample them down like mud in the streets."

Amos 3:1–2

Hear this word the Lord has spoken against you, O people of Israel—against the whole family I brought up out of Egypt: "You only have I chosen of all the families of the earth; therefore, I will punish you for all your sins."

Q What did the Hebrew prophets see as the chief transgressions of the Hebrew people? What do these selections tell you about the nature of the Hebrews as a "chosen" people?

of Israel to Assyria; twenty years later, Isaiah said the kingdom of Judah too would fall.

Out of the words of the prophets came new concepts that enriched the Jewish tradition and ultimately Western civilization, including a notion of universalism and a yearning for social justice. Although the Jews' religious practices gave them a sense of separateness from other peoples, the prophets transcended this by embracing a concern for all humanity. All nations would someday come to the God of Israel: "All the earth shall worship you." A universal community of all people under God would someday be established by Israel's effort. This vision encompassed the elimination of war and the establishment of peace for all the nations of the world. In the words of the prophet Isaiah: "He will judge between the nations and will settle disputes for many people. They will beat

Hebrew Law. Because of the supposed covenant between Yahweh and the Israelites, law became an important part of Jewish life. Seen here is a twelfth-century manuscript page of the *Mishneh Torah*, a fourteen-volume study of all of Jewish law by Moses Maimonides, the foremost Jewish philosopher of the Middle Ages.

their swords into plowshares and their spears into pruning hooks. Nation will not take up sword against nation, nor will they train for war anymore."[6]

The prophets also cried out against social injustice. They condemned the rich for causing the poor to suffer, denounced luxuries as worthless, and threatened Israel with prophecies of dire punishments for these sins. God's command was to live justly, share with one's neighbors, care for the poor and the unfortunate, and act with compassion. When God's command was not followed, the social fabric of the community was threatened. These proclamations by Israel's prophets became a source for Western ideals of social justice, even if they have never been perfectly realized.

Although the prophets ultimately developed a sense of universalism, the demands of the Jewish religion—the need to obey their God—encouraged a separation between the Jews and their non-Jewish neighbors. Unlike most other peoples of the Near East, Jews could not simply be amalgamated into a community by accepting the gods of their conquerors and their neighbors. To remain faithful to the demands of their God, they might even have to refuse loyalty to political leaders.

The Social Structure of the Hebrews

Originally, the Israelites had been organized along tribal lines, but by the time of the monarchy a new social structure had evolved as the Israelites settled in towns and villages, leaving them with conspicuous "divisions of the population."

SOCIAL PATTERNS The "men of rank and influence" formed a special group of considerable importance in Hebrew society. This group included officials of the king, military officers, civil officials, and governors. Although simply servants to the kings, they held a privileged position in the society at large. The common people, sometimes called "people of the land," remained a body of free people having basic civil rights. Their livelihood came mostly from the land and from various crafts. These peasants and artisans sold their own produce and products directly to buyers in markets in their local town or village squares, thus eliminating intermediaries or traders. There was no real merchant class in ancient Israel. Commerce was carried on by foreigners, such as the Phoenicians. Not until the **Diaspora** (dy-ASS-pur-uh), when Jews became scattered throughout the ancient world after their exile to Babylon, did they become merchants.

FAMILY The family was the central social institution in Hebrew life and consisted of individuals connected by common blood and a common living place. A family living in one house could comprise husband and wife, married sons and their wives, and their children. The Hebrew family was **patriarchal** (pay-tree-AR-kul). The husband-father was master of his wife and possessed absolute authority over his children, including the power of life and death.

MARRIAGE AND WOMEN Marriage was an important aspect of Hebrew family life. In ancient Israel, polygamy was an accepted form of marriage, especially for kings and wealthier citizens. Hebrew law limited kings to eighteen wives and citizens to four. In practice, only kings could afford a large harem. When others had more than one wife, it was usually because they desired more children; the first wife, for example, might be unable to have children or have produced only daughters.

Many Hebrews, however, believed that monogamy was the preferred form of marriage. Wives were honored for their faithfulness and dedication to their husbands. The Book of Proverbs in the Hebrew Bible provides a picture of what Hebrews considered a perfect wife:

> *A wife of noble character who can find? She is worth far more than rubies.*
> *Her husband has full confidence in her and lacks nothing of value.*
> *She brings him good, not harm, all the days of her life.*
> *She selects wool and flax and works with eager hands.*
> *She is like the merchant ships, bringing her food from afar.*
> *She gets up while it is still dark; she provides food for her family and portions for her servant girls.*
> *She considers a field and buys it; out of her earnings she plants a vineyard.*
> *She sets about her work vigorously; her arms are strong for her tasks. . . .*
> *She speaks with wisdom, and faithful instruction is on her tongue.*
> *She watches over the affairs of her household, and does not eat the bread of idleness.*
> *Her children arise and call her blessed; her husband also, and he praises her.*[7]

Women were greatly valued, but their work was obviously never done.

Although the Hebrew Bible, a male-edited work, reveals a society dominated by men, it also includes stories of women who played heroic roles in the early history of Israel. Deborah, for example, played a prominent role in the defeat of the Canaanites at Mount Tabor. After the same battle, Jael killed Sisera, the leader of the Canaanites. According to the Song of Deborah, "Most blessed of women be Jael, . . . most blessed of tent-dwelling women. . . . Her hand reached for the tent peg, her right hand for the workman's hammer. She struck Sisera, she crushed his head, she shattered and pierced his temple. At her feet he sank, he fell; there he lay."[8]

But these accounts are not the norm. In the Hebrew Bible, women are mostly dependent on men. It should not surprise us, then, to learn that a married woman was subject to her husband's authority. A married woman left her parents' home, lived with her husband's family, and became a member of their clan. Her children also belonged to the husband's clan. Since boys and girls were married at a relatively young age, parents took the responsibility for matchmaking. Wives were expected to remain faithful to their husbands, an ideal that would later have an impact on Christian attitudes toward women.

The primary goal of marriage was to produce children. They were the "crown of man," and sons, in particular, were desired. Daughters would eventually leave the family house, but sons carried on the family line. Mothers were in charge of the early education of children, especially in regard to basic moral principles. As boys matured, their fathers took over responsibility for their education, which remained largely informal. This included religious instruction as well as general education for life. The rod was not spared as a matter of principle. Since trades were usually hereditary, fathers also provided their sons' occupational education. As one rabbi (a Jewish teacher) warned, "He who does not teach his son a useful trade is bringing him up to be a thief."[9] Additional education for boys came from priests, whose sacred mission was to instruct people in the Torah. The only education girls received was from their mothers, who taught them the basic fundamentals of how to be good wives, mothers, and housekeepers.

Phoenician Plaque. The Phoenicians, a Semitic-speaking people dwelling in ancient Canaan, became the predominant sea traders of the ancient Near East. Ivory was one of the favorite materials of Phoenician artists of the ninth and eighth centuries B.C.E. This ivory plaque is one of a pair in the classic Phoenician style. It shows a lioness killing a Nubian; in the background are lilies and papyrus flowers.

The Neighbors of the Israelites

Focus Question: Who were the neighbors of the Israelites, and what was their significance?

The Israelites were not the only people living in Canaan. The Philistines, who invaded from the sea, established five towns on the coastal plain of the region. They settled down as farmers and eventually came into conflict with the Israelites. The Phoenicians (fuh-NEE-shunz) had resided in Canaan for some time but now found themselves with a new independence. A Semitic-speaking people, the Phoenicians resided along the Mediterranean coast on a narrow band of land 120 miles long. They had rebuilt their major cities, Byblos, Tyre, and Sidon, after destruction by the Sea Peoples. Their newfound political independence helped the Phoenicians expand the trade that was already the foundation of their prosperity. In fact, Byblos had been the principal distribution center for Egyptian papyrus outside Egypt (the Greek word for book, *biblos*, is derived from the name Byblos).

All three chief cities of Phoenicia were seaports, but they also served as distribution centers for the lands to the east in Mesopotamia. The Phoenicians themselves produced a number of goods for foreign markets, including purple dye, glass, wine, and lumber from the famous cedars of Lebanon. In addition, the Phoenicians improved their ships and became great international sea traders. They charted new routes, not only in the Mediterranean but also in the Atlantic Ocean, where they sailed south along the west coast of Africa. The Phoenicians established a number of colonies in the western Mediterranean, including settlements in southern Spain, Sicily, and Sardinia. Most of the Phoenician colonies were trading stations, not permanent settlements. A major exception was Carthage, the Phoenicians' most famous colony, located on the North African coast.

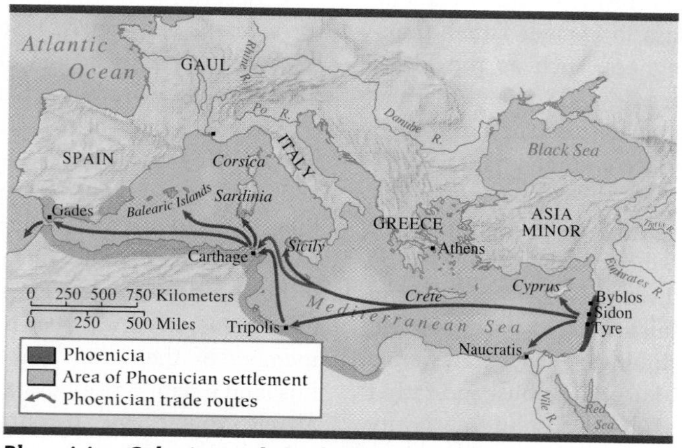

Phoenician Colonies and Trade Routes, c. 800 B.C.E.

Culturally, the Phoenicians are best known as transmitters. Instead of using pictographs or signs to represent whole words and syllables as the Mesopotamians and Egyptians did, the Phoenicians simplified their writing by using twenty-two different signs to represent the sounds of their speech. These twenty-two characters or letters could be used to spell out all the words in the Phoenician language. Although the Phoenicians were not the only people to invent an alphabet, theirs would have special significance because it was eventually passed on to the Greeks. From the Greek alphabet was derived the Roman alphabet that we still use today (see Table 2.1). The Phoenicians achieved much while independent, but they ultimately fell subject to the Assyrians, Chaldeans, and Persians.

TABLE 2.1 A Comparison of the Phoenician, Greek, and Latin Alphabets (Letters A–F)

Phoenician			Greek			Latin	
Phoenician	*Phoenician Name*	*Modern Symbol*	*Early Greek*	*Classical Greek*	*Greek Name*	*Early Latin*	*Classical Latin*
𐤀	'aleph	'	Α	Α	alpha	A	A
𐤁	beth	b	Β	Β	beta		B
𐤂	gimel	g	Γ	Γ	gamma		C
𐤃	daleth	d	Δ	Δ	delta	D	D
𐤄	he	h	Ε	Ε	epsilon	E	E
𐤅	waw	w	Ϝ		digamma	F	F

SOURCE: Andrew Robinson, *The Story of Writing* (London: Thames & Hudson, 1995), p. 170.

The Assyrian Empire

FOCUS QUESTION: What methods and institutions did the Assyrians use to amass and maintain their empire?

Independent states in Canaan flourished in the power void that followed the destruction of the Hittite kingdom and the weakening of the Egyptian empire. But this state of affairs did not last; new empires soon came to dominate vast stretches of the ancient Near East. The first of these empires emerged in Assyria, an area whose location on the upper Tigris River brought it into both cultural and political contact with southern Mesopotamia.

Although part of Mesopotamia, Assyria, with its hills and adequate, if not ample, rainfall, had a different terrain and climate. The Assyrians were a Semitic-speaking people; for much of their early history, they were vassals of foreign rulers, including Sargon of Akkad, the Third Dynasty of Ur, and the Babylonian King Hammurabi. From about 1650 to 1360 B.C.E., the Hurrian kingdom of Mitanni dominated Assyria (see Chapter 1). The Assyrians finally became independent when the Hittites destroyed Mitanni; we read in Hittite documents from about 1360 B.C.E. of the emergence of the "king of the land of Assyria." For the next 250 years, the Assyrians experienced alternating expansion and decline until the reassertion of Assyrian power under Tiglath-Pileser (TIG-lath-py-LEE-zur) I (1114–1076 B.C.E.), a brutal conqueror whose policy of deliberate terror set a pattern for later Assyrian rulers.

The Assyrian Empire created by Tiglath-Pileser was unable to maintain its strength after his death. A new phase of expansion did not begin until the ninth century with the conquests of Shalmaneser (shal-muh-NEE-zur) III (858–824 B.C.E.), who marched westward into Canaan and southward into Babylonia. Yet Assyrian power did not go unchallenged. The almost continuous warfare on these new frontiers did not end until the reigns of Tiglath-Pileser III (744–727 B.C.E.) and Sargon II (721–705 B.C.E.), who waged military campaigns almost every year, reestablishing control over Mesopotamia and completely subduing Canaan. The conquered territories were then incorporated into the empire as provinces. These two kings were also responsible for centralizing the system of government in order to increase the power of the king. By 700 B.C.E., the Assyrian Empire had reached the height of its power and included Mesopotamia, sections of Asia Minor, Syria, Canaan, and Egypt up to Thebes (see Map 2.2).

Ashurbanipal (ah-shur-BAH-nuh-pahl) (669–627 B.C.E.) was one of the strongest Assyrian rulers, but it was already becoming apparent during his reign that the Assyrian Empire was greatly overextended. Internal strife intensified as powerful Assyrian nobles gained control of vast territories and waged their own private military campaigns. Moreover, subject peoples greatly resented Assyrian rule. The hatred that the Babylonians felt after the brutal Assyrian sack of the city of Babylon in 689 B.C.E., for example, led them to rebel during the reign of Ashurbanipal. Soon after Ashurbanipal's death, the Assyrian Empire began to disintegrate. The capital city of Nineveh fell to a coalition of Chaldeans and Medes (see "The Neo-Babylonian Empire" later in this chapter) in 612 B.C.E., and in 605 B.C.E., the Neo-Babylonian Empire took over the rest of the empire.

Organization of the Empire

At its height, the Assyrian Empire was ruled by kings whose power was considered absolute. Under their leadership, the empire became well organized. By eliminating governorships held by nobles on a hereditary basis and instituting a new hierarchy of local officials directly responsible to the king, the Assyrian kings gained greater control over the resources of the empire. The relationship between the king and his officials was based on personal loyalty. Loyalty to the king was also expected of all people in Assyria. According to King Ashurbanipal, when his father King Esarhaddon appointed him as his successor, he "convened the people of Assyria, great and small, from coast to coast, made them swear a loyalty oath by the gods and established a binding agreement to protect my future kingship over Assyria."[10]

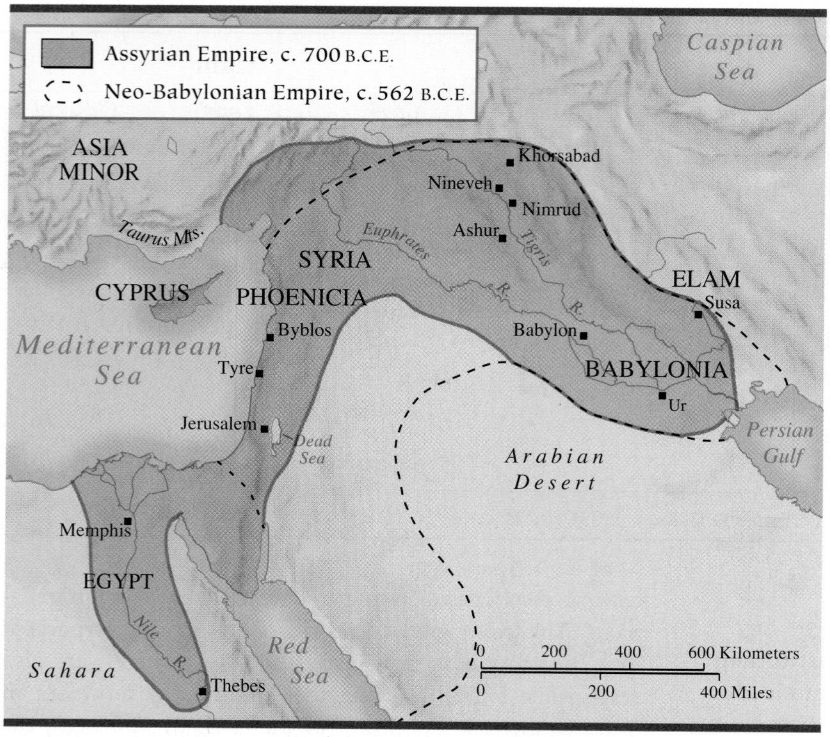

MAP 2.2 The Assyrian and Neo-Babylonian Empires. The Assyrian Empire expanded in large part due to its brutal military methods. It maintained its rule through use of a common language and religion, along with extremely violent suppression of internal revolts. It was overthrown by Chaldeans in Babylonia, leading to the Neo-Babylonian Empire epitomized by Nebuchadnezzar.

Why was control of Babylonia crucial to both empires?

View an animated version of this map or related maps on the CourseMate website.

The Assyrians also developed an efficient system of communication to administer their empire more effectively. They established a network of posting stages that used relays of horses (mules or donkeys in mountainous terrain) to carry messages throughout the empire. The system was so effective that a provincial governor anywhere in the empire (except Egypt) could send a question to the king in his palace and receive an answer within a week.

The Assyrian Military Machine

The ability of the Assyrians to conquer and maintain an empire derived from a combination of factors. Through years of practice, the Assyrians developed effective military leaders and fighters. They were able to enlist and deploy troops numbering in the hundreds of thousands, although most campaigns were not on such a large scale. In 845 B.C.E., Shalmaneser III led an army of 120,000 men across the Euphrates on a campaign. Size alone was not decisive, however. The Assyrian army was extremely well organized and disciplined. It included a standing army of infantry as its core, accompanied by cavalry and horse-drawn war chariots that were used as mobile platforms for shooting arrows. Moreover, the Assyrians had the advantage of having the first large armies equipped with iron weapons. The Hittites (see Chapter 1) had been the first to develop iron metallurgy, but iron came to be used extensively only after new methods for hardening it came into common use after 1000 B.C.E.

Another factor in the Assyrian army's success was its ability to use different kinds of military tactics. The army

British Museum, London//© Erich Lessing/Art Resource, NY

Ashurbanipal Destroys an Elamite City. Assyria was the first great empire to gain control over the ancient Near East in the first millennium B.C.E. The Assyrians had a highly efficient and well-organized military machine, capable of fighting under a variety of conditions. This relief depicts the army of King Ashurbanipal sacking an Elamite city in 647 B.C.E. Shown at the top are Assyrian soldiers destroying the city walls while below soldiers carry off the spoils of war.

was capable of waging guerrilla warfare in the mountains and set battles on open ground as well as laying siege to cities. The Assyrians were especially renowned for their siege warfare. They would hammer a city's walls with heavy, wheeled siege towers and armored battering rams while sappers dug tunnels to undermine the walls' foundations and cause them to collapse. The besieging Assyrian armies learned to cut off supplies so effectively that if a city did not fall to them, the inhabitants could be starved into submission.

Accounts of the Campaign of Sennacharib (701 B.C.E.)

A final factor in the effectiveness of the Assyrian military machine was its ability to create a climate of terror as an instrument of warfare, a policy that one historian has called "calculated frightfulness." The aim of the Assyrians was to encourage their enemies to surrender quickly rather face a series of atrocities. The Assyrians became famous for their terror tactics, although some historians believe they were no worse than other Near Eastern conquerors. As a matter of regular policy, the Assyrians laid waste to the land in which they were fighting, smashing dams, looting and destroying towns, setting crops on fire, and cutting down trees, particularly fruit trees. The Assyrians were especially known for their brutality toward their captives. King Ashurnasirpal (ah-shur-NAH-zur-pahl) II recorded this account of his treatment of prisoners:

> 3000 of their combat troops I felled with weapons.... Many of the captives taken from them I burned in a fire. Many I took alive; from some of these I cut off their hands to the wrist, from others I cut off their noses, ears, and fingers; I put out the eyes of many of the soldiers.... I burned their young men and women to death.

After conquering another city, the same king wrote: "I fixed up a pile of corpses in front of the city's gate. I flayed the nobles, as many as had rebelled, and spread their skins out on the piles.... I flayed many within my land and spread their skins out on the walls."[11] Note that this policy of extreme cruelty to prisoners was not used against all enemies but was reserved primarily for those who were already part of the empire and then rebelled against Assyrian rule (see the box on p. 44).

Assyrian Society and Culture

Unlike the Hebrews, the Assyrians were not fearful of mixing with other peoples. In fact, the Assyrian policy of deporting many prisoners of newly conquered territories to Assyria created a polyglot society in which ethnic differences were not very important. It has been estimated that over a period of three centuries, between 4 and 5 million people were deported to Assyria, resulting in a population that was racially and linguistically mixed. What gave identity to the Assyrians themselves was their language, although even that was akin to that of their southern neighbors in Babylonia. Religion was also a cohesive force. Assyria was literally "the land of Ashur," a reference to its chief god. The king, as the human representative of the god Ashur, brought order to his people and served as a final unifying focus.

Agriculture formed the principal basis of Assyrian life. Assyria was a land of farming villages with relatively few significant cities, especially in comparison with southern Mesopotamia. Unlike the river valleys, where farming required the minute organization of large numbers of people to control irrigation, Assyrian farms received sufficient moisture from regular rainfall.

King Ashurbanipal's Lion Hunt. This relief, sculptured on alabaster as a decoration for the northern palace in Nineveh, depicts King Ashurbanipal engaged in a lion hunt. Lion hunts were not conducted in the wild but were held under controlled circumstances. The king and his retainers faced lions released from cages in an arena. The purpose of the scene was to glorify the king as a conqueror of the king of beasts. Relief sculpture, one of the best-known forms of Assyrian art, reached its zenith under Ashurbanipal at about the time that the Assyrian Empire began to disintegrate.

Opposing VIEWPOINTS

The Governing of Empires: Two Approaches

Both the Assyrians and the Persians created large empires that encompassed large areas of the ancient Near East. Although both Assyrian and Persian rulers used military force and violence to attain their empires, their approaches to conquest and ruling sometimes differed. Assyrian rulers were known for their terror tactics and atrocities, as described in the first two selections. The kings of Persia had a reputation for less cruelty and more tolerance. Especially noteworthy was Cyrus, as is evident in this selection from a decree (known as the Cyrus Cylinder) that he issued in 538 B.C.E. The propaganda value of his words is also apparent, however.

King Sennacherib (704–681 B.C.E.) Describes His Siege of Jerusalem (701 B.C.E.)

As to Hezekiah, the Jew, he did not submit to my yoke, I laid siege to 46 of his strong cities, walled forts and to the countless small villages in their vicinity, and conquered them by means of well-stamped earth-ramps, and battering-rams brought thus near to the walls combined with the attack by foot soldiers, using mines, breaches as well as sapper work. I drove out of them 200,150 people, young and old, male and female, horses, mules, donkeys, camels, big and small cattle beyond counting, and considered them booty. Himself I made a prisoner in Jerusalem, his royal residence, like a bird in a cage. I surrounded him with earthwork in order to molest those who were leaving his city's gate.

King Ashurbanipal (669–627 B.C.E.) Describes His Treatment of Conquered Babylon

I tore out the tongues of those whose slanderous mouths had uttered blasphemies against my god Ashur and had plotted against me, his god-fearing prince; I defeated them completely. The others, I smashed alive with the very same statues of protective deities with which they had smashed my own grandfather Sennacherib—now finally as a belated burial sacrifice for his soul. I fed their corpses, cut into small pieces, to dogs, pigs, . . . vultures, the birds of the sky and also to the fish of the ocean. After I . . . thus made quiet again the hearts of the great gods, my lords, I removed the corpses of those whom the pestilence had felled, whose leftovers after the dogs and pigs had fed on them were obstructing the streets, filling the places of Babylon, and of those who had lost their lives through the terrible famine.

The Cyrus Cylinder

I am Cyrus, king of the world, great king, legitimate king, king of Babylon, king of Sumer and Akkad, king of the four corners of the earth. . . .

When I entered Babylon as a friend and when I established the seat of the government in the palace of the ruler under jubilation and rejoicing, Marduk, the great lord [the chief Babylonian god], caused the magnanimous inhabitants of Babylon to love me, and I was daily endeavoring to worship him. My numerous troops walked around in Babylon in peace. I did not allow anybody to terrorize any place of the country of Sumer and Akkad. I strove for peace in Babylon and in all his other sacred cities. As to the inhabitants of Babylon . . . I brought relief to their dilapidated housing, putting thus an end to their main complaints. . . .

As to the region from as far as Ashur and Susa . . . I returned to these sacred cities on the other side of the Tigris, the sanctuaries of which have been ruins for a long time, the images which used to live therein and established for them permanent sanctuaries. I also gathered all their former inhabitants and returned to them their dwellings.

Q Both Ashurbanipal and Cyrus entered Babylon as conquerors. How did their treatment of the conquered city differ? How do you explain the differences? Which method do you think was more effective? Why?

Trade was second to agriculture in economic importance. For internal trade, metals, such as gold, silver, copper, and bronze, were used as a medium of exchange. Various agricultural products also served as a form of payment or exchange. Because of their geographic location, the Assyrians served as intermediaries and participated in an international trade, importing timber, wine, and precious metals and stones while exporting textiles produced in palaces, temples, and private villas.

The culture of the Assyrian Empire was a hybrid. The Assyrians assimilated much of Mesopotamian civilization and saw themselves as guardians of Sumerian and Babylonian culture. Ashurbanipal, for example, amassed a large library at Nineveh that included the available works of Mesopotamian history. Assyrian religion also reflected this assimilation of other cultures. Although the Assyrians considered their own national god, Ashur, their chief deity, they recognized virtually all of the Mesopotamian gods and goddesses as well.

Among the best-known objects of Assyrian art are the relief sculptures found in the royal palaces in three of the Assyrian capital cities, Nimrud, Nineveh, and Khorsabad. These reliefs, which were begun in the ninth century and reached their high point in the reign of Ashurbanipal in the seventh century, depicted two different kinds of subject matter: ritual or ceremonial scenes revolving around the person of the king and scenes of hunting and war. The latter show realistic action scenes of the king and his warriors engaged in battle or hunting animals, especially lions. These reliefs depict a strongly masculine world where discipline, brute force, and toughness are the enduring values, indeed, the very values of the Assyrian military monarchy.

Ishtar Gate of Babylon. Nebuchadnezzar rebuilt Babylon as the center of his empire and adorned it with such architectural wonders as the Ishtar Gate, which was built of blue glazed bricks and opened onto the Triumphal Way. The bricks were made separately and then assembled on the gate walls. Figures of the dragon of Marduk (patron god of the city of Babylon, whose sacred animal was the dragon) and the bull of Adad (god of storms, whose sacred animal was the bull) alternate on the surfaces of the gate. Ishtar was the Babylonian goddess of war and sexual love. This picture shows the Ishtar Gate as it was rebuilt in the Pergamum Museum in Berlin.

The Neo-Babylonian Empire

Focus Question: What was the significance of the Neo-Babylonian Empire?

The Chaldeans, a Semitic-speaking people, had gained ascendancy in Babylonia by the seventh century and came to form the chief resistance to Assyrian control of Mesopotamia. The Chaldean king Nabopolassar (nab-uh-puh-LASS-ur) (626–605 B.C.E.), who joined forces with the Medes to capture the Assyrian capital Nineveh in 612 B.C.E., was responsible for establishing a new Babylonian monarchy. But it was his son Nebuchadnezzar II (605–562 B.C.E.) who achieved the final defeat of the Assyrian Empire. Under his rule, the Chaldeans defeated Egypt to gain control of Syria and Canaan, destroyed Jerusalem, carried the people of Judah into exile in Babylon, and in the process regained for Babylonia a position as the leading power in the ancient Near East (see Map 2.2).

During Nebuchadnezzar's reign, Babylonia was renowned for a prosperity based on lush agricultural lands, lucrative trade routes, and industries, especially textiles and metals. Nebuchadnezzar rebuilt Babylon as the center of his empire, giving it a reputation as one of the great cities of the ancient world. Babylon was surrounded by towering walls, 8 miles in length, encircled by a moat filled by the Euphrates River. The Ishtar Gate opened onto the Triumphal Way, which led to the sacred precincts of Marduk, the chief Babylonian god. Babylon was adorned with temples and palaces; most famous of all were the Hanging Gardens, renowned as one of the Seven Wonders of the ancient world. These were supposedly built to satisfy Nebuchadnezzar's wife, a princess from the land of Media, who missed the mountains of her homeland. A series of terraces led to a plateau, an artificial mountain, at the top of which grew the lush gardens irrigated by water piped to the top. According to the account of a first-century C.E. author, from a distance the gardens made a remarkable impression:

> On the top of the citadel are the hanging gardens, a wonder celebrated in the tales of the Greeks. . . . Columns of stone were set up to sustain the whole work, and on these was laid a floor of squared blocks, strong enough to hold the earth which is thrown upon it to a great depth, as well as the water with which they irrigate the soil; and the structure supports trees of such great size that the thickness of their trunks equals a measure of eight cubits [about 12 feet]. They tower to a height of fifty feet, and they yield as much fruit as if they were growing in their native soil. . . . To those who look upon the trees from a distance, real woods seem to be overhanging their native mountains.[12]

The splendor of the Neo-Babylonian Empire proved to be short-lived. Nabonidus (nab-uh-NY-duss) (555–539 B.C.E.) was the last king of the Chaldean dynasty. He had a great interest in history and encouraged scholars to collect Sumerian texts and study the Sumerian language. But his policies aroused considerable internal dissent. Among other things, Nabonidus neglected the cult of Marduk, instead worshiping the moon god, Sin. When Babylon fell to the Persian conqueror Cyrus in 539 B.C.E., the Babylonians welcomed him as a liberator.

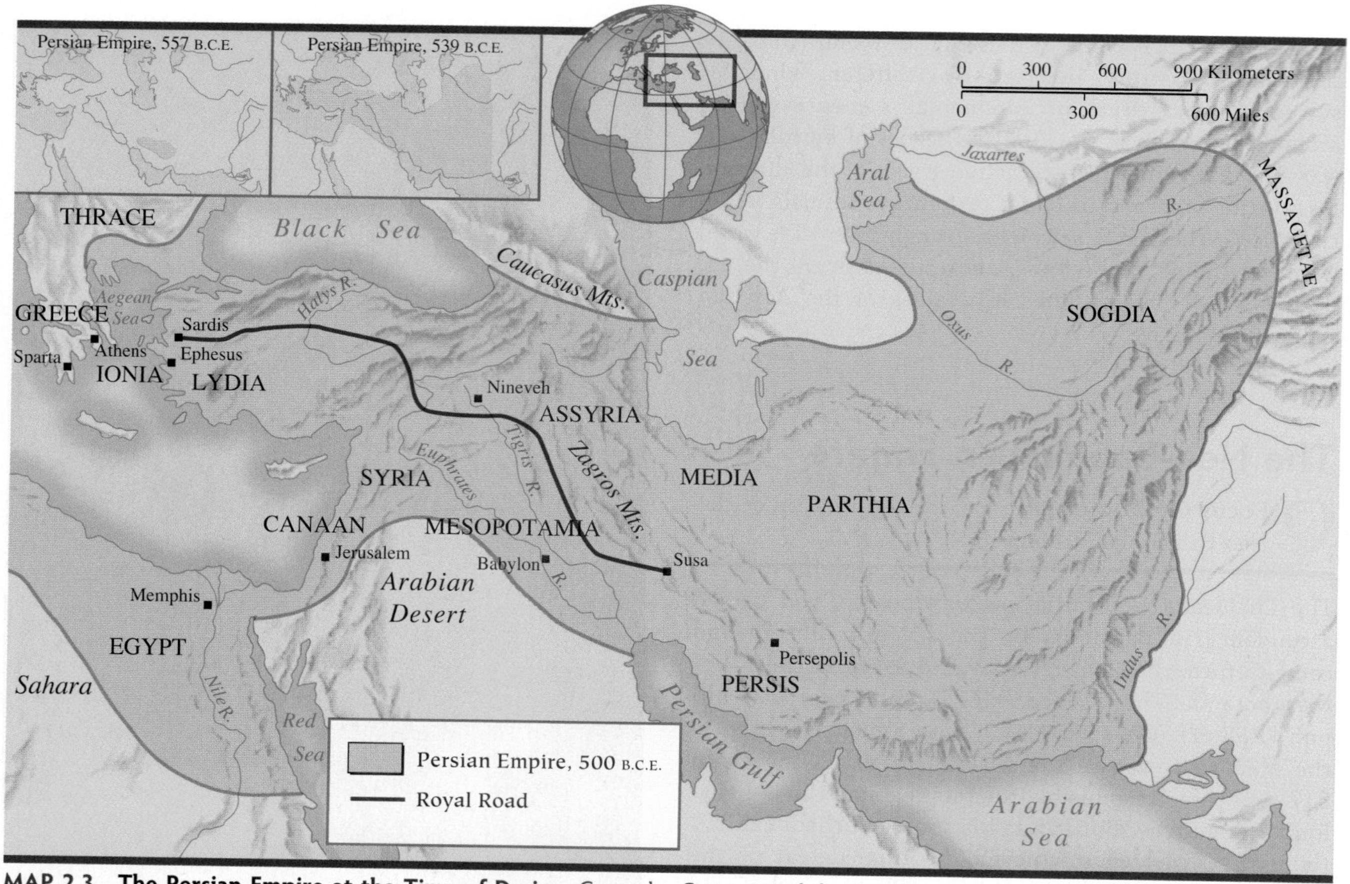

MAP 2.3 The Persian Empire at the Time of Darius. Cyrus the Great united the Persians and led them in the successful conquest of much of the Near East. By the time of Darius, the Persian Empire was the largest the world had yet seen. The Persians allowed a high degree of religious toleration and gave some government positions to natives of conquered territories.

Q ***How did Persian policies attempt to overcome the difficulties of governing far-flung provinces?***

The Persian Empire

Q **Focus Question**: What methods and institutions did the Persians use to amass and maintain their empire, and how did these methods and institutions differ from those of the Assyrians?

The Persians were an Indo-European-speaking people related to the Medes. Both peoples are mentioned in Assyrian documents in the ninth century B.C.E. and probably formed part of the great waves of Indo-European migrations into the Mediterranean, the Near East, and India. The Persians lived to the southeast of the Medes, who occupied the western Iranian plateau south of the Caspian Sea. Although these peoples grew some crops, lack of moisture made their lands more suitable for pasture. The Medes, in particular, were famous throughout the Near East for the quality of the horses they bred. Primarily nomadic, both Medes and Persians were organized in clans. Both peoples were led by petty kings assisted by a group of warriors who formed a class of nobles. Their populations also included both free and unfree people who worked the land, craftspeople, and slaves.

By 735 B.C.E., the Medes had begun to form a confederation of the various tribes, and sometime around the beginning of the seventh century, they became unified under a monarchy. The Persians did likewise under the Achaemenid (ah-KEE-muh-nud) dynasty established in Persis in southern Iran. About fifty years later, the Persians were made subject to the Medes. The Medes now constituted a powerful state and joined the Babylonians in attacking the Assyrians. After the capture of Nineveh in 612 B.C.E., King Cyaxares (si-AK-suh-reez) established a Median empire, the first Iranian empire known to the ancient Near East.

Cyrus the Great

In 559 B.C.E., Cyrus became the leader of the Persians, united them under his rule, and went on the offensive against the Medes. By 550 B.C.E. he had established Persian control over Media, making it the first Persian **satrapy** (province). Three years later, Cyrus defeated the prosperous Lydian kingdom in western Asia Minor, and Lydia became another Persian satrapy (see Map 2.3). Cyrus's forces then went on to conquer the Greek city-states that had been established on the Ionian coast of western Asia

The Fall of Babylon

Under the Chaldeans, Babylon became the center of an empire and gained a reputation as one of the great cities of the ancient world. But the Neo-Babylonian Empire did not last, and Babylon fell to the Persian forces under King Cyrus in 539 B.C.E. In his history of the Persian wars, the ancient Greek historian Herodotus described how Cyrus supposedly captured Babylon.

Herodotus, *The Persian Wars*

Cyrus, with the first approach of the ensuing spring, marched forward against Babylon. The Babylonians, encamped without their walls, awaited his coming. A battle was fought at a short distance from the city, in which the Babylonians were defeated by the Persian king, whereupon they withdrew within their defenses. Here they shut themselves up, and made light of his siege, having laid in a store of provisions for many years in preparation against this attack; for when they saw Cyrus conquering nation after nation, they were convinced that he would never stop, and that their turn would come at last.

Cyrus was now reduced to great perplexity, as time went on and he made no progress against the place. In this distress, either some one made the suggestion to him, or he thought himself of a plan, which he proceeded to put in execution. He placed a portion of his army at the point where the river enters the city and another body at the back of the place where it issues forth, with orders to march into the town by the bed of the stream, as soon as the water became shallow enough: he then himself drew off with the unwarlike portion of his host, and made for the place where Nitocris [supposedly a queen of Babylon] dug the basin for the river, where he did exactly what she had done formerly: he turned the Euphrates by a canal into the basin, which was then a marsh, on which the river sank to such an extent that the natural bed of the stream became fordable. Hereupon the Persians who had been left for the purpose at Babylon by the river-side, entered the stream, which had now sunk so as to reach about midway up a man's thigh, and thus got into the town. Had the Babylonians been apprised of what Cyrus was about, or had they noticed their danger, they would not have allowed the entrance of the Persians within the city, which was what ruined them utterly, but would have made fast all the streetgates which gave upon the river, and mounting upon the walls along both sides of the stream, would so have caught the enemy as it were in a trap. But, as it was, the Persians came upon them by surprise and so took the city. Owing to the vast size of the place, the inhabitants of the central parts (as the residents at Babylon declare) long after the outer portions of the town were taken, knew nothing of what had chanced, but as they were engaged in a festival, continued dancing and reveling until they learned of the capture but too certainly. Such, then, were the circumstances of the first taking of Babylon.

Q Do you think this is a realistic account of the fall of Babylon? What image do you have of Cyrus from this account?

Minor. Cyrus then turned eastward, subduing the eastern part of the Iranian plateau, Sogdia, and even western India. His eastern frontiers secured, Cyrus entered Mesopotamia in 539 and captured Babylon (see the box above). His treatment of Babylonia showed remarkable restraint and wisdom. Babylonia was made into a Persian province under a Persian **satrap,** or governor, but many government officials were kept in their positions. Cyrus took the title "King of All, Great King, Mighty King, King of Babylon, King of the Land of Sumer and Akkad, King of the Four Rims (of the Earth), the Son of Cambyses the Great King, King of Anshan"[13] and insisted that he stood in the ancient, unbroken line of Babylonian kings. By appealing to the vanity of the Babylonians, he won their loyalty. Cyrus also issued an edict permitting the Jews, who had been brought to Babylon in the sixth century B.C.E., to return to Jerusalem with their sacred temple objects and to rebuild their Temple as well.

Kurash (Cyrus) the Great, The Decree of Return for the Jews (c. 539 B.C.E.)

From 538 to 530 B.C.E., Cyrus consolidated his empire. Among other things, he constructed forts, especially in the northeast, to protect against nomadic incursions. It was there that he undertook his last campaign. In 530 B.C.E., he marched from Sogdia into the territory of the Massagetae, where he was killed in battle.

To his contemporaries, Cyrus the Great was deserving of his epithet. The Greek historian Herodotus recounted that the Persians viewed him as a "father," a ruler who was "gentle, and procured them all manner of goods."[14] Cyrus must have been an unusual ruler for his time, a man who demonstrated considerable wisdom and compassion in the conquest and organization of his empire (see the box on p. 44). Cyrus obtained the favor of the priesthoods in his conquered lands by restoring temples and permitting religious toleration. He won approval by using not only Persians but also native peoples as government officials in their own states. He allowed Medes to be military

Herodotus, Reports of Babylonia, Chaldea, and Assyria (c. 430 B.C.E.)

CHRONOLOGY The Empires

The Assyrians	
Tiglath-Pileser I	1114–1076 B.C.E.
Shalmaneser III	858–824 B.C.E.
Tiglath-Pileser III	744–727 B.C.E.
Sargon II	721–705 B.C.E.
Ashurbanipal	669–627 B.C.E.
Capture of Nineveh	612 B.C.E.
Assyrian Empire destroyed	605 B.C.E.
The Chaldeans	
Ascendancy in Babylonia	600s B.C.E.
Nabopolassar establishes Neo-Babylonian monarchy	626–605 B.C.E.
Height of empire under King Nebuchadnezzar II	605–562 B.C.E.
Fall of Babylon	539 B.C.E.
The Persians	
Unification of Persians	600s B.C.E.
Conquests of Cyrus the Great	559–530 B.C.E.
Cambyses II and conquest of Egypt	530–522 B.C.E.
Reign of Darius	521–486 B.C.E.

© The Art Archive/Gianni Dagli Orti

Darius, the Great King. Darius ruled the Persian Empire from 521 to 486 B.C.E. He is shown here on his throne in Persepolis, a new capital city that he built. In his right hand, Darius holds the royal staff. In his left hand, he grasps a lotus blossom with two buds, a symbol of royalty.

commanders. Unlike the Assyrian rulers of an earlier empire, he had a reputation for mercy. Medes, Babylonians, and Jews all accepted him as their legitimate ruler. Some peoples portrayed him as a great leader and peacemaker. Indeed, a Hebrew prophet regarded him as the anointed one of God: "I am the Lord who says of Cyrus, 'He is my shepherd and will accomplish all that I please'; he will say of Jerusalem, 'Let it be rebuilt'; and of the temple, 'Let its foundations be laid.' This is what the Lord says to his anointed, to Cyrus, whose right hand I take hold of to subdue nations before him."[15] Cyrus had a genuine respect for ancient civilizations—in building his palaces, he made use of Assyrian, Babylonian, Egyptian, and Lydian practices. Indeed, Cyrus believed that he was creating a "world empire" that included peoples who had ancient and venerable traditions and institutions.

Expanding the Empire

Upon Cyrus's death in 530 B.C.E., his son Cambyses (kam-BY-seez) II assumed power as the Great King. Four years later, Cambyses undertook the invasion of Egypt, the only kingdom in the Near East not yet brought under Persian control. Aided by the Phoenician fleet, he defeated and captured the pharaoh and the Egyptian forces. Egypt was made into a satrapy with Memphis as its capital. In the summer of 525 B.C.E., Cambyses took the title of pharaoh.

After the death of Cambyses in 522, Darius (duh-RY-uss) emerged as Great King after a year of intense civil war. Once in charge, Darius (521–486 B.C.E.) turned to the task of strengthening the empire. He codified Egyptian law and built a canal to link the Red Sea and the Mediterranean. A campaign into western India led to the creation of a new Persian province that extended to the Indus River. Darius also moved into Europe proper, conquering Thrace and making the Macedonian king a vassal. A revolt of the Ionian Greek cities in 499 B.C.E. resulted in temporary freedom for these communities in western Asia Minor. Aid from the Greek mainland, most notably from Athens, led to a brief invasion of Lydia by the Ionians and the burning of Sardis, center of the Lydian satrapy. This event led to Darius's involvement with the mainland Greeks. After reestablishing control of the Ionian Greek cities, Darius undertook an invasion of the Greek mainland, which culminated in the Athenian victory in the Battle of Marathon in 490 B.C.E. (see Chapter 3).

Governing the Empire

By the reign of Darius, the Persians had created the largest empire the world had yet seen. It not only included all the old centers of power in the Near East, Egypt, Mesopotamia, and Assyria but also extended into Thrace and Asia Minor in the west and into India in the east.

For administrative purposes, the empire had been divided into approximately twenty provinces called satrapies. Each province was ruled by a governor or satrap, literally a "protector of the kingdom." Although Darius had not introduced the system of satrapies, he did see that it was organized more rationally. He created a sensible system for calculating the tribute that each satrapy owed to the central government and gave satraps specific civil and military duties. They collected tributes, were responsible for justice and security, raised military levies, and normally commanded the military forces within their satrapies. In terms of real power, the satraps were miniature kings who established courts imitative of the Great King's.

From the time of Darius on, satraps were men of Persian descent. The major satrapies were given to princes of the king's family, and their positions became essentially hereditary. The minor satrapies were placed in the hands of Persian nobles. Their offices, too, tended to pass from father to son. The hereditary nature of the governors' offices made it necessary to provide some checks on their power. Consequently, some historians think that there were officials at the satrapal courts, such as secretaries and generals in charge of the garrison, who reported directly to the Great King, keeping him informed of what was going on within the various satrapal governments. It is also possible that an official known as the "king's eye" or "king's messenger" made annual inspections of each satrapy.

An efficient system of communication was considered crucial to sustaining the Persian Empire. Well-maintained roads facilitated the rapid transit of military and government personnel. One in particular, known as the Royal Road, stretched from Sardis, the center of Lydia in Asia Minor, to Susa, the chief capital of the Persian Empire (see Map 2.3). Like the Assyrians, the Persians established staging posts equipped with fresh horses for the king's messengers.

The Great King

In this vast administrative system, the Persian king occupied an exalted position. Although not considered a god like the Egyptian pharaoh, he was nevertheless the elect one or regent of the Persian god Ahuramazda (see "Persian Religion" later in this chapter). All subjects were the king's servants, and he was the source of all justice, possessing the power of life and death over everyone. Persian kings were largely secluded and not easily available. They resided in a series of splendid palaces. Darius in particular was a palace builder on a grand scale. His description of the construction of a palace in the chief Persian capital of Susa demonstrated what a truly international empire Persia was:

> This is the . . . palace which at Susa I built. From afar its ornamentation was brought. . . . The cedar timber was brought from a mountain named Lebanon; the Assyrians brought it to Babylon, and from Babylon the Carians and Ionians brought it to Susa. Teakwood was brought from Gandara and from Carmania. The gold which was used here was brought from Sardis and from Bactria. The stone—lapis lazuli and carnelian—was brought from Sogdiana. . . . The silver and copper were brought from Egypt. The ornamentation with which the wall was adorned was brought from Ionia. The ivory was brought from Ethiopia, from India, and from Arachosia. The stone pillars were brought from . . . Elam. The artisans who dressed the stone were Ionians and Sardians. The goldsmiths who wrought the gold were Medes and Egyptians. . . . Those who worked the baked brick [with figures] were Babylonians. The men who adorned the wall were Medes and Egyptians. At Susa here a splendid work was ordered; very splendid did it turn out.[16]

But Darius was unhappy with Susa. He did not really consider it his homeland, and it was oppressively hot in the summer months. He built another residence at Persepolis, a new capital located to the east of the old one and at a higher elevation.

The policies of Darius also tended to widen the gap between the king and his subjects. As the Great King himself said of all his subjects, "What was said to them by

Louvre, Paris//© Réunion des Musées Nationaux/Art Resource, NY

Archers of the Persian Guard. One of the main pillars supporting the Persian Empire was the military. This frieze, composed of enameled brick, depicts members of the famous infantry force known as the Immortals, so called because their number was never allowed to drop below ten thousand. Anyone killed would be replaced immediately. They carry the standard lance and bow and arrow of the infantry.

A Dinner of the Persian King

The Persian kings lived in luxury as a result of their conquests and ability to levy taxes from their conquered subjects. In this selection, we read a description of how a Persian king dined with his numerous guests.

Athenaeus, *The Deipnosophists,* 4:145–146

Heracleides of Cumae, author of the *Persian History,* writes in the second book of the work entitled *Equipment:* "All who attend upon the Persian kings when they dine first bathe themselves and then serve in white clothes, and spend nearly half the day on preparations for the dinner. Of those who are invited to eat with the king, some dine outdoors, in full sight of anyone who wishes to look on; others dine indoors in the king's company. Yet even these do not eat in his presence, for there are two rooms opposite each other, in one of which the king has his meal, in the other the invited guests. The king can see them through the curtain at the door, but they cannot see him. Sometimes, however, on the occasion of a public holiday, all dine in a single room with the king, in the great hall. And whenever the king commands a symposium [drinking-bout following the dinner] which he does often, he has about a dozen companions at the drinking. When they have finished dinner, that is the king by himself, the guests in the other room, these fellow-drinkers are summoned by one of the eunuchs; and entering they drink with him, though even they do not have the same wine; moreover, they sit on the floor, while he reclines on a couch supported by feet of gold, and they depart after having drunk to excess. In most cases the king breakfasts and dines alone, but sometimes his wife and some of his sons dine with him. And throughout the dinner his concubines sing and play the lyre; one of them is the soloist, the others sing in chorus. And so, Heracleides continues, the 'king's dinner,' as it is called, will appear prodigal to one who merely hears about it, but when one examines it carefully it will be found to have been got up with economy and even with parsimony; and the same is true of the dinners among other Persians of high station. For one thousand animals are slaughtered daily for the king; these comprise horses, camels, oxen, asses, deer, and most of the small animals; many birds are also consumed, including Arabian ostriches—and the creature is large—geese, and cocks. And of all these only moderate portions are served to each of the king's guests, and each of them may carry home whatever he leaves untouched at the meal. But the greater part of these meats and other foods are taken into the courtyard for the bodyguard and light-armed troopers maintained by the king; there they divide all the half-eaten remnants of meat and bread and share them in equal portions."

Q What does this description of a royal dinner tell you about the nature of Persian kingship?

me, night and day it was done."[17] Over a period of time, the Great Kings in their greed came to hoard immense quantities of gold and silver in the various treasuries located in the capital cities. Both their hoarding of wealth and their later overtaxation of their subjects are seen as crucial factors in the ultimate weakening of the Persian Empire (see the box above).

In its heyday, however, the empire stood supreme, and much of its power depended on the military. By the time of Darius, the Persian monarchs had created a standing army of professional soldiers. This army was truly international, composed of contingents from the various peoples who made up the empire. At its core was a cavalry force of ten thousand and an elite infantry force of ten thousand Medes and Persians known as the Immortals because they were never allowed to fall below ten thousand in number. When one was killed, he was immediately replaced. The Persians made effective use of their cavalry, especially for operating behind enemy lines and breaking up lines of communication. The Persian navy consisted of ships from subject states, including the Phoenicians, Egyptians, Anatolians, and Ionian Greeks.

Persian Religion

Of all the Persians' cultural contributions, the most original was their religion, **Zoroastrianism.** Zoroaster (ZOR-oh-ass-tur), or Zarathustra, was a semilegendary figure who, according to Persian tradition, was born in 660 B.C.E. After a period of wandering and solitude, he experienced revelations that caused him to be revered as a prophet of the "true religion." It is difficult to know what Zoroaster's original teachings were, since the sacred book of Zoroastrianism, the Zend Avesta, was not written down until the third century C.E. Scholars believe, however, that the earliest section of the Zend Avesta, known as the Yasna, consisting of seventeen hymns or *gathas,* contains the actual writings of Zoroaster. This enables us to piece together his message.

Like the Hebrews, Zoroaster taught a spiritual message of monotheism. To Zoroaster, the religion he preached was the only perfect one and Ahuramazda was the only God. Ahuramazda (the "Wise Lord") was the supreme deity who brought all things into being:

> *This I ask of You, O Ahuramazda; answer me well:*
> *Who at the Creation was the first father of Justice?—*

Who assigned their path to the sun and the stars?—
Who decreed the waxing and waning of the moon, if it was not You?— . . .
Who has fixed the earth below, and the heaven above
with its clouds that it might not be moved?—
Who has appointed the waters and the green things upon the earth?—
Who has harnessed to the wind and the clouds their steeds?— . . .
Thus do I strive to recognize in You, O Wise One,
Together with the Holy Spirit, the Creator of all things.[18]

According to Zoroaster, Ahuramazda also possessed abstract qualities or states that all humans should aspire to, such as Good Thought, Right, and Piety. Although Ahuramazda was supreme, he was not unopposed. Right is opposed by the Lie, Truth by Falsehood, Life by Death. At the beginning of the world, the good spirit of Ahuramazda was opposed by the evil spirit (in later Zoroastrianism identified with Ahriman).

Humans also played a role in this cosmic struggle between good and evil. Ahuramazda, the creator, gave all humans free will and the power to choose between right and wrong. The good person chooses the right way of Ahuramazda. Zoroaster taught that there would be an end to the struggle between good and evil. Ahuramazda would eventually triumph, and at the last judgment at the end of the world, the final separation of good and evil would occur. Individuals, too, would be judged. Each soul faced a final evaluation of its actions. A person who had performed good deeds would achieve paradise; the soul of a person who had performed evil deeds would be thrown into an abyss of torment.

The spread of Zoroastrianism was due to its acceptance by the Great Kings of Persia. The inscriptions of Darius make clear that he believed Ahuramazda was the only God. Although Darius himself may have been a monotheist, dramatic changes in Zoroastrianism occurred over time. Before Zoroaster, Persian religion had focused on the worship of powers of nature, such as the sun, moon, fire, and wind, with the aid of priests known as Magi. As the kings and Magi propagated Zoroaster's teachings on Ahuramazda. Zoroastrianism lost its monotheistic emphasis, and the old nature worship resurfaced. Soon Persian religion had returned to polytheism, with Ahuramazda the chief of a number of gods of light. Mithra, the sun god, became a helper of Ahuramazda and later, in Roman times, the source of another religion. Persian kings were also very tolerant of other religions, and gods and goddesses of those religions tended to make their way into the Persian pantheon. Moreover, Zoroaster's teachings, as frequently happens to the ideas of founders of religions, acquired concrete forms that he had never originally intended. The struggle between good and evil was taken beyond the abstractions of Zoroaster into a strong ethical dualism. The spirit of evil became an actual being who had to be warded off by the use of spells and incantations.

CHAPTER SUMMARY

By 1500 B.C.E., much of the creative impulse of the Mesopotamian and Egyptian civilizations was beginning to decline. And by 1200 B.C.E., the decline of the Hittites and Egyptians had created a power vacuum that allowed a patchwork of petty kingdoms and city-states to emerge, especially in the area of Syria and Canaan. One was that of the Phoenicians, who created a trading empire in the Mediterranean as well as an alphabet that was later adapted by the Greeks and the Romans.

Of these small states, however, perhaps the most important was that of the Israelites, who created a kingdom under Saul, David, and Solomon. By the tenth century B.C.E., the inhabitants of Israel had divided into a northern kingdom of Israel and a southern kingdom of Judah, but the rise of larger states in the region eventually led to their demise. Israel fell to the Assyrians at the end of the eighth century B.C.E. and Judah to the Chaldeans in the sixth century. Nevertheless, although the Israelites created no empire and were dominated by the Assyrians, Chaldeans, and eventually the Persians, they left a spiritual legacy that influenced much of the later development of Western civilization. The evolution of Hebrew monotheism created in Judaism one of the world's great religions; it influenced the development of both Christianity and Islam. When we speak of the Judeo-Christian heritage of Western civilization, we refer not only to the concept of monotheism but also to ideas of law, morality, and social justice that have become important parts of Western culture.

All of these small states were eventually overshadowed by the rise of the great empires of the Assyrians, Chaldeans, and Persians. The Assyrian Empire, built upon the effective use of military force, was the first to unite almost all of the ancient Near East. Nevertheless, after reaching the height of its power by 700 B.C.E., it succumbed gradually to internal dissension and was overrun by the armies

of the Medes and the Chaldeans near the end of the seventh century B.C.E. The latter created a Neo-Babylonian Empire, which in turn was short-lived and soon conquered by the Persians. Although the Persian Empire owed much to the administrative organization developed by the Assyrians, the Persian Empire had its own peculiar strengths. Persian rule was tolerant as well as efficient. Conquered peoples were allowed to keep their own religions, customs, and methods of doing business. The two centuries of relative peace that the Persian Empire brought to the Near East facilitated trade and the general well-being of its peoples. Many Near Eastern peoples, including the Israelites, expressed gratitude for being subjects of the Great Kings of Persia.

CHAPTER TIMELINE

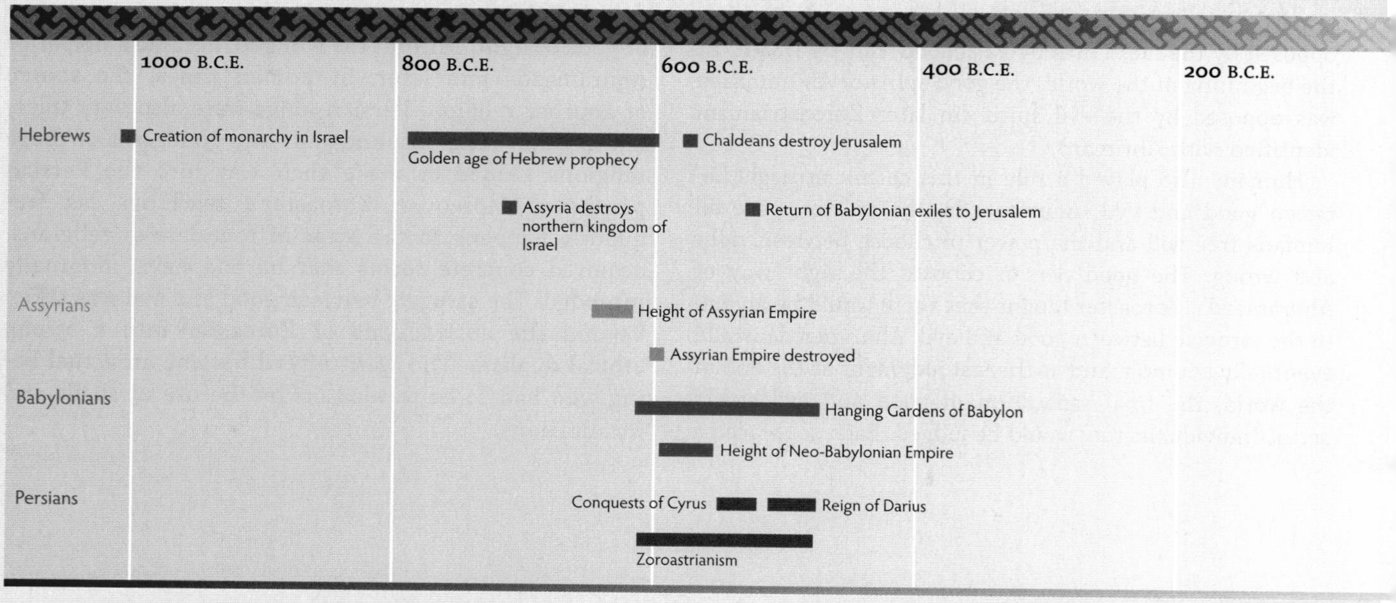

CHAPTER REVIEW

Upon Reflection

Q How did the Israelites establish a united state, and what became of it?

Q Compare and contrast the administrative and military structure and attitudes toward subject peoples of the Assyrian and Persian Empires.

Q If the large empires of the Assyrians, Chaldeans, and Persians dominated the entire Near East for centuries, why did the small state of the Israelites have a greater impact on Western civilization?

Key Terms

monotheism (p. 36)
Pentateuch (p. 36)
Torah (p. 36)
Diaspora (p. 39)
patriarchal (p. 39)
satrapy (p. 46)
satrap (p. 47)
Zoroastrianism (p. 50)

Suggestions for Further Reading

GENERAL SURVEYS For excellent general surveys of the material covered in this chapter, see **A. Kuhrt, *The Ancient Near East, c. 3000–330 B.C.*,** vol. 2 (London, 1995), and **M. van de Mieroop, *A History of the Ancient Near East, ca. 3000–323 B.C.*,** 2nd ed. (Oxford, 2006).

ANCIENT ISRAEL There is an enormous literature on ancient Israel. Two good studies on the archaeological aspects are **A. Mazar, *Archaeology of the Land of the Bible*** (New York, 1992), and **A. Ben-Tor, ed., *The Archaeology of Ancient Israel*** (New Haven, Conn., 1992). For an important revised view, see **I. Finkelstein** and **N. Silberman, *The Bible Unearthed: Archaeology's New Vision*** *of Ancient Israel* (New York, 2002). For historical narratives, see **J. M. Miller** and **J. H. Hayes, *A History of Ancient Israel and Judah*** (Philadelphia, 1986); **M. Grant, *The History of Ancient Israel*** (New York, 1984); and **H. Shanks, *Ancient Israel: A Short History from Abraham to the Roman Destruction of the Temple,*** rev. ed. (Englewood Cliffs, N.J., 1999). For another perspective, see **N. P. Lemche, *Ancient Israel: A New History of Israelite Society*** (Sheffield, England, 1988). On the origins of the Israelites, see **W. G. Dever, *Who Were the Early Israelites and Where Did They Come From?*** (Grand Rapids, Mich., 2003). On early Israelite kings, see **I. Finkelstein** and **N. Silberman, *David and Solomon: In Search of the Bible's Sacred Kings and the Roots of the Western Tradition*** (New York, 2006). On the controversies surrounding the history of the Israelites, see **J. M. Golden, *Ancient Canaan and Israel*** (Oxford, 2004). **R. de Vaux, *Ancient Israel: Its Life and Institutions*** (New York, 1961), is useful on the social institutions of ancient Israel. On women in ancient Israel, see **C. Meyers, *Discovering Eve: Ancient Israelite Women in Context*** (New York, 1988).

RELIGION OF ISRAEL For general studies on the religion of Israel, see **R. Albertz, *A History of Israelite Religion in the Old Testament Period*** (Louisville, Ky., 1994), and **W. J. Doorly, *The Religion of Israel*** (New York, 1997). The role of the prophets is examined in **J. Lindblom, *Prophecy in Ancient Israel*** (Oxford, 1962), and is given a new interpretation in **N. Podhoretz, *The Prophets*** (New York, 2002).

THE PHOENICIANS For a good account of Phoenician domestic and overseas expansion, see **D. Harden, *The Phoenicians,*** rev. ed. (Harmondsworth, England, 1980). See also **M. E. Aubet, *The Phoenicians and the West: Politics, Colonies and Trade,*** 2nd ed. (Cambridge, 2001), and **G. Markoe, *Phoenicians*** (London, 2000), on Phoenician society.

THE ASSYRIAN EMPIRE A detailed account of Assyrian political, economic, social, military, and cultural history is **H. W. F. Saggs, *The Might That Was Assyria*** (London, 1984). **A. T. Olmstead, *History of Assyria*** (Chicago, 1975), is a basic survey of the Assyrian Empire. The Neo-Babylonian Empire can be examined in **J. Oates, *Babylon*** (London, 1979), and **H. W. F. Saggs, *Babylonians*** (Norman, Okla., 1995).

THE PERSIAN EMPIRE The classic work on the Persian Empire is **A. T. Olmstead, *History of the Persian Empire*** (Chicago, 1948), but see also **L. Allen, *The Persian Empire*** (Chicago, 2005), and **J. M. Cook, *The Persian Empire*** (New York, 1983), for new material and fresh interpretations. On the history of Zoroastrianism, see **S. A. Nigosian, *The Zoroastrian Faith: Tradition and Modern Research*** (New York, 1993).

CHAPTER 3

Museo Pio Clementino, Vatican State// © Scala/Art Resource, NY

A bust of Pericles

The Civilization of the Greeks

CHAPTER OUTLINE AND FOCUS QUESTIONS

Early Greece

Q How did the geography of Greece affect Greek history?

The Greeks in a Dark Age (c. 1100–c. 750 B.C.E.)

Q Who was Homer, and why was his work used as the basis for Greek education?

The World of the Greek City-States (c. 750–c. 500 B.C.E.)

Q What were the chief features of the *polis,* or city-state, and how did the major city-states of Athens and Sparta differ?

The High Point of Greek Civilization: Classical Greece

Q What did the Greeks mean by *democracy,* and in what ways was the Athenian political system a democracy? What effect did the two great conflicts of the fifth century—the Persian Wars and the Peloponnesian War—have on Greek civilization?

Culture and Society of Classical Greece

Q Upon what ideals was Classical Greek art based, and how were these ideals expressed? What questions did the Greek philosophers pose, and what answers did they suggest?

CRITICAL THINKING

Q Why are the Greeks considered the cornerstone of the Western intellectual tradition?

IN 431 B.C.E., WAR ERUPTED in Greece as two very different Greek city-states—Athens and Sparta—fought for domination of the Greek world. The people of Athens felt secure behind their walls and in the first winter of the war held a public funeral to honor those who had died in battle. On the day of the ceremony, the citizens of Athens joined in a procession, with the relatives of the dead wailing for their loved ones. As was the custom in Athens, one leading citizen was asked to address the crowd, and on this day it was Pericles who spoke to the people. He talked about the greatness of Athens and reminded the Athenians of the strength of their political system. "Our constitution," he said, "is called a democracy because power is in the hands not of a minority but of the whole people. When it is a question of settling private disputes, everyone is equal before the law. Just as our political life is free and open, so is our day-to-day life in our relations with each other. . . . Here each individual is interested not only in his own affairs but in the affairs of the state as well."

In this famous Funeral Oration, Pericles gave voice to the ideal of democracy and the importance of the individual. It was the Greeks who created the intellectual foundations of our Western heritage. They asked some basic questions about human life that still dominate our own intellectual pursuits: What is the nature of the universe? What is the purpose of human existence? What is our relationship to divine forces? What constitutes a community? What constitutes a state? What is true education? What are the true sources of law? What is truth itself, and how do we realize it? Not only did the Greeks provide answers to these questions, but they created a system of logical, analytical thought to examine them. This rational outlook has remained an important feature of Western civilization.

The story of ancient Greek civilization is a remarkable one that begins with the first arrival of the Greeks around 2000 B.C.E. By the eighth century B.C.E., the characteristic institution of ancient Greek life, the *polis*, or city-state, had emerged. Greek civilization flourished and reached its height in the Classical era of the fifth century B.C.E., which has come to be closely identified with the achievements of Athenian democracy.

Early Greece

Focus Question: How did the geography of Greece affect Greek history?

Geography played an important role in the evolution of Greek history. Compared to the landmasses of Mesopotamia and Egypt, Greece occupied a small area, a mountainous peninsula that encompassed only 45,000 square miles of territory, about the size of the state of Louisiana. The mountains and the sea played especially significant roles in the development of Greek history. Much of Greece consists of small plains and river valleys surrounded by mountain ranges 8,000 to 10,000 feet high. The mountainous terrain had the effect of isolating Greeks from one another. Consequently, Greek communities tended to follow their own separate paths and develop their own way of life. Over a period of time, these communities became attached to their independence and were only too willing to fight one another to gain advantage. No doubt the small size of these independent Greek communities fostered participation in political affairs and unique cultural expressions, but the rivalry among these communities also led to the bitter warfare that ultimately devastated Greek society.

The sea also influenced the evolution of Greek society. Greece had a long seacoast, dotted by bays and inlets that provided numerous harbors. The Greeks also inhabited a number of islands to the west, the south, and particularly the east of the Greek mainland. It is no accident that the Greeks became seafarers who sailed out into the Aegean and Mediterranean seas, first to make contact with the outside world and later to establish colonies that would spread Greek civilization throughout the Mediterranean region.

Greek topography helped determine the major territories into which Greece was ultimately divided. South of the Gulf of Corinth was the Peloponnesus, virtually an island connected to the mainland by a narrow land bridge (see Map 3.1). Consisting mostly of hills, mountains, and small valleys, the Peloponnesus was the location of Sparta, as well as the site of Olympia, where athletic games were held. Northeast of the Peloponnesus was the Attic peninsula (or Attica), the home of Athens, hemmed in by mountains to the north and west and surrounded by the sea to the south and east. Northwest of Attica was Boeotia in central Greece, with its chief city of Thebes. To the north of Boeotia was Thessaly, which contained the largest plains and became a great producer of grain and horses. To the north of Thessaly lay Macedonia, which was not of much importance in Greek history until 338 B.C.E., when a Macedonian king, Philip II, conquered the Greeks.

Minoan Crete

The earliest civilization in the Aegean region emerged on the large island of Crete, southeast of the Greek mainland. A Bronze Age civilization that used metals, especially bronze, in making weapons had been established there by 2800 B.C.E. This civilization was discovered at the turn of the twentieth century by the English archaeologist Arthur Evans, who named it "Minoan" after Minos, a legendary king of Crete. In language and religion, the Minoans were not Greek, although they did have some influence on the peoples of the Greek mainland.

Evans's excavations on Crete led to the discovery of an enormous palace complex at Knossus, near modern Heracleion. The remains revealed a rich and prosperous culture with Knossus as the likely center of a far-ranging "sea empire," probably largely commercial. We know from archaeological remains that the people of Minoan Crete were accustomed to sea travel and had made contact with the more advanced civilization of Egypt. Egyptian products have been found in Crete and Cretan products in Egypt. Minoan Cretans also made contact with and exerted influence on the Greek-speaking inhabitants of the Greek mainland.

The Minoan civilization reached its height between 2000 and 1450 B.C.E. The palace at Knossus, the royal seat of the kings, demonstrates the prosperity and power of this civilization. It was an elaborate structure built around a central courtyard and included numerous private living rooms for the royal family and workshops for making decorated vases, small sculptures, and jewelry. Even bathrooms, with elaborate drains, formed part of the complex. The rooms were decorated with frescoes in bright colors showing sporting events and naturalistic scenes that have led some observers to conclude that the Cretans had a great love of nature. Storerooms in the palace held enormous jars of oil, wine, and grain, presumably paid as taxes to the king.

The centers of Minoan civilization on Crete suffered a sudden and catastrophic collapse around 1450 B.C.E. The cause of this destruction has been vigorously debated. Some historians believe that a tsunami triggered by a powerful volcanic eruption on the island of Thera was responsible for the devastation. Most historians, however, maintain that the destruction was the result of invasion and pillage by mainland Greeks known as the Mycenaeans.

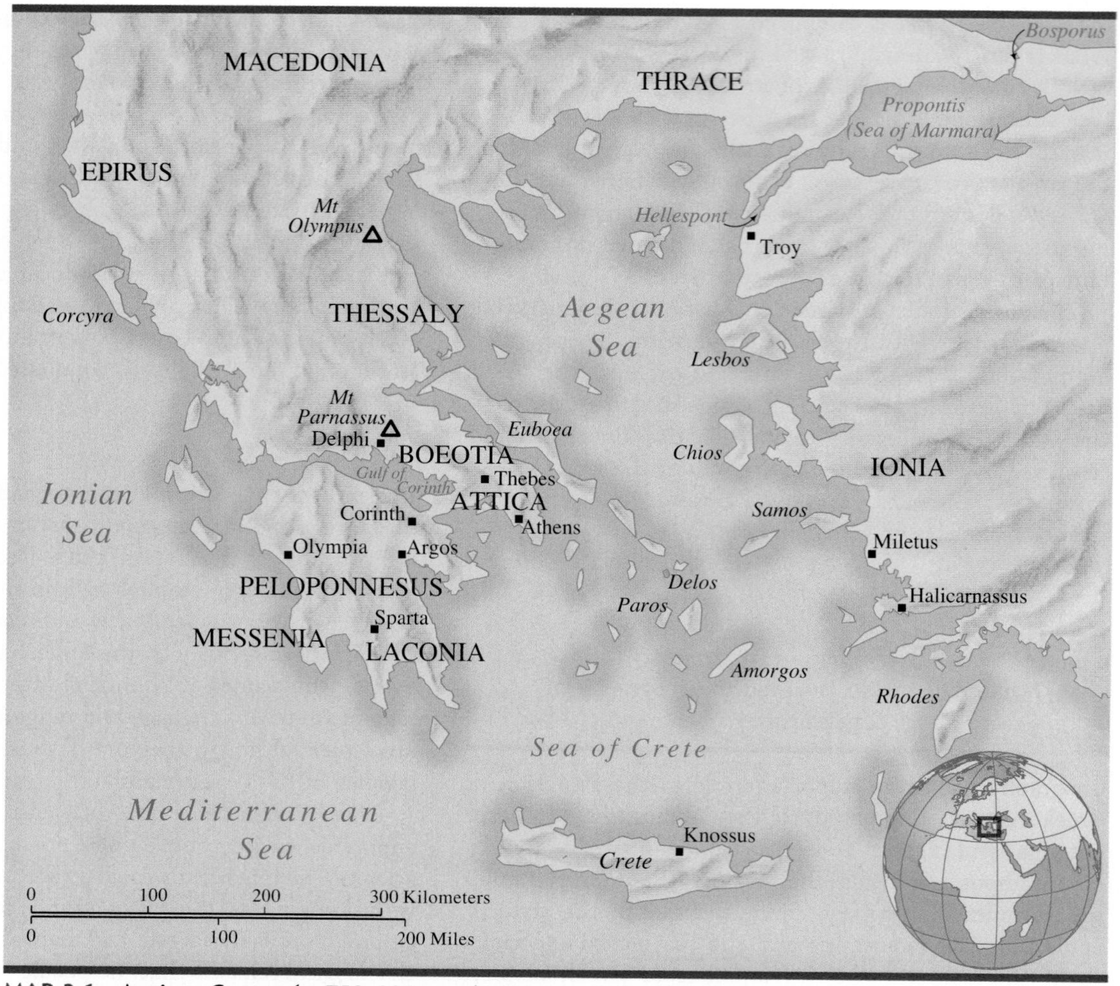

MAP 3.1 Ancient Greece (c. 750–338 B.C.E.). Between 750 and 500 B.C.E., Greek civilization witnessed the emergence of the city-state as the central institution in Greek life and the Greeks' colonization of the Mediterranean and Black seas. Classical Greece lasted from about 500 to 338 B.C.E. and encompassed the high points of Greek civilization in art, science, philosophy, and politics, as well as the Persian Wars and the Peloponnesian War.

Q ***How does the geography of Greece help explain the rise and development of the Greek city-state?***

The First Greek State: Mycenae

The term *Mycenaean* (my-suh-NEE-un) is derived from Mycenae, a remarkable fortified site first excavated by the amateur German archaeologist Heinrich Schliemann (HYN-rikh SHLEE-mahn). Mycenae was one center in a Mycenaean Greek civilization that flourished between 1600 and 1100 B.C.E. The Mycenaean Greeks were part of the Indo-European family of peoples (see Chapter 2) who spread from their original Central Asian location into southern and western Europe, India, and Iran. One group entered the territory of Greece from the north around 1900 B.C.E. and managed to gain control of the Greek mainland and develop a civilization.

Mycenaean civilization reached its high point between 1400 and 1200 B.C.E. It is especially noted for its fortified palace-centers, which were built on hills surrounded by gigantic stone walls. The royal families lived within the walls of these complexes, while the civilian populations lived in scattered locations outside the walls.

Mycenaean civilization consisted of a number of powerful monarchies centered in the palace complexes, such as those found at Mycenae, Tiryns, Pylos, and Orchomenos. These various centers of power probably formed a loose confederacy of independent states, with Mycenae the strongest. According to tablets written in an early form of Greek script called Linear B, a Mycenaean king used the title of *wanax*. Next in importance to the king were commanders of the army, priests, and

Minoan Crete and Mycenaean Greece

The Minoan Sport of Bull Leaping. Minoan bull games were held in the great palaces on the island of Crete. As seen in this fresco from the east wing of the palace at Knossus, women and men acrobats (the man in red) somersaulted over the back of the bull. Another person waited behind the bull to catch the leapers.

bureaucrats who kept careful records. The free citizenry included peasants, soldiers, and artisans, with the lowest rung of the social ladder consisting of serfs and slaves.

The Mycenaeans were above all a warrior people who prided themselves on their heroic deeds in battle. Archaeological evidence also indicates that the Mycenaean monarchies developed an extensive commercial network.

A Mycenaean Death Mask. This death mask of thin gold was one of several found by Heinrich Schliemann in his excavation of Grave Circle A at Mycenae. These masks are similar to the gold mummy masks used in Egyptian royal tombs. Schliemann claimed—incorrectly—that he had found the mask of Agamemnon, king of Mycenae in Homer's *Iliad.*

Mycenaean pottery has been found throughout the Mediterranean basin, in Syria and Egypt to the east and Sicily and southern Italy to the west. But some scholars believe that the Mycenaeans, led by Mycenae itself, also spread outward militarily, conquering Crete and making it part of the Mycenaean world. Some of the Aegean islands also fell subject to Mycenaean control. The most famous of all the Mycenaeans' supposed military adventures has come down to us in the epic poetry of Homer (discussed in the next section). Did the Mycenaeans, led by Agamemnon, king of Mycenae, sack the city of Troy on the northwestern coast of Asia Minor around 1250 B.C.E.? Scholars have debated this question ever since Schliemann began his excavations in 1870. Many believe that Homer's account does have a basis in fact, even if the details have become shrouded in mystery.

By the late thirteenth century, Mycenaean Greece was showing signs of serious trouble. Mycenae itself was torched around 1190 B.C.E., and other Mycenaean centers show similar patterns of destruction as new waves of Greek-speaking invaders moved into Greece from the north. By 1100 B.C.E., the Mycenaean culture was coming to an end, and the Greek world was entering a new period of considerable insecurity.

The Greeks in a Dark Age (c. 1100–c. 750 B.C.E.)

FOCUS QUESTION: Who was Homer, and why was his work used as the basis for Greek education?

After the collapse of the Mycenaean civilization, Greece entered a difficult period in which population declined and food production dropped. Because of the difficult

The Slaying of Hector. This scene from a late-fifth-century B.C.E. Athenian vase depicts the final battle between Achilles and the Trojan hero Hector. Achilles is shown lunging forward with his spear to deliver the fatal blow to the Trojan prince, a scene taken from Homer's *Iliad.* The *Iliad* is Homer's masterpiece and was important to later Greeks as a means of teaching the aristocratic values of courage and honor.

conditions and our lack of knowledge about the period, historians refer to it as the Dark Age. Not until 850 B.C.E. did farming revive. At the same time, some new developments were forming the basis for a revived Greece.

During the Dark Age, large numbers of Greeks left the mainland and migrated across the Aegean Sea to various islands and especially to the southwestern shore of Asia Minor, a strip of territory that came to be called Ionia. Based on their dialect, the Greeks who resided there were called Ionians. Two other major groups of Greeks settled in established parts of Greece. The Aeolian (ee-OH-lee-un) Greeks, located in northern and central Greece, colonized the large island of Lesbos and the adjacent territory on the northwestern coast of Asia Minor. The Dorians (DOR-ee-unz) established themselves in southwestern Greece, especially in the Peloponnesus, as well as on some of the southern Aegean islands, including Crete and Rhodes.

Other important activities occurred in this Dark Age as well. Greece saw a revival of some trade and some economic activity besides agriculture. Iron replaced bronze in the construction of weapons, making them affordable for more people. And farming tools made of iron helped reverse the decline in food production. At some point in the eighth century B.C.E., the Greeks adopted the Phoenician alphabet to give themselves a new system of writing. By reducing all words to a combination of twenty-four letters, the Greeks made learning to read and write simpler. Finally, near the end of this Dark Age appeared the work of Homer, who has come to be viewed as one of the great poets of all time.

Homer and Homeric Greece

The *Iliad* and the *Odyssey,* the first great epic poems of early Greece, were based on stories that had been passed on from generation to generation. It is generally assumed that early in the eighth century B.C.E., Homer made use of these oral traditions to compose the *Iliad,* his epic of the Trojan War. The war was sparked by Paris, a prince of Troy. By kidnapping Helen, wife of the king of the Greek state of Sparta, he outraged all the Greeks. Under the leadership of the Spartan king's brother, Agamemnon of Mycenae, the Greeks attacked Troy. Ten years later, the Greeks finally won and sacked the city.

Homer, *Iliad* Book 1 & *Odyssey* Book 1

But the *Iliad* is not so much the story of the war itself as it is the tale of the Greek hero Achilles and how the "wrath of Achilles" led to disaster. As is true of all great literature, the *Iliad* abounds in universal lessons. Underlying them all is the clear message, as one commentator has observed, that "men will still come and go like the generations of leaves in the forest; that [man] will still be weak, and the gods strong and incalculable; that the quality of a man matters more than his achievement; that violence and recklessness will still lead to disaster, and that this will fall on the innocent as well as on the guilty."[1]

The *Odyssey,* Homer's other masterpiece, is an epic romance that recounts the journeys of one of the Greek heroes, Odysseus, after the fall of Troy, and his ultimate return to his wife. But there is a larger vision here as well: the testing of the heroic stature of Odysseus until, by both cunning and patience, he prevails. In the course of this testing, the underlying moral message is "that virtue is a better policy than vice."[2]

Although the *Iliad* and the *Odyssey* supposedly deal with the heroes of the Mycenaean age of the thirteenth century B.C.E., many scholars believe that they really describe the social conditions of the Dark Age. According to the Homeric view, Greece was a society based on agriculture in which a landed warrior-aristocracy controlled much wealth and exercised considerable power. Homer's world reflects the values of aristocratic heroes.

Homer's Ideal of Excellence

The *Iliad* and the *Odyssey*, epics that the Greeks believed were written by Homer, were used as basic texts for the education of Greeks for hundreds of years in antiquity. This passage from the *Iliad,* describing a conversation between Hector, prince of Troy, and his wife, Andromache, illustrates the Greek ideal of gaining honor through combat. At the end of the passage, Homer also reveals what became the Greek attitude toward women: women are supposed to spin and weave and take care of their households and their children.

Homer, *Iliad*

Hector looked at his son and smiled, but said nothing. Andromache, bursting into tears, went up to him and put her hand in his. "Hector," she said, "you are possessed. This bravery of yours will be your end. You do not think of your little boy or your unhappy wife, whom you will make a widow soon. Some day the Achaeans [Greeks] are bound to kill you in a massed attack. And when I lose you I might as well be dead.... I have no father, no mother, now.... I had seven brothers too at home. In one day all of them went down to Hades' House. The great Achilles of the swift feet killed them all....

"So you, Hector, are father and mother and brother to me, as well as my beloved husband. Have pity on me now; stay here on the tower; and do not make your boy an orphan and your wife a widow...."

"All that, my dear," said the great Hector of the glittering helmet, "is surely my concern. But if I hid myself like a coward and refused to fight, I could never face the Trojans and the Trojan ladies in their trailing gowns. Besides, it would go against the grain, for I have trained myself always, like a good soldier, to take my place in the front line and win glory for my father and myself...."

As he finished, glorious Hector held out his arms to take his boy. But the child shrank back with a cry to the bosom of his girdled nurse, alarmed by his father's appearance. He was frightened by the bronze of the helmet and the horsehair plume that he saw nodding grimly down at him. His father and his lady mother had to laugh. But noble Hector quickly took his helmet off and put the dazzling thing on the ground. Then he kissed his son, dandled him in his arms, and prayed to Zeus and the other gods: "Zeus, and you other gods, grant that this boy of mine may be, like me, preeminent in Troy; as strong and brave as I; a mighty king of Ilium. May people say, when he comes back from battle, 'Here is a better man than his father.' Let him bring home the bloodstained armor of the enemy he has killed, and make his mother happy."

Hector handed the boy to his wife, who took him to her fragrant breast. She was smiling through her tears, and when her husband saw this he was moved. He stroked her with his hand and said: "My dear, I beg you not to be too much distressed. No one is going to send me down to Hades before my proper time. But Fate is a thing that no man born of woman, coward or hero, can escape. Go home now, and attend to your own work, the loom and the spindle, and see that the maidservants get on with theirs. War is men's business; and this war is the business of every man in Ilium, myself above all."

Q What important ideals for Greek men and women are revealed in this passage from the *Iliad?*

Homer's Enduring Importance

This, of course, explains the importance of Homer to later generations of Greeks. Homer did not record history; he made it. The Greeks regarded the *Iliad* and the *Odyssey* as authentic history as recorded by one poet, Homer. These masterpieces gave the Greeks an ideal past with a cast of heroes and came to be used as standard texts for the education of generations of Greek males. As one Athenian stated, "My father was anxious to see me develop into a good man...and as a means to this end he compelled me to memorize all of Homer."[3] The values Homer taught were essentially the aristocratic values of courage and honor (see the box above). A hero strives for excellence, which the Greeks called *arete*. In the warrior-aristocratic world of Homer, *arete* is won in a struggle or contest. Through his willingness to fight, the hero protects his family and friends, preserves his own honor and that of his family, and earns his reputation.

In the Homeric world, aristocratic women, too, were expected to pursue excellence. Penelope, for example, the wife of Odysseus, the hero of the *Odyssey,* remains faithful to her husband and displays great courage and intelligence in preserving their household during her husband's long absence. Upon his return, Odysseus praises her for her excellence: "Madame, there is not a man in the wide world who could find fault with you. For your fame has reached heaven itself, like that of some perfect king, ruling a populous and mighty state with the fear of god in his heart, and upholding the right."[4] Homer gave the Greeks a model of heroism, honor, and nobility. But in time, as a new world of city-states emerged in Greece, new values of cooperation and community also transformed what the Greeks learned from Homer.

The World of the Greek City-States (c. 750–c. 500 B.C.E.)

Focus Question: What were the chief features of the *polis,* or city-state, and how did the major city-states of Athens and Sparta differ?

In the eighth century B.C.E., Greek civilization burst forth with new energies, beginning the period that historians have called the Archaic Age of Greece. Two major developments stand out in this era: the evolution of the *polis* (POH-liss), or city-state, as the central institution in Greek life and the Greeks' colonization of the Mediterranean and Black seas.

The *Polis*

The Greek ***polis*** (plural, *poleis*) developed slowly during the Dark Age but by the eighth century B.C.E. had emerged as a unique and fundamental institution in Greek society. In a physical sense, the *polis* encompassed a town or city or even a village and its surrounding countryside. But the town or city or village served as the focus or central point where the citizens of the *polis* could assemble for political, social, and religious activities. In some *poleis,* this central meeting point was a hill, which could serve as a place of refuge during an attack and later in some locales came to be the religious center where temples and public monuments were erected. Below this *acropolis* would be an *agora,* an open space that served both as a place where citizens could assemble and as a market.

Poleis varied greatly in size, from a few square miles to a few hundred square miles. The larger ones were the product of consolidation. The territory of Attica, for example, had once had twelve *poleis* but eventually became a single *polis* (Athens) through a process of amalgamation. The population of Athens grew to about 250,000 by the fifth century B.C.E. Most *poleis* were much smaller, consisting of only a few hundred to several thousand people.

Although our word *politics* is derived from the Greek term *polis,* the *polis* itself was much more than just a political institution. It was, above all, a community of citizens in which all political, economic, social, cultural, and religious activities were focused. As a community, the *polis* consisted of citizens with political rights (adult males), citizens with no political rights (women and children), and noncitizens (slaves and resident aliens). All citizens of a *polis* possessed rights, but these rights were coupled with responsibilities. The Greek philosopher Aristotle argued that the citizen did not belong just to himself: "We must rather regard every citizen as belonging to the state." The unity of citizens was important and often meant that states would take an active role in directing the patterns of life. The loyalty that citizens had to their *poleis* also had a negative side, however. *Poleis* distrusted one another, and the division of Greece into fiercely patriotic sovereign units helped bring about its ruin. Greece was not a united country but a geographic location. The cultural unity of the Greeks did not mean much politically.

A NEW MILITARY SYSTEM: THE GREEK WAY OF WAR As the *polis* developed, so did a new military system. In earlier times, wars in Greece had been fought by aristocratic cavalry soldiers—nobles on horseback. These aristocrats, who were large landowners, also dominated the political life of their *poleis.* But at the end of the eighth century, a new military order came into being that was based on **hoplites** (HAHP-lyts), heavily armed infantrymen who wore bronze or leather helmets, breastplates, and greaves (shin guards). Each carried a round shield, a short sword, and a thrusting spear about 9 feet long. Hoplites advanced into battle as a unit, shoulder to shoulder, forming a **phalanx** (a rectangular formation) in tight order, usually eight ranks deep. As long as the hoplites kept their order, were not outflanked, and did not break, they either secured victory or, at the very least, suffered no harm. The phalanx was easily routed, however, if it broke its order. The safety of the phalanx thus depended on the solidarity and discipline of its members. As one seventh-century B.C.E. poet observed, a good hoplite was "a short man firmly placed upon his legs, with a courageous heart, not to be uprooted from the spot where he plants his legs."[5]

The hoplite force, which apparently developed first in the Peloponnesus, had political as well as military repercussions. The aristocratic cavalry was now outdated. Since each hoplite provided his own armor, men of property, both aristocrats and small farmers, made up the new phalanx. Initially, this created a bond between the aristocrats and peasants, which minimized class conflict and enabled the aristocrats to dominate their societies. In the long run, however, those who could become hoplites and fight for the state could also challenge aristocratic control.

In the new world of the Greek city-states, war became an integral part of the Greek way of life. The Greek philosopher Plato described war as "always existing by nature between every Greek city-state."[6] The Greeks created a tradition of warfare that became a prominent element of Western civilization. The Greek way of war exhibited a number of prominent features. The Greeks possessed excellent weapons and body armor, making effective use of technological improvements. Greek armies included a wide number of citizen-soldiers, who gladly accepted the need for training and discipline, giving them an edge over their opponents' often far-larger armies of mercenaries. Moreover, the Greeks displayed a willingness to engage the enemy head-on, thus deciding a battle quickly and with as few casualties as possible. Finally, the Greeks demonstrated the effectiveness of heavy infantry in determining the outcome of a battle. All of these features of Greek warfare remained part of Western warfare for centuries.

Museo Nazionale di Villa Giulia, Rome/© Scala/Art Resource, NY

The Hoplite Forces. The Greek hoplites were infantrymen equipped with large round shields and long thrusting spears. In battle, they advanced in tight phalanx formation and were dangerous opponents as long as this formation remained unbroken. This vase painting from the seventh century B.C.E. shows two groups of hoplite warriors engaged in battle. The piper on the left is leading another line of soldiers preparing to enter the fray.

Colonization and the Growth of Trade

Greek expansion overseas was another major development of the Archaic Age. Between 750 and 550 B.C.E., large numbers of Greeks left their homeland to settle in distant lands. Poverty and land hunger created by the growing gulf between rich and poor, overpopulation, and the development of trade were all factors that led to the establishment of colonies. Some Greek colonies were simply trading posts or centers for the transshipment of goods to Greece. Most were larger settlements that included fertile agricultural land taken from the native populations in those areas. Each colony was founded as a *polis* and was usually independent of the mother *polis* (*metropolis*) that had established it.

In the western Mediterranean, new Greek settlements were established along the coastline of southern Italy, including the cities of Tarentum (Taranto) and Neapolis (Naples) (see Map 3.2). So many Greek communities were established in southern Italy that the Romans later called it *Magna Graecia* (MAG-nuh GREE-shuh) ("Great Greece"). An important city was founded at Syracuse in eastern Sicily in 734 B.C.E. by the city-state of Corinth, one of the most active Greek states in establishing colonies. Greek settlements were also established in southern France (Massilia—modern Marseilles [mar-SAY]), eastern Spain, and northern Africa west of Egypt.

To the north, the Greeks set up colonies in Thrace, where they sought good agricultural lands to grow grains. Greeks also settled along the shores of the Black Sea and secured the approaches to it with cities on the Hellespont and Bosporus, most notably Byzantium, site of the later Constantinople (Istanbul). A trading post was established in Egypt, giving the Greeks access to both the products and the advanced culture of the East.

THE EFFECTS OF COLONIZATION The establishment of these settlements over such a wide area had important effects. For one thing, they contributed to the diffusion of Greek culture throughout the Mediterranean basin. The later Romans had their first contacts with the Greeks through the settlements in southern Italy. Furthermore, colonization helped the Greeks foster a greater sense of Greek identity. Before the eighth century, Greek communities were mostly isolated from one another, leaving many neighboring states on unfriendly terms. Once Greeks from different communities went abroad and encountered peoples with different languages and customs, they became more aware of their own linguistic and cultural similarities.

Colonization also led to increased trade and industry. The Greeks sent their pottery, wine, and olive oil to these areas; in return, they received grains and metals from the

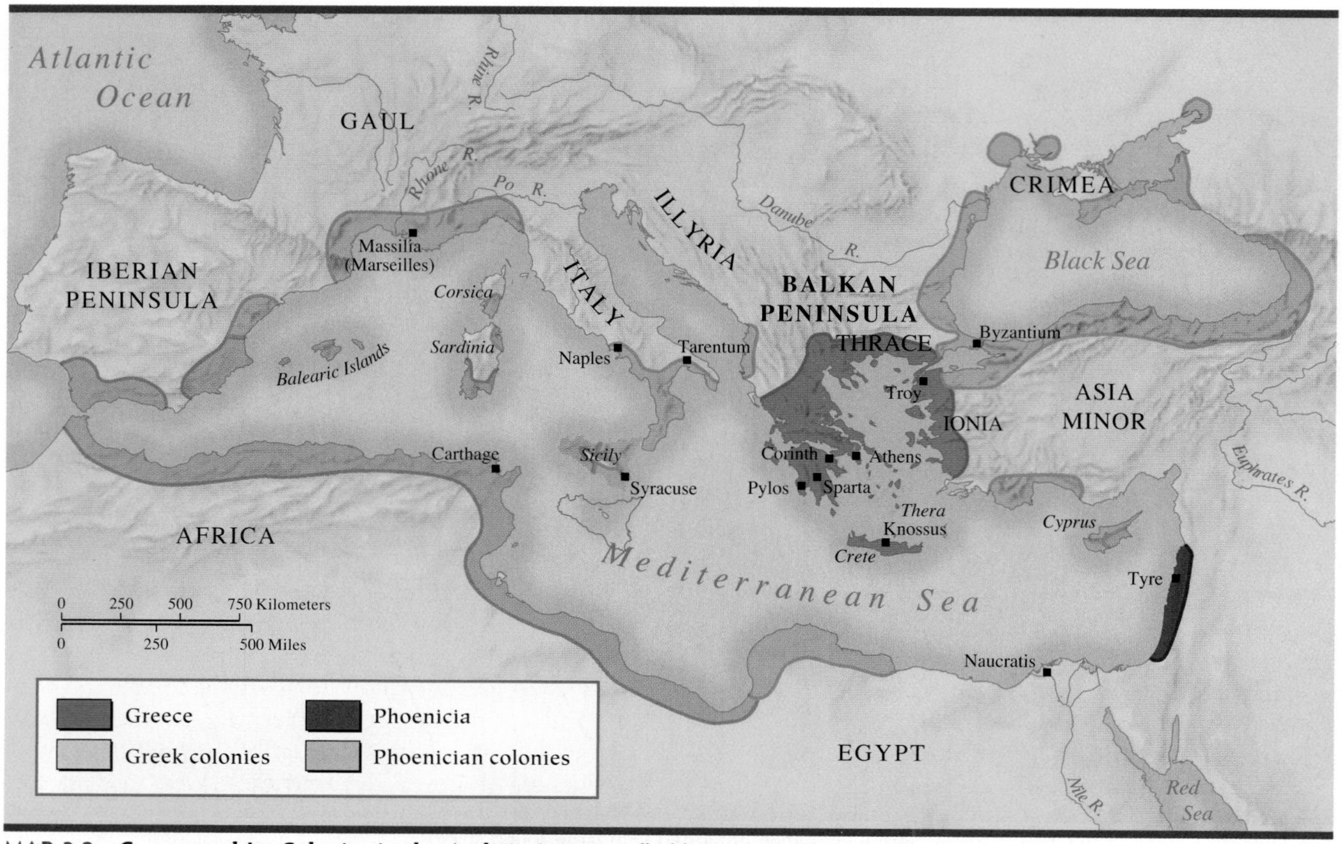

MAP 3.2 Greece and Its Colonies in the Archaic Age. Impelled by overpopulation and poverty, Greeks spread out from their homelands during the Archaic Age, establishing colonies in many parts of the Mediterranean. The colonies were independent city-states that traded with the older Greek city-states.

Q ***What aspects of the colonies' locations facilitated trade between them and city-states in Greece?***

west and fish, timber, wheat, metals, and slaves from the Black Sea region. In many *poleis,* the expansion of trade and industry created a new group of rich men who desired political privileges commensurate with their wealth but found them impossible to gain because of the power of the ruling aristocrats. The desire for change on the part of this group soon led to political crisis in many Greek states.

Tyranny in the Greek *Polis*

When the *polis* emerged as an important institution in Greece in the eighth century, monarchical power waned, and kings virtually disappeared in most Greek states or survived only as ceremonial figures with little or no real power. Instead, political power passed into the hands of local aristocracies. But increasing divisions between rich and poor and the aspirations of newly rising industrial and commercial groups in Greek *poleis* opened the door to the rise of **tyrants** in the seventh and sixth centuries B.C.E. They were not necessarily oppressive or wicked, as our word *tyrant* connotes. Greek tyrants were rulers who seized power by force and who were not subject to the law. Support for the tyrants came from the new rich, who made their money in trade and industry, as well as from poor peasants, who were in debt to landholding aristocrats. Both groups were opposed to the domination of political power by aristocratic oligarchies.

Tyrants usually achieved power by a local coup d'état and maintained it by using mercenary soldiers. Once in power, they built new marketplaces, temples, and walls that created jobs, glorified the city, and also enhanced their own popularity. Tyrants also favored the interests of merchants and traders by encouraging the founding of new colonies, developing new coinage, and establishing new systems of weights and measures. In many instances, they added to the prosperity of their cities. By their patronage of the arts, they encouraged cultural development.

THE EXAMPLE OF CORINTH One of the most famous examples of tyranny can be found in Corinth (KOR-inth). During the eighth and early seventh centuries B.C.E., Corinth had become one of the most prosperous states in Greece under the rule of an oligarchy led by members of the Bacchiad family. Their violent activities, however, made them unpopular and led Cypselus (SIP-suh-luss), a member of the family, to overthrow the oligarchy and assume sole control of Corinth.

Cypselus was so well liked that he could rule without a bodyguard. During his tyranny, Corinth prospered by exporting vast quantities of pottery and founding new colonies to expand its trade empire. Cypselus's son, Periander, took control of Corinth after his father's death but ruled with such cruelty that shortly after his death in 585 B.C.E., his own son, who succeeded him, was killed, and a new oligarchy soon ruled Corinth.

As in Corinth, tyranny elsewhere in Greece was largely extinguished by the end of the sixth century B.C.E. The children and grandchildren of tyrants, who tended to be corrupted by their inherited power and wealth, often became cruel and unjust rulers, making tyranny no longer seem such a desirable institution. Its very nature as a system outside the law seemed contradictory to the ideal of law in a Greek community. Tyranny did not last, but it played a significant role in the evolution of Greek history. The rule of narrow aristocratic oligarchies was destroyed. Once the tyrants were eliminated, the door was opened to the participation of more people in the affairs of the community. Although this trend culminated in the development of democracy in some communities, in other states expanded oligarchies of one kind or another managed to remain in power. Greek states exhibited considerable variety in their governmental structures; this can perhaps best be seen by examining the two most famous and most powerful Greek city-states, Sparta and Athens.

Sparta

The Greeks of Sparta and Athens spoke different dialects and developed different political systems. The Spartans sought stability and conformity and emphasized order. The Athenians allowed for individual differences and stressed freedom. Although the two states shared a common heritage, their differences grew so large in their own minds that they were ultimately willing to engage in a life-and-death struggle to support their separate realities. When they did so, the entire Greek world was the real loser.

Located in the southeastern Peloponnesus, in an area known as Laconia, the Spartans had originally occupied four small villages that eventually became unified into a single *polis* (a fifth soon joined the others). This unification made Sparta a strong community in Laconia and enabled the Spartans to conquer the neighboring Laconians. Many Laconians became ***perioikoi*** (per-ee-EE-koh-ee), free inhabitants but not citizens who were required to pay taxes and perform military service for Sparta. Other Laconians became known as **helots** (HEL-uts) (derived from a Greek word for "capture"). They were bound to the land and forced to work on farms and as household servants for the Spartans.

When the land in Laconia proved unable to maintain the growing number of Spartan citizens, the Spartans looked for land nearby and, beginning around 730 B.C.E., undertook the conquest of neighboring Messenia despite its larger size and population. Messenia possessed a spacious, fertile plain ideal for growing grain. After its conquest, which was not completed until the seventh century B.C.E., the Messenians were made helots and forced to work for the Spartans. To ensure control over their conquered Laconian and Messenian helots, the Spartans made a conscious decision to create a military state.

Sometime between 800 and 600 B.C.E., the Spartans instituted a series of reforms that are associated with the name of the lawgiver Lycurgus (see the box on p. 64). Although historians are not sure that Lycurgus ever existed, there is no doubt about the result of the reforms that were made: Sparta was transformed into a perpetual military camp.

THE NEW SPARTA The lives of Spartans were now rigidly organized. At birth, each child was examined by state officials who decided whether it was fit to live. Those judged unfit were exposed to the elements and left to die. Boys were taken from their mothers at the age of seven and put under control of the state. They lived in barracks, where they were subjected to harsh discipline to make them tough and given an education that stressed military training and obedience to authority. At twenty, Spartan males were enrolled in the army for regular military service. Although allowed to marry, they continued to live in the barracks and ate their meals in public dining halls with their fellow soldiers. Meals were simple; the famous Spartan black broth consisted of a piece of pork boiled in blood, salt, and vinegar, causing a visitor who ate in a public mess to remark that he now understood why Spartans were not afraid to die. At thirty, Spartan males were recognized as mature and allowed to vote in the assembly and live at home, but they remained in the army until the age of sixty.

While their husbands remained in military barracks until age thirty, Spartan women lived at home. Because of this separation, Spartan women had greater freedom of movement and greater power in the household than was common for women elsewhere in Greece. They were encouraged to exercise and remain fit to bear and raise healthy children. Like the men, Spartan women engaged in athletic exercises in the nude. At solemn feasts, the young women would march naked in processions, and in the presence of the young men, they would sing songs about those who had showed special gallantry or cowardice on the battlefield. Many Spartan women upheld the strict Spartan values, expecting their husbands and sons to be brave in war. The story is told that as a Spartan mother was burying her son, an old woman came up to her and said, "You poor woman, what a misfortune." "No," replied the other, "because I bore him so that he might die for Sparta and that is what has happened, as I wished."[7] Another Spartan woman saw her son off to war by telling him to come back carrying his shield or carried on it.

The Spartan social structure was rigidly organized. At the summit were the *Spartiates* (spar-tee-AH-teez)—full Spartan citizens. Each Spartan citizen owned a piece of

The Lycurgan Reforms

To maintain their control over the helots, the Spartans instituted the reforms that created their military state. In this account of the lawgiver Lycurgus, the Greek historian Plutarch discusses the effect of these reforms on the treatment and education of boys.

Plutarch, *Lycurgus*

Lycurgus was of another mind; he would not have masters bought out of the market for his young Spartans, . . . nor was it lawful, indeed, for the father himself to breed up the children after his own fancy; but as soon as they were seven years old they were to be enrolled in certain companies and classes, where they all lived under the same order and discipline, doing their exercises and taking their play together. Of these, he who showed the most conduct and courage was made captain; they had their eyes always upon him, obeyed his orders, and underwent patiently whatsoever punishment he inflicted; so that the whole course of their education was one continued exercise of a ready and perfect obedience. The old men, too, were spectators of their performances, and often raised quarrels and disputes among them, to have a good opportunity of finding out their different characters, and of seeing which would be valiant, which a coward, when they should come to more dangerous encounters. Reading and writing they gave them just enough to serve their turn; their chief care was to make them good subjects, and to teach them to endure pain and conquer in battle. To this end, as they grew in years, their discipline was proportionately increased; their heads were close-clipped, they were accustomed to go barefoot, and for the most part to play naked.

After they were twelve years old, they were no longer allowed to wear any undergarments, they had one coat to serve them a year; their bodies were hard and dry, with but little acquaintance of baths and unguents; these human indulgences they were allowed only on some few particular days in the year. They lodged together in little bands upon beds made of the rushes which grew by the banks of the river Eurotas, which they were to break off with their hands with a knife; if it were winter, they mingled some thistledown with their rushes, which it was thought had the property of giving warmth. By the time they were come to this age there was not any of the more hopeful boys who had not a lover to bear him company. The old men, too, had an eye upon them, coming often to the grounds to hear and see them contend either in wit or strength with one another, and this as seriously . . . as if they were their fathers, their tutors, or their magistrates; so that there scarcely was any time or place without some one present to put them in mind of their duty, and punish them if they had neglected it.

[Spartan boys were also encouraged to steal their food.] They stole, too, all other meat they could lay their hands on, looking out and watching all opportunities, when people were asleep or more careless than usual. If they were caught, they were not only punished with whipping, but hunger, too, being reduced to their ordinary allowance, which was but very slender, and so contrived on purpose, that they might set about to help themselves, and be forced to exercise their energy and address. This was the principal design of their hard fare.

Q What does this passage from Plutarch's account of Lycurgus tell you about the nature of the Spartan state? Why would the entire program have been distasteful to the Athenians?

land, worked by the helots, to provide economic sustenance. With their material needs provided for them, Spartan citizens could dedicate themselves to their duties as a ruling class. Below the *Spartiates* were the *perioikoi.* Though free, they did not possess the privileges of citizenship and served as small merchants and artisans. They were subject to military duty, however. At the bottom of the social scale were the helots, perpetually bound to the land. They were assigned to the lands of the Spartan citizens. The helots farmed the land and gave their masters half of the produce. According to one seventh-century Spartan poet, helots worked "like donkeys exhausted under heavy loads." A secret police force lived among them and was permitted to kill any helot considered dangerous. To legalize this murder, the state officially declared war on the helots at the beginning of each year.

THE SPARTAN STATE The so-called Lycurgan reforms also reorganized the Spartan government, creating an **oligarchy.** Two kings from different families were primarily responsible for military affairs and served as the leaders of the Spartan army on its campaigns. Moreover, the kings served as the supreme priests within the state religion and had some role in foreign policy.

The two kings shared power with a body called the *gerousia* (juh-ROO-see-uh), a council of elders. It consisted of twenty-eight citizens over the age of sixty, who were elected for life, and the two kings. The primary task of the *gerousia* was to prepare proposals that would be presented to the *apella* (uh-PELL-uh), an assembly of all male citizens. The assembly did not debate but only voted on the proposals put before it by the *gerousia;* rarely did the assembly reject these proposals. The assembly also elected the *gerousia* and another body known as the *ephors* (EFF-urz).

To balance the power of the kings and the *gerousia,* the Spartan state created a college of five *ephors.* Elected annually (all males over the age of thirty were eligible), their duties included convening the *gerousia* and supervising the education of youth and the conduct of all citizens. They also served as judges in all civil cases and could even bring charges against a king for wrongdoing.

To make their new military state secure, the Spartans deliberately turned their backs on the outside world. Foreigners, who might bring in new ideas, were discouraged from visiting Sparta. Nor were Spartans, except for military reasons, encouraged to travel abroad where they might pick up new ideas. Trade and commerce were likewise minimized. Spartan citizens were discouraged from pursuing philosophy, literature, the arts, or any subject that might foster novel thoughts dangerous to the stability of the state. The art of war and ruling was the Spartan ideal. All other arts were frowned on.

In the sixth century, Sparta used its military might and the fear it inspired to gain greater control of the Peloponnesus by organizing an alliance of almost all the Peloponnesian states. Sparta's strength enabled it to dominate this Peloponnesian League and determine its policies. By 500 B.C.E., the Spartans had organized a powerful military state that maintained order and stability in the Peloponnesus. Raised from early childhood to believe that total loyalty to the Spartan state was the basic reason for existence, the Spartans viewed their strength as justification for their militaristic ideals and regimented society.

Athens

By 700 B.C.E., Athens had established a unified *polis* on the peninsula of Attica. Although early Athens had been ruled by a monarchy, by the seventh century B.C.E. it had fallen under the control of its aristocrats. They possessed the best land and controlled political and religious life by means of a council of nobles called the Areopagus, assisted by a board of nine archons. Since the archons served only one year and entered the Areopagus afterward, the latter body held the real power. Although there was an *ecclesia* (ek-KLEE-zee-uh) or assembly of full citizens, it possessed few powers.

Near the end of the seventh century B.C.E., Athens faced political turmoil because of serious economic problems. Many Athenian farmers found themselves sold into slavery when they were unable to repay the loans they had borrowed from their aristocratic neighbors, pledging themselves as collateral. Over and over, there were cries to cancel the debts and give land to the poor. Athens seemed on the verge of civil war.

THE REFORMS OF SOLON Hoping to avoid tyranny, the ruling Athenian aristocrats responded to this crisis by choosing Solon (SOH-lun), a reform-minded aristocrat, as sole archon in 594 B.C.E. and giving him full power to make reforms. Solon canceled all current land debts, outlawed new loans based on humans as collateral, and freed people who had fallen into slavery for debt. He refused, however, to carry out the redistribution of the land and hence failed to deal with the basic cause of the economic crisis.

Like his economic reforms, Solon's political measures were also a compromise. Though by no means eliminating the power of the aristocracy, they opened the door to the participation of new people, especially the nonaristocratic wealthy, in the government. Wealth instead of birth now qualified people for holding political office, thus creating upward political mobility. Solon divided all Athenian citizens into four classes on the basis of wealth. Only men in the first two classes (the wealthiest classes) could hold the archonship and be members of the Areopagus. Men in the third class could be elected to a new council of four hundred called the *boule,* whose function was to prepare the agenda for the assembly. The fourth (and poorest) class, though not allowed to hold any political offices, could now vote in the assembly. Male citizens of all four classes could also sit in the new popular court (the *heliaea* [HEE-lee-ee]) instituted by Solon to hear appeals from cases tried before the archons. Moreover, any male citizen could bring to the new court charges against any magistrate suspected of a crime. Government officials were now answerable to all citizens. Indeed, Solon's laws created the principle that Athens would be directed by citizens working together, and in effect, Solon defined a citizen as a person who is involved in public affairs. This, however, did not include women.

THE MOVE TO TYRANNY Solon's reforms, though popular, did not solve Athens's problems. Aristocratic factions continued to vie for power, and the poorer peasants resented Solon's failure to institute land redistribution. Internal strife finally led to the very institution Solon had hoped to avoid—tyranny. Pisistratus (puh-SIS-truh-tuss), an aristocrat and a distant relative of Solon, seized power in 560 B.C.E. and made himself a tyrant.

Pisistratus did not tamper very much with the constitution. The assembly, councils, and courts continued to function while he made sure that his supporters were elected as magistrates and council members. Pisistratus curried favor with the small farmers by offering land and loans to the needy. His ambitious building program, aimed at beautifying the city, also created jobs. Pursuing a foreign policy that aided Athenian trade, Pisistratus also maintained the support of the mercantile and industrial classes. Pisistratus's mild tyranny was popular with many Athenians, but the policies of his son Hippias (527–510 B.C.E.) eventually produced a reaction, and the Athenians sent Hippias into exile and ended the tyranny. Although the aristocrats attempted to reestablish an aristocratic oligarchy, Cleisthenes (KLYSS-thuh-neez), an aristocratic reformer, opposed this plan and, with the backing of the Athenian people, gained the upper hand in 508 B.C.E.

CHRONOLOGY Archaic Greece: Sparta and Athens

Sparta	
Conquest of Messenia	c. 730–710 B.C.E.
Beginning of Peloponnesian League	c. 560–550 B.C.E.
Athens	
Solon's reforms	594–593 B.C.E.
Tyranny of Pisistratus	c. 560–556 and 546–527 B.C.E.
Deposition of Hippias—end of tyranny	510 B.C.E.
Cleisthenes' reforms	c. 508–501 B.C.E.

The reforms of Cleisthenes now established the basis for Athenian democracy.

THE REFORMS OF CLEISTHENES A major aim of Cleisthenes' reforms was to weaken the power of traditional localities and regions, which had provided the foundation for aristocratic strength. He made the *demes,* the villages and townships of Attica, the basic units of political life. Cleisthenes enrolled all the citizens of the demes in ten new tribes, each of which contained inhabitants located in the country districts of Attica, the coastal areas, and Athens itself. Each tribe thus contained a cross section of the population and reflected all of Attica, a move that gave local areas a basic role in the political structure. Each of the ten tribes chose fifty members by lot each year for a new Council of Five Hundred, which was responsible for the administration of both foreign and financial affairs and prepared the business that would be handled by the assembly. This assembly of all male citizens had final authority in the passing of laws after free and open debate; thus, Cleisthenes' reforms strengthened the central role of the assembly of citizens in the Athenian political system.

The reforms of Cleisthenes laid the foundations for Athenian democracy. More changes would come in the fifth century when the Athenians themselves would begin to use the word *democracy* (from the Greek words *demos,* "people," and *kratia,* "power"; thus, "power to the people") to describe their system. By 500 B.C.E., Athens was more united than it had been and was about to assume a more important role in Greek affairs.

Image © The Metropolitan Museum of Art/Art Resource, NY

Egyptian Museum, Cairo//© Scala/Art Resource, NY

Kouros. On the left is a statue of a young male nude from around 600 B.C.E., making it an early example of Greek *kouros* sculpture. Such statues, which were placed in temples along with companion figures of clothed young women, known as *korai,* were meant to be representations of the faithful dedicated to the gods. At the right is an early-seventh-century B.C.E. statue of an Egyptian nobleman that shows the influence of Egyptian sculpture on Greek art. Unlike the Egyptians, Greek sculptors preferred depicting nude male figures.

Greek Culture in the Archaic Age

The period after the Dark Age witnessed a revitalization of Greek life that is also evident in Greek art and literature. Some aspects of Archaic Greek culture, such as pottery and sculpture, were especially influenced by the East. Greek sculpture, particularly that of the Ionian Greek settlements in southwestern Asia Minor, demonstrates the impact of the considerably older Egyptian civilization. There we first see the life-size stone statues of young male nudes known as *kouros* (KOO-rohss) figures. The *kouros* bears considerable resemblance to Egyptian statues of the New Kingdom. The figures are not realistic but stiff, with a slight smile; one leg is advanced ahead of the other, and the arms are held rigidly at the sides of the body.

Greek literature of the seventh century is perhaps best known for its lyric poetry. The lyric is considerably shorter than epic poetry (such as Homer's) and focuses on personal emotions, usually the power of love and its impact on human lives. Later Greeks acknowledged Sappho as their greatest female lyric poet (see the box on p. 67). Born in the seventh century, Sappho lived on the island of Lesbos in the Aegean Sea, where she taught music and poetry to her young charges. Many of her poems are love songs to her female students. Our word *lesbian* is derived from Sappho's island of Lesbos. Sappho,

Sappho, Four Poems (7th century B.C.E.)

The Lyric Poetry of Sappho

These love poems are examples of the work of Sappho of Lesbos, regarded as one of the Greeks' greatest lyric poets. She wrote directly about her personal world of emotions. Sappho is an unusual figure, an independent woman in a world dominated by males. Her attitude toward the Trojan War, as seen in the poem *To Anaktoria,* is quite different from that found in Homer's *Iliad.*

Sappho, *To Anaktoria, Now a Soldier's Wife in Lydia*

Some say cavalry and some would claim
infantry or a fleet of long oars
is the supreme sight on the black earth.
I say it is

the girl you love. And easily proved.
Did not Helen, who was queen of mortal
beauty, choose as first among mankind
the very scourge

of Trojan honor? Haunted by Love
she forgot kinsmen, her own dear child
and wandered off to a remote country.
O weak and fitful

woman bending before any man:
so Anaktoria, although you are
far, do not forget your loving friends.
And I for one

would rather listen to your soft step
and see your radiant face—than watch
all the dazzling horsemen and armored
hoplites of Lydia.

To Atthis

So I shall never see Atthis again,
and really I long to be dead,
although she too cried bitterly

when she left and she said to me,
"Ah, what a nightmare we've suffered.
Sappho, I swear I go unwillingly."

And I answered, "Go, and be happy.
But remember me, for surely you
know how I worshiped you. If not,

then I want you to remember all
the exquisite days we too shared;
how when near me you would adorn

your hanging locks with violets and
tiny roses and your sapling throat
with necklets of a hundred blossoms;

how your young flesh was rich with kingly
myrrh as you leaned near my breasts on
the soft couch where delicate girls

served us all an Ionian could desire;
how we went to every hill, brook,
and holy place, and when early spring

filled the woods with noises of birds
and a choir of nightingales—we two
in solitude were wandering there."

Q Compare Sappho's *To Anaktoria* with the passage from Homer's *Iliad* (see p. 59). What does this comparison reveal about different forms of Greek literary expression, differences in Greek society, and the role of gender in the Greek description of emotion?

like many upper-class Greeks, accepted that homosexual and heterosexual feelings could exist in the same individual. Sappho was a wife and a mother who also wrote poems about love between men and between women.

Archaic Greece is also known for poets who reflected the lifestyles of both aristocrats and peasants. A wide gulf, however, separated the wealthy aristocrat with his large landed estates from the poor peasants and small farmers who eked out their existence as best they could. Hesiod, a poet from Boeotia in central Greece who lived around 700 B.C.E., wrote a lengthy epic poem titled *Works and Days.* Himself a farmer, Hesiod distrusted aristocrats and looked down on what he considered the aristocratic emphasis on pride and war. One of his aims was to show that the gods punished injustice and that the way to success was to work: "Famine and blight do not beset the just, who till their well-worked fields and feast. The earth supports them lavishly." Therefore:

. . . you must learn to organize your work
So you may have full barns at harvest time.
From working, men grow rich in flocks and gold
And dearer to the deathless gods. In work
There is no shame; shame is in idleness.
And if you work, the lazy man will soon
Envy your wealth: a rich man can become
Famous and good. No matter what your luck,
To work is better; turn your foolish mind
From other men's possessions to your own,
And earn your living, as I tell you to.[8]

Works and Days is the first known paean to work in Western literature.

Theognis of Megara described a way of life considerably different from Hesiod's. Theognis was an aristocrat who lived and wrote primarily in the sixth century B.C.E. As a result of revolutionary upheaval, he, like other aristocrats in sixth-century *poleis,* lost his position and probably his wealth. Sent into exile, he became a bitter man. In his poetry, he portrayed aristocrats as the only good people who are distinguished from others by their natural intelligence, virtue, honor, and moderation. The lower classes or common people were by nature bad and debased:

> *Only a fool does favors for the base;*
> *You'd do as well to sow the gray salt sea.*
> *No crop of corn would come up from the deep,*
> *No gratitude, no favors from the base.*
> *The scum are never sated. If you slip,*
> *Just once, their former friendship melts away.*
> *But put a gentleman once in your debt,*
> *You have a friend for life; he won't forget.*

Aristocrats, then, should associate only with other aristocrats: "Avoid low company, mix only with the better sort of men. . . . From them you will learn goodness. Men of little worth will spoil the natural beauty of your birth."[9] The poems of Theognis reveal the political views and biases of a typical sixth-century aristocrat.

The High Point of Greek Civilization: Classical Greece

Focus Questions: What did the Greeks mean by *democracy,* and in what ways was the Athenian political system a democracy? What effect did the two great conflicts of the fifth century—the Persian Wars and the Peloponnesian War—have on Greek civilization?

Classical Greece is the name given to the period of Greek history from around 500 B.C.E. to the conquest of Greece by the Macedonian king Philip II in 338 B.C.E. It was a period of brilliant achievement, much of it associated with the flowering of democracy in Athens under the leadership of Pericles. Many of the lasting contributions of the Greeks occurred during this period. The age began with a mighty confrontation between the Greek states and the mammoth Persian Empire.

The Challenge of Persia

As Greek civilization expanded throughout the Mediterranean region, it was inevitable that it would come into contact with the Persian Empire to the east. In his play *The Persians,* the Greek playwright Aeschylus (ESS-kuh-luss) reflected what some Greeks perceived to be the essential difference between themselves and the Persians. The Persian queen, curious to find out more about the Athenians, asks: "Who commands them? Who is shepherd of their host?" The chorus responds: "They are slaves to none, nor are they subject."[10] Thus, at least some Greeks saw the struggle with the Persians as a contest between freedom and slavery. To the Greeks, a person was a citizen of the state, not a subject.

The Ionian Greek cities in southwestern Asia Minor had already fallen subject to the Persian Empire by the mid-sixth century B.C.E. (see Chapter 2). An unsuccessful revolt by the Ionian cities in 499, assisted by the Athenian navy, led the Persian ruler Darius to seek revenge by attacking the mainland Greeks in 490. Darius may also have wished to expand his empire westward.

THE FIRST PERSIAN ATTACK The Persians sailed across the Aegean, captured Eretria (which had also aided the Ionian rebels) on the island of Euboea across from Attica, and then transferred their army to the plain of Marathon, only 26 miles from Athens (see Map 3.3). The Athenians, aided by the Plataeans (from a neighboring town in Boeotia), confronted the Persians without additional assistance. The two armies were quite different. The Persians, with their light-armed troops, were more mobile and flexible and relied heavily on missiles; the Greek hoplites were armed with heavy shields and relied on spear thrusts at close range. The Athenians and Plataeans were clearly outnumbered, but led by Miltiades, one of the Athenian leaders who insisted on attacking, the Greek hoplites charged across the plain of Marathon and crushed the Persian forces (see the box on p. 70). The Persians did not mount another attack against mainland Greece for ten years.

In the meantime, Athens had acquired a new leader, Themistocles, who persuaded his fellow citizens to pursue a new military policy, namely, the development of a navy. The Athenians used a newly discovered vein of silver from Laurium to finance the construction of ships and new port facilities. By 480 B.C.E., Athens had produced a navy of about two hundred vessels, primarily triremes (ships with three banks of oars).

A revolt in Egypt, compounded by the death of Darius in 486 B.C.E., kept the Persians from mounting another attack on Greece. Xerxes (ZURK-seez), the new Persian monarch, was bent on revenge and expansion, however. Some of the Greeks prepared by forming a defensive league under Spartan leadership, although many Greek states remained neutral; some even fought on the Persian side.

THE INVASION OF XERXES The Persians under Xerxes mounted their invasion in 480 B.C.E. Their military forces were massive: close to 150,000 troops, almost seven hundred naval ships, and hundreds of supply ships to feed their large army. The Persians crossed the Hellespont by forming a bridge of ships and then moved through Thrace and Macedonia on their way into Greece. The Greek plan,

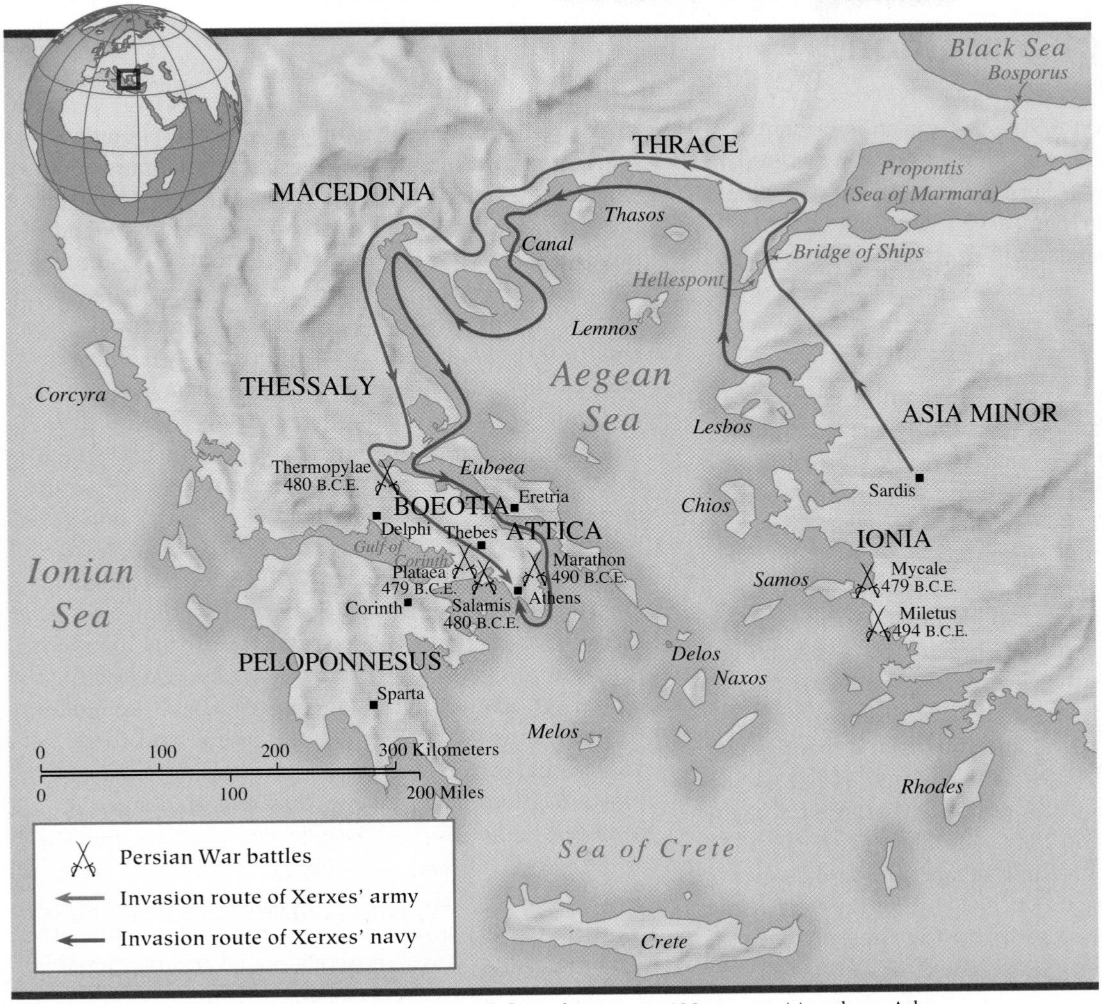

MAP 3.3 The Persian Wars. The Athenians defeated Persia in 490 B.C.E. at Marathon. Athens later led a coalition of Greek city-states that decisively defeated Xerxes' navy at the Battle of Salamis in 480 B.C.E., leading Xerxes to withdraw most of his troops back to Asia.

Q ***How far did the Persian army have to walk to get to Athens, and through what types of terrain?***

as it evolved, was to fight a holding action at the pass of Thermopylae (thur-MAHP-uh-lee) along the main road from Thessaly into Boeotia, probably to give the Greek fleet of three hundred ships at Artemisium, off northern Euboea, the chance to fight the Persian fleet (see the Film & History feature on p. 71). The Greeks knew that the Persian army depended on the fleet for supplies. A Greek force numbering close to nine thousand, under the leadership of the Spartan king Leonidas and his contingent of three hundred Spartans, held off the Persian army at Thermopylae for two days. The Spartan troops were especially brave. When told that Persian arrows would darken the sky in battle, one Spartan warrior supposedly responded, "That is good news. We will fight in the shade!" Unfortunately for the Greeks, a traitor told the Persians of a mountain path they could use to outflank the Greek force. King Leonidas and the three hundred Spartans fought to the last man.

The Athenians, now threatened by the onslaught of the Persian forces, decided to abandon Athens and evacuated the population of Attica to the offshore island of Salamis. Meanwhile, the Greek fleet remained in the straits off Salamis while the Persians sacked Athens. The Peloponnesians wanted the Greeks to retreat to the Peloponnesus and the Greek ships to move to the isthmus as well. Themistocles' refusal and his threat to withdraw the Athenian ships altogether if a fight was not made forced the ships to remain and set up the naval Battle of Salamis. Although the Greeks were outnumbered, they managed to outmaneuver the Persian fleet (mostly Phoenicians and Ionians) and decisively defeated them. The Persians still had their army and much of their fleet intact, but Xerxes, frightened at the prospect of another Ionian revolt, returned to Asia but left a Persian force in Thessaly.

Early in 479 B.C.E., the Greeks formed the largest Greek army seen up to that time. The Athenians forced the Spartans to move north of the Peloponnesus and take on the Persians at Plataea, northwest of Athens, where the Greek forces decisively defeated the Persian army.

The Battle of Marathon

The Battle of Marathon (490 B.C.E.) was an important event in the struggle between the Greeks and the Persians. The defeat of the mighty Persians gave Athenian confidence a tremendous boost. In *The Persian Wars,* the Greek historian Herodotus gave an account of this momentous battle.

Herodotus, *The Persian Wars*

So when the battle was set in array, and the victims showed themselves favorable, instantly the Athenians, so soon as they were let go, charged the barbarians at a run. Now the distance between the two armies was little short of a mile. The Persians, therefore, when they saw the Greeks coming on at speed, made ready to receive them, although it seemed to them that the Athenians were bereft of their senses, and bent upon their own destruction; for they saw a mere handful of men coming on at a run without either horsemen or archers. Such was the opinion of the barbarians; but the Athenians in close array fell upon them, and fought in a manner worthy of being recorded. They were the first of the Greeks, so far as I know, who introduced the custom of charging the enemy at a run, and they were likewise the first who dared to look upon the Median garb, and to face men clad in that fashion. Until this time the very name of the Medes had been a terror to the Greeks to hear.

The two armies fought together on the plain of Marathon for a length of time; and in the mid battle, where the Persians themselves and the Sacae had their place, the barbarians were victorious, and broke and pursued the Greeks into the inner country; but on the two wings the Athenians and the Plataeans defeated the enemy. Having so done, they suffered the routed barbarians to fly at their ease, and joining the two wings in one, fell upon those who had broken their own center, and fought and conquered them. These likewise fled, and now the Athenians hung upon the runaways and cut them down, chasing them all the way to the shore, on reaching which they laid hold of the ships and called for fire. . . .

After the full of the moon 2,000 Lacedaemonians [Spartans] came to Athens. So eager had they been to arrive in time, that they took but three days to reach Attica from Sparta. They came, however, too late for the battle; yet, as they had a longing to behold the Medes, they continued their march to Marathon and there viewed the slain. Then, after giving the Athenians all praise for their achievement, they departed and returned home.

Q How does this passage reflect Herodotus's pride in the Greeks?

The Greek Trireme. The trireme became the standard warship of ancient Greece. Highly maneuverable, fast, and outfitted with metal prows, Greek triremes were especially effective at ramming enemy ships. The bas-relief below shows a fifth-century B.C.E. Athenian trireme. The photo shows the *Olympias,* a trireme reconstructed by the Greek navy.

FILM & HISTORY

300 (2007)

300, directed by Zack Snyder, is an action film adapted from a graphic novel. The movie is a fictional portrayal of the Battle of Thermopylae in 480 B.C.E. in which the Greeks fought a delaying action against a much larger Persian army at the pass of Thermopylae along the main road from Thessaly into Boeotia. According to the movie, the Spartan king Leonidas (Gerard Butler), contrary to the wishes of the Spartan government, leads a group of three hundred Spartan warriors—"hard and strong"—to Thermopylae to defend the "freedom" of the Greeks against the Persian army, characterized by Leonidas as an army of slaves led by a despotic tyrant, King Xerxes (Rodrigo Santoro). The Spartans hold their own against the Persian army through a series of vividly constructed bloody encounters until a Spartan traitor informs the Persians of a secret path through the mountains that they can use to outflank the Spartans and surround them. The three hundred Spartans die courageously ("freedom comes with a high cost," as Leonidas says) but not before Leonidas sends one Spartan, Dilios (David Wenham), back to Sparta to tell of the bravery of the three hundred and the need to continue the struggle. The movie ends with a large Greek army of 30,000 men (including 10,000 Spartans) preparing to attack the Persians at the Battle of Plataea.

Warner Bros/Legendary Pictures/The KobalCollection

The three hundred Spartans prepare for battle.

300 is a strange mix of history and fantasy. Because the film is adapted from a graphic novel, it has a surreal quality in which special visual effects play a dominant role. Battle scenes rely on stylized violence using slow motion techniques, but they do capture the bloody nature of ancient warfare. The major historical events are accurate and so too are some of the prominent features of Spartan society. The Spartans were adamant about maintaining a code of honor based on martial values, but the film romanticizes that code by depicting the Spartan warriors with perfect physiques. As the film suggests, Spartan women also supported these martial values. The film uses the words of the Spartan mother who saw her son off to war by telling him to come back carrying his shield or carried on it, although they are incorrectly put in the mouth of Leonidas's wife as she sends him off to battle. Indeed, quotations and facts from ancient authors are sprinkled throughout the film, but they are usually misused or spoken by the wrong people. The film follows the ancient historian Herodotus in portraying the struggle between Greeks and Persians as a clash of civilizations, between free men and slaves.

The portrayal of the Persians and their subject soldiers as monsters, however, is a gross distortion of reality and reflects the world of graphic novel fantasy rather than history. This portrayal also angered current Iranian leaders who condemned the presentation of ancient Persians as barbaric and demonic monsters. Leonidas's putdown of Athenians as "boy lovers" is certainly misleading in view of the homosexual practices of Spartan warriors, practices that were encouraged by the Spartan educational system.

The remnants of the Persian forces retreated to Asia. At the same time, the Greeks destroyed much of the Persian fleet in a naval battle at Mycale in Ionia. The Greeks were overjoyed at their victory but remained cautious. Would the Persians try again?

The Growth of an Athenian Empire

After the defeat of the Persians, Athens stepped in to provide new leadership against the Persians by forming a confederation called the Delian League. Organized in the winter of 478–477 B.C.E., the Delian League was dominated by the Athenians from the beginning. Its main headquarters was the island of Delos, sacred to the Ionian Greeks, but its chief officials, including the treasurers and commanders of the fleet, were Athenians. Athens also provided most of the league's three hundred ships. While the larger states in the league, such as Lesbos, Samos, and Chios, contributed ships, the smaller communities made payments in money.

Under the leadership of the Athenians, the Delian League pursued the attack against the Persian Empire. Virtually all of the Greek states in the Aegean were liberated from

CHRONOLOGY The Persian Wars

Persian control of Greek cities in southwestern Asia Minor	By 540s B.C.E.
Rebellion of Greek cities in Asia Minor	499–494 B.C.E.
Battle of Marathon	490 B.C.E.
Xerxes invades Greece	480–479 B.C.E.
Battles of Thermopylae and Salamis	480 B.C.E.
Battles of Plataea and Mycale	479 B.C.E.

Persian control, and the Persian fleet and army were decisively defeated in 469 B.C.E. in southern Asia Minor. Arguing that the Persian threat was now over, some members of the Delian League wished to withdraw. Naxos did so in 470 and Thasos in 465 B.C.E. The Athenians responded vigorously. They attacked both states, destroyed their walls, took over their fleets, eliminated their liberty, and forced them to pay tribute. "No secession" became Athenian policy. The Delian League was rapidly becoming an instrument of Athenian imperialism and the nucleus of an Athenian empire.

THE AGE OF PERICLES At home, Athenians favored the new imperial policy, especially in the 450s B.C.E., when an aristocrat named Pericles (PER-i-kleez) began to play an important political role. Under Pericles, Athens embarked on a policy of expanding democracy at home while severing its ties with Sparta and expanding its new empire abroad. This period of Athenian and Greek history, which historians have subsequently labeled the Age of Pericles, witnessed the height of Athenian power and the culmination of its brilliance as a civilization.

During the Age of Pericles, the Athenians became deeply attached to their democratic system. The sovereignty of the people was embodied in the assembly (*ecclesia*), which consisted of all male citizens over eighteen years of age. In the 440s, that was probably a group of about 43,000. Meetings of the assembly were held on the hillside of the Pnyx, east of the Acropolis. Not all could attend, and the number present seldom exceeded 6,000, which was the capacity of the Pnyx. The assembly passed all laws and made final decisions on war and foreign policy. Although anyone could speak, usually only respected leaders did so, a feat that required considerable speaking ability in such a large crowd.

The reforms of Cleisthenes had introduced the Council of Five Hundred, elected by lot from the ten tribes. It prepared the agenda for the assembly and made recommendations for action. Thus, the council served as a control on the assembly. The council was divided into ten smaller groups of fifty called *prytanies*. Each prytany (PRIT-uh-nee) held office for one-tenth of the year to supervise the execution of the laws passed by the assembly.

Routine administration of public affairs was handled by a large body of city magistrates, usually chosen by lot without regard to class and usually serving only one-year terms. This meant that many male citizens held public office at some time in their lives. A board of ten officials known as generals (*strategoi* [strah-tay-GOH-ee]) was elected by public vote to guide affairs of state, although their power depended on the respect they had attained. Generals were usually wealthy aristocrats, even though the people were free to select otherwise. The generals could be reelected, enabling individual leaders to play an important political role. Pericles' frequent reelection (fifteen times) as one of the ten generals made him one of the leading politicians between 461 and 429 B.C.E.

All public officials were subject to scrutiny and could be deposed from office if they lost the people's confidence. After 488 B.C.E., the Athenians occasionally made use of a tactic called *ostracism*. This practice enabled the members of the assembly to write on a broken pottery fragment (*ostrakon* [AHSS-truh-kahn]) the name of the individual they most disliked or considered most harmful to the *polis*. Frequently, this was someone whose policy, approved at first by the assembly, had failed. A person who received a majority (if at least six thousand votes were cast) was exiled for ten years, although the practical Athenians often recalled a man from exile if they needed him.

Pericles expanded the Athenians' involvement in democracy, which was by now what Athenians had come to call their form of government (see the box on p. 73). Power was in the hands of the people: male citizens voted in the assemblies and served as jurors in the courts. Lower-class citizens were now eligible for public offices formerly closed to them. Pericles also introduced state pay for officeholders, including the widely held jury duty. This meant that even poor citizens could hold public office and afford to participate in public affairs. Nevertheless, although the Athenians developed a system of government that was unique in its time in which citizens had equal rights and the people were the government, aristocrats continued to hold the most important offices, and many people, including women, slaves, and foreigners residing in Athens, were not given the same political rights.

ATHENIAN IMPERIALISM The Athenian pursuit of democracy at home was coupled with increasing imperialism abroad as Athens attempted to create both a land empire in Greece and a maritime empire in the Aegean. As we have seen, after 470 B.C.E., Athenian policies had the effect of converting the voluntary allies of the Delian League into the involuntary subjects of an Athenian naval empire. After 462 B.C.E., Athens attempted to expand its empire on the Greek mainland as well. The creation of a land empire, however, overextended the Athenians and involved them in a series of skirmishes with Sparta and its allies known as the First Peloponnesian War (c. 460–445 B.C.E.). After a series of defeats in 445 B.C.E., the land empire of Athens disintegrated, and Athens agreed to a thirty years' peace with the Spartans in the following year. Athens consented to give up most of its land empire, and in return, Sparta recognized the existence of Athens's maritime empire.

While building its land empire, Athens continued its offensive against Persia and at the same time tightened its control over the Delian League. Citing the threat of the Persian fleet in the Aegean, the Athenians moved the

Athenian Democracy: The Funeral Oration of Pericles

In his *History of the Peloponnesian War*, the Greek historian Thucydides presented his reconstruction of the eulogy given by Pericles in the winter of 431–430 B.C.E. to honor the Athenians killed in the first campaigns of the Great Peloponnesian War. It is a magnificent, idealized description of the Athenian democracy at its height.

Thucydides, *History of the Peloponnesian War*

Our constitution is called a democracy because power is in the hands not of a minority but of the whole people. When it is a question of settling private disputes, everyone is equal before the law; when it is a question of putting one person before another in positions of public responsibility, what counts is not membership of a particular class, but the actual ability which the man possesses. No one, so long as he has it in him to be of service to the state, is kept in political obscurity because of poverty. And, just as our political life is free and open, so is our day-to-day life in our relations with each other. We do not get into a state with our next-door neighbor if he enjoys himself in his own way, nor do we give him the kind of black looks which, though they do no real harm, still do hurt people's feeling. We are free and tolerant in our private lives; but in public affairs we keep to the law. This is because it commands our deep respect.

We give our obedience to those whom we put in positions of authority, and we obey the laws themselves, especially those which are for the protection of the oppressed, and those unwritten laws which it is an acknowledged shame to break. . . . Here each individual is interested not only in his own affairs but in the affairs of the state as well: even those who are mostly occupied with their own business are extremely well-informed on general politics—this is a peculiarity of ours: we do not say that a man who takes no interest in politics is a man who minds his own business; we say that he has no business here at all. We Athenians, in our own persons, take our decisions on policy or submit them to proper discussions: for we do not think that there is an incompatibility between words and deeds; the worst thing is to rush into action before the consequences have been properly debated. . . . Taking everything together then, I declare that our city is an education to Greece, and I declare that in my opinion each single one of our citizens, in all the manifold aspects of life, is able to show himself the rightful lord and owner of his own person and do this, moreover, with exceptional grace and exceptional versatility. And to show that this is no empty boasting for the present occasion, but real tangible fact, you have only to consider the power which our city possesses and which has been won by those very qualities which I have mentioned.

Q In the eyes of Pericles, what are the ideals of Athenian democracy? In what ways does Pericles exaggerate his claims? Why would the Athenian passion for debate described by Pericles have been distasteful to the Spartans?

treasury of the league from the island of Delos to Athens itself, possibly in 454 B.C.E. Members were, in effect, charged a fee (tribute) for the protection that Athens claimed to provide. Pericles also used the treasury money of the league, without the approval of its members, to build new temples in Athens, a clear indication that the Delian League had become the Athenian empire. Henceforth, any protest by a league state against the tribute imposed by Athens could be heard only before an Athenian court. The pursuit of imperialism, both in Greece and abroad, took its toll, however. Pericles recognized the dangers of Athenian exhaustion and sought a lull. After peace was made with Sparta in 445 B.C.E., the Athenians had a breathing space in which to beautify Athens and enjoy the fruits of empire, but it was not long before all of Greece was plunged into a new and prolonged struggle.

The Great Peloponnesian War (431–404 B.C.E.)

In his classic *History of the Peloponnesian War*, the great Greek historian Thucydides (thoo-SID-uh-deez) pointed out that the fundamental, long-range cause of the war that began in 431 B.C.E. was the fear that Athens and its empire inspired in Sparta. The Spartans were especially concerned that Athens would use its superior naval power to weaken Sparta's control of the Peloponnesian League. The immediate causes of the war involved conflicts between Corinth and Athens and between Athens and Megara. When these two allies of Sparta threatened to withdraw from the Peloponnesian League if Sparta did not back them, the Spartans sent an ultimatum to Athens: if the Athenians did not back down in their disputes with Corinth and Megara, it would mean war. The Athenians refused to compromise when Pericles convinced them that if they accepted Sparta's ultimatum, they would be admitting that Sparta was the dominant power in Greece.

At the beginning of the war in 431 B.C.E., both sides believed they had winning strategies. The Athenian plan was based on the navy. The citizens of Attica would be brought in behind the protective walls of Athens and the port of Piraeus, while the overseas empire and the navy would keep them supplied (see Map 3.4). Pericles knew perfectly well that the Spartans and their allies could

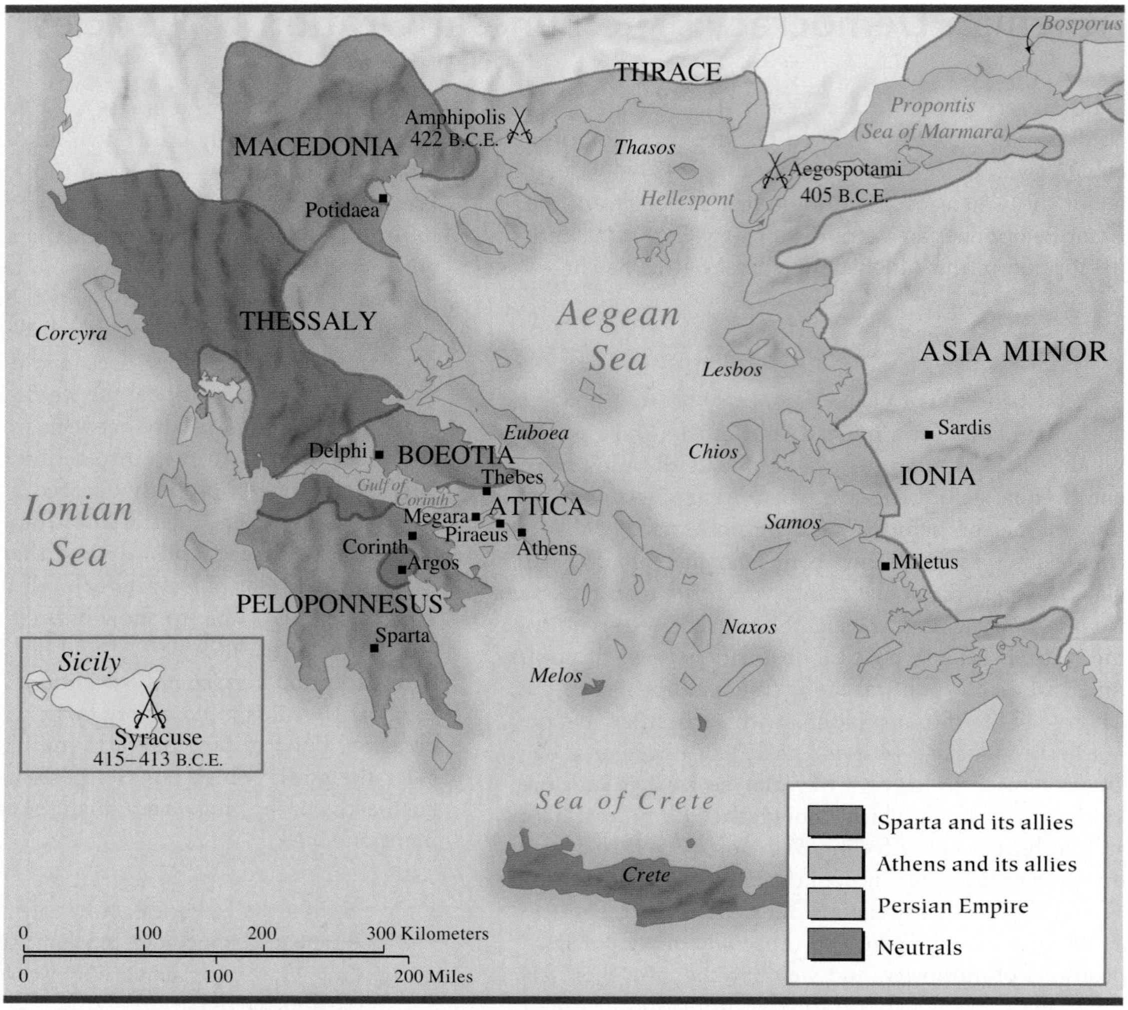

MAP 3.4 The Great Peloponnesian War (431–404 B.C.E.): Alliances and Battles. During much of the fifth century B.C.E., Athens sought to dominate Greece and the Aegean Sea. The Peloponnesian War ultimately saw Sparta and the Peloponnesian League defeat Athens and its allies, culminating in the destruction of Athens's navy and the dismantling of its empire in 404 B.C.E.

Q ***How did Athens use its proximity to the sea to forge and maintain its empire and to conduct the war?***

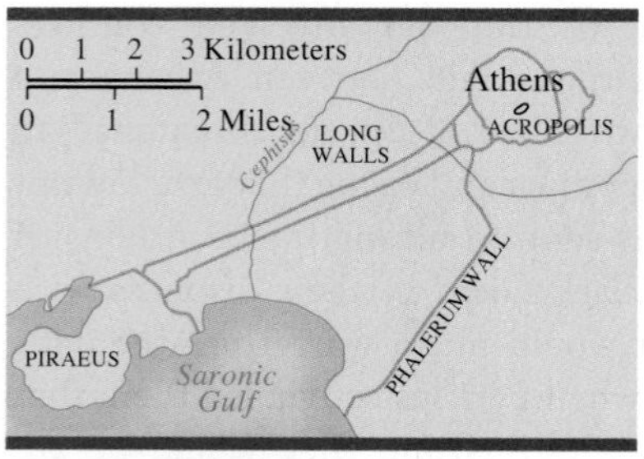

Piraeus and Athens

beat the Athenians in pitched battles, which, of course, formed the focus of the Spartan strategy. The Spartans and their allies invaded Attica and ravaged the fields and orchards, hoping that the Athenians would send out their army to fight beyond the walls. But Pericles was convinced that Athens was secure behind its walls and retaliated by sending out naval excursions to ravage the seacoast of the Peloponnesus. In the second year of the war, however, a plague devastated the crowded city of Athens and wiped out possibly one-third of the population. Pericles himself died the following year (429 B.C.E.), a severe loss to Athens. Dominance now passed to Cleon, leader of the war party, who was opposed by Nicias (NISS-ee-uss), head of a conservative faction that favored peace. Despite the losses from the plague, the Athenians fought on in a struggle that witnessed numerous instances of futile destruction. Cleon achieved some successes for the Athenians; Brasidas (BRASS-i-duss) came to be a dynamic general for the Spartans. At the Battle of Amphipolis in 422 B.C.E., both generals were killed, and the new Athenian leader, Nicias, negotiated the Peace of Nicias (421 B.C.E.). Although both parties agreed to keep the peace for fifty years, the truce did not solve the problems that had caused the war in the first place.

A second phase of the war began only six years after the fifty-year truce. This phase was initiated by Alcibiades (al-suh-BY-uh-deez), a nephew of Pericles. Elected to the

Disaster in Sicily

At the beginning of his *History of the Peloponnesian War*, the Greek historian Thucydides wrote, "The Peloponnesian War . . . not only lasted for a long time, but throughout its course brought with it unprecedented suffering for Greece. Never before had so many cities been captured and then devastated, . . . never had there been so many exiles; never such loss of life." The greatest defeat for Athens came in Sicily in 413 B.C.E. In his history, Thucydides described what happened to the captured Athenians.

Thucydides, *History of the Peloponnesian War*

The Syracusans and their allies now brought their forces together into one, took up the spoils and as many of the prisoners as they could, and went back to their city. They put the Athenian and allied prisoners whom they had taken into the stone quarries, thinking that this was the safest way of keeping them. . . .

Those who were in the stone quarries were treated badly by the Syracusans at first. There were many of them, and they were crowded together in a narrow pit, where, since there was no roof over their heads, they suffered first from the heat of the sun and the closeness of the air; and then, in contrast, came on the cold autumnal nights, and the change in temperature brought disease among them. Lack of space made it necessary for them to do everything on the same spot; and besides there were the bodies all heaped together on top of one another of those who had died from their wounds or from the change of temperature or other such causes, so that the smell was insupportable. At the same time they suffered from hunger and from thirst. During eight months the daily allowance for each man was half a pint of water and a pint of corn. In fact they suffered everything which one could imagine might be suffered by men imprisoned in such a place. For about ten weeks they lived like this all together; then, with the exception of the Athenians and any Greeks from Italy or Sicily who had joined the expedition, the rest were sold as slaves. It is hard to give the exact figure, but the whole number of prisoners must have been at least 7,000.

This was the greatest Hellenic action that took place during this war, and, in my opinion, the greatest action that we know of in Hellenic history—to the victors the most brilliant of successes, to the vanquished the most calamitous of defeats; for they were utterly and entirely defeated; their sufferings were on an enormous scale; their losses were, as they say, total; army, navy, everything was destroyed, and, out of many, only few returned. So ended the events in Sicily.

Q What happened to the Athenian soldiers captured in Sicily? In what way was this not typical of the Greek way of war? How would you explain this change?

generalship in 420 B.C.E., he proved to be a poor choice because of his recklessness and self-seeking. In 415 B.C.E., he convinced the Athenians to invade the island of Sicily, arguing that its conquest would give the Athenians a strong source of support to carry on a lengthy war. But the expedition was ill-fated. Alcibiades himself was removed from the leadership of the expedition on a charge of profaning the religious mysteries. Rather than stand trial, he fled to Sparta and advised the Spartans how to defeat Athens by getting help from Persia and assembling a navy with ships and money supplied by the Persians. The Spartans later followed his advice.

In the meantime, the Athenians pursued the Sicilian policy. A "great expedition" consisting of five thousand Athenian hoplites was sent out in 415 B.C.E. and reinforced two years later by an even larger army of Athenians and allies. All was in vain. The Athenians failed to take Syracuse and were captured during their retreat. All of the Athenians were killed or sold into slavery (see the box above). These heavy losses at Syracuse had immediate domestic repercussions. The democracy was weakened, and an aristocratic oligarchy was temporarily established (411–410 B.C.E.).

Despite the disaster, the Athenians refused to give up; they raised new armies and sent out new fleets. The final crushing blow, however, came in 405 B.C.E., when the Athenian fleet was destroyed at Aegospotami (ee-guh-SPAH-tuh-my) on the Hellespont. Athens was besieged and surrendered the next year. Its walls were torn down, the navy was disbanded, and the Athenian empire was dissolved. The great war was finally over.

The Decline of the Greek States (404–338 B.C.E.)

The next seventy years witnessed continuing warfare among the Greeks, with the leading roles shifting among Sparta, Athens, and a new Greek power, the city-state of Thebes. After the defeat of Athens in 404 B.C.E., the Spartans established their own control over Greece. The Athenian empire was no more. Oligarchies, headed by local ten-man boards in cooperation with Spartan garrisons, were placed in control of the states "liberated" from Athenian imperialism. But oligarchical control proved ineffective, especially in Athens, where the ruling oligarchical faction of thirty, set up by the Spartans, earned the nickname of "Thirty Tyrants" by executing about fifteen hundred of their democratic opponents. This led to a reaction in which the Athenians were able to

CHRONOLOGY **The Great Peloponnesian War**

Invasion of Attica	431 B.C.E.
Battle of Amphipolis	422 B.C.E.
Peace of Nicias	421 B.C.E.
Athenian invasion of Sicily	415–413 B.C.E.
Battle of Aegospotami	405 B.C.E.
Surrender of Athens	404 B.C.E.

reestablish their democracy in 403 B.C.E. They also rebuilt their navy and again became an important force in the Greek world.

To maintain its newly organized leadership in Greek affairs, Sparta encouraged a Panhellenic crusade against the Persians as a common enemy. The Persians had taken advantage of the Greeks' internal struggle to reimpose their control over the Greek states in western Asia Minor. The Spartans, under King Agesilaus (uh-jess-uh-LAY-uss), led a Greek expedition into Asia Minor in 396 B.C.E. But the Persians had learned the lessons of Greek politics and offered financial support to Athens, Thebes, and other Greek states to oppose Spartan power within Greece itself, thus beginning a new war, the Corinthian War (395–386 B.C.E.). The war ended when the Greek states, weary of the struggles, accepted the King's Peace, dictated by the Great King of Persia.

The city-state of Thebes, in Boeotia north of Athens, now began to exert its influence. Under their leader Epaminondas (i-PAM-uh-NAHN-duss), the Thebans dramatically defeated the Spartan army at the Battle of Leuctra in 371 B.C.E. Spartan power declined, to be replaced by the ascendancy of the Thebans. But Theban power was short-lived. After the death of Epaminondas in the Battle of Mantinea in 362 B.C.E., the Thebans could no longer dominate Greek politics. And yet the Greek states continued their petty wars, seemingly oblivious to the growing danger to the north, where King Philip II of Macedonia was developing a unified state that would finally end the destructive fratricide of the Greek states by imposing Macedonian authority.

Culture and Society of Classical Greece

FOCUS QUESTIONS: Upon what ideals was Classical Greek art based, and how were these ideals expressed? What questions did the Greek philosophers pose, and what answers did they suggest?

Classical Greece saw a period of remarkable intellectual and cultural growth throughout the Greek world. Historians agree, however, that Periclean Athens was the most important center of Classical Greek culture.

The Writing of History

History as we know it, the systematic analysis of past events, was a Greek creation. Herodotus (huh-ROD-uh-tuss) (c. 484–c. 425 B.C.E.), was the author of *The Persian Wars,* a work commonly regarded as the first real history in Western civilization. The Greek word *historia* (from which we derive our word *history*) means "research" or "investigation," and it is in the opening line of Herodotus's work that we find the first recorded use of the word:

> Here are presented the researches (*historiae*) carried out by Herodotus of Halicarnassus. The purpose is to prevent the traces of human events from being erased by time, and to preserve the fame of the important and remarkable achievements produced by both Greeks and non-Greeks; among the matters covered is, in particular, the cause of the hostilities between Greeks and non-Greeks.[11]

The central theme of Herodotus's work is the conflict between the Greeks and the Persians, which he viewed as a struggle between Greek freedom and Persian despotism. Herodotus traveled widely for his information and was dependent for his sources on what we today would call oral history. Although he was a master storyteller and sometimes included considerable fanciful material, Herodotus was also capable of exhibiting a critical attitude toward the materials he used. Regardless of its weaknesses, Herodotus's history is an important source of information on the Persians and our chief source on the Persian Wars themselves.

THUCYDIDES Thucydides (c. 460–c. 400 B.C.E.) was a far better historian; in fact, modern historians consider him the greatest of the ancient world. Thucydides was an Athenian and a participant in the Peloponnesian War. He had been elected a general, but a defeat in battle led the Athenian assembly to send him into exile. In *History of the Peloponnesian War,* he described his activities:

> I lived through the whole of it, being of an age to understand what was happening, and I put my mind to the subject so as to get an accurate view of it. It happened, too, that I was banished from my country for twenty years after my command at Amphipolis [422 B.C.E.]; I saw what was being done on both sides, particularly on the Peloponnesian side, because of my exile, and this leisure gave me rather exceptional facilities for looking into things.[12]

Unlike Herodotus, Thucydides was not concerned with underlying divine forces or gods as explanatory causal factors in history. He saw war and politics in purely rational terms, as the activities of human beings. He examined the long-range and immediate causes of the Peloponnesian War in a clear, methodical, objective fashion. Thucydides placed much emphasis on accuracy and the precision of his facts. As he stated:

> And with regard to my factual reporting of the events of the war I have made it a principle not to write down the first story that came my way, and not even to be guided by my own general impressions; either I was present myself at the

events which I have described or else I heard of them from eyewitnesses whose reports I have checked with as much thoroughness as possible.[13]

Thucydides also provided remarkable insight into the human condition. He believed that human nature was a constant: "It will be enough for me, however, if these words of mine are judged useful by those who want to understand clearly the events which happened in the past and which (human nature being what it is) will, at some time or other and in much the same ways, be repeated in the future."[14] He was not so naive as to believe in an exact repetition of events but felt that political situations recur in similar fashion and that the study of history is of great value in understanding the present.

Greek Drama

Drama as we know it was created by the Greeks and was clearly intended to do more than entertain. It was used to educate citizens and was supported by the state for that reason. Plays were presented in outdoor theaters as part of religious festivals. The form of Greek plays remained rather stable. Three male actors who wore masks acted all the parts. A chorus, also male, spoke the important lines that explained what was going on. Action was very limited because the emphasis was on the story and its meaning.

AESCHYLUS The first Greek dramas were tragedies, plays based on the suffering of a hero and usually ending in disaster. Aeschylus (525–456 B.C.E.) is the first tragedian whose plays are known to us. Although he wrote ninety tragedies, only seven have survived. As was customary in Greek tragedy, his plots are simple. The entire drama focuses on a single tragic event and its meaning. Greek tragedies were sometimes presented in a trilogy (a set of three plays) built around a common theme. The only complete trilogy we possess, called the *Oresteia* (uh-res-TY-uh), was composed by Aeschylus. The theme of this trilogy is derived from Homer. Agamemnon, the king of Mycenae, returns a hero from the defeat of Troy. His wife, Clytemnestra, avenges the sacrificial death of her daughter Iphigenia by murdering Agamemnon, who had been responsible for Iphigenia's death. In the second play of the trilogy, Agamemnon's son Orestes avenges his father by killing his mother. Orestes is now pursued by the avenging Furies, who torment him for killing his mother. Evil acts breed evil acts, and suffering is one's lot, suggests Aeschylus. But Orestes is put on trial and acquitted by Athena, the patron goddess of Athens. Personal vendetta has been eliminated, and law has prevailed.

Aeschylus, excerpt from *Agamemnon* (458 B.C.E.)

SOPHOCLES Another great Athenian playwright was Sophocles (SAHF-uh-kleez) (c. 496–406 B.C.E.), whose most famous play is *Oedipus the King.* The oracle of Apollo foretells that a man (Oedipus) will kill his own father and marry his mother. Despite all attempts at prevention, the tragic events occur. Although it appears that Oedipus suffered the fate determined by the gods, Oedipus also accepts that he himself as a free man must bear responsibility for his actions: "It was Apollo, friends, Apollo, that brought this bitter bitterness, my sorrows to completion. But the hand that struck me was none but my own."[15]

EURIPIDES The third outstanding Athenian tragedian, Euripides (uoo-RIP-i-deez) (c. 485–406 B.C.E.), moved beyond his predecessors in creating more realistic characters. His plots also became more complex, reflecting a greater interest in real-life situations. Perhaps the greatest of all his plays is *The Bacchae,* which deals with the introduction of the hysterical rites associated with Dionysus, god of wine. Euripides is often seen as a skeptic who questioned traditional moral and religious values. Euripides was also critical of the traditional view that war was glorious. He portrayed war as brutal and barbaric and expressed deep compassion for the women and children who suffered from it.

Greek tragedies dealt with universal themes that are still relevant in our day. They probed such problems as the

Louvre, Paris//© Erich Lessing/Art Resource, NY

Greek Tragedy: *The Eumenides.* A fourth-century B.C.E. Greek artist depicted this detail on a red-figured bell-krater from Apulia. Shown is a scene from *The Eumenides,* the third play of the *Oresteia* trilogy written by Aeschylus. In this play, Orestes is acquitted by Athena of the crime of killing his mother to avenge his father's death. The Furies, who had been pursuing Orestes for killing his mother, become instead the Eumenides—the "Kindly Ones." In this scene Apollo purifies Orestes with a piglet's blood while Orestes is shown holding the dagger with which he killed his mother. Clytemnestra is seen trying to awaken the sleeping Furies.

Athenian Comedy: Sex as an Antiwar Instrument

Aristophanes used his comedies to present political messages, especially to express his antiwar sentiments. The plot of *Lysistrata* centers on a sex strike by wives in order to get their husbands to end the Peloponnesian War. In this scene from the play, Lysistrata (whose name means "she who dissolves the armies") has the women swear a special oath.

Aristophanes, *Lysistrata*

LYSISTRATA: Lampito: all of you women: come, touch the bowl, and repeat after me: *I will have nothing to do with my husband or my lover*

KALONIKE: I will have nothing to do with my husband or my lover

LYSISTRATA: *Though he come to me in pitiful condition*

KALONIKE: Though he come to me in pitiful condition (Oh, Lysistrata! This is killing me!)

LYSISTRATA: *I will stay in my house untouchable*

KALONIKE: I will stay in my house untouchable

LYSISTRATA: *In my thinnest saffron silk*

KALONIKE: In my thinnest saffron silk

LYSISTRATA: *And make him long for me*

KALONIKE: And make him long for me

LYSISTRATA: *I will not give myself*

KALONIKE: I will not give myself

LYSISTRATA: *And if he constrains me*

KALONIKE: And if he constrains me

LYSISTRATA: *I will be as cold as ice and never move*

KALONIKE: I will be as cold as ice and never move

LYSISTRATA: *I will not lift my slippers toward the ceiling*

KALONIKE: I will not lift my slippers toward the ceiling

LYSISTRATA: *Or crouch on all fours like the lioness in the carving*

KALONIKE: Or crouch on all fours like the lioness in the carving

LYSISTRATA: *And if I keep this oath let me drink from this bowl*

KALONIKE: And if I keep this oath let me drink from this bowl

LYSISTRATA: *If not, let my own bowl be filled with water.*

KALONIKE: If not, let my own bowl be filled with water.

LYSISTRATA: You have all sworn?

MYRRHINE: We have.

Q How does this selection from Aristophanes illustrate the political use of comedy and male views of women in Classical Greece?

nature of good and evil, the conflict between spiritual values and the demands of the state or family, the rights of the individual, the nature of divine forces, and the nature of human beings. Over and over again, the tragic lesson was repeated: humans were free and yet could operate only within limitations imposed by the gods. The real task was to cultivate the balance and moderation that led to awareness of one's true position. But the pride in human accomplishment and independence is real. As the chorus chants in Sophocles' *Antigone:* "Is there anything more wonderful on earth, our marvelous planet, than the miracle of man?"[16]

GREEK COMEDY Greek comedy developed later than tragedy. The plays of Aristophanes (ar-is-STAH-fuh-neez) (c. 450–c. 385 B.C.E.), who used both grotesque masks and obscene jokes to entertain the Athenian audience, are examples of Old Comedy, which was used to attack or savagely satirize both politicians and intellectuals. In *The Clouds,* for example, Aristophanes characterizes the philosopher Socrates as the operator of a thought factory where people could learn deceitful ways to handle other people. Later plays give up the element of personal attack and focus on contemporary issues. Of special importance to Aristophanes was his opposition to the Peloponnesian War. *Lysistrata,* performed in 411 B.C.E., at a time when Athens was in serious danger of losing the war, has a comic but effective message against the war (see the box above).

The Arts: The Classical Ideal

The artistic standards established by the Greeks of the Classical period have largely dominated the arts of the Western world. Classical Greek art did not aim at experimentation for experiment's sake but was concerned with expressing eternally true ideals. Its subject matter was basically the human being, expressed harmoniously as an object of great beauty. The Classical style, based on the ideals of reason, moderation, symmetry, balance, and harmony in all things, was meant to civilize the emotions.

In architecture, the most important form was the temple dedicated to a god or goddess. Since Greek religious ceremonies were held at altars in the open air, temples were not used to enclose the faithful, as modern churches are. At the center of Greek temples were walled rooms that housed the statues of deities and treasuries in which gifts to the gods and goddesses were safeguarded. These central rooms were surrounded by a screen of columns that make Greek temples open structures rather than closed ones. The columns were originally made of wood but changed to limestone in the seventh century and to marble in the fifth century B.C.E. The most

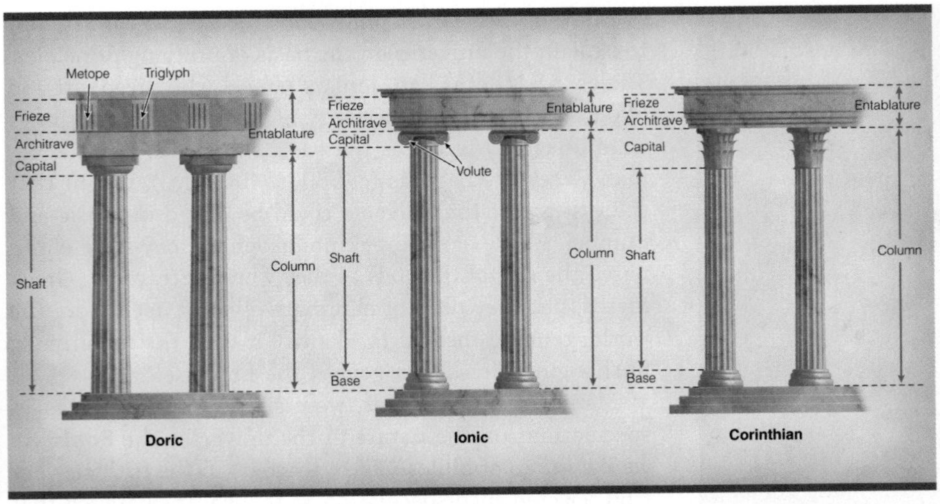

Doric, Ionic, and Corinthian Orders. The size and shape of a column constituted one of the most important aspects of Greek temple architecture. The Doric order, with plain capitals and no base, developed first in the Dorian Peloponnesus and was rather simple in comparison to the slender Ionic column, which had an elaborate base and spiral-shaped capitals, and the Corinthian column, which featured leaf-shaped capitals.

significant formal element in Greek temples was the shape and size of the columns in combination with the features above and below the column.

Some of the finest examples of Classical Greek architecture were built in fifth-century Athens. The development of Athenian architecture was aided tremendously by the massive rebuilding program funded from the treasury of the Delian League and instituted almost a half-century after the Persians destroyed Athens in the Persian Wars. Especially important was a series of constructions on the Acropolis begun in 448 B.C.E., which included a monumental entrance gate, a temple to Athena Nike (the Bringer of Victory), and the Erechtheum, a multilevel temple. These temples honored the gods and heroes who protected Athens.

The most famous building, regarded as the greatest example of the Classical Greek temple, was the Parthenon, built between 447 and 432 B.C.E. and consecrated to Athena, the patron goddess of Athens. The Parthenon typifies the principles of Classical architecture: the search for calm, clarity, and freedom from superfluous detail. The individual parts of the temple were constructed in accordance with certain mathematical ratios found in nature. The concern of the architects with these laws of proportion is paralleled by the attempt of Greek philosophers to understand the general laws of nature.

Greek sculpture also developed a Classical style that differed significantly from the artificial stiffness of the *kouros* figure of the Archaic Period. Statues of the male nude, the favorite subject of Greek sculptors, now exhibited more relaxed attitudes; their faces were self-assured, their bodies flexible and smooth-muscled. Although the figures possessed natural features that made them lifelike, Greek sculptors sought to achieve not realism but a standard of ideal beauty. Polyclitus (pahl-ee-KLY-tuss), a fifth-century sculptor, wrote a treatise (now lost) on a canon of proportions that he illustrated in a work known as the *Doryphoros* (doh-RIF-uh-rohss).

The Parthenon. The arts in Classical Greece were designed to express the eternal ideals of reason, moderation, symmetry, balance, and harmony. In architecture, the most important form was the temple, and the classic example of this kind of architecture is the Parthenon, built between 447 and 432 B.C.E. Located on the Acropolis in Athens, the Parthenon was dedicated to Athena, the patron goddess of the city, but it also served as a shining example of the power and wealth of the Athenian empire.

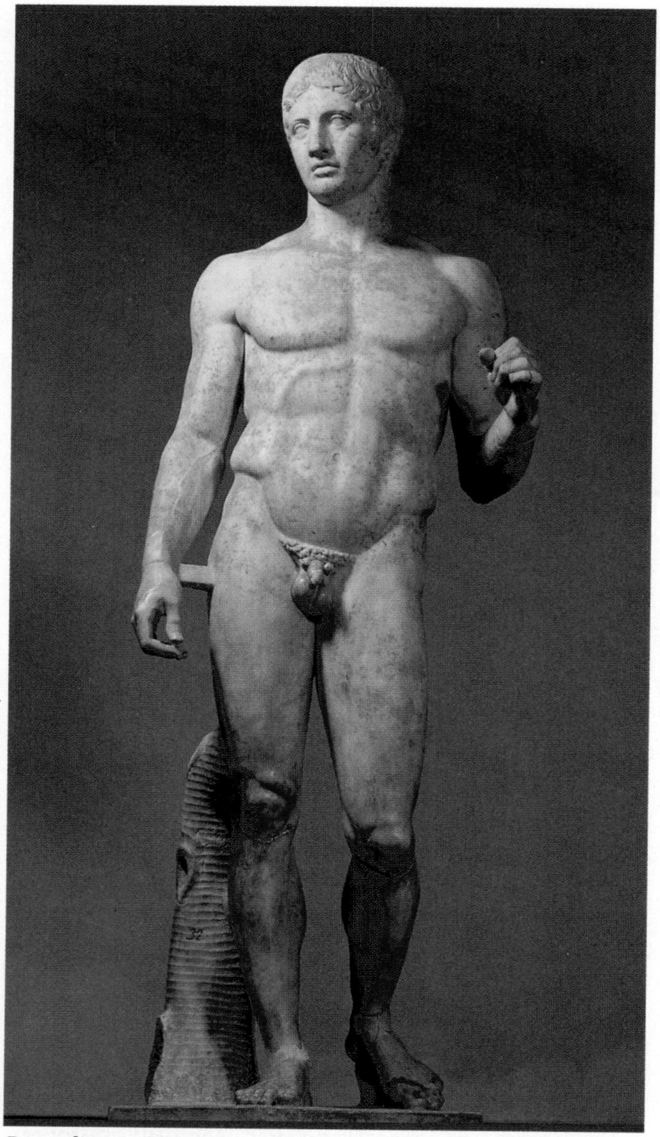

Doryphoros. This statue, known as the *Doryphoros,* or spear carrier, is a Roman copy of the original work by the fifth-century B.C.E. sculptor Polyclitus, who believed it illustrated the ideal proportions of the human figure. Classical Greek sculpture moved away from the stiffness of the *kouros* figure but retained the young male nude as the favorite subject matter. The statues became more lifelike, with relaxed poses and flexible, smooth-muscled bodies. The aim of sculpture, however, was not simply realism but rather the expression of ideal beauty.

His theory maintained that the use of ideal proportions, based on mathematical ratios found in nature, could produce an ideal human form, beautiful in its perfected and refined features. This search for ideal beauty was the dominant feature of the Classical standard in sculpture.

The Greek Love of Wisdom

Philosophy is a Greek word that literally means "love of wisdom." Early Greek philosophers were concerned with the development of critical or rational thought about the nature of the universe and the place of divine forces and souls in it.

Much of early Greek philosophy focused on the attempt to explain the universe on the basis of unifying principles. Thales of Miletus, an Ionian Greek who lived around 600 B.C.E., postulated the unity of the universe. All things were linked by water as the basic substance. Another Ionian Greek, Pythagoras (c. 580–c. 490 B.C.E.), taught that the essence of the universe could be found in music and number. These early Greek philosophers may have eliminated the role of the gods as they were portrayed in Greek myths, but they did not eliminate divinity itself from the world, tending instead to identify it with the underlying, unchanging forces that govern the universe.

Many Greeks, however, were simply not interested in speculations on the nature of the universe. The **Sophists** were a group of philosophical teachers in the fifth century who rejected such speculation as foolish; they argued that understanding the universe was beyond the reach of the human mind. It was more important for individuals to improve themselves, so the only worthwhile object of study was human behavior. The Sophists were wandering scholars who sold their services as professional teachers to the young men of Greece, especially those of Athens. The Sophists stressed the importance of **rhetoric** (the art of persuasive speaking) in winning debates and swaying an audience, a skill that was especially valuable in democratic Athens. To the Sophists, there was no absolute right or wrong—what was right for one individual might be wrong for another. True wisdom consisted of being able to perceive one's own good and to pursue its acquisition. Many people, however, viewed the Sophists as harmful to the traditional values of society and especially dangerous to the values of young people.

In Classical Greece, Athens became the foremost intellectual and artistic center. Its reputation is perhaps strongest of all in philosophy. After all, Socrates, Plato, and Aristotle raised basic questions that have been debated for more than two thousand years; these are still largely the same philosophical questions we wrestle with today.

SOCRATES Socrates (SAHK-ruh-teez) (469–399 B.C.E.) left no writings, but we know about him from his pupils, especially his most famous one, Plato. By occupation, Socrates was a stonemason, but his true love was philosophy. He taught a number of pupils, but not for pay, because he believed that the goal of education was only to improve the individual. He made use of a teaching method that is still known by his name. The **Socratic method** employs a question-and-answer technique to lead pupils to see things for themselves using their own reason. Socrates believed that all real knowledge is within each person; only critical examination was needed to call it forth. This was the real task of philosophy, since "the unexamined life is not worth living."

Socrates' questioning of authority and public demonstrations of others' lack of knowledge led him into trouble. Athens had had a tradition of free thought and inquiry, but its defeat in the Peloponnesian War created an environment intolerant of open debate and soul-searching. Socrates was accused and convicted of corrupting the youth of Athens by his teaching, and an Athenian jury sentenced him to death.

PLATO One of Socrates' disciples was Plato (PLAY-toh) (c. 429–347 B.C.E.), considered by many scholars the greatest philosopher of Western civilization. Unlike his master Socrates, who wrote nothing, Plato wrote a great deal. He was fascinated with the question of reality: How do we know what is real?

According to Plato, a higher world of eternal, unchanging Ideas or Forms has always existed. To know these Forms is to know truth. These ideal Forms constitute reality and can be apprehended only by a trained mind, which, of course, is the goal of philosophy. The objects that we perceive with our senses are simply reflections of the ideal Forms. Hence, they are shadows, while reality is found in the Forms themselves.

Plato's ideas of government were set out in a dialogue titled *The Republic*. Based on his experience in Athens, Plato had come to distrust the workings of democracy. It was obvious to him that individuals could not attain an ethical life unless they lived in a just and rational state. This insight led him to construct an ideal state in which the population was divided into three basic groups. At the top was an upper class, a ruling elite, the famous philosopher-kings: "Unless either philosophers become kings in their countries or those who are now called kings and rulers come to be sufficiently inspired with a genuine desire for wisdom; unless, that is to say, political power and philosophy meet together . . . there can be no rest from troubles . . . for states, nor yet, as I believe, for all mankind."[17] The second group consisted of the courageous; they would be the warriors who protected the society. All the rest made up the masses, essentially people driven not by wisdom or courage but by desire. They would be the producers of society—the artisans, tradesmen, and farmers.

Plato, *Republic*, Books 5 & 6 (360 B.C.E.)

In Plato's ideal state, each group fulfilled its assigned role, creating a society that functioned harmoniously. The needs of the community, rather than the happiness of the individual, were Plato's concern, and he focused on the need for the guardians or rulers, above all, to be removed from any concerns for wealth or prestige so that they could strive for what was best for the community. To rid the guardians of these desires, Plato urged that they live together, forgoing both private property and family life. Plato believed that women, too, could be rulers; in this he departed radically from the actual practices of the Greek states.

ARISTOTLE Plato established a school at Athens known as the Academy. One of his pupils, who studied there for twenty years, was Aristotle (AR-iss-tot-ul) (384–322 B.C.E.), who later became a tutor to Alexander the Great. Aristotle did not accept Plato's theory of ideal Forms. He believed that by examining individual objects, we can perceive their form and arrive at universal principles, but they do not exist as a separate higher world of reality beyond material things; rather they are a part of things themselves. Aristotle's interests, then, lay in analyzing and classifying things based on thorough research and investigation. His interests were wide-ranging, and he wrote treatises on an enormous number of subjects: ethics, logic, politics, poetry, astronomy, geology, biology, and physics.

Aristotle, *Politics*, Book 1 excerpts (350 B.C.E.)

Like Plato, Aristotle wished for an effective form of government that would rationally direct human affairs. Unlike Plato, he did not seek an ideal state based on embodiment of an ideal Form of justice; he tried to find the best form of government by a rational examination of existing governments. For his *Politics* (see the box on p. 82), Aristotle examined the constitutions of 158 states and arrived at general categories for organizing governments. He identified three good forms of government: monarchy, aristocracy, and constitutional government. But based on his examination, he warned that monarchy can easily turn into tyranny, aristocracy into oligarchy, and constitutional government into radical democracy or anarchy. He favored constitutional government as the best form for most people.

Aristotle's philosophical and political ideas played an enormous role in the development of Western thought during the Middle Ages (see Chapter 10). So did his ideas on women. Aristotle believed that marriage was meant to provide mutual comfort between man and woman and contributed to the overall happiness of a community: "The community needs both male and female excellences or it can only be half-blessed." Nevertheless, Aristotle maintained that women were biologically inferior to men: "A woman is, as it were, an infertile male. She is female in fact on account of a kind of inadequacy." Therefore, according to Aristotle, women must be subordinated to men, not only in the community but also in marriage: "The association between husband and wife is clearly an aristocracy. The man rules by virtue of merit, and in the sphere that is his by right; but he hands over to his wife such matters as are suitable for her."[18]

Greek Religion

Greek religion was intricately connected to every aspect of daily life; it was both social and practical. Public festivals, which originated from religious practices, served specific functions: boys were prepared to be warriors, girls to be mothers. Since religion was related to every aspect of life, citizens had to have a proper attitude toward the gods. Religion was a civic cult necessary for the well-being of the state. Temples dedicated to a god or goddess were the major buildings of Greek society.

The *Politics* of Aristotle

Aristotle was one of the great philosophers of ancient Athens. His philosophical and political ideas would play an important role in the evolution of Western thought during the Middle Ages. In this selection from his *Politics,* Aristotle examines the nature of political community and of the *polis.*

Aristotle, *Politics*

From these considerations it is evident that the *polis* belongs to the class of things that exist by nature, and that man is by nature an animal intended to live in a *polis.* He who is without a *polis,* by reason of his own nature and not of some accident, is either a poor sport of being, or a being higher than man: he is the man of whom Homer wrote in denunciation: "Clanless and lawless and hearthless is he." The man who is such by nature [unable to join in the society of a *polis*] at once plunges into a passion for war; he is in the position of a solitary advanced piece in a game of [checkers].

The reason why man is a being meant for political association, in a higher degree than bees or other gregarious animals can ever associate, is evident. Nature, according to our theory, makes nothing in vain; and man alone of the animals is furnished with the faculty of language. The mere making of sounds serves to indicate pleasure and pain, is thus a faculty that belongs to animals in general: their nature enables them to attain the point at which they have perceptions of pleasure and pain, and can signify those perceptions to one another. But language serves to declare what is advantageous and what is the reverse, and it therefore serves to declare what is just and what is unjust. It is the peculiarity of man, in comparison with the rest of the animal world, that he alone possesses perception of good and evil, of the just and the unjust, and of other similar qualities; and it is association in [a common perception of] these things which makes a family and a *polis.*

We now proceed to add that [though the individual and the family are prior in the order of time] the *polis* is prior in the order of nature to the family and the individual.

Q What do Aristotle's comments suggest about the importance of the *polis* to the ancient Greeks? How does Aristotle distinguish humans from other animals, and what is the relationship between humanity and the *polis*?

Homer gave an account of the gods that provided a definite structure to Greek religion. Over a period of time, most Greeks came to accept a common religion based on twelve chief gods who supposedly lived on Mount Olympus, the highest mountain in Greece. Among the twelve were Zeus, the chief deity and father of the gods; Athena, goddess of wisdom and crafts; Apollo, god of the sun and poetry; Aphrodite, goddess of love; and Poseidon, brother of Zeus and god of the seas and earthquakes.

The twelve Olympian gods were common to all Greeks, who thus shared a basic polytheistic religion. Each *polis* usually singled out one of the twelve Olympians as a guardian deity of its community. Athena was the patron goddess of Athens, for example. Because it was desirable to have the gods look favorably on one's activities, ritual assumed enormous proportions in Greek religion. Prayers were often combined with gifts to the gods based on the principle "I give so that you, the gods, will give in return." Ritual meant sacrifices, whether of animals or agricultural products. Animal victims were burned on an altar in front of a temple or on a small altar in front of a home.

Festivals also developed as a way to honor the gods and goddesses. Some of these (the Panhellenic celebrations) were important to all Greeks and were held at special locations, such as those dedicated to the worship of Zeus at Olympia, to Poseidon at the Isthmus of Corinth, and to Apollo at Delphi. The great festivals incorporated numerous events in honor of the gods, including athletic competitions to which all Greeks were invited. According to tradition, such games were first held at the Olympic festival in 776 B.C.E. and then held every four years thereafter to honor Zeus. Initially, the Olympic contests consisted of foot races and wrestling, but later boxing, javelin throwing, and various other contests were added. Competitions were always between individuals, not groups.

As another practical side of Greek religion, Greeks wanted to know the will of the gods. The most famous method of divining the will of the gods was the use of the *oracle,* a sacred shrine dedicated to a god or goddess who revealed the future. The most famous was the oracle of Apollo at Delphi, located on the side of Mount Parnassus, overlooking the Gulf of Corinth. At Delphi, a priestess listened to questions while in a state of ecstasy that was believed to be induced by Apollo. Her responses were interpreted by the priests and given in verse form to the person asking questions. Representatives of states and individuals traveled to Delphi to consult the oracle of Apollo. States might inquire whether they should undertake a military expedition; individuals might raise such questions as "Heracleidas asks the god whether he will have offspring from the wife he has now." Responses were often enigmatic and could be interpreted in more than one way. Croesus, the king of Lydia in Asia Minor who was known for his incredible wealth, sent messengers to the oracle at Delphi, asking whether he should go to war with

An Animal Sacrifice. Animal sacrifice was a regular part of Greek religious ritual. This painted wooden tablet, which was found in a cave near Corinth and dates from the sixth century B.C.E., depicts the beginning stage of an animal sacrifice performed at a small altar. After the sacrifice, the meat of the animal was cooked and shared by the participants.

the Persians. The oracle replied that if Croesus attacked the Persians, a mighty empire would be destroyed. Overjoyed to hear these words, Croesus made war on the Persians but was crushed by his enemy. A mighty empire was indeed destroyed—Croesus's own.

Greek religion, centered in ritual and a formal relationship with the gods, tended to lack a strong emotional component. It also offered no hope of life after death for most people. As a result, the Greeks sometimes turned to **mystery religions,** which included initiation into secret rites that promised a more emotional involvement with spiritual forces and a greater hope of immortality. The most important mysteries were those of the Eleusinian cult connected with the myth of Demeter. This was a fertility cult in which participants felt reborn and gained some hope for life after death.

Life in Classical Athens

The Greek city-state was, above all, a male community: only adult male citizens took part in public life. In Athens, this meant the exclusion of women, slaves, and foreign residents, or roughly 85 percent of the total population of Attica. In the fifth century, Athens had the largest population of all the Greek city-states. There were probably 150,000 citizens, of whom about 43,000 were adult males who exercised political power. Resident foreigners, known as **metics,** numbered about 35,000 and received the protection of the laws, but they were also subject to some of the responsibilities of citizens, namely, military service and the funding of festivals. The remaining social group, the slaves, numbered around 100,000.

SLAVERY AND THE ECONOMY Slavery was a common institution in the ancient world. Economic necessity dictated the desirability of owning at least one slave, although the very poor in Athens did not own any. A soldier on campaign usually took along one slave to carry his armor. The really wealthy might own large numbers of slaves, but those who did usually employed them in industry. Most often slaves in Athens performed domestic tasks as cooks and maids or worked in the fields. Few peasants could afford more than one or two. Other slaves worked as unskilled or skilled laborers. Slaves who worked in public construction were paid the same as metics or citizens.

The Athenian economy was largely agricultural but highly diversified. Athenian farmers grew grains, vegetables, and fruit for local consumption; cultivated vines and olives for wine and olive oil, which were exportable products; and raised sheep and goats for wool and milk products. Given the size of the population in Attica and the lack of abundant fertile land, Athens had to import between 50 and 80 percent of its grain, a staple in the Athenian diet. Trade was thus very important to the Athenian economy. The building of the port at Piraeus and the Long Walls (a series of defensive walls 41 miles long connecting Athens and Piraeus) created the physical conditions that made Athens the leading trade center in the fifth-century Greek world.

Athens did not have large numbers of artisans, but those it had were important to the economy. Athens was the chief producer of high-quality painted pottery in the fifth century. Other crafts had moved beyond the small workshop into the factory through the use of slave labor.

IMAGES OF EVERYDAY LIFE

Activities of Athenian Women

In Athens, women were considered citizens and could participate in religious cults and festivals, but they were barred from any political activity. Women were thought to belong in the house, caring for the children and the needs of the household. A principal activity of Greek women was the making of clothes. The scene on the left from the side of a fifth-century B.C.E. Greek vessel shows one woman spinning while another holds a small hand loom. The illustration on the right from a mid-sixth-century B.C.E. amphora shows another activity of Athenian women—participating in religious rituals. This scene shows a priestess dressed in an elaborate gown holding ceremonial branches and scattering holy water upon an altar while the men behind her are leading a bull to be sacrificed. It has recently been argued that the prominent position of the priestess standing in the center before the goddess Athena shows that the priestess was the chief supervisor of the sacrifice and, thus, is an indication that women as priestesses played important public roles in ancient Greece.

A SIMPLE LIFESTYLE The Athenian lifestyle was basically simple. Athenian houses were furnished with necessities bought from artisans, such as beds, couches, tables, chests, pottery, stools, baskets, and cooking utensils. Wives and slaves made clothes and blankets at home (see Images of Everyday Life above). The Athenian diet was rather plain. Basic foods consisted of barley, wheat, millet, lentils, grapes, figs, olives, almonds, bread made at home, vegetables, eggs, fish, cheese, and chicken. Olive oil was widely used, not only for eating but also for lighting lamps and for rubbing on the body after washing and exercise. Owners of country houses kept animals for reasons other than their flesh: oxen for plowing, sheep for wool, and goats for milk and cheese. Meat was consumed only on special occasions, such as festivals, when animals were sacrificed, cooked, and then eaten.

FAMILY AND RELATIONSHIPS The family was an important institution in ancient Athens. It was composed of husband, wife, and children (a nuclear family), although other dependent relatives and slaves were regarded as part of the family because of its economic unity. The family's primary social function was to produce new citizens. Strict laws of the fifth century had stipulated that a citizen must be the offspring of a legally acknowledged marriage between two Athenian citizens.

Women were citizens who could participate in most religious cults and festivals but were otherwise excluded from public life. They could not own property beyond personal items and always had a male guardian: if unmarried, a father or male relative; if married, a husband; if widowed, a son or male relative.

The function of the Athenian woman as wife was very clear. Her foremost obligation was to bear children, especially male children who would preserve the family line. The marriage formula that Athenians used put it succinctly: "I give this woman for the procreation of legitimate children." A wife was also expected to take care of her family and her house, either doing the household work herself or supervising the slaves who did the actual work (see the box on p. 85).

Women were kept under strict control. Since they were married at fourteen or fifteen, they were taught about their responsibilities at an early age. Although many managed to learn to read and play musical instruments, they were often cut off from any formal education. And women were expected to remain at home out of sight unless they attended funerals or festivals. If they left the house, they were to be accompanied.

Opposing VIEWPOINTS

Women in Athens and Sparta

In Classical Athens, a woman's place was in the home. She had two major responsibilities as a wife—bearing and raising children and managing the household. In the first selection, from a dialogue on estate management, Xenophon relates the instructions of an Athenian to his new wife. Although women in Sparta had the same responsibilities as women in Athens, they assumed somewhat different roles as a result of the Spartan lifestyle. The second, third, and fourth selections demonstrate these differences as seen in the accounts of three ancient Greek writers.

Xenophon, *Oeconomicus*

[Ischomachus addresses his new wife:] For it seems to me, dear, that the gods with great discernment have coupled together male and female, as they are called, chiefly in order that they may form a perfect partnership in mutual service. For, in the first place that the various species of living creatures may not fail, they are joined in wedlock for the production of children. Secondly, offspring to support them in old age is provided by this union, to human beings, at any rate. Thirdly, human beings live not in the open air, like beasts, but obviously need shelter. Nevertheless, those who mean to win stores to fill the covered place, have need of someone to work at the open-air occupations; since plowing, sowing, planting and grazing are all such open-air employments; and these supply the needful food.... For he made the man's body and mind more capable of enduring cold and heat, and journeys and campaigns; and therefore imposed on him the outdoor tasks. To the woman, since he had made her body less capable of such endurance, I take it that God has assigned the indoor tasks. And knowing that he had created in the woman and had imposed on her the nourishment of the infants, he meted out to her a larger portion of affection for newborn babes than to the man....

Your duty will be to remain indoors and send out those servants whose work is outside, and superintend those who are to work indoors, and to receive the incomings, and distribute so much of them as must be spent, and watch over so much as is to be kept in store, and take care that the sum laid by for a year be not spent in a month. And when wool is brought to you, you must see that cloaks are made for those that want them. You must see too that the dry corn is in good condition for making food. One of the duties that fall to you, however, will perhaps seem rather thankless: you will have to see that any servant who is ill is cared for.

Xenophon, *Constitution of the Spartans*

First, to begin at the beginning, I will start with the begetting of children. Elsewhere those girls who are going to have children and are considered to have been well brought up are nourished with the plainest diet which is practicable and the smallest amount of luxury good possible; wine is certainly not allowed them at all, or only if well diluted. Just as the majority of craftsmen are sedentary, the other Greeks expect their girls to sit quietly and work wool. But how can one expect girls brought up like this to give birth to healthy babies? Lycurgus (see p. 64) considered slave girls quite adequate to produce clothing, and thought that for free women the most important job was to bear children. In the first place, therefore, he prescribed physical training for the female sex no less than for the male; and next, just as for men, he arranged competitions of racing and strength for women also, thinking that if both parents were strong their children would be more robust.

Aristotle, *Politics*

Now, this license of the [Spartan] women, from the earliest times, was to be expected. For the men were absent from home for long periods of time on military expeditions, fighting the war against the Argives and again against the Arkadians and Messenians;.... And nearly two-fifths of the whole country is in the hands of women, both because there have been numerous heiresses, and because large dowries are customary. And yet it would have been better to have regulated them, and given none at all or small or even moderate ones. But at present it is possible for a man to give an inheritance to whomever he chooses.

Plutarch, *Lycurgus*

Since Lycurgus regarded education as the most important and finest duty of the legislator, he began at the earliest stage by looking at matters relating to marriages and births.... For he exercised the girls' bodies with races and wrestling and discus and javelin throwing, so that the embryos formed in them would have a strong start in strong bodies and develop better, and they would undergo their pregnancies with vigor and would cope well and easily with childbirth. He got rid of daintiness and sheltered upbringing and effeminacy of all kinds, by accustoming the girls no less than the young men to walking naked in processions and dancing and

(continued)

singing at certain festivals, when young men were present and watching. . . . The nudity of the girls had nothing disgraceful in it for modesty was present and immorality absent, but rather it made them accustomed to simplicity and enthusiastic as to physical fitness, and gave the female sex a taste of noble spirit, in as much as they too had a share in valor and ambition.

Q In what ways were the lifestyles of Athenian and Spartan women the same? In what ways were they different? How did the Athenian and Spartan views of the world shape their conceptions of gender and gender roles, and why were those conceptions different?

Women in Athens served males in other ways as well. Prostitution flourished in Classical Athens. Most female prostitutes were slaves in brothels run as a business or trade by an Athenian citizen. Another class of prostitutes in Athenian society occupied a more favorable position; these more refined courtesans were known as ***hetairai*** (huh-TY-ree), literally "female companions." Usually ex-slaves or foreigners, these women were more sophisticated than ordinary prostitutes and were known for their intellectual and musical achievements as well as their physical ones. Athenian males continued the aristocratic practice of the *symposium,* a sophisticated drinking party, where *hetairai* were often present. Symposia were held in the men's dining rooms, and wives were not present. *Hetairai* danced, played musical instruments, and provided entertainment, including sex. Some *hetairai* achieved fortune and considerable renown. Aspasia was the most famous. A friend of Socrates and known for her learning, she was the mistress of Pericles and eventually became his wife.

Male homosexuality was also a prominent feature of Classical Athens. It was widely practiced and tolerated. Athenian law disenfranchised a citizen who had prostituted his body to another male, but nothing was done to males who engaged in homosexual love with male prostitutes or other adult males for love or pleasure. The law did not eliminate male prostitution but ensured that male prostitutes would be foreigners, not Athenian citizens.

The Greek homosexual ideal was a relationship between a mature man and a young male. It is likely that this was primarily an aristocratic ideal. While the relationship was frequently physical, the Greeks also viewed it as educational. The older male (the "lover") won the love of his "beloved" by his value as a teacher and by the devotion he demonstrated in training his charge. In a sense, this love relationship was seen as a way of initiating young males into the male world of political and military dominance. The Greeks did not feel that the coexistence of homosexual and heterosexual predilections created any special problems for individuals or their society.

CHAPTER SUMMARY

The earliest Greek-speaking people migrated into Greece about 2000 B.C.E., and by 1600 B.C.E. they had established a Greek civilization, known as Mycenaean civilization from Mycenae, one of its major cities.

After its collapse in the twelfth century B.C.E., Greece entered a Dark Age. With the end of the Dark Age around 800 B.C.E., the era of the *polis,* or city-state, began. The *polis* was a community of citizens ruled by its male citizens. The two most famous city-states were Sparta, a militaristic *polis* ruled by an oligarchy, and Athens, which became known for its democratic institutions in spite of the fact that slaves and women had no political rights.

The Greek city-states flourished and reached their height in the Classical era of the fifth century B.C.E. The century began with the Persian Wars, which temporarily unified the Greeks, who were victorious against the powerful Persian Empire. But the growth of an Athenian empire led to a mighty conflict between Athens and Sparta—the Great Peloponnesian War—that weakened the Greek city-states and ultimately opened the door to an invasion by Philip II of Macedonia that put an end to their freedom in 338 B.C.E.

The civilization of the ancient Greeks was the fountainhead of Western culture. Socrates, Plato, and Aristotle established the foundations of Western philosophy. Herodotus and Thucydides created the discipline of history. Our literary forms are largely derived from Greek poetry and drama. Greek notions of

harmony, proportion, and beauty have remained the touchstones for all subsequent Western art and architecture. A rational method of inquiry, so important to modern science, was conceived in ancient Greece. Many of our political terms are Greek in origin, and so are our concepts of the rights and duties of citizenship, especially as they were conceived in Athens, which gave the idea of democracy to the Western world. Especially during the Classical period, the Greeks raised and debated fundamental questions about the purpose of human existence, the structure of human society, and the nature of the universe that have concerned Western thinkers ever since. Although the Greeks did not conceive of Western civilization as a cultural entity, their artistic, intellectual, and political contributions were crucial to the foundations of Western civilization.

All of these achievements came from a group of small city-states in ancient Greece. And yet there remains an element of tragedy about Greek civilization. For all of their brilliant accomplishments, the Greeks were unable to rise above the divisions and rivalries that caused them to fight each other and undermine their own civilization. Luckily, their contributions to Western civilization survived their political struggles.

CHAPTER TIMELINE

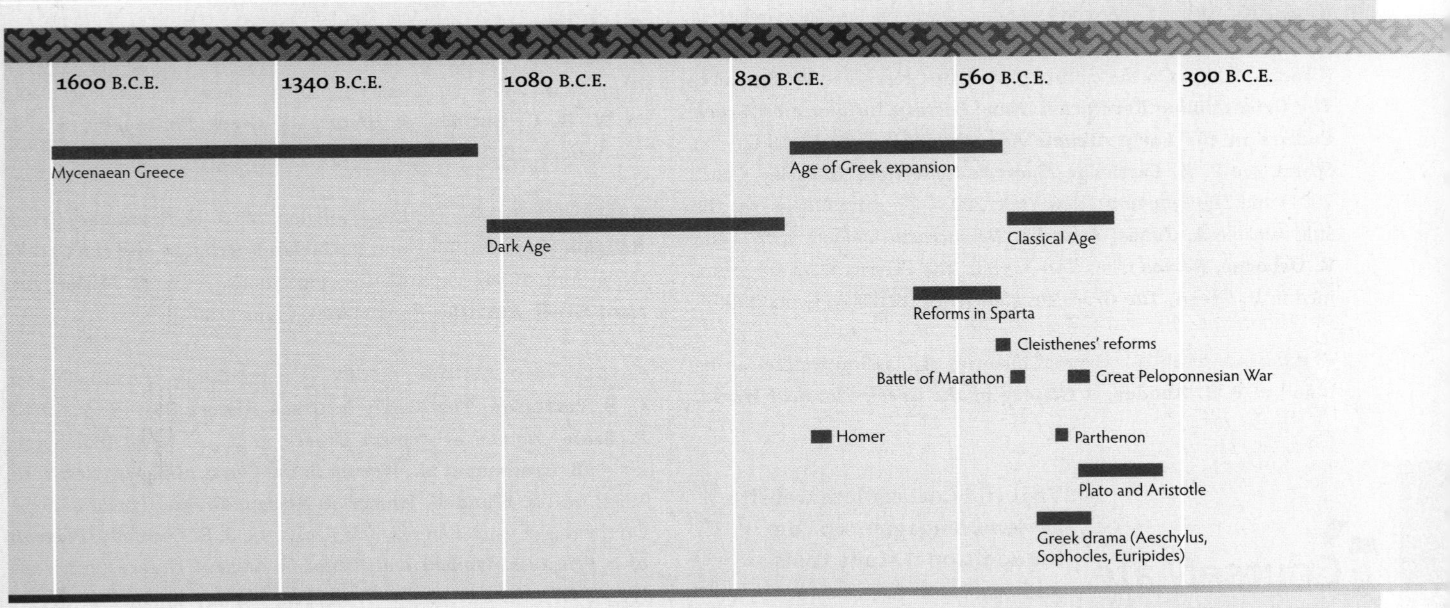

CHAPTER REVIEW

Upon Reflection

Q What was the *polis,* and why is it considered by many historians to be an important development in the political history of Western civilization?

Q Discuss the organization of the Athenian political system. Was it a democracy? In what ways was Athenian democracy similar to U.S. democracy? In what ways was it different?

Q The Classical Age in Greece is known for its literary, artistic, and intellectual achievements. What basic characteristics of Greek culture are reflected in the major achievements of the Greeks in the writing of history, drama, the arts, and philosophy? What universal human concerns did these same achievements reflect?

Key Terms

polis (p. 60)
hoplites (p. 60)
phalanx (p. 60)
tyrants (p. 62)
perioikoi (p. 63)
helots (p. 63)
oligarchy (p. 64)
Sophists (p. 80)
rhetoric (p. 80)
Socratic method (p. 80)
mystery religions (p. 83)
metics (p. 83)
hetairai (p. 86)

Suggestions for Further Reading

GENERAL WORKS Good general introductions to Greek history include **T. R. Martin, *Ancient Greece*** (New Haven, Conn., 1996); **P. Cartledge, *The Cambridge Illustrated History of Ancient Greece*** (Cambridge, 1998); and **W. Donlan et al., *Ancient Greece: A Political, Social, and Cultural History*** (New York, 1998). On the Greek way of war, see **V. D. Hanson, *The Wars of the Ancient Greeks,*** rev. ed. (London, 2006).

EARLY GREEK HISTORY Early Greek history is examined in **O. Murray, *Early Greece,*** 2nd ed. (Cambridge, Mass., 1993); and **J. L. Fitton, *The Discovery of the Greek Bronze Age*** (Cambridge, 1995). On the Trojan War, see **B. Strauss, *The Trojan War: A New History*** (New York, 2006).

ARCHAIC GREECE A good general work on Archaic Greece is **J. Hall, *History of the Archaic Greek World, c. 1200–479 B.C.*** (London, 2006). On the culture of Archaic Greece, see **W. Burkert, *The Orientalizing Revolution: Near Eastern Influence on Greek Culture in the Early Archaic Age*** (Cambridge, Mass., 1992). On Sparta, see **P. A. Cartledge, *Spartan Reflections*** (Berkeley, Calif., 2001) and ***The Spartans*** (New York, 2003). On early Athens, see the still valuable **A. Jones, *Athenian Democracy*** (London, 1957), and **R. Osborne, *Demos*** (New York, 1985). The Persian Wars are examined in **P. Green, *The Greco-Persian Wars*** (Berkeley, Calif., 1996).

CLASSICAL GREECE General histories of Classical Greece can be found in **P. J. Rhodes, *A History of the Greek Classical World, 478–323 B.C.*** (London, 2006), and **S. Hornblower, *The Greek World, 479–323 B.C.,*** 3rd ed. (London, 2002). Valuable works on Athens include **D. Kagan, *Pericles of Athens and the Birth of Democracy*** (New York, 1991), and **K. A. Raaflaub et al., *Origins of Democracy in Ancient Greece*** (Berkeley, Calif., 2007). On the development of the Athenian empire, see **M. F. McGregor, *The Athenians and Their Empire*** (Vancouver, 1987). Recent accounts of the Great Peloponnesian War include **D. Kagan, *The Peloponnesian War*** (New York, 2003); **J. F. F. Lazenby, *The Peloponnesian War*** (New York, 2004); and **V. D. Hanson, *A War Like No Other*** (New York, 2006).

GREEK CULTURE For a history of Greek art, see **M. Fullerton, *Greek Art*** (Cambridge, 2000). On sculpture, see **A. Stewart, *Greek Sculpture: An Exploration*** (New Haven, Conn., 1990). On Greek drama, see the general work by **J. De Romilly, *A Short History of Greek Literature*** (Chicago, 1985). On Greek history writing, see **D. Shanske, *Thucydides and the Philosophical Origin of History*** (Cambridge, 2006). On Greek philosophy, a detailed study is available in **W. K. C. Guthrie, *A History of Greek Philosophy,*** 6 vols. (Cambridge, 1962–81).

GREEK RELIGION On Greek religion, see **J. N. Bremmer, *Greek Religion*** (Oxford, 1994), and **R. Garland, *Religion and the Greeks*** (New York, 1994). On athletic competitions, see **S. G. Miller, *Ancient Greek Athletics*** (New Haven, Conn., 2004).

FAMILY AND GENDER ISSUES On the family and women, see **C. B. Patterson, *The Family in Greek History*** (New York, 1998); **P. Brule, *Women of Ancient Greece,*** trans. A. Nevill (Edinburgh, 2004); **E. Fantham et al., *Women in the Classical World*** (New York, 1994); and **S. Blundell, *Women in Ancient Greece*** (London, 1995). On the role of women in religious rituals, see **J. B. Connelly, *Portrait of a Priestess: Women and Ritual in Ancient Greece*** (Princeton, N.J., 2007). On slavery, see **Y. Garlan, *Slavery in Ancient Greece*** (Ithaca, N.Y., 1988), and **N. R. E. Fisher, *Slavery in Classical Greece*** (New York, 1995).

CourseMate

Visit the CourseMate website at www.cengagebrain.com for additional study tools and review materials for this chapter.

CHAPTER 4

Louvre, Paris//© Reunion des Musees Nationaux/Art Resource, NY

Roman statuette of Alexander the Great wearing a helmet

The Hellenistic World

CHAPTER OUTLINE AND FOCUS QUESTIONS

Macedonia and the Conquests of Alexander

Q How was Alexander able to amass his empire, and what might his rule have been like if he had lived longer?

The World of the Hellenistic Kingdoms

Q What were the main features of the political and military organization of the Hellenistic kingdoms, and how did the new political systems differ from those of the Greek city-states?

Hellenistic Society

Q What were the main social developments in the Hellenistic world?

Culture in the Hellenistic World

Q What achievements in literature, art, science, medicine, and philosophy occurred during the Hellenistic period?

Religion in the Hellenistic World

Q Which religions were prominent during the Hellenistic period, and what does their popularity suggest about Hellenistic society?

CRITICAL THINKING

Q How was the Hellenistic period different from the Greek Classical Age?

IN 334 B.C.E., Alexander the Great led an army of Macedonians and Greeks into western Asia to launch his attack on the Persian Empire. Years of campaigning resulted in the complete defeat of the Persians, and in 327 B.C.E., Alexander and his troops pushed eastward into India. But two more years of fighting in an exotic and difficult terrain exhausted his troops, who rebelled and refused to go on. Reluctantly, Alexander turned back, leading his men across the arid lands of southern Persia. Conditions in the desert were appalling; the blazing sun and lack of water led to thousands of deaths. At one point, when a group of his soldiers found a little water, they scooped it up in a helmet and gave it to Alexander. Then, according to Arrian, an ancient Greek historian, Alexander, "with a word of thanks for the gift, took the helmet and, in full view of his troops, poured the water on the ground. So extraordinary was the effect of this action that the water wasted by Alexander was as good as a drink for every man in the army." Ever the great military leader, Alexander had found yet another way to inspire his troops.

Alexander the Great was the son of King Philip II of Macedonia, who in 338 B.C.E. defeated the Greeks and established his control over the Greek peninsula. After Philip's death, Alexander became king and led the Macedonians and Greeks on a spectacular conquest of the Persian Empire, opening the door to the spread of Greek culture throughout the ancient Near East. Greek settlers poured into these lands as bureaucrats, traders, soldiers, and scholars. Alexander's triumph created a new series of kingdoms that blended the achievements of the eastern world with the cultural outlook and attitudes of the Greeks. We use the term **Hellenistic** to designate this new order. The Hellenistic world was the world of Greeks and non-Greek easterners, and it resulted, in its own way, in a remarkable series of accomplishments that are sometimes underestimated. They form the story of this chapter.

Macedonia and the Conquests of Alexander

FOCUS QUESTION: How was Alexander able to amass his empire, and what might his rule have been like if he had lived longer?

While the Greek city-states were continuing their fratricidal warfare, to their north a new and ultimately powerful kingdom was emerging in its own right. The Macedonians were probably not Greek; scholars are still unsure whether the Macedonian language was an archaic dialect of Greek or an altogether separate language. The Greeks certainly viewed the Macedonians as barbarians but did allow them to participate as "Greeks" in the Olympic games beginning in the fifth century B.C.E.

Unlike the Greeks, the Macedonians were mostly rural folk and were organized in tribes, not city-states. Not until the end of the fifth century B.C.E., during the reign of King Archelaus (c. 413–399 B.C.E.) did Macedonia emerge as an important kingdom. But his reign was followed by decades of repeated foreign invasions and internal strife until King Philip II (359–336 B.C.E.) took control and turned Macedonia into the chief power of the Greek world.

Philip and the Conquest of Greece

Philip had spent three years as a hostage in Thebes, where he had gained a great admiration for Greek culture and absorbed the latest Greek military developments. Philip understood the importance of having an efficient army if Macedonia was to be a strong state. He used Macedonian countrymen, sturdy peasants and shepherds, as the core of his phalanx of infantrymen. From the gold mines of Mount Pangaeus, he obtained the wealth to pay these soldiers and establish a standing professional army that could fight year round.

Philip also instituted military reforms that transformed Macedonia into a major military power. He created a new phalanx of infantrymen who were more lightly armed than Greek hoplites; each carried a smaller shield and a shorter sword. Instead, the Macedonian infantryman's chief weapon was a long thrusting spear—18 feet in length, or twice as long as the Greek hoplite's spear. In this way, Macedonian infantrymen could impale an opposing hoplite force before the hoplites could even reach them. The Macedonian phalanx was supported by strong cavalry contingents that helped to break the opposing line of battle and create disorder in the enemy's ranks. Philip also recognized the value of technological improvements in warfare and created a group of engineers to design new catapults to destroy an enemy's fortifications. Finally, Philip strengthened the bonds between the army and its leaders. Even the king shared directly in the dangers of battle, as is evident from his many wounds. Philip's new army defeated the Illyrians to the west and the Thracians to the north and east and was then drawn into the Greeks' interstate conflicts.

The Greeks had mixed reactions to Philip's growing strength. Many Athenians, especially the orator Demosthenes (duh-MAHSS-thuh-neez), came to have a strong distrust of the Macedonian leader's intentions. Demosthenes delivered a series of orations, known as the *Philippics,* in which he portrayed Philip as ruthless, deceitful, treacherous, and barbaric and called on the Athenians to undertake a struggle against him. Other Athenians, such as Isocrates (eye-SAHK-ruh-teez), a teacher of rhetoric, viewed Philip as a savior who would rescue the Greeks from themselves by uniting them and organizing the entire Greek world in a crusade against the common enemy, the Persians (see the box on p. 91).

Demosthenes, "The First Philippic" (4th century B.C.E.)

Demosthenes' repeated calls for action, combined with Philip's rapid expansion, finally spurred Athens into action. Allied with Thebes and some other smaller states, Athens fought the Macedonians at the Battle of Chaeronea (ker-uh-NEE-uh), near Thebes, in 338 B.C.E. The Macedonian army crushed the Greek allies, and Philip was now free to consolidate his control over the Greek peninsula. While Thebes was punished severely, Athens was treated leniently out of respect for its past and expected cooperation in the future. The Greek states were joined together in an alliance that we call the Corinthian League because they met at Corinth. All members took an oath of loyalty: "I swear by Zeus, Earth, Sun, Poseidon, Athena, Ares, and all the gods and goddesses. I will abide by the peace, and I will not break the agreements with Philip the Macedonian, nor will I take up arms with hostile intent against any one of those who abide by the oaths either by land or by sea."[1]

Though based on the principle of self-governing, independent states, the league did have an army and a council. Philip of Macedon was recognized as *hegemon* (HEJ-uh-mun) (leader) of the league and its army. Although Philip allowed the Greek city-states autonomy in domestic affairs, he retained the general direction of their foreign affairs. Many Greeks still objected to being subject to the less civilized master from the north, but Philip insisted that the Greek states end their bitter rivalries and cooperate with him in a war against Persia.

Before Philip could undertake his invasion of Asia, however, he was assassinated, leaving the task to his son

Opposing ≷ VIEWPOINTS

Demosthenes and Isocrates Address Philip of Macedonia

Among the Greeks, Demosthenes reacted most strongly to the growing strength and expansionary policies of the Macedonian king Philip II. Demosthenes delivered a series of orations to the Athenian assembly in which he portrayed Philip as a ruthless and barbaric man. The first selection is from Demosthenes' *Third Philippic,* delivered around 341 B.C.E. Isocrates, an Athenian teacher of rhetoric, saw Philip in a different light and appealed to him to lead both Greeks and Macedonians in a war against the Persians. The second selection is from Isocrates' *Address to Philip,* written in 346 B.C.E.

Demosthenes, *The Third Philippic*

I observe, however, that all men, and you first of all, have conceded to him something which has been the occasion of every war that the Greeks have ever waged. And what is that? The power of doing what he likes, of calmly plundering and stripping the Greeks one by one, and of attacking their cities and reducing them to slavery. Yet your hegemony in Greece lasted seventy-three years, that of Sparta twenty-nine, and in these later times Thebes too gained some sort of authority after the battle of Leuctra. But neither to you nor to the Thebans nor to the Spartans did the Greeks ever yet, men of Athens, concede the right of unrestricted action, or anything like it. On the contrary, when you, or rather the Athenians of that day, were thought to be showing a want of consideration in dealing with others, all felt it their duty, even those who had no grievance against them, to go to war in support of those who had been injured.... Yet all the faults committed by the Spartans in those thirty years, and by our ancestors in their seventy years of supremacy, are fewer, men of Athens, than the wrongs which Philip has done to the Greeks in the thirteen incomplete years in which he has been coming to the top—or rather, they are not a fraction of them.... Ay, and you know this also, that the wrongs which the Greeks suffered from the Spartans or from us, they suffered at all events at the hands of true-born sons of Greece, and they might have been regarded as the acts of a legitimate son, born to great possessions, who should be guilty of some fault or error in the management of his estate: so far he would deserve blame and reproach, yet it could not be said that it was not one of the blood, not the lawful heir who was acting thus. But if some slave or illegitimate bastard had wasted and squandered what he had no right to, heavens! how much more monstrous and exasperating all would have called it! Yet they have no such qualms about Philip and his present conduct, though he is not only no Greek, nor related to the Greeks, but not even a barbarian from any place that can be named with honor, but a pestilent knave from Macedonia, from where it was never yet possible to buy a decent slave.

Isocrates, *Address to Philip*

I chose to address to you what I have to say... I am going to advise you to champion the cause of concord among the Hellenes and of a campaign against the barbarians; and as persuasion will be helpful in dealing with the Hellenes, so compulsion will be useful in dealing with the barbarians....

I affirm that, without neglecting any of your own interests, you ought to make an effort to reconcile Argos and Sparta and Thebes and Athens; for if you can bring these cities together, you will not find it hard to unite the others as well....

You see how utterly wretched these states have become because of their warfare, and how like they are to men engaged in a personal encounter; for no one can reconcile the parties to a quarrel while their wrath is rising; but after they have punished each other badly, they need no mediator, but separate of their own accord. And that is just what I think these states also will do unless you first take them in hand....

Now regarding myself, and regarding the course which you should take toward the Hellenes, perhaps no more need be said. But as to the expedition against Asia, we shall urge upon the cities which I have called upon you to reconcile that it is their duty to go to war with the barbarians.

Q What are Demosthenes' criticisms of Philip II? What appeal does Isocrates make to Philip? What do these documents tell you about the persistent factionalism and communal tensions within the Greek world? In light of subsequent events, who—Demosthenes or Isocrates—made the stronger argument? Why?

Alexander. Although Alexander justly deserves credit for the destruction of the Persian Empire, it was Philip who really paved the way for the conquest. He had unified Macedonia, created a powerful military machine, and subdued the Greeks.

Alexander the Great

Alexander was only twenty when he became king of Macedonia. In the next twelve years, he achieved so much that he has ever since been called Alexander the Great.

The illustrious conqueror was in many ways groomed for kingship by his father, who had taken Alexander along on military campaigns and at the important Battle of Chaeronea had given him control of the cavalry. After his father's assassination, Alexander moved quickly to assert his authority, securing the Macedonian frontiers and smothering a rebellion in Greece by sacking the city of Thebes, killing most of its male inhabitants, and selling the women and children into slavery. He then turned to his father's dream, the invasion of the Persian Empire.

Plutarch, *Life of Alexander* (75 C.E.)

ALEXANDER'S CONQUESTS There is no doubt that Alexander was taking a chance in attacking the Persian Empire. Although weakened in some respects, it was still a strong state. Alexander's fleet was inferior to the Persian navy, which drew its ships from the Phoenicians and other coastal peoples of western Asia, and his finances were shaky at best. His army would have to live off the countryside and win quick victories to gain the resources needed to continue the struggle. In the spring of 334 B.C.E., Alexander entered Asia Minor with an army of some 37,000 men. About half were Macedonians, the rest Greeks and other allies. The cavalry, which would play an important role as a strike force, numbered about five thousand. Architects, engineers, historians, and scientists accompanied the army, a clear indication of Alexander's grand vision and positive expectations at the beginning of his campaign.

Alexander the Great. This marble head of Alexander the Great was made in the second or first century B.C.E. The long hair and tilt of his head reflect the descriptions of Alexander in the literary sources of the time. This portrait shows a youthful and even godlike appearance. Alexander claimed to be descended from Heracles, a Greek hero worshiped as a god, and as pharaoh of Egypt, he gained recognition as a living deity. It is reported that one statue, now lost, showed Alexander gazing at Zeus. At the base of the statue were the words "I place the earth under my sway; you, O Zeus, keep Olympus."

His first confrontation with the Persians, at the Granicus River in 334 B.C.E. (see Map 4.1), nearly cost him his life but resulted in a major victory. By the following spring, the entire western half of Asia Minor was in Alexander's hands, and the Ionian Greek cities of southwestern Asia Minor had been "liberated" from the Persian oppressor. Not all of them wished to be liberated, however, and many regarded Alexander simply as their new master.

Meanwhile, the Persian king, Darius III, mobilized his forces to stop Alexander's army. Although the Persian troops outnumbered Alexander's, the Battle of Issus was fought on a narrow field that canceled the advantage of superior numbers and resulted in another Macedonian success. (The Persian cause was not helped when Darius made a spectacular exit from the battlefield before it was even clear who would be victorious.) After his victory at Issus in 333 B.C.E., Alexander laid siege to the port cities of Tyre and Gaza to prevent Persian control of the sea. The siege of Tyre provides an example of Alexander's military and engineering skills. Tyre stood on an island just off the coast. Lacking adequate naval resources to attack the city from the sea, Alexander built a causeway from the coast to the city, a project that took six months but enabled him to bring forward his siege machines. After seven months, the city finally fell to Alexander's forces. Six thousand of the inhabitants were killed and 30,000 sold into slavery.

Egypt surrendered without a fight, and by the winter of 332 B.C.E., Syria, Palestine, and Egypt were under Alexander's domination. He took the traditional title of pharaoh of Egypt and was hailed as the "son of Amon," to the Greeks the equivalent of being called the son of Zeus. Alexander also built the first of a series of cities named after him (Alexandria) as the Greek administrative capital of Egypt. It became (and remains today) one of the most important cities in the Mediterranean world.

In the meantime, Darius indicated his willingness to make a peace settlement, offering to cede all land west of the Euphrates River to Alexander. Alexander refused and renewed the offensive. He moved now into the territory of the ancient Mesopotamian kingdoms and fought a decisive battle with the Persians at Gaugamela (gaw-guh-MEE-luh) in the summer of 331 B.C.E. At Gaugamela, Alexander's men were clearly outnumbered by the Persian forces, which had established the battle site on a broad, open plain where their war chariots could maneuver to best advantage. Alexander was able to break through the center of the Persian line with his heavy cavalry, followed

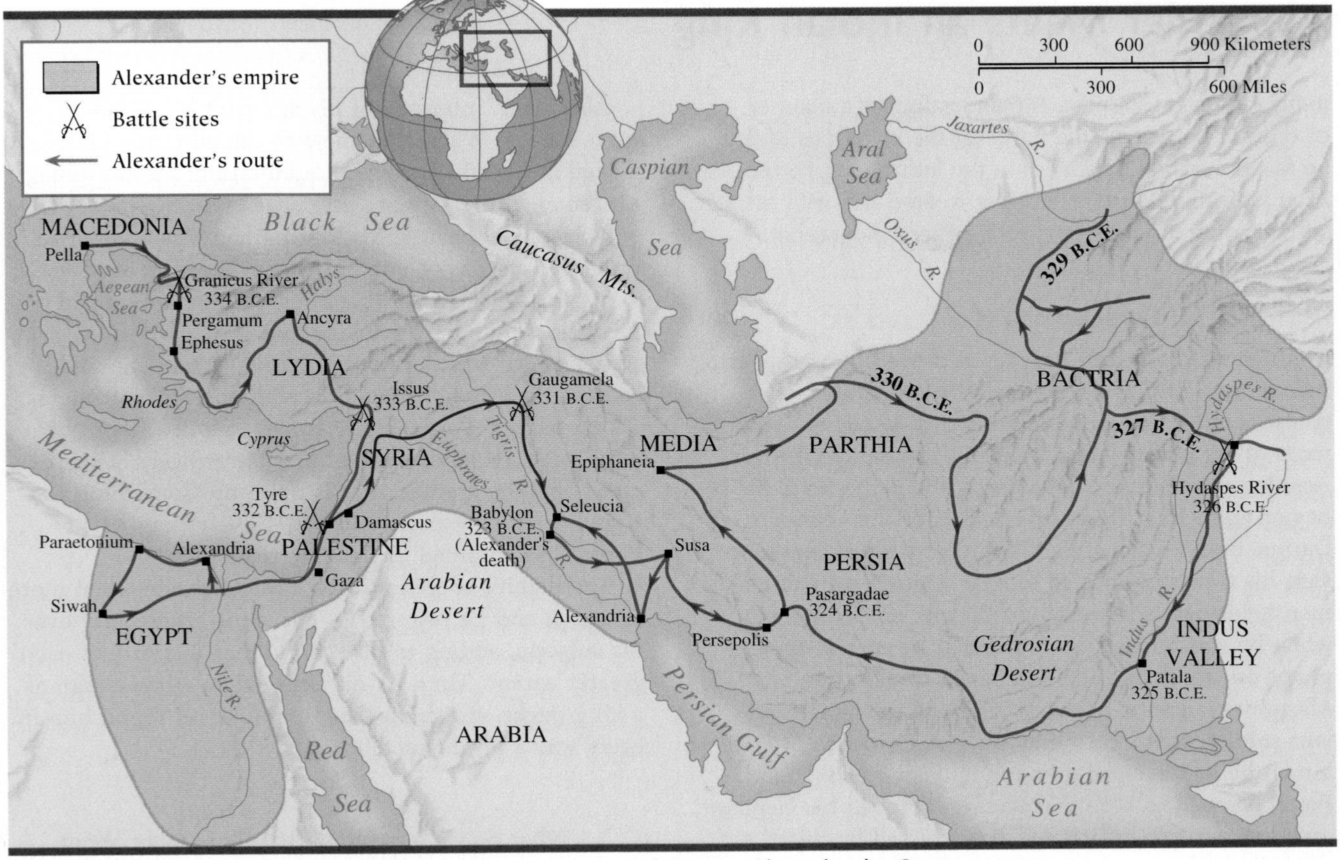

MAP 4.1 The Conquests of Alexander the Great. In just twelve years, Alexander the Great conquered vast territories. Dominating lands from west of the Nile to east of the Indus, he brought the Persian Empire, Egypt, and much of the Middle East under his control and laid the foundations for the Hellenistic world.

Q ***Approximately how far did Alexander and his troops travel during those twelve years?***

Museo Archeologico Nazionale, Naples//© Erich Lessing/Art Resource, NY

Alexander and Darius at the Battle of Issus. This late-second or early-first-century B.C.E. mosaic from the floor of a Roman villa at Pompeii is thought to be a copy of a panel painting made by Philoxenos of Eretria about 310 B.C.E. The mosaic depicts the battle between Alexander and Darius III, king of Persia, at Issus in 333 B.C.E. Alexander is seen at the left on horseback, recklessly leading his troops into battle. Darius is shown in his chariot, already turning around to flee from the enemy.

Alexander Meets an Indian King

In his campaigns in India, Alexander fought a number of difficult battles. At the Battle of the Hydaspes River, he faced a strong opponent in the Indian king Porus. After defeating Porus, Alexander treated him with respect, according to Arrian, Alexander's ancient biographer.

Arrian, *The Campaigns of Alexander*

Throughout the action Porus had proved himself a man indeed, not only as a commander but as a soldier of the truest courage. When he saw his cavalry cut to pieces, most of his infantry dead, and his elephants killed or roaming riderless and bewildered about the field, his behavior was very different from that of the Persian King Darius: unlike Darius, he did not lead the scramble to save his own skin, but so long as a single unit of his men held together, he fought bravely on. It was only when he was himself wounded that he turned the elephant on which he rode and began to withdraw. . . . Alexander, anxious to save the life of this great and gallant soldier, sent . . . [to him] an Indian named Meroes, a man he had been told had long been Porus' friend. Porus listened to Meroes' message, stopped his elephant, and dismounted; he was much distressed by thirst, so when he had revived himself by drinking, he told Meroes to conduct him with all speed to Alexander.

Alexander, informed of his approach, rode out to meet him. . . . When they met, he reined in his horse and looked at his adversary with admiration: he was a magnificent figure of a man, over seven feet high and of great personal beauty; his bearing had lost none of its pride; his air was of one brave man meeting another, of a king in the presence of a king, with whom he had fought honorably for his kingdom.

Alexander was the first to speak. "What," he said, "do you wish that I should do with you?" "Treat me as a king ought," Porus is said to have replied. "For my part," said Alexander, pleased by his answer, "your request shall be granted. But is there not something you would wish for yourself? Ask it." "Everything," said Porus, "is contained in this one request."

The dignity of these words gave Alexander even more pleasure, and he restored to Porus his sovereignty over his subjects, adding to his realm other territory of even greater extent. Thus, he did indeed use a brave man as a king ought, and from that time forward found him in every way a loyal friend.

Q What do we learn from Arrian's account about Alexander's military skills and Indian methods of fighting?

by the infantry. The battle turned into a rout, although Darius managed to escape. After his victory, Alexander entered Babylon and then proceeded to the Persian capitals at Susa and Persepolis, where he acquired the Persian treasuries and took possession of vast quantities of gold and silver.

By 330 B.C.E., Alexander was again on the march. After Darius was killed by one of his own men, Alexander took the title and office of the Great King of the Persians. But he was not content to rest with the spoils of the Persian Empire. Over the next three years, he moved east and northeast, as far as modern Pakistan. By the summer of 327 B.C.E., he had entered India, which at that time was divided into a number of warring states. In 326 B.C.E., Alexander and his armies arrived in the plains of northwestern India. At the Battle of the Hydaspes River, Alexander won a brutally fought battle (see the box above). When Alexander made clear his determination to march east to conquer more of India, his soldiers, weary of campaigning year after year, mutinied and refused to go further. Alexander surrendered to their demands and agreed to return, leading his troops through southern Persia across the Gedrosian Desert, where they suffered heavy losses from appalling desert conditions. Alexander and the remnant of his army went to Susa and then Babylon, where he planned more campaigns.

CHRONOLOGY Macedonia and the Conquests of Alexander

Reign of Philip II	359–336 B.C.E.
Battle of Chaeronea; Philip II conquers Greece	338 B.C.E.
Reign of Alexander the Great	336–323 B.C.E.
Alexander invades Asia; Battle of Granicus River	334 B.C.E.
Battle of Issus	333 B.C.E.
Battle of Gaugamela	331 B.C.E.
Fall of Persepolis, the Persian capital	330 B.C.E.
Alexander enters India	327 B.C.E.
Battle of Hydaspes River	326 B.C.E.
Death of Alexander	323 B.C.E.

But in June 323 B.C.E., weakened from wounds, fever, and probably excessive alcohol, he died at the young age of thirty-two (see the Film & History feature on p. 95).

ALEXANDER'S MILITARY SUCCESS Historians, both ancient and modern, generally agree that Alexander was an outstanding military leader. How do they explain his

Alexander (2004)

Alexander is a product of director Oliver Stone's lifelong fascination with Alexander, the king of Macedonia who conquered the Persian Empire in the fourth century B.C.E. and initiated the Hellenistic era. Stone's epic film cost $150 million, which resulted in an elaborate and in places visually beautiful film. Narrated by the aging Ptolemy (Anthony Hopkins), Alexander's Macedonian general who took control of Egypt after his death, the film tells the story of the life of Alexander (Colin Farrell) through an intermix of battle scenes, scenes showing the progress of Alexander and his army through the Middle East and India, and flashbacks to his early years. Stone portrays Alexander's relationship with his mother, Olympias (Angelina Jolie), as instrumental in his early development while also focusing on his rocky relationship with his father, King Philip II (Val Kilmer). The movie elaborates on the major battle at Gaugamela in 331 B.C.E., where the Persian leader Darius is forced to flee, and then follows Alexander as he conquers the rest of the Persian Empire and continues east into India. After his troops begin to mutiny, Alexander finally returns to the Persian capital of Babylon, where he dies on June 10, 323 B.C.E.

The enormous amount of money spent on the film enabled Stone to achieve a stunning visual spectacle, but as history the film leaves much to be desired. The character of Alexander is never developed in depth. He is shown at times as a weak character who is plagued by doubts over his own decisions and often seems obsessed with his desire for glory. Alexander is also portrayed as an idealistic leader who believed that the people he conquered wanted change, that he was "freeing the people of the world," and that Asia and Europe would grow together into a single world. But was Alexander an idealistic dreamer, as Stone apparently believes, or was he a military leader who, following the dictum that "fortune favors the bold," ran roughshod over the wishes of his soldiers in order to follow his dream and was responsible for mass slaughter in the process? The latter is a perspective that Stone glosses over, but Ptolemy probably expresses the more realistic notion that "none of us believed in his dream." The movie also does not elaborate upon Alexander's wish to be a god. Certainly, Alexander aspired to divine honors; at one point he sent instructions to the Greek cities to "vote him a god." Stone's portrayal of Alexander is perhaps most realistic in presenting Alexander's drinking binges and his bisexuality, which was common in the Greco-Roman world. The movie shows not only his marriage to Roxane (Rosario Dawson), daughter of a Bactrian noble, but also his love for his lifelong companion Hephaestion (Jared Leto) and his sexual relationship with the Persian male slave Bagoas (Francisco Bosch).

Warner Bros/The Kobal Collection/Jaap Buitendijk

Alexander (Colin Farrell) on Bucephalus, reviewing the troops before the Battle of Gaugamela.

The film contains a number of inaccurate historical details. Alexander's first encounters with the Persian royal princesses and Bagoas did not occur when he entered Babylon for the first time. Alexander did not kill Cleitas in India, and he was not wounded in India at the Battle of Hydaspes but at the siege of Malli. Specialists in Persian history have also argued that the Persian military forces were much more disciplined than they are depicted in the movie.

success? For one thing, Alexander demonstrated superb tactical skills. His success in his numerous battles was based to a large extent on his ability to assess the topography of the battlefield and make plans that took advantage of the strengths and weaknesses of his enemy's forces as well as his own. Within hours after arriving at a potential battlefield, Alexander was able to plan troop formations and tactics appropriate to the landscape on which he was fighting. Then, too, if something went wrong after the battle began, he was quick to adapt to changing circumstances.

Alexander pushed his troops mercilessly, often catching his enemy by surprise as a result of a quick march. But he also maintained a personal interest in his troops and for the most part, until the campaign in India, kept their intense loyalty. His willingness to lead by personal example inspired his troops, although it often led to risks that endangered his own life. He did not hesitate to lead cavalry attacks into the ranks of his enemies. In India, he was injured when he led his troops up a ladder in their assault on the Mallians. He was, in fact, wounded eight times in battle.

Alexander also paid attention to details. All aspects of his campaigns were well organized, from obtaining supplies and reinforcements to doing advanced planning for excursions into little known territories. As the number of Macedonian troops declined from deaths in battle or from being assigned to occupy new conquests, Alexander recruited Persian troops. He also took advantage of his father's technical developments and made good use of siege warfare.

But there is also an uglier side to Alexander's military greatness. Did he become accustomed, as some historians have recently argued, to killing his enemies on a scale that far outstripped what was usual in Greek and Macedonian warfare?

ALEXANDER'S IDEALS Certainly, Alexander is one of the most puzzling great figures in history. Historians relying on the same sources give vastly different pictures of him. Some portray him as an idealistic visionary and others as a ruthless Machiavellian. How did Alexander view himself? We know that he sought to imitate Achilles, the warrior-hero of Homer's *Iliad*. Alexander kept a copy of the *Iliad*—and a dagger—under his pillow. He also claimed to be descended from Heracles, the Greek hero who came to be worshiped as a god. No doubt Alexander aspired to divine honors; as pharaoh of Egypt, he became a living god according to Egyptian tradition and at one point even sent instructions to the Greek cities to "vote him a god."

Some historians have argued that Alexander believed in an ideal of universal humanity. As evidence they cite the fact that he urged his soldiers to marry native women, and at Susa in 324 B.C.E. he celebrated the marriages of ten thousand of them en masse to local women. Alexander himself married easterners—Stateira, daughter of Darius, and Roxane, daughter of a Bactrian baron. Was Alexander pursuing a lofty ideal, or was he simply looking for a realistic way to unify his newly won domains? Early on in his conquests, he adopted aspects of Persian rule. He called himself the Great King and asked his subjects to bow before him in the Persian fashion. He wore Persian dress, used Persians as administrators, and trained native youths in Macedonian military methods. His fellow Macedonians objected to these trappings of eastern despotism and the equal treatment he accorded Persians. Some even went so far as to attempt his assassination. But Alexander must have felt a need to fuse the Macedonians, Greeks, and Persians into a ruling class that would enable him to control such an extensive empire. One is left with the impression that he aspired to autocratic monarchy rather than a lofty vision of the unity of humankind.

ALEXANDER'S LEGACY Regardless of his ideals, motives, or views about himself, one fact stands out: Alexander created a new age, the Hellenistic era. The word *Hellenistic* is derived from a Greek word meaning "to imitate Greeks." It is an appropriate way to describe an age that saw the extension of the Greek language and ideas to the non-Greek world of the ancient Near East. Alexander's destruction of the Persian monarchy had extended Greco-Macedonian rule over an enormous area. It created opportunities for Greek engineers, intellectuals, merchants, soldiers, and administrators. While the Greeks on the mainland might remain committed to the ideals of their city-states, those who followed Alexander and his successors participated in a new political unity based on the principle of monarchy. Alexander had transformed his army from a Macedonian force into an international one, owing loyalty only to himself. His successors used force to establish military monarchies that dominated the Hellenistic world after his death. Autocratic power, based on military strength and pretensions of divine rule, became a regular feature of those Hellenistic monarchies and was part of Alexander's political legacy to the Hellenistic world. His vision of empire no doubt inspired the Romans, who were, of course, the real heirs of Alexander's legacy.

But Alexander also left a cultural legacy. As a result of his conquests, Greek language, art, architecture, and literature spread throughout the Near East. The urban centers of the Hellenistic Age, many founded by Alexander and his successors, became springboards for the diffusion of Greek culture. Alexander had established a number of cities and military colonies named Alexandria to guard strategic points and supervise wide areas. Most of the settlers were Greek mercenaries. It has been estimated that in the course of his campaigns, Alexander summoned some 60,000 to 65,000 additional mercenaries from Greece, at least 36,000 of whom took up residence in the garrisons and new cities. While the Greeks spread their culture in the east, they were also inevitably influenced by eastern ways. Thus, Alexander's legacy became one of the hallmarks of the Hellenistic world: the clash and fusion of different cultures.

The World of the Hellenistic Kingdoms

Q **FOCUS QUESTION**: What were the main features of the political and military organization of the Hellenistic kingdoms, and how did the new political systems differ from those of the Greek city-states?

The united empire that Alexander created by his conquests disintegrated after his death. All too soon, Macedonian military leaders were engaged in a struggle for power. By 301 B.C.E., any hope of unity was dead.

Hellenistic Monarchies

Eventually, four Hellenistic kingdoms emerged as the successors to Alexander: Macedonia under the Antigonid (an-TIG-uh-nid) dynasty, Syria and the east under the Seleucids (suh-LOO-sids), the Attalid (AT-uh-lid) kingdom of Pergamum (PURR-guh-mum), and Egypt under the Ptolemies (TAHL-uh-meez) (see Map 4.2).

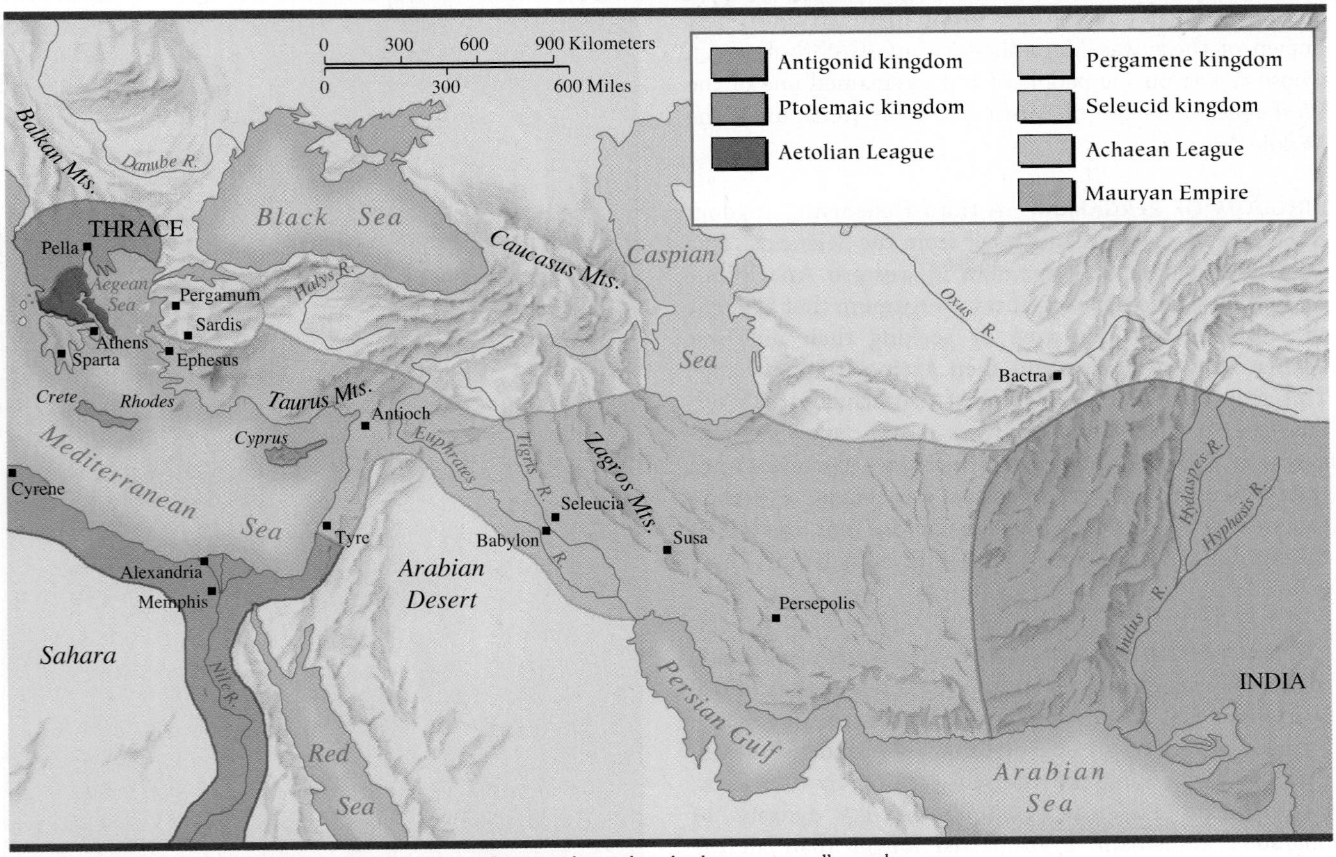

MAP 4.2 The World of the Hellenistic Kingdoms. Alexander died unexpectedly at the age of thirty-two and did not designate a successor. Upon his death, his generals struggled for power, eventually establishing four monarchies that spread Hellenistic culture and fostered trade and economic development.

Q ***Which kingdom encompassed most of the old Persian Empire?***

ANTIGONID KINGDOM OF MACEDONIA In Macedonia, the struggles for power led to the extermination of Alexander the Great's dynasty. Not until 276 B.C.E. did Antigonus Gonatus (an-TIG-oh-nuss guh-NAH-tuss), the grandson of one of Alexander's generals, succeed in establishing the Antigonid dynasty as rulers of Macedonia. The Antigonids viewed control of Greece as essential to their power but did not see outright conquest as necessary. Macedonia was, of course, also important to the Greeks. As one ancient commentator noted, "It is in the interest of the Greeks that the Macedonian dominion should be humbled for long, but by no means that it should be destroyed. For in that case . . . [the Macedonians] would very soon experience the lawless violence of the Thracians and Gauls, as they had on more than one occasion."[2] But the Greeks, like the Macedonians, eventually fell subject to Roman power.

SELEUCID KINGDOM Another Hellenistic monarchy was founded by the general Seleucus (suh-LOO-kuss), who established the Seleucid dynasty of Syria. This was the largest of the Hellenistic kingdoms and controlled much of the old Persian Empire from Turkey in the west to India in the east, although the Seleucids found it increasingly difficult to maintain control of the eastern territories. In fact, an Indian ruler named Chandragupta Maurya (chun-druh-GOOP-tuh MOWR-yuh) (324–301 B.C.E.) created a new Indian state, the Mauryan Empire, and drove out the Seleucid forces. His grandson Asoka (uh-SOH-kuh) (269–232 B.C.E.) extended the empire to include most of India and is considered the greatest ruler in India's history. Asoka, a pious Buddhist, sought to convert the remaining Greek communities in northwestern India to his religion and even sent Buddhist missionaries to Greek rulers.

The Seleucid rulers maintained relations with the Mauryan Empire. Trade was fostered, especially in such luxuries as spices and jewels. Seleucus also sent Greek

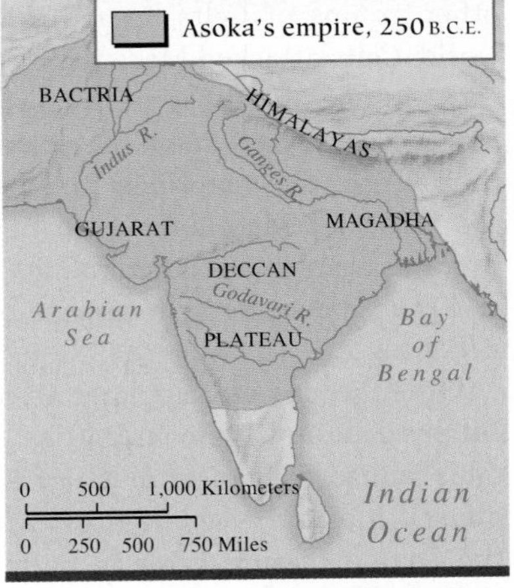

The Mauryan Empire Under Asoka

and Macedonian ambassadors to the Mauryan court. Best known of these was Megasthenes (muh-GAS-thuh-neez), whose report on the people of India remained one of the West's best sources of information on India until the Middle Ages.

KINGDOM OF PERGAMUM A third Hellenistic kingdom came into being by freeing itself from the Seleucids. This was the kingdom of Pergamum in western Asia Minor under the Attalid dynasty. It was Pergamum that brought the Romans into the area by seeking their aid first against the Antigonids and then against the Seleucids. This led to the Roman defeat of Antiochus (an-TY-uh-kuss) III, probably the strongest of the Seleucid monarchs, in 191 B.C.E. The Seleucids declined thereafter until their small remaining territory was made a Roman province in 63 B.C.E. Seventy years before that, the last of the Attalid dynasty had bequeathed his kingdom to Rome in his will.

PTOLEMAIC KINGDOM OF EGYPT The fourth Hellenistic monarchy was Egypt, which had come under the control of Ptolemy (TAHL-uh-mee), another Macedonian general. Named governor of Egypt after Alexander's death, Ptolemy had established himself as king by 305 B.C.E., creating the Ptolemaic (tahl-uh-MAY-ik) dynasty of pharaohs. Hellenistic Egypt lasted longer than all the other Hellenistic monarchies; it was not until the reign of Cleopatra VII, who allied herself with the wrong side in the Roman civil wars (see Chapter 5), that Egypt fell to the Romans in 30 B.C.E.

A Gaul and His Wife: Monument to the Victory of a Hellenistic King. This statue of a Gaulish chieftain and his wife is a Roman copy of a bronze original that was part of a larger monument erected around 230–220 B.C.E. to commemorate the victory of Attalus I of Pergamum over the Gauls, a victory that gave Pergamum control over much of Asia Minor. In this scene, the defeated Gaulish leader plunges a sword into his chest just after he has killed his wife to prevent her from being sold into slavery.

The Threat from the Celts

The Celts, also known as the Gauls, were a people who had occupied large areas of Europe north of the Alps during the Early Iron Age (c. 800–500 B.C.E.), especially the region to the south and west of the Rhine River, west of the Alps, and north of the Pyrenees (a region known as Gaul).

At the end of the fifth century B.C.E., possibly as a result of overpopulation, Celtic peoples began to migrate south and east. One group sacked the city of Rome in 390 B.C.E. (see Chapter 5). After the death of Alexander the Great, other groups of Celts began to threaten the Hellenistic world. Celts attacked Macedonia early in the third century B.C.E., as one ancient writer reported: "When the defeated Macedonians had fixed themselves within the walls of their cities, the victorious Brennus ravaged the fields of the whole of Macedonia with no one to oppose him."[3] Brennus also led a group of 30,000 Celts into Greece itself and caused considerable damage before being defeated in 278 B.C.E.

Other groups of Celts later attacked Asia Minor, where Attalus I bested them in 230 B.C.E. After his victory, Attalus gained control of much of Asia Minor and declared himself king of Pergamum. As a result of these attacks, the Celts, or Gauls, came to be feared everywhere in the Hellenistic world.

Political and Military Institutions

The Hellenistic monarchies created a semblance of stability for several centuries, even though Hellenistic kings refused to accept the new status quo and periodically engaged in wars to alter it. At the same time, an underlying strain always existed between the new Greco-Macedonian ruling class and the native populations. Together, these factors created a certain degree of tension that was never truly ended until the vibrant Roman state to the west stepped in and imposed a new order.

The Hellenistic kingdoms shared a common political system that represented a break with their Greek past. To the Greeks, monarchy was an institution for barbarians, associated in their minds with people like the Persians. Although they retained democratic forms of government in their cities, the Greeks of the Hellenistic world were forced to accept monarchy as a new fact of political life.

Although Alexander the Great had apparently planned to fuse Greeks and easterners, Hellenistic monarchs relied primarily on Greeks and Macedonians to form the new ruling class. It has been estimated that in the Seleucid kingdom, for example, only 2.5 percent of the people in authority were non-Greek, and most of them were commanders of local military units. Those who did advance to important administrative posts had learned Greek (all government business was transacted in Greek) and had become Hellenized in a cultural sense. The policy of excluding non-Greeks from leadership positions was due not to the incompetence of the natives but to the determination of the Greek ruling class to maintain its privileged position. It was the Greco-Macedonian ruling class that provided the only unity in the Hellenistic world.

Since the Hellenistic monarchs created and maintained their kingdoms by military force, warfare continued to be an integral part of the Hellenistic world. The phalanx—still composed of heavily armed infantry with 18-foot-long spears—and cavalry continued to form the core of the Hellenistic forces. But Hellenistic warfare also saw some innovations. Most noticeable were the elephants, "the tanks of ancient warfare," which were especially prominent in the army of the Seleucids, who procured theirs from India, and the Ptolemies, who obtained them from North Africa. But even more important, since armies quickly learned tricks that neutralized the elephants, was the development of new siege machinery, especially the catapult and siege towers. In Classical times, cities with good walls were virtually impregnable; Alexander and later Hellenistic rulers could capture cities by using their new equipment. Hellenistic rulers also had the resources to build larger warships with twenty and even thirty banks of oars.

Museo Nazionale di Villa Giulia, Rome //© Scala/Art Resource, NY

Greek War Elephants. Some of the armies in the Hellenistic world made use of elephants obtained from North Africa and India. Pictured on this Italian plate is a Greek war elephant that was brought to the Mediterranean by one of Alexander's successors. The battle fortress on the back of the elephant was a Greek innovation.

Hellenistic Cities

Cities played an especially important role in the Hellenistic kingdoms. Throughout his conquests, Alexander had founded a series of new cities and military settlements, and Hellenistic kings did likewise. The new population centers varied considerably in size and importance. Military settlements were meant to maintain order and might consist of only a few hundred men heavily dependent on the king. But there were also new independent cities with thousands of inhabitants. Alexandria in Egypt was the largest city in the Mediterranean region by the first century B.C.E. Seleucus was especially active in founding new cities, according to one ancient writer: "The other kings have exulted in destroying existing cities; he, on the other hand, arranged to build cities which did not yet exist. He established so many . . . that they were enough to carry the names of towns in Macedonia as well as the names of those in his family. . . . One can go to Phoenicia to see his cities; one can go to Syria and see even more."[4]

Hellenistic rulers encouraged this massive spread of Greek colonists to the Near East because of their intrinsic value to the new monarchies. Greeks (and Macedonians) provided not only a recruiting ground for the army but also a pool of civilian administrators and workers who would contribute to economic development. Even architects, engineers, dramatists, and actors were in demand in the new Greek cities. Many Greeks and Macedonians were quick to see the advantages of moving to the new urban centers and gladly sought their fortunes in the Near East. Greeks of all backgrounds joined the exodus until around 250 B.C.E., when the outpouring began to slow significantly.

Within the Hellenistic cities, the culture was primarily Greek. The political institutions of the cities were modeled after those of the Greek *polis*. Greeks of the Classical period would easily have recognized the councils, magistracies, assemblies, and codes of law. The physical layout of the new cities was likewise modeled on those of the Greek homeland. Using the traditional rectilinear grid, cities were laid out with temples, altars, and stone theaters.

Many of the new urban centers were completely dominated by Greeks, while the native populations remained cut off from all civic institutions. The Greeks commissioned purely Greek sculpture, read literature of the Classical period, and had separate law courts for themselves. Complaints from resentful natives have been recorded. An Egyptian camel driver, for example, complained bitterly that he was not paid regularly because he did "not know how to behave like a Greek." Not only was it difficult for easterners to enter the ranks of the ruling class, but those who did so had to become thoroughly Hellenized. This often required alienation from one's own culture.

The Greeks' belief in their own cultural superiority provided an easy rationalization for their political dominance of the eastern cities. But Greek control of the new cities was also necessary because the kings frequently used the cities as instruments of government, enabling them to rule considerable territory without an extensive bureaucracy. At the same time, for security reasons, the Greeks needed the support of the kings. After all, the Hellenistic cities were islands of Greek culture in a sea of non-Greeks. The relationship between rulers and cities, therefore, was a symbiotic one that bore serious consequences for the cities.

In their political system, religious practices, and architecture, the Greeks tried to re-create the *poleis* of their homeland in their new cities. But it was no longer possible to do so. The new cities were not autonomous entities and soon found themselves dependent on the power of the Hellenistic monarchies. Although the kings did not rule the cities directly, they restricted the cities' freedom in other ways. City administrators knew they could not conduct an independent foreign policy and did not try to do so. The kings also demanded tribute, which could be a heavy burden.

The Greek cities of the era were the chief agents for the spread of Hellenistic culture in the Near East, as far, in fact, as modern Afghanistan and India. These Greek cities were also remarkably vibrant despite their subordination to the Hellenistic monarchies and persisted in being a focal point for the loyalty of their citizens. Their continuing vitality is perhaps most evident on the Greek mainland, where the Greek cities formed two important leagues, the Aetolian League in central Greece and the Achaean League in the Peloponnesus.

Economic Trends

Agriculture was still of primary importance to both the native populations and the new Greek cities of the Hellenistic world. The Greek cities continued their old agrarian patterns. A well-defined body of citizens owned land and worked it with the assistance of slaves. But their farms were isolated units in a vast area of land ultimately owned by the king or assigned to large estate owners and worked by native peasants dwelling in villages. Overall, then, neither agricultural patterns nor methods of production underwent significant changes.

Few new products or manufacturing methods were introduced in the Hellenistic period, but the centers of manufacturing shifted significantly. Industry spread from Greece to the east—especially to Asia Minor, Rhodes, and Egypt. New textile centers were set up at Pergamum, and glass and silver crafts were developed in Syria. Leading all cities in manufacturing was Alexandria in Egypt, which became the center for the production of parchment, textiles, linens, oil, metalwork, and glass.

Commerce expanded considerably in the Hellenistic era. Indeed, trading contacts linked much of the Hellenistic world. The decline in the number of political barriers encouraged more commercial traffic. Although Hellenistic monarchs still fought wars, the conquests of Alexander and the policies of his successors made possible greater trade between east and west. Two major trade routes connected the east with the Mediterranean. The central route was the major one and led by sea from India to the Persian Gulf, up the Tigris River to Seleucia on the Tigris, which replaced Babylon as the center for waterborne traffic from the Persian Gulf and overland caravan routes as well. Overland routes from Seleucia then led to Antioch and Ephesus. A southern route wound its way from India by sea but went around Arabia and up the Red Sea to Petra or later Berenice. Caravan routes then led overland to Coptos on the Nile, thence to Alexandria and the Mediterranean.

An incredible variety of products were traded: gold and silver from Spain; iron from northern Armenia; salt from Asia Minor; timber from Macedonia; purple dye from Tyre; ebony, gems, ivory, and spices from India; frankincense (used on altars) from Arabia; slaves from Thrace, Syria, and Asia Minor; fine wines from Syria and western Asia Minor; olive oil from Athens; and numerous exquisite foodstuffs, such as the famous prunes of Damascus. The greatest trade, however, was in the basic staple of life—grain. The great exporting areas were Egypt, Sicily, and the Black Sea region, while Rhodes and Delos served as the major depots for the international grain trade.

Hellenistic Society

Focus Question: What were the main social developments in the Hellenistic world?

One of the noticeable features of social life in the Hellenistic world was the emergence of new opportunities for women—at least for upper-class women. No doubt this was related to the changes in Hellenistic society itself, since the subordination of the cities to the kings altered the way men related to their *polis* and to each other. Some historians maintain that the visible role of Hellenistic queens may also have contributed to a new model for upper-class women.

New Opportunities for Upper-Class Women

The creation of the Hellenistic monarchies, which represented a considerable departure from the world of the city-state, gave new scope to the role played by the monarchs' wives, the Hellenistic queens. In Macedonia, a pattern of alliances between mothers and sons provided openings for women to take an active role in politics, especially in political intrigue. In Egypt, opportunities for royal women were even greater after the Ptolemaic rulers adopted the Egyptian custom of kings marrying their own

Queen Arsinoë II. Arsinoë II, sister and wife of King Ptolemy II, played an active role in Egyptian political affairs. Arsinoë was the first Egyptian queen whose portrait appeared on coins with her husband, as is evident in the illustration at the left showing the queen on the reverse side of a gold coin from the kingdom of Egypt in 263 B.C.E. The illustration at the right shows a third-century B.C.E. cameo relief made in Alexandria. It depicts Ptolemy II and Arsinoë as Greek gods.

sisters. Of the first eight Ptolemaic rulers, four wed their sisters. Ptolemy II and his sister-wife Arsinoë (ahr-SIN-oh-ee) II were both worshiped as gods in their lifetimes. Arsinoë played an energetic role in government and was involved in the expansion of the Egyptian navy. She was also the first Egyptian queen whose portrait appeared on coins with her husband. Hellenistic queens also showed an intense interest in culture. They wrote poems, collected art, and corresponded with intellectuals.

The most notable gains for upper-class women came in the economic area. Documents show increasing numbers of women involved in managing slaves, selling property, and making loans. Even then, legal contracts made by women had to include their official male guardians, although in numerous instances these men no longer played an important role but were listed only to satisfy legal requirements. In Sparta, women were allowed to own land and manage their own economic affairs. As many of their husbands were absent or had died in war, many Spartan women became wealthy; females owned 40 percent of the privately held land in Sparta.

Spartan women, however, were an exception, especially on the Greek mainland. Women in Athens, for example, still remained highly restricted and supervised. Although a few philosophers welcomed female participation in men's affairs, many philosophers rejected equality between men and women and asserted that the traditional roles of wives and mothers were most satisfying for women. In her treatise "On Chastity," Phintys (FIN-tiss) wrote that "serving as generals, public officials, and statesmen is appropriate for men," but "keeping house, remaining within, and taking care of husbands belongs to women."[5]

But the opinions of philosophers did not prevent upper-class women from making gains in areas other than the economic sphere (see the box on p. 102). New possibilities for females arose when women in some parts of the Hellenistic world were allowed to pursue education in the fields of literature, music, and even athletics. Education, then, provided new opportunities for women: female poets appeared again in the third century B.C.E., and there are instances of women involved in both scholarly and artistic pursuits.

Some wealthy aristocratic women even became politically active and participated in running their cities. In the second century B.C.E., a number of cities passed decrees honoring women for their service to the community. Cyme, in Asia Minor, for example, paid homage to Archippe for her enormous financial contributions. In return, some women were given political rights and in a few instances were allowed to hold office as city magistrates. But often economic motives were attached to this generosity. When Phile of Priene was made a magistrate of her city, it was probably with the understanding that she would donate funds for public works. Once in office, she did build an aqueduct and a reservoir for the community.

Improvements in the position of females were largely restricted to upper-class women. A large group of women

A New Autonomy for Women?

There were noticeable gains for upper-class women in Hellenistic society. But even in the lives of ordinary women, a new assertiveness came to the fore despite the continuing domination of society by men. The first selection is taken from the letter of a wife to her husband, complaining about his failure to return home. In the second selection, a father complains that his daughter has abandoned him, contrary to Egyptian law providing that children who have been properly raised should support their parents.

Letter from Isias to Hephaistion, 168 B.C.E.

If you are well and other things are going right, it would accord with the prayer that I make continually to the gods. I myself and the child and all the household are in good health and think of you always. When I received your letter from Horos, in which you announce that you are in detention in the Serapeum at Memphis, for the news that you are well I straightway thanked the gods, but about your not coming home, when all the others who had been secluded there have come, I am ill-pleased, because after having piloted myself and your child through such bad times and been driven to every extremity owing to the price of wheat, I thought that now at least, with you at home, I should enjoy some respite, whereas you have not even thought of coming home nor given any regard to our circumstances, remembering how I was in want of everything while you were still here, not to mention this long lapse of time and these critical days, during which you have sent us nothing. As, moreover, Horos who delivered the letter has brought news of your having been released from detention, I am thoroughly ill-pleased. Notwithstanding, as your mother also is annoyed, for her sake as well as for mine please return to the city, if nothing more pressing holds you back. You will do me a favor by taking care of your bodily health. Farewell.

Letter from Ktesikles to King Ptolemy, 220 B.C.E.

I am wronged by Dionysios and by Nike my daughter. For though I raised her, my own daughter, and educated her and brought her to maturity, when I was stricken with bodily ill-health and was losing my eyesight, she was not minded to furnish me with any of the necessities of life. When I sought to obtain justice from her in Alexandria, she begged my pardon, and in the eighteenth year she swore me a written royal oath to give me each month twenty drachmas, which she was to earn by her own bodily labor. . . . But now corrupted by Dionysios, who is a comic actor, she does not do for me anything of what was in the written oath, despising my weakness and ill-health. I beg you, therefore, O King, not to allow me to be wronged by my daughter and by Dionysios the actor who corrupted her, but to order Diophanes the strategus [provincial administrator] to summon them and hear us out; and if I am speaking the truth, let Diophanes deal with her corrupter as seems good to him and compel my daughter Nike to do justice to me. If this is done I shall no longer be wronged but by fleeing to you, O King, I shall obtain justice.

Q What specific complaints are contained in each letter? What do these complaints reveal about some women in the Hellenistic world? Judging by the content of these letters, what freedoms did Hellenistic women enjoy? How autonomous were they? Based on your knowledge of gender and gender roles in shaping earlier cultures, how did Hellenistic civilization differ in its conceptions of what was "proper" for men and women?

condemned to the practice of prostitution faced a harsher reality. Inscriptional evidence indicates that small families were common in the Hellenistic world; boys were preferred, and rarely was more than one daughter raised. Unwanted girl babies were often exposed to the elements and left to die. Some of these infants were gathered up by eager entrepreneurs and raised to be slave prostitutes. Only the most beautiful and luckiest prostitutes came to be the companions (the *hetairai*) of upper-class men.

The Role of Slavery

The Hellenistic world witnessed the migration of large numbers of people from one area to another. Greeks and Macedonians went into the Hellenistic kingdoms of the east as administrators, mercenaries, engineers, scholars, artists, teachers, and merchants. Moreover, significantly large numbers of non-Greeks moved around for economic and military purposes. But the largest number of uprooted people were slaves. Slavery was viewed as a normal part of life in the Hellenistic world and in antiquity in general.

Slaves were obtained from four chief sources: the children of slaves; children who were sold by their parents or abandoned to perish; persons kidnapped by pirates; and, perhaps the largest source of all, prisoners of war. Delos, a major trading center, could handle ten thousand slaves a day in its markets. Although slaves came from everywhere, Thracians and Syrians were the most numerous. Slaves varied in price; Macedonians, Thracians, and Italians drew the highest prices.

Treatment of Slaves in the Egyptian Gold Mines

Slavery was a common practice throughout antiquity. In both Classical Greece and the Hellenistic world, the worst-treated slaves were those who worked in the mines. The Egyptians were especially notorious for their treatment of slaves in the gold mines in Nubia, described in this account by Diodorus of Sicily, who lived in the first century B.C.E. His account was based on the now lost work of the second-century writer Agatharchides.

Diodorus of Sicily, *Library of History*

And those who have been condemned in this way—and they are a great multitude and are all bound in chains—work at their task unceasingly both by day and throughout the entire night, enjoying no respite and being carefully cut off from any means of escape; since guards of foreign soldiers who speak a language different from theirs stand watch over them, so that not a man, either by conversation or by some contact of a friendly nature, is able to corrupt one of his keepers.... And the entire operations are in charge of a skilled worker who distinguishes the stone and points it out to the laborers; and of those who are assigned to this unfortunate task the physically strongest break the quartz-rock with iron hammers, applying no skill to the task but only force, and cutting tunnels through the stone, not in a straight line but wherever the seam of gleaming rock may lead. Now these men, working in darkness as they do because of the bending and winding of the passages, carry lamps bound on their foreheads; and since much of the time they change the position of their bodies to follow the particular character of the stone they throw the blocks, as they cut them out, on the ground, and at this task they labor without ceasing beneath the sternness and blows of an overseer.

The boys there who have not yet come to maturity, entering through the tunnels into the galleries formed by the removal of the rock, laboriously gather up the rock as it is cast down piece by piece and carry it out into the open to the place outside the entrance. Then those who are above thirty years of age take this quarried stone from them and with iron pestles pound a specified amount of it in stone mortars, until they have worked it down to a smaller size. Thereupon the women and older men receive from them the rock of this size and cast it into mills of which a number stand there in a row, and taking their places in groups of two or three at the spoke or handle of each mill they grind it until they have worked down the amount given them to the consistency of the finest flour. And since no opportunity is afforded any of them to care for his body and they have no garment to cover their shame, no man can look upon the unfortunate wretches without feeling pity for them because of the exceeding hardships they suffer. For no leniency or respite of any kind is given to any man who is sick, or maimed or aged, or in the case of a woman for her weakness, but all without exception are compelled by blows to persevere in their labors, until through ill-treatment they die in the midst of their tortures. Consequently the poor unfortunates believe, because their punishment is so excessively severe, that the future will always be more terrible than the present and therefore look forward to death as more to be desired than life.

Q Compare the treatment of slaves in the Egyptian gold mines with the treatment of slaves in Classical Athens. What does your comparison reveal about the nature of slavery in the Greek world?

Slaves were put to work in numerous ways in the Hellenistic world. States employed slaves as servants for government officials and in government-run industries such as weaving. Most slaves were used in domestic service, farming, and mines, but the situation could vary from state to state. Egypt had no slave class in the countryside, nor was there much domestic slavery outside Alexandria. But the Egyptians did use slave labor in state-run textile factories and made especially brutal use of them in mining operations (see the box above). Women were also sold as slaves to be concubines for Greek and Macedonian soldiers and civilians.

The effects of slavery could also be important. The employment of large numbers of slaves in the Hellenistic kingdoms contributed to the Hellenizing process. Slaves working in homes, farms, or factories had opportunities to absorb Greek ways. This is especially evident in the case of the slave-wives of Hellenistic soldiers.

The Transformation of Education

In the Hellenistic world, education underwent a significant transformation. In the Classical period of Greek history, education had been left largely to private enterprise. Greek cities now began to supervise education in new ways. The Greek **gymnasium,** which had been primarily an athletic institution, evolved into a secondary school. The curriculum centered on music, physical exercise, and literature, especially the poetry of Homer. Wealthy individuals often provided the money for the schools and also specified how it should be spent. An inscription from the city of Teos in Asia Minor specified that Polythroos "gave 34,000 drachmas... for there to be appointed each year... three grammar-masters to teach the boys and the girls; . . . for two gymnastics-masters to be appointed, . . . for a lyre—or harp—player to be appointed . . . [to] teach music and lyre—or harp—playing to the children."[6]

The school in Teos was unusual, however, in that education was ordinarily for upper-class male children. An official known as the *gymnasiarch* served as the head of a gymnasium. This was a civic position of considerable prestige. He was not paid and was expected to provide money for sacrifices, competitions, entertainment, and even school repairs. Many cities passed decrees awarding praise and a "gold crown" to the gymnasiarch for his "munificence toward the people." The educational year culminated with various musical, academic, and athletic contests in which students competed for the honor of having their names inscribed on a victory column.

Hellenistic kings also served as patrons of gymnasia, recognizing their importance in training youths who might serve later as administrators of the state. The institution of the gymnasium played a significant role in the diffusion of Greek culture throughout the Hellenistic world. Whether an upper-class Greek youth lived on the Greek mainland, in Alexandria, or in another city in the east, he could imbibe Greek culture and maintain that sense of superiority that characterized the Greek overlords of the Hellenistic kingdoms.

Culture in the Hellenistic World

Focus Question: What achievements in literature, art, science, medicine, and philosophy occurred during the Hellenistic period?

Although the Hellenistic kingdoms encompassed vast areas and many diverse peoples, the Greeks provided a sense of unity as a result of the diffusion of Greek culture throughout the Hellenistic world. The Hellenistic era was a period of considerable cultural accomplishment in many fields—literature, art, science, medicine, and philosophy. Although these achievements occurred throughout the Hellenistic world, certain centers, especially the great Hellenistic cities of Alexandria and Pergamum, stood out. In both cities, cultural developments were encouraged by the rulers themselves. Rich Hellenistic kings had considerable resources with which to patronize culture.

The Ptolemies in Egypt made Alexandria an especially important cultural center. The library became the largest in ancient times, with more than half a million scrolls. The museum (literally, "temple of the Muses") created a favorable environment for scholarly research. Alexandria became home to poets, writers, philosophers, and scientists—scholars of all kinds.

New Directions in Literature

The Hellenistic Age produced an enormous quantity of literature, most of which has not survived. Hellenistic monarchs, who held literary talent in high esteem, subsidized writers on a grand scale. The Ptolemaic rulers of Egypt were particularly lavish. The combination of their largess and the famous library drew a host of scholars and authors to Alexandria, including a circle of poets. Theocritus (thee-AHK-ruh-tuss) (c. 315–250 B.C.E.), originally a native of the island of Sicily, wrote "little poems" or idylls dealing with erotic themes, lovers' complaints, and above all, pastoral themes expressing his love of nature and his appreciation of nature's beauty (see the box on p. 105).

In the Hellenistic era, Athens remained the theatrical center of the Greek world. Though little remained of tragedy, a new kind of comedy developed that completely rejected political themes and sought only to entertain and amuse. The Athenian playwright Menander (muh-NAN-dur) (c. 342–291 B.C.E.) was perhaps the best representative of New Comedy. Plots were simple: typically, a hero falls in love with a not-really-so-bad prostitute who turns out eventually to be the long-lost daughter of a rich neighbor. The hero marries her, and they live happily ever after.

The Hellenistic period saw a great outpouring of historical and biographical literature. The chief historian of the Hellenistic Age was Polybius (puh-LIB-ee-uss) (c. 203–c. 120 B.C.E.), a Greek who lived for some years in Rome. He is regarded by many historians as second only to Thucydides among Greek historians. His major work consisted of forty books narrating the history of the "inhabited Mediterranean world" from 221 to 146 B.C.E. Only the first five books are extant, although long extracts from the other books survive. His history focuses on the growth of Rome from a city-state to a vast empire. It is apparent that Polybius understood the significance of the Romans' achievement. He followed Thucydides in seeking rational motives for historical events. He also approached his sources critically and used firsthand accounts.

Hellenistic Art

In addition to being patrons of literary talent, the Hellenistic monarchs were eager to spend their money to beautify and adorn the cities in their states. The founding of new cities and the rebuilding of old ones provided numerous opportunities for Greek architects and sculptors. The structures of the Greek homeland—gymnasia, baths, theaters, and temples—lined the streets of these cities. Most noticeable in the construction of temples was the use of the more ornate Corinthian order (see Chapter 3), which became especially popular during the Hellenistic era.

Sculptors were patronized by Hellenistic kings and rich citizens. Thousands of statues, many paid for by their subjects, were erected in towns and cities all over the Hellenistic world. Hellenistic sculptors traveled widely, attracted by the material rewards offered by wealthy patrons. While maintaining the technical skill of the Classical period, Hellenistic sculptors moved away from the idealism of fifth-century classicism to a more emotional

The Pastoral Idyll of Theocritus

Little is known of the poet Theocritus (c. 315–250 B.C.E.). Born in Syracuse on the island of Sicily, he also lived in Miletus, Cos, and Alexandria. He is best known as the creator of pastoral idylls that portray his great love of nature. This selection is from the famous *Seventh Idyll* (called the "queen of pastorals"), which describes a delightful day on the island of Cos.

Theocritus, *The Seventh Idyll*

This I sang, and Lykidas laughed
again pleasantly, and gave me his stick
in fellowship of the Muses,
and turned left, taking the road
to Pyxa, but Eukritos
and handsome Amyntas and I
turned off at Phrasidamos's
and happily laid ourselves down
on beds of sweet grass and vine-leaves,
freshly picked. Overhead, many elms
and poplars rustled, and nearby
the sacred waters splashed down
from the Nymphs' cave. Brown cicadas
shrilled from the shady branches,
and far off the tree-frog whined
in the heavy underbrush.
Lark and finches sang, doves crooned,
and bees hummed about the spring.
Everything smelled of rich summer
and rich fruits. Pears lay at our feet,
apples in plenty rolled beside us,
and branches loaded down with plums
bent to the ground. And we broke
the four-year seals on the wine-jars.
Nymphs of Kastalia that live
on the slopes of Parnassos, tell me,
was it such a cup old Chiron
offered Herakles in Pholos'
rocky cave? Was it a drink like this
set Polyphemos dancing,
that mighty shepherd who grazed
his flocks beside the Anapos
and pelted ships with mountains—
such nectar as you mixed for us,
you Nymphs, that day by the altar
of Demeter of the Harvest?
May I plant the great winnowing-fan
another time in her grain-heaps,
while she stands and smiles at us
with wheat-sheaves and poppies in her hand.

Q What images does Theocritus create in his poem? What does his poetry tell us about the poet's interests and values?

and realistic art, seen in numerous statues of old women, drunks, and little children at play. They also placed a new emphasis on the female nude.

Alexander's incursion into the western part of India also resulted in some Greek cultural influences there, especially during the Hellenistic era. During the first century B.C.E., Indian sculptors began to create statues of the Buddha. The impact of Greek statues is especially evident in the Buddhist statues done in Gandhara, which today is part of Pakistan.

A Golden Age of Science and Medicine

The Hellenistic era witnessed a more conscious separation of science from philosophy. In Classical Greece, what we would call the physical and life sciences had been divisions of philosophical inquiry. Nevertheless, the Greeks, by the time of Aristotle, had already established an important principle of scientific investigation—empirical research, or systematic observation, as the basis for generalization. In the Hellenistic Age, the sciences tended to be studied in their own right.

One of the traditional areas of Greek science was astronomy, and two Alexandrian scholars continued this exploration. Aristarchus (ar-iss-TAR-kus) of Samos (c. 310–230 B.C.E.) developed a *heliocentric* view of the universe, contending that the sun and the fixed stars remain stationary while the earth rotates around the sun in a circular orbit. He also argued that the earth rotates around its own axis. This view was not widely accepted, and most scholars clung to the earlier *geocentric* view of the Greeks, which held that the earth was at the center of the universe. Another astronomer, Eratosthenes (er-uh-TAHSS-thuh-neez) (c. 275–194 B.C.E.), determined that the earth was round and calculated the earth's circumference at 24,675 miles, an estimate that was within 200 miles of the actual figure.

A third Alexandrian scholar was Euclid (YOO-klid), who lived around 300 B.C.E. He established a school in Alexandria but is primarily known for his work titled *Elements*. This was a systematic organization of the fundamental elements of geometry as they had already been worked out; it became the standard textbook of plane geometry and was used up to modern times.

ARCHIMEDES The most famous of the scientists of the Hellenistic period, Archimedes (ahr-kuh-MEE-deez) (287–212 B.C.E.), came from the western Mediterranean region. Archimedes was especially important for his work on the

Museo Pio Clementino, Vatican State//© Scala/Art Resource, NY

Laocoön and His Sons. Three sculptors from Rhodes created this famous piece. This version is probably a Roman copy of the original. The scene illustrates an episode from the Trojan War when the gods sent serpents into Troy to kill the Trojan priest Laocoön and his sons. The intense struggles of the figures are reflected in the pained expressions on their faces.

Musei Capitolini, Rome//© Araldo de Luca/CORBIS

Drunken Old Woman. Hellenistic sculptors no longer tried to capture ideal beauty in their sculpture, a quest that characterized Greek classicism, but moved toward a more emotional and realistic art. This statue of a drunken old woman is typical of this new trend in art. Old and haggard, mired in poverty, she struggles just to go on living.

geometry of spheres and cylinders, for establishing the value of the mathematical constant pi, and for creating the science of hydrostatics. Archimedes was also a practical inventor. He may have devised the so-called Archimedean screw used to pump water out of mines and to lift irrigation water, as well as a compound pulley for transporting heavy weights. During the Roman siege of his native city of Syracuse, he constructed a number of devices to thwart the attackers. According to Plutarch's account, the Romans became so frightened "that if they did but see a little rope or a piece of wood from the wall, instantly crying out, that there it was again, Archimedes was about to let fly some engine at them, they turned their backs and fled."[7]

Archimedes' accomplishments inspired a wealth of semilegendary stories. Supposedly, he discovered specific gravity by observing the water he displaced in his bath and became so excited by his realization that he jumped out of the water and ran home naked, shouting, "Eureka!" ("I have found it!"). He is said to have emphasized the importance of levers by proclaiming to the king of Syracuse: "Give me a lever and a place to stand on, and I will move the earth." The king was so impressed that he encouraged Archimedes to lower his sights and build defensive weapons instead.

MEDICINE The scientific foundations of medicine also made considerable strides in the Hellenistic period. This represents a continuation from the fifth century when Hippocrates, a contemporary of Socrates, is credited with having been the "first to separate medicine from philosophy" by stressing natural explanations and natural cures for disease. Herophilus (huh-ROF-uh-luss) and Erasistratus (er-uh-SIS-truh-tuss), both well-known physicians, were active in Alexandria in the first half of the third century B.C.E. Both were interested in anatomy and used dissection and vivisection (the dissection of living bodies) to expand their knowledge, or so the Roman author Celsus claimed:

> Moreover, as pains, and also various kinds of diseases, arise in the more internal parts, they hold that no one can apply remedies for these who is ignorant about the parts themselves; hence it becomes necessary to lay open the bodies of the dead and to scrutinize their viscera and intestines. They hold that Herophilus and Erasistratus did this in the best way by far, when they laid open men while alive—criminals received out of prison from the kings—and while these were still breathing, observed parts which beforehand nature had concealed, their position, color, shape, size, arrangement, hardness, softness, smoothness, relation, processes and depressions of each, and whether any part is inserted into or is received into another.[8]

Herophilus added significantly to the understanding of the brain, eye, liver, and the reproductive and nervous systems. Erasistratus made discoveries in the process of digestion.

Hellenistic Sculpture and a Greek-Style Buddha. Greek architects and sculptors were highly valued throughout the Hellenistic world. Shown on the left is a terra-cotta statuette of a draped young woman, made as a tomb offering near Thebes, probably around 300 B.C.E. The incursion of Alexander into the western part of India resulted in some Greek cultural influences there. During the first century B.C.E., Indian sculptors in Gandhara began to make statues of the Buddha in a style that combined Indian and Hellenistic artistic traditions, evident in the stone sculpture of the Buddha on the right. Note the wavy hair topped by a bun tied with a ribbon, also a feature of earlier statues of Greek deities. This Buddha is also seen wearing a Greek-style toga.

It would be misleading to think of medicine in the Hellenistic world only in terms of scientific advances. Alongside these developments, a wide range of alternative methods of healing continued to exist. These included magical practices, such as the use of amulets to cast off evil spirits, herbal remedies, and the healing powers of deities, especially those of Asclepius, the god of healing (see the box on p. 108).

Philosophy: New Schools of Thought

While Alexandria and Pergamum became the renowned cultural centers of the Hellenistic world, Athens remained the prime center for philosophy and continued to attract the most illustrious philosophers from the Greek world who chose to establish their schools there. New schools of philosophical thought—the Epicureans and Stoics—reinforced Athens's reputation as a philosophical center.

EPICUREANISM Epicurus (ep-i-KYOOR-uss) (341–270 B.C.E.), the founder of **Epicureanism** (ep-i-kyoo-REE-uh-ni-zum), established a school in Athens near the end of the fourth century B.C.E. Epicurus's famous belief in a doctrine of "pleasure" began with his view of the world. Although he did not deny the existence of the gods, he did not believe they played any active role in the world. The universe ran on its own. This left human beings free to follow self-interest as a basic motivating force. Happiness was the goal of life, and the means to achieve it was the pursuit of pleasure, the only true good. But the pursuit of pleasure was not meant in a physical, hedonistic sense:

Diogenes Laertius, *Lives of the Eminent Philosophers, Life of Epicurus*

> When, therefore, we maintain that pleasure is the end, we do not mean the pleasures of profligates and those that consist in sensuality, as is supposed by some who are either ignorant or disagree with us or do not understand, but freedom from pain in the body and from trouble in the mind. For it is not continuous drinkings and revelings, nor the satisfaction of lusts, nor the enjoyment of fish and other luxuries of the wealthy table, which produce a pleasant life, but sober reasoning, searching out the motives for all choice and avoidance, and banishing mere opinions, to which are due the greatest disturbance of the spirit.

Pleasure was not satisfying one's desire in an active, gluttonous fashion but rather freedom from emotional turmoil, freedom from worry, the freedom that came from a mind at rest. To achieve this passive pleasure, one had to free oneself from public activity: "We must release ourselves from the prison of affairs and politics." They were too strenuous to give peace of mind. But this was not a renunciation of all social life, for to Epicurus, a life could be complete only when it was centered on the basic ideal of friendship: "Of all the things which wisdom acquires to produce the blessedness of the complete life, far the greatest is the possession of friendship."[9] Epicurus's own life in Athens was an embodiment of his teachings. He and his friends created their own private community where they could pursue their ideal of true happiness.

STOICISM Epicureanism was eventually overshadowed by another school of thought known as **Stoicism** (STOH-i-siz-um), which became the most popular philosophy of the Hellenistic world and persisted in the Roman Empire as well. It was the product of a teacher named Zeno (335–263 B.C.E.), who came to Athens and began to teach in a public colonnade known as the Painted Portico (the *Stoa Poikile*—hence the name Stoicism). Like Epicureanism, Stoicism was concerned with how individuals find happiness. But Stoics took a radically different approach. To them, happiness, the supreme good, could be

Miraculous Cures

Although all gods and goddesses were believed to have healing powers, special curative powers were attributed to Asclepius, the god of healing. A cult of supernatural healing came to be associated with him. Dreams that people experienced when they slept in a sanctuary dedicated to Asclepius supposedly had curative powers, as these texts demonstrate.

Texts on the Miraculous Cures at Epidaurus

A man with the fingers of his hand paralyzed except for one came as a suppliant to the god, and when he saw the tablets in the sanctuary he would not believe the cures and was rather contemptuous of the inscriptions, but when he went to sleep he saw a vision: he thought that as he was playing dice below the sanctuary and was about to throw the dice, the god appeared, sprang on his hand and stretched out his fingers, and when the god moved away, the man thought he bent his hand and stretched out the fingers one by one. When he had straightened them all out, the god asked him whether he still did not believe the inscriptions on the tablets in the sanctuary, and the man said he did. The god said: "Since previously you would not believe them, although they are not incredible, in future let [your name] be 'Incredulous.'" When day came he went away cured.

Ambrosia from Athens, blind in one eye. She came as a suppliant to the god, and as she walked about the sanctuary she ridiculed some of the cures as being incredible and impossible, that persons who were lame and blind should be restored to health merely by seeing a dream. But when she went to sleep she saw a vision: she thought the god was standing next to her and saying that he would restore her to health, but she must dedicate in the sanctuary as a reward a silver pig, as a memorial of her stupidity. Having said this he split open the diseased eye and poured in a medicine. When day came she went away cured.

Q What does this selection reveal about medical practices in the Hellenistic world? How might a modern psychologist explain these cures?

© DEA/G. Dagli Orti//Getty Images

Portrait of Epicurus. Epicurus was the founder of the Epicurean school of philosophy, which became very popular during the Hellenistic period. He maintained an "atomic" theory of the universe—that the only things that exist are atoms moving through the void—and an ethical theory based on the pursuit of pleasure.

found only in virtue, which meant essentially living in harmony with divine will: "And this very thing constitutes the virtue of the happy man and the smooth current of life, when all actions promote the harmony of the spirit dwelling in the individual man with the will of him who orders the universe."[10] One achieved happiness by choosing to follow divine will through the free exercise of one's own will. To the Stoics, divine will was the same as the will of nature, since nature was simply a manifestation or expression of the gods. "Living according to nature," therefore, meant following divine will or the natural laws that the gods established to run the universe.

Virtuous living, then, was living in accordance with the laws of nature or submitting to divine will (see the box on p. 109). This led to the acceptance of whatever one received in life, since divine will for us was by its very nature good. By accepting divine law, people mastered themselves and gained inner peace. Life's problems could not disturb such individuals, and they could bear whatever life offered (hence our word *stoic*).

Unlike Epicureans, Stoics did not believe in the need to separate oneself from the world and politics. Public service was regarded as noble. The real Stoic was a good citizen and could even be a good government official. Because Stoics believed that a divine principle was present throughout the universe, each human being also contained a divine spark. This led to a belief in the oneness of humanity. The world constituted a single society of equal human beings. Although humans were not equal in the outer world, the divine spark in each meant that all were free to follow divine will (what was best for each

The Stoic Ideal of Harmony with God

The Stoic Cleanthes (331–232 B.C.E.) succeeded Zeno as head of this school of philosophy. One historian of Hellenistic civilization has called this work by Cleanthes the greatest religious hymn in Greek literature. Certainly, it demonstrates that Stoicism, unlike Epicureanism, did have an underlying spiritual foundation. This poem has been compared to the great psalms of the Hebrews.

Cleanthes, *Hymn to Zeus*

Nothing occurs on the earth apart from you, O God,
nor in the heavenly regions nor on the sea,
except what bad men do in their folly;
but you know to make the odd even,
and to harmonize what is dissonant; to you the alien is akin.
And so you have wrought together into one all things that are good and bad,
So that there arises one eternal logos [rationale] of all things,
Which all bad mortals shun and ignore,
Unhappy wretches, ever seeking the possession of good things
They neither see nor hear the universal law of God,
By obeying which they might enjoy a happy life.

Q Based on Cleanthes' poem, what are some of the beliefs of the Stoics? How do they differ from the beliefs of the Epicureans?

individual). All persons, then, even slaves, though unfree in body, were equal at the level of the soul.

Epicureanism and especially Stoicism appealed to large numbers of people in the Hellenistic world. Both of these philosophies focused primarily on the problem of human happiness. Their popularity would suggest a fundamental change in the character of the Greek lifestyle. In the Classical Greek world, the happiness of individuals and the meaning of life were closely associated with the life of the *polis*. One found fulfillment within the community. In the Hellenistic kingdoms, although the *polis* continued to exist, the sense that one could find satisfaction and fulfillment through life in the *polis* had weakened. Not only did individuals seek new philosophies that offered personal happiness, but in the cosmopolitan world of the Hellenistic states, with their mixtures of peoples, a new openness to thoughts of universality could also emerge. For some people, Stoicism embodied this larger sense of community. The appeal of new philosophies in the Hellenistic era can also be explained by the apparent decline in certain aspects of traditional religion.

Religion in the Hellenistic World

Q **Focus Question**: Which religions were prominent during the Hellenistic period, and what does their popularity suggest about Hellenistic society?

When the Greeks spread throughout the Near East, they took their gods with them. Hellenistic cities increased the number of public festivals and celebrated them with great magnificence. But as time went on, there was a noticeable decline in the vitality of the traditional Greek Olympian religion. The civic cults based on the traditional gods no longer seemed sufficient to satisfy people's emotional needs.

This left Greeks receptive to the numerous religious cults of the eastern world. The Greeks were always tolerant of other existing religious institutions. Hence, in the Hellenistic cities of the Near East, the traditional civic cults of their own gods and foreign cults existed side by side. Alexandria had cults of the traditional Greek gods, Egyptian deities such as Isis and Horus, the Babylonian Astarte, and the Syrian Atargatis.

But for many people, the search for personal meaning remained unfulfilled. Among educated Greeks, the philosophies of Epicureanism and especially Stoicism offered help. Another source of solace came in the form of **mystery religions.**

Mystery Religions

Mystery cults, with their secret initiations and promises of individual salvation, were not new to the Greek world. But the Greeks of the Hellenistic era were also strongly influenced by eastern mystery cults, such as those of Egypt, which offered a distinct advantage over the Greek mystery religions. The latter had usually been connected to specific locations (such as Eleusis), which meant that a would-be initiate had to undertake a pilgrimage in order to participate in the rites. In contrast, the eastern mystery religions were readily available since temples to their gods and goddesses were located throughout the Greek cities of the east.

All of the mystery religions were based on the same fundamental premises. Individuals could pursue a path to salvation and achieve eternal life by being initiated into a union with a savior god or goddess who had died and risen again. The ritual of initiation, by which the seeker identified with the god or goddess, was no doubt a highly emotional experience.

The Egyptian cult of Isis was one of the most popular of the mystery religions. The cult of Isis was very ancient but

The Cult of Isis. The cult of Isis was one of the most popular mystery religions in the Hellenistic world. This fresco from Herculaneum in Italy depicts a religious ceremony in front of the temple of Isis. At the top a priest holds a golden vessel, while below him another priest leads the worshipers with a staff. A third priest fans the flames at the altar.

became truly universal in Hellenistic times. Isis was the goddess of women, marriage, and children, as one of her hymns states: "I am she whom women call goddess. I ordained that women should be loved by men: I brought wife and husband together, and invented the marriage contract. I ordained that women should bear children."[11] Isis was also portrayed as the giver of civilization who had brought laws and letters to all humankind. The cult of Isis offered a precious commodity to its initiates—the promise of eternal life. In many ways, the mystery religions of the Hellenistic era helped pave the way for Christianity.

The Jews in the Hellenistic World

In observing the similarities among their gods and goddesses, Greeks and easterners tended to assume that the deities were the same beings with different names, giving rise to a process of **syncretism.** But a special position was occupied in the Hellenistic world by the Jews, whose monotheistic religion was exclusive and did not permit this kind of fusion of spiritual beings.

The Jewish province of Judaea was ruled by the Ptolemies until it fell under the control of the Seleucids by 200 B.C.E. In the reign of the Seleucid king Antiochus IV (175–163 B.C.E.), conflict erupted in Judaea. Hellenistic monarchs were generally tolerant of all religions, but problems with Rome prompted Antiochus to try to impose more cultural and religious unity in Judaea. When he sent troops to Jerusalem and seized the Temple, he sparked a Jewish uprising led by Judas Maccabaeus (JOO-dus mak-uh-BEE-uss). In 164 B.C.E., the rebels succeeded in recapturing the Temple, a joyous event that has been celebrated every year since in the Jewish holiday of Hanukkah (HAH-nuh-kuh) (Hebrew for "rededication"). Although the conflict in Judaea continued, the Seleucids ultimately made concessions and allowed the Jews considerable freedom.

But since the Diaspora (see Chapter 2), large numbers of Jews no longer lived in Judaea. There was a large Jewish population in Egypt, particularly in Alexandria, as well as Jewish settlements throughout the cities of Asia Minor and Syria. In each city, Jews generally set up a synagogue and formed a private association for worship as other foreigners did. Some city authorities also allowed the Jews to form a political corporation that gave them greater rights than other resident aliens. Most important, they gained the privilege to live by their own laws and their own judicial system. The Jews were not really interested in citizenship in the cities in which they resided because full citizenship meant worship of the city's gods, anathema to Jews who believed only in Yahweh.

CHAPTER SUMMARY

While the Greek city-states were pursuing their squabbles, to their north a new and powerful kingdom—Macedonia—emerged. Under King Philip II, the Macedonians undertook military reforms, defeated a Greek allied army in 338 B.C.E., and then consolidated their control over the Greek peninsula. Although the independent Greek city-states lost their freedom when they were conquered by the Macedonians, Greek culture did not die, and a new age, known as the Hellenistic era, eventually came into being.

That era began with the conquest of the Persian Empire by Alexander the Great, the young successor to his father, Philip II. Alexander, vowing to avenge the Persian attacks on Greece, crossed into Asia Minor with his army in 334 B.C.E. By 330 B.C.E., the Persian Empire had been defeated, but Alexander, never at rest, moved eastward into India, where a mutiny by his exhausted troops forced him to return to Babylon, where he died in 323 B.C.E. Though a great military leader, Alexander was not a good political administrator. He failed to establish any definite structure for the empire he had conquered, and four Hellenistic kingdoms eventually emerged as his successors.

Within those kingdoms, the resulting society is known as *Hellenistic,* meaning Greek-like or "to imitate Greeks." The Greek language became dominant throughout the area as Greek ideas became influential. Greek merchants, artists, philosophers, and soldiers found opportunities and rewards throughout the Near East, now a world of kingdoms rather than independent city-states.

The Hellenistic period was, in its own way, a vibrant one. New cities rose and flourished. New philosophical doctrines—such as Epicureanism and Stoicism—captured the minds of many. Sculptors and architects found many opportunities under the patronage of kings and other wealthy individuals. Significant achievements occurred in literature and science, as is evident in the work of Polybius, Euclid, and Archimedes. Greek culture spread throughout the Near East and made an impact wherever it was carried. In some areas of the Hellenistic world, queens played an active role in political life, and many upper-class women found new avenues for expressing themselves. Commerce increased, and women often played significant roles in economic activities. Although the Hellenistic era achieved a degree of political stability, by the late third century B.C.E., signs of decline were beginning to multiply, and the growing power of Rome eventually endangered the Hellenistic world.

CHAPTER TIMELINE

CHAPTER REVIEW

Upon Reflection

Q What role did Alexander the Great play in the creation of the Hellenistic kingdoms?

Q What were the main achievements of the Hellenistic kingdoms, and why did they fail to bring any lasting order to the lands of the Near East?

Q It can be said that the Hellenistic Age witnessed a shift from the *polis* to the *cosmopolis*. What does this mean, and what effects did it have on Greek life?

Key Terms

Hellenistic (p. 90)
gymnasium (p. 103)
Epicureanism (p. 107)
Stoicism (p. 107)
mystery religions (p. 109)
syncretism (p. 110)

Suggestions for Further Reading

GENERAL WORKS For a general introduction to the Hellenistic era, see **P. Green, *The Hellenistic Age: A Short History*** (New York, 2007). The best general surveys are **F. W. Walbank, *The Hellenistic World,*** rev. ed. (Cambridge, Mass., 2006), and **G. Shipley, *The Greek World After Alexander, 323–30 B.C.*** (London, 2000). See also **A. Erskine, ed., *A Companion to the Hellenistic World*** (Oxford, 2005).

EARLY HISTORY OF MACEDONIA For a good introduction to the early history of Macedonia, see **E. N. Borza, *In the Shadow of Olympus: The Emergence of Macedon*** (Princeton, N.J., 1990), and **R. M. Errington, *A History of Macedonia*** (Berkeley, Calif., 1990).

ALEXANDER There are considerable differences of opinion on Alexander the Great. Good biographies include **R. L. Fox, *Alexander the Great*** (London, 1973); **P. Cartledge, *Alexander the Great*** (New York, 2004); **N. G. L. Hammond, *The Genius of Alexander the Great*** (Chapel Hill, N.C., 1997); **P. Green, *Alexander of Macedon*** (Berkeley, Calif., 1991); and **G. M. Rogers, *Alexander: The Ambiguity of Greatness*** (New York, 2004).

HELLENISTIC MONARCHIES Studies on the various Hellenistic monarchies include **N. G. L. Hammond** and **F. W. Walbank, *A History of Macedonia, vol. 3, 336–167 B.C.*** (Oxford, 1988); **S. Sherwin-White** and **A. Kuhrt, *From Samarkand to Sardis: A New Approach to the Seleucid Empire*** (Berkeley, Calif., 1993); **N. Lewis, *Greeks in Ptolemaic Egypt*** (Oxford, 1986); and **R. E. Allen, *The Attalid Kingdom*** (Oxford, 1983). See also the collection of essays in **C. Habicht, *Hellenistic Monarchies*** (Ann Arbor, Mich., 2006). On warfare, see **A. Chaniotis, *War in the Hellenistic World: A Social and Cultural History*** (Oxford, 2005).

THE CELTS On the Celts, see **B. Cunliffe, *The Ancient Celts*** (London, 1997), and the beautifully illustrated brief study by **J. Davies, *The Celts*** (London, 2000).

HELLENISTIC WOMEN Hellenistic women are examined in two works by **S. B. Pomeroy, *Goddesses, Whores, Wives, and Slaves: Women in Classical Antiquity*** (New York, 1975), pp. 120–148, and ***Women in Hellenistic Egypt*** (New York, 1984).

HELLENISTIC CULTURE For a general introduction to Hellenistic culture, see **J. Onians, *Art and Thought in the Hellenistic Age*** (London, 1979). On art, see **J. J. Pollitt, *Art in the Hellenistic Age*** (New York, 1986). On Hellenistic philosophy, see **R. W. Sharples, *Stoics, Epicureans, and Skeptics: An Introduction to Hellenistic Philosophy*** (London, 1996). A superb work on Hellenistic science is **G. E. R. Lloyd, *Greek Science After Aristotle*** (London, 1973).

HELLENISTIC RELIGION On various facets of Hellenistic religion, see **L. Martin, *Hellenistic Religions: An Introduction*** (New York, 1987); **R. E. Witt, *Isis in the Graeco-Roman World*** (London, 1971); **J. D. Mikalson, *Religion in Hellenistic Athens*** (Berkeley, Calif., 1998); and **A. Tripolitis, *Religions of the Hellenistic-Roman Age*** (Ann Arbor, Mich., 2001).

ROME AND THE HELLENISTIC WORLD On the entry of Rome into the Hellenistic world, see the basic work by **E. S. Gruen, *The Hellenistic World and the Coming of Rome,*** 2 vols. (Berkeley, Calif., 1984).

CourseMate

Visit the CourseMate website at www.cengagebrain.com for additional study tools and review materials for this chapter.

CHAPTER 5

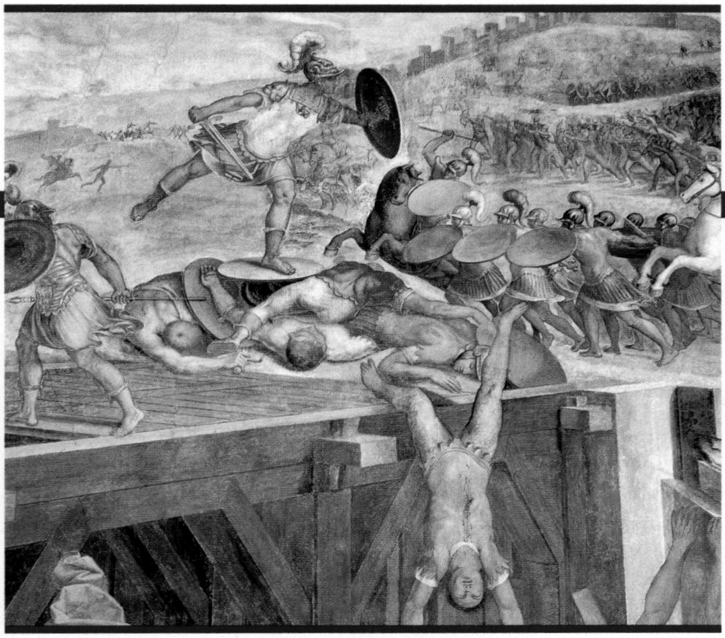

Art Library

Horatius defending the bridge as envisioned by Tommaso Laureti, a sixteenth-century Italian painter

The Roman Republic

CHAPTER OUTLINE AND FOCUS QUESTIONS

The Emergence of Rome

Q What impact did geography have on the history of Rome, and what influence did the Etruscans and Greeks have on early Roman history?

The Roman Republic (c. 509–264 B.C.E.)

Q What were the major political institutions of the Roman Republic, and what policies and institutions help explain the Romans' success in conquering Italy?

The Roman Conquest of the Mediterranean (264–133 B.C.E.)

Q How did Rome achieve its empire from 264 to 133 B.C.E., and what is meant by the phrase "Roman imperialism"?

Society and Culture in the Roman Republic

Q How did the acquisition of an empire affect Roman religious, social, and economic institutions, values and attitudes, law, and art and literature?

The Decline and Fall of the Roman Republic (133–31 B.C.E.)

Q What were the main problems Rome faced during the last century of the Republic, and how were they ultimately resolved?

CRITICAL THINKING

Q What did the Roman poet Horace mean when he wrote, "Captive Greece took captive her rude conqueror"?

EARLY ROMAN HISTORY is filled with legendary tales of the heroes who made Rome great. One of the best known is the story of Horatius at the bridge. Threatened by attack from the neighboring Etruscans, Roman farmers abandoned their fields and moved into the city, where they would be protected by the walls. One weak point in the Roman defenses, however, was a wooden bridge over the Tiber River. Horatius was on guard at the bridge when a sudden assault by the Etruscans caused many Roman troops to throw down their weapons and flee. Horatius urged them to make a stand at the bridge to protect Rome; when they hesitated, as a last resort he told them to destroy the bridge behind him while he held the Etruscans back. Astonished at the sight of a single defender, the confused Etruscans threw their spears at Horatius, who caught them on his shield and barred the way. By the time the Etruscans had regrouped and were about to overwhelm the lone defender, the Roman soldiers brought down the bridge. When Horatius heard the bridge crash into the river behind him, he dived fully armed into the water and swam safely to the other side through a hail of arrows. Rome had been saved by the courageous act of a Roman who knew his duty and was determined to carry it out. Courage, duty, determination—these qualities would also serve the many Romans who believed that it was their mission to rule nations and peoples.

In the first millennium B.C.E., a group of Latin-speaking people established a small community on the plain of Latium on the Italian peninsula. This community, called Rome, was one of numerous Latin-speaking communities in Latium, and the Latin speakers, in turn, constituted only some of the many peoples in Italy. Roman history is basically the story of the Romans' conquest of the plain of Latium, then Italy, and finally the entire Mediterranean world. Why were the Romans able to do this? The Romans made the right decisions at the right time; in other words, the Romans had political wisdom.

The Romans were also practical. Unlike the Greeks, who reserved their citizenship for small, select groups, the Romans often offered citizenship to the peoples they conquered, thus laying the basis for a strong, integrated empire. The Romans also did not hesitate to borrow ideas and culture from the Greeks. Roman strength lay in government, law, and engineering. The Romans knew how to govern people, establish legal structures, and construct the roads that took them to the ends of the known world. Throughout their empire, they carried their law, their political institutions, their engineering skills, and their Latin language. And even after the Romans were gone, those same gifts continued to play an important role in the continuing saga of Western civilization.

The Emergence of Rome

Focus Question: What impact did geography have on the history of Rome, and what influence did the Etruscans and Greeks have on early Roman history?

Not much is known about the prehistoric peoples who lived in Italy. We do know that Indo-European peoples moved into Italy during the second half of the second millennium B.C.E. By the first millennium B.C.E., other peoples had also settled in Italy, the two most notable being the Greeks and the Etruscans (i-TRUSS-kunz). Before examining these peoples, however, we need to consider the influence geography had on the historical development of the peoples on the Italian peninsula.

Geography of the Italian Peninsula

Geography had a major impact on Roman history. Italy is a narrow peninsula extending about 750 miles from north to south but averaging only about 120 miles across (see Map 5.1). The Apennine Mountains traverse the peninsula from north to south, forming a ridge down the middle that divides west from east. Nevertheless, Italy has some fairly large fertile plains ideal for farming. Most important were the Po valley in the north, probably the most fertile agricultural area; the plain of Latium (LAY-shee-um), on which Rome was located; and Campania to the south of Latium. To the east of the Italian peninsula is the Adriatic Sea, and to the west, the Tyrrhenian Sea and the large islands of Corsica and Sardinia. Sicily lies just west of the toe of the boot-shaped peninsula.

Although the Apennines bisect Italy, they are less rugged than the mountain ranges of Greece and so did not divide the peninsula into many small isolated communities. Italy also possessed considerably more productive farmland than Greece, enabling it to support a large population. Rome's location was favorable from a geographic point of view. Located 18 miles inland on the Tiber River, Rome had access to the sea but was far enough inland to be safe from pirates. Built on seven hills, it was easily defended, and because it was situated where the Tiber could be readily forded, Rome became a natural crossing point for north-south traffic in western Italy. All in all, Rome had a good central location in Italy from which to expand.

Moreover, the Italian peninsula juts into the Mediterranean Sea, making it an important crossroads between the western and eastern Mediterranean. Once Rome had unified Italy, involvement in Mediterranean affairs was natural. And after the Romans had conquered their Mediterranean empire, Italy's central location made their task of governing that empire considerably easier.

The Greeks

The Greeks arrived on the Italian peninsula in large numbers during the age of Greek colonization (750–550 B.C.E.; see Chapter 3). Initially, the Greeks settled in southern Italy. They founded Cumae on the Bay of Naples, Naples itself, and Tarentum and then crept around the coast and up the peninsula as far as Brindisi. They also occupied the eastern two-thirds of Sicily. In establishing their colonies, the Greeks planned permanent communities, secured the coastal plains for agriculture, and built walled cities with harbors to carry on trade. Ultimately, the Greeks had considerable influence on Rome. They cultivated the olive and the vine, passed on their alphabetic system of writing, and provided artistic and cultural models through their sculpture, architecture, and literature. Indeed, many historians view Roman culture as a continuation of Greek culture. While Greek influence initially touched Rome indirectly through the Etruscans, the Romans' conquest of southern Italy and Sicily brought them into direct contact with the Greeks.

The Etruscans

The initial development of Rome was influenced most by a people known as the Etruscans, who had settled north of Rome in Etruria. They were a city-dwelling people who established their towns in commanding positions and fortified them with walls. Numerous inscriptions in tombs show that the Etruscans adopted alphabetic writing from the Greeks before 600 B.C.E.

The origins of the Etruscans are not clear, but after 650 B.C.E., they expanded in Italy and became the dominant cultural and economic force in a number of areas. To the

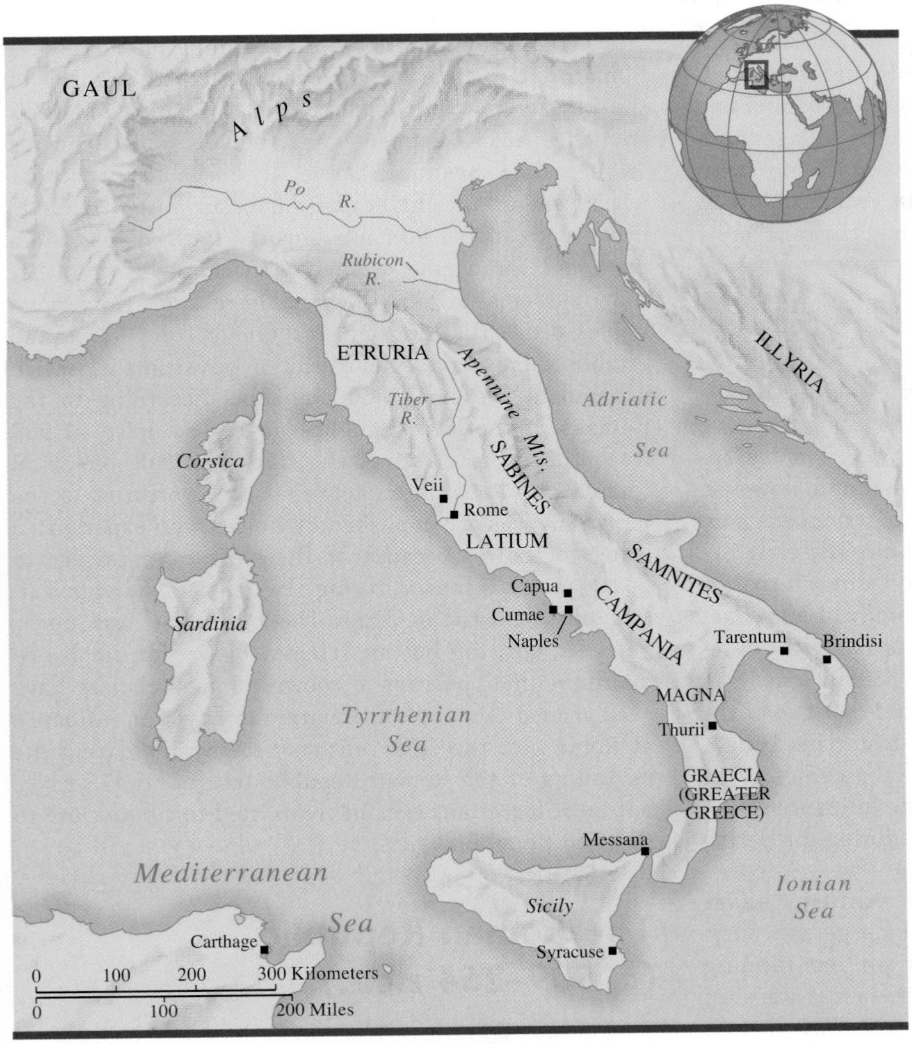

MAP 5.1 Ancient Italy. Ancient Italy was home to several groups. Both the Etruscans in the north and the Greeks in the south had a major influence on the development of Rome.

Once Rome had conquered the Etruscans, Sabines, Samnites, and other local groups, what aspects of the Italian peninsula helped make it defensible against outside enemies?

View an animated version of this map or related maps on the CourseMate website.

north, they moved into north-central Italy. To the south, according to Roman tradition and archaeological evidence, they controlled Rome and possibly all of Latium. From Latium they moved south into Campania, founded a settlement at Capua, and came into direct contact with Greek colonists in southern Italy. In the sixth century B.C.E., the Etruscans were at the height of their power. But by 480 B.C.E., their power had begun to decline, and

Tomb of the Leopards, Tarquinia//© Scala/Art Resource, NY

Etruscan Tomb Mural. Like the Egyptians, the Etruscans filled their tombs with furniture, bowls, and other objects of daily life, as well as murals showing diversions experienced in life and awaiting the dead in the afterlife. Shown in this mural found in an Etruscan tomb at Tarquinia are servants and musicians at a banquet. This mural was painted in the first half of the fifth century B.C.E.

by 400 B.C.E., they were again limited to Etruria itself. Later they were invaded by the Gauls and then conquered by the Romans. But by then the Etruscans had already made an impact. By transforming villages into towns and cities, they brought urbanization to northern and central Italy (the Greeks brought urbanization to southern Italy). Rome was, of course, the Etruscans' most famous creation.

Early Rome

According to Roman legend, Rome was founded by the twin brothers Romulus and Remus in 753 B.C.E. Of course, the Romans invented this story to provide a noble ancestry for their city. Archaeologists have found, however, that by the eighth century there was a settlement consisting of huts on the tops of Rome's hills. The early Romans, basically a pastoral people, spoke Latin, which, like Greek, belongs to the Indo-European family of languages (see Table 1.2 in Chapter 1). The Roman historical tradition also maintained that early Rome (753–509 B.C.E.) had been under the control of seven kings and that two of the last three had been Etruscans. Some historians believe that the king list may have some historical accuracy. What is certain is that Rome did fall under the influence of the Etruscans for about one hundred years during the period of the kings.

By the beginning of the sixth century, under Etruscan influence, Rome began to emerge as a city. The Etruscans were responsible for an outstanding building program. They constructed the first roadbed of the chief street through Rome—the Sacred Way—before 575 B.C.E. and oversaw the development of temples, markets, shops, streets, and houses. By 509 B.C.E., supposedly when the monarchy was overthrown, a new Rome had emerged, essentially a product of the fusion of Etruscan and native Roman elements. After Rome had expanded over its seven hills and the valleys in between, the Servian Wall was built in the fourth century B.C.E. to surround the city.

The Etruscans had an impact on Roman civilization in numerous ways, both large and small. The Romans adopted Etruscan dress—the toga and short cloak. The insignia of the Etruscan kings became the insignia of Roman magistrates. Most impressive was the *fasces,* an ax surrounded by a bundle of rods used as a symbol for the power to scourge and execute, hence to rule. The Romans were also indebted to the Etruscans for the alphabet. The Latin alphabet was a modification of the Etruscan one derived from the Greeks.

The Romans traditionally associated the end of both monarchy and Etruscan domination with the rape of Lucretia, a Roman noblewoman of great virtue. Raped by a son of the king, Lucretia told her father, husband, and their friends what had happened and then committed suicide "rather than be an example of unchastity to other wives," as an ancient Roman historian put it. Lucretia became the model Roman woman: a faithful wife and a pure and courageous woman who chose death rather than be seen as lacking in virtue. In revenge, the Roman nobles drove the king and his family from Rome and established a republican form of government, which ushered in the era of the Republic. According to the Romans of the late Republic, all this occurred in 509 B.C.E. Though interesting, the story has little historical foundation. It is more likely that the overthrow of the monarchy was accomplished by nobles who experienced a loss of power because of the shift from cavalry to heavy-armed infantry during the reign of Servius Tullius, the next-to-last king. The overthrow was not a patriotic uprising but an attempt by Roman nobles to maintain their position of power. Some scholars have even argued that the continuation of Etruscan influence at Rome into the fifth century necessitates dating the beginning of the Roman Republic to around 475 B.C.E., but most historians remain committed to a date close to the traditional 509 B.C.E.

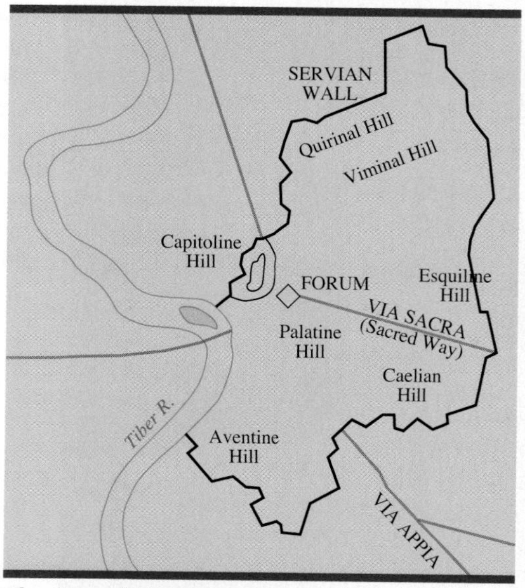

The City of Rome

The Roman Republic (c. 509–264 B.C.E.)

Focus Question: What were the major political institutions of the Roman Republic, and what policies and institutions help explain the Romans' success in conquering Italy?

The transition from monarchy to republican government was not easy. Rome felt threatened by enemies from every direction and in meeting these threats embarked on a course of military expansion that led to the conquest of the entire Italian peninsula. During this period of expansion in Italy, the Roman Republic developed political institutions that were in many ways determined by the social divisions that existed within the community.

The Roman State

In politics and law, as in conquest, the Romans took a practical approach and fashioned political institutions in response to problems as they arose. Hence, it is important to remember that the political institutions we will discuss evolved over a period of centuries.

POLITICAL INSTITUTIONS The Romans had a clear concept of executive authority, embodied in their word ***imperium*** (im-PEE-ree-um), or "the right to command." Invested with *imperium,* the chief magistrates of the Roman state exercised a supreme power that was circumscribed only by extraneous means—officials held office for a limited term and could be tried for offenses committed in office once their term ended. While political institutions changed, the concept of *imperium* did not, and it is the one factor that gives Roman constitutional history continuity and unity.

The chief executive officers of the Roman Republic who possessed *imperium* were the consuls and praetors. After the monarchy was overthrown, two **consuls** (KAHN-sulls), chosen annually, administered the government and led the Roman army into battle. In 366 B.C.E., a new office, that of the **praetor** (PREE-tur), was created. The praetor also possessed *imperium* and could govern Rome when the consuls were away from the city and could also lead armies. The praetor's primary function, however, was the execution of justice. He was in charge of the civil law as it applied to Roman citizens. In 242 B.C.E., reflecting Rome's growth, another praetor was added to judge cases in which one or both parties were noncitizens.

As Rome expanded into the Mediterranean, additional praetors were established to govern the newly conquered provinces (two in 227, two more in 197 B.C.E.). But as the number of provinces continued to grow, the Romans devised a new system in which ex-consuls and ex-praetors who had served their one-year terms were given the title of *proconsul* and *propraetor,* respectively, and sent out as provincial governors. This demonstrates once again the Romans' practical solution to an immediate problem. It was reasonable to assume that officials with governmental experience would make good provincial administrators, although this was not always true in practice due to the opportunities for financial corruption in the provinces.

Periodically, the Republic also created an extraordinary executive. In an emergency, the consuls would resign, and a **dictator** with unlimited power would be chosen to run the state. This office was supposed to last only for the duration of the emergency, the usual limit being six months. The Roman state also had administrative officials with specialized duties. **Quaestors** (KWES-turs) assisted consuls and praetors in the administration of financial affairs. **Aediles** (EE-dylz) supervised the public games and watched over the grain supply of the city, a major problem for a rapidly growing urban community that came to rely on imported grain to feed its population.

The Roman **senate** came to hold an especially important position in the Republic. The senate or council of elders was a select group of about three hundred men who served for life. The senate was not a legislative body and could only advise the magistrates. The advice of the senate was not taken lightly, however, and by the third century B.C.E. had virtually the force of law. No doubt the prestige of the senate's members furthered this development. But it also helped that the senate met continuously, while the chief magistrates changed annually and the popular assemblies operated slowly and met only periodically.

The Roman Republic possessed a number of popular assemblies. By far the most important was the **centuriate assembly,** essentially the Roman army functioning in its political role. Organized by classes based on wealth, it was structured in such a way that the wealthiest citizens always had a majority. The centuriate assembly elected the chief magistrates and passed laws. It is important to remember, however, that the Romans passed few statutory laws and simply left much governance to magisterial authority. As a result of the struggle between the orders, another assembly, the council of the plebs, came into being in 471 B.C.E.

The government of the Roman Republic, then, consisted of three major elements. Two consuls and later other elected officials served as magistrates and ran the state. An assembly of adult males (the centuriate assembly), controlled by the wealthiest citizens, elected these officials, while the senate, a small group of large landowners, advised them. Thus, the Roman state was an aristocratic republic controlled by a relatively small group of privileged people.

Mostra Augustea, Rome//© Alinari/Art Resource, NY

Lictors with *Fasces.* Pictured are lictors bearing the *fasces,* an ax surrounded by a bundle of rods tied with a red thong, an insignia borrowed from the Etruscan kings. The *fasces* was a symbol of the power to rule, and the consuls, the chief executives of the Roman Republic, were always preceded by twelve lictors bearing the *fasces.*

SOCIAL ORGANIZATION The family was the basis of Roman society. At its head was the ***paterfamilias*** (pay-tur-fuh-MEEL-yus), who theoretically had unlimited power over his family. With the *paterfamilias* at the head, the family resembled a kind of miniature state within the state. When a father died, his sons became heads of their own families. Families were often grouped into social units known as *gentes* (GEN-tayz) or clans, descended from the same ancestor and bearing the same family name.

In the early Republic, a Roman citizen had two names, but three names became more common later in the Republic. Each man had a *praenomen* (pree-NOH-mun), or forename, which was his personal name. There were only a limited number of personal names, such as Gaius or Marcus, and these were usually abbreviated in writing (C. for Gaius or M. for Marcus). The *praenomen* was followed by the *nomen* (NOH-mun), which was the name of the group of families or clan (*gens*) to which the person belonged. Thus, the full name of the politician and writer Cicero was Marcus Tullius Cicero, Tullius referring to the clan Tullia. The third name, in this case Cicero, was the *cognomen* (kahg-NOH-mun), which was an extra personal name, sometimes even a nickname by which the person was known. Eventually, the *cognomen* became a hereditary family name, enabling people to identify different branches of the same clan. Women usually had one name, the feminine form of the father's *nomen.* Thus, the daughter of Marcus Tullius Cicero was called Tullia. Names were important to the Romans because they signified a person's place in Roman society.

Closely associated with clan and family was the practice of clientage. Clients constituted a dependent class; they were people who did not have the means to protect themselves or their families without the assistance of a patron. The patron, usually a wealthy member of the upper classes, gave protection and especially legal assistance to his clients. In return, clients provided their patrons with certain services, such as field labor, military assistance, and, especially important in the Republic, votes in the assemblies.

The most noticeable element in the social organization of early Rome was the division between two groups—the **patricians** and the **plebeians.** The word *patrician* is derived from *patres*—the fathers—as the members of the Roman senate were called. The patrician class in Rome consisted of families descended from the original senators appointed during the period of the kings. Their initial prominence was probably due to their wealth as great landowners. Thus, the patricians constituted an aristocratic governing class. They alone could be consuls, other magistrates, and senators. Through their patronage of large numbers of dependent clients, they could control the centuriate assembly and many other facets of Roman life.

The plebeians constituted the considerably larger group of "independent, unprivileged, poorer and vulnerable men" as well as nonpatrician large landowners, less wealthy landholders, artisans, merchants, and small farmers. Although they were citizens, the plebeians did not possess the same rights as the patricians, and at the beginning of the fifth century B.C.E., they began a struggle to rectify that situation. The plebeians who led the struggle for plebeian rights were large landowners who were equal in wealth to many patricians and therefore considered themselves equally qualified to enjoy the same privileges.

THE STRUGGLE OF THE ORDERS Two major problems that existed in the fifth century probably fueled the struggle between the patricians and the plebeians. Both patricians and plebeians could vote, but only the patricians could be elected to governmental offices. Both had the right to make legal contracts and marriages, but intermarriage between patricians and plebeians was forbidden. The wealthy plebeians wanted political equality with the patricians, namely, the right to hold office, and social equality in the form of the right of intermarriage.

The first success for the plebeians came in 494 B.C.E., when they withdrew physically from the state. The patricians, realizing that they could not defend Rome by themselves, were forced to compromise. Two new officials known as **tribunes of the plebs** were instituted (later the number was raised to five and then ten). These tribunes were given the power to protect plebeians against arrest by patrician magistrates. Moreover, after a new popular assembly for plebeians only, called the **council of the plebs,** was created in 471 B.C.E., the tribunes became responsible for convoking it and placing proposals before it. If adopted, these measures became ***plebiscita*** (pleb-i-SEE-tuh) ("it is the opinion of the plebs"), but they were binding only on the plebeians, not on the patricians. Nevertheless, the plebeian council gave the plebeians considerable political leverage.

The next step for the plebeians involved the law. The plebeians came to realize that if they were to increase their power, they needed knowledge of the law and the legal and governmental procedures carefully guarded by the patricians. Due to plebeian pressure, a special commission of ten officials known as the *decemviri* (duh-SEM-vuh-ree) ("ten men") was created with the task of regularizing and publishing the laws. This action resulted in the publication in 450 B.C.E. of the Twelve Tables of Law, which included the legal procedures for going to court; provisions on family, women, and divorce; regulations concerning private property; rules governing relationships and injuries to others; and a provision prohibiting intermarriage between patricians and plebeians (see the box on p. 119). This publication of the laws led to further agitation from the plebeians between 450 and 445 since they could now see how disadvantaged they were. In particular, they demanded the right of intermarriage and admission to the chief magistracies, especially the consulship. In 445 B.C.E., the Canuleian law allowed patricians and plebeians to intermarry. Once this was permitted, the division between the two groups became less important, and the solidarity of the patrician class against plebeian gains began to falter. But it was not until 367 B.C.E. that the consulship was opened to plebeians. The Licinian-Sextian laws stipulated that one consul could now be a plebeian. From 366 to

The Twelve Tables (451–450 B.C.E.)

The Twelve Tables

The Twelve Tables were the first formal codification of Roman laws and customs. The code was inscribed on bronze plaques, which were eventually destroyed. These selections are taken from reconstructions of the code preserved in the works of later writers.

Selections from the Twelve Tables

Table III: Execution; Law of Debt

When a debt has been acknowledged, or judgment about the matter has been pronounced in court, thirty days must be the legitimate time of grace. After that, the debtor may be arrested by laying on of hands. Bring him into court. If he does not satisfy the judgment, or no one in court offers himself as surety in his behalf, the creditor may take the defaulter with him. He may bind him either in stocks or in fetters....

Unless they make a settlement, debtors shall be held in bond for sixty days. During that time they shall be brought before the praetor's court in the meeting place on three successive market days, and the amount for which they are judged liable shall be announced; on the third market day they shall suffer capital punishment or be delivered up for sale abroad, across the Tiber.

Table IV: Rights of Head of Family

Quickly kill... a dreadfully deformed child.

If a father three times surrenders a son for sale, the son shall be free from the father.

A child born ten months after the father's death will not be admitted into legal inheritance.

Table V: Guardianship; Succession

Females shall remain in guardianship even when they have attained their majority.

If a man is raving mad, rightful authority over his person and chattels shall belong to his agnates [nearest male relatives] or to his clansmen.

A spendthrift is forbidden to exercise administration over his own goods.... A person who, being insane or a spendthrift, is prohibited from administering his own goods shall be under trusteeship of agnates.

Table VII: Rights Concerning Land

Branches of a tree may be lopped off all round to a height of more than 15 feet.... Should a tree on a neighbor's farm be bent crooked by a wind and lean over your farm, action may be taken for removal of that tree.

It is permitted to gather up fruit falling down on another man's farm.

Table VIII: Torts or Delicts

If any person has sung or composed against another person a song such as was causing slander or insult to another, he shall be clubbed to death.

If a person has maimed another's limb, let there be retaliation in kind unless he makes agreement for settlement with him.

Any person who destroys by burning any building or heap of corn deposited alongside a house shall be bound, scourged, and put to death by burning at the stake, provided that he has committed the said misdeed with malice aforethought, but if he shall have committed it by accident, that is, by negligence, it is ordained that he repair the damage, or, if he be too poor to be competent for such punishment, he shall receive a lighter chastisement.

Table IX: Public Law

The penalty shall be capital punishment for a judge or arbiter legally appointed who has been found guilty of receiving a bribe for giving a decision.

Table XI: Supplementary Laws

Intermarriage shall not take place between plebeians and patricians.

Q What do the selections from the Twelve Tables reveal about Roman society? In what ways do these points of law differ from those found in the Code of Hammurabi? In what ways are they similar?

361 B.C.E., however, only two plebeians were elected to the consulship, and from 361 to 340, only three, a clear indication that only the most prominent plebeian families could obtain the office. In 342 B.C.E., another law stipulated that both consuls could be plebeians but at least one had to be a plebeian.

The chief landmark in Roman constitutional history—and the climax of the struggle between the orders—came in 287 B.C.E. with the Hortensian law. Henceforth all *plebiscita* passed by the plebeian assembly had the force of law and were binding on the entire community, both plebeians and patricians. Moreover, unlike the laws passed by the centuriate assembly, these *plebiscita* did not need the approval of the senate.

The struggle between the orders, then, had a significant impact on the development of the Roman constitution. Plebeians could hold the highest offices of state, they could intermarry with the patricians, and they

CHRONOLOGY The Struggle of the Orders

First secession of the plebeians; creation of tribunes of the plebs	494 B.C.E.
Creation of the council of the plebs	471 B.C.E.
Publication of the Twelve Tables of Law	450 B.C.E.
Canuleian law: Right of plebeians to marry patricians	445 B.C.E.
Licinian-Sextian laws: One consul may be a plebeian	367 B.C.E.
Both consuls may be plebeians; one must be	342 B.C.E.
Hortensian law: Laws passed by plebeian assembly are binding on all Romans	287 B.C.E.

could help pass laws binding on the entire Roman community. Although the struggle had been long, the Romans had handled it by compromise, not violent revolution. Theoretically, by 287 B.C.E. all Roman citizens were equal under the law, and all could strive for political office. But in reality, as a result of the right of intermarriage, a select number of wealthy patrician and plebeian families formed a new senatorial aristocracy called the *nobiles* (no-BEE-layz), which came to dominate the political offices. The Roman Republic had not become a democracy.

The Roman Conquest of Italy

At the beginning of the Republic, Rome was surrounded by enemies, including the Etruscans to the north and the Sabines, Volscians, and Aequi to the east and south. The Latin communities on the plain of Latium posed an even more immediate threat. After the expulsion of the Etruscan kings, a league of Latin allies formed and challenged Roman leadership in Latium. But in 493 B.C.E., the Romans established an alliance with the Latin communities, which provided for a common defense of Latium.

Rome was under constant pressure from its neighbors for the next hundred years. If we are to believe Livy, one of the chief ancient sources for the history of the early Roman Republic, Rome was engaged in almost continuous warfare with its neighbors.

In his account of these years, Livy provided a detailed narrative of Roman efforts. Many of Livy's stories were legendary in character and indeed were modeled on events in Greek history. But Livy, writing in the first century B.C.E., used these stories to teach Romans the moral values and virtues that had made Rome great. These included tenacity, duty, courage, and especially discipline (see the box on p. 121). Indeed, Livy recounted stories of military leaders who executed their own sons for leaving their place in battle, a serious offense because the success of the hoplite infantry depended on maintaining a precise order. These stories had little basis in fact, but like the story of George Washington and the cherry tree in American history, they provided mythic images to reinforce Roman patriotism.

Livy (59 B.C.E.–17 C.E.), *Histories*, Book 1, Chapters I–VIII

CHRONOLOGY The Roman Conquest of Italy

Alliance with Latin states	493 B.C.E.
Latin revolt	340–338 B.C.E.
Creation of the Roman confederation	338 B.C.E.
Samnite Wars	343–290 B.C.E.
Pyrrhic War	281–267 B.C.E.

In 340 B.C.E., Rome had to deal with a revolt of the Latin states in Latium, which had come to resent Rome's increasing domination of their alliance. The Romans crushed the revolt and established complete supremacy in Latium. Between 343 and 290 B.C.E., the Romans waged a fierce struggle with the Samnites, a hill people from the central Apennines, some of whom had settled in Campania, south of Rome. The conquest of the Samnites gave Rome considerable control over a large part of Italy and also brought it into direct contact with the Greek communities of southern Italy. Soon the Romans were involved in hostilities with some of these Greek cities. The Greek communities were primarily commercial cities and had no standing armies. They were accustomed to hiring mercenaries to fight their battles for them. Consequently, they bought the aid of King Pyrrhus (PEER-uss) of Epirus (approximately modern-day Epirus in Greece), who crossed the Adriatic with 20,000 troops and defeated the Romans twice. In both battles, however, Pyrrhus experienced heavy losses, leading him to comment that one more victory would ruin him—hence our phrase "Pyrrhic (PEER-ik) victory". After a diversion to Sicily, Pyrrhus came back for one more battle with the Romans and this time was decisively defeated. By 267 B.C.E., the Romans completed their conquest of southern Italy. After crushing the remaining Etruscan states to the north, Rome had conquered all of Italy, except the extreme north, by 264 B.C.E.

To rule Italy, the Romans devised the Roman confederation in 338 B.C.E. Under this system, Rome allowed some peoples—especially the Latins—to have full Roman citizenship. Most of the remaining communities were made allies. They remained free to run their own local affairs but were required to provide soldiers for Rome. Moreover, the Romans made it clear that loyal allies could improve their status and even aspire to becoming Roman citizens. Thus, the Romans had found a way to give conquered states a stake in Rome's success.

In the course of their expansion throughout Italy, the Romans pursued consistent policies that help explain their success. The Romans excelled at making the correct diplomatic decisions; they were superb diplomats. Though firm and even cruel when necessary—rebellions were

Cincinnatus Saves Rome: A Roman Morality Tale

There is perhaps no better account of how the virtues of duty and simplicity enabled good Roman citizens to prevail during the travails of the fifth century B.C.E. than Livy's account of Cincinnatus. He was chosen dictator, supposedly in 457 B.C.E., to defend Rome against the attacks of the Aequi. The position of dictator was a temporary expedient used only in emergencies; the consuls would resign, and a leader with unlimited power would be appointed for a limited period (usually six months). In this account, Cincinnatus did his duty, defeated the Aequi, and returned to his simple farm in just fifteen days.

Livy, *The Early History of Rome*

The city was thrown into a state of turmoil, and the general alarm was as great as if Rome herself were surrounded. Nautius was sent for, but it was quickly decided that he was not the man to inspire full confidence; the situation evidently called for a dictator, and, with no dissenting voice, Lucius Quinctius Cincinnatus was named for the post.

Now I would solicit the particular attention of those numerous people who imagine that money is everything in this world, and that rank and ability are inseparable from wealth: let them observe that Cincinnatus, the one man in whom Rome reposed all her hope of survival, was at that moment working a little three-acre farm . . . west of the Tiber, just opposite the spot where the shipyards are today. A mission from the city found him at work on his land—digging a ditch, maybe, or plowing. Greetings were exchanged, and he was asked—with a prayer for divine blessing on himself and his country—to put on his toga and hear the Senate's instructions. This naturally surprised him, and, asking if all were well, he told his wife Racilia to run to their cottage and fetch his toga. The toga was brought, and wiping the grimy sweat from his hands and face he put it on; at once the envoys from the city saluted him, with congratulations, as Dictator, invited him to enter Rome, and informed him of the terrible danger of Municius's army. A state vessel was waiting for him on the river, and on the city bank he was welcomed by his three sons who had come to meet him, then by other kinsmen and friends, and finally by nearly the whole body of senators. Closely attended by all these people and preceded by his lictors he was then escorted to his residence through streets lined with great crowds of common folk who, be it said, were by no means so pleased to see the new Dictator, as they thought his power excessive and dreaded the way in which he was likely to use it.

[Cincinnatus proceeds to raise an army, march out, and defeat the Aequi.]

In Rome the Senate was convened by Quintus Fabius the City Prefect, and a decree was passed inviting Cincinnatus to enter in triumph with his troops. The chariot he rode in was preceded by the enemy commanders and the military standards, and followed by his army loaded with its spoils. . . . Cincinnatus finally resigned after holding office for fifteen days, having originally accepted it for a period of six months.

Q What values did Livy emphasize in his account of Cincinnatus? How important were those values to Rome's success? Why did Livy say he wrote his history? As a writer during the Augustan Age (see Chapter 6), would he have pleased or displeased Augustus by writing a history with such a purpose?

crushed without mercy—they were also shrewd in extending their citizenship and allowing autonomy in domestic affairs. Once at war, the Romans were not only good soldiers but also persistent ones. The loss of an army or a fleet did not cause them to quit but spurred them on to build new armies and new fleets. Finally, the Romans had a practical sense of strategy. As they conquered, they settled Romans and Latins in new communities outside Latium. By 264 B.C.E., the Romans had established colonies—fortified towns—at all strategic locations. By building roads to these settlements and connecting them, the Romans assured themselves of an impressive military and communications network that enabled them to rule effectively and efficiently. By insisting on military service from the allies in the Roman confederation, Rome essentially mobilized the entire military manpower of all Italy for its wars.

The Roman Conquest of the Mediterranean (264–133 B.C.E.)

Q **Focus Question**: How did Rome achieve its empire from 264 to 133 B.C.E., and what is meant by the phrase "Roman imperialism"?

After their conquest of the Italian peninsula, the Romans found themselves face to face with a formidable Mediterranean power—Carthage (KAR-thij). Founded around 800 B.C.E. by Phoenicians from Tyre, Carthage was located in a favorable position for commanding Mediterranean trade routes and had become an important commercial center (see Map 5.2).

In the sixth century B.C.E., Carthage was governed by two judges, who were elected annually. They were usually men of wealth from prominent families. Separately

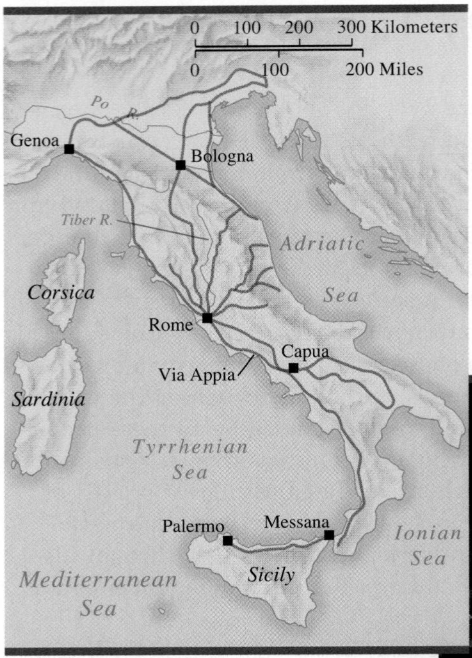

Roman Roads in Italy. The Romans built a remarkable system of roads. After laying a foundation with gravel, which allowed for drainage, the Roman builders placed flagstones, closely fitted together. Unlike other peoples who built similar kinds of roads, the Romans did not follow the contours of the land but made their roads as straight as possible to facilitate communications and transportation, especially for military purposes. Seen here is a view of the Via Appia (Appian Way), built in 312 B.C.E. under the leadership of the censor and consul Appius Claudius (Roman roads were often named after the great Roman families who encouraged their construction). The Via Appia (shown on the map) was constructed to make it easy for Roman armies to march from Rome to the newly conquered city of Capua, a distance of 152 miles.

elected generals led the military forces, which consisted primarily of mercenaries recruited from different parts of the western Mediterranean. There was also a senate composed of several hundred prominent men chosen for life. Ordinary citizens had little power, although a group of 104 judges examined the activities of officials and generals and prevented anyone from either group from establishing a tyranny.

Carthage gradually became a strong military state. By the third century B.C.E., its empire included the coast of North Africa, southern Spain, Sardinia, Corsica, and western Sicily. With its monopoly of western Mediterranean trade, Carthage was the largest and richest state in the area. The presence of Carthaginians (kar-thuh-JIN-ee-unz) in Sicily made the Romans apprehensive about Carthaginian encroachment on the Italian coast. In 264 B.C.E., mutual suspicions drove the two powers into a lengthy struggle for control of the western Mediterranean.

The Struggle with Carthage

The First Punic (PYOO-nik) War (264–241 B.C.E.)—the Latin word for Phoenician was *Punicus*—began when the Romans decided to intervene in a struggle between two Sicilian cities and sent an army to Sicily. The Carthaginians, who considered Sicily within their own sphere of influence, regarded this as just cause for war. In going to war, both sides determined on the conquest of Sicily. The Romans realized that the war would be long and drawn out if they could not supplement land operations with a navy and promptly developed a substantial fleet. The Carthaginians, however, had difficulty finding mercenaries to continue the fight. After a long struggle in which both sides lost battles in North Africa and Sicily, a Roman fleet defeated the Carthaginian navy off Drepana, Sicily, in 242 B.C.E. The cities of western Sicily that had been controlled by Carthage capitulated. Carthage sued for peace, and the war ended in 241 B.C.E. Carthage gave up all rights to Sicily and had to pay an indemnity. Three years later, Rome took advantage of Carthage's problems with its mercenaries to seize the islands of Sardinia and Corsica. This act so angered the Carthaginians that, according to one story, their leading general, Hamilcar Barca, made his nine-year-old son swear that he would hate Rome ever after. The son's name was Hannibal (HAN-uh-bul).

HANNIBAL AND THE SECOND PUNIC WAR Between the wars, Carthage made an unexpected recovery under the

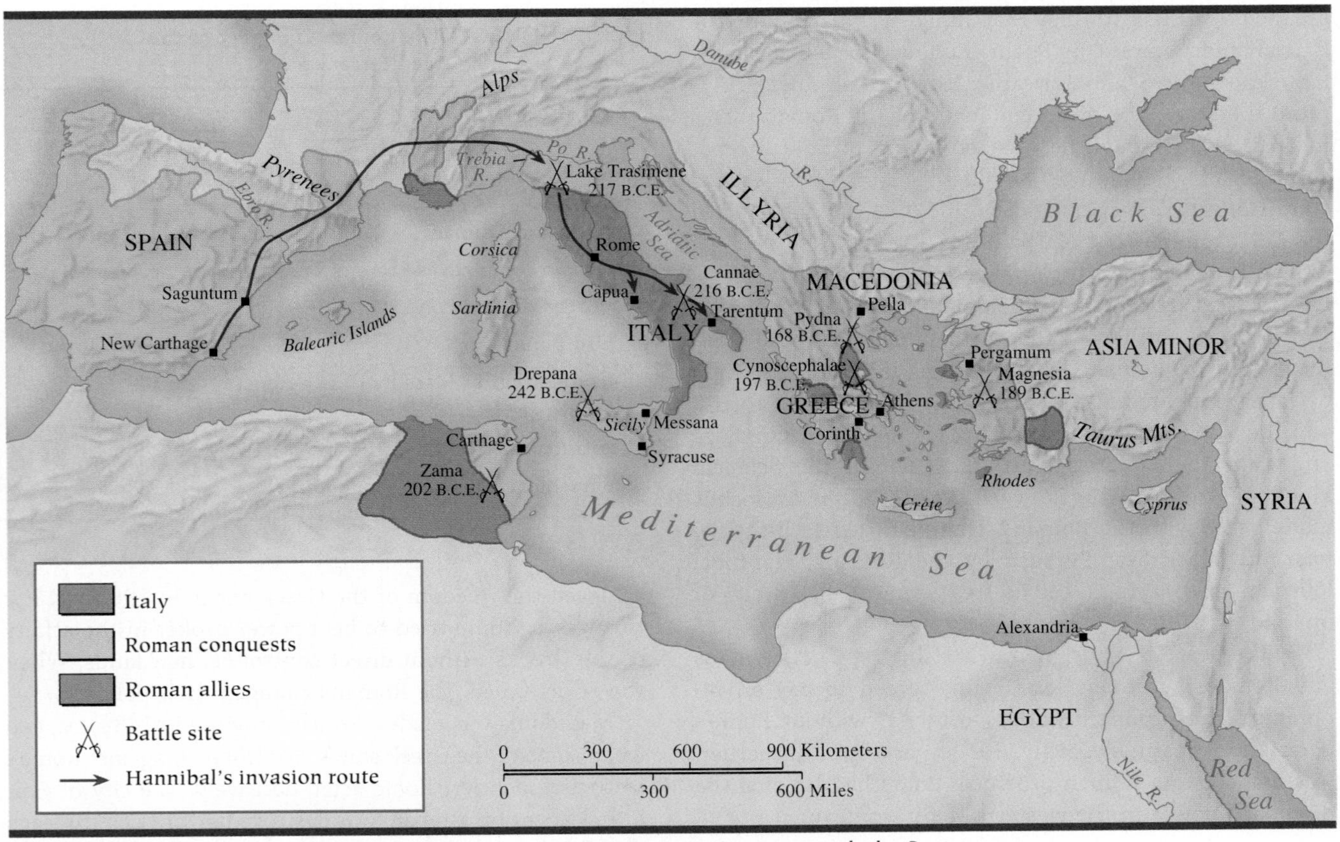

MAP 5.2 Roman Conquests in the Mediterranean, 264–133 B.C.E. Beginning with the Punic Wars, Rome expanded its holdings, first in the western Mediterranean at the expense of Carthage and later in Greece and western Asia Minor.

Q ***What aspects of Mediterranean geography, combined with the territorial holdings and aspirations of Rome and the Carthaginians, made the Punic Wars more likely?***

leadership of the general who had been briefly successful in Sicily in the First Punic War, Hamilcar Barca. Hamilcar extended Carthage's domains in Spain to compensate for the territory lost to Rome. A major goal in creating the Spanish empire was to get manpower for Carthage. The Spanish natives made great soldiers, being physically strong and possessing excellent swords. Hamilcar and his successors proceeded to build up a formidable land army in the event of a second war with Rome because they realized that Carthage's success depended on defeating Rome on land. In 221 B.C.E., Hamilcar's son Hannibal, now twenty-five, took over the direction of Carthaginian policy. Within three years, Rome and Carthage were again at war.

Carthage and Rome had agreed to divide Spain into respective spheres of influence. Although Saguntum was located in the Carthaginian sphere, Rome made an alliance with the city and encouraged its inhabitants in anti-Carthaginian activities. Thoroughly provoked by the Roman action, Hannibal attacked Saguntum, and the Romans declared war on Carthage in 218 B.C.E. This time the Carthaginian strategy aimed at bringing the war home to the Romans and defeating them in their own backyard. In an amazing march, Hannibal crossed the Alps with an army of 30,000 to 40,000 men and 6,000 horses and elephants and advanced into northern Italy. After defeating the Romans at the Trebia River, he added thousands of Gauls to his army and proceeded into central Italy. At Lake Trasimene in Etruria, he again defeated the Romans. In desperation, the Romans elected as consul Quintus Fabius Maximus, who became known as the "Delayer" because of his tactics of following and delaying Hannibal's army without risking a pitched battle. Hannibal hoped to destroy the Roman confederation and win Italian cities away from Rome. The policy failed; virtually all remained loyal to Rome.

In 216 B.C.E., the Romans decided to meet Hannibal head-on. It was a serious mistake. At Cannae, Hannibal's forces devastated a Roman army, killing as many as 40,000 soldiers. At last, some of the southern Italian cities rebelled against Roman rule and went over to Hannibal. Rome seemed on the brink of disaster but refused to give up and raised yet another army.

Rome gradually recovered. Although Hannibal remained free to roam in Italy, he had neither the men nor the equipment to lay siege to the major cities, including Rome itself. The Romans began to reconquer some of the rebellious Italian cities. More important, the Romans pursued a Spanish strategy that aimed at undermining the Carthaginian empire in Spain. Publius Cornelius Scipio, later known as Scipio Africanus (SEE-pee-oh af-ree-KAY-nuss) the Elder, was given command of the Roman forces in Spain even though he was too young to hold the position legally. But he was a brilliant general who learned from Hannibal's tactics, and by 206 B.C.E. he had pushed the Carthaginians out of Spain.

The Romans then took the war directly to Carthage. Late in 204 B.C.E., Scipio led a Roman army from Sicily into North Africa and forced the Carthaginians to recall Hannibal from Italy. At the Battle of Zama in 202 B.C.E., Scipio decisively defeated Hannibal and the Carthaginian forces, and the war was over. Eventually, Hannibal left Carthage and went to help Antiochus, the ruler of the Seleucid kingdom, in his struggle with Rome. After Antiochus made peace with the Romans, Hannibal fled to Bithynia, near the Black Sea. Pursued by the Romans, Hannibal killed himself saying, "Let us free Rome of her dread of one old man."

By the peace treaty signed in 201 by the Carthaginians and Romans, Carthage lost Spain, agreed to pay an indemnity, and promised not to go to war without Rome's permission. Spain, like Sicily, Corsica, and Sardinia earlier, was made into a Roman province. Rome had become the dominant power in the western Mediterranean.

THE DESTRUCTION OF CARTHAGE But some Romans wanted even more. A number of prominent Romans, especially the conservative politician Cato, advocated the complete destruction of Carthage. Cato ended every speech he made to the senate with the words, "And I think Carthage must be destroyed." When the Carthaginians technically broke their peace treaty with Rome by going to war against one of Rome's North African allies that had been encroaching on Carthage's home territory, the Romans declared war. Led by Scipio Aemilianus (SEE-pee-oh ee-mil-YAY-nuss) Africanus the Younger, Roman forces undertook their third and last war with Carthage (149–146 B.C.E.). This time, Carthage was no match for the Romans, who seized the opportunity to carry out the final destruction of Carthage (see the box on p. 125). The territory of Carthage was made a province called Africa.

The Eastern Mediterranean

During the Punic Wars, Rome had become acutely aware of the Hellenistic states of the eastern Mediterranean when the king of Macedonia made an alliance with Hannibal after the Roman defeat at Cannae. But the Romans were preoccupied with the Carthaginians, and it was not until after the defeat of Carthage that Rome became involved in the world of Hellenistic politics as an advocate for the freedom of the Greek states. This support of the Greeks brought the Romans into conflict with both Macedonia and the kingdom of the Seleucids. Roman military victories and diplomatic negotiations rearranged the territorial boundaries of the Hellenistic kingdoms and achieved the freedom of the Greek states in 196 B.C.E. For fifty years, Rome tried to be a power broker in the affairs of the Greeks without direct control of their lands. When the effort failed, the Romans changed their policy.

Macedonia was made a Roman province in 148 B.C.E., and when some of the Greek states rose in revolt against Rome's restrictive policies, Rome acted decisively. The city of Corinth, leader of the revolt, was destroyed in 146 B.C.E. to teach the Greeks a lesson, and Greece was placed under the control of the Roman governor of Macedonia. Thirteen years later, in 133 B.C.E., the king of Pergamum deeded his kingdom to Rome, giving Rome its first province in Asia. Rome was now master of the Mediterranean Sea.

CHRONOLOGY The Roman Conquest of the Mediterranean

First Punic War	264–241 B.C.E.
Rome seizes Corsica and Sardinia	238 B.C.E.
Second Punic War	218–201 B.C.E.
Battle of Cannae	216 B.C.E.
Scipio completes seizure of Spain	206 B.C.E.
Battle of Zama	202 B.C.E.
Third Punic War	149–146 B.C.E.
Incorporation of Macedonia as a Roman province	148 B.C.E.
Destruction of Carthage	146 B.C.E.
Roman acquisition of Pergamum	133 B.C.E.

The Nature of Roman Imperialism

Rome's empire was built in three stages: the conquest of Italy, the conflict with Carthage and expansion into the western Mediterranean, and the involvement with and domination of the Hellenistic kingdoms in the eastern Mediterranean. The Romans did not have a master plan for the creation of an empire. Much of their expansion was opportunistic; once involved in a situation that threatened their security, the Romans did not hesitate to act. And the more they expanded, the more threats to their security appeared on the horizon, involving them in yet more conflicts. Indeed, the Romans liked to portray themselves as declaring war only for defensive reasons or to protect allies. That is only part of the story, however. It is likely, as some historians have suggested, that at some point a group of Roman aristocratic leaders emerged who favored expansion both for the glory it offered and for the economic benefits it provided. Certainly, by the second century B.C.E., aristocratic senators perceived new opportunities for lucrative foreign commands, enormous spoils of war, and an abundant supply of slave labor for their growing landed estates. By that same time, as the destruction of Corinth and Carthage indicates, Roman imperialism had become more arrogant and brutal as well. Rome's foreign success also had

The Destruction of Carthage

The Romans used a technical breach of Carthage's peace treaty with Rome as a pretext to undertake a third and final war with Carthage (149–146 B.C.E.). Although Carthage posed no real threat to Rome's security, the Romans still remembered the traumatic experiences of the Second Punic War when Hannibal had ravaged much of their homeland. The hard-liners gained the upper hand in the senate and called for the complete destruction of Carthage. The city was razed, the survivors were sold into slavery, and the land was made a province of Rome. In this passage, the historian Appian of Alexandria describes the final destruction of Carthage by the Romans under the command of Scipio Aemilianus.

Appian, *Roman History*

Then came new scenes of horror. The fire spread and carried everything down, and the soldiers did not wait to destroy the buildings little by little, but pulled them all down together. So the crashing grew louder, and many fell with the stones into the midst dead. Others were seen still living, especially old men, women, and young children who had hidden in the inmost nooks of the houses, some of them wounded, some more or less burned, and uttering horrible cries. Still others, thrust out and falling from such a height with the stones, timbers, and fire, were torn asunder into all kinds of horrible shapes, crushed and mangled. Nor was this the end of their miseries, for the street cleaners, who were removing the rubbish with axes, mattocks, and boathooks, and making the roads passable, tossed with these instruments the dead and the living together into holes in the ground, sweeping them along like sticks and stones or turning them over with their iron tools, and man was used for filling up a ditch. Some were thrown in head foremost, while their legs, sticking out of the ground, writhed a long time. Others fell with their feet downward and their heads above the ground. Horses ran over them, crushing their faces and skulls, not purposely on the part of the riders, but in their headlong haste. Nor did the street cleaners either do these things on purpose; but the press of war, the glory of approaching victory, the rush of the soldiery, the confused noise of heralds and trumpeters all round, the tribunes and centurions changing guard and marching the cohorts here and there—all together made everybody frantic and heedless of the spectacle before their eyes.

Six days and nights were consumed in this kind of turmoil, the soldiers being changed so that they might not be worn out with toil, slaughter, lack of sleep, and these horrid sights. . . .

Scipio, beholding this city, which had flourished 700 years from its foundation and had ruled over so many lands, islands, and seas, as rich in arms and fleets, elephants, and money as the mightiest empires, but far surpassing them in hardihood and high spirit . . . now come to its end in total destruction—Scipio, beholding this spectacle, is said to have shed tears and publicly lamented the fortune of the enemy. After meditating by himself a long time and reflecting on the inevitable fall of cities, nations, and empires, as well as of individuals, upon the fate of Troy, that once proud city, upon the fate of the Assyrian, the Median, and afterwards of the great Persian empire, and, most recently of all, of the splendid empire of Macedon, either voluntarily or otherwise the words of the poet [Homer, *Iliad*] escaped his lips:

The day shall come in which our sacred Troy
And Priam, and the people over whom
Spear-bearing Priam rules, shall perish all.

Being asked by Polybius in familiar conversation (for Polybius had been his tutor) what he meant by using these words, Polybius says that he did not hesitate frankly to name his own country, for whose fate he feared when he considered the mutability of human affairs. And Polybius wrote this down just as he heard it.

Q What does this description of Rome's destruction of Carthage reveal about the nature of Roman imperialism? What features seem more rhetorical than realistic? Why?

enormous repercussions for the internal development of the Roman Republic.

Evolution of the Roman Army

By the fourth century B.C.E., the Roman army consisted of four legions, each made up of 4,000 to 5,000 men; each legion had about 300 cavalry and the rest infantry. The infantry consisted of three lines of battle. The *hastati* (hahs-TAH-tee) (spearmen), consisting of the youngest recruits, formed the front line; they were armed with heavy spears and short swords, and protected by a large oval shield, helmet, breastplate, and greaves (shin guards). The *principes* (prin-KI-payz *or* prin-SI-payz) (chief men), armed and protected like the *hastati,* formed the second line. The third line of battle was formed by the *triarii* (tri-AR-ee-ee) (third-rank men), who knelt behind the first two lines, ready to move up and fill any gaps. A fourth group of troops, poor citizens who wore cloaks but no armor and were lightly armed, functioned as skirmishers who usually returned to the rear lines after their initial contact with the enemy to form backup reserves.

Roman Legionaries. Roman legionaries, famed for their courage and tenacity, made possible Roman domination of the Mediterranean Sea. At the time of the Punic Wars, a Roman legionary wore chain-mail armor and a plumed helmet and carried an oval shield, as in the bronze statue from the second or first century B.C.E. shown at the left. Heavy javelins and swords were their major weapons. This equipment remained standard until the time of Julius Caesar. The illustration on the right shows a Roman legion on the march from Trajan's column, erected in the second century C.E.

In the early Republic, the army was recruited from citizens between the ages of eighteen and forty-six who had the resources to equip themselves for battle. Since most of them were farmers, they enrolled only for a year, campaigned during the summer months, and returned home in time for the fall harvest. Later, during the Punic Wars of the third century B.C.E., the period of service had to be extended, although this was resisted by farmers whose livelihoods could be severely harmed by a long absence. Nevertheless, after the disastrous battle of Cannae in 216 B.C.E., the Romans were forced to recruit larger armies, and the number of legions rose to twenty-five.

The ancient historian Polybius believed that the fact that in the early centuries of the Republic the Roman army was basically a citizen army led by the Republic's elected magistrates was one of the reasons that the Romans were so successful militarily. An army of citizens who wanted to defend their homeland would be braver and fight harder than hired mercenaries. Roman military success may also have been due to the aggressive behavior of the Roman military leaders, although this could be detrimental at sea. According to Polybius,

> The Romans, to speak generally, rely on force in all their enterprises, and think it is incumbent on them to carry out their projects in spite of all, and that nothing is impossible when they have once decided on it. They owe their success in many cases to this spirit, but sometimes they conspicuously fail by reason of it and especially at sea. For on land they are attacking men and the works of man and are usually successful, as there they are employing force against forces of the same nature.... But when they come to encounter the sea and the atmosphere and choose to fight them by force they meet with signal defeats.[1]

Major changes in the military would not come until the first century B.C.E. with the military reforms of Marius (see "Marius and the New Roman Army" later in this chapter).

Society and Culture in the Roman Republic

Q **FOCUS QUESTION:** How did the acquisition of an empire affect Roman religious, social, and economic institutions, values and attitudes, law, and art and literature?

One of the most noticeable aspects of Roman society and culture is the impact of the Greeks. The Romans had experienced Greek influence early on through the Greek cities in southern Italy. By the end of the third century B.C.E., however, Greek civilization played an ever-increasing role in Roman culture. Greek ambassadors, merchants, and artists traveled to Rome and spread Greek thought and practices. After their conquest of the Hellenistic kingdoms, Roman military commanders shipped Greek manuscripts and art back to Rome. Multitudes of educated Greek slaves were used in Roman households. Greek models affected virtually every area of Roman life, from literature and philosophy to religion and education. Wealthy Romans hired Greek tutors and sent their sons to Athens to study. As the Roman poet Horace said, "Captive Greece took captive her rude conqueror." Greek thought captivated the less sophisticated Roman minds, and the Romans became willing transmitters of Greek culture—not, however, without some resistance from Romans who had nothing but contempt for Greek politics and feared the end of old Roman values. Even those who favored Greek culture, such as Scipio Aemilianus, blamed the Greeks for Rome's new vices, including luxury and homosexual practices.

Roman Religion

Every aspect of Roman society was permeated with religion. The official state religion focused on the worship of a pantheon of gods and goddesses, including Juno, the patron goddess of women; Minerva, the goddess of craftspeople; Mars, the god of war; and Jupiter Optimus Maximus (JOO-puh-tur AHP-tuh-muss MAK-suh-muss) ("best and greatest"), who became the patron deity of Rome and assumed a central place in the religious life of the city. As Rome developed and came into contact with other peoples and gods, the community simply adopted new deities. Hence, the Greek Hermes became the Roman Mercury, and the Greek Demeter, Ceres. Eventually, a complete amalgamation of Greek and Roman religion occurred, giving the Romans and the Greeks essentially the same "Greco-Roman" religion. The Romans were generally tolerant of new religious cults and only occasionally outlawed them.

Forum Boarium, Rome //© Scala/Art Resource, NY

Temple of Portunus. The Romans considered the proper worship of the gods an important key to success. Typical of Roman religious architecture was the small urban temple located in the midst of a crowded commercial center. Pictured here is a rectangular temple built in Rome in the late second or early first century B.C.E. and dedicated to Portunus, the god of harbors. The temple was located in the cattle market close to the Tiber River.

THE IMPORTANCE OF RITUAL Roman religion focused on the worship of the gods for a very practical reason—human beings were thought to be totally dependent on them. The exact performance of ritual was crucial to establishing a right relationship with the gods. What was true for individuals was also valid for the state: it also had to observe correct ritual in order to receive its reward. Consequently, accurate performance of ritual was important, and the Romans established a college of priests or *pontiffs* to carry out that responsibility. Initially three in number, by the first century B.C.E., they had increased to sixteen. At the head of the pontiffs was the *pontifex maximus* (PAHN-ti-feks MAK-si-muss) (chief pontiff), a powerful figure who controlled the state religion. First Julius Caesar and later all emperors until 381 C.E. held this position. The *pontifex maximus* also chose six girls between the ages of six and ten to serve as Vestal Virgins (see the box on p. 128).

The pontiffs were in charge of what the Romans called the divine law, maintaining the right relationship between the state and the gods. The pontiffs performed all public religious acts and supervised magistrates in the correct ritual for public political acts. If the rituals were performed correctly, the Romans would obtain the "peace of the gods." The Romans' success in creating an empire was no doubt taken as confirmation of divine favor. As Cicero, the first-century B.C.E. politician and writer, claimed, "We have overcome all the nations of the world, because we have realized that the world is directed and governed by the gods."[2]

THE USE OF OMENS In addition to the college of pontiffs, a college of *augurs* (AW-gurz) existed whose responsibility was to interpret the *auspices* (AWSS-puh-sizz)—signs or warnings that the gods gave to men through such phenomena as unusual changes in the weather or the migratory pattern of birds. Before every important act of state, a magistrate with *imperium* took the auspices to make sure the gods approved. The Romans attributed great importance to this—if the omens were unfavorable, the act was invalid or the planned action was

The Vestal Virgins

The Vestal Virgins guarded the fire on the state hearth in the temple of Vesta (goddess of the hearth) in Rome. To the Romans, the extinguishing of the fire was a warning of the destruction of the city. It was also a sign that a Vestal Virgin had lost her virginity, an act that was punished harshly, as is explained in this selection from the historian Dionysius of Halicarnassus, a Greek who lived in Rome and published his *Roman Antiquities* near the end of the first century B.C.E.

Dionysius of Halicarnassus, *Roman Antiquities*

Originally there were four virgins who served the goddess Vesta. They were chosen by the king in accordance with the regulations which Numa established. Because of the numerous sacred duties which they perform, their number was increased to six, and six it has remained up to our own time. The virgins live in the sanctuary of the goddess, and no one can be prevented from entering there in the day if he so wishes, but it is forbidden for any man to stay there at night.

The priestesses remain pure and unmarried for 30 years, offering sacrifices, and performing other religious rituals in accordance with the law. They learn these rituals in the first ten years, and for the second ten years they perform them, and during the remaining ten years they must teach them to their successors. When the 30 years have been completed, nothing prohibits those who want to from putting aside their headbands and other insignia of their service and getting married. But only a few have done that, and their lives for their remaining years were neither enviable nor very happy. Therefore, taking what has happened to those unhappy few as a warning, the rest of the virgins remain in service to the goddess until their deaths, at which time another virgin is appointed by the priests to take the place of the one who has died.

They receive many splendid honors from the city, and therefore they do not want children or marriage. And anyway, there are heavy penalties for misbehavior. Misdeeds are investigated and punished by priests according to the law. They whip those who have committed some lesser offense, but those who have lost their virginity are sentenced to a shameful and pitiful death. While they are still alive they are carried in a funeral procession. Their friends and relatives join the procession and mourn for them as though for someone deceased. They are taken as far as the Colline gate, and interred (alive) in an underground cell which has been built within the walls of the gate. They are dressed in funeral clothes but they receive no monument or funeral offering or any of the other rites which are customary at funerals.

There are said to be many clues which indicate that a priestess who is performing a holy ritual is no longer a virgin, but the principal clue is that the fire goes out, something which the Romans fear more than all catastrophes, since they believe that whatever was the cause of the fire going out, it warns of the destruction of the city. They reintroduce the fire with many rituals of atonement.

Q What was the importance of the Vestal Virgins? Why were any violations of the rules treated with such harsh punishments?

not auspicious. As Cicero later commented, the augurs had "the highest and most important authority in the State" because "no act of any magistrate at home or in the field can have any validity for any person without their authority."[3] Auspices were taken by observing the flights of birds, lightning and other natural phenomena, and the behavior of certain animals.

HOUSEHOLD CULTS Just as the state had an official cult, so did families. Because the family was regarded as a small state within the state, it had its own household cults, which included Janus, the spirit of the doorway; Vesta, the goddess of the hearth; and the Penates, the spirits of the storehouse. Here, too, proper ritual was important, and it was the responsibility of the *paterfamilias* as head of the family to ensure that the religious obligations were properly fulfilled.

One of the most important ceremonies involved purification. In his manual *On Agriculture,* Marcus Cato the Elder spelled out the proper ritual for purification of a landed estate. The ceremony included these words, addressed to Mars, the god of vegetation as well as war:

> Father Mars, I beg and entreat you to be of good will and favorable to me and to our house and household, for which purpose I have ordered the swine-sheep-bull procession to be led around my land and fields and farm. And [I beg] that you will check, thrust back, and avert diseases seen and unseen, crop failure and crop destruction, sudden losses and storms, and that you will permit the annual crops, the grain crops, the vineyards, and tree and vine slips to grow and turn out well. And [that you] keep safe the shepherds and the flocks and give good health and strength to me and to our house and household: with these purposes in view . . . receive the honor of this suckling swine-sheep-bull sacrifice.[4]

Proper observance of the ritual was so crucial that any error necessitated a repetition of the entire ritual.

RELIGIOUS FESTIVALS Religious festivals were an important part of Roman religious practice. There were two kinds: public festivals ordained and paid for by the state and private festivals celebrated by individuals and families. By the mid-second century B.C.E., six public festivals were celebrated annually, each lasting several days.

The practice of holding games also grew out of religious festivals. The games were inaugurated in honor of Jupiter Optimus Maximus but had become annual events by 366 B.C.E. In the late Republic, both the number of games and the number of days they lasted were increased. Consequently, state funds became inadequate for the magnificence expected, and the aediles, who were in charge of the games and hoped to use their office as a stepping-stone to higher political offices, paid additional expenses out of their own pocket. Originally, the games consisted of chariot racing in the Circus Maximus; later, animal hunts and theatrical performances were added. In the empire, gladiatorial contests would become the primary focus (see Chapter 6).

Education: The Importance of Rhetoric

The Romans did not possess a system of public education. In the early Republic, the family provided training in the various skills needed by a Roman citizen. Boys were expected to master the basic elements of farming, develop the physical skills needed to be good soldiers, learn the traditions of the state through the legends of heroic Roman ancestors, and become acquainted with public affairs. Girls were supposed to learn the skills needed to be good wives and mothers. Every upper-class Roman boy or girl was expected to learn to read.

Through contact with the Greek world, Roman education took on new ideals in the third and second centuries B.C.E. The wealthy classes wanted their children exposed to Greek studies and were especially attracted to the training in **rhetoric** and philosophy that would prepare their sons for a successful public career. For upper-class males, rhetoric—the art of persuasive speaking—was an especially important part of their education. To pursue a public career, they needed to learn good speaking skills that would enable them to win elections and lawsuits in the courts. By winning lawsuits, a person could make a name for himself and build political support.

Since knowledge of Greek was a crucial ingredient in education, schools taught by professional teachers emerged to supply this need. Those who could afford to might provide Greek tutors for their children, but less well endowed families could turn to private schools where most of the instructors were educated slaves or freedmen, usually of Greek origin. After several years of primary instruction, whose aim was simply to teach the basics of reading, writing, and arithmetic, the pupil went to a secondary school run by a *grammaticus,* or grammarian. These schools had a standard curriculum based on the liberal arts: literature, dialectic (logic), arithmetic, geometry, astronomy, and music. The core of the liberal arts and the curriculum, however, was Greek literature. As a result, by the second and first centuries B.C.E., educated Romans had become increasingly bilingual.

Rheinisches Landesmuseum, Trier//© Erich Lessing/Art Resource, NY

Schoolmaster and Pupils. In the third and second centuries B.C.E., wealthy Romans sought to prepare their sons for successful public careers with a thorough education in rhetoric and philosophy. Pictured here from a relief on a stele is a teacher with his two pupils, one of whom is reading from a papyrus scroll.

The Growth of Slavery

Slavery was a common institution throughout the ancient world, but no people possessed more slaves or relied so much on slave labor as the Romans eventually did. Before the third century B.C.E., a small Roman farmer might possess one or two slaves who would help farm his few acres and perform domestic chores. These slaves would most likely be from Italy and be regarded as part of the family household. Only the very rich would have large numbers of slaves.

The Roman conquest of the Mediterranean brought a drastic change in the use of slaves. Large numbers of foreign slaves were brought back to Italy. During the Republic, then, the chief source of slaves was from capture in war, followed by piracy. Of course, the children of slaves also became slaves. Although some Roman generals brought back slaves to be sold to benefit the public treasury, ambitious generals of the first century, such as Pompey and Caesar, made personal fortunes by treating slaves captured by their armies as private property.

Slaves were used in many ways in Roman society. The rich, of course, owned the most and the best. In the late Republic, it became a badge of prestige to be attended by many slaves. Greeks were in much demand as tutors, musicians, doctors, and artists. Roman businesses would employ them as shop assistants or craftspeople. Slaves were also used as farm laborers; the large landed estates known as ***latifundia*** (lat-i-FOON-dee-uh) were worked by huge gangs of slaves living in pitiful conditions. Cato the Elder argued that it was cheaper to work slaves to death and then replace them than to treat them well. Many slaves of all nationalities were used as menial household workers, such as cooks, valets, waiters, cleaners, and gardeners. Contractors used slave labor to build roads, aqueducts, and other public facilities. The total number of slaves is difficult to judge—estimates range from one-fourth to one-half the number of free people.

It is also difficult to generalize about the treatment of Roman slaves. There are numerous instances of humane treatment by masters and situations in which slaves even protected their owners from danger out of gratitude and esteem. But slaves were also subject to severe punishments, torture, abuse, and hard labor that drove some to run away or even revolt against their owners. The Republic had stringent laws against aiding a runaway slave. The murder of a master by a slave usually meant the execution of all the other household slaves. Near the end of the second century B.C.E., large-scale slave revolts occurred in Sicily, where enormous gangs of slaves were subjected to horrible working conditions on large landed estates. Slaves were branded, beaten, fed inadequately, worked in chains, and housed at night in underground prisons. One revolt of 70,000 slaves lasted three years (135–132 B.C.E.) before it was crushed, and the great revolt on Sicily (104–101 B.C.E.) involved most of the island and required a Roman army of 17,000 men to suppress. The most famous revolt on the Italian peninsula occurred in 73 B.C.E. Led by a Thracian gladiator named Spartacus (SPAR-tuh-kuss), the revolt broke out in southern Italy and involved 70,000 slaves. Spartacus managed to defeat several Roman armies before he was finally trapped and killed in southern Italy in 71 B.C.E. Six thousand of his followers were crucified, the traditional form of execution for slaves (see the Film & History feature on p. 131).

The Roman Family

At the heart of the Roman social structure stood the family, headed by the *paterfamilias*—the dominant male. The household also included the wife, sons with their wives and children, unmarried daughters, and slaves. As we have seen, a family was virtually a small state within the state, and the power of the *paterfamilias* paralleled that of the state magistrates over citizens. He held absolute authority over his children; he could sell them or have them put to death. Like the Greeks, Roman males believed that the weakness of the female sex necessitated male guardians (see the box on p. 132). The *paterfamilias* exercised that authority; on his death, sons or the nearest male relatives assumed the role of guardians. By the late Republic, however, although the rights of male guardians remained legally in effect, many upper-class women had found numerous ways to circumvent the power of their guardians.

MARRIAGE Fathers arranged the marriages of daughters, although there are instances of mothers and daughters influencing the choice. In the Republic, women married *cum manu* (koom MAH-noo), "with legal control" passing from father to husband. By the mid-first century B.C.E., the dominant practice had changed to *sine manu* (sy-nee MAH-noo), "without legal control," which meant that married daughters officially remained within the father's legal power. Since the fathers of most married women were dead, not being in the "legal control" of a husband made possible independent property rights that forceful women could translate into considerable power within the household and outside it. Traditionally, Roman marriages were intended to be for life, but divorce was introduced in the third century and became relatively easy to obtain since either party could initiate it and no one needed to prove the breakdown of the marriage. Divorce became especially prevalent in the first century B.C.E.—a period of political turmoil—when marriages were used to cement political alliances.

Some parents in upper-class families provided education for their daughters. Some girls had private tutors, and others may have gone to primary schools. But at the age when boys were entering secondary schools, girls were pushed into marriage. The legal minimum age was twelve; fourteen was a more common age in practice. Although some Roman doctors warned that early pregnancies could be dangerous to young girls, early marriages persisted due to the desire to benefit from dowries as soon as possible and the reality of early mortality. A good example is Tullia, Cicero's beloved daughter. She was married at sixteen, widowed at twenty-two, remarried one year later, divorced at twenty-eight, remarried at twenty-nine, and divorced at thirty-three. She died at thirty-four, not unusual for females in Roman society.

UPPER-CLASS WOMEN In contrast to upper-class Athenian women, upper-class Roman women were not

A Roman Woman. Roman women, especially those of the upper class, had more freedom than women in Classical Athens despite the persistent male belief that women required guardianship. This portrait of a Roman woman is from a Roman mosaic dating from the first century B.C.E.

FILM & HISTORY

Spartacus (1960)

Spartacus, directed by Stanley Kubrick, focuses on the major events in the life of the gladiator who led a major rebellion against the Romans. Kirk Douglas stars as a Thracian slave who was bought and trained as a gladiator by Batiatus, a role played by Peter Ustinov, who won an Oscar for Best Supporting Actor for his performance. Spartacus leads a revolt in the gladiatorial camp in Capua run by Batiatus, flees with the other gladiators, and then brings together a large number of escaped slaves as they move through southern Italy. The gladiators among them are able to create the semblance of a trained army, and they are initially successful in defeating a force sent from the city of Rome. Eventually, however, they are defeated by the army of Crassus (Laurence Olivier), who is aided by the unexpected arrival of the forces of two other Roman generals. Many of the leaders of the revolt, including Spartacus, are crucified as punishment for their rebellion. Nevertheless, the movie has a typical Hollywood ending that is entirely fictional. Varinia, a slave woman (Jean Simmons) who has married Spartacus and given birth to his son, bids a final farewell to the crucified Spartacus, who sees his son and is assured by Varinia that he will live as a free man.

Freedom is the key word for this entire movie. Spartacus is portrayed as a man who dreamed of the death of slavery, thousands of years before its death (although he would be disappointed to know that it still survives in some corners of the world today). The film rings with the words of freedom: "we only want our freedom," "we must stay true to ourselves; we are brothers and we are free," and "I pray for a son who must be born free." Indeed, freedom was also on the minds of the film's creators. The film appeared in 1960, only a few years after Senator Joseph McCarthy's anti-Communist crusade in the 1950s had led to an exaggerated fear of Communists. Both Howard Fast, the author of the novel *Spartacus* on which the film was based, and Dalton Trumbo, the screenwriter for the film, had been blacklisted from working in Hollywood as a result of McCarthy's charges that they were Communists or Communist sympathizers. The film was a statement of Hollywood's determination to allow both men to work freely and openly. The speeches about freedom also evoke the rhetoric of free world versus communism that was heard frequently during the height of the Cold War in the 1950s.

Bryna/Universal/The Kobal Collection

Spartacus (Kirk Douglas) collects booty and followers as he leads his army south.

Although the general outlines of the film are historically accurate (there was a slave rebellion in southern Italy from 73 to 71 B.C.E. led by Spartacus that was ended by Roman troops commanded by Crassus), it also contains a number of historical inaccuracies. Although many slave leaders were crucified, Spartacus was not one of them. He was killed in the final battle, and his body was never found. Crassus, the general who crushed the slave rebellion, was not seeking dictatorial power as the film insists. The character of Gracchus is depicted as a mob-loving popular senatorial leader, although the Gracchi brothers had died some fifty years before the revolt. Julius Caesar had nothing to do with Spartacus, nor was he made prefect of the city, a position that did not yet exist.

segregated from males in the home. Wives were appreciated as enjoyable company and were at the center of household social life. Women talked to visitors and were free to shop, visit friends, and go to games, temples, and theaters. Nevertheless, they were not allowed to participate in public life, although there are examples of women exerting considerable political influence through their husbands. In fact, while upper-class men served the government abroad or in the military, they depended on their wives and mothers to manage their estates and protect their political interests.

Cato the Elder on Women

During the Second Punic War, the Romans enacted the Oppian law, which limited the amount of gold women could possess and restricted their dress. In 195 B.C.E., an attempt was made to repeal the law, and women demonstrated in the streets on behalf of the effort. According to the Roman historian Livy, the conservative Roman official Cato the Elder spoke against repeal and against the women favoring it. His words reflect a traditional male Roman attitude toward women.

Livy, *The History of Rome*

"If each of us, citizens, had determined to assert his rights and dignity as a husband with respect to his own spouse, we should have less trouble with the sex as a whole; as it is, our liberty, destroyed at home by female violence, even here in the Forum is crushed and trodden underfoot, and because we have not kept them individually under control, we dread them collectively.... But from no class is there not the greatest danger if you permit them meetings and gatherings and secret consultations....

"Our ancestors permitted no woman to conduct even personal business without a guardian to intervene in her behalf; they wished them to be under the control of fathers, brothers, husbands; we (Heaven help us!) allow them now even to interfere in public affairs, yes, and to visit the Forum and our informal and formal sessions. What else are they doing now on the streets and at the corners except urging the bill of the tribunes and voting for the repeal of the law? Give loose rein to their uncontrollable nature and to this untamed creature and expect that they will themselves set no bounds to their license. Unless you act, this is the least of the things enjoined upon women by custom or law and to which they submit with a feeling of injustice. It is complete liberty or rather, if we wish to speak the truth, complete license that they desire.

"If they win in this, what will they not attempt? Review all the laws with which your forefathers restrained their license and made them subject to their husbands; even with all these bonds you can scarcely control them. What of this? If you suffer them to seize these bonds one by one and wrench themselves free and finally to be placed on a parity with their husbands, do you think you will be able to endure them? The moment they begin to be your equals, they will be your superiors....

"Now they publicly address other women's husbands, and, what is more serious, they beg for a law and votes, and from various men they get what they ask. In matters affecting yourself, your property, your children, you, Sir, can be importuned; once the law has ceased to set a limit to your wife's expenditures you will never set it yourself. Do not think, citizens, that the situation which existed before the law was passed will ever return."

Q What particular actions of the women protesting this law have angered Cato? What more general concerns does he have about Roman women? What was Cato's attitude toward women? Compare and contrast this selection with the one by Xenophon in Chapter 3.

The Evolution of Roman Law

One of Rome's chief gifts to the Mediterranean world of its day and to succeeding generations of Western civilization was its development of law. After the Twelve Tables of 450 B.C.E., there was no complete codification of Roman law until the reign of the Byzantine emperor Justinian in the sixth century C.E. (see Chapter 7). The Twelve Tables, though inappropriate for later times, were never officially abrogated and were still memorized by schoolboys in the first century B.C.E. Civil law, or *ius civile* (YOOSS see-VEE-lay), derived from the Twelve Tables proved inadequate for later Roman needs, however, and gave way to corrections and additions by the praetors. On taking office, a praetor issued an edict listing his guidelines for dealing with different kinds of legal cases. The praetors were knowledgeable in law, but they also relied on Roman jurists—amateur law experts—for advice in preparing their edicts. The interpretations of the jurists, often embodied in the edicts of the praetors, created a body of legal principles.

In 242 B.C.E., the Romans appointed a second praetor who was responsible for examining suits between a Roman and a non-Roman as well as between two non-Romans. The Romans found that although some of their rules of law could be used in these cases, special rules were often needed. These rules gave rise to a body of law known as the *ius gentium* (YOOSS GEN-tee-um)—the law of nations—defined by the Romans as "that part of the law which we apply both to ourselves and to foreigners." But the influence of Greek philosophy, primarily Stoicism, led Romans in the late Republic to develop the idea of *ius naturale* (YOOSS nah-too-RAH-lay)—natural law—or universal divine law derived from right reason. The Romans came to view their law of nations as derived from or identical to this natural law, thus giving Roman jurists a philosophical justification for systematizing Roman law according to basic principles.

The Development of Literature and Art

The Romans produced little literature before the third century B.C.E., and the Latin literature that emerged in

Roman Comedy

This excerpt is a scene from one of the plays of Plautus. While Plautus made use of Greek New Comedy, his devious plots and earthiness were original. His farcical humor and buffoonery made his plays exceedingly popular, especially with the masses. This excerpt is from *Miles Gloriosus* ("The Swaggering Soldier"). This opening scene features a pompous general and a parasitical bootlicker. Plautus loved to create fantastic names for his characters. Pyrgopolynices means "Often victorious over fortresses," and Artotrogus means "Bread eater."

Plautus, *The Swaggering Soldier*

PYRGOPOLYNICES: My shield, there—have it burnished brighter than the bright splendor of the sun on any summer's day. Next time I have occasion to use it in the press of battle, it must flash defiance into the eyes of the opposing foe. My sword, too, I see, is pining for attention; poor chap, he's quite disheartened and cast down, hanging idly at my side so long; he's simply itching to get at an enemy and carve him into little pieces. . . . Where's Artotrogus?

ARTOTROGUS: Here, at his master's heels, close to his hero, his brave, his blessed, his royal, his doughty warrior—whose valor Mars himself could hardly challenge or outshine.

PYRGOPOLYNICES [*reminiscent*]: Ay—what of the man whose life I saved on the Curculionean field, where the enemy was led by Bumbomachides Clytomestoridysarchides, a grandson of Neptune?

ARTOTROGUS: I remember it well. I remember his golden armor, and how you scattered his legions with a puff of breath, like a wind sweeping up leaves or lifting the thatch from a roof.

PYRGOPOLYNICES [*modestly*]: It was nothing much, after all.

ARTOTROGUS: Oh, to be sure, nothing to the many more famous deeds you did—[*aside*] or never did. [*He comes down, leaving the captain attending to his men.*] If anyone ever saw a bigger liar or more conceited braggart than this one, he can have me for keeps. . . . The only thing to be said for him is, his cook makes a marvelous olive salad. . . .

PYRGOPOLYNICES [*missing him*]: Where have you got to, Artotrogus?

ARTOTROGUS [*obsequiously*]: Here I am, sir. I was thinking about that elephant in India, and how you broke his ulna with a single blow of your fist.

PYRGOPOLYNICES: His ulna, was it?

ARTOTROGUS: His femur, I should have said.

PYRGOPOLYNICES: It was only a light blow, too.

ARTOTROGUS: By Jove, yes, if you had really hit him, your arm would have smashed through the animal's hide, bones, and guts.

PYRGOPOLYNICES [*modestly*]: I'd rather not talk about it, really.

Q What kind of comedy does Plautus employ in *The Swaggering Soldier*? Why do you think Roman audiences would have found this hysterically funny? Where might you see this kind of comedy today?

that century was strongly influenced by Greek models. The demand for plays at public festivals eventually led to a growing number of native playwrights. The best known were Plautus (PLAW-tuss) and Terence.

PLAUTUS Plautus (c. 254–184 B.C.E.) used plots from Greek New Comedy (see Chapter 4) for his own plays (see the box above). The actors wore Greek costumes and Greek masks and portrayed the same stock characters: dirty old men, clever slaves, prostitutes, and young men in love, whose pains are recounted in this brief excerpt:

Not the throes of all mankind
Equal my distracted mind.
I strain and I toss
On a passionate cross:
Love's goad makes me reel,
I whirl on Love's wheel,
In a swoon of despair
Hurried here, hurried there—
Torn asunder, I am blind
With a cloud upon my mind.[5]

Though indebted to the Greeks, Plautus managed to infuse his plays with his own earthy Latin quality, incorporating elements that appealed to the Romans: drunkenness, gluttony, and womanizing. Plautus wrote for the masses and became a very popular playwright in Rome.

TERENCE A second playwright of distinction was Terence (185–159 B.C.E.), who was born in Carthage and brought to Rome as a slave by a Roman senator who freed him. Terence died at an early age after he had written six plays. He also used plots from Greek New Comedy, but his plays contained less slapstick than those of Plautus. Terence was more concerned with the subtle portrayal of character and the artistry of his language. His refined Latin style appealed more to a cultivated audience than to the masses. In the prologue to *The Brothers,* he stated, "The author . . . takes it as a high compliment if he can win the approval of men who themselves find favor with you all and with the general public, men whose services in war, in peace, and in your private affairs, are given at the right moment, without ostentation, to be available for each one of you."[6] Terence wrote for Rome's aristocracy.

Pompeii//© CM Dixon/HIP/The Image Works

Roman Theater. The eruption of Mount Vesuvius in 79 C.E. buried Pompeii under volcanic ash and preserved works of art that were later discovered when the city was excavated (see Chapter 6). Shown here is a mosaic pavement created by Dioscurides of Samos and found in the so-called villa of Cicero. The mosaic shows musicians and masked actors in a play. Roman actors wore masks to show the character of the figures they represented. Plays were a popular entertainment in Pompeii, where the local theater could seat five thousand people.

LATIN PROSE Latin prose developed later than poetry and playwriting and was often the product of Rome's ruling elite. These upper classes were interested in history as a means of exalting their ideals and in oratory because it could be an important instrument for effective statecraft. Hence, their emphasis in writing prose was on creating works of a practical value. This is a prominent feature of the oldest existing work of Latin prose, Cato the Elder's treatise *On Agriculture*. In effect, this was a technical manual reminiscent of the practical handbooks produced in the Hellenistic world.

Despite their attraction to the Greek world, Romans were generally repelled by much of Greek philosophy with the exception of Stoicism. The latter's emphasis on virtuous conduct and performance of duty (see Chapter 4) fit well with Roman ideals and the practical bent of the Roman character.

ROMAN ART The Romans were also dependent on the Greeks for artistic inspiration. During the third and second centuries B.C.E., they adopted many features of the Hellenistic style of art (see Chapter 4). The Romans excelled in architecture, a highly practical art. In addition to their justly famous highways, they built sturdy bridges and aqueducts that made use of the arch. They also developed the technique of using concrete in construction projects, which enabled them to erect giant amphitheaters, public baths, and the high-rise tenement buildings that housed Rome's exploding population in the late second and first centuries B.C.E.

The Romans developed a taste for Greek statues, which they placed not only in public buildings but in their homes as well. When demand outstripped the supply of original works, reproductions of Greek statues became fashionable. The Romans' own portrait sculpture was characterized by an intense realism that included even unattractive physical details.

VALUES AND ATTITUDES The Romans were by nature a conservative people. They were very concerned about maintaining the *mos maiorum* (MOHSS my-YOR-um), the customs or traditions of their ancestors. The Romans emphasized parental authority and, above all, their obligations to the state. The highest virtue was *pietas*—the dutiful execution of one's obligations to one's fellow citizens, to the gods, and to the state.

By the second century B.C.E., however, the creation of an empire had begun to weaken the old values. The Romans began to place greater stress on affluence, status, and material possessions. There was also more emphasis on individualism and less on collective well-being, on the old public spirit that had served Rome so well. Romans who worried about the decline of the old values blamed it on different causes. Some felt that after the destruction of Carthage, the Romans no longer had any strong enemies to challenge them. Others believed that the Romans had simply been overwhelmed by the affluence created by the new empire. And finally, there were those who blamed everything on the Greeks for importing ideas and practices baneful to the Romans.

Of course, Romans responded differently to the changes brought by the creation of an empire. Two examples from the second century demonstrate this well. Marcus Cato the Elder (234–149 B.C.E.) was a Roman praetor, consul, and member of the ruling class who assumed the office of censor in 184. Cato scorned the "Greeklings"—people who followed Greek ways and read Greek philosophy and literature. He even introduced a decree to force all Greek philosophers to leave Rome. He wrote to his son:

> I shall speak about those Greek fellows in their proper place, son Marcus, and point out the results of my inquiries at Athens, and convince you what benefit comes from dipping

> into their literature, and not making a close study of it. They are a quite worthless people, and an intractable one, and you must consider my words prophetic. When that race gives us its literature it will corrupt all things.[7]

But Cato was not stupid. He not only learned Greek himself but also allowed his own son to study in Athens. He knew only too well that, like it or not, Greek was becoming a necessity for Roman political life.

Scipio Aemilianus (185–129 B.C.E.) was a member of a patrician family and a brilliant general who easily achieved the top offices of the Roman state. Scipio was also concerned about the traditional Roman values, but he was much more inclined to accept Rome's growing urbanization as it became the center of the Mediterranean world and was consequently more open to the Greeks as well. He was an admirer of Greek philosophy and literature. He created a group of intellectuals dedicated to Greek thought, which included Polybius, Terence, and Panaetius. While desirous of maintaining old Roman virtues, Scipio was well aware that the acquisition of an empire had created a new world with new demands and values.

The Decline and Fall of the Roman Republic (133–31 B.C.E.)

Focus Question: What were the main problems Rome faced during the last century of the Republic, and how were they ultimately resolved?

By the mid-second century B.C.E., Roman domination of the Mediterranean Sea was well established. Yet the process of building an empire had weakened and threatened the internal stability of Rome. This internal instability characterizes the period of Roman history from 133 until 31 B.C.E., when Octavian defeated Mark Antony and stood supreme over the Roman world. By that time, the constitution of the Roman Republic was in shambles.

Background: Social, Economic, and Political Problems

By the second century B.C.E., the senate had become the effective governing body of the Roman state. It had achieved this position through its own initiative—not through law, but by custom. As always, it comprised some three hundred men drawn primarily from the landed aristocracy who remained senators for life and held the chief magistracies of the Republic. During the wars of the third and second centuries, the senate came to exercise enormous power. It directed the wars and took control of both foreign and domestic policy, including financial affairs. The advice of the senate to the consuls had come to have the force of law.

Moreover, the magistracies and senate were increasingly controlled by a relatively select circle of wealthy and powerful families—both patrician and plebeian—called the ***nobiles*** ("nobles"). The *nobiles* were essentially the men whose families were elected to the more important political offices of the Republic. In the hundred years from 233 to 133 B.C.E., 80 percent of the consuls came from twenty-six families; 50 percent came from only ten families. Hence, the *nobiles* constituted a governing oligarchy that managed, through landed wealth, patronage, and intimidation, to maintain its hold over the magistracies and senate and thus guide the destiny of Rome while running the state in its own interests. When a new man—a *novus homo* (NOH-vuss HOH-moh)—did win a consulship, he and his descendants became members of this select oligarchy.

DIVISION OF THE ARISTOCRATS By the end of the second century B.C.E., two types of aristocratic leaders, called the ***optimates*** (ahp-tuh-MAH-tayz) ("the best men") and the ***populares*** (PAWP-oo-lahr-ayss) ("favoring the people"), became prominent. These were not political parties or even individual cliques but leaders who followed two different approaches to politics. *Optimates* and *populares* were terms of political rhetoric that were used by individuals within the aristocracy against fellow aristocratic rivals to distinguish one set of tactics from another. The *optimates* tended to be the *nobiles* who controlled the senate and wished to maintain their oligarchical privileges, while the *populares* were usually other ambitious aristocrats who used the people's assemblies, especially the council of the plebs, as instruments to break the domination of the *optimates*. The conflicts between these aristocratic leaders and their supporters engulfed the first century B.C.E. in political turmoil.

ROLE OF THE EQUESTRIANS Another social group in Rome also became entangled in this political turmoil—the *equites* (EK-wuh-teez) or **equestrians,** a name derived from the fact that they had once formed Rome's cavalry. Many equestrians had become extremely wealthy through a variety of means, often related to the creation of the empire. Some, for example, were private contractors who derived their wealth from government contracts for the collection of taxes, the outfitting of armies, and the construction of fleets and public works. In 218 B.C.E., the senate enacted a law that forbade senators to bid for state contracts or engage in commerce. The law effectively barred the equestrians from high office, since to serve in the senate they would have to give up their livelihoods. By the end of the second century B.C.E., the equestrians were seeking real political power commensurate with their financial stake in the empire. They would play an important role in the political turmoil that brought an end to the Republic.

THE LAND PROBLEM Of course, equestrians and aristocrats together formed only a tiny minority of the Roman people. The backbone of the Roman state and army had traditionally been the small farmers who tilled their little plots of land and made up the chief source of recruits for the army. But economic changes that began in the period of the Punic Wars increasingly undermined the position of that group. This occurred for several reasons. Their lands had been severely damaged during the Second Punic War when Hannibal invaded Italy. Moreover, in order to win the wars, Rome had to increase the term of military service to six years. The Roman army was never meant to serve in distant wars but was called out for the "war season," after which the soldiers returned to their farms. Now when the soldiers returned home after many years of service abroad, they found their farms so deteriorated that they chose to sell out instead of remaining on the land. By this time, capitalistic agriculture was also increasing rapidly. Landed aristocrats had been able to develop large estates (*latifundia*) by taking over state-owned land and by buying out small peasant owners. These large estates relied on slave and tenant labor and frequently concentrated on cash crops, such as grapes for wine, olives, and sheep for wool, which small farmers could not afford to do. Thus, the rise of *latifundia* contributed to the decline in the number of small citizen farmers. Since the latter group traditionally formed the basis of the Roman army—Romans conscripted only people with a financial stake in the community—the number of men available for military service declined. Many of the newly landless families stayed in the countryside, finding agricultural work as best they could. Some of them, however, drifted to the cities, especially Rome, forming a large class of day laborers who possessed no property. This new class of urban proletariat formed a highly unstable mass with the potential for much trouble in depressed times. Thus, Rome's economic, social, and political problems were serious and needed attention. In 133 B.C.E., a member of the aristocracy proposed a solution that infuriated his fellow aristocrats.

The Reforms of Tiberius and Gaius Gracchus

Tiberius Gracchus (ty-BEER-ee-uss GRAK-us) (163–133 B.C.E.) was a member of the *nobiles* who ruled Rome. Although concerned with the immediate problem of a shortage of military recruits, Tiberius believed that the underlying cause of Rome's problems was the decline of the small farmers. Tiberius was not a revolutionary, and his proposals for reform, drafted with the help of several prominent senators, were essentially conservative; he was looking back to what had constituted the foundation of Rome's greatness.

Tiberius Gracchus was elected one of the tribunes of the plebs for 133 B.C.E. Without consulting the senate, where he knew his rivals would oppose his proposal, Tiberius took his legislation directly to the council of the plebs, which passed his land reform bill. It authorized the government to reclaim public land held by large landowners and to distribute it to landless Romans. Many senators, themselves large landowners whose estates included large tracts of public land, were furious, and a group of them took the law into their own hands and assassinated Tiberius.

The efforts of Tiberius Gracchus were continued by his brother Gaius (GY-uss) (153–121 B.C.E.), who was elected tribune for both 123 and 122 B.C.E. Like Tiberius, Gaius pushed for the rapid distribution of land to displaced farmers, but he also broadened his reform program to appeal to more people disenchanted with the current senatorial leadership. To win the support of the *equites*, he replaced the senators on the jury courts that tried provincial governors accused of extortion with members of the equestrian order and opened the new province of Asia to equestrian tax collectors. Thus, Gaius gave the *equites* two instruments of public power: control over the jury courts that often tried provincial governors and control over provincial taxation. Fellow senators, hostile to Gaius's reforms and fearful of his growing popularity, made use of a constitutional innovation, a "final decree of the senate," which encouraged the consuls to "do everything possible to prevent any misfortune befalling the Republic." As a result, Gaius and many of his followers were killed in 121 B.C.E. The attempts of the Gracchus brothers to bring reforms by using the tribuneship and council of the plebs had opened the door to more instability and further violence and marked the beginning of the breakdown of the republican form of government.

Marius and the New Roman Army

In the closing years of the second century B.C.E., a series of military disasters gave rise to a fresh outburst of popular anger against the old leaders of the senate and resulted in the rise of Marius (MAR-ee-uss) (157–86 B.C.E.).

Marius came to prominence during the war in North Africa against Jugurtha and the Numidians. The senate had badly bungled the war effort. Marius had served as legate to the senate-appointed commanding general Metellus but quarreled with his superior, returned to Rome, and ran for the consulship with "Win the War" as his campaign slogan. Despite being from the equestrian order, Marius won and became a consul for 107 B.C.E. The council of the plebs then voted to give Marius command of the army in Africa, a definite encroachment on the senate's right to conduct wars. Generals no longer needed to be loyal to the senate.

Marius brought the Jugurthine War to a successful conclusion in 105 B.C.E. and was then called on to defeat the Celtic tribes (or Gauls, as the Romans called them), who had annihilated a Roman army and threatened an invasion of Italy. Marius was made consul for five years, from 104 to 100 B.C.E., raised a new army, and decisively defeated the Celts, leaving him in a position of personal ascendancy in Rome.

In raising a new army, Marius initiated military reforms that proved to have drastic consequences. The Roman army had traditionally been a conscript army of small landholders—basically a citizen army, as described earlier. Marius recruited volunteers from both the urban and the rural proletariat who possessed no property. These volunteers, who were now trained more thoroughly, swore an oath of loyalty to the general, not the senate, and thus inaugurated a professional-type army that might no longer be subject to the state. Moreover, to recruit these men, a general would promise them land, so generals had to play politics to get legislation passed that would provide the land for their veterans. Marius left a powerful legacy. He had created a new system of military recruitment that placed much power in the hands of the individual generals. Roman republican politics was entering a new and potentially dangerous stage.

The Role of Sulla

After almost a decade of relative quiet, the Roman Republic was threatened with another crisis—the Italian or Social War (90–88 B.C.E.). This war resulted from Rome's unwillingness to deal constructively with the complaints of its Italian allies. These allies had fought loyally on Rome's side but felt they had not shared sufficiently in the lands and bonuses given to Roman veterans. In 90 B.C.E., the Italians rebelled and formed their own confederation. Two years of bitter fighting left Italy devastated and took an enormous number of lives. The Romans managed to end the rebellion but only by granting full rights of Roman citizenship to all free Italians. "Rome was now Italy, and Italy Rome."[8] This influx of new voters into the popular assemblies drastically altered the voting power structure in favor of the *populares,* who had earlier favored enfranchisement of the Italians.

During this war, a new figure came into prominence—Lucius Cornelius Sulla (138–78 B.C.E.), a member of the *nobiles.* Sulla (SULL-uh) had been made a consul for 88 B.C.E. and been given command by the senate of the war against Mithridates, the king of Pontus in Asia Minor, who had rebelled against Roman power. Now, however, Marius, who had retired from Roman politics, returned to the scene. The council of the plebs, contradicting the senate's wishes, transferred command of the war against Mithridates to Marius. Considering this action illegal, Sulla marched on Rome with his army. Marius fled, and Sulla reestablished his command. After Sulla left again for the east, Marius joined forces with the consul Cinna, marched on Rome, seized control of the government, outlawed Sulla, and killed many of Sulla's supporters. Civil war had become a fact of life in Roman politics.

Marius soon died, but Cinna continued to use his forces to remain as consul. His control, however, really depended on the fortunes of Sulla and his army. After defeating Mithridates in the east, Sulla returned to Rome, crushed the armies opposing him in Italy, and seized Rome itself in 82 B.C.E. He forced the senate to grant him the title of dictator to "reconstitute the Republic." After conducting a reign of terror to wipe out all opposition, Sulla revised the constitution to restore power to the senate. He eliminated most of the powers of the popular assemblies and the tribunes of the plebs and restored the senators to the jury courts. He also enlarged the senate by adding men of the equestrian order. In 79 B.C.E., believing that he had restored the traditional Republic governed by a powerful senate, he resigned his office of dictator, retired, and soon died, leaving a power vacuum. But his real legacy was quite different from what he had intended. His example of how an army could be used to seize power would prove most attractive to ambitious men.

The Death of the Republic

For the next fifty years, Roman history would be characterized by two important features: the jostling for power by a number of powerful individuals and the civil wars generated by their conflicts.

THE RISE OF POMPEY Not long after Sulla's attempts to revive senatorial power, the senate made two extraordinary military appointments that raised to prominence two very strong personalities—Crassus (KRASS-uss) (c. 112–53 B.C.E.) and Pompey (PAHM-pee) (106–48 B.C.E.). Crassus had fought for Sulla and had also become extremely rich—it was said that he "owned most of Rome." In 73 B.C.E.,

Museo Archeologico, Venice//© Bildarchiv Preussischer Kulturbesitz/Art Resource, NY

Pompey. A popular and powerful figure of the late Republic, Pompey was a successful general who joined with Caesar and Crassus in a coalition known as the First Triumvirate in order to secure his reorganization of the east and to obtain lands for his veterans. He later opposed Caesar during the civil war and was killed in Egypt in 48 B.C.E. Pictured is a marble bust of Pompey; in keeping with Roman artistic practices, the portrait is quite realistic.

the senate gave Crassus a military command against the slave rebellion led by Spartacus, which he successfully completed. Pompey had also fought for Sulla and was given an important military command in Spain in 77 B.C.E. When he returned six years later, he was hailed as a military hero.

Despite their jealousy of one another, Pompey and Crassus joined forces and were elected consuls for 70 B.C.E. Although both men had been supporters of Sulla, they undid his work. They restored the power of the tribunes and helped put *equites* back on the jury courts, thereby reviving the *populares* as a path to political power.

With their power reestablished by this action, friendly plebeian tribunes now proposed legislation that gave two important military commands to Pompey. In 67 B.C.E., he cleared the Mediterranean Sea of the pirates who were harassing Roman commerce. After this success, he was put in charge of the campaign against Mithridates, who thought he could take advantage of Rome's internal troubles to pursue his plans of conquest. Pompey defeated Mithridates and reorganized the east, winning immense success and prestige as well as enormous wealth. When he returned to Rome, he disbanded his army, expecting that the senate would automatically ratify his eastern settlement and give land to his veterans. But new forces and new personalities had risen to prominence during his absence, and his requests encountered complications.

Galleria degli Uffizi, Florence//© Scala/Art Resource, NY

Cicero. The great orator Marcus Tullius Cicero, whose writings provide much information about politics and upper-class life, rose to the highest offices in the Republic due to his oratorical skills. He was a supporter of the senate and wished to establish a "concord of the orders," cooperative rule by the equestrians and the senators. This realistic portrait, typical of Republican Rome, gives a sense of Cicero's rigid character.

THE ROLE OF CICERO Marcus Tullius Cicero (106–43 B.C.E.) was one of these new personalities. A *novus homo* ("new man") from the equestrian order and the first of his family to achieve the consulship, Cicero (SIS-uh-roh) made a name for himself as a lawyer, using his outstanding oratorical skills to defend people accused of crimes and to prosecute others, including a corrupt provincial governor. He became consul in 63 B.C.E. and upheld the interests of the senate. While consul, he added to his reputation by acting forcefully to suppress a political conspiracy led by a desperate and bankrupt aristocrat named Catiline. Cicero was one of the few prominent politicians who attempted to analyze the problems of the Republic systematically. He believed in a "concord of the orders," meaning the cooperation of the equestrians and senators. In effect, Cicero harked back to the days of collective rule, a time when political leaders were motivated to work together for the good of the Roman state. But collective rule was no longer meaningful to ambitious men seeking personal power. Cicero himself had few military skills and could not command an army. He realized that the senate needed the support of a powerful general if the concord of the orders was to be made a reality. In 62 B.C.E., he saw Pompey as that man. But a large element in the senate felt that Pompey had become too powerful, and they now refused to grant his wishes after his return from the east. This same element in the senate treated Julius Caesar in a similar fashion when he returned from Spain. That turned out to be a big mistake.

THE STRUGGLE BETWEEN POMPEY AND CAESAR Julius Caesar (100–44 B.C.E.) had been a spokesman for the *populares* from the beginning of his political career, an alliance that ran in the family—Marius was his uncle by marriage. Caesar pursued political power by appealing to many of the same groups who had supported Marius. After serving as aedile and praetor, he sought a military command and was sent to Spain. He returned from Spain in 60 B.C.E. and requested a special dispensation so that he could both celebrate a triumph with his troops and run for the consulship, which would place him in the highest rank within the senate. Rival senators blocked his request. Consequently, Caesar joined with two fellow senators, Crassus and Pompey, who were also being stymied by the senate. Historians call their coalition the First Triumvirate. Though others had made political deals before, the combined wealth and power of these three men was enormous, enabling them to dominate the political scene. Caesar was elected consul for 59 B.C.E. and used the popular assemblies to achieve the basic aims of the triumvirs: Pompey received his eastern settlement and lands for his veterans; equestrian allies of Crassus were given a reduction on tax contracts for which they had overbid; and Caesar was granted a special military command in Gaul (modern France, Belgium, and parts of the Netherlands) for five years.

Plutarch, *Life of Caesar* (75 C.E.)

Caesar did so well in Gaul that Crassus and Pompey realized anew the value of military command. They became

Museo Archeologico Nazionale, Naples//© Scala/Art Resource, NY

Caesar. Conqueror of Gaul and member of the First Triumvirate, Julius Caesar is perhaps the best-known figure of the late Republic. Caesar became dictator of Rome in 47 B.C.E. and after his victories in the civil war was made dictator for life. Some members of the senate who resented his power assassinated him in 44 B.C.E. Pictured is a marble copy of a bust of Caesar.

consuls again for 55 B.C.E. and garnered more benefits for the coalition: Caesar was given a five-year extension in Gaul; Crassus, a command in Syria; and Pompey, one in Spain. When Crassus was killed in battle in 53 B.C.E., his death left two powerful men with armies in direct competition. Caesar had used his time in Gaul to gain fame and military experience. He had waged numerous campaigns, costing the lives, it has been estimated, of almost 2 million men, women, and children. As a military leader, Caesar had always been willing to face great personal danger. One ancient writer said that Caesar's soldiers were astonished that:

> he should undergo toils beyond his body's apparent power of endurance. . . . because he was of a spare habit, had soft and white skin, suffered from epileptic fits. . . . Nevertheless, he did not make his feeble health an excuse for soft living, but rather his military service a cure for his feeble health, since by wearisome journeys, simple diet, continuously sleeping in the open air, and enduring hardships he fought off his trouble and kept his body strong against its attacks.[9]

Caesar's wars had also enabled him to amass enough booty and slaves to pay off all of the debts he had accumulated in gaining political offices. Moreover, he now had an army of seasoned veterans who were loyal to him. No doubt most senators would have preferred both Pompey and Caesar to lay down their commands and give up their armies. Since both refused, the leading senators fastened on Pompey as the less harmful to their cause and voted for Caesar to lay down his command and return as a private citizen to Rome. Such a step was intolerable to Caesar, as it would leave him totally vulnerable to his enemies (see the box on p. 140). He chose to keep his army and moved into Italy by crossing the Rubicon, the river that formed the southern boundary of his province, on January 10, 49 B.C.E. (The phrase "crossing the Rubicon" is still used today to mean being unable to turn back.) According to his ancient biographer Suetonius, Caesar said to his troops, "Even now we could turn back; but once we cross that tiny bridge, then everything will depend on armed force."[10]

Pompey and his followers fled to Greece, where they raised a new army. Meanwhile it took Caesar until the end of 49 to raise a fleet and ship his troops to Greece. The next spring, at the Battle of Pharsalus, Caesar's veterans carried the day against Pompey's forces. The defeated Pompey fled to Egypt, where the king was one of his foreign clients, but one of the king's advisers had Pompey killed. The war continued, however, since some of the senators on his side, including Cato the Younger, had recruited new troops. After victories in North Africa and Spain, Caesar returned triumphant to Rome in 45 B.C.E.

No doubt Caesar realized that the old order of unfettered political competition could not be saved. He was unwilling to take the title of king, which was intensely disliked by the Roman upper classes, but he had no intention of giving up his control. Caesar had officially been made dictator in 47 B.C.E., and in 44 B.C.E. he was made dictator for life. He continued to hold elections for offices but saw to it that his supporters chose the people he recommended. As Rome's new ruler, he quickly instituted a number of ambitious reforms. He increased the senate to nine hundred members by filling it with many of his followers. He granted citizenship to a number of people in the provinces who had provided assistance to him. By establishing colonies of Roman citizens in North Africa, Gaul, and Spain, he initiated a process of Romanization in those areas. He tried to reorganize the administrative structures of cities in Italy in order to create some sense of rational order in their government.

Caesar was a generous victor and pardoned many of the republican leaders who had opposed him, allowing them to return to Rome. He also replaced the Roman calendar with the Egyptian solar year of 365 days (this so-called Julian calendar, with later changes made in 1582, became the basis of our modern calendar). He planned much more in the way of building projects and military adventures in the east but was not able to carry them out. In 44 B.C.E., a group of leading senators who resented his domination assassinated him, believing that the old republican system would now return (see the box on p. 142). In truth, however, they had set the stage for another civil war that delivered the death blow to the Republic.

THE FINAL STRUGGLE: OCTAVIAN VERSUS ANTONY A new struggle for power soon ensued. Caesar's heir and adopted son, his grandnephew Octavian (ahk-TAY-vee-un),

Opposing ≷ VIEWPOINTS

The End of the Republic: Three Views

Although Rome stood supreme over the Mediterranean world by 133 B.C.E., the internal structure of the Republic had begun to disintegrate. During the next hundred years, the Republic was afflicted with mob violence, assassinations, civil wars, and unscrupulous politicians who seized every opportunity to advance their own interests. The Roman historian Sallust (86–35 B.C.E.), who lived through many of these crises, reflected on the causes of Rome's problems. In the first selection below, he discusses the moral decline that set in after the destruction of Carthage in 146 B.C.E. Sallust presented a broad, philosophical view of the problem, but some figures directly involved in the struggles of the last century—namely, Caesar and Cicero—had their own ideas about the immediate crisis that led to the end of the Republic. In the second selection, taken from *The Civil Wars,* Caesar presents a defense of his decision to move into Italy with his troops. In his letter to his friend Atticus, Cicero indicates what he thinks of Caesar's action.

Sallust, *The War with Catiline*

Good morals were cultivated at home and in the field; [in the early Republic] there was the greatest harmony and little or no avarice; justice and honesty prevailed among them, thanks not so much to laws as to nature. Quarrels, discord, and strife were reserved for their enemies; citizen vied with citizen only for the prize of merit. They were lavish in their offerings to the gods, frugal in the home, loyal to their friends. By practicing these two qualities, boldness in warfare and justice when peace came, they watched over themselves and their country. . . .

But when our country had grown great through toil and the practice of justice, when great kings had been vanquished in war, savage tribes and mighty people subdued by force of arms, when Carthage, the rival of Rome's sway, had perished root and branch, and all seas and lands were open, then Fortune began to grow cruel and to bring confusion into all our affairs. Those who had found it easy to bear hardships and dangers, anxiety and adversity, found leisure and wealth, desirable under other circumstances, a burden and a curse. Hence the lust for power first, then for money, grew upon them; these were, I may say, the root of all evils. For avarice destroyed honor, integrity, and all other noble qualities; taught in their place insolence, cruelty, to neglect the gods, to set a price on everything. Ambition drove many men to become false; to have one thought locked in the breast, another ready on the tongue; to value friendships and enmities not on their merits but by the standard of self-interest, and to show a good front rather than a good heart. At first these vices grew slowly; from time to time they were punished; finally, when the disease had spread like a deadly plague, the state was changed and a government second to none in justice and excellence became cruel and intolerable.

Caesar, *The Civil Wars*

Having called the senate together, he [Caesar, who refers to himself in the third person] recounts the wrongs done him by his personal enemies. He explains that he had sought no extraordinary office, but, waiting for the legitimate time of his consulship, had been content with privileges open to all the citizens. . . . He sets forth his own patience when under no pressure he had made the request about the disbandment of the armies, a point in which he was ready to make a personal sacrifice of dignity and position. He tells them of the bitterness of his foes who refused in his case what they demanded in the other, and preferred utter confusion to the surrender of military power and armed force. He tells of their injustice in robbing him of his legions, of their cruelty and insolence in infringing the rights of the tribunes; he enumerates the terms that he had offered, the conferences asked for and refused. On these considerations he exhorts and charges them to take up the burden of state and administer it with his help; but if they shrink through fear he will not burden them, and will administer the state himself. Envoys should be sent to Pompey to effect a settlement, nor was he afraid of the remark made by Pompey a little before in the senate, to the effect that undue influence is attributed to those to whom envoys are sent and fear argued on the part of those that send them. Such considerations seemed to belong to a poor and weak spirit. His own wish was to be superior to others in justice and equity as he had striven to surpass them in action.

Cicero, *Letter to Atticus*

Pray, what's all this? What is going on? I am in the dark. Is it a Roman general or Hannibal we are talking of? Deluded wretch, with never in his [Caesar's] life a glimpse of even the shadow of Good! And he says he is doing all this for his honor's sake! Where is honor without moral good? And is it good to have an army without public authority, to seize Roman towns by way of opening the road to the mother city, to plan debt

(continued)

(Opposing Viewpoints continued)

cancellations, recall of exiles, and a hundred other villainies "all for that first of deities, Sole Power"? He is welcome to his greatness. I would rather a single hour with you, warming myself in that "bonus" sunshine of yours, than all such autocracies, or rather I had sooner die a thousand deaths than entertain one such thought.

Q How did Caesar view the steps he had taken? How did Cicero view those steps? What do the differences between Caesar and Cicero tell you about the end of the Republic? How do the views of Caesar and Cicero give support to Sallust's argument? What do these three selections have in common in regard to the fall of the Republic? How do they differ?

though only nineteen, took command of some of Caesar's legions. After forcing the senate to name him consul, he joined forces with Mark Antony, Caesar's ally and assistant, and Marcus Lepidus, who had been commander of Caesar's cavalry. Together, the three formed the Second Triumvirate, which was legally empowered to rule Rome. Their first act was to restore Sulla's policy of proscription, as described by the ancient historian Appian:

> As soon as they were on their own, the three drew up a list of those who were to die. They put on the list, both then and later, those of whom they were suspicious because of their ability, as well as their personal enemies, trading with each other for the lives of their own relations and friends. They decreed death and confiscation of property for about 300 senators and 2,000 equestrians, among them their own brothers and uncles, as well as senior officers serving under them who had had cause to offend them or their own colleagues.[11]

In addition to proscribing their enemies at home (Cicero was one of those killed), the three commanders pursued Caesar's assassins, who had in the meantime raised an army, and defeated them at Philippi in Macedonia. Lepidus was soon shunted aside, and Octavian and Antony then divided the Roman world between them—Octavian taking the west and Antony the east. To seal their bargain, Antony married Octavia, Octavian's sister.

But the empire of the Romans, large as it was, was still too small for two masters, and Octavian and Antony eventually came into conflict. Antony abandoned Octavia and allied himself with the Egyptian queen Cleopatra VII, with whom, like Caesar before him, he fell deeply in love. Octavian began a propaganda campaign, accusing Antony of catering to Cleopatra and giving away Roman territory to this "whore of the east." Finally, at the Battle of Actium in Greece in 31 B.C.E., Octavian's forces smashed the army and navy of Antony and Cleopatra. Both fled to Egypt, where, according to the Roman historian Florus, they committed suicide a year later:

> Antony was the first to commit suicide, by the sword. Cleopatra threw herself at Octavian's feet, and tried her best to attract his gaze: in vain, for his self-control was impervious to her beauty. It was not her life she was after, for that had already been granted, but a portion of her kingdom. When she realized this was hopeless and that she had been earmarked to feature in Octavian's triumph in Rome, she took advantage of her guard's carelessness to get herself into the mausoleum, as the royal tomb is called. Once there, she put on the royal robes which she was accustomed to wear, and lay down in a richly perfumed coffin beside her Antony. Then she applied poisonous snakes to her veins and passed into death as though into a sleep.[12]

CHRONOLOGY The Decline and Fall of the Roman Republic

Reforms of Tiberius Gracchus	133 B.C.E.
Reforms of Gaius Gracchus	123–122 B.C.E.
Jugurthine War	111–105 B.C.E.
Marius: First consulship	107 B.C.E.
Marius: Consecutive consulships	104–100 B.C.E.
Italian or Social War	90–88 B.C.E.
Sulla's march on Rome	88 B.C.E.
Sulla as dictator	82–79 B.C.E.
Pompey's command in Spain	77–71 B.C.E.
Campaign of Crassus against Spartacus	73–71 B.C.E.
Consulship of Crassus and Pompey	70 B.C.E.
First Triumvirate (Caesar, Pompey, Crassus)	60 B.C.E.
Caesar in Gaul	59–49 B.C.E.
Crassus and Pompey as consuls	55 B.C.E.
Crassus killed by Parthians	53 B.C.E.
Caesar crosses the Rubicon	49 B.C.E.
Battle of Pharsalus; Pompey killed in Egypt	48 B.C.E.
Caesar as dictator	47–44 B.C.E.
Assassination of Caesar	44 B.C.E.
Second Triumvirate (Octavian, Antony, Marcus Lepidus); Cicero killed	43 B.C.E.
Caesar's assassins defeated at Philippi	42 B.C.E.
Octavian defeats Antony at Actium	31 B.C.E.

Octavian, at the age of thirty-two, stood supreme over the Roman world (see Map 5.3). The civil wars had ended. And so had the Republic.

Literature in the Late Republic

The last century of the Roman Republic witnessed the completion of the union of Greek and Roman culture in a truly Greco-Roman civilization. Greek was now the language not just of Greece but of the entire Hellenistic world of the eastern Mediterranean, which Rome had conquered, and educated, upper-class Romans spoke it fluently. The influence of Greece would continue to be felt in the development of Latin literature.

The Assassination of Julius Caesar

When it became apparent that Julius Caesar had no intention of restoring the Republic as they conceived it, about sixty senators, many of them his friends or pardoned enemies, formed a conspiracy to assassinate the dictator. It was led by Gaius Cassius and Marcus Brutus, who naively imagined that this act would restore the traditional Republic. The conspirators set the Ides of March (March 15) of 44 B.C.E. as the date for the assassination. Caesar was in the midst of preparations for a campaign in the eastern part of the empire. Although warned about a plot against his life, he chose to disregard it. This account of Caesar's death is taken from his biography by the Greek writer Plutarch.

Plutarch, *Life of Caesar*

Fate, however, is to all appearance more unavoidable than unexpected. For many strange prodigies and apparitions are said to have been observed shortly before this event.... One finds it also related by many that a soothsayer bade him [Caesar] prepare for some great danger on the Ides of March. When this day was come, Caesar, as he went to the senate, met this soothsayer, and said to him mockingly, "The Ides of March are come," who answered him calmly, "Yes, they are come, but they are not past...."

All these things might happen by chance. But the place which was destined for the scene of this murder, in which the senate met that day, was the same in which Pompey's statue stood, and was one of the edifices which Pompey had raised and dedicated with his theater to the use of the public, plainly showing that there was something of a supernatural influence which guided the action and ordered it to that particular place. Cassius, just before the act, is said to have looked toward Pompey's statue, and silently implored his assistance.... When Caesar entered, the senate stood up to show their respect to him, and of Brutus's confederates, some came about his chair and stood behind it, others met him, pretending to add their petitions to those of Tillius Cimber, in behalf of his brother, who was in exile; and they followed him with their joint applications till he came to his seat. When he sat down, he refused to comply with their requests, and upon their urging him further began to reproach them severely for their demand, when Tillius, laying hold of his robe with both his hands, pulled it down from his neck, which was the signal for the assault. Casca gave him the first cut in the neck, which was not mortal nor dangerous, as coming from one who at the beginning of such a bold action was probably very much disturbed; Caesar immediately turned about, and laid his hand upon the dagger and kept hold of it. And both of them at the same time cried out, he that received the blow, in Latin, "Vile Casca, what does this mean?" and he that gave it, in Greek to his brother, "Brother, help!" Upon this first onset, those who were not privy to the design were astonished, and their horror and amazement at what they saw were so great that they dared not fly nor assist Caesar, nor so much as speak a word. But those who came prepared for the business enclosed him on every side, with their naked daggers in their hands. Which way soever he turned he met with blows, and saw their swords leveled at his face and eyes, and was encompassed like a wild beast in the toils on every side. For it had been agreed they should each of them make a thrust at him, and flesh themselves with his blood: for which reason Brutus also gave him one stab in the groin. Some say that he fought and resisted all the rest, shifting his body to avoid the blows, and calling out for help, but that when he saw Brutus's sword drawn, he covered his face with his robe and submitted, letting himself fall, whether it were by chance or that he was pushed in that direction by his murderers, at the foot of the pedestal on which Pompey's statue stood, and which was thus wetted with his blood. So that Pompey himself seemed to have presided, as it were, over the revenge done upon his adversary, who lay here at his feet, and breathed out his soul through his multitude of wounds, for they say he received three-and-twenty. And the conspirators themselves were many of them wounded by each other while they all leveled their blows at the same person.

Q What does this account of Caesar's assassination reveal about the character of Julius Caesar? Based on this selection, what lessons did Classical historians intend their readers to take from their accounts of great and dramatic political events?

In the last century of the Republic, the Romans began to produce a new poetry, less dependent on epic themes and more inclined to personal expression. Latin poets now took to using various Greek forms to express their own feelings about people, social and political life, and love. The finest example is the work of Catullus (kuh-TULL-uss) (c. 87–54 B.C.E.), the best lyric poet Rome produced and one of the greatest in world literature.

CATULLUS Like most of the great Roman writers of the first century B.C.E., Catullus was not from Rome. He grew up in northern Italy but came to Rome, where he joined a group of carefree, youthful aristocrats. He became a master at adapting and refining Greek forms of poetry to express emotions. He wrote a variety of poems on, among other themes, political figures, social customs, the use of language, the death of his brother, and the travails of love.

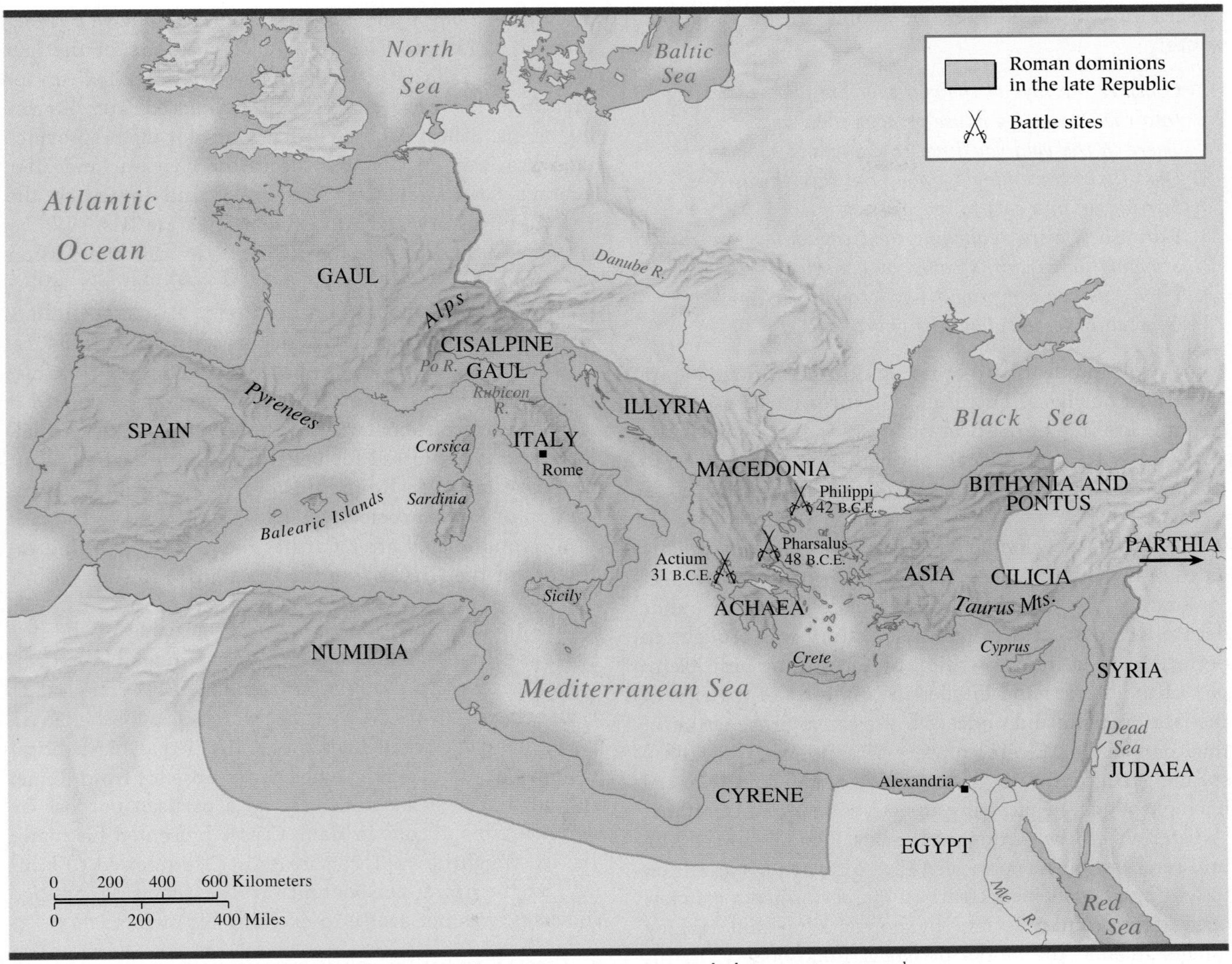

MAP 5.3 Roman Dominions in the Late Republic, 31 B.C.E. Rome expanded its empire not only in response to military threats on its borders but also for increased access to economic resources and markets, in addition to the vanity of conquest itself. For comparison, look back at Map 5.2.

In what areas did the Romans gain the greatest amount of territory, and how?

View an animated version of this map or related maps on the CourseMate website.

Catullus became infatuated with Clodia, the promiscuous sister of a tribune and wife of a provincial governor, and addressed a number of poems to her (he called her Lesbia), describing his passionate love and hatred for her (Clodia had many other lovers besides Catullus):

You used to say that you wished to know only Catullus,
Lesbia, and wouldn't take even Jove before me!
I didn't regard you just as my mistress then: I cherished you
as a father does his sons or his daughters' husbands.
Now that I know you, I burn for you even more fiercely,
though I regard you as almost utterly worthless.
How can that be, you ask? It's because such cruelty forces
lust to assume the shrunken place of affection.[13]

The ability of Catullus to express in simple fashion his intense feelings and curiosity about himself and his world had a noticeable impact on later Latin poets.

LUCRETIUS Another important poet of the late Republic was Lucretius (loo-KREE-shus) (c. 94–55 B.C.E.), who followed an old Greek tradition of expounding philosophy in the form of poetry. Although Stoicism was the Greek school of philosophy that the Romans found most congenial, the philosophy of Epicurus also enjoyed a period of intense popularity between 60 and 40 B.C.E. Lucretius's lengthy poem *On the Nature of the Universe* played a role in furthering that philosophy. In this work, Lucretius attempted to set out poetically Epicurus's idea that the world and all its creatures had been created by an accidental combination of atoms and not by the operation of divine forces. Two themes are repeated: divine forces have no effect on us, and death is of no real consequence because the soul, like the body, is material and after death also dissolves into atoms. Lucretius was especially adept at using vivid imagery.

Describing the movement of atoms in the void, he wrote:

Consider the rays of the sun that are always stealing
Into the shade of a house to pour their light.
There in the void you'll notice many and sundry
Dust flecks that mingle among the rays themselves,
Stirring up in a sort of ceaseless strife
Skirmishes, wars, realigning their squadrons, never
Stopping for breath, assailed by alliance, secession;
From this you can project how atoms are
Constantly tossed along the gulf of space.[14]

If the gods and death are of no significance, how then are we to lead our lives? Lucretius's Epicurean argument that a simple life free of political worries was the highest good ran counter to Roman ideals but had an obvious appeal to Romans sick of the civil discord of the first century B.C.E.

CICERO The development of Roman prose was greatly aided by the practice of oratory. Romans had great respect for oratory, for the ability to persuade people in public debate led to success in politics. Oratory was brought to perfection in a literary fashion by Cicero, the best exemplar of the literary and intellectual interests of the elite of the late Republic and, indeed, the greatest prose writer of that period. For Cicero, oratory was not simply skillful speaking. An orator was a statesman, a man who achieved his highest goal by pursuing an active life in public affairs.

Later, when the turmoil of the late Republic forced him into semiretirement politically, Cicero turned his attention to writing philosophical treatises. He performed a valuable service for Roman society by popularizing and making understandable the works of Greek philosophers. In his philosophical works, Cicero, more than anyone else, transmitted the Classical intellectual heritage to the Western world. Cicero's original contributions to Western thought came in the field of politics. His works *On the Laws* and *On the Republic* provided fresh insights into political thought, including the need for a mixed constitution: "A moderate and well-balanced form of government which is a combination of the three simple good forms (monarchy, aristocracy, and democracy) is preferable even to monarchy."[15] Centuries later his emphasis on the need to pursue an active life to benefit and improve humankind would greatly influence the Italian Renaissance.

SALLUST Rome's upper classes continued to have a strong interest in history. The best-known historian of the late Republic is Sallust (86–35 B.C.E.), who established an approach to historical studies that influenced later Roman historians. Sallust, who served as governor of the province of Africa, was on Caesar's side in the civil war and after Caesar's death went into retirement and turned to the writing of history. His two extant works are *War with Jugurtha,* which discusses the Roman war with the African king from 111 to 105 B.C.E., and *War with Catiline,* an account of the conspiracy of the disaffected aristocrat Catiline, whom Cicero had opposed during his consulship in 63 B.C.E.

Sallust modeled his style after that of the Greek historian Thucydides, whose historical work experienced a sudden wave of popularity in the 50s and 40s B.C.E. Sallust's works expressed his belief that the most important causative factor in Roman history was the moral degeneration of Roman society, which he attributed to the lack of a strong enemy after Carthage and the corrupting influence of the Greeks (see the box on p. 140).

CAESAR Brief mention should also be made of the historical writing of Julius Caesar. Most famous is his *Commentaries on the Gallic War,* an account of his conquest of Gaul between 58 and 51 B.C.E. The work was published in 51 B.C.E., at a time when Caesar was afraid that his political enemies would take advantage of his absence from Rome. Although the *Commentaries* served a partisan purpose by defending his actions in Gaul, Caesar presented his material in straightforward, concise prose. He referred to himself in the third person and, as the following passage indicates, was not averse to extolling his own bravery:

> Caesar saw that the situation was critical, and there was no reserve to throw in. He snatched a shield from a soldier in the rear—he had not brought one himself—and moved to the front line; he called upon the centurions by name, encouraged the men to advance, and directed them to open their lines out to give freer play to their swords. His coming inspired the men with hope and gave them new heart. Even in a desperate situation each man was anxious to do his utmost when his general was looking on, and the enemy's onset was somewhat slowed down.[16]

Caesar's work reminds us that some of the best prose of the late Republic was written by politicians who were concerned with enhancing their own position in a world of civil conflict.

CHAPTER SUMMARY

Sometime in the eighth century B.C.E., a group of Latin-speaking people built a small community called Rome on the Tiber River in Italy. Between 509 and 264 B.C.E., this city expanded and united almost all of Italy under its control. Diplomacy was as important as the Roman armies in this achievement, and the Romans made their rule acceptable by allowing local autonomy and gradually granting Roman citizenship to non-Romans. During this time of conquest, Rome also developed the political institutions of a republic ruled by an aristocratic oligarchy.

Although Rome had no master plan for expansion, its relationship with its neighbors outside Italy soon led to

involvement in new wars. Its first challenge was Carthage and the Carthaginian empire in Spain and Africa. Rome was victorious after the three long and bloody Punic Wars. In the east, Rome conquered Macedonia and also took control of the Greek states. Thus, between 264 and 133 B.C.E., Rome expanded to the west and east and became master of the Mediterranean Sea.

Religion and law permeated Roman life. Ritual was at the focus of religion, for ritual established the correct relationship with the gods, both for individuals and for the state. Roman law was among Rome's most enduring accomplishments. The early laws, written in the Twelve Tables, constituted civil law for Romans. As Rome expanded, the Romans developed a new body of law, the law of nations, that applied to Romans and non-Romans alike. Republican Rome was also influenced by Hellenistic Greece, especially in literature, art, and philosophy.

In the second century B.C.E., the conservative, traditional values of Rome declined as affluence and individualism increased. After 133 B.C.E., Rome's republican institutions proved inadequate for the task of ruling an empire. In the breakdown that ensued, ambitious individuals such as Pompey, Crassus, and Caesar saw opportunities for power unparalleled in Roman history and succumbed to the temptations. The military reforms of Marius at the beginning of the first century had made possible the creation of professional armies that were loyal to the generals who recruited them, rather than to the state. Bloody civil war ensued as powerful individuals jockeyed for power. Peace was finally achieved when Octavian defeated Antony and Cleopatra. Octavian, who came to be known by the title of Augustus, would soon create a new system of government that seemed to preserve the Republic while establishing the basis for a new system that would rule the empire in an orderly fashion.

CHAPTER TIMELINE

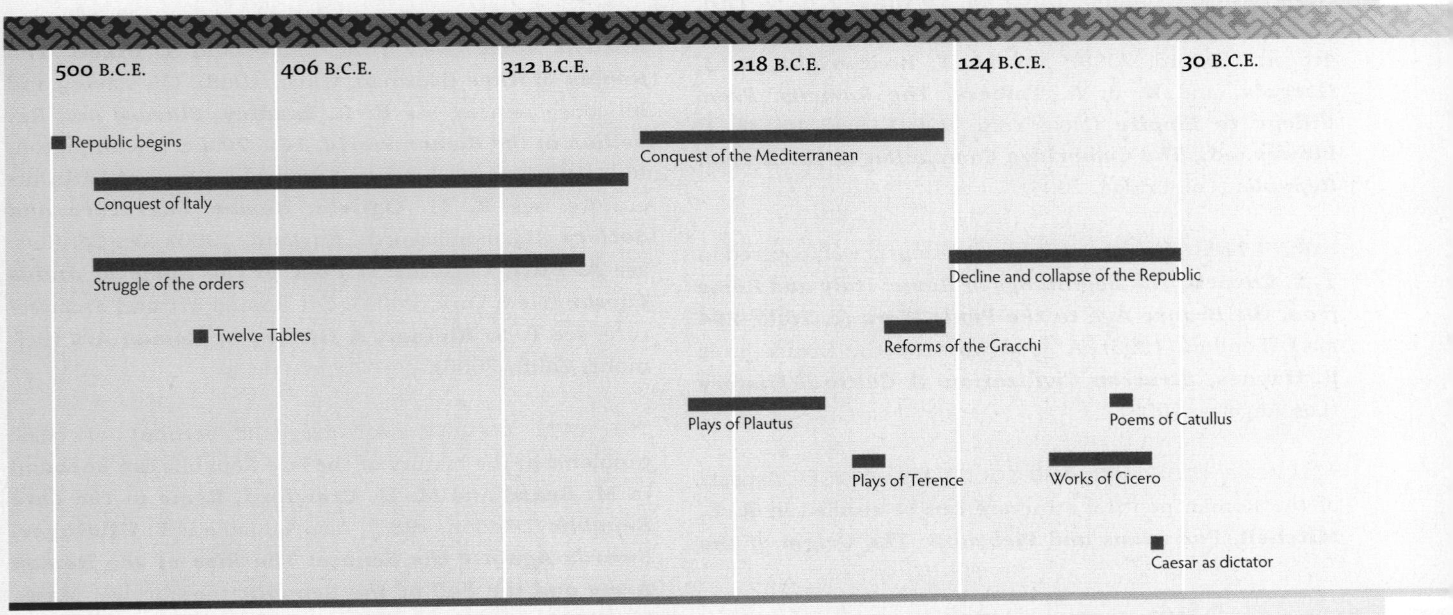

CHAPTER REVIEW

Upon Reflection

Q How did Rome's contact with the Hellenistic world affect Roman civilization in the second and first centuries B.C.E.?

Q How did Rome achieve its empire from 264 to 133 B.C.E., and in the course of its expansion, what happened to the political structure and the political values of the Roman Republic?

Q Was the fall of the Roman Republic due to systemic institutional weaknesses or the personal ambitions of generals and politicians? Explain your answer.

Key Terms

imperium (p. 117)
consul (p. 117)
praetor (p. 117)

dictator (p. 117)
quaestor (p. 117)
aedile (p. 117)
senate (p. 117)
centuriate assembly (p. 117)
paterfamilias (p. 117)
patricians (p. 118)
plebeians (p. 118)
tribunes of the plebs (p. 118)
council of the plebs (p. 118)
plebiscita (p. 118)
rhetoric (p. 129)
latifundia (p. 129)
nobiles (p. 135)
optimates (p. 135)
populares (p. 135)
equestrians (p. 135)

Suggestions for Further Reading

GENERAL SURVEYS Good surveys of Roman history include **C. S. Mackay, *Ancient Rome: A Military and Political History*** (Cambridge, 2004); **M. H. Crawford, *The Roman Republic,*** 2nd ed. (Cambridge, Mass., 1993); **H. H. Scullard, *History of the Roman World, 753–146 B.C.,*** 4th ed. (London, 1978) and ***From the Gracchi to Nero,*** 5th ed. (London, 1982); **M. Le Glay, J.-L. Voisin,** and **Y. Le Bohec, *A History of Rome,*** trans. **A. Nevill,** 4th ed. (Oxford, 2009); and **M. T. Boatwright, D. J. Gargola,** and **R. J. A. Talbert, *The Romans: From Village to Empire*** (New York, 2004). See also **H. I. Flower, ed., *The Cambridge Companion to the Roman Republic*** (Cambridge, 2004).

EARLY ROME The history of early Rome is well covered in **T. J. Cornell, *The Beginnings of Rome: Italy and Rome from the Bronze Age to the Punic Wars (c. 1000–264 B.C.)*** (London, 1995). A good work on the Etruscans is **S. Haynes, *Etruscan Civilization: A Cultural History*** (Los Angeles, 2005).

POLITICAL, ECONOMIC, AND SOCIAL STRUCTURE Aspects of the Roman political structure can be studied in **R. E. Mitchell, *Patricians and Plebeians: The Origin of the Roman State*** (Ithaca, N.Y., 1990). Changes in Rome's economic life can be examined in **A. H. M. Jones, *The Roman Economy*** (Oxford, 1974). On the Roman social structure, see **G. Alföldy, *The Social History of Rome*** (London, 1985).

THE EXPANSION OF ROME On the conquest of Italy, see **J.-M. David, *The Roman Conquest of Italy,*** trans. **A. Nevill** (Oxford, 1996). On Rome's struggle with Carthage, see **N. Bagnall, *The Punic Wars*** (Oxford, 2002), and **A. Goldsworthy, *The Punic Wars*** (New York, 2001). Especially important works on Roman expansion and imperialism include **W. V. Harris, *War and Imperialism in Republican Rome*** (Oxford, 1979), and **E. Badian, *Roman Imperialism in the Late Republic*** (Oxford, 1968). On Roman military forces, see **A. Goldsworthy, *The Complete Roman Army*** (London, 2003).

ROMAN SOCIETY AND CULTURE Roman religion can be examined in **E. M. Orlin, *Temples, Religion, and Politics in the Roman Republic*** (New York, 2002), and **H. H. Scullard, *Festivals and Ceremonies of the Roman Republic*** (Ithaca, N.Y., 1981). A general study of daily life in Rome is available in **F. Dupont, *Daily Life in Ancient Rome*** (Oxford, 1994). On the Roman family, see **S. Dixon, *The Roman Family*** (Baltimore, 1992). Roman women are examined in **R. Baumann, *Women and Politics in Ancient Rome*** (New York, 1995); and **S. Dixon, *The Roman Mother*** (Norman, Okla., 1988). On slavery and its consequences, see **K. R. Bradley, *Slavery and Rebellion in the Roman World, 140–70 B.C.*** (Bloomington, Ind., 1989). For a brief and readable survey of Latin literature, see **R. M. Ogilvie, *Roman Literature and Society*** (Harmondsworth, England, 1980). On Catullus, see **A. Burl, *Catullus: A Poet in the Rome of Julius Caesar*** (New York, 2004). On Roman art and architecture, see **F. S. Kleiner, *A History of Roman Art*** (Belmont, Calif., 2006).

THE LATE REPUBLIC An excellent account of basic problems in the history of the late Republic can be found in **M. Beard** and **M. H. Crawford, *Rome in the Late Republic*** (London, 1985). Also valuable is **E. Hildinger, *Swords Against the Senate: The Rise of the Roman Army and the Fall of the Republic*** (Cambridge, Mass., 2002). Numerous biographies provide many details on the politics of the period. Especially worthwhile are **D. Stockton, *The Gracchi*** (Oxford, 1979); **A. Goldsworthy, *Caesar: Life of a Colossus*** (New Haven, Conn., 2006); **R. Seager, *Pompey: A Political Biography*** (Berkeley, Calif., 1980); and **A. Everitt, *Cicero*** (New York, 2001).

CourseMate

Visit the CourseMate website at www.cengagebrain.com for additional study tools and review materials for this chapter.

CHAPTER 6

Art Library

A second-century Roman marble bust of Hadrian

The Roman Empire

CHAPTER OUTLINE AND FOCUS QUESTIONS

The Age of Augustus (31 B.C.E.–14 C.E.)

Q In his efforts to solve the problems Rome had faced during the late Republic, what changes did Augustus make in Rome's political, military, and social institutions?

The Early Empire (14–180)

Q What were the chief features of the Roman Empire at its height during the second century?

Roman Culture and Society in the Early Empire

Q What were the chief intellectual, artistic, and social developments in the Early Empire? How did these differ from the intellectual, artistic, and social developments of the Republic?

Transformation of the Roman World: Crises in the Third Century

Q What political, military, economic, and social problems did the Roman Empire face during the third century?

Transformation of the Roman World: The Rise of Christianity

Q What characteristics of Christianity enabled it to grow and ultimately to triumph?

CRITICAL THINKING

Q How did Christianity transform the Roman Empire?

WITH THE VICTORIES OF OCTAVIAN, peace finally settled on the Roman world. Although civil conflict still erupted occasionally, the new imperial state constructed by Octavian experienced a period of remarkable stability for the next two hundred years. The Romans imposed their peace on the largest empire established in antiquity. Indeed, Rome's writers proclaimed that "by heaven's will my Rome shall be capital of the world."[1] Rome's writers were not quite accurate, but few Romans were aware of the Han Empire, which flourished at the same time (202 B.C.E.–221 C.E.) and extended from Central Asia to the Pacific. Although there was little contact between them, the Han and Roman empires had remarkable similarities: they lasted for centuries, they had remarkable success in establishing centralized control, and they maintained their law and political institutions, their technical skills, and their languages throughout the empire.

To the Romans, their divine mission was clearly to rule nations and peoples. Hadrian, one of the emperors of the second century C.E., was but one of many Roman rulers who believed in Rome's mission. He was a strong and intelligent ruler who took his responsibilities quite seriously. Between 121 and 132, he visited all of the provinces in the empire. According to his Roman biographer, Aelius Spartianus, "Hardly any emperor ever traveled with such speed over so much territory." When he arrived in a province, Hadrian dealt firsthand with any problems and bestowed many favors on the local population. He also worked to establish the boundaries of the provinces and provide for their defense. New fortifications, such as the 80-mile-long Hadrian's Wall across northern Britain, were built to defend the borders. Hadrian insisted on rigid discipline for frontier armies and demanded that the soldiers be kept in training "just as if war were imminent." He also tried to lead by personal example; according to his biographer, he spent time with the troops and "cheerfully ate out of doors such camp food as bacon, cheese, and vinegar." Moreover, he "would walk as much as twenty miles fully armed." By the third century C.E., however, Rome's ability to rule nations and people began to weaken as the Roman Empire began to experience renewed civil war, economic chaos, and invasions. In the meantime, the growth of Christianity, one of the remarkable success stories of Western civilization, led to the emergence of a new and vibrant institution.

The Age of Augustus (31 B.C.E.–14 C.E.)

FOCUS QUESTION: In his efforts to solve the problems Rome had faced during the late Republic, what changes did Augustus make in Rome's political, military, and social institutions?

In 27 B.C.E., Octavian proclaimed the "restoration of the Republic." He understood that only traditional republican forms would satisfy the senatorial aristocracy. At the same time, Octavian was aware that the Republic could not be fully restored and managed to arrive at a compromise that worked, at least during his lifetime. In 27 B.C.E., the senate awarded him the title of Augustus—"the revered one." He preferred the title *princeps* (PRIN-keps *or* PRIN-seps), meaning chief citizen or first among equals. The system of rule that Augustus established is sometimes called the **principate,** conveying the idea of a constitutional monarch as coruler with the senate. But while Augustus worked to maintain this appearance, in reality, power was heavily weighted in favor of the *princeps.*

The New Order

In the new constitutional order that Augustus created, the basic governmental structure consisted of the *princeps* (Augustus) and an aristocratic senate. Augustus retained the senate as the chief deliberative body of the Roman state. Its decrees, screened in advance by the *princeps,* now had the effect of law. The title of *princeps*—first citizen of the state—carried no power in itself, but each year until 23 B.C.E., Augustus held the office of consul, which gave him *imperium,* or the right to command (see Chapter 5). When Augustus gave up the consulship in 23 B.C.E., he was granted *maius imperium* (MY-yoos im-PEE-ree-um)—greater *imperium* than all others. The consulship was now unnecessary. Moreover, very probably in 23 B.C.E., Augustus was given the power of a tribune without actually holding the office itself; this power enabled him to propose laws and veto any item of public business. Although officials continued to be elected, Augustus's authority ensured that his candidates for office usually won. This situation caused participation in elections to decline. Consequently, the popular assemblies, shorn of any real role in elections and increasingly overshadowed by the senate's decrees, gradually declined in importance.

Braccio Nuovo, Vatican State/© Scala/Art Resource, NY

Augustus. Octavian, Caesar's adopted son, emerged victorious from the civil conflict that rocked the Republic after Caesar's assassination. The senate awarded him the title Augustus. This marble statue from Prima Porta is an idealized portrait, based on Greek rather than Roman models. The statue was meant to be a propaganda piece, depicting a youthful general addressing his troops. At the bottom stands Cupid, the son of Venus, goddess of love, meant to be a reminder that the Julians, Caesar's family, claimed descent from Venus, thus emphasizing the ruler's divine background.

The Achievements of Augustus

This excerpt is taken from a text written by Augustus and inscribed on a bronze tablet at Rome. Copies of the text in stone were displayed in many provincial capitals. Called "the most famous ancient inscription," the *Res Gestae* of Augustus summarizes his accomplishments in three major areas: his offices, his private expenditures on behalf of the state, and his exploits in war and peace. Though factual in approach, it is a highly subjective account.

Augustus, *Res Gestae*

Below is a copy of the accomplishments of the deified Augustus by which he brought the whole world under the empire of the Roman people, and of the moneys expended by him on the state and the Roman people, as inscribed on two bronze pillars set up in Rome.

1. At the age of nineteen, on my own initiative and at my own expense, I raised an army by means of which I liberated the Republic, which was oppressed by the tyranny of a faction [Mark Antony and his supporters]. . . .
2. Those who assassinated my father [Julius Caesar, his adoptive father] I drove into exile, avenging their crime by due process of law; and afterwards when they waged war against the state, I conquered them twice on the battlefield.
3. I waged many wars throughout the whole world by land and by sea, both civil and foreign, and when victorious I spared all citizens who sought pardon. . . .
5. The dictatorship offered to me . . . by the people and the senate, both in my absence and in my presence, I refused to accept. . . .
17. Four times I came to the assistance of the treasury with my own money, transferring to those in charge of the treasury 150,000,000 sesterces. And in the consulship of Marcus Lepidus and Lucius Arruntius I transferred out of my own patrimony 170,000,000 sesterces to the soldiers' bonus fund, which was established on my advice for the purpose of providing bonuses for soldiers who had completed twenty or more years of service. . . .
20. . . . I repaired the conduits of the aqueducts which were falling into ruin in many places because of age. . . .
22. I gave a gladiatorial show three times in my own name, and five times in the names of my sons or grandsons; at these shows about 10,000 fought. . . .
25. I brought peace to the sea by suppressing the pirates. In that war I turned over to their masters for punishment nearly 30,000 slaves who had run away from their owners and taken up arms against the state. . . .
26. I extended the frontiers of all the provinces of the Roman people on whose boundaries were peoples not subject to our empire. . . .
27. I added Egypt to the empire of the Roman people. . . .
28. I established colonies of soldiers in Africa, Sicily, Macedonia, in both Spanish provinces, in Achaea, Asia, Syria, Narbonese Gaul, and Pisidia. Italy, moreover, has twenty-eight colonies established by me, which in my lifetime have grown to be famous and populous. . . .
35. When I held my thirteenth consulship, the senate, the equestrian order, and the entire Roman people gave me the title of "father of the country" and decreed that this title should be inscribed in the vestibule of my house, in the Julian senate house, and in the Augustan Forum on the pedestal of the chariot which was set up in my honor by decree of the senate. At the time I wrote this document I was in my seventy-sixth year.

Q What were the achievements of Augustus? To what extent did these accomplishments create the "job" of being emperor? In what sense could this document be called a piece of propaganda?

Augustus proved highly popular. As the Roman historian Tacitus commented, "Indeed, he attracted everybody's goodwill by the enjoyable gift of peace. . . . Opposition did not exist."[2] The ending of the civil wars had greatly bolstered Augustus's popularity (see the box above). At the same time, his continuing control of the army, while making possible the Roman peace, was a crucial source of his power.

The Army

As a result of the civil wars of the first century B.C.E., the Roman army had increased in size and had become more professional with legionaries who served a longer period. Under the empire, the shift to a professional army was completed when early emperors created a bureaucracy that could train and administer such an army. The peace of the Roman Empire depended on the army, and so did the security of the *princeps*. Though primarily responsible for guarding the frontiers of the empire, the army was also used to maintain domestic order within the provinces. Moreover, the army played an important social role. It was an agent of upward mobility for both officers and recruits and provided impetus for **Romanization** wherever the legions were stationed. The colonies of veterans established by Augustus

Louvre, Paris//© Réunion des Musées Nationaux/Art Resource, NY

The Praetorian Guard. Augustus was responsible for setting up the praetorian guard as an imperial bodyguard of elite troops. Pictured in this second-century relief are members of the praetorian guard. Their body armor resembled that of the legionaries, although the cohort serving in the palace wore togas.

throughout the empire proved especially valuable in Romanizing the provinces.

Augustus maintained a standing army of twenty-eight legions. Since each legion at full strength numbered 5,400 soldiers, the Roman Empire had an army of about 150,000 men, certainly not large either by modern standards or in terms of the size of the empire itself (the population of the empire was probably close to 50 million). Roman legionaries served twenty years and were recruited only from the citizenry and, under Augustus, largely from Italy. Augustus also maintained a large contingent of auxiliary forces enlisted from the subject peoples. They served as both light-armed troops and cavalry and were commanded by Roman officers as well as tribal leaders. During the principate of Augustus, the **auxiliaries** numbered around 130,000. They were recruited only from noncitizens, served for twenty-four years, and along with their families received citizenship after their terms of service.

Augustus was also responsible for establishing the **praetorian guard.** These "nine cohorts of elite troops," roughly nine thousand men, had the important task of guarding the person of the *princeps*. They were recruited from Roman citizens in Italy and served for sixteen years. Eventually, the praetorian guard would play an important role in making and deposing emperors.

The role of the *princeps* as military commander gave rise to a title by which this ruler eventually came to be known. When victorious, a military commander was acclaimed by his troops as *imperator* (im-puh-RAH-tur). Augustus was so acclaimed on a number of occasions. *Imperator* is our word *emperor*. Although such a title was applied to Augustus and his successors, Augustus still preferred to use the title *princeps*.

Roman Provinces and Frontiers

Augustus inaugurated a new system for governing the provinces. Under the Republic, the senate had appointed the provincial governors. Now certain provinces were allotted to the *princeps*, who assigned deputies known as *legates* to govern them. These legates were from the senatorial class and held office as long as the emperor chose. The senate continued to designate the governors of the remaining provinces, but the authority of Augustus gave him the power to overrule the senatorial governors and thus to establish a unified imperial policy.

Since a governor had relatively few administrative officials to assist him, effective government of the provinces necessitated considerable cooperation from local authorities. By supporting the power of local elites—the upper classes—in return for their cooperation, Roman policy encouraged a substantial degree of self-government and local autonomy in the cities. By fostering municipal life, Rome essentially made cities and city-states the basic units of imperial administration. City councils of leading citizens made for stable local government, and leading city officials were rewarded for their administrative services with Roman citizenship.

FRONTIER POLICY Augustus added more territory to the Roman Empire than any other single Roman. In the east, instead of creating new provinces, Augustus encouraged the establishment of client kingdoms, a policy that enabled him to minimize the Roman military presence in the east so that he could use his forces elsewhere. After the final pacification of Spain in 19 B.C.E., the *princeps* expended his greatest military efforts along the northern frontiers of the Roman Empire. He conquered the central and maritime Alps and then expanded Roman control of the Balkan peninsula up to the Danube River.

The extension of Roman power to the Danube now opened the door for Augustus's major military project—expansion into Germany. After 15 B.C.E., Roman forces advanced across the Rhine and by 9 B.C.E. had reached the Elbe River in eastern Germany. In 6 C.E., the Romans began another advance between the Elbe and the Danube but encountered a series of difficulties, including the great catastrophe of 9 C.E. when three Roman legions under Varus were massacred in the Teutoburg Forest by a coalition of German tribes led by Arminius, a German tribal leader who had served in the Roman auxiliary forces and had even received Roman citizenship. Roman historians blamed Varus for the disaster: "He [Varus] entertained the notion that the Germans were a people who were men only in voice and limbs.... With this purpose in mind, he entered the heart of Germany as though he were going among a people enjoying the blessings of peace."[3] The defeat severely dampened Augustus's enthusiasm for continued expansion in central Europe. Thereafter, the Romans were content to use the Rhine as the frontier between the Roman province of Gaul and the German tribes to the east. In fact, the difficulties had convinced Augustus that "the empire should not be extended beyond its present frontiers."[4] His defeats in Germany taught Augustus that Rome's power was limited. They also left him devastated; for months he would beat his head against a door and shout, "Varus, give me back my legions!"

Augustan Society

Society in the Early Roman Empire was characterized by a system of social stratification, inherited from the Republic, in which Roman citizens were divided into three basic classes: the senatorial, equestrian, and lower classes.

THE SOCIAL ORDER Augustus had accepted the senatorial order as a ruling class for the empire. Senators filled the chief magistracies of the Roman government, held the most important military posts, and governed the provinces. One needed to possess property worth 1 million sesterces (an unskilled laborer in Rome received 3 sesterces a day; a Roman legionary, 900 sesterces a year in pay) to belong to the senatorial order. When Augustus took charge, the senate had more than a thousand members. Augustus revised the senatorial list and reduced its size to six hundred but also added new men from wealthy families throughout Italy. Overall, Augustus was successful in winning the support of the senatorial class for his new order.

The equestrian order was expanded under Augustus and given a share of power in the new imperial state. The order was open to all Roman citizens of good standing who possessed property valued at 400,000 sesterces. They could now hold military and governmental offices, but the positions open to them were less important than those held by the senatorial order. At the end of his career, an equestrian might be rewarded by membership in the senatorial order.

Citizens not of the senatorial or equestrian orders belonged to the lower classes, who made up the overwhelming majority of the free citizens. The diminution of the power of the Roman assemblies ended whatever political power they may have possessed earlier in the Republic. Many of these people were provided with free grain and public spectacles to keep them from creating disturbances. Nevertheless, by gaining wealth and serving as lower officers in the Roman legions, it was sometimes possible for them to advance to the equestrian order.

AUGUSTUS'S REFORMS Augustus was very concerned about certain aspects of Rome's social health. He believed that the civil strife of the first century B.C.E. had sapped the strength of public religion, which he considered the cornerstone of a strong state. Therefore, he restored traditional priesthoods that had fallen into disuse in the late Republic, rebuilt many ruined temples and shrines, and constructed new ones to honor the Roman gods.

Augustus also instituted a new religious cult to strengthen the empire. Since the Roman state was intimately tied to Roman religion, an imperial cult served as a unifying instrument for the Roman world. Augustus did not claim to be a god, but he did permit the construction of temples to his deified adoptive father, Julius Caesar. Augustus also permitted the building of temples to Augustus and Roma, the personification of the Roman state. The worship of Augustus and Roma became the foundation of the imperial cult. Its development was furthered when Augustus was acclaimed as a god upon his death.

Augustus's belief that Roman morals had been corrupted during the late Republic led him to initiate social legislation to arrest the decline. He thought that increased luxury had undermined traditional Roman frugality and simplicity and caused a decline in morals, evidenced by easy divorce, a falling birthrate among the upper classes, and lax behavior manifested in hedonistic parties and the love affairs of prominent Romans with fashionable women and elegant boys.

Through his new social legislation, Augustus hoped to restore respectability to the upper classes and reverse the declining birthrate as well. Expenditures for feasts were limited, and other laws made adultery a criminal offense. In fact, Augustus exiled his own daughter Julia for adultery—a rather hypocritical act in view of Augustus's numerous sexual affairs. Augustus also revised the tax laws to penalize bachelors, widowers, and married persons who had fewer than three children.

A Golden Age of Latin Literature

The high point of Latin literature was reached in the time of Augustus. The literary accomplishments of the Augustan Age were such that the period has been called the golden age of Latin literature.

VIRGIL The most distinguished poet of the Augustan Age was Virgil (VUR-jul) (70–19 B.C.E.). The son of a small landholder in northern Italy, he welcomed the rule of

Augustus and wrote his greatest work in the emperor's honor. Virgil's masterpiece was *The Aeneid,* an epic poem clearly meant to rival the work of Homer. The connection between Troy and Rome is made explicitly. Aeneas, the son of Anchises of Troy, survives the destruction of Troy and eventually settles in Latium; thus, Roman civilization is linked to Greek history. The character of Aeneas is portrayed in terms that remind us of the ideal Roman—his virtues are duty, piety, and faithfulness. Virgil's overall purpose was to show that Aeneas had fulfilled his mission to establish the Romans in Italy and thereby start Rome on its divine mission to rule the world:

Virgil, *The Aeneid,* Book 1 (29–19 B.C.E)

Let others fashion from bronze more lifelike, breathing
images—
For so they shall—and evoke living faces from marble;
Others excel as orators, others track with their
instruments
The planets circling in heaven and predict when stars
will appear.
But, Romans, never forget that government is your
medium!
Be this your art:—to practice men in the habit of
peace,
Generosity to the conquered, and firmness against
aggressors.[5]

As Virgil expressed it, ruling was Rome's gift.

HORACE Another prominent Augustan poet was Horace (HOR-uss) (65–8 B.C.E.), a friend of Virgil. Horace was a very sophisticated writer whose overriding concern seems to have been to point out to his contemporaries the "follies and vices of his age." In the *Satires,* a medley of poems on a variety of subjects, Horace is revealed as a detached observer of human weaknesses. He directed his attacks against movements, not living people, and took on such subjects as sexual immorality, greed, and job dissatisfaction ("How does it happen, Maecenas, that no man alone is content with his lot?"[6]). Horace mostly laughs at the weaknesses of humankind and calls for forbearance: "Supposing my friend has got liquored and wetted my couch. . . . Is he for such a lapse to be deemed less dear as a friend, or because when hungry he snatched up before me a chicken from my side of the dish?"[7] In his final work, the *Epistles,* Horace used another Greek form—the imaginary letter in verse—to provide a portrait of his friends and society and the things he held most dear: a simple life, good friends, and his beloved countryside.

OVID Ovid (OH-vid) (43 B.C.E.–18 C.E.) was the last of the great poets of the golden age. He belonged to a privileged group of Roman youths who liked to ridicule old Roman values. In keeping with the spirit of this group, Ovid wrote a frivolous series of love poems known as the *Amores.* Intended to entertain and shock, they achieved their goal. Ovid's most popular work was the *Metamorphoses,* a series of fifteen complex mythological tales involving transformations of shapes, such as the change of chaos into order. A storehouse of mythological information, the *Metamorphoses* inspired many Western painters, sculptors, and writers, including Shakespeare.

Another of Ovid's works was *The Art of Love.* This was essentially a takeoff on didactic poems. Whereas authors of earlier didactic poems had written guides to farming, hunting, or some such subject, Ovid's work was a handbook on the seduction of women (see the box on p. 153). *The Art of Love* appeared to applaud the loose sexual morals of the Roman upper classes at a time when Augustus was trying to clean them up. The *princeps* was not pleased. Ovid chose to ignore the wishes of Augustus and paid a price for it. In 8 C.E., Ovid was implicated in a sexual scandal, possibly involving the emperor's daughter Julia. He was banished to a small town on the coast of the Black Sea and died in exile.

LIVY The most famous Latin prose work of the golden age was written by the historian Livy (LIV-ee) (59 B.C.E.–17 C.E.). Livy's masterpiece was a history of Rome from the foundation of the city to 9 B.C.E., written in 142 books, although only 35 of the books have survived. Livy perceived history in terms of moral lessons. He stated in the preface:

Livy (59 B.C.E.–17 C.E.), *Histories,* Book 1, Chapters I–VIII

> The study of history is the best medicine for a sick mind; for in history you have a record of the infinite variety of human experience plainly set out for all to see; and in that record you can find for yourself and your country both examples and warnings: fine things to take as models, base things, rotten through and through, to avoid.[8]

For Livy, human character was the determining factor in history.

Livy's history celebrated Rome's greatness. He built scene upon scene that not only revealed the character of the chief figures but also demonstrated the virtues that had made Rome great. Of course, he had serious weaknesses as a historian. He was not always concerned about the factual accuracy of his stories and was not overly critical of his sources. But he did tell a good tale, and his work remained the standard history of Rome for centuries.

Significance of the Augustan Age

The Augustan Age was a lengthy one. Augustus died in 14 C.E. after dominating the Roman world for forty-five years. He had created a new order while placating the old by restoring and maintaining traditional values, a fitting combination for a leader whose favorite maxim was "Make haste slowly." By the time of his death, his new order was so well established that few Romans agitated for an alternative. Indeed, as the Roman historian Tacitus (TASS-i-tuss) pointed out, "Actium had been won before the

Ovid and the Art of Love

Ovid has been called the last great poet of the Augustan golden age of literature. One of his most famous works was *The Art of Love,* a guidebook for the seduction of women. Unfortunately for Ovid, the work appeared at a time when Augustus was anxious to improve the morals of the Roman upper class. Augustus considered the poem offensive, and Ovid soon found himself in exile.

Ovid, *The Art of Love*

Now I'll teach you how to captivate and hold the woman of your choice. This is the most important part of all my lessons. Lovers of every land, lend an attentive ear to my discourse; let goodwill warm your hearts, for I am going to fulfill the promises I made you.

First of all, be quite sure that there isn't a woman who cannot be won, and make up your mind that you will win her. Only you must prepare the ground. Sooner would the birds cease their song in the springtime, or the grasshopper be silent in the summer, ... than a woman resist the tender wooing of a youthful lover....

Now the first thing you have to do is to get on good terms with the fair one's maid. She can make things easy for you. Find out whether she is fully in her mistress's confidence, and if she knows all about her secret dissipations. Leave no stone unturned to win her over. Once you have her on your side, the rest is easy....

In the first place, it's best to send her a letter, just to pave the way. In it you should tell her how you dote on her; pay her pretty compliments and say all the nice things lovers always say.... And promise, promise, promise. Promises will cost you nothing. Everyone's a millionaire where promises are concerned....

If she refuses your letter and sends it back unread, don't give up; hope for the best and try again....

Don't let your hair stick up in tufts on your head; see that your hair and your beard are decently trimmed. See also that your nails are clean and nicely filed; don't have any hair growing out of your nostrils; take care that your breath is sweet, and don't go about reeking like a billy-goat....

When you find yourself at a feast where the wine is flowing freely, and where a woman shares the same couch with you, pray to that god whose mysteries are celebrated during the night, that the wine may not overcloud your brain. 'Tis then you may easily hold converse with your mistress in hidden words whereof she will easily divine the meaning....

By subtle flatteries you may be able to steal into her heart, even as the river insensibly overflows the banks which fringe it. Never cease to sing the praises of her face, her hair, her taper fingers and her dainty foot....

Tears, too, are a mighty useful resource in the matter of love. They would melt a diamond. Make a point, therefore, of letting your mistress see your face all wet with tears. Howbeit, if you can't manage to squeeze out any tears—and they won't always flow just when you want them to—put your finger in your eyes.

Q What were Ovid's principles of love? Why do you think Augustus found *The Art of Love* so offensive?

younger men were born. Even most of the older generation had come into a world of civil wars. Practically no one had ever seen truly Republican government.... Political equality was a thing of the past; all eyes watched for imperial commands."[9] The Republic was now only a memory and, given its last century of warfare, an unpleasant one at that. The new order was here to stay.

The Early Empire (14–180)

Q **Focus Question**: What were the chief features of the Roman Empire at its height during the second century?

There was no serious opposition to Augustus's choice of successor, his stepson Tiberius (ty-BEER-ee-uss). By designating a family member as *princeps,* Augustus established the Julio-Claudian dynasty; the next four rulers were related either to his own family or to that of his wife, Livia.

The Julio-Claudians (14–68)

The Julio-Claudian rulers varied greatly in ability. Tiberius (14–37) was a competent general and an able administrator who tried initially to involve the senate in government. Caligula (kuh-LIG-yuh-luh) (37–41) was a grandnephew of Tiberius and great-grandson of Augustus. He exhibited tyrannical behavior and was extremely erratic. Claudius (KLAW-dee-uss) (41–54) had been mistreated by his family because of a physical disability due to partial paralysis, but he was intelligent, well educated, and competent. He was followed by Nero (NEE-roh) (54–68), who was only sixteen when he came to power. Nero's interest in the arts caused him to neglect affairs of state, especially the military, and that proved to be his undoing.

Several major tendencies emerged during the reigns of the four Julio-Claudians. In general, more and more of the responsibilities that Augustus had given to the senate tended to be taken over by the emperors. Moreover, an imperial bureaucracy was instituted under Claudius.

The Fate of Cremona in the Year of the Four Emperors

After the death of Nero in 68 C.E., a power struggle ensued that resulted in a year of confusion with four different emperors, each the leader of a field army. Galba replaced Nero and was succeeded by Otho, who was then defeated by Vitellius. Finally, Vespasian established a new dynasty. Some of the Italian cities suffered greatly in these struggles between Roman legions loyal to their commanders. This excerpt is from Tacitus's account of the destruction of Cremona by the forces that had declared for Vespasian.

Tacitus, *The Histories*

Forty thousand armed men forced their way into the city.... Neither rank nor years saved the victims from an indiscriminate orgy in which rape alternated with murder and murder with rape. Graybeards and frail old women, who had no value as loot, were dragged off to raise a laugh. But any full-grown girl or good-looking lad who crossed their path was pulled this way and that in a violent tug-of-war between the would-be captors, and finally drove them to destroy each other. A single looter trailing a hoard of money or temple-offerings of massive gold was often cut to pieces by others who were stronger. Some few turned up their noses at the obvious finds and inflicted flogging and torture on the owners in order to rummage after hidden valuables and dig for buried treasure. In their hands they held firebrands, which, once they had got their spoil away, they wantonly flung into the empty houses and rifled temples. It is not surprising that, in an army of varied tongues and conventions, including Romans, allies and foreigners [auxiliaries], there was a diversity of wild desires, differing conceptions of what was lawful, and nothing barred. Cremona lasted them four days. While all its buildings, sacred and secular, collapsed in flames, only the temple of Melitis [goddess of pestilential vapors] outside the walls remained standing, defended by its position or the power of the divinity.

Q What does this selection from Tacitus tell you about the nature of the civil war in the Roman Empire? What were its results?

He rationalized the central government by developing bureaucratic departments with talented freedmen as their chiefs. This practice further undermined the authority of the senators, who had previously shared in these responsibilities.

As the Julio-Claudian successors of Augustus began to behave openly like real rulers rather than "first citizens of the state," the opportunity for arbitrary and corrupt acts increased. Caligula, who became mentally unbalanced, wanted to be hailed as a god and neglected affairs of state while indulging his passions. Nero freely eliminated people he wanted out of the way, including his own mother, whom he had murdered. Without troops, the senators proved unable to oppose these excesses. Only the praetorian guard established by Augustus seemed capable of interfering with these rulers but did so in a manner that did not bode well for future stability. Caligula proved so capricious that the officers of the praetorian guard hatched a plot and assassinated him before he had ruled for four complete years. Afterward, they chose Claudius, uncle of Caligula, as the next emperor and forced the senate to confirm their act, thereby demonstrating the power of the military units stationed around Rome.

The downfall of the Julio-Claudian dynasty came during the reign of Nero. His early reign had been quite successful. The young emperor worked hard and with the assistance of his childhood tutor, the philosopher Seneca (SEN-uh-kuh), gave the empire a sound government. But Nero soon tired of his duties and began to pursue other interests, including singing, acting, horse racing, and sexual excesses. After Seneca resigned his position in disgust in 62, Nero's rule deteriorated. His obsession with singing and acting in public was greeted with contempt by the senatorial class. At the same time, he aroused animosity by executing a number of prominent figures, including a popular general, on charges of treason. His actions finally led to a conspiracy, not by the praetorian guard, but by the Roman legions themselves. In 68, Galba (GAHL-buh), governor of one of the Spanish provinces, rose in revolt and secured the principate for himself. Nero, abandoned by his guards, chose to commit suicide by stabbing himself in the throat after uttering his final words, "What an artist the world is losing in me."

The Flavians (69–96)

Galba, however, was not readily accepted by the other provincial armies, which led to civil wars in 69, known as the year of the four emperors (see the box above). Finally, Vespasian (vess-PAY-zhun), commander of the legions in the east, established himself as sole ruler and his family as a new dynasty known as the Flavians. The significance of the year 69 was summed up precisely by Tacitus when he stated that "a well-hidden secret of the principate had been revealed: it was possible, it seemed, for an emperor to be chosen outside Rome"[10]—chosen, of course, by members of the Roman army.

The accession of Vespasian to the imperial power demonstrated that it was no longer necessary to be descended from an ancient aristocratic family to be emperor.

In fact, the family of Vespasian (69–79) was from the equestrian order. Once in control, he managed to reestablish the economy on a sound basis after the extravagances of Nero and the destruction wrought by the civil wars of 69. More important, Vespasian had no compunctions whatever about establishing the principle of dynastic succession for the principate. He was followed by his sons Titus (TY-tuss) (79–81) and Domitian (doh-MISH-un) (81–96). The Flavians, especially Domitian, dropped the pretense of the word *princeps* and began to use the title of *imperator,* emperor, freely. The emperor was rapidly becoming an absolute monarch.

The Five "Good Emperors" (96–180)

Many historians see the ***Pax Romana*** (the "Roman peace") and the prosperity it engendered as the chief benefits of Roman rule during the first and second centuries C.E. These benefits were especially noticeable during the reigns of the five so-called **good emperors.** These rulers treated the ruling classes with respect, cooperated with the senate, ended arbitrary executions, maintained peace in the empire, and supported domestic policies generally beneficial to the empire. Though absolute monarchs, they were known for their tolerance and diplomacy.

The first of the five good emperors was Nerva (NUR-vuh) (96–98), chosen by the senate after the assassination of Domitian. By chance, Nerva and his next three successors had no sons and had to resort to adoption to obtain heirs. According to one Roman historian, "Nerva, therefore, finding himself held in such contempt by reason of his old age, ascended the Capital and said in a loud voice: 'May good success attend the Roman senate and people and myself: I hereby adopt Marcus Ulpius Nerva Trajan.'"[11] Trajan (TRAY-jun) (98–117) was a capable man who was also acceptable to the army, an increasingly important requirement. He had been born in Spain to an old Roman family and was the first emperor born outside Italy.

Trajan was succeeded by his second cousin Hadrian (HAY-dree-un) (117–138), who spent years inspecting the provinces and restoring the military forces to good order. Hadrian adopted as his successor Antoninus Pius (an-tuh-NY-nuss PY-uss) (138–161), who achieved a reputation as the most beneficent of the five good emperors. It was said of him that "one should behave in all things like a pupil of Antoninus: his energy on behalf of what was done in accord with reason, his equability everywhere, his serene expression, his sweetness, his disdain of glory, his ambition to grasp affairs."[12] Unlike Hadrian, who traveled extensively in the provinces, Antoninus Pius stayed in Rome and made even greater use of the senate. He in turn adopted Marcus Aurelius (MAR-kuss aw-REE-lee-uss) (161–180), who has been viewed as a philosopher-king of the sort Plato envisioned (see Chapter 3). Highly influenced by Stoicism, Marcus Aurelius wrote his *Meditations,* reflecting on the ideal of Stoic duty as a religious concept.

CHRONOLOGY **Rulers of the Early Empire**

Julio-Claudian Dynasty	
Augustus	31 B.C.E.–14 C.E.
Tiberius	14–37
Caligula	37–41
Claudius	41–54
Nero	54–68
Flavian Dynasty	
Vespasian	69–79
Titus	79–81
Domitian	81–96
Five Good Emperors	
Nerva	96–98
Trajan	98–117
Hadrian	117–138
Antoninus Pius	138–161
Marcus Aurelius	161–180

Under the five good emperors, the powers of the emperor continued to expand at the expense of the senate. Increasingly, imperial officials appointed and directed by the emperor took over the running of the government. The five good emperors also extended the scope of imperial administration to areas previously untouched by the imperial government. Trajan established a program that provided state funds to assist poor parents in raising and educating their children. He was not motivated simply by benevolence, as he believed that such assistance would materially aid in creating a larger pool of young men in Italy eligible for military service.

The five good emperors were widely praised by their subjects for their extensive building programs. Trajan and Hadrian were especially active in constructing public works—aqueducts, bridges, roads, and harbor facilities—throughout the provinces and in Rome. Trajan built a new forum in Rome to provide a setting for his celebrated victory column. Hadrian's Pantheon, a temple of "all the gods," is one of the grandest ancient buildings surviving in Rome.

The Roman Empire at Its Height: Frontiers and Provinces

At its height in the second century, the Roman Empire (see Map 6.1) covered about 3.5 million square miles and had a population, like that of Han China, estimated at more than 50 million. While the emperors and the imperial administration provided a degree of unity, considerable leeway was given to local customs, and the privileges of Roman citizenship were extended to many people throughout the empire. In 212 C.E., the emperor Caracalla completed the process by giving Roman citizenship to every free inhabitant of the empire. Latin was

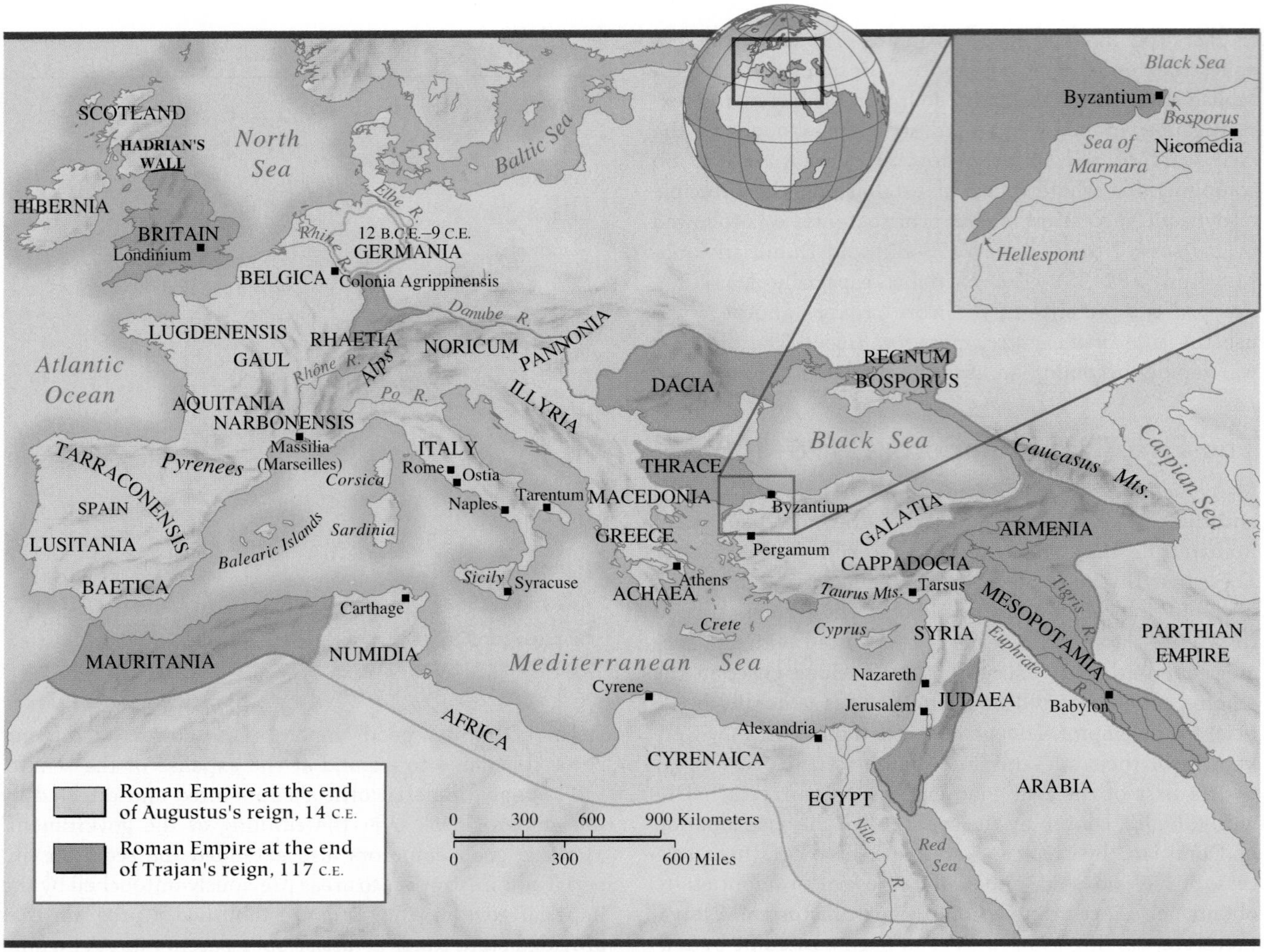

MAP 6.1 The Roman Empire from Augustus Through Trajan (14–117). Augustus and later emperors continued the expansion of the Roman Empire, adding more resources but also increasing the tasks of administration and keeping the peace. Compare this map with Map 5.3.

Q ***Which territories were conquered by Augustus, and which were added by the end of Trajan's reign?***

View an animated version of this map or related maps on the CourseMate website.

the language of the western part of the empire, while Greek was used in the east. Although Roman culture spread to all parts of the empire, there were limits to Romanization since local languages persisted and many of the empire's residents spoke neither Latin nor Greek.

ROMAN FRONTIERS With the exception of Claudius's annexation of Britain, the first-century successors of Augustus had largely followed his advice to curb expansion and remain within the natural frontiers of the empire—the ocean to the west, the rivers in the north, and the desert in the east and south.

Although Trajan broke with Augustus's policy of defensive imperialism by extending Roman rule into Dacia (modern Romania), Mesopotamia, and the Sinai peninsula, his conquests represent the high-water mark of Roman expansion. His successors recognized that the empire was overextended and pursued a policy of retrenchment. Hadrian withdrew Roman forces from much of Mesopotamia. Although he retained Dacia and Arabia, he went on the defensive in his frontier policy, reinforcing the fortifications along a line connecting the Rhine and Danube rivers and building a defensive wall 80 miles long across northern Britain. By the end of the second century, the vulnerability of the empire had become apparent. Frontiers were stabilized, and the Roman forces were established in permanent bases behind the frontiers. But when one frontier was attacked, troops had to be drawn from other frontiers, leaving them vulnerable. The empire lacked a real strategic reserve, and its weakness would become ever more apparent.

THE ARMY AND ROMANIZATION The Roman army was the primary instrument for the defense of the Roman frontiers. In 14 C.E., it numbered twenty-eight legions but had increased to thirty by the time of Trajan.

© DeA Picture Library (M. Borchi)/Art Resource, NY

Rome in Germany. The Roman army helped bring Roman culture and institutions to the provinces. Local production and trade grew up around the military camps to meet the soldiers' needs, and cities often developed from the bases themselves or from colonies located nearby. Pictured are the remains of the imperial thermal baths in the Roman city of Augusta Treverorum (modern Trier). Trier became the headquarters of the imperial procurator of Belgica and the two Germanies and flourished as one of the most significant cities in the western Roman Empire. Public baths were a prominent feature of any Roman city.

The auxiliaries were increased correspondingly, creating a Roman army of about 400,000 by the end of the second century. Since legionaries had to be Roman citizens, most recruits in Augustus's time were from Italy. Over the course of the first century, however, the Italians' reluctance to serve in the military led to the recruitment of citizens from the provinces. By 100 C.E., only one in five legionaries was Italian.

In addition to defense and protection, the Roman army also served as an important instrument for Romanizing the provinces. Roman military camps became centers for the spread of the Latin language and Roman institutions and ways of thought and conduct. The presence of large numbers of troops and their dependent women and slaves encouraged the development of trade and local production to meet the army's need for supplies. Urban centers developed around army bases or nearby colonies. Many cities along the Rhine had their roots in legionary bases or auxiliary forts. The city of Cologne, for example, grew out of the military colony the Romans called Colonia Agrippinensis. Since many veterans, when they retired, chose to remain in the new towns, establishing families and new businesses, the towns served to pass on Roman culture and attitudes to the people in the provinces.

CITIES AND ROMANIZATION The administration and cultural life of the Roman Empire depended greatly on cities and towns. A provincial governor's staff was not large, so it was left to local city officials to act as Roman agents in carrying out many government functions, especially those related to taxes. Most towns and cities were not large by modern standards. The largest was Rome, but there were also some large cities in the east: Alexandria in Egypt numbered over 300,000 inhabitants, Ephesus in Asia Minor had 200,000, and Antioch in Syria had around 150,000. In the west, cities were usually small, with only a few thousand inhabitants. Cities were important in the spread of things Roman. They were also uniform in physical appearance, with similar temples, markets, amphitheaters, and other public buildings.

Magistrates and town councillors chosen from the ranks of the wealthy upper classes directed municipal administration. These municipal offices were unsalaried but were nevertheless desired by wealthy citizens because the offices conferred prestige and power at the local level as well as Roman citizenship. Roman municipal policy effectively tied the upper classes to Roman rule and ensured that these classes would retain control over the rest of the population.

The process of Romanization in the provinces was reflected in significant changes in the governing classes of the empire. In the course of the first century, there was a noticeable decline in the number of senators from Italian families. By the end of the second century, Italian senators made up less than half the total. Increasingly, the Roman senate was being recruited from wealthy provincial equestrian families. The provinces also provided many of the legionaries for the Roman army and, beginning with Trajan, supplied many of the emperors.

The extent and speed of Romanization also varied widely in different areas of the empire. In the western areas where Greeks and Phoenicians had established cities centuries before, such as Spain, Africa, and parts of Gaul, Romanization occurred quickly. Temples, aqueducts, amphitheaters, and the Latin language all became a regular part of life in these areas.

The process of Romanization was less developed in other parts of the empire, especially in Asia, where towns and cities had their own traditions free of Roman influence. Their common language was Greek, not Latin, and many people outside the urban areas spoke neither Latin nor Greek. Even more important than geography in determining the degree of Romanization, however, was class status. By 200 C.E., the upper classes everywhere in the empire had become Romanized, sharing a common culture as well as similar economic and social interests.

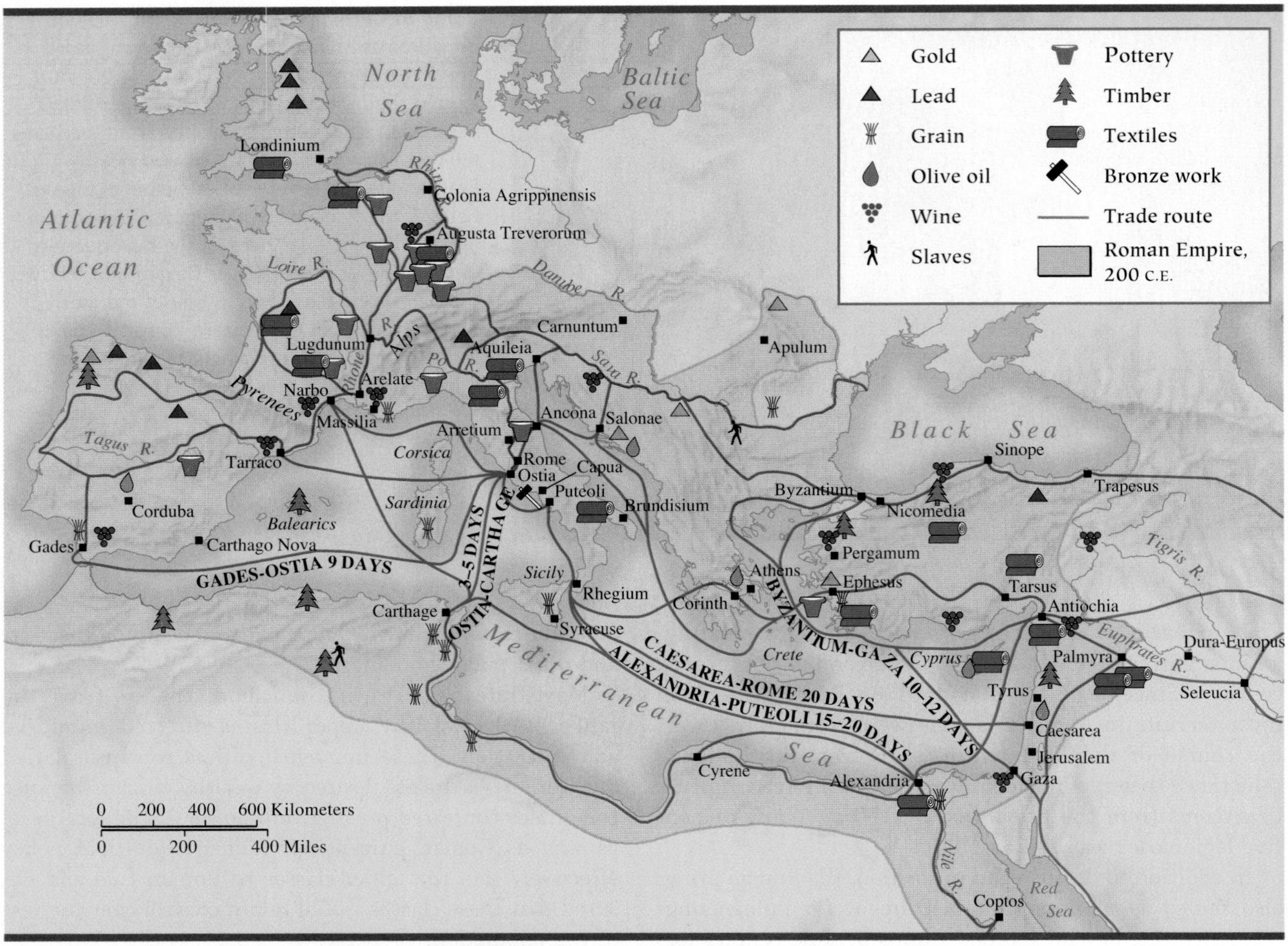

MAP 6.2 Trade Routes and Products in the Roman Empire, c. 200. Although still primarily an agrarian economy, the Roman Empire provided the single currency and stable conditions necessary for an expansion of trade in various commodities and products. An extensive system of roads and shipping routes also facilitated trade.

Q ***What truth is there to the statement "All roads lead to Rome"?***

ROMAN LAW AND ROMANIZATION As Roman citizenship spread in the cities, the new citizens became subject to Roman law, which in itself became an important instrument in the process of Romanization. The Early Empire experienced great progress in the study and codification of law. The second and third centuries C.E. witnessed the "classical age of Roman law," a period in which a number of great jurists classified and compiled basic legal principles that have proved valuable to the Western world. Most jurists emphasized the emperor as the source of law: "What has pleased the emperor has the force of law."

During the classical age of Roman law, the identification of the law of nations with natural law led to a concept of natural rights. According to the jurist Ulpian (d. 228), natural rights implied that all men are born equal and should therefore be equal before the law. In practice, however, the principle was not applied.

The Romans did, however, establish standards of justice, applicable to all people, that included principles that we would immediately recognize. A person was considered innocent until proved otherwise. People accused of wrongdoing were allowed to defend themselves before a judge. A judge was expected to weigh evidence carefully before arriving at a decision. These principles lived on in Western civilization long after the fall of the Roman Empire.

For Roman citizens, Roman law provided a uniform system of principles by which they conducted their affairs and led their lives. When the emperor Caracalla extended Roman citizenship to every free person in the empire in 212 C.E., Roman law became an even more significant factor in binding the entire empire together.

Prosperity in the Early Empire

The Early Empire was a period of considerable prosperity. Internal peace resulted in unprecedented levels of trade (see Map 6.2). Merchants from all over the empire came to

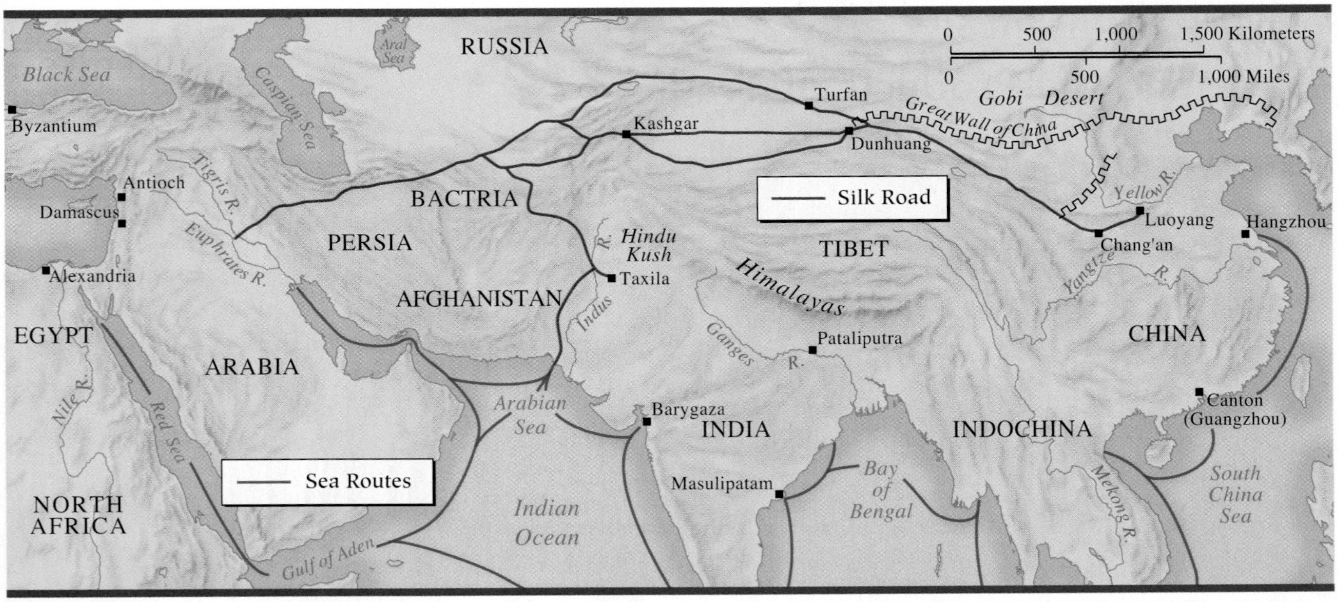

The Silk Road

the chief Italian ports of Puteoli on the Bay of Naples and Ostia at the mouth of the Tiber. The importation of large quantities of grain to feed the populace of Rome and an incredible quantity of luxury items for the wealthy upper classes in the west led to a steady drain of gold and silver coins from Italy and the west to the eastern part of the empire (see Images of Everyday Life on p. 160).

Long-distance trade beyond the Roman frontiers also flourished during the Early Empire. Developments in both the Roman and Chinese empires helped foster the growth of this trade. Although both empires built roads chiefly for military purposes, the roads also facilitated trade. Moreover, by creating large empires, the Romans and Chinese not only established internal stability but also pacified bordering territories, thus reducing the threat that bandits posed to traders. As a result, merchants developed a network of trade routes that brought these two great empires into commercial contact. Most important was the overland Silk Road, a regular caravan route between West and East (see the spot map on the Silk Road above).

The Silk Road received its name from the Chinese export of silk cloth, which became a popular craze among Roman elites, leading to a vast outpouring of silver from Rome to China and provoking the Roman emperor Tiberius to grumble that "the ladies and their baubles are transferring our money to foreigners." The silk trade also stimulated a degree of mutual curiosity between the two great civilizations, but not much mutual knowledge or understanding. So far as is known, no personal or diplomatic contacts between the two civilizations ever took place. But two great empires at the extremes of the Eurasian supercontinent had for the first time been linked together in a commercial relationship.

The increased trade helped stimulate manufacturing. The cities of the east still produced the items made in Hellenistic times (see Chapter 4). The first two centuries of the empire also witnessed the high point of industrial development in Italy. Some industries became concentrated in certain areas, such as bronze work in Capua and pottery in Arretium in Etruria. Other industries, such as brickmaking, were pursued in rural areas on large landed estates. Much industrial production remained small-scale and was done by individual artisans, usually freedmen or slaves. In the course of the first century, Italian centers of industry experienced increasing competition from the provinces.

Despite the prosperity from trade and commerce, agriculture remained the chief occupation of most people and the underlying basis of Roman prosperity. While the large landed estates, the *latifundia,* still dominated agriculture, especially in southern and central Italy, small peasant farms persisted, particularly in Etruria and the Po valley. Although large estates concentrating on sheep and cattle raising used slave labor, the lands of some *latifundia* were worked by free tenant farmers called ***coloni*** (kuh-LOH-nee). The *colonus* was essentially a sharecropper who paid rent in labor, produce, or sometimes cash.

In considering the prosperity of the Roman world, it is important to remember the enormous gulf between rich and poor underlying it (see the box on p. 161). The development of towns and cities, so important to the creation of any civilization, is based to a large degree on the agricultural surpluses of the countryside. In ancient times, the margin of surplus produced by each farmer was relatively small. Therefore, the upper classes and urban populations had to be supported by the labor of a large number of agricultural producers who never found it easy to produce much more than enough for themselves. In lean years, when there were no surpluses, the townspeople often took what they wanted, leaving little for the peasants.

Trade and the Products of Trade

© The Art Archive/Bardo Museum, Tunis/Gianni Dagli Orti

Museo Civico, Albenga//© Scala/Art Resource, NY

Trade was an important component in the prosperity of the Early Roman Empire. Although Roman roads were excellent, most goods traveled by boat throughout the Mediterranean and beyond. This third-century C.E. Roman mosaic from Sousse, Tunisia, shows workers unloading a cargo of iron ore from a ship. Vast numbers of amphoras, large two-handled pottery jars, were used to transport olive oil and wine, as well as such luxury items as pepper, cloves, and incense. As can be seen in the illustration at the right from excavations done near Pisa, amphoras could be stacked to transport large quantities of goods. Roman merchant ships could stack between 5,000 and 10,000 amphoras in their holds. Rome itself became, as one Greek observed, "the warehouse of the world," where "whatever is raised or manufactured by every people is always here in superabundance." In addition to the imported grain that fed the populace, numerous luxury goods were available in the shops. Since many Romans despised trade, most shops were run by slaves or freedmen. The stone relief from Ostia in the second century C.E. shows a shopkeeper selling groceries and livestock. In addition to the local produce, two monkeys from overseas are available as pets.

Museo Ostiense, Ostia//© Erich Lessing/

Roman Culture and Society in the Early Empire

Focus Questions: What were the chief intellectual, artistic, and social developments in the Early Empire? How did these differ from the intellectual, artistic, and social developments of the Republic?

The shift from Republic to empire not only transformed the Roman political world, but also affected its cultural and social life. Intellectuals found ways to accommodate the autocratic rule of emperors while Roman architects created massive buildings befitting an empire. Gladiatorial games and slavery increased dramatically in the Early Empire, while upper-class women acquired greater independence.

The Silver Age of Latin Literature

In the history of Latin literature, the century and a half after Augustus is often labeled the "silver age" to indicate

The Daily Life of an Upper-Class Roman

There was an enormous gulf between rich and poor in Roman society. The upper classes lived lives of great leisure and luxury in their villas and on their vast estates. Pliny the Younger (c. 62–c. 113) was an upper-class Roman who rose to the position of governor of Bithynia in Asia Minor. In this excerpt from one of his letters, Pliny describes a typical day vacationing at one of his Italian villas. Although Pliny owned four villas in Italy, we should note that he did not belong to the ranks of the really rich in Roman society.

Pliny, Letter to Fuscus Salinator

You want to know how I plan the summer days I spend in Tuscany. I wake when I like, usually about sunrise, often earlier but rarely later. My shutters stay closed, for in the stillness and darkness I feel myself surprisingly detached from any distractions and left to myself in freedom. . . . If I have anything on hand I work it out in my head, choosing and correcting the wording, and the amount I achieve depends on the ease or difficulty with which my thoughts can be marshaled and kept in my head. Then I call my secretary, the shutters are opened, and I dictate what I have put into shape; he goes out, is recalled, and again dismissed. Three or four hours after I first wake (but I don't keep to fixed times) I betake myself according to the weather either to the terrace or the covered arcade, work out the rest of my subject, and dictate it. I go for a drive, and spend the time in the same way as when walking or lying down; my powers of concentration do not flag and are in fact refreshed by the change. After a short sleep and another walk I read a Greek or Latin speech aloud and with emphasis, not so much for the sake of my voice as my digestion, though of course both are strengthened by this. Then I have another walk, am oiled, take exercise, and have a bath. If I am dining alone with my wife or with a few friends, a book is read aloud during the meal and afterward we listen to a comedy or some music; then I walk again with the members of my household, some of whom are educated. Thus, the evening is prolonged with varied conversations, and even when the days are at their longest, comes to a satisfying end.

Sometimes I vary this routine, for, if I have spent a long time on my couch or taking a walk, after my siesta and reading I go out on horseback instead of a carriage so as to be quicker and take less time. Part of the day is given up to friends who visit me from neighboring towns and sometimes come to my aid with a welcome interruption when I am tired. Occasionally I go hunting, but not without my notebooks so that I shall have something to bring home even if I catch nothing. I also give some time to my tenants (they think it should be more) and the boorishness of their complaints gives fresh zest to our literary interests and the more civilized pursuits of town.

Q What does Pliny's letter tell you about the lifestyle of upper-class Romans? Could this lifestyle be related to the decline of the Roman Empire? Why or why not?

that the literary efforts of the period, while good, were not equal to the high standards of the Augustan "golden age." The popularity of rhetorical training encouraged the use of clever literary expressions, often at the expense of original and meaningful content. A good example of this trend can be found in the works of Seneca.

SENECA Educated in Rome, Seneca (c. 4 B.C.E.–65 C.E.) became strongly attached to the philosophy of Stoicism (see Chapter 4). After serving as tutor to Nero, he helped run the government during the first five years of Nero's reign. Seneca began to withdraw from politics after Nero took a more active role in government. In 65, he was charged with involvement in a conspiracy against Nero and committed suicide at Nero's command.

In letters written to a young friend, Seneca expressed the basic tenets of Stoicism: living according to nature, accepting events dispassionately as part of the divine plan, and a universal love for all humanity. Thus, "the first thing philosophy promises us is the feeling of fellowship, of belonging to mankind and being members of a community. . . . Philosophy calls for simple living, not for doing penance, and the simple way of life need not be a crude one."[13] Viewed in retrospect, Seneca displays some glaring inconsistencies. While preaching the virtues of simplicity, he amassed a fortune and was ruthless at times in protecting it. His letters show humanity, benevolence, and fortitude, but his sentiments are often undermined by an attempt to be clever with words.

TACITUS The greatest historian of the silver age was Tacitus (c. 56–120). His main works included the *Annals* and the *Histories*, which presented a narrative account of Roman history from the reign of Tiberius through the assassination of Domitian in 96. Tacitus believed that history had a moral purpose: "It seems to me a historian's foremost duty to ensure that merit is recorded, and to confront evil deeds and words with the fear of posterity's denunciations."[14] As a member of the senatorial class, Tacitus was disgusted with the abuses of power perpetrated by the emperors and was determined that the "evil deeds" of wicked men would not be forgotten. Many historians

Tacitus, *Annals of Imperial Rome*, three excerpts

© PictureNet/CORBIS

© David Buffington/Photodisc/Getty Images

The Pantheon. Shown here is the Pantheon, one of Rome's greatest buildings. Constructed of brick, six kinds of concrete, and marble, it was a stunning example of the Romans' engineering skills. The outside porch of the Pantheon contained eighteen Corinthian granite columns, but it was the inside of the temple that amazed onlookers. The interior is a large circular space topped by a huge dome. A hole in the center of the roof was the only source of light. The dome, built up layer by layer, was made of concrete, weighing 5,000 tons. The walls holding the dome are almost 20 feet thick.

believe he went too far in projecting the evils of his own day back into his account of the past. Tacitus's work *Germania* is especially important as a source of information about the early Germans. But it too is colored by his attempt to show the Germans as noble savages in contrast to the decadent Roman upper classes.

JUVENAL By the second century C.E., though still influenced by the familiar Greek models, Latin authors were increasingly imitating the great Latin writers of earlier ages. This was evident in the work of Juvenal (JOO-vuh-nul), the best poet of the silver age. Juvenal (c. 55–c. 128) wrote five books of satires in which he pilloried the manners and vices of his generation. He attacked the affectations of Roman women, the abuse of slaves, the excesses of emperors, the eastern and Greek immigrants, his own poverty, and the inequities of Roman society. For example: "They demand that the teacher shall mold these tender minds. . . . 'See to it,' you're told, and when the school year's ended, you'll get as much as a jockey makes from a single race."[15] But Juvenal was not a reformer. Though he attacked many vices, he offered no basic critique of his society.

Art in the Early Empire

The Romans contributed little that was original to painting and sculpture. Much work was done by Greek artists and craftspeople who adhered to the Roman desire for realism and attention to details. Wall paintings and frescoes in the houses of the rich realistically depicted landscapes, portraits, and scenes from mythological stories.

In architecture, the Romans continued to imitate Greek styles and made use of colonnades, rectangular structures, and post-and-lintel construction. But the Romans were innovative in their own way. They made considerable use of curvilinear forms: the arch, vault, and dome. The Romans were the first people in antiquity to use concrete on a massive scale. By combining concrete and curvilinear forms, they were able to construct massive buildings—public baths, such as those of Caracalla, and amphitheaters, the most famous of which was the Colosseum in Rome. These large buildings were made possible by Roman engineering skills. These same skills were put to use in constructing roads (the Romans built a network of 50,000 miles of roads throughout their empire), aqueducts (in Rome, almost a dozen aqueducts kept the population supplied with water), and bridges.

Roman Aqueduct. The engineering skills of the Romans enabled them to build massive constructions, including aqueducts such as this one in southern France, known as the Pont du Gard. The Pont du Gard is a three-story bridge built of blocks of stone without cement, at the top of which was a channel that carried water. Nîmes received its water from a source 30 miles away. Since gravity kept the water flowing, channels holding the water had to have a gradual decline from the source of the water to its final destination. The Pont du Gard, which crosses the Gardon River outside Nîmes, was built to the exact height needed to maintain the flow of water into the city.

Imperial Rome

At the center of the colossal Roman Empire was the ancient city of Rome (see Map 6.3). Truly a capital city, Rome had the largest population of any city in the empire. It is estimated that its population was close to one million by the time of Augustus. For anyone with ambitions, Rome was the place to be. A magnet to many people, Rome was extremely cosmopolitan. Nationalities from all over the empire resided there, with entire neighborhoods inhabited by specific groups, such as Greeks and Syrians.

Rome was no doubt an overcrowded and noisy city. Because of the congestion, cart and wagon traffic was banned from the streets during the day. The noise from the resulting vehicular movement at night often made sleep difficult. Evening pedestrian travel was dangerous. Although Augustus had organized a police force, lone travelers might be assaulted, robbed, or soaked by filth thrown out of the upper-story windows of Rome's massive apartment buildings.

An enormous gulf existed between rich and poor in the city of Rome. While the rich had comfortable villas, the poor lived in apartment blocks called *insulae,* which might be six stories high. Constructed of concrete, they were often poorly built and prone to collapse. The use of wooden beams in the floors and movable stoves, torches, candles, and lamps for heat and light created a constant danger of fire. Once started, fires were extremely difficult to put out. The famous conflagration of 64, which Nero was unjustly accused of starting, devastated a good part of the city. Besides the hazards of collapse and fire, living conditions were miserable. High rents forced entire

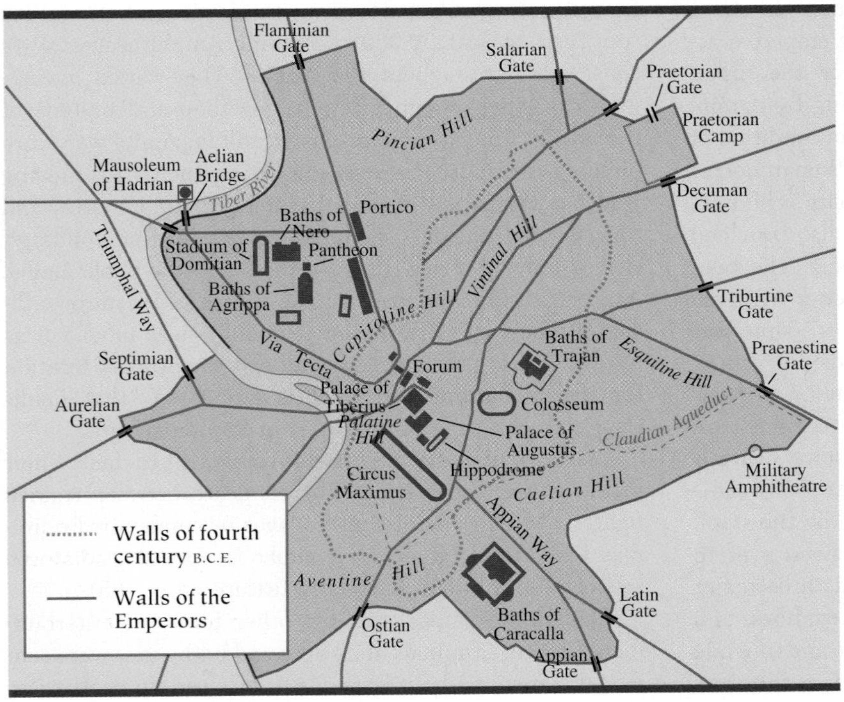

MAP 6.3 Imperial Rome. A large, overcrowded, and dirty city, Rome was the political, economic, social, and cultural hub of the Roman Empire. Squalid and desperate living conditions for the poor contrasted dramatically with the city's magnificent architectural works.

Q ***How did roads from outside enter Rome, and what could possibly explain this?***

© Thomas S. England/Photo Researchers, Inc.

Interior of the Colosseum of Rome. The Colosseum was a large amphitheater constructed under the emperor Vespasian and his son Titus. Such amphitheaters, in which gladiatorial contests were held, were built throughout the empire. They varied in size, but the one at Rome was the largest. The Colosseum was named after the Colossus of Nero, a large statue of the first-century C.E. emperor that stood nearby. The scene of many bloody gladiatorial combats, the Colosseum could be used for other spectacles as well. It was flooded for a spectacular naval battle when the emperor Titus held the first games there.

families into one room. In the absence of plumbing and central heating, conditions were so uncomfortable that poorer Romans spent most of their time outdoors in the streets.

Fortunately for these people, Rome boasted public buildings unequaled anywhere in the empire. Its temples, forums, markets, baths, theaters, triumphal arches, governmental buildings, and amphitheaters gave parts of the city an appearance of grandeur and magnificence.

Though the center of a great empire, Rome was also a great parasite. Beginning with Augustus, the emperors accepted responsibility for providing food for the urban populace, with about 200,000 people receiving free grain. But even the free grain did not relieve the grim condition of the poor. Early in the second century C.E., a Roman doctor claimed that rickets was common among the city's children.

In addition to food, entertainment was also provided on a grand scale for the inhabitants of Rome. The poet Juvenal said of the Roman masses: "Nowadays, with no vote to sell, their motto is 'Couldn't care less.' Time was when their vote elected generals, heads of state, commanders of legions: but now they've pulled in their horns, there's only two things that concern them: Bread and Circuses."[16] The emperor and other state officials provided public spectacles as part of the great festivals—most of them religious in origin—celebrated by the state. More than one hundred days a year were given over to these public holidays. The festivals included three major types of entertainment. At the Circus Maximus, horse and chariot races attracted hundreds of thousands, while dramatic and other performances were held in theaters. But the most famous of all the public spectacles were the gladiatorial shows.

The Gladiatorial Shows

The gladiatorial shows were an integral part of Roman society. They took place in amphitheaters; the first permanent one was constructed in Rome in 29 B.C.E. Perhaps the most famous was the Flavian amphitheater, called the Colosseum, constructed in Rome under Vespasian and his son Titus to seat 50,000 spectators. Amphitheaters were constructed throughout the empire. They varied in size, with capacities ranging from a few thousand to tens of thousands. Considerable resources and ingenuity went into building them, especially in the arrangements for moving wild beasts efficiently into the arena. In most cities and towns, amphitheaters came to be the biggest buildings, rivaled only by the circuses for races and the public baths. As we shall see repeatedly in the course of Western civilization, where a society invests its money gives an idea of its priorities. Since the amphitheater was the primary location for the gladiatorial games, it is fair to say that public slaughter was an important part of Roman culture.

Gladiatorial games were held from dawn to dusk. Their main features were contests to the death between trained fighters. Most gladiators were slaves or condemned criminals who were trained for combat in special gladiatorial schools (see the Film & History feature on p. 165).

Gladiatorial games included other forms of entertainment as well. Criminals of all ages and both sexes were sent into the arena without weapons to face certain death from

FILM & HISTORY

Gladiator (2000)

The film *Gladiator,* directed by Ridley Scott, is a fictional story set in the Roman Empire near the end of the second century C.E. In the movie, Emperor Marcus Aurelius (Richard Harris) informs his son Commodus (Joaquin Phoenix) that he intends to turn over imperial power to his successful and respected general, Maximus (Russell Crowe), in the hope that this decent and honest man can restore the Roman senate and revive the Republic. Commodus reacts by killing his father, assuming the position of emperor, and ordering the deaths of Maximus, his wife, and son. Maximus escapes but returns too late to Spain to save his wife and child. He is captured and then sold into slavery to Proximo (Oliver Reed), who trains him to be a gladiator. Maximus is eventually sent to Rome, where he becomes a superhero in the gladiatorial games in the Roman Colosseum, all the while awaiting an opportunity to avenge the death of his wife and son by killing Commodus. Maximus becomes involved in a plot with Lucilla (Connie Nielsen), the emperor's sister, and Gracchus (Derek Jacobi), a Roman senator, to rejoin his army, march on Rome, and overthrow the emperor. When Commodus discovers the plot, he challenges the captured Maximus to a duel in the Colosseum but stabs him first to ensure his own success. Despite his injury, Maximus kills the emperor in combat.

Gladiator is a relatively exciting story, but how much of it is based on historical facts? With the exception of Marcus Aurelius, Commodus, and Lucilla, all of the characters are fictional. Marcus Aurelius was a kind emperor with a love of philosophy and died in 180, probably from plague, and certainly not by his son's hands, as depicted in the film. Commodus ruled from 180 to 192, although he was only eighteen when he became emperor, not in his late twenties as in the movie; and he had blond hair, not dark hair. Commodus was an unstable and cruel young man who was strongly attracted to gladiatorial contests. He was obsessed with performing in the arena, especially with slaughtering animals. He was not killed in the Colosseum, however, but strangled by his wrestling partner on the last day of 192.

Contrary to the movie, Marcus Aurelius had no intention of restoring the Republic; by 180, most Romans had become well accustomed to the empire. In fact, Marcus Aurelius had already made his son Commodus a joint ruler in 177. Nor had Marcus Aurelius banned gladiatorial games, as the movie claims. And although Commodus's sister Lucilla did enter into a plot with some senators to assassinate her brother, the plot of 182 failed, and the conspirators, including Lucilla, were executed.

Maximus (Russell Crowe) triumphs in the Roman Colosseum.

Although *Gladiator* shows little concern for historical facts, the movie did demonstrate that many people are still interested in ancient history. It became one of the highest earning films of 2000 and won numerous awards including Academy Awards for Best Picture and Best Actor for Russell Crowe. Moreover, the film helped to renew interest in Roman history—sales of biographies of historical Roman figures and of Marcus Aurelius's *Meditations* increased noticeably in the years after the movie was released.

wild animals who would tear them to pieces. Numerous kinds of animal contests were also held: wild beasts against each other, such as bears against buffalo; staged hunts with men shooting safely from behind iron bars; and gladiators in the arena with bulls, tigers, and lions. Reportedly, five thousand beasts were killed in one day of games when the emperor Titus inaugurated the Colosseum in 80 C.E. Enormous resources were invested in capturing and shipping wild animals for slaughter, and whole species were hunted to extinction in parts of the empire.

These bloodthirsty spectacles were extremely popular with the Roman people. Tacitus reported, "Few indeed are to be found who talk of any other subjects in their homes, and whenever we enter a classroom, what else is the

The Eruption of Mount Vesuvius

Pliny the Younger, whose description of his villa we read in the box on p. 161, also wrote a letter to the Roman historian Tacitus describing the death of his uncle, Pliny the Elder, as a result of the eruption of Mount Vesuvius. Pliny the Elder was the commander of a fleet at Misenum. When the eruption occurred, his curiosity led him to take a detachment from his fleet to the scene. He landed at Stabiae, where he died from the toxic fumes.

Pliny, Letter to Cornelius Tacitus

Thank you for asking me to send you a description of my uncle's death so that you can leave an accurate account of it for posterity.... It is true that he perished in a catastrophe which destroyed the loveliest regions of the earth, a fate shared by whole cities and their people, and one so memorable that it is likely to make his name live for ever....

My uncle was stationed at Misenum, in active command of the fleet. On 24 August, in the early afternoon, my mother drew his attention to a cloud of unusual size and appearance.... He called for his shoes and climbed up to a place which would give him the best view of the phenomenon. It was not clear at that distance from which mountain the cloud was rising (it was afterwards known to be Vesuvius); its general appearance can best be expressed as being like an umbrella pine, for it rose to a great height on a sort of trunk and then split off into branches, I imagine because it was thrust upwards by the first blast and then left unsupported as the pressure subsided, or else it was borne down by its own weight so that it spread out and gradually dispersed. In places it looked white, elsewhere blotched and dirty, according to the amount of soil and ashes it carried with it. My uncle's scholarly acumen saw at once that it was important enough for a closer inspection, and he ordered a boat to be made ready....

[Unable to go further by sea, he lands at Stabiae.]

Meanwhile on Mount Vesuvius broad sheets of fire and leaping flames blazed at several points, their bright glare emphasized by the darkness of night. My uncle tried to allay the fears of his companions by repeatedly declaring that these were nothing but bonfires left by the peasants in their terror, or else empty houses on fire in the districts they had abandoned....

They debated whether to stay indoors or take their chance in the open, for the buildings were now shaking with violent shocks, and seemed to be swaying to and fro as if they were torn from their foundations. Outside on the other hand, there was the danger of falling pumice-stones, even though these were light and porous; however, after comparing the risks they chose the latter. In my uncle's case one reason outweighed the other, but for the others it was a choice of fears. As a protection against falling objects they put pillows on their heads tied down with cloths.

Elsewhere there was daylight by this time, but they were still in darkness, blacker and denser than any ordinary night, which they relieved by lighting torches and various kinds of lamp. My uncle decided to go down to the shore and investigate on the spot the possibility of any escape by sea, but he found the waves still wild and dangerous. A sheet was spread on the ground for him to lie down, and he repeatedly asked for cold water to drink. Then the flames and smell of sulphur which gave warning of the approaching fire drove the others to take flight and roused him to stand up. He stood leaning on two slaves and then suddenly collapsed, I imagine because the dense fumes choked his breathing by blocking his windpipe which was constitutionally weak and narrow and often inflamed. When daylight returned on the 26th—two days after the last day he had seen—his body was found intact and uninjured, still fully clothed and looking more like sleep than death.

Q What do you think were the reactions of upper-class Romans to this event? How do you think lower-class Romans reacted?

conversation of the youths."[17] But the gladiatorial games served a purpose beyond mere entertainment. Like the other forms of public entertainment, the games fulfilled both a political and a social function. Certainly, the games served to divert the idle masses from political unrest. It was said of the emperor Trajan that he understood that although the distribution of grain and money satisfied the individual, spectacles were necessary for the "contentment of the masses."

Disaster in Southern Italy

Gladiatorial spectacles were contrived by humans, but the Roman Empire also experienced some horrific natural spectacles. One of the greatest was the eruption of Mount Vesuvius on August 24, 79. Although known to be a volcano, Vesuvius was thought to be extinct, its hillsides green with flourishing vineyards. Its eruption threw up thousands of tons of lava and ash. Toxic fumes killed many people, and the nearby city of Pompeii was quickly buried under volcanic ash. To the west, Herculaneum and other communities around the Bay of Naples were submerged beneath a mud flow (see the box above). Not for another 1,700 years were systematic excavations begun on the buried towns. The examination of their preserved remains has enabled archaeologists to reconstruct the everyday life and art of these Roman towns. Their discovery in the eighteenth century was an important force in stimulating both scholarly and public interest in Classical antiquity and helped give rise to the Neoclassical style of that century.

The Art of Medicine

Although early Romans had no professional physicians, they did possess an art of medicine. Early Roman medicine was essentially herbal. The *paterfamilias* would prepare various remedies to heal wounds and cure illnesses. Knowledge of the healing properties of plants was passed down from generation to generation. This traditional approach to medicine continued in the Early Empire. Of course, numerous recipes for nonillnesses, such as remedies to prevent baldness, were also passed on. One such formula consisted of wine, saffron, pepper, vinegar, *laserpicium* (the queen of Roman medicinal plants, now extinct), and rat dung.

As in other areas of Roman life, Greek influence was also felt in medicine. At the end of the third century B.C.E., scientific medicine entered the Roman world through professional practitioners from the Hellenistic world. Doctors became fashionable in Rome, although prejudice against them was never completely abandoned. Many were Greek slaves who belonged to the households of large aristocratic families. The first public doctors in Rome were attached to the Roman army. Military practices were then extended to imperial officials and their families in the provinces and included the establishment of public hospitals. Gladiatorial schools had their own resident doctors as well. In fact, one of the most famous physicians, the Greek Galen (129–199), emerged from the ranks of gladiatorial doctors to become court physician to the emperor Marcus Aurelius. Roman scientific medicine also witnessed the development of numerous specialists. For example, Alcon, the famous surgeon of the Flavian age, specialized in bone diseases and hernia operations.

Slaves and Their Masters

The number of slaves had increased dramatically in the Roman Republic as the empire was expanded through warfare. Consequently, slaves were highly visible in the Early Empire. The residences of the rich were filled with slaves. Possessing a large number of slaves was a status symbol; a single household might include dozens of slaves, serving as hairdressers, footmen, messengers, accountants, secretaries, carpenters, plumbers, librarians, goldsmiths, and doctors as well as ordinary domestic servants. The reliance on slaves, especially as skilled craftspeople, undoubtedly created unemployment among the free population. Some slaves worked at high-status jobs as architects and managers of businesses, while some imperial slaves held positions in the government bureaucracy. Slaves were also used on landed estates.

But the number of slaves probably peaked in the Early Empire. The defensive imperial policies pursued after Augustus led to a decline in the supply of slaves from foreign conquest. Manumission also contributed to the decline in the number of slaves. It had been customary in Rome for "good masters" to free their slaves, especially well-educated ones or good workers. Although freedmen became Roman citizens, they were not given full rights of citizenship. They could vote but not run for office.

Many authors have commented on the supposed advance in humanitarian attitudes toward slaves in the Early Empire, especially in the second century. They argue that the philosophy of Stoicism, with its emphasis on the universality of humanity, had an influence in this direction. Seneca stressed the need for kindness to slaves. Very likely, however, the practical Romans were as much, if not more, concerned about the usefulness of their slaves than about any humanitarian attitudes. New laws in the second century moralized more than they actually improved the condition of slaves. Hadrian, for example, forbade the sale of slaves for immoral or gladiatorial purposes. Such laws had little impact, however, on how masters actually treated their slaves. Despite the changes, there were still instances of slaves murdering their owners, and Romans continued to live in unspoken fear of their slaves (see the box on p. 168).

The Upper-Class Roman Family

By the second century C.E., significant changes were occurring in the Roman family. The foundations of the authority of the *paterfamilias* over his family, which had already begun to weaken in the late Republic, were further undermined. The *paterfamilias* no longer had absolute authority over his children; he could no longer sell his children into slavery or have them put to death. Moreover, the husband's absolute authority over his wife also disappeared, a process that had begun in the late Republic. In the Early Empire, the idea of male guardianship continued to weaken significantly, and by the late second century, it had become a mere formality.

Upper-class Roman women in the Early Empire had considerable freedom and independence. They had acquired the right to own, inherit, and dispose of property. Upper-class women could attend races, the theater, and events in the amphitheater, although in the latter two places they were forced to sit in separate female sections. Moreover, ladies of rank were still accompanied by maids and companions when they went out. Some women operated businesses, such as shipping firms. Women still could not participate in politics, but the Early Empire saw a number of important women who influenced politics through their husbands or sons, including Livia, the wife of Augustus; Agrippina, the mother of Nero; and Plotina, the wife of Trajan.

At the end of the first century and beginning of the second, there was a noticeable decline in the number of children among the upper classes, a trend that had already begun in the late Republic. Especially evident was

The Roman Fear of Slaves

The lowest stratum of the Roman population consisted of slaves. They were used extensively in households and the court, as craftspeople in industrial enterprises, as business managers, and in numerous other ways. Although some historians have argued that slaves were treated more humanely during the Early Empire, these selections by the Roman historian Tacitus and the Roman statesman Pliny indicate that slaves still rebelled against their masters because of mistreatment. Many masters continued to live in fear of their slaves, as witnessed by the saying "as many enemies as you have slaves."

Tacitus, *The Annals of Imperial Rome*

The City Prefect, Lucius Pedanius Secundus, was murdered by one of his slaves [in 61 C.E.]. Either Pedanius had refused to free the murderer after agreeing to a price, or the slave, in a homosexual infatuation, found competition from his master intolerable. After the murder, ancient custom required that every slave residing under the same roof must be executed. But a crowd gathered, eager to save so many innocent lives; and rioting began. The senate-house was besieged. Inside, there was feeling against excessive severity, but the majority opposed any change. Among the latter was Gaius Cassius Longinus, who when his turn came spoke as follows. . . .

"An ex-consul has been deliberately murdered by a slave in his own home. None of his fellow-slaves prevented or betrayed the murderer, though the senatorial decree threatening the whole household with execution still stands. Exempt them from the penalty if you like. But then, if the City Prefect was not important enough to be immune, who will be? Who will have enough slaves to protect him if Pedanius's 400 were too few? Who can rely on his household's help if even fear for their own lives does not make them shield us?" [The sentence of death was carried out.]

Pliny, Letter to Acilius

This horrible affair demands more publicity than a letter—Larcius Macedo, a senator and expraetor, has fallen a victim to his own slaves. Admittedly he was a cruel and overbearing master, too ready to forget that his father had been a slave, or perhaps too keenly conscious of it. He was taking a bath in his house at Formiae when suddenly he found himself surrounded; one slave seized him by the throat while the others struck his face and hit him in the chest and stomach and—shocking to say—in his private parts. When they thought he was dead they threw him on to the hot pavement, to make sure he was not still alive. Whether unconscious or feigning to be so, he lay there motionless, thus making them believe that he was quite dead. Only then was he carried out, as if he had fainted with the heat, and received by his slaves who had remained faithful, while his concubines ran up, screaming fanatically. Roused by their cries and revived by the cooler air he opened his eyes and made some movement to show that he was alive, it being now safe to do so. The guilty slaves fled, but most of them have been arrested and a search is being made for the others. Macedo was brought back to life with difficulty, but only for a few days; at least he died with the satisfaction of having revenged himself, for he lived to see the same punishment meted out as for murder. There you see the dangers, outrages, and insults to which we are exposed. No master can feel safe because he is kind and considerate; for it is their brutality, not their reasoning capacity, which leads slaves to murder masters.

Q What do these selections reveal about the practice of slavery in the Roman Empire? What were Roman attitudes toward the events discussed in these documents?

an increase in childless marriages. Despite imperial laws aimed at increasing the number of children, the low birthrate persisted. Not only did **infanticide** continue to be practiced, but upper-class Romans also used contraception and abortion to limit their families. There were numerous techniques for contraception. Though highly touted, amulets, magical formulas, and potions to induce temporary sterility proved ineffective, as did the rhythm method, since Roman medical writers believed that a woman was most fertile just when menstruation was ending. A more dependable practice involved the use of oils, ointments, and soft wool to obstruct the opening of the uterus. Contraceptive techniques for males were also advocated. An early version of a condom used the bladder of a goat, but it was prohibitively expensive. Although the medical sources do not mention it, the Romans may also have used the ubiquitous coitus interruptus. Abortion was practiced, using drugs or surgical instruments. Ovid chastises Corinna: "Ah, women, why will you thrust and pierce with the instrument, and give dire poisons to your children yet unborn?"[18]

Women also faced great dangers in childbirth. They gave birth at home with the assistance of a midwife and a few female relatives. Fathers-to-be and other males were not present. Although exact numbers are not available, we do know that many upper-class women between the ages of sixteen and thirty-five died in childbirth. Prominent women who died in childbirth or soon after due to complications include Cicero's daughter Tullia and Caesar's daughter Julia.

Transformation of the Roman World: Crises in the Third Century

Focus Question: What political, military, economic, and social problems did the Roman Empire face during the third century?

During the reign of Marcus Aurelius, the last of the five good emperors, a number of natural catastrophes struck Rome. Floods of the Tiber, famine, and plague brought back from the east by the army led to considerable loss of population and a shortage of military manpower. To many Romans, these natural disasters seemed to portend an ominous future for Rome. New problems arose soon after the death of Marcus Aurelius.

Political and Military Woes

Unlike the first four good emperors, who chose capable successors by adopting competent men as their sons, Marcus Aurelius allowed his own son, Commodus (KAHM-uh-duss) (180–192), to become emperor. A cruel man, Commodus was a poor choice, and his assassination led to a brief renewal of civil war until Septimius Severus (sep-TIM-ee-uss se-VEER-uss) (193–211), who was born in North Africa and spoke Latin with an accent, used his legions to seize power. On his deathbed, Septimius Severus advised his sons, "Live in harmony, make the soldiers rich, and don't give a damn for anything else." His advice set the tone for the new dynasty he established. The Severan rulers (193–235) began to create a military monarchy. The army was expanded, soldiers' pay was increased, and military officers were appointed to important government positions. A new stability seemed at hand, but the increased power of the military led new military leaders to aspire to become emperor, and the military monarchy of the Severan rulers degenerated into military anarchy.

For the next fifty years (235–284), the empire was mired in the chaos of continual civil war. Contenders for the imperial throne found that bribing soldiers was an effective way to become emperor. In these five decades, there were twenty-two emperors, only two of whom did not meet a violent end. At the same time, the empire was beset by a series of invasions, no doubt encouraged by the internal turmoil. In the east, the Sassanid Persians made inroads into Roman territory. A fitting symbol of Rome's crisis was the capture of the Roman emperor, Valerian (253–260), by the Persians and his death in captivity, an event unprecedented in Roman history. Valerian's body was displayed in the chief towns of Persia. Germanic

Antikensammlung, Berlin//© Bildarchiv Preussischer Kulturbesitz/Art Resource, NY

Septimius Severus and His Family. This portrait, which was painted on wood about 200 C.E. and found in Egypt, is the only existing painted likeness of a Roman emperor. The emperor is portrayed with gray hair and beard in memory of Marcus Aurelius. To legitimize his authority, Septimius Severus had himself adopted into the Antonine dynasty, calling himself the son of Marcus Aurelius. The emperor stands next to his wife with their two sons in front of them. The face of his son Geta has been blotted out, no doubt by order of the other son standing next to him, Caracalla, who had his brother killed when he succeeded to the throne.

tribes also poured into the empire. The Goths overran the Balkans and moved into Greece and Asia Minor. The Franks advanced into Gaul and Spain. Not until the reign of Aurelian (aw-REEL-yun) (270–275) were most of the boundaries restored. Although he abandoned the Danubian province of Dacia, Aurelian reconquered Gaul and reestablished order in the east and along the Danube. He also built a new defensive wall around Rome to defend the city against invaders. Grateful citizens hailed him as "restorer of the world."

As civil wars and invasions wore down the central government, provinces began to break away from the empire. A military commander named Postumus seized control of Gaul and then gained the support of Britain and Spain. He defended his "Gallic empire" until he was killed by his own soldiers in 269. In the east, Zenobia (zuh-NOH-bee-uh), the wife of the ruler of Syria, seized power after his death and then in 270 extended her control over Egypt and much of Asia Minor. In 272, Emperor Aurelian ended this threat to imperial power by defeating Zenobia and her forces in Syria.

Economic and Social Crises

Invasions, civil wars, and a recurrence of the plague came close to causing an economic collapse of the Roman Empire in the third century. The population declined drastically, possibly by as much as one-third. There was a significant decline in trade and small industry. The manpower shortage created by the plague affected both military recruiting and the economy. Farm production deteriorated as fields were ravaged by barbarians and even more often by the defending Roman armies. Many farmers complained that Roman commanders and their soldiers were confiscating produce and livestock. Provincial governors seemed powerless to stop these depredations, and some even joined in the frenzy.

The monetary system began to show signs of collapse as a result of debased coinage and the onset of serious inflation. Gold coins disappeared from circulation, and silver coins were diluted. The standard coin, the denarius, was now worth less than half of its first-century value. After further decline, it was replaced by new coins of even less value. Goods began to replace money as a medium of exchange.

Armies were needed more than ever, but financial strains made it difficult to enlist and pay the necessary soldiers. Short of cash, the imperial government paid its soldiers with produce, causing bitter resentment. Whereas in the second century the Roman army had been recruited among the inhabitants of frontier provinces, by the mid-third century, the state had to rely on hiring barbarians to fight under Roman commanders. These soldiers had no understanding of Roman traditions and no real attachment to either the empire or the emperors. By the end of the third century, a new form of political structure would emerge (see Chapter 7).

Transformation of the Roman World: The Rise of Christianity

Focus Question: What characteristics of Christianity enabled it to grow and ultimately to triumph?

The advent of Christianity marks a fundamental break with the dominant values of the Greco-Roman world. Christian views of God, human beings, and the world were quite different from those of the Greeks and Romans. Nevertheless, to understand the rise of Christianity, we must first examine both the religious environment of the Roman world and the Jewish background from which Christianity emerged.

The Religious World of the Roman Empire

Augustus had taken a number of steps to revive the Roman state religion, which had declined during the turmoil of the late Republic. The official state religion focused on the worship of a pantheon of Greco-Roman gods and goddesses, including Jupiter, Juno, Minerva, and Mars. Observance of proper ritual by state priests theoretically brought the Romans into proper relationship with the gods and guaranteed security, peace, and prosperity. The polytheistic Romans were extremely tolerant of other religions. The Romans allowed the worship of native gods and goddesses throughout their provinces and even adopted some of the local gods. In addition, the imperial cult of Roma and Augustus was developed to bolster support for the emperors. After Augustus, dead emperors deified by the Roman senate were included in the official imperial cult.

The desire for a more emotional spiritual experience led many people to the mystery religions of the Hellenistic east, which flooded into the western Roman world during the Early Empire. The mystery religions offered secret teachings that supposedly brought special benefits. They promised their followers advantages unavailable through Roman religion: an entry into a higher world of reality and the promise of a future life superior to the present one. They also featured elaborate rituals with deep emotional appeal. By participating in their ceremonies and performing their rites, an adherent could achieve communion with spiritual beings and undergo purification that opened the door to life after death.

Many mystery cults were vying for the attention of the Roman world. The cults of Cybele or the Great Mother and the Egyptian Isis had many followers, especially among the urban poor who gained little from the prosperity of the Early Empire. The cult of Isis, an Egyptian mother goddess, had become especially widespread throughout the empire by the first century C.E. Isis, seen in her role as the loving mother of Horus, appealed especially to women. Initiation into the cult of Isis came with a promise of immortality after death.

Perhaps the most important mystery cult was Mithraism. Mithra was the chief agent of Ahuramazda, the supreme god of light in Persian Zoroastrianism (see Chapter 2). In the Roman world, Mithra came to be identified with the sun god and was known by his Roman title of the Unconquered Sun. Mithraism had spread rapidly in Rome and the western provinces by the second century C.E. and was especially favored by soldiers, who viewed Mithra as their patron deity. It was a religion for men only and featured an initiation ceremony in which devotees were baptized in the blood of a sacrificed bull. Mithraists paid homage to the sun on the first day of the week (Sunday), commemorated the sun's birthday around December 25, and celebrated ceremonial meals.

The Jewish Background

Christianity emerged out of Judaism, and so it is to the Jewish political-religious world that we must turn to find the beginnings of Christianity. In Hellenistic times, the Jewish people had enjoyed considerable independence under their Seleucid rulers (see Chapter 4). Roman involvement with the Jews began in 63 B.C.E., and by 6 C.E., Judaea had been made a province and placed under the direction of a Roman procurator. But unrest continued, augmented by divisions among the Jews themselves. The Sadducees favored a rigid adherence to Hebrew law, rejected the possibility of personal immortality, and favored cooperation with the Romans. The Pharisees adhered strictly to Jewish ritual and, although they wanted Judaea to be free from Roman control, did not advocate violent means to achieve this goal. The Essenes were a Jewish sect that lived in a religious community near the Dead Sea. As revealed in the Dead Sea Scrolls, a collection of documents first discovered in 1947, the Essenes, like many other Jews, awaited a Messiah who would save Israel from oppression, usher in the kingdom of God, and establish a paradise on earth. A fourth group, the Zealots, were militant extremists who advocated the violent overthrow of Roman rule. A Jewish revolt in 66 C.E. was crushed by the Romans four years later. The Jewish Temple in Jerusalem was destroyed, and Roman power once more stood supreme in Judaea.

The Origins of Christianity

Jesus of Nazareth (c. 6 B.C.E.–30 C.E.) was a Palestinian Jew who grew up in Galilee, an important center of the militant Zealots. He began his itinerant public preaching as a young adult amid the confusion and conflict in Judaea. Jesus's message was basically simple. He reassured his fellow Jews that he did not plan to undermine their traditional religion: "Do not think that I have come to abolish the Law or the Prophets; I have not come to abolish them but to fulfill them."[19] According to Jesus, what was important was not strict adherence to the letter of the law and attention to rules and prohibitions but the transformation of the inner person: "So in everything, do to others what you would have them do to you, for this sums up the Law and the Prophets."[20] God's command was simply to love God and one another: "Love the Lord your God with all your heart and with all your soul and with all your mind and with all your strength. The second is this: Love your neighbor as yourself."[21] In the Sermon on the Mount (see the box on p. 172), Jesus presented the ethical concepts—humility, charity, and brotherly love—that would form the basis for the value system of medieval Western civilization. As we have seen, these were not the values of Classical Greco-Roman civilization.

Although some Jews welcomed Jesus as the Messiah who would save Israel from oppression and establish God's kingdom on earth, Jesus spoke of a heavenly kingdom, not an earthly one: "My kingdom is not of this world."[22] Consequently, he disappointed the radicals. At the same time, conservative religious leaders believed Jesus was another false Messiah who was undermining

Catacomb of S. Domitilla, Rome//© Scala/Art Resource, NY

Jesus and His Apostles. Pictured is a fourth-century fresco from a Roman catacomb depicting Jesus and his apostles. Catacombs were underground cemeteries where early Christians buried their dead. Christian tradition holds that in times of imperial repression, Christians withdrew to the catacombs to pray and hide.

Christian Ideals: The Sermon on the Mount

Christianity was simply one of many religions competing for attention in the Roman Empire during the first and second centuries. The rise of Christianity marked a fundamental break with the value system of the upper-class elites who dominated the world of Classical antiquity. As these excerpts from the Sermon on the Mount in the Gospel of Matthew illustrate, Christians emphasized humility, charity, brotherly love, and a belief in the inner being and a spiritual kingdom superior to this material world. These values and principles were not those of Classical Greco-Roman civilization as exemplified in the words and deeds of its leaders.

The Gospel According to Matthew

Now when he saw the crowds, he went up on a mountainside and sat down. His disciples came to him, and he began to teach them saying:

Blessed are the poor in spirit: for theirs is the kingdom of heaven.
Blessed are those who mourn: for they will be comforted.
Blessed are the meek: for they will inherit the earth.
Blessed are those who hunger and thirst for righteousness: for they will be filled.
Blessed are the merciful: for they will be shown mercy.
Blessed are the pure in heart: for they will see God.
Blessed are the peacemakers: for they will be called sons of God.
Blessed are those who are persecuted because of righteousness: for theirs is the kingdom of heaven. . . .

You have heard that it was said, "Eye for eye, and tooth for tooth." But I tell you, Do not resist an evil person. If someone strikes you on the right cheek, turn to him the other also. . . .

You have heard that it was said, "Love your neighbor, and hate your enemy." But I tell you, Love your enemies and pray for those who persecute you. . . .

Do not store up for yourselves treasures on earth, where moth and rust destroy, and where thieves break in and steal. But store up for yourselves treasures in heaven, where moth and rust do not destroy, and where thieves do not break in and steal. For where your treasure is, there your heart will be also. . . .

No one can serve two masters. Either he will hate the one and love the other, or he will be devoted to the one and despise the other. You cannot serve both God and Money.

Therefore I tell you, do not worry about your life, what you will eat or drink; or about your body, what you will wear. Is not life more important than food, and the body more important than clothes? Look at the birds of the air; they do not sow or reap to store away in barns, and yet your heavenly Father feeds them. Are you not much more valuable than they? . . . So do not worry, saying, What shall we eat? or What shall we drink? or What shall we wear? For the pagans run after all these things, and your heavenly Father knows that you need them. But seek first his kingdom and his righteousness, and all these things will be given to you as well.

Q What were the ideals of early Christianity? How do they differ from the values and principles of Classical Greco-Roman civilization?

respect for traditional Jewish religion. To the Roman authorities of Palestine and their local allies, the Nazarene was a potential revolutionary who might transform Jewish expectations of a messianic kingdom into a revolt against Rome. Therefore, Jesus found himself denounced on many sides and was given over to the Roman authorities. The procurator Pontius Pilate ordered his crucifixion. But that did not solve the problem. A few loyal disciples of Jesus spread the story, common to mystery cults (see Chapter 4), that he had overcome death, been resurrected, and then ascended into heaven. The belief in Jesus's resurrection became an important tenet of Christian doctrine. Jesus was now hailed by his followers as the "anointed one" (*Christ* in Greek), the Messiah who would return and usher in the kingdom of God on earth.

THE IMPORTANCE OF PAUL Christianity began, then, as a religious movement within Judaism and was viewed that way by Roman authorities for many decades. Although tradition holds that one of Jesus's disciples, Peter, founded the Christian church at Rome, the most important figure in early Christianity after Jesus was Paul of Tarsus (c. 5–c. 67). Paul reached out to non-Jews and transformed Christianity from a Jewish sect into a broader religious movement.

Called the "second founder of Christianity," Paul was a Jewish Roman citizen who had been strongly influenced by Hellenistic Greek culture. He believed that the message of Jesus should be preached not only to Jews but to Gentiles (non-Jews) as well. Paul was responsible for founding Christian communities throughout Asia Minor and along the shores of the Aegean.

It was Paul who provided a universal foundation for the spread of Jesus's ideas. He taught that Jesus was, in effect, a savior-God, the son of God, who had come to earth to save all humans, who were basically sinners as a result of Adam's original sin of disobedience against God. By his death, Jesus had atoned for the sins of all humans and made it possible for all men and women to experience a new beginning with the potential for individual salvation. By accepting Jesus as their savior, they, too, could be saved.

THE SPREAD OF CHRISTIANITY At first, Christianity spread slowly. Although the teachings of early Christianity were mostly disseminated by the preaching of convinced Christians, written materials also appeared. Paul had written a series of letters, or epistles, outlining Christian beliefs for different Christian communities. Some of Jesus's disciples may also have preserved some of the sayings of the master in writing and would have passed on personal memories that became the basis of the written gospels—the "good news" concerning Jesus of Matthew, Mark, Luke, and John—which by the end of the first century C.E. became the authoritative record of Jesus's life and teachings and formed the core of the New Testament. Recently, some scholars have argued that other gospels, such as that of Thomas, were rejected because they deviated from the beliefs about Jesus held by the emerging church leaders.

Although Jerusalem was the first center of Christianity, its destruction by the Romans in 70 C.E. left individual Christian churches with considerable independence. By 100, Christian churches had been established in most of the major cities of the east and in some places in the western part of the empire. Many early Christians came from the ranks of Hellenized Jews and the Greek-speaking populations of the east. But in the second and third centuries, an increasing number of followers were Latin-speaking people. A Latin translation of the Greek New Testament that appeared soon after 200 aided this process.

EARLY CHRISTIAN COMMUNITIES Early Christian groups met in private homes in the evening to share a common meal called an *agape* or love feast and to celebrate what became known as the sacrament of the **Eucharist** or Lord's Supper—the communal celebration of Jesus's Last Supper:

> While they were eating, Jesus took bread, gave thanks and broke it, and gave it to the disciples, saying, Take and eat; this is my body. Then he took the cup, gave thanks, and offered it to them, saying, Drink from it, all of you. This is my blood of the covenant, which is poured out for many for the forgiveness of sins.[23]

Early Christian communities were loosely organized, with both men and women playing significant roles. Some women held important positions, often as preachers. Local churches were under the leadership of boards of elders (*presbyters*), but by the beginning of the second century, officials known as *bishops* came to exercise considerable authority over the presbyters. These bishops based their superior position on apostolic succession—as the successors to Jesus's original twelve apostles (disciples), they were living representatives of Jesus's power. As Ignatius of Antioch wrote in 107, "It is clear that we must regard a bishop as the Lord Himself.... Your clergy... are attuned to their bishop like the strings of a harp, and the result is a hymn of praise to Jesus Christ from minds that are in unison."[24] Bishops were invariably men, a clear indication that by the second century C.E., most Christian communities were following the views of Paul that Christian women should be subject to Christian men.

Although some of the fundamental values of Christianity differed markedly from those of the Greco-Roman world, the Romans initially did not pay much attention to the Christians, whom they regarded at first as simply another sect of Judaism. The structure of the Roman Empire itself aided the growth of Christianity. Christian missionaries, including some of Jesus's original twelve apostles, used Roman roads to travel throughout the empire spreading their "good news."

THE CHANGING ROMAN VIEW OF CHRISTIANITY As the popular appeal of Christianity grew, the Roman attitude toward it began to change. As we have seen, the Romans were tolerant of other religions except when they threatened public order or public morals. Many Romans came to view Christians as harmful to the order of the Roman state. These views were often based on misperceptions. The celebration of the Lord's Supper, for example, led to rumors that Christians practiced horrible crimes, such as the ritualistic murder of children. Although we know these rumors are untrue, some Romans believed them and used them to incite people against the Christians during times of crisis. Moreover, because Christians held their meetings in secret and seemed to be connected to Christian groups in distant areas, the government could view them as potentially dangerous to the state.

Some Romans felt that Christians were overly exclusive and hence harmful to the community and public order. The Christians did not recognize other gods and therefore abstained from public festivals honoring the popular deities. Finally, Christians refused to participate in the worship of the state gods and the imperial cult. Since the Romans regarded these as important to the state, the Christians' refusal undermined the security of the state and hence constituted an act of treason, punishable by death. It was also proof of atheism (disbelief in the gods) and subject to punishment on those grounds. But to the Christians, who believed there was only one real God, the worship of state gods and the emperors was idolatry and would endanger their own salvation.

Roman persecution of Christians in the first and second centuries was never systematic but only sporadic and local. Persecution began during the reign of Nero. After the fire that destroyed much of Rome, the emperor used the Christians as scapegoats, accusing them of arson and hatred of the human race and subjecting them to cruel deaths in Rome. In the second century, Christians were often ignored as harmless (see the box on p. 174). By the end of the reigns of the five good emperors, Christians still represented a small minority, but one of considerable

Opposing ≶VIEWPOINTS

Roman Authorities and a Christian on Christianity

At first, Roman authorities were uncertain how to deal with the Christians. In the second century, as seen in the following exchange between Pliny the Younger and the emperor Trajan, Christians were often viewed as harmless and yet were subject to persecution if they persisted in being Christians. Pliny was governor of the province of Bithynia in northwestern Asia Minor (present-day Turkey). He wrote to the emperor for advice about how to handle people accused of being Christians. Trajan's response reflects the general approach toward Christians by the emperors of the second century. The final selection is taken from *Against Celsus,* written about 246 by Origen of Alexandria. In it, Origen defended the value of Christianity against Celsus, a philosopher who had written an attack on Christians and their teachings.

An Exchange Between Pliny and Trajan

Pliny to Trajan

It is my custom to refer all my difficulties to you, Sir, for no one is better able to resolve my doubts and to inform my ignorance.

I have never been present at an examination of Christians. Consequently, I do not know the nature of the extent of the punishments usually meted out to them, nor the grounds for starting an investigation and how far it should be pressed. . . .

For the moment this is the line I have taken with all persons brought before me on the charge of being Christians. I have asked them in person if they are Christians, and if they admit it, I repeat the question a second and third time, with a warning of the punishment awaiting them. If they persist, I order them to be led away for execution; for, whatever the nature of their admission, I am convinced that their stubbornness and unshakable obstinacy ought not to go unpunished. There have been others similarly fanatical who are Roman citizens. I have entered them on the list of persons to be sent to Rome for trial.

Now that I have begun to deal with this problem, as so often happens, the charges are becoming more widespread and increasing in variety. An anonymous pamphlet has been circulated which contains the names of a number of accused persons. . . .

I have therefore postponed any further examination and hastened to consult you. The question seems to me to be worthy of your consideration, especially in view of the number of persons endangered; for a great many individuals of every age and class, both men and women, are being brought to trial, and this is likely to continue. It is not only the towns, but villages and rural districts too which are infected through contact with this wretched cult. I think though that it is still possible for it to be checked and directed to better ends, for there is no doubt that people have begun to throng the temples which had been almost entirely deserted for a long time; the sacred rites which had been allowed to lapse are being performed again, and flesh of sacrificial victims is on sale everywhere, though up till recently scarcely anyone could be found to buy it. It is easy to infer from this that a great many people could be reformed if they were given an opportunity to repent.

Trajan to Pliny

You have followed the right course of procedure, my dear Pliny, in your examination of the cases of persons charged with being Christians, for it is impossible to lay down a general rule to a fixed formula. These people must not be hunted out; if they are brought before you and the charge against them is proved, they must be punished, but in the case of anyone who denies that he is a Christian, and makes it clear that he is not by offering prayers to our gods, he is to be pardoned as a result of his repentance however suspect his past conduct may be. But pamphlets circulated anonymously must play no part in any accusation. They create the worst sort of precedent and are quite out of keeping with the spirit of our age.

Origen, *Against Celsus*

He [Celsus] says that Christians perform their rites and teach their doctrines in secret, and they do this with good reason to escape the death penalty that hangs over them. He compares the danger to the risks encountered for the sake of philosophy as by Socrates. . . . I reply to this that in Socrates' cases the Athenians at once regretted what they had done, and cherished no grievance against him. . . . But in the case of the Christians the Roman Senate, the contemporary emperors, the army, . . . and the relatives of believers fought against the gospel and would have hindered it; and it would have been defeated by the combined force of so many unless it had overcome and risen above the opposition by divine power, so that it has conquered the whole world that was conspiring against it. . . .

He [also] ridicules our teachers of the gospel who try to elevate the soul in every way to the Creator of the universe. . . . He compares them [Christians] to wool-workers in houses, cobblers, laundry-workers, and the

(continued)

most obtuse yokels, as if they called children quite in infancy and women to evil practices, telling them to leave their father and teachers and to follow them. But let Celsus . . . tell us how we make women and children leave noble and sound teaching, and call them to wicked practices. But he will not be able to prove anything of any kind against us. On the contrary, we deliver women from licentiousness and from perversion caused by their associates, and from all mania for theaters and dancing, and from superstition, while we make boys self-controlled when they come to the age of puberty and burn with desires for sexual pleasure, showing them not only the disgrace of their sins, but also what a state these pleasures produce in the souls of bad men, and what penalties they will suffer and how they will be punished.

Q What were Pliny's personal opinions of Christians? Why was he willing to execute them? What was Trajan's response, and what were its consequences for the Christians? What major points did Origen make about the benefits of the Christian religion? Why did the Roman authorities consider these ideas dangerous to the Roman state?

strength. That strength lay in their conviction of the rightness of their path, a conviction that had been reinforced by the willingness of the first Christians to become martyrs for their faith.

CHRISTIAN MARTYRS From its beginning, Christianity was characterized by the willingness of many of its followers to accept death for their faith. In 177, a group of fifty Christians in Lyon were sacrificed to wild beasts. In Asia, Polycarp, the bishop of Smyrna, when told to renounce his faith, replied, "I have served [Christ] for eighty-six years and he has done me no wrong. How can I blaspheme my king and my savior?" Polycarp, who had played an important role in spreading Christian teachings in Asia, was burned at the stake as "an offering ready and acceptable to God." In Africa, in 180, a small group of Christian men and women from near Carthage were put on trial and condemned to die: "having confessed that they live according to the Christian religion, since they obstinately persisted when given the opportunity of returning to Roman ways, [they] are to be executed by the sword." The Christians responded, "We give thanks to God."[25]

For many Christians, martyrdom meant achieving salvation by following the example of Jesus's sacrificial suffering and death on the cross. Indeed, Tertullian (tur-TULL-yun) (c. 160–c. 225), a Christian writer from Carthage, declared that Christian martyrs were "witnesses to the Grace of God." By imitating Jesus, the Christian martyrs established a model to be followed by other Christians. Said Tertullian, "No one would want to be killed unless possessed of the truth," making the blood of martyrs "the seed of the church."[26]

The Growth of Christianity

The sporadic persecution of Christians by the Romans in the first and second centuries did nothing to stop the growth of Christianity. In fact, it served to strengthen Christianity as an institution in the second and third centuries by causing it to shed the loose structure of the first century and move toward a more centralized organization of its various church communities. Crucial to this change was the emerging role of the bishops. Though still chosen by the community, bishops began to assume more control, with the bishop serving as leader and the presbyters emerging as clergy subject to the bishop's authority. By the third century, bishops were nominated by the clergy, simply approved by the congregation, and then officially ordained into office. The Christian church was creating a well-defined hierarchical structure in which the bishops and clergy were salaried officers separate from the laity or regular church members.

CHRISTIANITY AND GRECO-ROMAN CULTURE Many early Christians expressed considerable hostility toward the pagan culture of the Classical world. Tertullian had proclaimed: "What has Jerusalem to do with Athens, the Church with the Academy, the Christian with the heretic? . . . After Jesus Christ we have no need of speculation, after the Gospel no need of research."[27] To many early Christians, the Bible contained all the knowledge anyone needed.

Others, however, thought it was not possible to separate Christian theological thought from Classical traditions and education and encouraged Christians to absorb the Classical heritage. As it spread in the eastern Roman world, Christianity adopted Greek as its language. The New Testament was written in Greek. Christians also turned to Greek thought for help in expressing complicated theological concepts. An especially important influence was Neoplatonism, a revival of Platonic thought that reached its high point in the third century C.E. Neoplatonists believed that one could use reason to perceive the link between the invisible spiritual world and the visible material world. Christian theologians used Neoplatonic concepts to explain doctrines on Jesus, especially the distinction between his human and divine natures. In many ways, then, Christianity served to preserve Greco-Roman culture.

THE APPEAL OF CHRISTIANITY Christianity grew slowly in the first century, took root in the second, and had spread widely by the third. Why was Christianity able to attract so many followers? Historians are not really sure but have offered several answers. Certainly, the Christian message had much to offer the Roman world. The promise of salvation, made possible by Jesus's death and resurrection, had immense appeal in a world full of suffering and injustice. Christianity seemed to imbue life with a meaning and purpose beyond the simple material things of everyday reality. Second, Christianity was not entirely unfamiliar. It could be viewed as simply another eastern mystery religion, offering immortality as the result of the sacrificial death of a savior-god. At the same time, it offered advantages that the other mystery religions lacked. Jesus had been a human figure, not a mythological one, such as Isis or Mithra. Moreover, Christianity had universal appeal. Unlike Mithraism, it was not restricted to men. Furthermore, it did not require a difficult or expensive initiation rite as other mystery religions did. Initiation was accomplished simply by baptism—a purification by water—by which one entered into direct communion with Jesus. In addition, Christianity gave new meaning to life and offered what the Roman state religions could not—a personal relationship with God and a link to higher worlds.

Finally, Christianity fulfilled the human need to belong. Christians formed communities bound to one another in which people could express their love by helping each other and offering assistance to the poor, sick, widows, and orphans. Christianity satisfied the need to belong in a way that the huge, impersonal, and remote Roman Empire could never do.

Christianity proved attractive to all classes. The promise of eternal life was for all—rich, poor, aristocrats, slaves, men, and women. As Paul stated in his Epistle to the Colossians: "And [you] have put on the new self, which is being renewed in knowledge in the image of its Creator. Here there is no Greek nor Jew, circumcised or uncircumcised, barbarian, Scythian, slave or free, but Christ is all, and is in all."[28] Although it did not call for revolution or social upheaval, Christianity emphasized a sense of spiritual equality for all people.

WOMEN AND EARLY CHRISTIANITY As we have seen, first-century C.E. Christian communities had allowed both men and women to play significant roles. By the second century, however, men had gained control of church organization and subjected women to secondary roles. Women, as Paul had argued, should be subject to men.

Nevertheless, many women found that Christianity offered them new roles and new forms of companionship with other women. Christian women fostered the new religion in their own homes and preached their convictions to other people in their towns and villages. Many also died for their faith. Perpetua (d. 203) was an aristocratic woman who converted to Christianity. Her pagan family begged her to renounce her new faith, but she refused. Arrested by the Roman authorities, she chose instead to die for her faith and was one of a group of Christians who were slaughtered by wild beasts in the arena at Carthage on March 7, 203.

PERSECUTION As the Christian church became more organized, two emperors in the third century responded with more systematic persecutions. The emperor Decius (DEE-she-uss) (249–251) blamed the Christians for the disasters befalling the Roman Empire in the terrible third century: their refusal to acknowledge the state gods had brought the gods' retribution against the Romans. Moreover, as the administrative organization of the church grew, Christianity appeared to Decius even more like a state within a state that was undermining the empire. Accordingly, he initiated the first systematic persecution of Christians. All citizens were required to appear before their local magistrates and offer sacrifices to the Roman gods. Christians, of course, refused to do so. Decius's scheme, however, failed to work. Not only did local officials fail to cooperate, but Decius's reign was not very long. The last great persecution was by Diocletian (dy-uh-KLEE-shun) at the beginning of the fourth century, but by then it was too late. Christianity had become too strong to be eradicated by force.

CHAPTER SUMMARY

The Roman Republic had created one of the largest empires in antiquity, but its republican institutions had proved inadequate for the task of ruling an empire. After a series of bloody civil wars, Augustus created a new order that began the Roman Empire. Although he never declared the Republic dead and continued to give the senate a role in governing, most political power remained in the hands of the *princeps,* or chief citizen, as he called himself. Significantly, the army swore loyalty to him, and the restoration of peace soon made the new political order acceptable to most people in the empire.

Augustus established the Julio-Claudian dynasty, which lasted until 68. In 69, Vespasian, a successful general, founded the Flavian dynasty after a year of civil war. This dynasty began to openly use the title of *imperator,* or emperor. In the second century, the five "good emperors" maintained a period of peace and prosperity in which trade flourished and the provinces were governed efficiently. Within their empire, the Romans were responsible for a remarkable series of achievements that were bequeathed to the future.

These achievements were fundamental to the development of Western civilization, a civilization that would arise for the most part in the lands in Europe conquered by the Romans, where Roman culture and political ideals were gradually spread. The Romance languages of today (French, Italian, Spanish, Portuguese, and Romanian) are based on Latin. Western practices of impartial justice and trial by jury owe much to Roman law. As great builders, the Romans left monuments to their skills throughout Europe, some of which, including aqueducts and roads, are still in use today. Other monuments provided models for public buildings in the West for hundreds of years. Aspects of Roman administrative practices survived in the Western world for centuries. The Romans also preserved the intellectual heritage of the Greco-Roman world of antiquity.

By the third century, however, the Roman world was suffering an era of decline. Generals fought each other in civil wars. Between the years 235 and 284, there were twenty-two emperors, and only two of them did not suffer a violent end. German tribes and Persian armies invaded the empire. There were plagues, population decline, and economic problems. At the same time, a new religion—Christianity—was spreading throughout the empire. Beginning among the followers of Jesus of Nazareth, Christianity, with its promise of salvation, its similarity to many mystery religions, and its universality as a religion for all—rich and poor, men and women, Greek and Roman—slowly gained acceptance. As we shall see in the next chapter, the response to the crises of the third century and the rise of Christianity would gradually bring a transformation of the Roman Empire in the fourth and fifth centuries.

CHAPTER TIMELINE

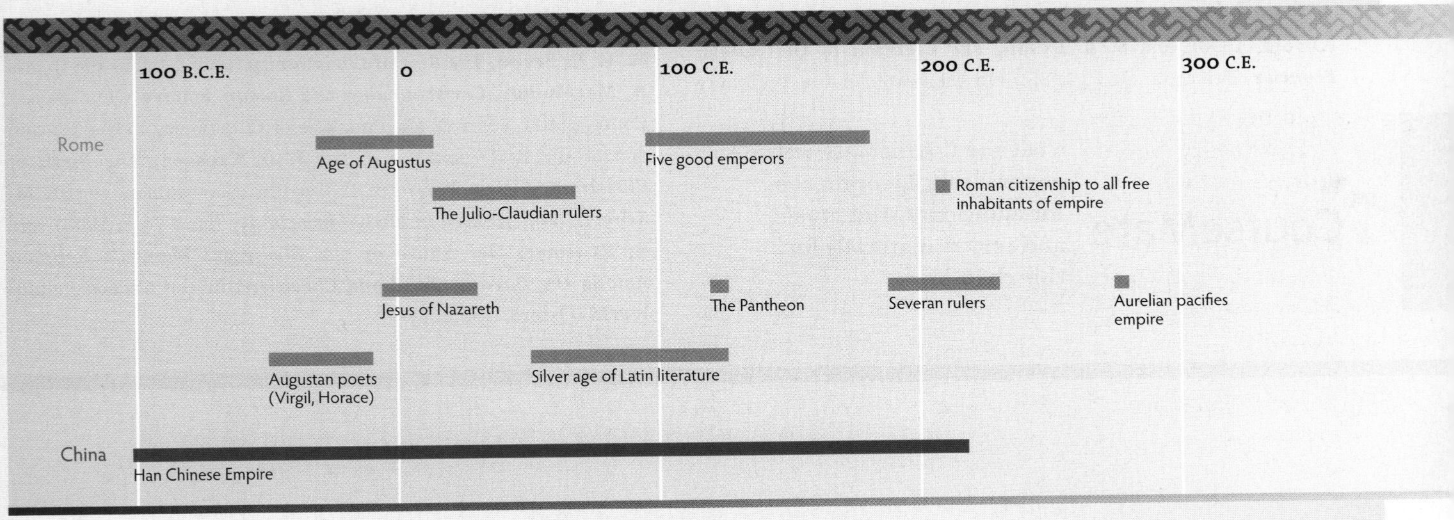

CHAPTER REVIEW

Upon Reflection

Q Was Augustus the last of the republicans or the first of the emperors? Why do you think so?

Q In what ways was the rule of the Roman emperors in the first and second centuries C.E. an improvement over the Republic of the first century B.C.E.? In what ways was their rule not an improvement over the last century of the Republic?

Q How do you explain the spread of Christianity in the Roman Empire?

Key Terms

principate (p. 148)
Romanization (p. 149)
auxiliaries (p. 150)
praetorian guard (p. 150)
Pax Romana (p. 155)
good emperors (p. 155)
coloni (p. 159)
infanticide (p. 168)
Eucharist (p. 173)

Suggestions for Further Reading

GENERAL HISTORIES OF THE ROMAN EMPIRE Good surveys of the Early Empire include **P. Garnsey** and **R. P. Saller, *The Roman Empire: Economy, Society and Culture*** (London, 1987); **C. Wells, *The Roman Empire,*** 2nd ed. (London, 1992); and **M. Goodman, *The Roman World, 44 B.C.–A.D. 180*** (London, 1997). On the crises of the third century, see **D. S. Potter, *The Roman Empire at Bay, A.D. 180–395*** (New York, 2004).

ROMAN EMPERORS Studies of Roman emperors of the first and second centuries include **A. Everitt, *Augustus: Life of Rome's First Emperor*** (New York, 2006); **R. Seager, *Tiberius,*** 2nd ed. (London, 2005); **S. Wilkinson, *Caligula*** (London, 2005); **E. Champlin, *Nero*** (Cambridge, Mass., 2003); **E. Speller, *Following Hadrian*** (Oxford, 2003); and **M. Hammond, *The Antonine Monarchy*** (Rome, 1959). See **P. Matyszak, *The Sons of Caesar: Imperial Rome's First Dynasty*** (London, 2006) on the Julio-Claudian rulers. On the wife of Augustus, see **A. A. Barrett, *Livia: First Lady of Imperial Rome*** (New Haven, Conn., 2002).

ROMAN ARMY AND PROVINCES The Roman army is examined in **J. B. Campbell, *The Emperor and the Roman Army*** (Oxford, 1984). On warfare, see **A. Goldsworthy, *Roman Warfare*** (New York, 2005). On the provinces and Roman foreign policy, see **B. Isaac, *The Limits of Empire: The Roman Empire in the East*** (Oxford, 1990); and **S. L. Dyson, *The Creation of the Roman Frontier*** (Princeton, N.J., 1985). On the battle in the Teutoburg Forest, see **P. S. Wells, *The Battle That Stopped Rome: Emperor Augustus, Arminius and the Slaughter of the Legions in the Teutoburg Forest*** (New York, 2003).

ROMAN CULTURE A good survey of Roman literature can be found in **R. M. Ogilvie, *Roman Literature and Society*** (Harmondsworth, England, 1980). A survey of Roman art can be found in **F. S. Kleiner, *A History of Roman Art*** (Belmont, Calif., 2006). Architecture is covered in the standard work by **J. B. Ward-Perkins, *Roman Imperial Architecture,*** rev. ed. (Harmondsworth, England, 1992). On the importance of concrete in Roman architecture, see **L. C. Lancaster, *Concrete Vaulted Construction in Imperial Rome*** (Cambridge, 2005).

ROMAN SOCIETY Various aspects of Roman society are covered in **L. Adkins** and **R. A. Adkins, *Handbook to Life in Ancient Rome*** (New York, 1994). Also useful on urban life is **J. E. Stambaugh, *The Ancient Roman City*** (Baltimore, 1988). On the gladiators, see **F. Meijer, *The Gladiators: History's Most Deadly Sport*** (Boston, 2005). Studies on Roman women include **S. Dixon, *Reading Roman Women*** (London, 2001), and **A. Fraschetti, *Roman Women,*** trans. **L. Lappan** (Chicago, 1999). On slavery, see **K. Bradley, *Slavery and Society at Rome*** (New York, 1994). On the poor, see **M. Atkins** and **R. Osborne, eds., *Poverty in the Roman World*** (Cambridge, 2006).

EARLY CHRISTIANITY Useful works on early Christianity include **W. H. C. Frend, *The Rise of Christianity*** (Philadelphia, 1984), and **R. MacMullen, *Christianizing the Roman Empire*** (New Haven, Conn., 1984). For a detailed analysis of Christianity in the 30s and 40s of the first century C.E., see **J. D. Crossan, *The Birth of Christianity*** (New York, 1998). On Christian women, see **D. M. Scholer, ed., *Women in Early Christianity*** (New York, 1993), and **R. Kraemer, *Her Share of the Blessings: Women's Religion Among the Pagans, Jews and Christians in the Graeco-Roman World*** (Oxford, 1995).

Kharbine-Tapabor/Collection Jean Vigne

A fifteenth-century manuscript illustration of Clovis, his wife Clotilde, and their four sons

CHAPTER 7

Late Antiquity and the Emergence of the Medieval World

CHAPTER OUTLINE AND FOCUS QUESTIONS

The Late Roman Empire

Q What reforms did Diocletian and Constantine institute, and to what extent were the reforms successful?

The Germanic Kingdoms

Q What changes did the Germanic peoples make to the political, economic, and social conditions of the Western Roman Empire? What were the main features of Germanic law and society, and how did they differ from those of the Romans?

Development of the Christian Church

Q How and why did the organization of the Christian church and its relations with the state change during the fourth and fifth centuries? What were the chief characteristics of Benedictine monasticism, and what role did monks play in both the conversion of Europe to Christianity and the intellectual life of the Germanic kingdoms?

The Byzantine Empire

Q How did the Byzantine Empire that had emerged by the eighth century differ from the empire of Justinian and from the Germanic kingdoms in the west?

The Rise of Islam

Q What was the basic message of Islam, and why was it able to expand so successfully?

CRITICAL THINKING

Q In what ways were the Byzantine and Islamic civilizations different from the civilization developing in western Europe? In what ways were they similar?

BY THE THIRD CENTURY, the Roman Empire was experiencing a number of problems as well as witnessing the growth of a new religion—Christianity. To restore the empire, the emperors Diocletian and Constantine initiated a number of reforms that created the so-called Late Empire. Constantine also converted to Christianity, starting a process that gave the Late Empire a new state religion.

After Constantine, the Late Roman Empire survived, but in the west it increasingly faced incursions of Germanic tribes. By the second half of the fifth century, new political arrangements were taking shape that brought the collapse of the old imperial structure in the west and the emergence of a series of Germanic kingdoms in western Europe that would form the basis of a new civilization. In these kingdoms, the Christian church also played a role as it drew these Germanic tribes to its faith.

The conversion to Christianity of the pagan leaders of the Germanic tribes was sometimes dramatic, at least as reported by the sixth-century historian Gregory of Tours. Clovis (KLOH-viss), leader of the Franks, married Clotilde, daughter of the king of the Burgundians. She was a Christian, but Clovis refused her pleas to become a Christian, telling her, "Your god can do nothing." But during a battle with the Alemanni, when Clovis's army was close to utter destruction, "he saw the danger; his heart was stirred; and he raised his eyes to heaven, saying, 'Jesus Christ, I beseech the glory of your aid. If you shall grant me victory over these enemies, I will believe in you and be baptized in your name.'" When he had uttered these words, the Alemanni began to flee. Clovis kept his vow and became a Christian.

While the Germanic kingdoms were putting down roots in the west, the eastern part of the old Roman Empire, increasingly Greek in culture, continued as the Byzantine Empire. Serving as a buffer between Europe and the peoples to the east, the Byzantine or Eastern Roman Empire also preserved the intellectual and legal accomplishments of Greek and Roman antiquity. At the same time, a new culture centered on Islam emerged in the east; it spread through large parts of the old Roman Empire, preserved much of Greek culture, and created its own flourishing civilization. This chapter, then, concerns the transformation of the Roman world in late antiquity, the heirs of the Roman Empire, and the new world—the medieval world—they began to create.

The Late Roman Empire

Focus Question: What reforms did Diocletian and Constantine institute, and to what extent were the reforms successful?

At the end of the third century and the beginning of the fourth, the Roman Empire gained a new lease on life through the efforts of two strong emperors, Diocletian and Constantine, who restored order and stability. The empire was virtually transformed into a new state, the Late Roman Empire, which included a new governmental structure, a rigid economic and social system, and a new state religion—Christianity.

The Reforms of Diocletian and Constantine

Diocletian had risen through the ranks to become a prominent military leader. After the murder of the emperor Numerian by his praetorian prefect, Diocletian executed the prefect and was then hailed as emperor by his soldiers. Diocletian's own rise to power led him to see the need for a new system for ruling the Roman Empire.

POLITICAL REFORMS Diocletian (284–305) created a new administrative system for a restructured empire. The number of provinces was increased to almost one hundred by creating smaller districts superintended by more officials. The provinces were in turn grouped into twelve dioceses, each headed by an official called a vicar. The twelve dioceses were grouped into four prefectures (see Map 7.1), and the entire Roman Empire was divided into two parts, east and west. Each part contained two prefectures and was ruled by an "Augustus." Diocletian ruled the east, and Maximian (mak-SIM-ee-un), a strong military commander, the west. Each Augustus was assisted by a chief lieutenant or "vice-emperor" called a "Caesar," who theoretically would eventually succeed to the position of Augustus. This new system was called the **tetrarchy** (rule by four). Diocletian had obviously come to believe that one man was incapable of ruling such an enormous empire, especially in view of the barbarian invasions of the third century. Each of the four tetrarchs—two Augusti and two Caesars—resided in a different administrative capital. Diocletian, for example, established his base at Nicomedia in Bithynia. Despite the appearance of four-man rule, however, it is important to note that Diocletian's military seniority enabled him to claim a higher status and hold the ultimate authority.

Soon after Diocletian's retirement in 305, a new struggle for power ensued. The victory of Constantine (306–337) in 312 led to his control of the entire west, although he continued to share imperial authority with Licinius (ly-SIN-ee-uss), a fellow emperor. Twelve years later, in 324, Constantine's army routed Licinius's forces, and Constantine established himself as the sole ruler.

Constantine continued and even expanded the autocratic policies of Diocletian. Under these two rulers, the Roman Empire was transformed into a system in which the emperor had far more personal power than Augustus, Trajan, or any of the other emperors had had during the *Pax Romana*. The emperor, now clothed in jewel-bedecked robes of gold and blue, was seen as a divinely sanctioned monarch whose will was law. Government officials were humble servants required to kneel before the emperor and kiss his robe. The Roman senate was stripped of any power and became merely the city council for Rome.

Diocletian and Constantine greatly strengthened and enlarged the administrative bureaucracies of the Roman Empire. Henceforth, civil and military bureaucracies were sharply separated. Each contained a hierarchy of officials who exercised control at the various levels. The emperor presided over both hierarchies and served as the only link between them. New titles of nobility—such as *illustres* (ee-loo-STRAYSS) ("illustrious ones") and *illustrissimi* (ee-loo-STREE-see-mee) ("most illustrious ones")—were instituted to dignify the holders of positions in the civil and military bureaucracies.

MILITARY REFORMS Additional military reforms were also instituted. The army was enlarged to 400,000 men, including units filled with Germans. By the end of Constantine's reign, a new organization of the army had also been put in place. Military forces were divided into two kinds: garrison troops, which were located on the frontiers and intended as a first line of defense against invaders, and mobile units, which were located behind the frontier but could be quickly moved to support frontier troops when the borders were threatened. This gave the empire greater flexibility in responding to invasion.

ECONOMIC AND SOCIAL TRENDS The political and military reforms of Diocletian and Constantine greatly

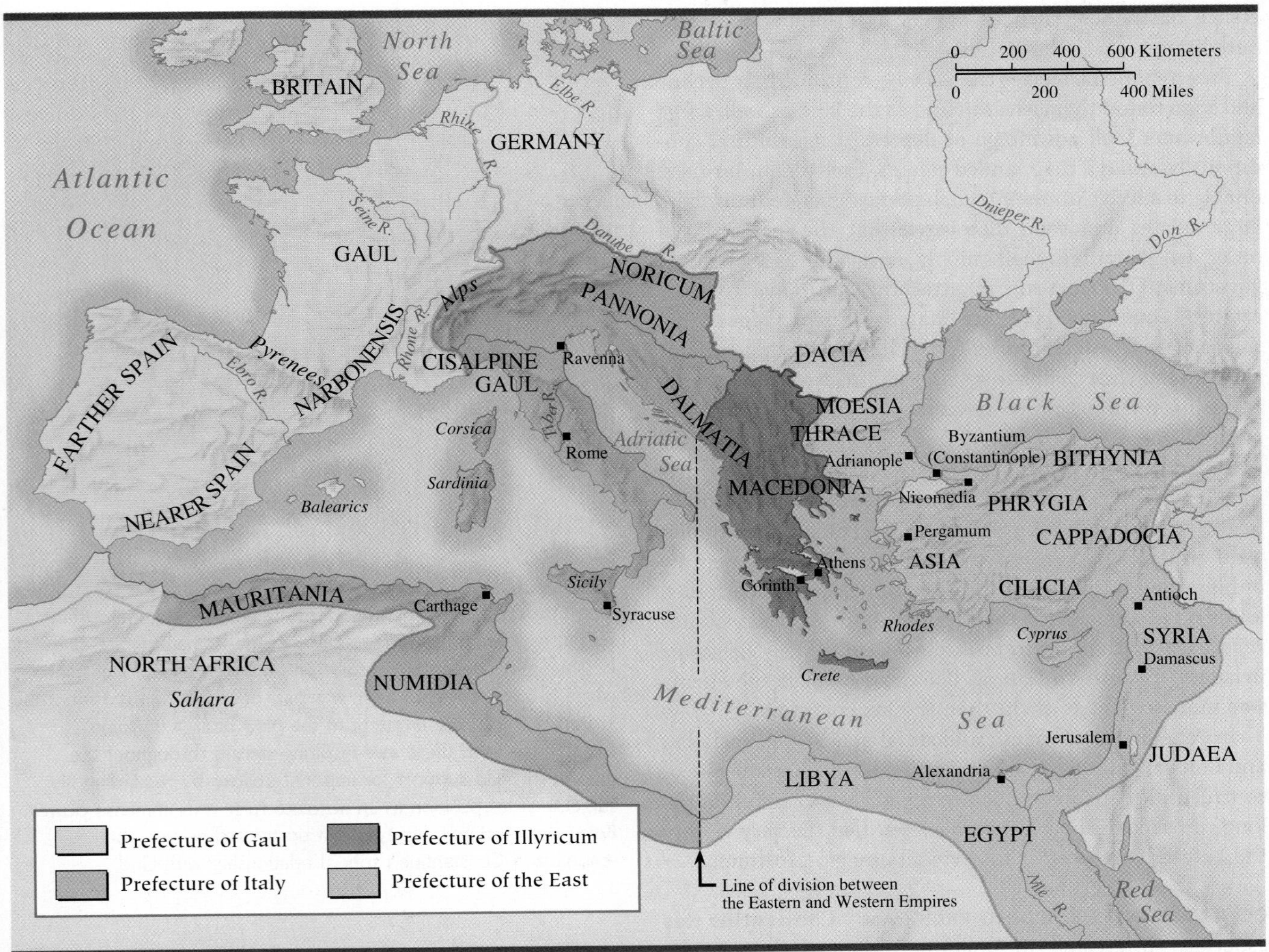

MAP 7.1 Divisions of the Late Roman Empire, c. 300. Diocletian imposed order and a new economic and administrative structure on the Late Empire. He divided the Roman Empire into four regions, each ruled by either an "Augustus" or a "Caesar," although Diocletian retained supreme power.

Q ***Compare this map with Map 6.1. How much territory had been lost by the time of Diocletian?***

enlarged two institutions—the army and the civil service—that drained most of the public funds. Although more revenues were needed to pay for the military and the bureaucracy, the population was not growing, so the tax base could not be expanded. Diocletian and Constantine devised new economic and social policies to deal with these financial burdens. Like their political policies, these economic and social policies were all based on coercion and loss of individual freedom.

To fight **inflation,** in 301 Diocletian resorted to issuing an edict that established maximum wages and prices for the entire empire. It was applied mostly in the east, but despite severe penalties, like most wage and price controls, it was largely unenforceable. The decline in the coins in circulation forced Diocletian to collect taxes and make government payments in produce. Constantine, however, managed to introduce a new gold coin, the solidus, and new silver coins that remained in circulation during his reign.

In the third century, the city councils, which had formed one of the most important administrative units of the empire, had begun to decline. Since the ***curiales*** (KUR-ee-all-ayss) (the city councillors) were forced to pay expenses out of their own pocket when the taxes they collected were insufficient, the wealthy no longer wanted to serve in these positions. Diocletian and Constantine responded by issuing edicts that forced the rich to continue in their posts as *curiales,* making the positions virtually hereditary. Some *curiales* realized that their fortunes would be wiped out and fled the cities to escape the clutches of the imperial bureaucracy. If caught, however, they were returned to their cities like runaway slaves and forced to resume their duties.

Coercion also came to form the underlying basis for numerous occupations in the Late Roman Empire. To maintain the tax base and keep the empire going despite the shortage of labor, the emperors issued edicts that forced people to remain in their designated vocations.

Hence basic jobs, such as bakers and shippers, became hereditary.

Free tenant farmers—the *coloni*—continued to decline and soon found themselves bound to the land as well. Large landowners took advantage of depressed agricultural conditions to enlarge their landed estates. Free tenant farmers, unable to survive on their own, became dependent on these large estates and soon discovered that the landlords, in order to guarantee their supply of labor, had obtained government cooperation in attaching the *coloni* to their estates. One imperial edict stated: "And as for *coloni* themselves, it will be proper for such as contemplate flight to be bound with chains to a servile status, so that by virtue of such condemnation to servitude they may be compelled to fulfill the duties that befit free men."[1]

In addition to facing increased restrictions on their freedom, the lower classes were burdened with enormous taxes, since the wealthiest classes in the Late Roman Empire were either exempt from paying taxes or evaded them by bribing the tax collectors. These tax pressures undermined lower-class support for the regime. A fifth-century writer reported that the Roman peasants welcomed the Visigothic invaders of southern Gaul as liberators because the enemy was more lenient to them than the tax collectors.

In general, the economic and social policies of Diocletian and Constantine were based on an unprecedented degree of control and coercion. Though temporarily successful, in the long run such authoritarian policies stifled the very vitality the Late Empire needed to revive its sagging fortunes.

Palazzo dei Conservatori, Rome/© Scala/Art Resource, NY

The Emperor Constantine. Constantine played an important role in restoring order and stability to the Roman Empire at the beginning of the fourth century. This marble head of Constantine, which is 8 feet 6 inches high, was part of an enormous 30-foot-tall seated statue of the emperor in the New Basilica in Rome. Constantine used these awe-inspiring statues throughout the empire to build support for imperial policies by reminding his subjects of his position as an absolute ruler with immense power. Being depicted with his eyes cast up toward heaven also emphasized Constantine's special relationship with God.

CONSTANTINE'S BUILDING PROGRAM Constantine was especially interested in building programs despite the strain they placed on the budget. Much of the construction took place in the provinces, since Rome had become merely a symbolic capital. It was no longer an imperial administrative center, as it was considered too far from the frontiers. Between 324 and 330, Constantine engaged in his biggest project, the construction of a new capital city in the east, on the site of the Greek city of Byzantium, on the shores of the Bosporus. Named the "city of Constantine," or Constantinople (modern Istanbul), it was developed for defensive reasons; it had an excellent strategic location. Calling it his "New Rome," Constantine endowed the city with a forum, large palaces, and a vast amphitheater. It was officially dedicated on May 11, 330, "by the commandment of God," and in the following years, many Christian churches were built there.

Constantine did not entirely forget Rome. Earlier he was responsible for building public baths and the triumphal Arch of Constantine, erected between 312 and 315. Constantine was also the first emperor to build churches for the Christian faith in Rome, including the first basilica dedicated to Saint Peter, built on the supposed site of Saint Peter's burial. Constantine also gave grants to Christian leaders in Rome, enabling them to assume a more conspicuous role in the city. These acts by Constantine are a reminder of the new role Christianity was beginning to play in the Late Empire.

The Empire's New Religion

In the fourth century, Christianity flourished as never before, and the emperor Constantine played an important role in its new status.

THE CONVERSION OF CONSTANTINE Constantine's support for Christianity supposedly began in 312, when his army was about to fight a crucial battle against the forces of Maxentius (mak-SEN-shuss) at the Milvian Bridge, which crossed the Tiber River just north of the city of Rome. According to the traditional story, before the battle, Constantine saw a vision of a Christian cross with the words, "In this sign you will conquer." Having won the battle, the story goes, Constantine was convinced of the power of the Christian God. Although he was not baptized until the end of his life, in 313 he issued the famous Edict of Milan, which officially tolerated the existence of Christianity.

After Constantine, all of the emperors were Christian with the exception of Julian (360–363), who tried briefly to restore the traditional Greco-Roman polytheistic religion. But he died in battle, and his reign was too short to make a difference. Under Theodosius (thee-uh-DOH-shuss) I "the Great" (379–395), Christianity was made the official religion of the Roman Empire. Once in control, Christian leaders used their influence and power to outlaw pagan religious practices. Christianity had triumphed.

ORGANIZATION AND RELIGIOUS DISPUTES By the fourth century, the Christian church had developed a system of government based on a territorial plan borrowed from Roman administration. The Christian community in each city was headed by a bishop, whose area of jurisdiction was known as a bishopric or diocese. The bishoprics of each Roman province were clustered together under the direction of an archbishop. The bishops of four great cities, Rome, Jerusalem, Alexandria, and Antioch, held positions of special power in church affairs because the churches in these cities all asserted that they had been founded by the original apostles sent out by Jesus.

One reason the church needed a more formal organization was the problem of **heresy.** As Christianity developed and spread, contradictory interpretations of important doctrines emerged. Heresy came to be viewed as a teaching different from the official "catholic" or universal beliefs of the church. In a world where people were concerned about salvation, the question of whether Jesus's nature is divine or human took on great significance. These doctrinal differences also became political issues, creating political factions that actually warred with one another. It is highly unlikely, though, that ordinary people understood the issues in these debates.

One of the major heresies of the fourth century was **Arianism,** which was a product of the followers of Arius, a priest from Alexandria in Egypt. Arius postulated that Jesus had been human and thus not truly God. Arius was opposed by Athanasius, a bishop of Alexandria, who argued that Jesus was human but also truly God. Emperor Constantine, disturbed by the controversy, called the first ecumenical council of the church, a meeting composed of representatives from the entire Christian community. The Council of Nicaea, held in 325, condemned Arianism and stated that Jesus was of "the same substance" as God: "We believe in one God the Father All-sovereign, maker of all things visible and invisible; And in one Lord Jesus Christ, the Son of God, begotten of the Father, only-begotten, that is, of the substance of the Father, God of God, Light of Light, true God of true God, begotten not made, of one substance with the Father."[2] The Council of Nicaea did not end the controversy, however; not only did Arianism persist in some parts of the Roman Empire for many years, but even more important, many of the Germanic Goths who established states in the west converted to Arian Christianity (see "The Germanic Kingdoms" later in this chapter). As a result of these fourth-century religious controversies, the Roman emperor came to play an increasingly important role in church affairs.

The End of the Western Empire

Constantine had reunited the Roman Empire and restored a semblance of order. After his death, however, the empire continued to divide into western and eastern parts as fighting erupted on a regular basis between elements of the Roman army backing the claims of rival emperors. By 395, the western and eastern parts of the empire had become virtually two independent states. In the course of the fifth century, while the empire in the east remained intact under the Roman emperor in Constantinople (see "The Byzantine Empire" later in this chapter), the administrative structure of the empire in the west collapsed and was replaced by an assortment of Germanic kingdoms. The process was a gradual one, involving the movement of Germans into the empire, military failures, struggles for power on the part of both Roman and German military leaders, and the efforts of wealthy aristocrats to support whichever side seemed to offer them greater security.

THE GERMANS During the first and second centuries C.E., the Romans had established the Rhine and Danube rivers as the empire's northern boundary. The Romans called all the peoples to the north of the rivers "Germans" and regarded them as uncivilized barbarians. In fact, the Germans comprised several different groups with their own customs and identities, but these constantly changed as tribes broke up and came together in new configurations. At times they formed larger confederations under strong warrior leaders. The Germans lived by herding and farming and also traded with people living along the northern frontiers of the Roman Empire. Their proximity to the Romans also led to some Romanization of the tribes. They were familiar with the Roman use of coins rather than barter and also gained some knowledge of both the Latin language and Roman military matters.

Although the Romans had established a series of political frontiers along the Rhine and Danube rivers, Romans and Germans often came into contact across these boundaries. For some time, the Romans had hired Germanic tribes to fight other Germanic tribes that threatened Rome or enlisted groups of Germans to fight for Rome. In any case, until the fourth century, the empire had proved capable of absorbing these people without harm to its political structure. In the second half of the fourth century, this situation began to change.

GERMAN MIGRATIONS In the late fourth century, the Germanic tribes came under new pressure when the Huns, a fierce tribe of nomads from the steppes of Asia (see the box on p. 184), moved into the Black Sea region, possibly attracted by the riches of the empire to its south. One of the groups displaced by the Huns was the Visigoths (VIZ-uh-gathz), who in 376 asked the Roman emperor Valens (VAY-linz) (364–378) to allow them to cross the Danube and farm in the Balkans in return for providing troops for the Roman military. But the Roman military commanders mistreated them, as one ancient German historian recounted:

> [They] crossed the Danube and settled Dacia Ripensis, Moesia, and Thrace by permission of the Emperor. Soon famine and want came upon them.... Their leaders ... begged the Roman commanders to open a market. But to what will not the "cursed lust for gold" compel men to assent? The generals, swayed by greed, sold them at a high price not only the flesh of sheep and oxen, but even the carcasses of dogs and unclean animals.... When their goods and chattels failed,

Opposing VIEWPOINTS

Two Views of the Huns

The first selection is a description of the Huns by Ammianus Marcellinus (c. 330–c. 393), who has been called the "last great Roman historian." Ammianus wrote a history of Rome from 96 C.E. to his own day. Only the chapters that deal with the period from 354 to 378 have survived. Historians believe that his account of the Huns is largely based on stereotypes. The second selection is taken from an account by Priscus, an envoy from the Eastern Roman Empire to the court of Attila, king of the Huns from 434 to 453. His description of the Huns in 448 is quite different from that of Ammianus Marcellinus.

Ammianus Marcellinus, *The Later Roman Empire*

The Huns . . . are quite abnormally savage. From the moment of their birth they make deep gashes in their children's cheeks, so that when in due course hair appears its growth is checked by the wrinkled scars. . . . They have squat bodies, strong limbs, and thick necks, and are so prodigiously ugly and bent that they might be two-legged animals, or the figures crudely carved from stumps which are seen on the parapets of bridges. Still, their shape, however disagreeable, is human; but their way of life is so rough that they have no use for fire or seasoned food, but live on the roots of wild plants and the half-raw flesh of any sort of animal, which they warm a little by placing it between their thighs and the backs of their horses. They have no buildings to shelter them, but avoid anything of the kind; . . . not so much as a hut thatched with reeds is to be found among them. . . . They wear garments of linen or of the skins of field-mice stitched together, and there is no difference between their clothing whether they are at home or abroad. Once they have put their necks in some dingy shirt they never take it off or change it till it rots and falls to pieces from incessant wear. They have round caps of fur on their heads, and protect their hairy legs with goatskins. Their shapeless shoes . . . make it hard to walk easily. In consequence they are ill-fitted to fight on foot, and remain glued to their horses, hardy but ugly beasts, on which they sometimes sit like women to perform their everyday business. Buying or selling, eating or drinking, are all done by day or night on horseback, and they even bow forward over their beasts' narrow necks to enjoy a deep and dreamy sleep. . . .

They sometimes fight by challenging their foes to single combat, but when they join battle they advance in packs, uttering their various warcries. Being lightly equipped and very sudden in their movements they can deliberately scatter and gallop about at random, inflicting tremendous slaughter; their extreme nimbleness enables them to force a rampart or pillage an enemy's camp before one catches sight of them. . . . None of them plows or ever touches a plow-handle. They have no fixed abode, no home or law or settled manner of life, but wander like refugees with the wagons in which they live. In these their wives weave their filthy clothing, mate with their husbands, and give birth to their children, and rear them to the age of puberty.

Priscus, *An Account of the Court of Attila the Hun*

[We were invited to a banquet with Attila.] When the hour arrived we went to Attila's palace, along with the embassy from the western Romans, and stood on the threshold of the hall in the presence of Attila. The cupbearers gave us a cup, according to the national custom, that we might pray before we sat down. Having tasted the cup, we proceeded to take our seats, all the chairs being ranged along the walls of the room on either side. Attila sat in the middle on a couch; a second couch was set behind him, and from it steps led up to his bed, which was covered with linen sheets and coverlets. . . .

[First the king and his guests pledged one another with the wine.] When this ceremony was over the cupbearers retired and tables, large enough for three or four, or even more, to sit at, were placed next the table of Attila, so that each could take of the food on the dishes without leaving his seat. The attendant of Attila first entered with a dish full of meat, and behind him came the other attendants with bread and other dishes, which they laid on the tables. A luxurious meal, served on silver plate, had been made ready for us and the other guests, but Attila ate nothing but meat on a wooden platter. In everything else, too, he showed himself temperate; his cup was of wood, while to the guests were given goblets of gold and silver. His dress, too, was quite simple, affecting only to be clean.

Q What motives may have prompted Ammianus Marcellinus to describe the Huns so harshly? How does the account of Priscus differ, and what strategies of the Huns do you detect here to impress and overawe foreigners? How reliable do you think these descriptions of the Huns are? Why?

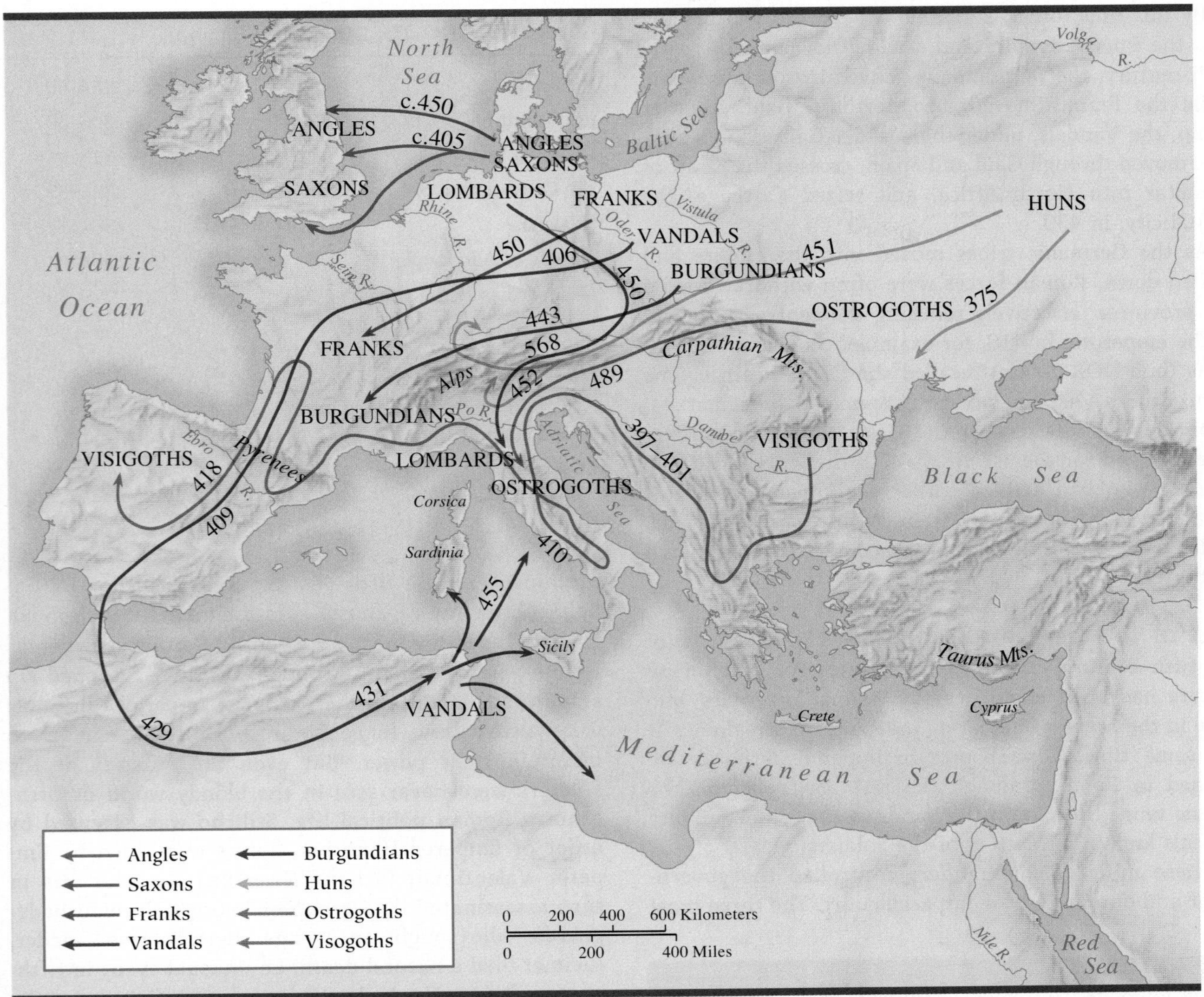

MAP 7.2 German Migration Routes. In the fifth century, various groups of Germans migrated throughout the Western Roman Empire. Pressure from Huns in the east forced some tribes to move west into the empire, and many tribes already in the empire experienced conflict. Some fought the Roman forces, while others were induced to move to the empire's far regions.

How far did the Vandals travel in what period of time?

View an animated version of this map or related maps on the CourseMate website.

> the greedy traders demanded their sons in return for the necessities of life. And the parents consented even to this.[3]

Outraged at the Romans' behavior, the Visigoths revolted. In 378, Emperor Valens and an army of 40,000 soldiers confronted the Visigoths at Adrianople. The emperor was killed, and two-thirds of the Roman army was left dead on the battlefield.

The loss was not fatal, although the new emperor, Theodosius I, resettled the Visigoths and incorporated many of their soldiers into the Roman army. Some of the Visigoths even became army leaders. By the second half of the fourth century, Roman policy allowed Roman army units to be composed entirely of Germanic tribes, known as **federates,** or allies of Rome.

THE THREAT OF THE GERMANS The existence of such military groups proved dangerous to the Late Empire. This was especially evident after Alaric (AL-uh-rik) became the leader of the Visigoths. Between 395 and 401, Alaric and his soldiers moved through the Balkans and then into Italy, seeking food and cash payments from Roman officials. When the city of Rome refused his demands in 408, Alaric marched to the gates and besieged the city, causing the senate of Rome to agree to pay 5,000 pounds of gold and 30,000 pounds of silver for his withdrawal. Two years later, frustrated in his demand that the Visigoths be given part of northern Italy, Alaric and his forces sacked Rome for three days. Alaric died soon after, and his Visigothic followers left Italy, crossed the Alps, and moved into Spain and southern Gaul as Roman allies (see Map 7.2).

By this time, other Germanic tribes were also passing into the Roman Empire and settling down. In the early fifth century, the Burgundians arrived in southern Gaul, while the Franks moved into northern Gaul. Another group, the Vandals, under their leader Gaiseric (GY-zuh-rik), moved through Gaul and Spain, crossed the Strait of Gibraltar into North Africa, and seized Carthage, the capital city, in 439.

As the Germanic tribes moved into the empire and settled down, Roman forces were often withdrawn from the provinces, effectively reducing the central authority of the emperors. In 410, for example, the emperor Honorius (hoh-NOR-ee-uss) recalled the last Roman legions from Britain. As one ancient commentator remarked, "Honorius sent letters to the cities in Britain, urging them to fend for themselves."[4] With the withdrawal, the Saxons, who had arrived earlier as Roman allies, now expanded their control in Britain. Within another decade, both Spain and Gaul had also become free of imperial authority.

CHRONOLOGY The Late Roman Empire

Diocletian	284–305
Constantine	306–337
Edict of Milan	313
Construction of Constantinople	324–330
Valens	364–378
Battle of Adrianople	378
Theodosius I "the Great"	379–395
Division of the empire	395
Alaric and Visigoths sack Rome	410
Roman legions abandon Britain	410
Vandals sack Rome	455
Odoacer deposes Romulus Augustulus	476

ROLE OF MASTERS OF THE SOLDIERS By the middle of the fifth century, the western provinces of the Roman Empire had been taken over by Germanic peoples who were in the process of creating independent kingdoms. At the same time, a semblance of imperial authority remained in Rome, although the real power behind the throne tended to rest in the hands of important military officials known as Masters of the Soldiers.

These military commanders controlled the government and dominated the imperial court. The three most prominent in the fifth century were Stilicho (STIL-i-koh), Aetius (ay-EE-shuss), and Ricimer (RISS-uh-mur). Stilicho and Ricimer were both Germans, whereas Aetius was a Roman. Athough all three propped up emperors to maintain the fiction of imperial rule, they were also willing to cooperate with the Germans to maintain their power. But even the Masters of the Soldiers were never safe in the bloody world of fifth-century Roman political life. Stilicho was executed by order of Emperor Honorius. Aetius was killed by Emperor Valentinian (val-en-TIN-ee-un) III, who was in turn assassinated by a group of Aetius's German bodyguards, who sought to avenge their betrayed leader. Ricimer died a natural death, an unusual event in fifth-century Rome. No doubt, the constant infighting at the center of the Western Empire added to the instability of imperial rule.

Stilicho, a German Master of the Soldiers. Half-Vandal and half-Roman, Stilicho was the power behind the imperial throne from 395 to 408. Emperor Honorius ordered his execution in 408. These ivory panels show Stilicho at the right, in Vandal clothing, with his wife and son at the left.

By the mid-fifth century, imperial authority in the west was still operating only in Italy and small parts of Gaul. Even Rome itself was not safe. In 455, after the Romans broke a treaty that they had made with Gaiseric, leader of the Vandals, Gaiseric sent a Vandal fleet to Italy and sacked the undefended city of Rome. Twenty-one years later, in 476, Odoacer (oh-doh-AY-sur), a new Master of the Soldiers, himself of German origin, deposed the Roman emperor, the boy Romulus Augustulus (RAHM-yuh-luss ow-GOOS-chuh-luss). To many historians, the deposition of Romulus signaled the end of the Roman Empire. Of course, this is only a symbolic date, since much of direct imperial rule had already been lost in the course of the fifth century. Even then the empire remained, as Odoacer presented himself as a German king obedient in theory to the Roman emperor Zeno (ZEE-noh) in Constantinople.

By the end of the fifth century, Roman imperial authority in the west had ceased. Nevertheless, the intellectual, governmental, and cultural traditions of the Late Roman Empire continued to live on in the new Germanic kingdoms.

The Germanic Kingdoms

Focus Questions: What changes did the Germanic peoples make to the political, economic, and social conditions of the Western Roman Empire? What were the main features of Germanic law and society, and how did they differ from those of the Romans?

By 500, the Western Roman Empire was being replaced politically by a series of kingdoms ruled by German kings (see Map 7.3). Although the Germans now ruled, they were greatly outnumbered by the Romans, who still controlled most of the economic resources. Both were Christian, but many of the Germans were Arian Christians, considered heretics by Romans who belonged to the Christian church in Rome, which had become known as the Roman Catholic Church. Gradually, the two groups merged into a common culture, although the pattern of settlement and the fusion of the Romans and Germans took different forms in the various Germanic kingdoms.

The Ostrogothic Kingdom of Italy

Zeno, the Roman emperor in Constantinople, was not pleased with Odoacer's actions and plotted to unseat him. In his desire to act against the German leader, Zeno brought another German tribe, the Ostrogoths (AHSS-truh-gahthss), into Italy. The Ostrogoths had recovered from a defeat by the Huns in the fourth century and under their king Theodoric (thee-AHD-uh-rik) (493–526) had attacked Constantinople. To divert them, Emperor Zeno invited Theodoric to act as his deputy to defeat Odoacer and bring Italy back into the empire. Theodoric accepted the challenge, marched into Italy, killed Odoacer, and then, contrary to Zeno's wishes, established himself as ruler of Italy in 493.

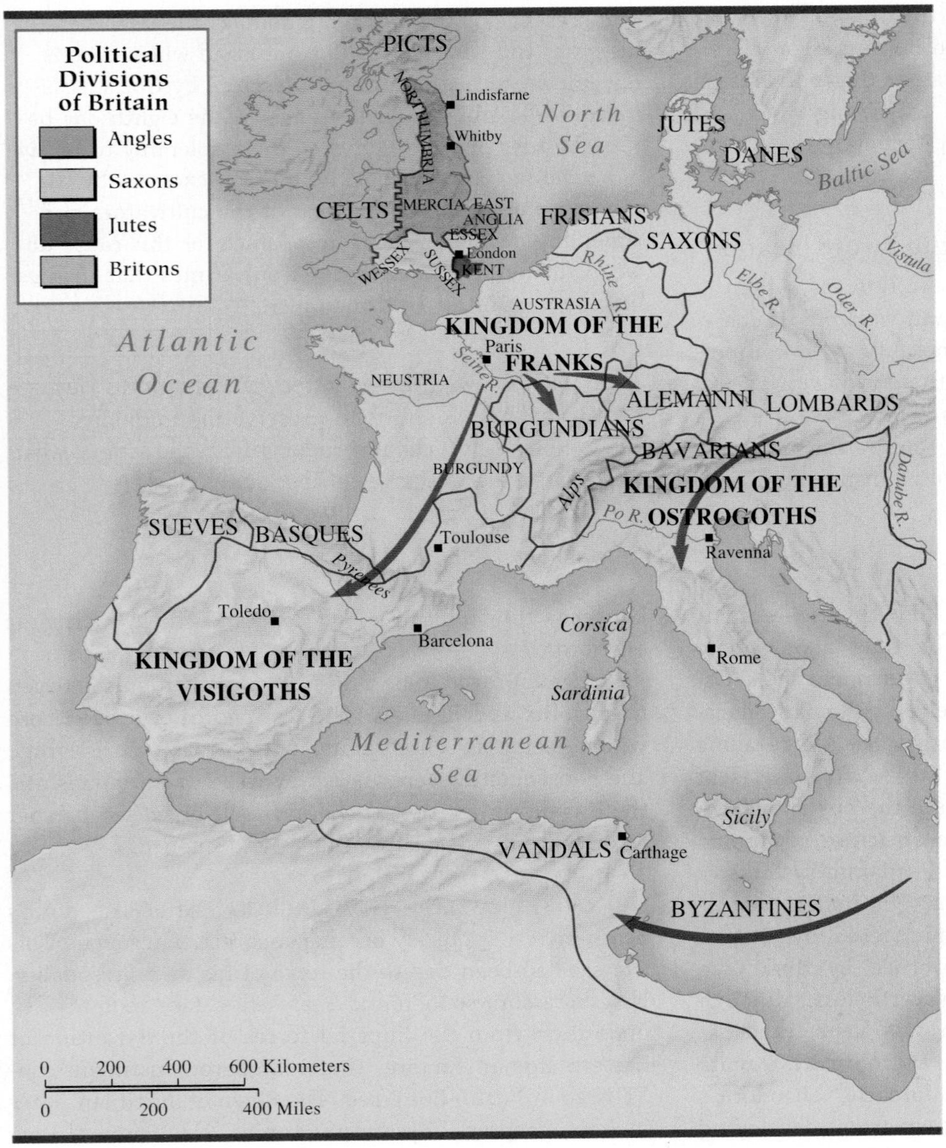

MAP 7.3 The Germanic Kingdoms of the Old Western Empire. The Germanic tribes filled the power vacuum created by the demise of the Roman Empire, building states that blended elements of Germanic customs and laws with those of Roman culture, including large-scale conversions to Christianity. The Franks established the most durable of these Germanic states.

How did the movements of the Franks during this period correspond to the borders of present-day France?

Theodoric and Ostrogothic Italy

The Ostrogothic king Theodoric (493–526), who had been educated in Constantinople, was determined to maintain Roman culture rather than destroy it. His attempt to preserve *civilitas,* the traditional Roman civic culture, was well expressed in the official letters written in his name by Cassiodorus, who became master of offices in 525. Theodoric's efforts were largely undone by opposition from the Roman nobility and especially by Justinian's reconquest of the Italian peninsula shortly after Theodoric's death.

Letters of Cassiodorus

King Theodoric to Colossaeus

We delight to entrust our mandates to persons of approved character. . . .

Show forth the justice of the Goths, a nation happily situated for praise, since it is theirs to unite the forethought of the Romans and the virtue of the Barbarians. Remove all ill-planted customs, and impress upon all your subordinates that we would rather that our Treasury lost a suit than that it gained one wrongfully, rather that we lost money than the taxpayer was driven to suicide.

King Theodoric to Unigis, the Sword-Bearer

We delight to live after the law of the Romans, whom we seek to defend with our arms; and we are as much interested in the maintenance of morality as we can possibly be in war. For what profit is there in having removed the turmoil of the Barbarians, unless we live according to law? . . . Let other kings desire the glory of battles won, of cities taken, of ruins made; our purpose is, God helping us, so to rule that our subjects shall grieve that they did not earlier acquire the blessing of our dominion.

King Theodoric to All the Jews of Genoa

The true mark of *civilitas* is the observance of law. It is this which makes life in communities possible, and which separates man from the brutes. We therefore gladly accede to your request that all the privileges which the foresight of antiquity conferred upon the Jewish customs shall be renewed to you, for in truth it is our great desire that the laws of the ancients shall be kept in force to secure the reverence due to us. Everything which has been found to conduce to *civilitas* should be held fast with enduring devotion.

King Theodoric to All the Goths Settled in Picenum and Samnium

The presence of the Sovereign doubles the sweetness of his gifts, and that man is like one dead whose face is not known to his lord. Come therefore by God's assistance, come all into our presence on the eighth day before the Ides of June [June 7], there solemnly to receive our royal largesse. But let there be no excesses by the way, no plundering the harvest of the cultivators nor trampling down their meadows, since for this cause do we gladly defray the expense of our armies that *civilitas* may be kept intact by armed men.

Q In what ways do the letters of Cassiodorus illustrate Theodoric's efforts to preserve the traditional Roman civic culture? Judging from the letters, what were the obstacles to Theodoric's goal?

THEODORIC'S RULE More than any other Germanic state, the Ostrogothic kingdom of Italy managed to maintain the Roman tradition of government. The Ostrogothic king, Theodoric, had received a Roman education while a hostage in Constantinople. After taking control of Italy, he was eager to create a synthesis of Ostrogothic and Roman practices (see the box above). In addition to maintaining the entire structure of Roman imperial government, he established separate systems of rule for the Ostrogoths and Romans. The Italian population lived under Roman law administered by Roman officials. The Ostrogoths were governed by their own customs and their own officials. Nevertheless, although the Roman administrative system was kept intact, it was the Ostrogoths alone who controlled the army. Despite the apparent success of this "dual approach," Theodoric's system was unable to keep friction from developing between the Italian population and their Germanic overlords.

Religion proved to be a major source of trouble between Ostrogoths and Romans. The Ostrogoths had been converted earlier to Christianity, but to Arian Christianity, and consequently were viewed by western Christians and the Italians as heretics. Theodoric's rule grew ever harsher as discontent with Ostrogothic rule deepened.

END OF THE OSTROGOTHIC KINGDOM After Theodoric's death in 526, it quickly became apparent that much of his success had been due to the force of his own personality. His successors soon found themselves face to face with opposition from the imperial forces of the Byzantine or Eastern Roman Empire. Under Emperor Justinian (juh-STIN-ee-un) (527–565) (see "The Reign of Justinian" later in this chapter), Byzantine armies reconquered Italy between 535 and 552, devastating much of the peninsula in the process and destroying Rome as one of the great urban centers of the Mediterranean world. The Byzantine reconquest proved ephemeral, however. Another German tribe, the Lombards, invaded Italy in 568 and conquered much of northern and central Italy. Unlike the Ostrogoths, the Lombards were harsh rulers and cared little for Roman structures and traditions. The Lombards' fondness for fighting each other enabled the Byzantines to retain control of some parts of Italy, especially the area around Ravenna, which became the capital of imperial government in the west.

The Visigothic Kingdom of Spain

The Visigothic kingdom in Spain demonstrated a number of parallels to the Ostrogothic kingdom of Italy. Both favored coexistence between the Roman and German populations, both featured a warrior caste dominating a larger native population, and both continued to maintain much of the Roman structure of government while largely excluding Romans from power. There were also noticeable differences, however. Perceiving that their Arianism was a stumbling block to good relations, the Visigothic rulers in the late sixth century converted to Latin or Catholic Christianity and ended the tension caused by this heresy. Laws preventing intermarriage were dropped, and the Visigothic and Hispano-Roman peoples began to fuse together. A new body of law common to both peoples also developed.

The kingdom possessed one fatal weakness, however—the Visigoths fought constantly over the kingship. The Visigoths had no hereditary monarchy and no established procedure for choosing new rulers. Church officials tried to help develop a sense of order, as this canon from the Fourth Council of Toledo in 633 illustrates: "No one of us shall dare to seize the kingdom; no one shall arouse sedition among the citizenry; no one shall think of killing the king." Church decrees failed to stop the feuds, however, and assassinations remained a way of life in Visigothic Spain. In 711, Muslim invaders destroyed the Visigothic kingdom itself (see "The Rise of Islam" later in this chapter).

The Frankish Kingdom

Only one of the German states on the European continent proved long-lasting—the kingdom of the Franks. The establishment of a Frankish kingdom was the work of Clovis (c. 482–511), the leader of one group of Franks who eventually became king of them all.

THE RULE OF CLOVIS Around 500, Clovis became a Catholic Christian. He was not the first German king to convert to Christianity, but the others had joined the Arian sect of Christianity. The Roman Catholic Church regarded the Arians as heretics, people who believed in teachings that departed from the official church doctrine. Clovis found that his conversion to Catholic Christianity gained him the support of the Roman Catholic Church, which was only too eager to obtain the friendship of a major Germanic ruler who was a Catholic Christian. The conversion of the king also paved the way for the conversion of the Frankish peoples. Finally, Clovis could pose as a defender of the orthodox Catholic faith in order to justify his expansion at the beginning of the sixth century. He defeated the Alemanni (al-uh-MAH-nee) in southwest Germany and the Visigoths in southern Gaul. By 510, Clovis had established a powerful new Frankish kingdom stretching from the Pyrenees in the west to German lands in the east (modern-day France and western Germany).

The Conversion of Clovis (c. 500 C.E.), two accounts

Clovis was thus responsible for establishing a Frankish kingdom under the Merovingian (meh-ruh-VIN-jee-un) dynasty, a name derived from Merovech, their semilegendary ancestor. Clovis came to rely on his Frankish followers to rule in the old Roman city-states under the title of count. Often these officials were forced to share power with the Gallo-Roman Catholic bishops, producing a gradual fusion of Latin and German cultures, with the church serving to preserve the Latin culture. Clovis spent the last years of his life ensuring the survival of his dynasty by killing off relatives who were leaders of other groups of Franks.

THE SUCCESSORS OF CLOVIS After the death of Clovis, his sons divided the newly created kingdom, as was the Frankish custom. During the sixth and seventh centuries, the once-united Frankish kingdom came to be partitioned into three major areas: Neustria (NOO-stree-uh) in northern Gaul; Austrasia (au-STRY-zhuh), consisting of the ancient Frankish lands on both sides of the Rhine; and the former kingdom of Burgundy. All three were ruled by members of the Merovingian dynasty. Within the three territories, members of the dynasty were assisted by powerful nobles. Frankish society possessed a ruling class that gradually intermarried with the old Gallo-Roman senatorial class to form a new nobility. These noble families took advantage of their position to expand their own lands and wealth at the expense of the monarchy. Within the royal household, the position of ***major domus*** (my-YOR DOH-moos), or mayor of the palace, the chief officer of the king's household, began to overshadow the king. Essentially, both nobles and mayors of the palace were expanding their power at the expense of the kings.

At the beginning of the eighth century, the most important political development in the Frankish kingdom was the rise of Charles Martel, who served as mayor of the palace of Austrasia beginning in 714. Charles Martel led troops that defeated the Muslims near Poitiers in 732 and by the time of his death in 741 had become virtual ruler of the three Merovingian kingdoms. Though he was not king, Charles Martel's dynamic efforts put his family on the verge of creating a new dynasty that would establish an even more powerful Frankish state (see Chapter 8).

CHRONOLOGY The Germanic Kingdoms

Theodoric establishes an Ostrogothic kingdom in Italy	493
Frankish king Clovis converts to Christianity	c. 500
Reconquest of Italy by Byzantines	535–552
Lombards begin conquest of Italy	568
Muslims shatter Visigoths in Spain	711
Charles Martel defeats Muslims	732

During the sixth and seventh centuries, the Frankish kingdom witnessed a process of fusion between Gallo-Roman and Frankish cultures and peoples, a process accompanied by a significant decline in Roman standards of civilization and commercial activity. The Franks were warriors and did little to encourage either urban life or trade. Commerce declined in the interior, though seacoast towns maintained some activity. By 750, Frankish Gaul was basically an agricultural society in which the old Roman *latifundia* system of the Late Empire continued unimpeded. Institutionally, however, Germanic concepts of kingship and customary law had replaced the Roman governmental structure.

Anglo-Saxon England

The barbarian pressures on the Western Roman Empire had forced the emperors to withdraw the Roman armies and abandon Britain by the beginning of the fifth century. This opened the door to the Angles and Saxons, Germanic tribes from Denmark and northern Germany. Although these same peoples had made plundering raids for a century, the withdrawal of the Roman armies enabled them to make settlements instead. They met with resistance from the Celtic Britons, however, who still controlled the western regions of Cornwall, Wales, and Cumberland at the beginning of the seventh century (see Map 7.3). The German invaders eventually succeeded in carving out small kingdoms throughout the island, Kent in southeast England being one of them. This wave of German invaders would eventually be converted to Christianity by new groups of Christian missionaries (see "The Conversion of England" later in this chapter).

The Society of the Germanic Kingdoms

As the Germans infiltrated the Roman Empire, they were influenced by the Roman society they encountered. Consequently, the Germanic peoples of the fifth, sixth, and seventh centuries were probably quite different from the Germans that the forces of Augustus encountered in the first century C.E. Moreover, there was a meaningful fusion of Roman and German upper classes in the new kingdoms. In Merovingian Frankish lands, upper-class Gallo-Romans intermarried with Frankish nobles to produce a new ruling class. Each influenced the other. Franks constructed Roman-style villas; Gallo-Romans adopted Frankish weapons.

The crucial social bond among the Germanic peoples was the family, especially the extended or patriarchal family of husbands, wives, children, brothers, sisters, cousins, and grandparents. In addition to working the land together and passing it down to succeeding generations, the extended family provided protection, which was sorely needed in the violent atmosphere of Merovingian times.

GERMANIC LAW The German conception of family and kinship affected the way Germanic law treated the problem of crime and punishment. In the Roman system, as in our own, a crime such as murder was considered an offense against society or the state and was handled by a court that heard evidence and arrived at a decision. Germanic law tended to be personal. An injury by one person against another could lead to a blood feud in which the family of the injured party took revenge on the kin of the wrongdoer. Feuds could result in savage acts of revenge, such as hacking off hands or feet, gouging out eyes, or slicing off ears and noses. Since this system had a tendency to get out of control and allow mayhem to multiply, an alternative system arose that made use of a fine called ***wergeld*** (WURR-geld). This was the amount paid by a wrongdoer to the family of the person who had been injured or killed. *Wergeld,* which means "money for a man," was the value of a person in monetary terms. That value varied considerably according to social status. The law of the Salic Franks, which was first written down under Roman influence at the beginning of the sixth century, stated, "If any one shall have killed a free Frank, or a barbarian living under the Salic law, and it have been proved on him, he shall be sentenced to 8,000 denars.... But if any one has slain a man who is in the service of the king, he shall be sentenced to 24,000 denars."[5] An offense against a noble obviously cost considerably more than one against a free person or a slave.

Under German customary law, compurgation and the ordeal were the two most commonly used procedures for determining whether an accused person was guilty and should have to pay *wergeld.* Compurgation was the swearing of an oath by the accused person, backed up by a group of "oathhelpers," numbering twelve or twenty-five, who would also swear that the accused person should be believed. The ordeal functioned in a variety of ways, all of which were based on the principle of divine intervention; divine forces (whether pagan or Christian) would not allow an innocent person to be harmed (see the box on p. 191).

THE FRANKISH FAMILY AND MARRIAGE For the Franks, like other Germanic peoples of the Early Middle Ages, the extended family was at the center of social organization. The Frankish family structure was quite simple. Males were dominant and made all the important decisions. A woman obeyed her father until she married and then fell under the legal domination of her husband. A widow,

Germanic Customary Law: The Ordeal

In Germanic customary law, the ordeal came to be a means by which accused persons might clear themselves. Although the ordeal took different forms, all involved a physical trial of some sort, such as holding a red-hot iron. It was believed God would protect the innocent and allow them to come through the ordeal unharmed. This sixth-century account by Gregory of Tours describes an ordeal by hot water.

Gregory of Tours, *An Ordeal of Hot Water* (c. 580)

An Arian priest disputing with a deacon of our religion made venomous assertions against the Son of God and the Holy Ghost, as is the habit of that sect [the Arians]. But when the deacon had discoursed a long time concerning the reasonableness of our faith and the heretic, blinded by the fog of unbelief, continued to reject the truth, . . . the former said: "Why weary ourselves with long discussions? Let acts approve the truth; let a kettle be heated over the fire and someone's ring be thrown into the boiling water. Let him who shall take it from the heated liquid be approved as a follower of the truth, and afterward let the other party be converted to the knowledge of the truth. And do you also understand, O heretic, that this our party will fulfill the conditions with the aid of the Holy Ghost; you shall confess that there is no discordance, no dissimilarity in the Holy Trinity [belief that God, Jesus (son of God), and Holy Spirit (Ghost) are three manifestations of the same unique Deity]." The heretic consented to the proposition and they separated after appointing the next morning for the trial. But the fervor of faith in which the deacon had first made this suggestion began to cool through the instigation of the enemy. Rising with the dawn he bathed his arm in oil and smeared it with ointment. But nevertheless he made the round of the sacred places and called in prayer on the Lord. . . . About the third hour they met in the marketplace. The people came together to see the show. A fire was lighted, the kettle was placed upon it, and when it grew very hot the ring was thrown into the boiling water. The deacon invited the heretic to take it out of the water first. But he promptly refused, saying, "You who did propose this trial are the one to take it out." The deacon all of a tremble bared his arm. And when the heretic saw it besmeared with ointment he cried out: "With magic arts you have thought to protect yourself, that you have made use of these salves, but what you have done will not avail." While they were thus quarreling there came up a deacon from Ravenna named Iacinthus and inquired what the trouble was about. When he learned the truth he drew his arm out from under his robe at once and plunged his right hand into the kettle. Now the ring that had been thrown in was a little thing and very light so that it was thrown about by the water as chaff would be blown about by the wind; and searching for it a long time he found it after about an hour. Meanwhile the flame beneath the kettle blazed up mightily so that the greater heat might make it difficult for the ring to be followed by the hand; but the deacon extracted it at length and suffered no harm, protesting rather that at the bottom the kettle was cold while at the top it was just pleasantly warm. When the heretic beheld this he was greatly confused and audaciously thrust his hand into the kettle saying, "My faith will aid me." As soon as his hand had been thrust in all the flesh was boiled off the bones clear up to the elbow. And so the dispute ended.

Q What was the purpose of the ordeal of hot water? What does it reveal about the nature of the society that used it? What conception of justice do you think was held by this society?

however, could hold property without a male guardian. In Frankish law, the *wergeld* of a wife of childbearing age—of value because she could produce children—was considerably higher than that of a man. The Salic law stated: "If any one killed a free woman after she had begun bearing children, he shall be sentenced to 24,000 denars. . . . After she can have no more children, he who kills her shall be sentenced to 8,000 denars."[6]

Since marriage affected the extended family group, fathers or uncles could arrange marriages for the good of the family without considering their children's wishes. Most important was the engagement ceremony in which a prospective son-in-law made a payment symbolizing the purchase of paternal authority over the bride. The essential feature of the marriage itself involved placing the married couple in bed to achieve their physical union. In first marriages, it was considered important that the wife be a virgin so as to ensure that any children would be the husband's. A virgin symbolized the ability of the bloodline to continue. For this reason, adultery was viewed as pollution of the woman and her offspring, poisoning the future. Adulterous wives were severely punished (an adulterous woman could be strangled or even burned alive); adulterous husbands were not. Divorce was relatively simple and was initiated primarily by the husband. Divorced wives simply returned to their families.

For most women in the new Germanic kingdoms, their legal status reflected the material conditions of their lives. Archaeological evidence suggests that most women had life expectancies of only thirty or forty years and that about 10 to 15 percent of women died in their childbearing years, no doubt due to complications associated with childbirth. For most women, life consisted of domestic labor: providing food and clothing for the household, caring for the children, and assisting with numerous farming chores. Of all the duties of women, the most important was childbearing because it was crucial to the maintenance of the family and its properties.

Development of the Christian Church

Focus Questions: How and why did the organization of the Christian church and its relations with the state change during the fourth and fifth centuries? What were the chief characteristics of Benedictine monasticism, and what role did monks play in both the conversion of Europe to Christianity and the intellectual life of the Germanic kingdoms?

By the end of the fourth century, Christianity had become the predominant religion of the Roman Empire. As the official Roman state disintegrated, the Christian church played an increasingly important role in the new civilization built on the ruins of the old Roman Empire.

The Church Fathers

A number of intellectuals in the early church who wrote in Latin profoundly influenced the development of Christian thought in the west. They came to be known as the Latin Fathers of the Catholic Church.

THE WORK OF AUGUSTINE Saint Augustine (AW-guh-steen) (354–430) was the most prominent of the Latin Fathers. His work provides one of the best examples of how Christian theologians used pagan culture in the service of Christianity.

Born in North Africa, Augustine was reared by his mother, an ardent Christian. He eventually became a professor of rhetoric at Milan in 384. But two years later, after experiencing a profound and moving religious experience, Augustine gave up his teaching position and went back to North Africa, where he served as bishop of Hippo from 396 until his death in 430.

Augustine's two most famous works are the *Confessions* and *The City of God*. Written in 397, the *Confessions* was a self-portrait not of Augustine's worldly activities but of the "history of a heart," an account of his own personal and spiritual experiences, written to help others with their search. Augustine describes how he struggled throughout his early life to find God until in his thirty-second year he experienced a miraculous conversion (see the box on p. 193).

St. Augustine, *Confessions*, Books 1 & 3 excerpt (397–398 C.E.)

The City of God, Augustine's other major work, was a profound expression of a Christian philosophy of government and history. In it, Augustine theorized on the ideal relations between two kinds of societies existing throughout time—the City of God and the City of the World. Those who loved God would be loyal to the City of God, whose ultimate location was the kingdom of heaven. Earthly society would always be insecure because of human beings' imperfect nature and inclination to violate God's commandments. And yet the City of the World was still necessary, for it was the duty of rulers to curb the depraved instincts of sinful humans and maintain the peace necessary for Christians to live in the world. Hence, Augustine posited that secular government and authority were necessary for the pursuit of the true Christian life on earth; in doing so, he provided a justification for secular political authority that would play an important role in medieval thought.

Augustine was also important in establishing the Christian church's views on sexual desire. Many early Christians had seen **celibacy** (SELL-uh-buh-see), or complete abstinence from sexual activity, as the surest way to holiness. Augustine, too, believed Christians should reject sex, but he maintained that many Christians were unable to do so. For them, marriage was a good alternative, but with the understanding that even in marriage, sex between a man and woman had to serve a purpose—the procreation of children. It was left to the clergy of the church to uphold the high ideal of celibacy.

JEROME AND THE BIBLE Another Latin Father was Jerome (345–420), who pursued literary studies in Rome and became a master of Latin prose. Jerome had mixed feelings about his love for liberal studies, however, and like Augustine experienced a spiritual conversion, after which he tried to dedicate himself more fully to Jesus. He had a dream in which Jesus appeared as his judge:

> Asked who and what I was, I replied: "I am a Christian." But He who presided said: "You lie, you are a follower of Cicero, not of Christ. For where your treasure is, there will your heart be also." Instantly, I became dumb.... Accordingly I made oath and called upon His name, saying: "Lord, if ever again I possess worldly books [the classics], or if ever again I read such, I have denied You."

After this dream, Jerome determined to "read the books of God with a zeal greater than I had previously given to the books of men."[7]

Ultimately, Jerome found a compromise by purifying the literature of the pagan world and then using it to further the Christian faith. Jerome was the greatest scholar among the Latin Fathers, and his extensive knowledge of both Hebrew and Greek enabled him to translate the Old and New Testaments into Latin. In the process, he created the so-called Latin Vulgate, or common text, of the Scriptures that became the standard edition for the Catholic Church in the Middle Ages.

The *Confessions* of Augustine

Saint Augustine's spiritual and intellectual autobiography is a revealing self-portrait of the inner struggles of one of the intellectual giants of early Christianity. The first excerpt is taken from Book 8, in which Augustine describes how he heard a voice from heaven and was converted from his old habits. In the second excerpt, from Book 9, Augustine expresses joy and gratitude for his conversion.

Augustine, *Confessions*

From Book 8

So was I speaking and weeping in the most bitter contrition of my heart, when, lo! I heard from a neighboring house a voice as of boy or girl, I know not, chanting, and oft repeating, "Take up and read; Take up and read." Instantly, my countenance altered, I began to think most intently whether children were wont in any kind of play to sing such words: nor could I remember ever to have heard the like. So checking the torrent of my tears, I arose; interpreting it to be no other than a command from God to open the book, and read the first chapter I should find. For I had heard of Antony, that coming in during the reading of the Gospel, he received the admonition, as if what was being read was spoken to him: Go, sell all that you have, and give to the poor, and you shall have treasure in heaven, and come and follow me: and by such oracle he was forthwith converted unto You. Eagerly then I returned to the place where Alypius was sitting; for there I had laid the volume of the Apostle [Paul] when I arose thence. I seized, opened, and in silence read that section on which my eyes first fell: Not in rioting and drunkenness, not in chambering and wantonness, not in strife and envying; but put you on the Lord Jesus Christ, and make not provision for the flesh. . . . No further would I read; nor need I: for instantly at the end of this sentence, by a light as it were of serenity infused into my heart, all the darkness of doubt vanished away.

From Book 9

O Lord I am your servant; I am your servant, and the son of your handmaid: You have broken my bonds in sunder. I will offer to You the sacrifice of praise. Let my heart and my tongue praise You; yea, let all my bones say, O Lord, who is like unto You? Let them say, and answer You me, and say unto my soul, I am your salvation. Who am I, and what am I? What evil have not been either my deeds, or if not my deeds, my words, or if not my words, my will? But You, O Lord, are good and merciful, and your right hand had respect unto the depth of my death, and from the bottom of my heart emptied that abyss of corruption.

Q What was the nature of Augustine's conversion experience? How did it affect his life and teaching?

The Power of the Pope

In the early centuries of Christianity, the churches in the larger cities had great influence in the administration of the church. It was only natural, then, that the bishops of those cities would also exercise considerable power. One of the far-reaching developments in the history of the Christian church was the emergence of one bishop—that of Rome—as the recognized leader of the western Christian church.

The doctrine of **Petrine supremacy,** based on the belief that the bishops of Rome occupied a preeminent position in the church, was grounded in Scripture. According to the Gospel of Matthew, when Jesus asked his disciples, "Who do you say I am?" Simon Peter answered:

> You are the Christ, the Son of the living God. Jesus replied, Blessed are you, Simon, son of Jonah, for this was not revealed by man, but by my Father in heaven. And I tell you that you are Peter, and on this rock I will build my church, and the gates of hell will not overcome it. I will give you the keys of the kingdom of heaven; whatever you bind on earth will be bound in heaven; and whatever you loose on earth will be loosed in heaven.[8]

According to church tradition, Jesus had given the keys to the kingdom of heaven to Peter, who was considered the chief apostle and the first bishop of Rome. Subsequent bishops of Rome were considered Peter's successors and later the "vicars of Christ" on earth. Though this exalted view of the bishops of Rome was by no means accepted by all early Christians, Rome's position as the traditional capital of the Roman Empire served to buttress this claim.

By the end of the fourth century, the bishops of Rome were using the title of *papa,* "father" (which became the English *pope*). Pope Leo I (440–461) was especially energetic in systematically expounding the doctrine of Petrine supremacy. He portrayed himself as the heir of Peter, whom Jesus had chosen to be head of the Christian church. But state authorities were also claiming some power over the church.

Church and State

Once the Roman emperors became Christians, they came to play a significant role in the affairs of the church. Christian emperors viewed themselves as God's representatives on earth. They not only built churches and influenced the structure of the church's organization but also became involved in church government and doctrinal controversies.

While emperors were busying themselves in church affairs, the spiritual and political vacuum left by the disintegration of the Roman state allowed bishops to play a more active role in imperial government. Increasingly, they served as advisers to Christian Roman emperors. Moreover, as imperial authority declined, bishops often played a noticeably independent political role. Ambrose (c. 339–397) of Milan was an early example of a strong and independent bishop. Through his activities and writings, Ambrose created an image of the ideal Christian bishop. Among other things, this ideal bishop would defend the independence of the church against the tendency of imperial officials to oversee church policy: "Exalt not yourself, but if you would reign the longer, be subject to God. It is written, God's to God and Caesar's to Caesar. The palace is the Emperor's, the Churches are the Bishop's."[9] When Emperor Theodosius I ordered the massacre of many citizens in Thessalonika for refusing to obey his commands, Ambrose denounced the massacre and refused to allow the emperor to take part in church ceremonies. Theodosius finally agreed to do public penance in the cathedral of Milan for his dastardly deed. Ambrose proved himself a formidable advocate of the position that spiritual authority should take precedence over temporal power, at least in spiritual matters.

The weakness of the political authorities on the Italian peninsula also contributed to the church's independence in that area. In the Germanic kingdoms, the kings controlled both churches and bishops. But in Italy, a different tradition prevailed, fed by semilegendary accounts of papal deeds. Pope Leo I, for example, supposedly caused Attila the Hun to turn away from Rome in 452. Although Attila's withdrawal was probably due more to plague than to papal persuasion, the pope got the credit. Popes, then, played significant political roles in Italy, which only added to their claims of power vis-à-vis the secular authorities. Pope Gelasius (juh-LAY-shuss) I (492–496) could write to the emperor at Constantinople:

> There are two powers, august Emperor, by which this world is ruled from the beginning: the consecrated authority of the bishops, and the royal power. In these matters the priests bear the heavier burden because they will render account, even for rulers of men, at the divine judgment. Besides, most gracious son, you are aware that, although you in your office are the ruler of the human race, nevertheless you devoutly bow your head before those who are leaders in things divine and look to them for the means of your salvation.[10]

According to Gelasius, though there were two ruling powers, spiritual and temporal, with different functions, the church was ultimately the higher authority because all men, including emperors, must look to the church "for the means of . . . salvation."

Pope Gregory the Great

Although western Christians came to accept the bishop of Rome as head of the church, there was no unanimity on the extent of the powers the pope possessed as a result of his position. Nevertheless, the emergence in the sixth century of a strong pope, Gregory I, known as Gregory the Great, set the papacy and the Roman Catholic Church on an energetic path that enabled the church in the seventh and eighth centuries to play an increasingly prominent role in civilizing the Germans and aiding the emergence of a distinctly new European civilization.

As pope, Gregory I (590–604) assumed direction of Rome and its surrounding territories, which had suffered enormously from the Ostrogothic-Byzantine struggle and the Lombard invasion of the sixth century. Gregory described the conditions in a sermon to the people of Rome:

> What Rome herself, once deemed the Mistress of the World, has now become, we see—wasted away with afflictions grievous and many, with the loss of citizens, the assaults of enemies,

Pope Gregory I. Pope Gregory the Great became one of the most important popes of the Early Middle Ages. As a result of his numerous writings, he is considered the last of the Latin Fathers of the church. This twelfth-century manuscript illustration shows Gregory dictating a work to a monk. On Gregory's shoulder is a dove, symbol of the Holy Spirit, which is providing divine inspiration for what he is dictating.

The Life of Saint Anthony

In the third and early fourth centuries, the lives of martyrs had provided important models for early Christianity. But in the course of the fourth century, monks who attempted to achieve spiritual perfection through asceticism, the denial of earthly life, and the struggle with demons became the new spiritual ideal for Christians. Consequently, spiritual biographies of early monks became a significant new form of Christian literature. Especially noteworthy was *The Life of Saint Anthony* by Saint Athanasius, the defender of Catholic orthodoxy against the Arians. His work had been translated into Latin before 386. This excerpt describes how Anthony fought off the temptations of Satan.

Athanasius, *The Life of Saint Anthony*

Now when the Enemy [Satan] saw that his craftiness in this matter was without profit, and that the more he brought temptation into Saint Anthony, the more strenuous the saint was in protecting himself against him with the armor of righteousness, he attacked him by means of the vigor of early manhood which is bound up in the nature of our humanity. With the goadings of passion he sued to trouble him by night, and in the daytime also he would vex him and pain him with the same to such an extent that even those who saw him knew from his appearance that he was waging war against the Adversary. But the more the Evil One brought unto him filthy and maddening thoughts, the more Saint Anthony took refuge in prayer and in abundant supplication, and amid them all he remained wholly chaste. And the Evil One was working upon him every shameful deed according to his wont, and at length he even appeared unto Saint Anthony in the form of a woman; and other things which resembled this he performed with ease, for such things are a subject for boasting to him.

But the blessed Anthony knelt down upon his knees on the ground, and prayed before Him who said, "Before you criest unto Me, I will answer you," and said, "O my Lord, this I entreat you. Let not Your love be blotted out from my mind, and behold, I am, by Your grace, innocent before You." And again the Enemy multiplied in him the thoughts of lust, until Saint Anthony became as one who was being burned up, not through the Evil One, but through his own lusts; but he girded himself about with the threat of the thought of the Judgment, and of the torture of Gehenna [Hell], and of the worm which does not die. And while meditating on the thoughts which could be directed against the Evil One, he prayed for thoughts which would be hostile to him. Thus, to the reproach and shame of the Enemy, these things could not be performed; for he who imagined that he could be God was made a mock of by a young man, and he who boasted over flesh and blood was vanquished by a man who was clothed with flesh.

Q Based on this account by Athanasius, how would you characterize the ascetic ideals of early Christian monks? How important were those ideals to the growth of early Christianity? What do you think would be the broader cultural effects of a Christian hatred of the human body?

> the frequent fall of ruined buildings.... Where is the Senate? Where is the people? The bones are all dissolved, the flesh is consumed, all the pomp of the dignities of this world is gone.[11]

Gregory took charge and made Rome and its surrounding area into an administrative unit that eventually came to be known as the Papal States. Although historians disagree about Gregory's motives in establishing papal temporal power, no doubt Gregory was probably only doing what he felt needed to be done: provide for the defense of Rome against the Lombards, establish a government for Rome, and feed the people. Gregory remained loyal to the empire and continued to address the Byzantine emperor as the rightful ruler of Italy.

Gregory also pursued a policy of extending papal authority over the Christian church in the west. He intervened in ecclesiastical conflicts throughout Italy and corresponded with the Frankish rulers, urging them to reform the church in Gaul. He successfully initiated the efforts of missionaries to convert England to Christianity and was especially active in converting the pagan peoples of Germanic Europe. His primary instrument was the monastic movement.

The Monks and Their Missions

A **monk** (Latin *monachus,* meaning "someone who lives alone") was a man who sought to live a life divorced from the world, cut off from ordinary human society, in order to pursue an ideal of godliness or total dedication to the will of God. Christian **monasticism,** which developed first in Egypt, was initially based on the model of the solitary hermit who forsakes all civilized society to pursue spirituality. Saint Anthony (c. 250–350) was a prosperous Egyptian peasant who decided to follow Jesus's injunction in the Gospel of Mark: "Go your way, sell whatsoever you have, and give to the poor, and you shall have treasure in heaven: and come, take up the cross, and follow me."[12] Anthony gave his 300 acres of land to the poor and went into the desert to pursue his ideal of holiness (see the box above). Others did likewise, often to extremes. Saint Simeon the Stylite lived for three decades in a basket atop a pillar more than 60 feet high. These spiritual gymnastics established a new ideal for Christianity. Whereas the early Christian model had been the martyr who died for the faith and achieved eternal life in the process, the new ideal was the monk who died to the world and achieved spiritual life through denial, asceticism, and mystical experience of God.

These early monks, however, soon found themselves unable to live in solitude. Their feats of holiness attracted followers on a wide scale, and as the monastic ideal spread throughout the east, a new form of monasticism, based on the practice of communal life, soon became the dominant form. Monastic communities soon came to be seen as the ideal Christian society that could provide a moral example to the wider society around them.

Saint Benedict. Benedict was the author of a set of rules that was instrumental in the development of monastic groups in the Catholic Church. In this thirteenth-century Latin manuscript, Benedict is shown handing the rules of the Benedictine order to a group of nuns and a group of monks.

BENEDICTINE MONASTICISM Saint Benedict of Nursia (c. 480–c. 543), who founded a monastic house for which he wrote a set of rules sometime between 520 and 530, established the fundamental form of monastic life in the western Christian church. Benedict's rules largely rejected the ascetic ideals of eastern monasticism, which had tended to emphasize such practices as fasting and self-inflicted torments (such as living atop pillars for thirty years), in favor of an ideal of moderation. In Chapter 40 of the rules, on the amount of drink a monk should imbibe, this sense of moderation becomes apparent:

> "Every man has his proper gift from God, one after this manner, another after that." And therefore it is with some misgiving that we determine the amount of food for someone else. Still, having regard for the weakness of some brothers, we believe that a hemina [a quarter liter] of wine per day will suffice for all. Let those, however, to whom God gives the gift of abstinence, know that they shall have their proper reward. But if either the circumstances of the place, the work, or the heat of summer necessitates more, let it lie in the discretion of the abbot to grant it. But let him take care in all things lest satiety or drunkenness supervene.

At the same time, moderation did not preclude a hard and disciplined existence based on the ideals of poverty, chastity, and obedience.

Benedict's rules divided each day into a series of activities with primary emphasis on prayer and manual labor. Physical work of some kind was required of all monks for several hours a day because "idleness is the enemy of the soul." At the very heart of community practice was prayer, the proper "work of God." While this included private meditation and reading, all monks gathered together seven times during the day for common prayer and chanting of psalms. A Benedictine life was a communal one; monks ate, worked, slept, and worshiped together.

Each Benedictine monastery was strictly ruled by an **abbot,** or "father" of the monastery, who had complete authority over the monks, who bent unquestioningly to the will of the abbot. Each Benedictine monastery owned lands that enabled it to be a self-sustaining community, isolated from and independent of the world surrounding it. Within the monastery, however, monks were to fulfill their vow of poverty: "Let all things be common to all, as it is written, lest anyone should say that anything is his own or arrogate it to himself."[13] By the eighth century, Benedictine monasticism had spread throughout the west.

Women, too, sought to withdraw from the world to dedicate themselves to God. Already in the third century, groups of women abandoned the cities to form communities in the deserts of Egypt and Syria. The first monastic rules for western women were produced by Caesarius of Arles for his sister in the fifth century. They strongly emphasized a rigid cloistering of female religious, known as **nuns,** to preserve them from dangers. Later in the west, in the seventh and eighth centuries, the growth of double monasteries allowed monks and nuns to reside close by and follow a common set of rules. Not all women pursued the celibate life in the desert, however. In a number of cities in the fourth century, women organized religious communities in their own homes.

Monasticism played an indispensable role in early medieval civilization. Monks became the new heroes of Christian civilization. Their dedication to God became the highest ideal of Christian life. Moreover, the monks played an increasingly significant role in spreading Christianity to all of Europe.

IRISH MONKS AS MISSIONARIES Ireland had remained a Celtic outpost beyond the reach of the Roman Empire and the Germanic invaders. The most famous of the Christian missionaries to Ireland in the fifth century was Saint Patrick (c. 390–461). Son of a Romano-British Christian,

Irish Monasticism and the Penitential

Irish monasticism became well known for its ascetic practices. Much emphasis was placed on careful examination of conscience to determine if one had committed a sin against God. To facilitate this examination, penitentials were developed that listed possible sins with appropriate penances. Penance usually meant fasting a number of days each week, taking only bread and water. Although these penitentials were eventually used throughout Christendom, they were especially important in Irish Christianity. This excerpt from the penitential of Cummean, an Irish abbot, was written about 650 and demonstrates a distinctive feature of the penitentials, an acute preoccupation with sexual sins.

The Penitential of Cummean

A bishop who commits fornication shall be degraded and shall do penance for twelve years.

A priest or a deacon who commits natural fornication, having previously taken the vow of a monk, shall do penance for seven years. He shall ask pardon every hour; he shall perform a special fast during every week except in the days between Easter and Pentecost.

He who defiles his mother shall do penance for three years, with perpetual pilgrimage.

So shall those who commit sodomy do penance every seven years.

He who merely desires in his mind to commit fornication, but is not able, shall do penance for one year, especially in the three forty-day periods.

He who is willingly polluted during sleep shall arise and sing nine psalms in order, kneeling. On the following day, he shall live on bread and water.

A cleric who commits fornication once shall do penance for one year on bread and water; if he begets a son he shall do penance for seven years as an exile; so also a virgin.

He who loves any woman, but is unaware of any evil beyond a few conversations, shall do penance for forty days.

He who is in a state of matrimony ought to be continent during the three forty-day periods and on Saturday and on Sunday, night and day, and in the two appointed week days [Wednesday and Friday], and after conception, and during the entire menstrual period.

After a birth he shall abstain, if it is a son, for thirty-three [days]; if a daughter, for sixty-six [days].

Boys talking alone and transgressing the regulations of the elders [in the monastery], shall be corrected by three special fasts.

Children who imitate acts of fornication, twenty days; if frequently, forty.

But boys of twenty years who practice masturbation together and confess [shall do penance] twenty or forty days before they take communion.

Q What does the penitential of Cummean reveal about the nature of Irish monasticism? What do you think was the theory of human sexuality held by early Irish Christianity?

Patrick was kidnapped as a young man by Irish raiders and kept as a slave in Ireland. After his escape to Gaul, he became a monk and chose to return to Ireland to convert the Irish to Christianity. Irish tradition ascribes to Patrick the title of "founder of Irish Christianity," a testament to his apparent success.

Since Ireland had not been part of the Roman world and was fairly isolated from the European continent even after its conversion, Irish Christianity tended to develop along lines somewhat different from Roman Christianity. Whereas Catholic ecclesiastical structure had followed Roman government models, the absence of these models in Ireland engendered a different pattern of church organization. Rather than bishoprics, monasteries became the fundamental units of church organization, and abbots, the heads of the monasteries, exercised far more control over the Irish church than bishops did.

By the sixth century, Irish monasticism was a flourishing institution with its own striking characteristics. It was strongly ascetic. Monks performed strenuous fasts, prayed and meditated frequently under extreme privations, and confessed their sins on a regular basis to their superiors. In fact, Irish monasticism gave rise to the use of penitentials or manuals that provided a guide for examining one's life to see what offenses against the will of God one had committed (see the box above).

A great love of learning also characterized Irish monasticism. The Irish eagerly absorbed both Latin and Greek culture and fostered education as a major part of their monastic life. Irish monks were preserving Classical Latin at the same time spoken Latin was being corrupted on the Continent into new dialects that eventually became the Romance languages, such as Italian, French, and Spanish. Irish monasteries produced extraordinary illuminated manuscripts illustrated with abstract geometric patterns.

The emphasis on asceticism led many Irish monks to go into voluntary exile. This "exile for the love of God" was not into isolation, however, but into missionary activity. Irish monks became fervid missionaries. Saint Columba (521–597) left Ireland in 565 as a "pilgrim for Christ" and founded a highly influential monastic community off the coast of Scotland on the island of Iona. From there Irish missionaries went to northern England to begin the

The Book of Kells. Art historians use the term *Hiberno-Saxon* (Hibernia was the ancient name for Ireland) or *Insular* to refer to works produced primarily in the monasteries of the British Isles, especially Ireland. The best example of Hiberno-Saxon art is *The Book of Kells,* a richly decorated illuminated manuscript of the Christian gospels. Though owned by the monastery of Kells, the work was produced by the monks of Iona, who combined Celtic and Anglo-Saxon abstract designs with elaborate portrayals of human figures and animals. A twelfth-century priest who viewed it observed: "Look . . . keenly at it and you . . . will make out intricacies, so delicate and subtle, so exact and compact, so full of knots and links, with colors so fresh and vivid, that you might say that all this was the work of an angel, and not of a man." This page from the Gospel of Luke shows the devil tempting Jesus to cast himself down from the Temple.

process of converting the Angles and Saxons. Aidan of Iona, for example, founded the island monastery of Lindisfarne (LIN-dis-farn) in the Anglo-Saxon kingdom of Northumbria. Lindisfarne in turn became a training center for monks who spread out to different parts of Anglo-Saxon England. Meanwhile, other Irish monks traveled to the European mainland. New monasteries founded by the Irish became centers of learning wherever they were located.

THE CONVERSION OF ENGLAND At the same time the Irish monks were busy bringing their version of Christianity to the Anglo-Saxons of Britain, Pope Gregory the Great had set in motion his own effort to convert England to Roman Christianity. His most important agent was Augustine, a monk from Saint Andrew's monastery in Rome, who arrived in England in 597. England at that time had a number of Germanic kingdoms. Augustine went first to Kent, where he converted King Ethelbert, whereupon most of the king's subjects followed suit. Pope Gregory's conversion techniques emphasized persuasion rather than force, and as seen in this excerpt from one of his letters, he was willing to assimilate old pagan practices in order to coax the pagans into the new faith:

> We wish you [Abbot Mellitus] to inform him [Augustine] that we have been giving careful thought to the affairs of the English, and have come to the conclusion that the temples of the idols among that people should on no account be destroyed. The idols are to be destroyed, but the temples themselves are to be sprinkled with holy water, altars set up in them, and relics deposited there. For if these temples are well-built, they must be purified from the worship of demons and dedicated to the service of the true God. In this way, we hope that the people, seeing that their temples are not destroyed, may abandon their error and, flocking more readily to their accustomed resorts, may come to know and adore the true God.[14]

Freed of their pagan past, temples became churches, as one Christian commentator noted with joy: "The dwelling place of demons has become a house of God. The saving light has come to shine, where shadows covered all. Where sacrifices once took place and idols stood, angelic choirs now dance. Where God was angered once, now God is made content."[15]

Likewise, old pagan feasts were given new names and incorporated into the Christian calendar. No doubt Gregory was aware that early Christians had done the same. The Christian feast of Christmas, for example, was held on December 25, the day of the pagan celebration of the winter solstice.

As Roman Christianity spread northward in Britain, it encountered Irish Christianity moving southward. Soon arguments arose over the differences between Celtic and Roman Christianity, especially over matters of discipline. At the Synod of Whitby, held in the kingdom of Northumbria in 664, the king of Northumbria accepted the arguments of the representatives of Roman Christianity and decided the issue in favor of Roman practices. A gradual fusion of Celtic and Roman Christianity now ensued. Despite its newfound unity and loyalty to Rome, the English church retained some Irish features. Most important was the concentration on monastic culture with special emphasis on learning and missionary work. By 700, the English clergy had become the best trained and most learned in western Europe.

Following the Irish example, English monks journeyed to the European continent to carry on the work of conversion (see Map 7.4). Most important was Boniface (c. 675–754), who undertook the conversion of pagan Germans in Frisia, Bavaria, and Saxony. By 740, Saint Boniface, the "Apostle of the Germans," had become the most famous churchman in Europe. Fourteen

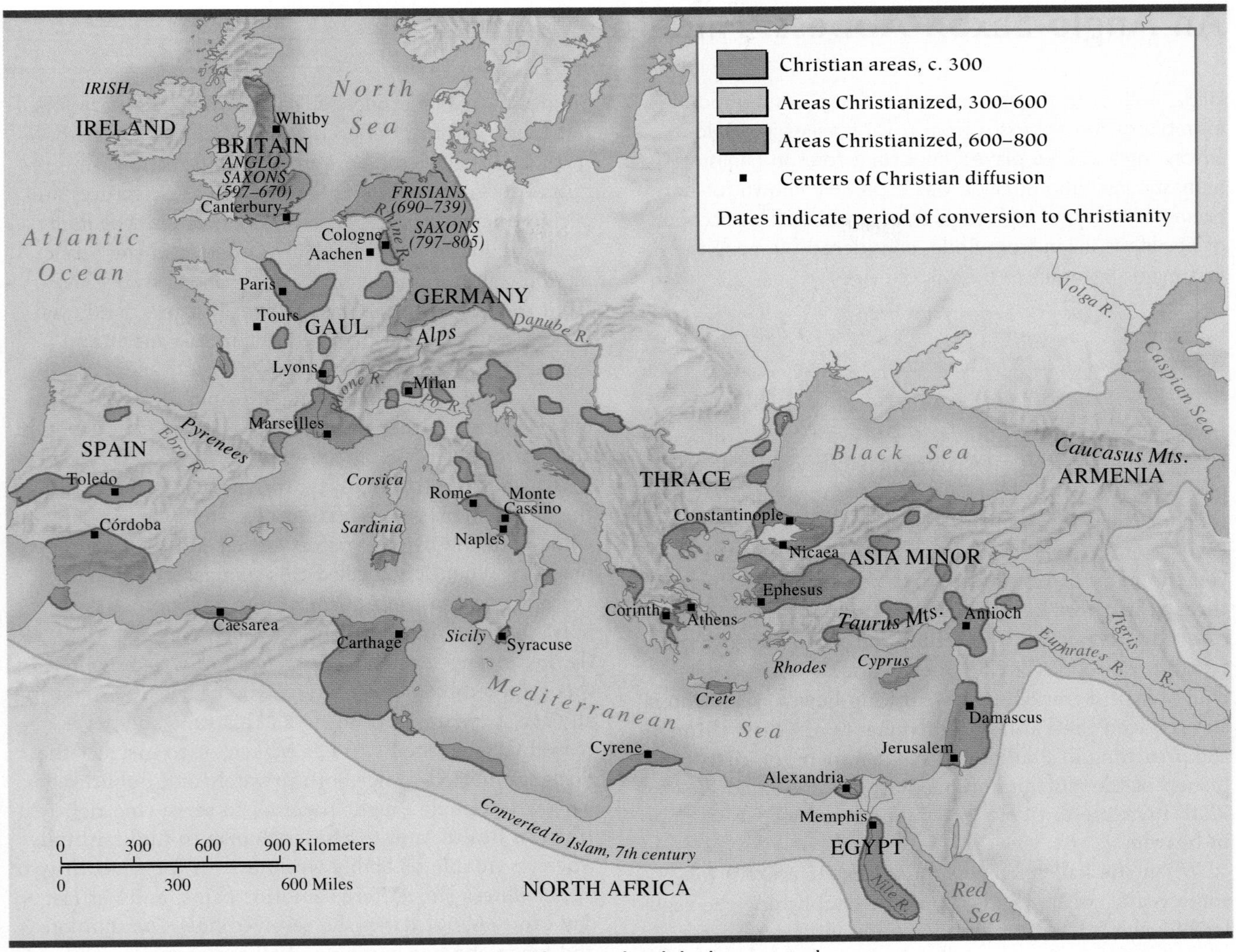

MAP 7.4 The Spread of Christianity, 400–800. The Christian church had penetrated much of the Roman Empire by the end of the fifth century. It emerged as a major base of power after the fall of the empire, and it pushed its influence into new areas through the activities of missionaries.

What aspects of geography help explain the relatively late conversions of the Anglo-Saxons in Britain and the Frisians and Saxons east of the Rhine River?

View an animated version of this map or related maps on the CourseMate website.

years later, he was killed while trying to convert the pagan Frisians. Boniface was a brilliant example of the numerous Irish and English monks whose tireless efforts made Europe the bastion of the Roman Catholic faith.

WOMEN AND MONASTICISM Women, too, played an important role in the monastic missionary movement and the conversion of the Germanic kingdoms. Double monasteries, where monks and nuns lived in separate houses but attended church services together, were found in both the English and Frankish kingdoms. The monks and nuns followed common rules under a common head—frequently an **abbess** rather than an abbot. Many of these abbesses belonged to royal houses, especially in Anglo-Saxon England. In the kingdom of Northumbria, for example, Saint Hilda founded the monastery of Whitby in 657. As abbess, she was responsible for giving learning an important role in the life of the monastery; five future bishops were educated under her tutelage (see the box on p. 200). For female intellectuals, monasteries offered opportunities for learning not found elsewhere in the society of their day.

Nuns of the seventh and eighth centuries were not always as heavily cloistered as they once had been and were therefore able to play an important role in the spread of Christianity. The great English missionary Boniface relied on nuns in England for books and money. He also asked the abbess of Wimborne to send groups of nuns to establish convents in newly converted German lands. A nun named Leoba established the first convent in Germany at Bischofsheim.

An Anglo-Saxon Abbess: Hilda of Whitby

Hilda, abbess of the monastery of Whitby, is a good example of the abbesses from royal families in Anglo-Saxon England who played important roles in English monastic institutions. Hilda was especially known for her exemplary life and high regard for learning. This account of her life is taken from Bede, considered by many the first major historian of the Middle Ages.

Bede, *The Ecclesiastical History of the English People*

In the following year, that is the year of our Lord 680, Hilda, abbess of the monastery of Whitby, a most religious servant of Christ, passed away to receive the reward of eternal life on the seventeenth of November at the age of sixty-six, after a life full of heavenly deeds. Her life fell into two equal parts, for she spent thirty-three years most nobly in secular occupations, and dedicated the remainder of her life even more nobly to our Lord in the monastic life. She was nobly born, the daughter of Hereric, nephew to King Edwin, with whom she received the Faith and sacraments of Christ through the preaching of Paulinus of blessed memory, first bishop of the Northumbrians, and she preserved this Faith inviolate until she was found worthy to see him in heaven. . . .

When she had ruled this monastery (Heruteu) for some years, constantly occupied in establishing the regular life, she further undertook to found or organize a monastery at a place known as Streaneshalch, and carried out this appointed task with great energy. She established the same regular life as in her former monastery, and taught the observance of justice, devotion, purity, and other virtues, but especially in peace and charity. After the example of the primitive Church, no one there was rich or poor, for everything was held in common, and none possessed any personal property. So great was her prudence that not only ordinary folk, but kings and princes used to come and ask her advice in their difficulties. Those under her direction were required to make a thorough study of the Scriptures and occupy themselves in good works, in order that many might be found fitted for Holy Orders and the service of God's altar. Subsequently, five bishops were chosen from this monastery—Bosa, Hedda, Oftfor, John, and Wilfrid—all of them men of outstanding merit and holiness. . . .

Christ's servant Abbess Hilda, whom all her acquaintances called Mother because of her wonderful devotion and grace, was not only an example of holy life to members of her own community, for she also brought about the amendment and salvation of many living far distant, who heard the inspiring story of her industry and goodness. . . . When Hilda ruled this monastery for many years, it pleased the Author of our salvation to try her holy soul by a long sickness, in order that, like the Apostle, her strength might be perfected in weakness. She was attacked by a burning fever that racked her continually for six years; but during all this time she never ceased to give thanks to her Maker, or to instruct the flock committed to her both privately and publicly. For her own example taught them all to serve God rightly when in health, and to render thanks to him faithfully when in trouble or bodily weakness. In the seventh year of her illness she suffered interior pains, and her last day came. About dawn she received holy Communion, and when she had summoned all the servants of Christ in the monastery, she urged them to maintain the gospel peace among themselves and with others. And while she was still speaking, she joyfully welcomed death, and in the words of our Lord, passed from death to life.

Q What kind of portrait does Bede present of Hilda? What moral lessons is he trying to teach?

THE PATH OF CELIBACY The monastic movement enabled some women to pursue a new path to holiness. Cloisters for both men and women offered the ideal place to practice the new Christian ideal of celibacy. This newfound emphasis on abstaining from sexual relations, especially evident in the emphasis on virginity, created a new image of the human body in late antiquity. To many Greeks and Romans, the human body had been a source of beauty, joy, and enjoyment, an attitude evident in numerous works of art. Many Christians, however, viewed the body as a hindrance to a spiritual connection with God. The refusal to have sex was a victory over the desires of the flesh and thus an avenue to holiness.

In the fourth and fifth centuries, a cult of virginity also moved beyond the walls of monasteries and convents. Throughout the Mediterranean world, groups of women met together to study the importance and benefits of celibacy. In Rome, a woman named Marcella supported a group of aristocratic women who studied the teachings about celibacy and also aided Jerome, the church father, with his work in translating the Bible into Latin.

Christian Intellectual Life in the Germanic Kingdoms

Although the Christian church came to accept Classical culture, it was not easy to do so in the new Germanic kingdoms. Nevertheless, some Christian scholars managed to keep learning alive.

CASSIODORUS Most prominent was Cassiodorus (c. 490–585), who came from an aristocratic Roman family and served as an official of the Ostrogothic king Theodoric (see the box on p. 188). The conflicts that erupted after the death of Theodoric led Cassiodorus to withdraw from public life and retire to his landed estates in southern Italy, where he wrote his final work, *Divine and Human Readings,* a compendium of the literature of both Christian and pagan antiquity. Cassiodorus accepted the advice of earlier Christian intellectuals to make use of Classical works while treasuring the Scriptures above all else.

Cassiodorus continued the tradition of late antiquity of classifying knowledge according to certain subjects. In assembling his compendium of authors, he followed the works of late ancient authors in placing all secular knowledge into the categories of the seven **liberal arts,** which were divided into two major groups: the ***trivium,*** consisting of grammar, rhetoric, and dialectic or logic, and the ***quadrivium,*** consisting of arithmetic, geometry, astronomy, and music. The seven liberal arts would remain the cornerstone of Western education for nearly twelve hundred years.

BEDE The Venerable Bede (BEED) (c. 672–735) was a scholar and product of Christian Anglo-Saxon England. He entered a monastery at Jarrow as a small boy and remained there most of the rest of his life. His *Ecclesiastical History of the English People,* completed in 731, was a product of the remarkable flowering of English ecclesiastical and monastic culture in the eighth century. His history of England begins with the coming of Christianity to Britain. Although Bede shared the credulity of his age in regard to stories of miracles, he had a remarkable sense of history. He used his sources so judiciously that they remain our chief source of information about early Anglo-Saxon England (see the box on p. 200). His work was a remarkable accomplishment for a monk from a small corner of England and reflects the high degree of intellectual achievement in England in the eighth century.

The Byzantine Empire

FOCUS QUESTION: How did the Byzantine Empire that had emerged by the eighth century differ from the empire of Justinian and from the Germanic kingdoms in the west?

As noted earlier, in the fourth century, a separation between the western and eastern parts of the Roman Empire began to occur. Even as the Germans moved into the western part of the empire and established various kingdoms over the course of the fifth century, the Roman Empire in the east, centered on Constantinople, solidified and prospered.

The Reign of Justinian (527–565)

In the sixth century, the empire in the east came under the control of one of its most remarkable rulers, the emperor Justinian. As the nephew and heir of the previous emperor, Justinian had been well trained in imperial administration. He was determined to reestablish the Roman Empire in the entire Mediterranean world and began his attempt to reconquer the west in 533.

Justinian's army under Belisarius (bell-uh-SAH-ree-uss), probably the best general of the late Roman world, presented a formidable force. Belisarius sailed to North Africa and quickly destroyed the Vandals in two major battles. From North Africa, he led his forces onto the Italian peninsula after occupying Sicily in 535. But it was not until 552 that the Ostrogoths were finally defeated. The struggle devastated Italy, which suffered more from Justinian's reconquest than from all of the previous barbarian invasions.

Justinian has been criticized for overextending his resources and bankrupting the empire. Historians now think, however, that a devastating plague in 542 and long-term economic changes were far more damaging to the Eastern Roman Empire than Justinian's conquests. Before he died, Justinian appeared to have achieved his goals. He had restored the imperial Mediterranean world; his empire included Italy, part of Spain, North Africa, Asia Minor, Palestine, and Syria (see Map 7.5). But the conquest of the Western Empire proved fleeting. Only three years after Justinian's death, the Lombards entered Italy. Although the Eastern Empire maintained the fiction of Italy as a province, its forces were limited to southern and central Italy, Sicily, and coastal areas, such as the territory around Ravenna.

THE CODIFICATION OF ROMAN LAW Though his conquests proved short-lived, Justinian made a lasting contribution to Western civilization through his codification of Roman law. The Eastern Empire was heir to a vast quantity of materials connected to the development of Roman law. These included laws passed by the senate and assemblies, legal commentaries of jurists, decisions of praetors, and the edicts of emperors. Justinian had been well trained in imperial government and was thoroughly acquainted with Roman law. He wished to codify and simplify this mass of materials.

To accomplish his goal, Justinian authorized the jurist Trebonian to make a systematic compilation of imperial edicts. The result was the Code of Law, the first part of the *Corpus Iuris Civilis* (KOR-pus YOOR-iss SIV-i-liss) (Body of Civil Law), completed in 529. Four years later, two other parts of the *Corpus* appeared: the *Digest,* a compendium of writings of Roman jurists, and the *Institutes,* a brief summary of the chief principles of Roman law that could be used as a textbook on Roman law. The fourth part of the *Corpus* was the *Novels,* a compilation of the most important new edicts issued during Justinian's reign.

S. Vitale, Ravenna//© Scala/Art Resource, NY

The Emperor Justinian and His Court. As the seat of Byzantine power in Italy, the town of Ravenna was adorned with many examples of Byzantine art. The Church of San Vitale at Ravenna contains some of the finest examples of sixth-century Byzantine mosaics. Small pieces of colored glass were set in mortar on the wall to form these figures and their surroundings. The emperor is seen as both head of state (he wears a jeweled crown and a purple robe) and head of the church (he carries a gold bowl symbolizing the body of Jesus.)

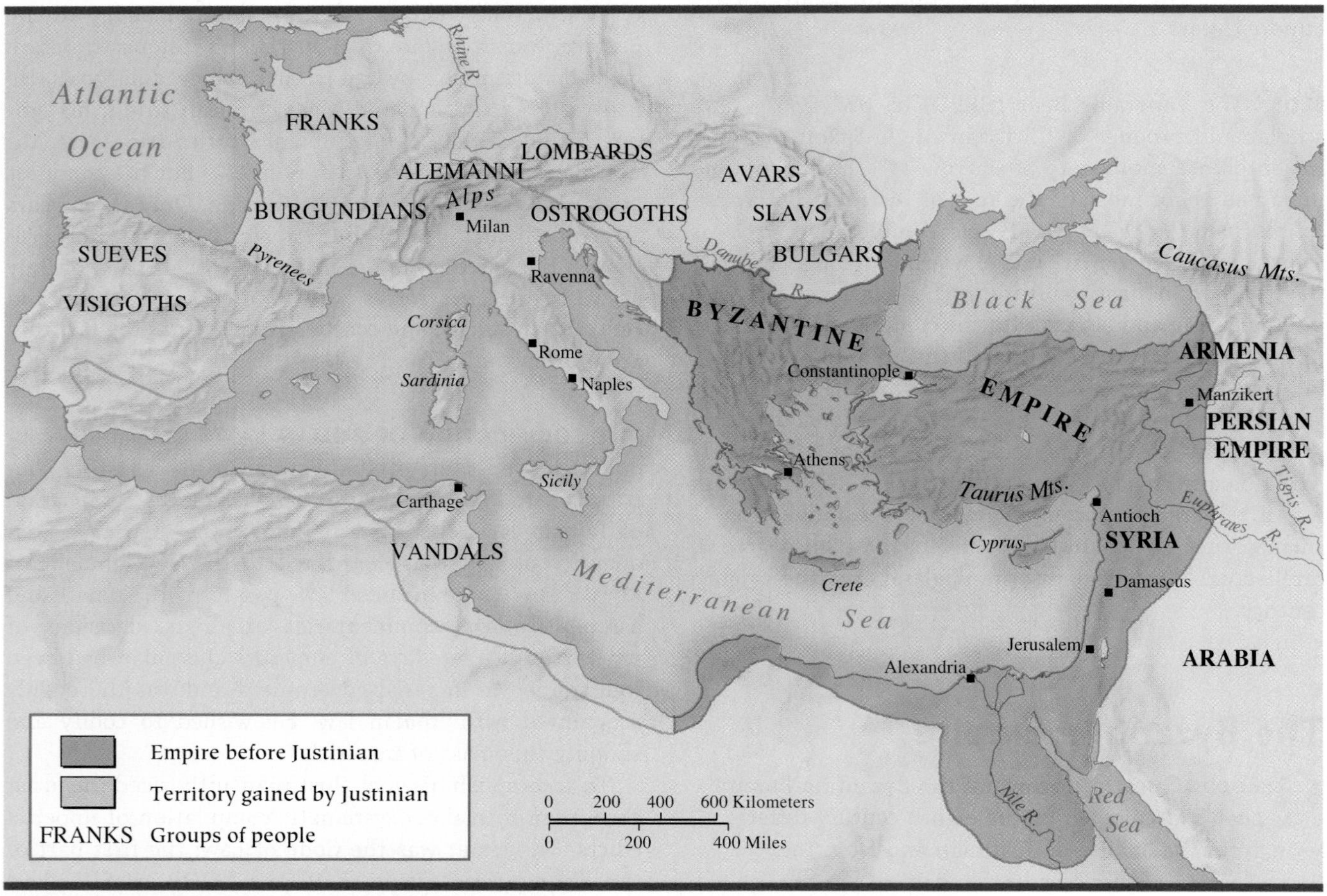

MAP 7.5 The Byzantine Empire in the Time of Justinian. The Byzantine emperor Justinian briefly restored much of the Mediterranean portion of the old Roman Empire. His general Belisarius quickly conquered the Vandals in North Africa but wrested Italy from the Ostrogoths only after a long and devastating struggle.

Q ***Look back at Map 6.1. What former Roman territories remained outside Justinian's control?***

View an animated version of this map or related maps on the CourseMate website.

S. Vitale, Ravenna/© Scala/Art Resource, NY

The Empress Theodora and Her Attendants. This mosaic, located on the south wall of the apse of the Church of San Vitale (Justinian is on the north wall), depicts Theodora and her attendants. Her presence on the wall of this church indicates the important role she played in the Byzantine state. At the bottom of her robe is a scene of the three Wise Men, an indication that Theodora was special enough to have belonged in the company of the three kings who visited the newborn Jesus.

Justinian's codification of Roman law became the basis of imperial law in the Byzantine Empire until its end in 1453. More important, however, since it was written in Latin (it was, in fact, the last product of eastern Roman culture to be written in Latin, which was soon replaced by Greek), it was also eventually used in the west and in fact became the basis of the legal system of all of continental Europe.

INTELLECTUAL LIFE UNDER JUSTINIAN The intellectual life of the Eastern Roman Empire was highly influenced by the traditions of Classical civilization. Scholars actively strived to preserve the works of the ancient Greeks while basing a great deal of their own literature on Classical models. Initially, however, the most outstanding literary achievements of the Eastern Empire were historical and religious works.

The best known of the historians was Procopius (pruh-KOH-pee-uss) (c. 500–c. 562), court historian during the reign of Justinian. Procopius served as secretary to the great general Belisarius and accompanied him on his wars on behalf of Justinian. Procopius's best historical work, the *Wars,* is a firsthand account of Justinian's wars of reconquest in the western Mediterranean and his wars against the Persians in the east. Deliberately modeled after the work of his hero, the Greek historian Thucydides (see Chapter 3), Procopius's narrative features vivid descriptions of battle scenes, clear judgment, and noteworthy objectivity.

Procopius also wrote a work that many historians consider mostly scandalous gossip, his infamous *Secret History.* At the beginning of this work, Procopius informed his readers that "what I shall write now follows a different plan, supplementing the previous formal chronicle with a disclosure of what really happened throughout the Roman Empire."[16] What he revealed constituted a scathing attack on Justinian and his wife Theodora for their alleged misdeeds.

Procopius, *Secret History,* excerpt

THE EMPRESS THEODORA Theodora (thee-uh-DOR-uh) was the daughter of the "keeper of bears" for the games at Constantinople, who died when she was a child. Theodora followed in her mother's footsteps by becoming an actress, which at that time was considered a lowborn activity. Often actresses also worked as prostitutes, and Theodora was no exception. At the age of twenty-five, she met Justinian, who was forty. His uncle, the Emperor Justin, had to change the law to allow an aristocratic senator to marry a woman who had been an actress. After his uncle died in 527, Justinian became emperor and Theodora empress, a remarkable achievement for a woman from the lower classes.

Justinian and Theodora were close and loving companions. She also influenced her husband in both church and state affairs. A strong-willed and intelligent woman, she proved especially valuable in 532, when the two

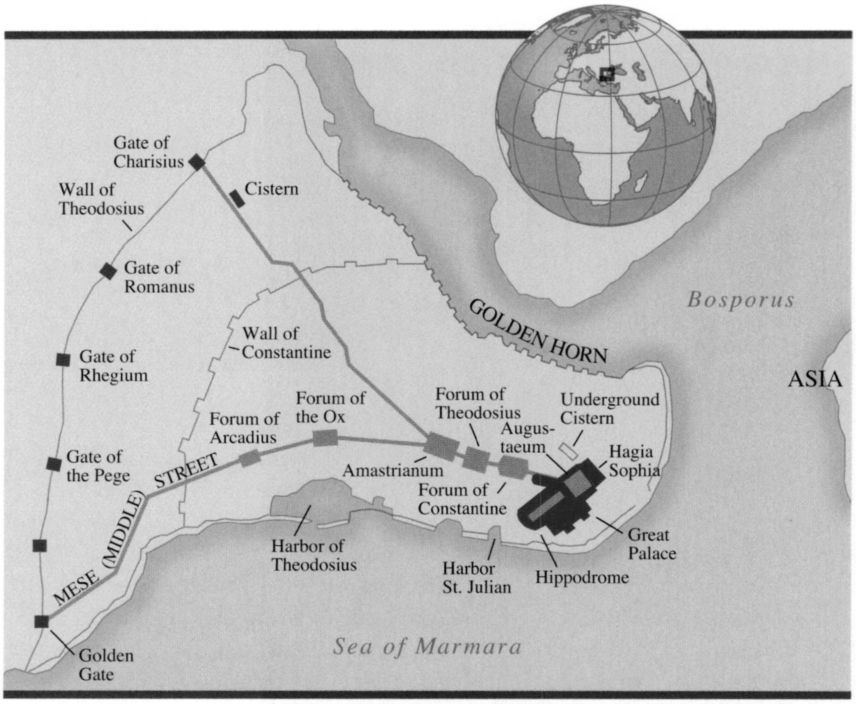

MAP 7.6 Constantinople. Constantinople was the largest city in Europe, and until the twelfth century, it was the nexus of trade between east and west. Emperor Justinian oversaw a massive building program that produced important architectural monuments such as Hagia Sophia.

Q ***What natural and human-built aspects of the city helped protect it from invasion?***

View an animated version of this map or related maps on the CourseMate website.

factions of charioteer supporters in Constantinople joined forces and rioted against the emperor. The riots soon became a revolt as the rioters burned and looted the center of the city, shouting "*Nika!*" ("win"), a word normally used to cheer on their favorite chariot teams. Justinian seemed ready to flee, but Theodora strengthened his resolve by saying, "My opinion then is that the present time, above all others, is inopportune for flight, even though it bring safety.... For one who has been emperor it is unendurable to be a fugitive, ... and may I not live that day on which those who meet me shall not address me as mistress."[17] On hearing her words, Justinian resolved to stay and fight. Many of the protesters were killed, and the so-called Nika Revolt was ended.

THE EMPEROR'S BUILDING PROGRAM After the riots destroyed much of Constantinople, Justinian rebuilt the city and gave it the appearance it would keep for almost a thousand years (see Map 7.6). Earlier, Emperor Theodosius II (408–450) had constructed an enormous defensive wall to protect the city on its land side. The city was dominated by an immense palace complex, a huge arena known as the Hippodrome, and hundreds of churches. No residential district was particularly fashionable; palaces, tenements, and slums ranged alongside one another. Justinian added many new buildings. His public works projects included roads, bridges, walls, public baths, law courts, and colossal underground reservoirs to hold the city's water supply. He also built hospitals, schools, monasteries, and churches. Churches were his special passion, and in Constantinople alone he built or rebuilt thirty-four of them. His greatest achievement was the famous Hagia Sophia, the Church of the Holy Wisdom.

Completed in 537, Hagia Sophia was designed by a Greek architect who departed radically from the simple, flat-roofed basilica of Western architecture. The center of Hagia Sophia consisted of four huge piers crowned by an enormous dome, which seemed to be floating in space. This effect was emphasized by Procopius, the court historian, who, at Justinian's request, wrote a treatise on the emperor's building projects: "From the lightness of the building, it does not appear to rest upon a solid foundation, but to cover the place beneath as though it were suspended from heaven by the fabled golden chain." In part, this impression was created by putting forty-two windows around the base of the dome, which allowed an incredible play of light within the cathedral. Light served to remind the worshipers of God; as Procopius commented:

> Whoever enters there to worship perceives at once that it is not by any human strength or skill, but by the favor of God that this work has been perfected; his mind rises sublime to commune with God, feeling that He cannot be far off, but must especially love to dwell in the place which He has chosen; and this takes place not only when a man sees it for the first time, but it always makes the same impression upon him, as though he had never beheld it before.[18]

As darkness is illumined by invisible light, so too it was believed the world is illumined by invisible spirit.

The royal palace complex, Hagia Sophia, and the Hippodrome were the three greatest buildings in Constantinople. This last was a huge amphitheater, constructed of brick covered by marble, holding as many as 60,000 spectators. Although gladiator fights were held there, the main events were the chariot races; twenty-four would usually be presented in one day. The citizens of Constantinople were passionate fans of chariot racing. Successful charioteers were acclaimed as heroes and honored with public statues. Crowds in the Hippodrome also took on political significance. Being a member of the

Interior View of Hagia Sophia. Pictured here is the interior of the Church of the Holy Wisdom in Constantinople (modern Istanbul), constructed under Justinian by Authemius of Tralles and Isidore of Milan. Some of the stones used in the construction of the church had been plundered from the famous Classical Temple of Diana, near Ephesus, in Asia Minor. This view gives an idea of how the windows around the base of the dome produced a special play of light within the cathedral. The pulpits and plaques bearing inscriptions from the Qur'an were introduced when the Turks converted this church to a mosque in the fifteenth century.

two chief factions of charioteers—the Blues or the Greens—was the only real outlet for political expression. Even emperors had to be aware of their demands and attitudes: the loss of a race in the Hippodrome frequently resulted in bloody riots, and rioting could threaten the emperor's power.

From Eastern Roman to Byzantine Empire

Justinian's accomplishments had been spectacular, but when he died, he left the Eastern Roman Empire with serious problems: too much distant territory to protect, an empty treasury, a smaller population after the plague, and renewed threats to the frontiers. In the first half of the seventh century, during the reign of Heraclius (610–641), the empire faced attacks from the Persians to the east and the Slavs to the north.

CHRONOLOGY The Byzantine Empire

Protective walls of Theodosius II	408–450
Justinian codifies Roman law	529–533
Reconquest of Italy by the Byzantines	535–552
Completion of Hagia Sophia	537
Attacks on the empire in reign of Heraclius	610–641
Defeat by the Arabs at Yarmuk	636
Defeat by the Bulgars; losses in the Balkans	679

The empire was left exhausted by these struggles. In the midst of them, it had developed a new system of defense by creating a new administrative unit, the *theme,* which combined civilian and military offices in the hands of the same person. Thus, the civil governor was also the military leader of the area. Although this innovation helped the empire survive, it also fostered an increased militarization of the empire. By the mid-seventh century, it had become apparent that a restored Mediterranean empire was simply beyond the resources of the Eastern Empire, which now increasingly turned its back on the Latin west. A renewed series of external threats in the second half of the seventh century strengthened this development.

The most serious challenge to the Eastern Empire was the rise of Islam, which unified the Arab tribes and created a powerful new force that swept through the east (see "The Rise of Islam" later in this chapter). The defeat of an eastern Roman army at Yarmuk in 636 meant the loss of the provinces of Syria and Palestine. The Arabs also moved into the old Persian Empire and conquered it. An Arab attempt to besiege Constantinople failed, in large part due to the use of Greek fire against the Arab fleets. Greek fire was a petroleum-based compound containing quicklime and sulfur. Because it would burn under water, the Byzantines created the equivalent of modern flamethrowers by using tubes to blow Greek fire onto wooden ships, with frightening effect. Arabs and eastern Roman forces now faced each other along a frontier in southern Asia Minor.

Problems also arose along the northern frontier, especially in the Balkans, where an Asiatic people known as the Bulgars had arrived earlier in the sixth century. In 679, the Bulgars defeated the eastern Roman forces and took possession of the lower Danube valley, setting up a strong Bulgarian kingdom.

By the beginning of the eighth century, the Eastern Roman Empire was greatly diminished in size, consisting only of the eastern Balkans and Asia Minor. It was now an eastern Mediterranean state. These external challenges had important internal repercussions as well. By the eighth century, the Eastern Roman Empire had been transformed into what historians call the Byzantine Empire, a civilization with its own unique character that would last until 1453 (Constantinople was built on the site of an older city named Byzantium—hence the term *Byzantine*).

THE BYZANTINE EMPIRE IN THE EIGHTH CENTURY The Byzantine Empire was a Greek state. Justinian's *Corpus Iuris Civilis* had been the last official work published in Latin. Increasingly, Latin fell into disuse as Greek became not only the common language of the Byzantine Empire but its official language as well.

The Byzantine Empire, c. 750

The Byzantine Empire was also a Christian state, built on a faith in Jesus that was shared in a profound way by almost all its citizens. An enormous amount of artistic talent was poured into the construction of churches, church ceremonies, and church decoration. Spiritual principles deeply permeated Byzantine art. The importance of religion to the Byzantines explains why theological disputes took on an exaggerated form. The most famous of these disputes, the so-called iconoclastic controversy, threatened the stability of the empire in the first half of the eighth century.

Beginning in the sixth century, the use of religious images, especially in the form of icons or pictures of sacred figures, became so widespread that charges of idolatry, the worship of images, began to be heard. The use of images or icons had been justified by the argument that icons were not worshiped but were simply used to help illiterate people understand their religion. This argument failed to stop the **iconoclasts,** as the opponents of icons were called.

Iconoclasm was not unique to the Byzantine Empire. In the neighboring Islamic empire (see "The Rise of Islam" later in the chapter), religious art did not include any physical representations of Muhammad. Iconoclasm would also play a role among some of the new religious groups that emerged in the Protestant Reformation in sixteenth-century Europe (see Chapter 13).

Beginning in 730, the Byzantine emperor Leo III (717–741) outlawed the use of icons. Strong resistance ensued, especially from monks. Leo also used the iconoclastic controversy to add to the prestige of the patriarch of Constantinople, the highest church official in the east and second in dignity only to the bishop of Rome. The Roman popes were opposed to the iconoclastic edicts, and their opposition created considerable dissension between the popes and the Byzantine emperors. Late in the eighth century, the Byzantine rulers reversed their stand on the use of images, but not before considerable damage had been done to the unity of the Christian church. Although the final separation between Roman Catholicism and Greek Orthodoxy (as the Christian church in the Byzantine Empire was called) did not occur until 1054, the iconoclastic controversy was important in moving both sides in that direction.

The emperor occupied a crucial position in the Byzantine state. Portrayed as chosen by God, the Byzantine emperor was crowned in sacred ceremonies, and his subjects were expected to prostrate themselves in his presence. His power was considered absolute and was limited in practice only by deposition or assassination. Because the emperor appointed the patriarch, he also exercised control over both church and state. The Byzantines believed that God had commanded their state to preserve the true faith—Orthodox Christianity. Emperor, clergy, and civic officials were all bound together in service to this ideal. It can be said that spiritual values truly held the Byzantine state together.

Because of their many foreign enemies, Byzantine emperors spent considerable energy on war and preparations for war. Byzantine literature included many manuals on war, instructing people in the ways of fighting. Byzantine armies, often led by the emperors, were well trained and well equipped with the latest weapons. The Byzantines, however, often preferred to use diplomacy rather than fight. Our word *byzantine*—often defined as "extremely complicated or carried on by underhand methods"—stems from the complex and crafty instructions that Byzantine rulers sent to their envoys.

By 750, it was apparent that two of Rome's heirs, the Germanic kingdoms and the Byzantine Empire, were moving in different directions. Nevertheless, Byzantine influence on the Western world was significant. The images of a Roman imperial state that continued to haunt the west lived on in Byzantium. The legal system of the west came to owe much to Justinian's codification of Roman law. In addition, the Byzantine Empire served in part as a buffer state, protecting the west for a long time from incursions from the east. Although the Byzantine Empire would continue to influence the west until its demise in 1453, it went its own unique way.

LIFE IN CONSTANTINOPLE: THE IMPORTANCE OF TRADE With a population estimated in the hundreds of thousands, Constantinople was the largest city in Europe during the Middle Ages. It viewed itself as the center of an empire and a special Christian city. The Byzantines believed that the city was under the protection of God and the Virgin Mary. One thirteenth-century Byzantine said: "About our city you shall know: until the end she will fear no nation whatsoever, for no one will entrap or capture her, not by any means, for she has been given to the Mother of God and no one will snatch her out of Her hands. Many nations will break their horns against her walls and withdraw with shame."[19]

Until the twelfth century, Constantinople was Europe's greatest commercial center. The city was the chief entrepôt for the exchange of products between west and east, and trade formed the basis for its fabulous prosperity. This trade, however, was largely carried on by foreign merchants. As one contemporary said:

> All sorts of merchants come here from the land of Babylon, from . . . Persia, Media, and all the sovereignty of the land of Egypt, from the lands of Canaan, and from the empire of Russia, from Hungaria, Kharzaria, and the land of Lombardy and Sepharad. It is a busy city, and merchants come to it from every country by sea or land, and there is none like it in the world except Baghdad, the great city of Islam.[20]

Highly desired in western Europe were the products of the east: silk from China, spices from Southeast Asia and India, jewelry and ivory from India (the latter used by artisans for church items), wheat and furs from southern Russia, and flax and honey from the Balkans. Many of these eastern goods were shipped from Constantinople to the Mediterranean area and northern Europe. Despite the Germanic incursions, European trade did not entirely end.

Moreover, imported raw materials were used in Constantinople for local industries. During Justinian's reign, two Christian monks smuggled silkworms from China to begin a silk industry. The state had a monopoly on the production of silk cloth, and the workshops themselves were housed in Constantinople's royal palace complex. European demand for silk cloth made it the city's most lucrative product. It is interesting to note that the upper classes, including emperors and empresses, were not discouraged from making money through trade and manufacturing. Indeed, one empress even manufactured perfumes in her bedroom.

The Rise of Islam

Focus Question: What was the basic message of Islam, and why was it able to expand so successfully?

The Arabs were a Semitic-speaking people of southwestern Asia with a long history. In Roman times, the Arabian peninsula came to be dominated by Bedouin nomads who moved constantly to find water and food for their animals. In early times, the Bedouins had supported themselves primarily by sheepherding or by raiding passing caravans, but after the domestication of the camel during the second millennium B.C.E., the Bedouins began to participate in the caravan trade themselves and became major carriers of goods between the Persian Gulf and the Mediterranean Sea.

Although these early Arabs were polytheistic, there was a supreme God named Allah (AH-lah) (Arabic for "God") who ruled over the other gods. There was no priesthood; all members of the tribe were involved in the practice of the faith. Allah was symbolized by a sacred stone, and each tribe had its own stone. All tribes, however, worshiped a massive black meteorite—the Black Stone, which had been placed in a central shrine called the *Ka'ba* (KAH-buh) in the city of Mecca.

In the fifth and sixth centuries C.E., the Arabian peninsula took on new importance. As a result of political disorder in Mesopotamia and Egypt, the usual trade routes in the region began to change. A new trade route—from the Mediterranean through Mecca to Yemen and then by ship across the Arabian Sea and the Indian Ocean—became more popular, and communities in that part of the Arabian peninsula, such as Mecca, began to prosper from this caravan trade. As a result, tensions arose between the Bedouins in the desert and the increasingly wealthy merchant classes in the towns. Into this intense world came Muhammad (moh-HAM-mud *or* moo-HAM-mud).

Muhammad

Born in Mecca to a merchant family, Muhammad (c. 570–632) was orphaned at the age of five. He grew up to become a caravan manager and eventually married a rich widow who was also his employer. In his middle years, he began to experience visions that he believed were inspired by Allah. Muhammad believed that although Allah had already revealed himself in part through Moses and Jesus—and thus through the Hebrew and Christian traditions—the final revelations were now being given to him. Out of these revelations, which were eventually written down, came the Qur'an (kuh-RAN *or* kuh-RAHN) or Koran, which contained the guidelines by which followers of Allah were to live. Muhammad's teachings formed the basis for the religion known as Islam, which means "submission to the will of Allah." Allah was the all-powerful being who had created the universe and everything in it. Humans must subject themselves to Allah if they wished to achieve everlasting life. His followers were called Muslims, meaning "practitioners of Islam."

After receiving the revelations, Muhammad set out to convince the people of Mecca that the revelations were true. At first, many thought he was insane, and others feared that his attacks on the corrupt society around him would upset the established social and political order. Discouraged by the failure of the Meccans to accept his message, in 622 Muhammad and some of his closest supporters left the city and moved north to the rival city of Yathrib, later renamed Medina ("city of the Prophet"). The year of the journey to Medina, known in history as the *Hegira* (hee-JY-ruh) ("departure"), became year 1 in the official calendar of Islam.

Muhammad, who had been invited to Medina by a number of prominent residents, soon began to win support from people in the town as well as from members of Bedouin tribes in the surrounding countryside. From these groups, he formed the first Muslim community. Muslims saw no separation between political and religious authority; submission to the will of Allah meant submission to his Prophet, Muhammad. Muhammad soon became both a religious and a political leader. His political and military skills enabled him to put together a reliable military force, with which he returned to Mecca in 630, conquering the city and converting the townspeople to the new faith. From Mecca, Muhammad's ideas spread quickly across the Arabian peninsula and within a relatively short time had resulted in both the religious and the political unification of Arab society.

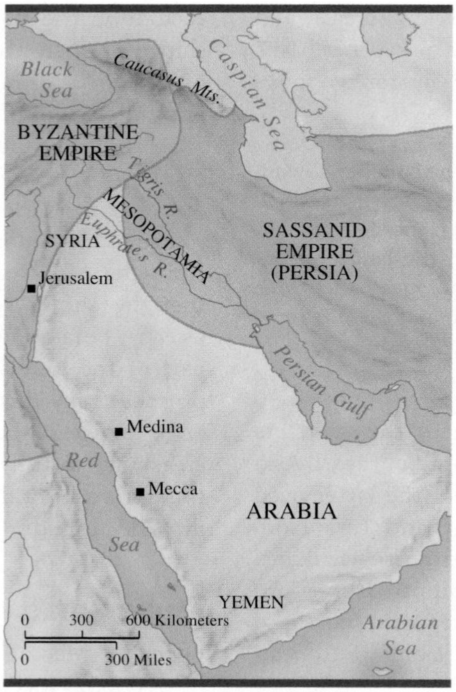

Arabia in the Time of Muhammad

The Teachings of Islam

At the heart of Islam was its sacred book, the Qur'an, with its basic message that there is no God but Allah and Muhammad is his Prophet. Essentially, the Qur'an contains Muhammad's revelations of a heavenly book written down by secretaries. Consisting of 114 chapters, the Qur'an recorded the beliefs of the Muslims and served as their code of ethics and law.

Islam was a direct and simple faith, emphasizing the need to obey the will of Allah. This meant following a basic ethical code consisting of the **Five Pillars of Islam:** belief in Allah and Muhammad as his Prophet; standard prayer five times a day and public prayer on Friday at midday to worship Allah; observance of the holy month of Ramadan (the ninth month on the Muslim calendar) by fasting from dawn to sunset; making a pilgrimage—known as the *hajj* (HAJ)—to Mecca in one's lifetime, if possible (see the box on p. 209); and giving alms to the poor and unfortunate. The faithful who observed the law were guaranteed a place in an eternal paradise.

Islam was not just a set of religious beliefs but a way of life as well. After the death of Muhammad, Muslim scholars drew up a law code, called the *Shari'a* (shah-REE-uh), to provide believers with a set of prescriptions to regulate their daily lives. Much of the *Shari'a* was drawn from the Qur'an. Believers' behavior was subject to strict guidelines. In addition to the Five Pillars, Muslims were forbidden to gamble, to eat pork, to drink alcoholic beverages, and to engage in dishonest behavior. Sexual practices were also strict. Marriages were to be arranged by parents, and contacts between unmarried men and women were discouraged. In accordance with Bedouin custom, males were permitted to have more than one wife, but Muhammad attempted to limit the practice by restricting the number of wives to four.

The Spread of Islam

The death of Muhammad presented his followers with a dilemma. Although Muhammad had not claimed to be divine, Muslims saw no separation between religious and political authority. Submission to the will of Allah was the same thing as submission to his Prophet, Muhammad.

Muslims Celebrate the End of Ramadan. Ramadan is the holy month of Islam during which all Muslims must fast from dawn to sunset. Observance of this holy month is regarded as one of the Five Pillars of the faith. Muhammad instituted the fast during his stay at Medina. It was designed to replace the single Jewish Day of Atonement. This Persian miniature depicts Muslims on horseback celebrating the end of Ramadan.

The Qur'an: The Pilgrimage

The Qur'an is the sacred book of the Muslims, comparable to the Bible in Christianity. This selection from Chapter 22, titled "Pilgrimage," discusses the importance of making a pilgrimage to Mecca, one of the Five Pillars of Islam. The pilgrim's final destination was the *Ka'ba* at Mecca, containing the Black Stone.

Qur'an, Chapter 22: "Pilgrimage"

Exhort all men to make the pilgrimage. They will come to you on foot and on the backs of swift camels from every distant quarter; they will come to avail themselves of many a benefit, and to pronounce on the appointed days the name of God over the cattle which He has given them for food. Eat of their flesh, and feed the poor and the unfortunate.

Then let the pilgrims tidy themselves, make their vows, and circle the Ancient House. Such is God's commandment. He that reveres the sacred rites of God shall fare better in the sight of his Lord.

The flesh of cattle is lawful for you, except for that which has been specified before. Guard yourselves against the filth of idols; and avoid the utterance of falsehoods.

Dedicate yourselves to God, and serve none besides Him. The man who serves other deities besides God is like him who falls from heaven and is snatched by the birds or carried away by the wind to some far-off region. Even such is he.

He that reveres the offerings made to God shows the piety of his heart. Your cattle are useful to you in many ways until the time of their slaughter. Then they are offered for sacrifice at the Ancient House.

For every community We have ordained a ritual, that they may pronounce the name of God over the cattle which He has given them for food. Your God is one God; to Him surrender yourselves. Give good news to the humble, whose hearts are filled with awe at the mention of God; who endure adversity with fortitude, attend to their prayers, and give in alms from what We gave them.

We have made the camels a part of God's rites. They are of much use to you. Pronounce over them the name of God as you draw them up in line and slaughter them; and when they have fallen to the ground eat of their flesh and feed the uncomplaining beggar and the demanding supplicant. Thus have We subjected them to your service, so that you may give thanks.

Their flesh and blood does not reach God; it is your piety that reaches Him. Thus has He subjected them to your service, so that you may give glory to God for guiding you.

Give good news to the righteous. God will ward off evil from true believers. God does not love the treacherous and the thankless.

Q What is the key purpose of undertaking a pilgrimage to Mecca? What is the historical importance of the sacred stone?

According to the Qur'an: "Whoever obeys the messenger obeys Allah." But Muhammad had never named a successor, and although he had several daughters, he left no sons. In a male-oriented society, who would lead the community of the faithful? Shortly after Muhammad's death, a number of his closest followers selected Abu Bakr (ah-bu BAHK-ur), a wealthy merchant who was Muhammad's father-in-law, as **caliph,** or temporal leader, of the Islamic community.

Muhammad and the early caliphs who succeeded him took up the Arab tribal custom of the *razzia* or raid in the struggle against their enemies. Some have called this activity a *jihad* (ji-HAHD), which they misleadingly interpret as a holy war. ***Jihad*** actually means "striving in the way of the Lord" to achieve personal betterment, although it can also mean fair, defensive fighting to preserve one's life and one's faith. Arab conquests were not carried out to convert others, since conversion to Islam was purely voluntary. Those who did not convert were required only to submit to Muslim rule and pay taxes.

Once the Arabs had become unified under Abu Bakr, they began to direct the energy they had once expended against each other outward against neighboring peoples. The Byzantines and the Persians were the first to feel the strength of the newly united Arabs. At Yarmuk in 636, the Muslims defeated the Byzantine army, and by 640, they had taken possession of the province of Syria (see Map 7.7). To the east, the Arabs defeated Persian forces in 637 and then went on to conquer the entire Persian Empire by 650. In the meantime, Egypt and other areas of northern Africa had been added to the new Muslim empire. Led by a series of brilliant generals, the Arabs had put together a large and highly motivated army, whose valor was enhanced by the belief that Muslim warriors were guaranteed a place in paradise if they died in battle.

Al-Baladhuri, The Battle of Yarmuk (636 C.E.) and After

Early caliphs, ruling from Medina, organized their newly conquered territories into taxpaying provinces. By the mid-seventh century, problems arose again over the succession to the Prophet until Ali, Muhammad's son-in-law, was assassinated and the general Muawiya (moo-AH-wee-yah), the governor of Syria and one of Ali's

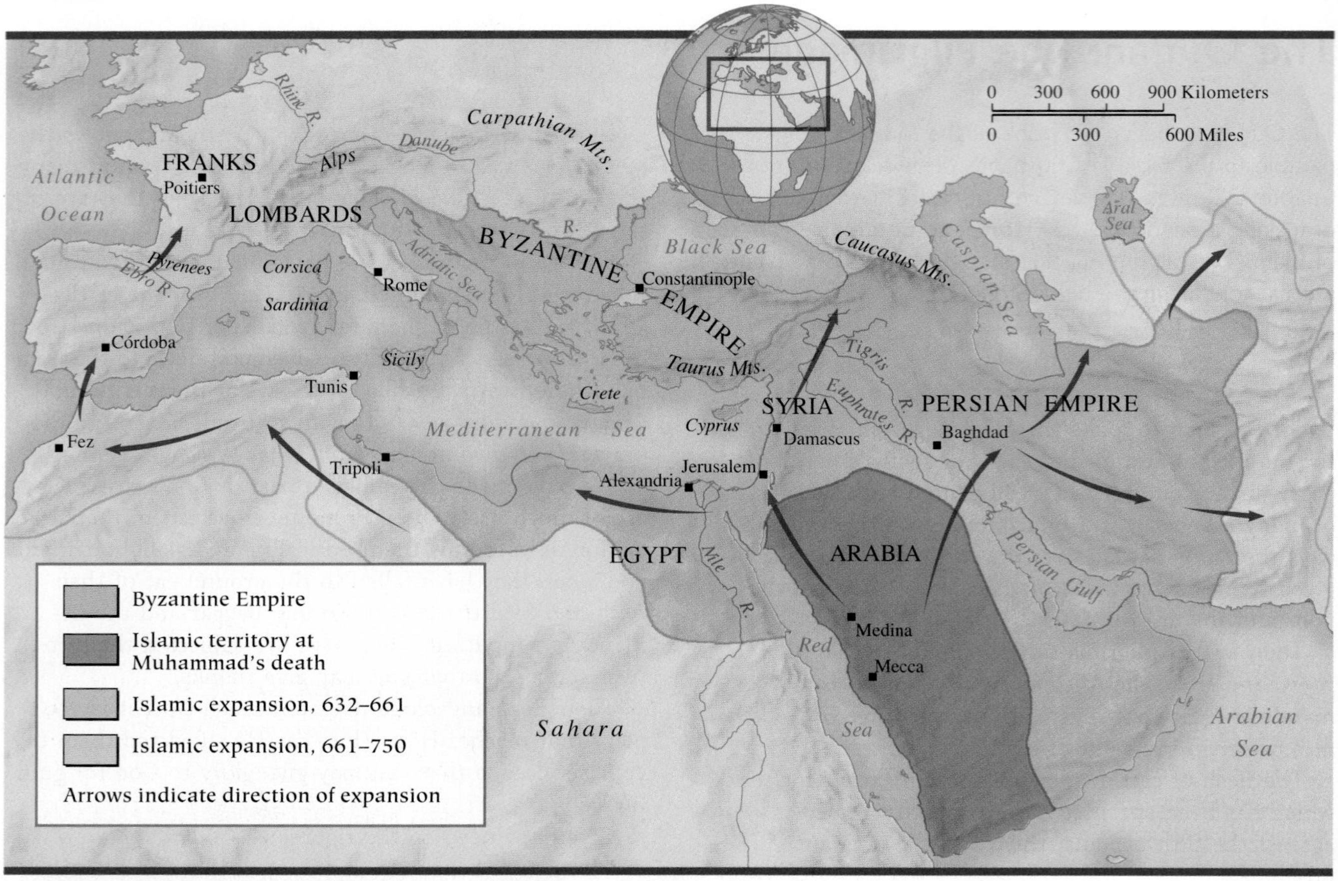

MAP 7.7 The Expansion of Islam. Muhammad, the prophet of Islam, engaged in warfare against neighboring tribes. Militaristic expansion continued with great zeal under the Prophet's successors. Islamic rule spread rapidly in the decades after Muhammad's death, stopped finally by the Byzantine Empire and the Franks.

Q ***Why was the continuance of the Byzantine Empire a key factor in stopping the spread of Islam into Europe?***

View an animated version of this map or related maps on the CourseMate website.

chief rivals, became caliph in 661. Muawiya was known for one outstanding virtue: he used force only when necessary. As he said, "I never use my sword when my whip will do, nor my whip when my tongue will do."[21] Muawiya moved quickly to make the caliphate hereditary in his own family, thus establishing the Umayyad dynasty. As one of their first actions, the Umayyads moved the capital of the Muslim empire from Medina to Damascus in Syria. This internal dissension over the caliphate created a split in Islam between the Shi'ites, or those who accepted only the descendants of Ali, Muhammad's son-in-law, as the true rulers, and the Sunnites, who claimed that the descendants of the Umayyads were the true caliphs. This seventh-century split in Islam has lasted until the present day.

Internal dissension did not stop the expansion of Islam, however. At the beginning of the eighth century, new attacks were made at both the western and eastern ends of the Mediterranean. After sweeping across North Africa, the Muslims crossed the Strait of Gibraltar and moved into Spain around 710. The Visigothic kingdom collapsed, and by 725, most of Spain had become a Muslim state with its center at Córdoba. In 732, a Muslim army, making a foray into southern France, was defeated at the Battle of Tours near Poitiers. Muslim expansion in Europe came to a halt.

Meanwhile, in 717, another Muslim force had launched a naval attack on Constantinople with the hope of destroying the Byzantine Empire. In the spring of 718, the Byzantines destroyed the Muslim fleet and saved the Byzantine Empire and indirectly Christian Europe, since the fall of Constantinople would no doubt have opened the door to Muslim invasion of eastern Europe. The Byzantine Empire and Islam now established an uneasy frontier in southern Asia Minor.

The Arab advance had finally come to an end, but not before the southern and eastern Mediterranean portions of the old Roman Empire had been conquered.

CHRONOLOGY The Rise of Islam

Birth of Muhammad	c. 570
Muhammad's flight from Mecca (*Hegira*)	622
Death of Muhammad	632
Defeat of Byzantines at Yarmuk	636
Defeat of Persians	637–650
Seizure of Byzantine provinces of Syria and Egypt	640–642
Invasion of Spain	c. 710
Arab failure to capture Constantinople	717–718
Defeat of Muslims near Poitiers	732

Islam had truly become heir to much of the old Roman Empire. That part of the empire had been a prosperous one, and the new Arab Empire benefited greatly from its conquest.

The Umayyad dynasty at Damascus now ruled an enormous empire. While expansion had conveyed untold wealth and new ethnic groups into the fold of Islam, it also brought contact with Byzantine and Persian civilization. As a result, the new Arab Empire would be influenced by Greek culture as well as the older civilizations of the ancient Near East. The children of the conquerors would be educated in new ways and produce a brilliant culture that would eventually influence western Europe intellectually.

CHAPTER SUMMARY

The period from the mid-third century to the mid-eighth century was both chaotic and creative. During late antiquity, the Roman world of the Mediterranean was gradually transformed. Diocletian and Constantine restored an aura of stability to the Late Empire by increasing the size of the bureaucracy and the army, establishing price controls, raising taxes, and making occupations hereditary. Nevertheless, even their efforts proved ultimately to be in vain as the empire stumbled along. With fewer resources and little resolve, the government was less able to repel the German migrants who moved into the western part of the empire. In 476, the last western emperor was deposed.

As the western part of the Roman Empire disintegrated, a new civilization slowly emerged, formed by the coalescence of three major elements: the Germanic peoples who moved into the western part of the empire and established new kingdoms, the continuing attraction of the Greco-Roman cultural legacy, and the Christian church. Politically, the Roman Empire in the west was replaced by a new series of Germanic kingdoms, including the Ostrogoths in Italy, the Visigoths in Spain, several Anglo-Saxon kingdoms in Britain, and a Frankish kingdom in Gaul. Each of these kingdoms fused Roman and Germanic elements to create a new society.

Beginning in the fourth century, Christianity had become the official religion of the Roman Empire. The Christian church (or Roman Catholic Church, as it came to be called in the west) played a crucial role in the growth of a new civilization. The church developed an organized government under the leadership of the bishop of Rome, who became known as the pope. One of the most significant popes was Gregory I the Great, who established claims to both religious and political power. The church also assimilated the Classical tradition and through its clergy brought Christianized civilization to the Germanic tribes. Especially important were the monks and nuns who led the way in converting the Germanic peoples in Europe to Christianity.

But the Germanic kingdoms were not the only heir to Roman civilization. In the east, Greek and eastern elements of late antiquity were of more consequence as the Eastern Roman Empire was transformed into the Byzantine Empire. Although the Germanic kingdoms of the west and the Byzantine civilization of the east came to share a common bond in Christianity, it proved incapable of keeping them in harmony politically as the two civilizations continued to move apart.

The rise of Islam, Rome's third heir, resulted in the loss of the southern and eastern Mediterranean portions of the old Roman Empire to a religious power that was neither Roman nor Christian. The new Islamic empire forced Europe proper back upon itself, and slowly, a new civilization emerged that became the heart of what we know as Western civilization.

CHAPTER TIMELINE

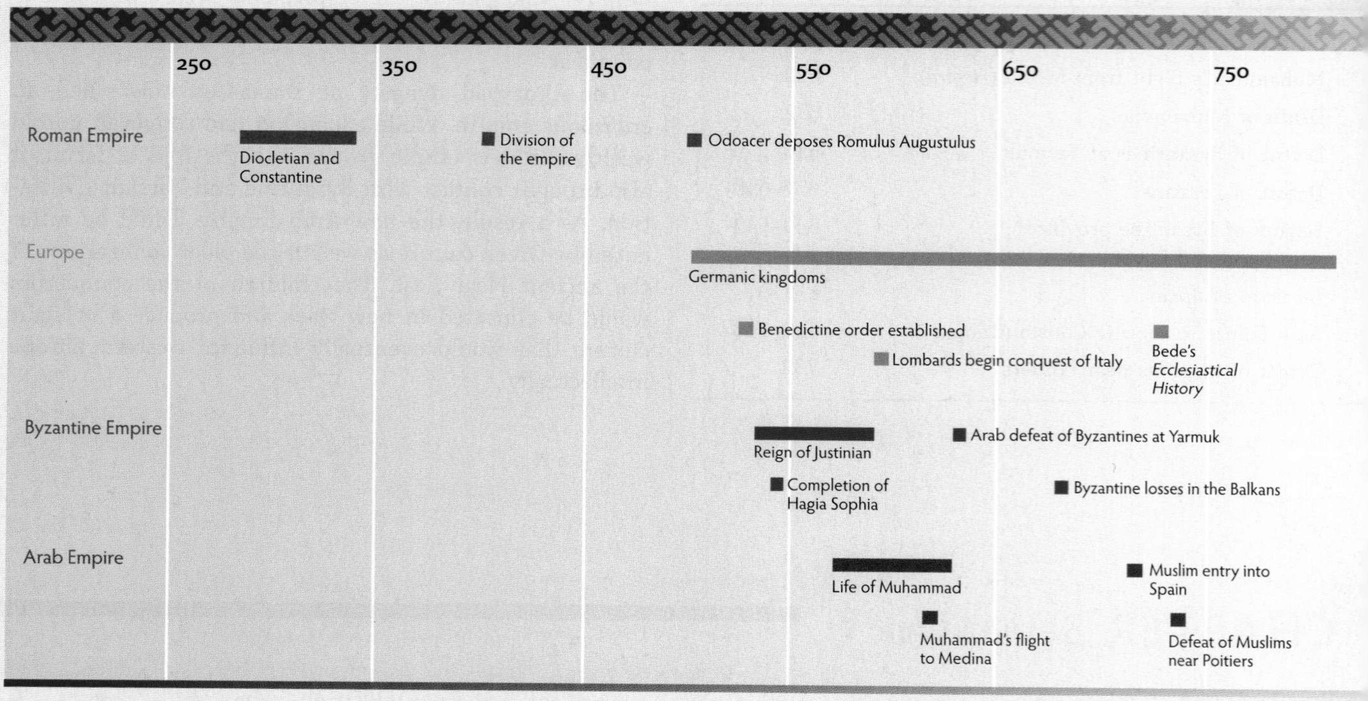

CHAPTER REVIEW

Upon Reflection

Q What role did monks and nuns play in early medieval society?

Q What contributions did the Germanic peoples make to the political, economic, and social conditions of early medieval society?

Q What impact did Christianity have on the intellectual life of early medieval society?

Key Terms

tetrarchy (p. 180)
inflation (p. 181)
curiales (p. 181)
heresy (p. 183)
Arianism (p. 183)
federates (p. 185)
major domus (p. 189)
wergeld (p. 190)
celibacy (p. 192)
Petrine supremacy (p. 193)
monks (p. 195)
monasticism (p. 195)
abbot (p. 196)
nuns (p. 196)
abbess (p. 199)
liberal arts (p. 201)
trivium (p. 201)
quadrivium (p. 201)
iconoclasts (p. 206)
iconoclasm (p. 206)
Five Pillars of Islam (p. 208)
caliph (p. 209)
jihad (p. 209)

Suggestions for Further Reading

GENERAL WORKS ON LATE ANTIQUITY For good introductions to late antiquity, see **P. Brown, *The World of Late Antiquity, A.D. 150–750*** (New York, 1989); **J. Moorhead, *The Roman Empire Divided, 400–700*** (London, 2001); **A. Cameron, *The Mediterranean World in Late Antiquity, A.D. 395–600*** (London, 1993); and **J. J. O'Donnell, *The Ruin of the Roman Empire: A New History*** (New York, 2008). There is an excellent collection of essays and encyclopedic entries in **G. W. Bowersock, P. Brown,** and **O. Grabar, *Late Antiquity: A Guide to the Postclassical World*** (Cambridge, Mass., 1999).

LATE ROMAN EMPIRE On the Late Roman Empire, see **S. Mitchell, *History of the Later Roman Empire, A.D. 284–641*** (Oxford, 2006); **R. M. Errington, *Roman Imperial Policy from Julian to Theodosius*** (Chapel Hill, N.C., 2006); and **A. Cameron, *The Later Roman Empire*** (Cambridge, Mass., 1993). For new perspectives on the fall of the Western Roman Empire, see **P. Heather, *The Fall of the***

Roman Empire: A New History of Rome and the Barbarians (Oxford, 2006); **B. Ward-Perkins, *The Fall of Rome and the End of Civilization*** (Oxford, 2005); and **Adrian Goldsworthy, *How Rome Fell*** (New Haven, Conn., 2009).

THE GERMANIC PEOPLES For surveys of the German tribes and their migrations, see **T. S. Burns, *A History of the Ostrogoths*** (Bloomington, Ind., 1984); **P. Heather, *Goths and Romans*** (Oxford, 1991); **E. James, *The Franks*** (Oxford, 1988); **H. Wolfram, *The Goths,*** trans. **T. J. Dunlop** (Berkeley, Calif., 1988); and **M. Todd, *The Early Germans,*** 2nd ed. (Oxford, 2004). On the relationship between the Romans and the Germans, see **T. S. Burns, *Rome and the Barbarians, 100 B.C.–A.D. 400*** (Baltimore, 2003), and **M. Kulikowski, *Rome's Gothic Wars*** (New York, 2007).

EARLY CHRISTIANITY For a superb introduction to early Christianity, see **P. Brown, *The Rise of Western Christendom: Triumph and Adversity, A.D. 200–1000,*** 2nd ed. (Oxford, 2002). For a good account of early monasticism, see **C. H. Lawrence, *Medieval Monasticism,*** 3rd ed. (London, 2000). For women in monastic life, see **M. T. Malone, *Women and Christianity,*** vol. 1 (New York, 2001). On women in general, see **G. Clark, *Women in Late Antiquity: Pagan and Christian Life-Styles*** (Oxford, 1993). A survey of the development of the papacy can be found in **J. Richards, *The Popes and the Papacy in the Early Middle Ages, 476–752*** (Boston, 1979). On Pope Gregory the Great, see **J. Moorhead, *Gregory the Great*** (London, 2005).

THE BYZANTINE EMPIRE Brief but good introductions to Byzantine history can be found in **J. Haldon, *Byzantium: A History*** (Charleston, S.C., 2000); **A. Cameron, *The Byzantines*** (Oxford, 2006); and **W. Treadgold, *A Concise History of Byzantium*** (London, 2001). For a comprehensive survey of the Byzantine Empire, see **W. Treadgold, *A History of the Byzantine State and Society*** (Stanford, Calif., 1997). On Justinian, see **J. Moorhead, *Justinian*** (London, 1995). On Theodora, see **P. Cesavetti, *Theodora, Empress of Byzantium,*** trans. **R. M. Frongia** (New York, 2001). On Constantinople, see **J. Harris, *Constantinople: Capital of Byzantium*** (London, 2007).

THE ISLAMIC MIDDLE EAST On the rise of Islam, see **F. E. Peters, *Muhammad and the Origins of Islam*** (Albany, N.Y., 1994); **M. Lings, *Muhammad: His Life Based on the Earliest Sources*** (New York, 1983); **K. Armstrong, *Muhammad: A Prophet for Our Time*** (New York, 2006); and **F. Donner, *The Early Islamic Conquests*** (Princeton, N.J., 1980).

CourseMate

Visit the CourseMate website at www.cengagebrain.com for additional study tools and review materials for this chapter.

A fifteenth-century French manuscript illustration of the coronation of Charlemagne by Pope Leo III

CHAPTER 8

European Civilization in the Early Middle Ages, 750–1000

CHAPTER OUTLINE AND FOCUS QUESTIONS

Europeans and the Environment

Q What were the main features of the physical environment of the Early Middle Ages?

The World of the Carolingians

Q What was the significance of Charlemagne's coronation as emperor? In what ways did the political, intellectual, and daily life in the Carolingian Empire represent a fusion of Gallo-Roman, Germanic, and Christian practices?

Disintegration of the Carolingian Empire

Q What impact did the Vikings have on the history and culture of medieval Europe?

The Emerging World of Lords and Vassals

Q What was fief-holding, and how was it related to manorialism?

The Zenith of Byzantine Civilization

Q What were the chief developments in the Byzantine Empire between 750 and 1000?

The Slavic Peoples of Central and Eastern Europe

Q What patterns of development occurred in central and eastern Europe as a result of the Slavic peoples?

The Expansion of Islam

Q What were the chief developments in the Islamic world between 750 and 1000?

CRITICAL THINKING

Q Why can it be said that Islamic civilization was more advanced than the civilization of western Europe in the ninth and tenth centuries?

IN 800, CHARLEMAGNE, the king of the Franks, journeyed to Rome to help Pope Leo III, who was barely clinging to power in the face of rebellious Romans. On Christmas Day, Charlemagne and his family, attended by Romans, Franks, and visitors from the Byzantine Empire, crowded into Saint Peter's Basilica to hear Mass. Quite unexpectedly, according to a Frankish writer, "as the king rose from praying before the tomb of the blessed apostle Peter, Pope Leo placed a golden crown on his head." In keeping with ancient tradition, the people in the church shouted, "Long life and victory to Charles Augustus, crowned by God the great and pacific Emperor of the Romans." Seemingly, the Roman Empire in the west had been reborn, and Charles had become the first western emperor since 476. But this "Roman emperor" was actually a German king, and he had been crowned by the head of the western Christian church. In truth, the coronation of Charlemagne was a sign not of the rebirth of the Roman Empire but of the emergence of a new European civilization.

By the year of Charlemagne's coronation, the contours of this new European civilization were beginning to emerge in western Europe. Increasingly, Europe would become the focus and center of Western civilization. Building on a fusion of Germanic, Greco-Roman, and Christian elements, the medieval European world first became visible in the Carolingian Empire of Charlemagne. The agrarian foundations of the eighth and ninth centuries proved inadequate to maintain a large monarchical system, however, and a new political and military order based on the decentralization of political power subsequently evolved to become an integral part of the political world of the Middle Ages.

European civilization began on a shaky and uncertain foundation, however. In the ninth century, Vikings, Magyars, and Muslims posed threats that could easily have stifled the new society. But the Vikings and Magyars were assimilated, and recovery slowly began to set in. By 1000, European civilization was ready to embark on a period of dazzling vitality and expansion.

Europeans and the Environment

FOCUS QUESTION: What were the main features of the physical environment of the Early Middle Ages?

The number of people in early medieval Europe is a matter of considerable uncertainty. In all probability, the population of the eighth century still had not recovered from the losses caused by the plagues of the sixth and seventh centuries. Historians generally believe that in the Early Middle Ages, Europe was a sparsely populated landscape dotted with villages and clusters of villages of farmers and warriors. Although rivers, such as the Loire, Seine, Rhine, Elbe, and Oder, served as major arteries of communication, villages were still separated from one another by forests, swamps, and mountain ridges. Forests, which provided building and heating materials as well as game, covered the European landscape. In fact, it has been estimated that less than 10 percent of the land was cultivated, a figure so small that some economic historians believe that Europe had difficulty feeding even its modest population. Thus, hunting and fishing were necessary to supplement the European diet.

Farming

The cultivation of new land proved especially difficult in the Early Middle Ages. Given the crude implements of the time, it was not easy to clear forests and prepare the ground for planting. Moreover, German tribes had for centuries considered trees sacred and resisted cutting them down to make room for farms. Even conversion to Christianity did not entirely change these attitudes. In addition, the heavy soils of northern Europe were not easily plowed. Agricultural methods also worked against significant crop yields. Land was allowed to lie fallow (unplanted) every other year to regain its fertility, but even so it produced low yields. Evidence indicates that Frankish estates yielded incredibly low ratios of two measures of grain to one measure of seed.

The Climate

Climatic patterns show that European weather began to improve around 700 after several centuries of wetter and colder conditions. Nevertheless, natural disasters were always a threat, especially since the low yields meant that little surplus could be saved for bad times. Drought or too much rain could mean meager harvests, famine, and dietary deficiencies that made people susceptible to a wide range of diseases. This was a period of low life expectancy. One study of Hungarian graves found that of every five skeletons, one was a child below the age of one, and two were children between one and fourteen; more than one in five was a woman below the age of twenty. Overall, then, the picture of early medieval Europe is of a relatively small population subsisting on the basis of a limited agricultural economy and leading, in most cases, a precarious existence.

The World of the Carolingians

FOCUS QUESTIONS: What was the significance of Charlemagne's coronation as emperor? In what ways did the political, intellectual, and daily life in the Carolingian Empire represent a fusion of Gallo-Roman, Germanic, and Christian practices?

By the eighth century, the Merovingian dynasty was losing its control of the Frankish lands. Charles Martel, the Carolingian mayor of the palace of Austrasia, became the virtual ruler of these territories. When Charles Martel died in 741, his son, Pepin (PEP-in *or* pay-PANH), deposed the Merovingians and assumed the kingship of the Frankish state for himself and his family. Pepin's actions, which were approved by the pope, created a new form of Frankish kingship. Pepin (751–768) was crowned king and formally anointed by a representative of the pope with holy oil in imitation of an Old Testament practice. The anointing not only symbolized that the kings had been entrusted with a sacred office but also provides yet another example of how a Germanic institution fused with a Christian practice in the Early Middle Ages.

Charlemagne and the Carolingian Empire (768–814)

Pepin's death in 768 brought to the throne of the Frankish kingdom his son, a dynamic and powerful ruler known to history as Charles the Great or Charlemagne (*Carolus magnus* in Latin—hence our word *Carolingian*). Charlemagne was a determined and decisive man, intelligent and inquisitive. A fierce warrior, he was also a wise patron of learning and a resolute statesman (see the box on p. 216). He greatly expanded the territory of the Carolingian Empire during his lengthy rule.

EXPANSION OF THE CAROLINGIAN EMPIRE In the tradition of Germanic kings, Charlemagne was a determined

The Achievements of Charlemagne

Einhard, the biographer of Charlemagne, was born in the valley of the Main River in Germany about 775. Raised and educated in the monastery of Fulda, an important center of learning, he arrived at the court of Charlemagne in 791 or 792. Although he did not achieve high office under Charlemagne, he served as private secretary to Louis the Pious, Charlemagne's son and successor. Einhard's *Life of Charlemagne*, written between 817 and 830, was modeled on *Lives of the Caesars* by the Roman author Suetonius, especially his biography of Augustus. In this selection, Einhard discusses some of Charlemagne's accomplishments.

Einhard, *Life of Charlemagne*

Such are the wars, most skillfully planned and successfully fought, which this most powerful king waged during the forty-seven years of his reign. He so largely increased the Frank kingdom, which was already great and strong when he received it at his father's hands, that more than double its former territory was added to it.... He subdued all the wild and barbarous tribes dwelling in Germany between the Rhine and the Vistula, the Ocean and the Danube, all of which speak very much the same language, but differ widely from one another in customs and dress....

He added to the glory of his reign by gaining the good will of several kings and nations; so close, indeed, was the alliance that he contracted with Alfonso, King of Galicia and Asturias, that the latter, when sending letters or ambassadors to Charles, invariably styled himself his man.... The Emperors of Constantinople [the Byzantine emperors] sought friendship and alliance with Charles by several embassies; and even when the Greeks [the Byzantines] suspected him of designing to take the empire from them, because of his assumption of the title Emperor, they made a close alliance with him, that he might have no cause of offense. In fact, the power of the Franks was always viewed with a jealous eye, whence the Greek proverb, "Have the Frank for your friend, but not for your neighbor."

This King, who showed himself so great in extending his empire and subduing foreign nations, and was constantly occupied with plans to that end, undertook also very many works calculated to adorn and benefit his kingdom, and brought several of them to completion. Among these, the most deserving of mention are the basilica of the Holy Mother of God at Aix-la-Chapelle, built in the most admirable manner, and a bridge over the Rhine River at Mainz, half a mile long, the breadth of the river at this point.... Above all, sacred buildings were the object of his care throughout his whole kingdom; and whenever he found them falling to ruin from age, he commanded the priests and fathers who had charge of them to repair them, and made sure by commissioners that his instructions were obeyed.... Thus did Charles defend and increase as well as beautify his kingdom....

He cherished with the greatest fervor and devotion the principles of the Christian religion, which had been instilled into him from infancy. Hence it was that he built the beautiful church at Aix-la-Chapelle, which he adorned with gold and silver and lamps, and with rails and doors of solid brass. He had the columns and marbles for this structure brought from Rome and Ravenna, for he could not find such as were suitable elsewhere. He was a constant worshiper at this church as long as his health permitted, going morning and evening, even after nightfall, besides attending Mass....

He was very forward in caring for the poor, so much so that he not only made a point of giving in his own country and his own kingdom, but when he discovered that there were Christians living in poverty in Syria, Egypt, and Africa, at Jerusalem, Alexandria, and Carthage, he had compassion on their wants, and used to send money over the seas to them.... He sent great and countless gifts to the popes, and throughout his whole reign the wish that he had nearest at heart was to reestablish the ancient authority of the city of Rome under his care and by his influence, and to defend and protect the Church of St. Peter, and to beautify and enrich it out of his own store above all other churches.

Q Based on Einhard's account, discuss the strengths and weaknesses of Charlemagne. Which characteristics help explain Charlemagne's success as a ruler? Does Einhard exaggerate Charlemagne's strengths? What might motivate him to do that?

warrior who undertook fifty-four military campaigns. Even though the Frankish army was relatively small—only eight thousand men gathered each spring for campaigning—supplying it and transporting it to distant areas could still present serious problems. The Frankish army comprised mostly infantry, with some cavalry armed with swords and spears.

Charlemagne's campaigns took him to many areas of Europe. In 773, he led his army into Italy, crushed the Lombards, and took control of the Lombard state. Although his son was crowned king of Italy, Charlemagne was its real ruler. Four years after subduing Italy, Charlemagne and his forces advanced into northern Spain. This campaign proved disappointing; not only did the Basques harass his army as it crossed the Pyrenees on the way home, but they also ambushed and annihilated his rear guard.

Einhard, *Life of Charlemagne*, selected topics

Charlemagne was considerably more successful with his eastern campaigns into Germany, especially against the Saxons, who had settled between the Elbe River and the North Sea. As Einhard, Charlemagne's biographer, recounted it:

> No war ever undertaken by the Frank nation was carried on with such persistence and bitterness, or cost so much labor, because the Saxons, like almost all the tribes of Germany, were a fierce people, given to the worship of devils, and hostile to our religion, and did not consider it dishonorable to transgress and violate all law, human and divine.[1]

Charlemagne's insistence that the Saxons convert to Christianity simply fueled their resistance. Not until 804, after eighteen campaigns, was Saxony finally pacified and added to the Carolingian domain.

CHRONOLOGY The Carolingian Empire

Pepin crowned king of the Franks	751
Reign of Charlemagne	768–814
Campaign in Italy	773–774
Campaign in Spain	778
Conquest of Bavarians	787–788
Charlemagne crowned emperor	800
Final conquest of Saxons	804
Reign of Louis the Pious	814–840
Treaty of Verdun divides Carolingian Empire	843

Louvre, Paris//© Réunion des Musées Nationaux/Art Resource, NY

Bronze Equestrian Statue of Charlemagne. This small bronze statue is believed to represent the emperor Charles the Great, although some scholars believe it is his grandson, Charles the Bald. The figure dates from the ninth century, but the horse is a sixteenth-century restoration. The attire on the figure accords with Einhard's account of how Charlemagne dressed. The imperial crown rests on his head, and in his left hand he grasps a globe, a symbol of world power and a reminder that the power of the Roman Empire had been renewed.

Charlemagne invaded the lands of the Bavarians in southeastern Germany in 787 and had incorporated them into his empire by the following year, an expansion that brought him into contact with the southern Slavs and the Avars. The latter disappeared from history after their utter devastation at the hands of Charlemagne's army. Now at its height, Charlemagne's empire covered much of western and central Europe (see Map 8.1); not until the time of Napoleon in the nineteenth century would an empire of this size be seen again in Europe.

GOVERNING THE EMPIRE Charlemagne continued the efforts of his father in organizing the Carolingian kingdom. Because there was no system of public taxation, Charlemagne was dependent on the royal estates for the resources he needed to govern his empire. Food and goods derived from these lands provided support for the king, his household staff, and officials. To keep the nobles in his service, Charlemagne granted part of the royal lands as lifetime holdings to nobles who assisted him.

Besides the household staff, the administration of the empire depended on counts, who were the king's chief representatives in local areas, although in dangerous border districts officials known as margraves (literally, *mark graf,* count of the border district) were used. Counts were members of the nobility who had already existed under the Merovingians. They had come to control public services in their own lands and thus acted as judges, military leaders, and agents of the king. Gradually, as the rule of the Merovingian kings weakened, many counts had simply attached the royal lands and services performed on behalf of the king to their own family possessions.

In an effort to gain greater control over his kingdom, Charlemagne attempted to limit the power of the counts. They were required to serve outside their own family lands and were moved about periodically rather than being permitted to remain in a county for life. By making the offices appointive, Charlemagne tried to prevent the counts' children from automatically inheriting their offices. Moreover, as another check on the counts, Charlemagne instituted the *missi dominici* (MISS-ee doh-MIN-i-chee) ("messengers of the lord king"), two men, one lay lord and one church official, who were sent out to local districts to

MAP 8.1 The Carolingian Empire. Charlemagne inherited the Frankish kingdom from his father, Pepin. He expanded his territories in several directions, creating an empire that would not be rivaled in size until the conquests of Napoleon in the early nineteenth century.

Q ***How might Charlemagne's holdings in northern Italy have influenced his relationship with the pope?***

ensure that the counts were executing the king's wishes. The counts also had assistants, but they were members of their households, not part of a bureaucratic office.

The last point is an important reminder that we should not think of Carolingian government in the modern sense of government offices run by officials committed to an impersonal ideal of state service. The Carolingian system was glaringly inefficient. Great distances had to be covered on horseback, making it impossible for Charlemagne and his household staff to exercise much supervision over local affairs. What held the system together was personal loyalty to a single ruler who was strong enough to ensure loyalty by force when necessary.

Charlemagne also realized that the Catholic Church could provide valuable assistance in governing his kingdom. By the late seventh century, the system of ecclesiastical government within the Christian church that had been created in the Late Roman Empire had largely disintegrated. Many church offices were not filled or were held by grossly unqualified relatives of the royal family. Both Pepin and his son Charlemagne took up the cause of church reform by creating new bishoprics and archbishoprics, restoring old ones, and seeing to it that the clergy accepted the orders of their superiors and executed their duties. Charlemagne also insisted that church officials restore churches that had fallen into disrepair, a clear indication of his close attention to church affairs.

CHARLEMAGNE AS EMPEROR As Charlemagne's power grew, so did his prestige as the most powerful Christian ruler; one monk even wrote of his empire as the "kingdom of Europe." Charlemagne acquired a new title—emperor of the Romans—in 800, but substantial controversy surrounds this event, and it can only be understood within the context of the relationship between the papacy and the Frankish monarchs.

Already during the reign of Pepin, a growing alliance had emerged between the kingdom of the Franks and the papacy. The popes welcomed this support, and in the course of the second half of the eighth century, they severed more and more of their ties with the Byzantine Empire and drew closer to the Frankish kingdom. Charlemagne encouraged this development. In 799, after a rebellion against his authority, Pope Leo III (795–816) managed to escape from Rome and flee to safety at Charlemagne's court. Charlemagne offered assistance, and when he went to Rome in November 800 to settle affairs, he was received by the pope like an emperor. On Christmas Day in 800, after Mass, Pope Leo placed a crown on Charlemagne's head and proclaimed him emperor of the Romans.

THE SIGNIFICANCE OF CHARLEMAGNE The significance of this imperial coronation has been much debated by historians. We are not even sure whether the pope or Charlemagne initiated the idea when they met in the summer of 799 in Paderborn in German lands or whether Charlemagne was pleased or displeased. His biographer Einhard claimed that "at first [he] had such an aversion that he declared that he would not have set foot in the Church the day that [it was] conferred, although it was a great feast-day, if he could have foreseen the design of the Pope."[2] But Charlemagne also perceived the usefulness of the imperial title; after all, he was now on a level of equality with the Byzantine emperor, a status he did not reject. Moreover, the papacy now had a defender of great stature, although later popes in the Middle Ages would become involved in fierce struggles with emperors over who possessed the higher power.

In any case, Charlemagne's coronation as Roman emperor certainly demonstrated the strength, even after three hundred years, of the concept of an enduring Roman Empire. More important, it symbolized the fusion of Roman, Christian, and Germanic elements. Did this fusion constitute the foundations of European civilization? A Germanic king had been crowned emperor of the Romans by the spiritual leader of western Christendom. Charlemagne had created an empire that stretched from the North Sea in the north to Italy in the south, and from France in western Europe to Vienna in central Europe. This empire differed significantly from the Roman Empire, which encompassed much of the Mediterranean world. Had a new civilization emerged? And should Charlemagne be seen, as one recent biographer has argued, as the "father of Europe"?[3]

The Carolingian Intellectual Renewal

Charlemagne had a strong desire to revive learning in his kingdom, an attitude that stemmed from his own intellectual curiosity as well as the need to provide educated clergy for the church and literate officials for the government. His efforts led to a revival of learning and culture that some historians have labeled a Carolingian Renaissance, or "rebirth" of learning.

For the most part, the revival of Classical studies and the efforts to preserve Latin culture took place in the monasteries, many of which had been established by the Irish and English missionaries of the seventh and eighth centuries (see Chapter 7). By the ninth century, the work required of Benedictine monks was the copying of manuscripts. Monasteries established **scriptoria** (skrip-TOR-ee-uh), or writing rooms, where monks copied not only the works of early Christianity, such as the Bible and the treatises of the church fathers, but also the works of Classical Latin authors.

Following the example of the Irish and English monks, their Carolingian counterparts developed new ways of producing books. Their texts were written on pages made of parchment or sheepskin rather than papyrus and then bound in covers decorated with jewels and precious metals. The use of parchment made books very expensive; an entire herd of sheep could be required to make a Bible.

The Monk as Copyist. The copying of manuscripts was a major task of monastic establishments in the Middle Ages. The work took place in a scriptorium or writing room. This medieval manuscript illustration from the fourteenth century shows a monk at work in the scriptorium of a monastery. To copy an entire book was considered a work of special spiritual merit. Copying the Bible was especially important because it was considered a sacred object. The monk in this illustration had the benefit of wearing eyeglasses, first introduced in the thirteenth century and refined in the fourteenth.

Charlemagne's Chapel at Aachen. Construction of the palace chapel at Aachen, which is modeled loosely after the Church of San Vitale in Ravenna, began in the early 790s. Charlemagne's throne was placed on the second floor. From there he could look down at the main altar. The chapel maintains its original design, although extensive remodeling has altered much of its decoration.

(Papyrus was no longer available because Egypt was in Muslim hands, and the west could no longer afford to import it.) Carolingian monastic scribes also developed a new writing style called the Carolingian minuscule (see the illustration on p. 225). This was really hand printing rather than cursive writing and was far easier to read than the Merovingian script.

The production of manuscripts, some of which were illustrated, in Carolingian monastic scriptoria was a crucial factor in the preservation of the ancient legacy. About eight thousand manuscripts survive from Carolingian times. Some 90 percent of the ancient Roman works that we have today exist because they were copied by Carolingian monks.

Charlemagne personally promoted learning by establishing a palace school and encouraging scholars from all over Europe to come to the Carolingian court. These included men of letters from Italy, Spain, Germany, and Ireland. Best known was Alcuin (AL-kwin), called by Einhard the "greatest scholar of that day." He was from the famous school at York that was a product of the great revival of learning in the Anglo-Saxon kingdom of Northumbria. From 782 to 796, while serving at Charlemagne's court as an adviser on ecclesiastical affairs, Alcuin also provided the leadership for the palace school. He concentrated on teaching Classical Latin and adopted Cassiodorus's sevenfold division of knowledge known as the liberal arts (see Chapter 7), which became the basis for all later medieval education.

Charlemagne's official seal carried the words "renewal of the Roman Empire." For Charlemagne, who made a number of visits to Italy, this included a revival of the arts, which meant looking to Italy for inspiration. Charlemagne encouraged his own artists to look to the arts of ancient Rome and the Byzantine Empire. The chapel he built at Aachen was modeled after the Church of San Vitale in Ravenna, a church that had been built by the emperor Justinian after his reconquest of much of Italy (see Chapter 7). All in all, the Carolingian Renaissance played an important role in keeping the Classical heritage alive.

Life in the Carolingian World

In daily life as well as intellectual life, the Europe of the Carolingian era witnessed a fusion of Roman, Germanic, and Christian practices. The last in particular seem to have exercised an ever-increasing influence.

THE FAMILY AND MARRIAGE By Carolingian times, the Catholic Church had begun to make a significant impact on Frankish family life and marital and sexual attitudes. Marriages in Frankish society were arranged by fathers or uncles to meet the needs of the extended family. Although wives were expected to be faithful to their husbands, Frankish aristocrats often kept concubines, either slave girls or free women from their estates. Even the "most Christian king" Charlemagne had a number of concubines.

To limit such sexual license, the church increasingly emphasized its role in marriage and attempted to Christianize it. Although marriage was a civil arrangement, priests tried to add their blessings and strengthen the concept of a special marriage ceremony. Moreover, the church tried to serve as the caretaker of marriage by stipulating that a girl over fifteen must give her consent to her guardian's choice of a husband or her marriage would not be valid in the eyes of the church.

To stabilize marriages, the church also began to emphasize **monogamy** and permanence. A Frankish church council in 789 stipulated that marriage was an "indissoluble sacrament" and condemned the practice of concubinage and easy divorce; during the reign of Emperor Louis the Pious (814–840), the church finally established the right to prohibit divorce. Now a man who married was expected to remain with his wife "even though she were sterile, deformed, old, dirty, drunken, a frequenter of bad company, lascivious, vain, greedy, unfaithful, quarrelsome, abusive . . . for when that man was free, he freely engaged himself."[4] This was not easily accepted, since monogamy and indissoluble marriages were viewed as obstacles to the well-established practice of concubinage. Not until the thirteenth century was divorce largely stamped out among both the common people and the nobility.

Advice from a Carolingian Mother

The wife of a Carolingian aristocrat bore numerous responsibilities. She was entrusted with the management of the household and even the administration of extensive landed estates while her husband was absent in the royal service or on a military campaign. A wife was also expected to bear large numbers of children and to supervise their upbringing. This selection by Dhouda, wife of Bernard, marquis of Septimania (in southern France), is taken from a manual she wrote to instruct her son on his duties to his new lord, King Charles the Bald (840–877).

Dhouda, *Handbook for William*

Direction on your comportment toward your lord.

You have Charles as your lord; you have him as lord because, as I believe, God and your father, Bernard, have chosen him for you to serve at the beginning of your career, in the flower of your youth. Remember that he comes from a great and noble lineage on both sides of his family. Serve him not only so that you please him in obvious ways, but also as one clearheaded in matters of both body and soul. Be steadfastly and completely loyal to him in all things. . . .

This is why, my son, I urge you to keep this loyalty as long as you live, in your body and in your mind. For the advancement that it brings you will be of great value both to you and to those who in turn serve you. May the madness of treachery never, not once, make you offer an angry insult. May it never give rise in your heart to the idea of being disloyal to your lord. There is harsh and shameful talk about men who act in this fashion. I do not think that such will befall you or those who fight alongside you because such an attitude has never shown itself among your ancestors. It has not been seen among them, it is not seen now, and it will not be seen in the future.

Be truthful to your lord, my son William, child of their lineage. Be vigilant, energetic, and offer him ready assistance as I have said here. In every matter of importance to royal power take care to show yourself a man of good judgment—in your own thoughts and in public—to the extent that God gives you strength. Read the sayings and the lives of the holy Fathers who have gone before us. You will there discover how you may serve your lord and be faithful to him in all things. When you understand this, devote yourself to the faithful execution of your lord's commands. Look around as well and observe those who fight for him loyally and constantly. Learn from them how you may serve him. Then, informed by their example, with the help and support of God, you will easily reach the celestial goal I have mentioned above. And may your heavenly Lord God be generous and benevolent toward you. May he keep you safe, be your kind leader and your protector. May he deign to assist you in all your actions and be your constant defender.

Q What advice does Dhouda of Septimania give her son? What does this selection tell us about aristocratic women in the Early Middle Ages and their relationship with power?

The acceptance and spread of the Catholic Church's views on the indissolubility of marriage encouraged the development of the **nuclear family** at the expense of the extended family. Although the kin was still an influential social and political force, the conjugal unit came to be seen as the basic unit of society. The new practice of young couples establishing their own households had a significant impact on women (see the box above). In the extended family, the eldest woman controlled all the other female members; in the nuclear family, the wife was still dominated by her husband, but at least she now had control of her own household and children.

CHRISTIANITY AND SEXUALITY The early church fathers had stressed that celibacy and complete abstinence from sexual activity constituted an ideal state superior to marriage. Subsequently, the early church gradually developed a case for clerical celibacy, although it proved impossible to enforce in the Early Middle Ages.

The early fathers had also emphasized, however, that not all people had the self-discipline to remain celibate. It was thus permissible to marry, as Paul had indicated in his first epistle to the Corinthians: "It is good for a man not to touch a woman. Nevertheless, to avoid fornication, let every man have his own wife, and let every woman have her own husband. . . . I say therefore to the unmarried and widows, It is good for them if they abide even as I. But if they cannot contain, let them marry: for it is better to marry than to burn [with passion]."[5] The church thus viewed marriage as the lesser of two evils; it was a concession to human weakness and fulfilled the need for companionship, sex, and children. Although marriage was the subject of much debate in the early medieval church, it was generally agreed that marriage gave the right to indulge in sexual intercourse. Sex, then, was permissible within marriage, but only so long as it was used for the purpose of procreation, or the begetting of children, not for pleasure.

Saint Paul, First Epistle to the Corinthians

Because the church developed the tradition that sexual relations between man and wife were legitimate only if engaged in for procreation, it condemned all forms of contraception. The church accepted only one way to limit children: abstinence from intercourse, either periodic or total. The church also strongly condemned abortion, although its prohibition failed to stop the practice. Various herbal potions, whose formulas appear in writings from Roman and Byzantine doctors, were available to prevent conception or cause abortion.

The church's condemnation of sexual activity outside marriage also included homosexuality. Neither Roman religion nor Roman law had recognized any real difference between homosexual and heterosexual eroticism, and the Roman Empire had taken no legal measures against the practice of homosexuality between adults. Later, in the Byzantine Empire, Emperor Justinian in 538 condemned homosexuality, emphasizing that such practices brought down the wrath of God ("we have provoked Him to anger") and endangered the welfare of the state:

> For because of such crimes, there are famines, earthquakes, and pestilences; wherefore we admonish men to abstain from the aforesaid unlawful acts, that they may not lose their souls.... We order the most illustrious prefect of the capital to arrest those who persist in the aforesaid lawless and impious acts after they have been warned by us, and to inflict on them the extreme punishments, so that the city and the state may not come to harm by reason of such wicked deeds.[6]

Justinian recommended that the guilty parties be punished by castration. Although the early medieval church similarly condemned homosexuality, it also pursued a flexible policy in its treatment of homosexuals. In the Early Middle Ages, homosexuals were treated less harshly than married couples who practiced contraception.

NEW ATTITUDES TOWARD CHILDREN The Catholic Church also had an impact on another aspect of family life—children. The ancient Romans had limited their family size through infanticide, primarily the exposure of unwanted children, which was accepted in Classical society. The Romans then paid much attention to the children chosen to survive, as is especially evident in the education of upper-class children. In the emerging early medieval world, German practices of child rearing became influential. As we saw in Chapter 7, the Germanic law codes listed *wergelds,* whose size represented a crude evaluation of a person's importance. According to a Visigothic code of the mid-seventh century, for example, male children were valued at 60 solidi. At the age of twenty, when they had become warriors, the *wergeld* increased fivefold to 300 solidi, where it remained until the adult male reached fifty, after which it again declined. The value of females was only half that of males, although it also jumped tremendously (to 250 solidi) for women between the ages of fifteen and forty because of their importance as bearers of children.

Although the Christian church condemned infanticide, it was not able to eliminate the practice, especially among the poor and among victims of seduction who did not want to keep their illegitimate offspring. Nevertheless, priests tried to discourage such practices by urging people to abandon unwanted children in churches. Often such children were taken in by monasteries and convents and raised to be monks and nuns. Following the example of Jesus's love for children, monks and nuns tended to respect and preserve the virtues of childhood. As children grew older, however, it was thought necessary to use strict discipline to control what was considered the natural inclination of children to sin, especially by disobeying their elders.

TRAVEL AND HOSPITALITY Monasteries served another important function in the early medieval world as providers of hospitality. Both monasteries and aristocratic households were expected to provide a place to stay for weary travelers, who were ever at risk from thieves or violence of many kinds. Indeed, Burgundian law stipulated that "anyone who refused to offer a visitor shelter and warmth shall pay a fine of three solidi."[7] Hospitality, then, was a sacred duty, and monasteries were especially active in providing it. It was customary for monasteries to have two guest houses, one for the rich and another for the poor. The plan for the monastery of Saint Gall, for example, provided pilgrims and paupers with a house containing benches, two dormitories, and outbuildings. For travelers of high rank, there was a separate guest house with two heated rooms, servants' bedrooms, and stables for horses. One could not always be sure of hospitality in the Early Middle Ages, however. The famous English missionary to Germany, Saint Boniface, reported that female pilgrims to Rome had been forced to become prostitutes in every town along their route in order to obtain their sustenance and reach their goal. The church responded by forbidding females to go on such pilgrimages.

DIET For both rich and poor, the main staple of the Carolingian diet was bread. The aristocratic classes, as well as the monks, consumed it in large quantities. Ovens at the monastery of Saint Gall were able to bake a thousand loaves of bread. Sometimes a gruel made of barley and oats was substituted for bread in the peasant diet.

The upper classes in Carolingian society enjoyed a much more varied diet than the peasants. Pork was the major meat. Domestic pigs, allowed to run wild in the forests to find their own food, were collected and slaughtered in the fall, then smoked and salted to be eaten during the winter months. Because Carolingian aristocrats were especially fond of roasted meat, hunting wild game became one of their favorite activities. They ate little beef or mutton, however, because cattle were kept as dairy cows and oxen to draw plows, and sheep were raised for wool.

Dairy products became prevalent in the Carolingian diet. Milk, which spoiled rapidly, was made into cheese and butter. Chickens were raised for their eggs. Vegetables also formed a crucial part of the diet of both rich and poor. These included legumes, such as beans, peas, and lentils, and roots, such as garlic, onions, and carrots.

The Carolingian diet, especially of the upper classes, was also heavily dependent on honey and spices. Honey was used as a sweetener, both for foods and for many drinks, including wine and ale. Spices included domestic varieties that were grown in home gardens, such as thyme, sage, and chives, and more exotic—and outrageously expensive—varieties imported from the East, such as pepper, cumin, cloves, and cinnamon. Aristocrats were especially fond of spicy dishes, not just for their taste but as a sign of prestige and wealth; spices were also believed to aid the digestion.

Both gluttony and drunkenness were vices shared by many people in Carolingian society. Monastic rations were greatly enlarged in the eighth century to include a daily allotment of 3.7 pounds of bread (nuns were permitted 3 pounds), 11.2 quarts of wine or ale, 2 or 3 ounces of cheese, and 8 ounces of vegetables (4 ounces for nuns). These rations provided a total of 6,000 calories a day, and since only heavy and fatty foods—bread, milk, and cheese—were considered nourishing, we begin to understand why some Carolingians were known for their potbellies. Malnutrition, however, remained a widespread problem for common people in this period.

Everyone in Carolingian society, including abbots and monks, drank heavily and often to excess. Taverns became a regular feature of life and were found everywhere: in marketplaces, at pilgrimage centers, and on royal, episcopal, and monastic estates. Drinking contests were not unusual; one penitential stated: "Does drunken bravado encourage you to attempt to outdrink your friends? If so, thirty days' fast."

The aristocrats and monks favored wine above all other beverages, and much care was lavished on its production, especially by monasteries. Although ale was considered inferior in some quarters, it was especially popular in the northern and eastern parts of the Carolingian world. Water was also drunk as a beverage, but much care had to be taken to obtain pure sources from wells or clear streams. Monasteries were particularly active in going to the sources of water and building conduits to bring it to the cloister or kitchen fountains.

Water was also used for bathing. Although standards of personal hygiene were not high, medieval people did not ignore cleanliness. A royal palace, such as Charlemagne's, possessed both hot and cold baths. Carolingian aristocrats changed clothes and bathed at least once a week, on Saturdays. The Saturday bath was also a regular practice in many Carolingian monasteries. To monks, bathing more than once a week seemed an unnecessary luxury; to aristocrats, it often seemed desirable.

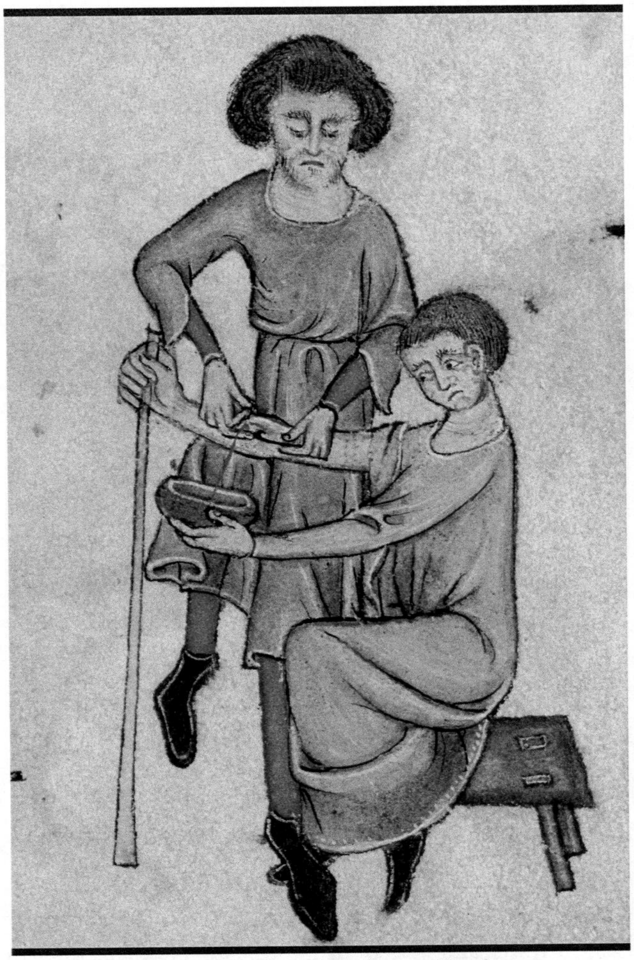

Bloodletting in Early Medieval Medicine. Bleeding was a regular part of medieval medical practice. It involved the withdrawing of blood from a person in the belief that doing so would bring balance to the body and thus heal a diseased condition. This fourteenth-century manuscript illustration shows a physician bleeding his patient with a cut in the arm. As the physician squeezes the arm, the blood spurts into a bowl; the patient seems to be quite anxious about the procedure.

HEALTH Medical practice in Carolingian times stressed the use of medicinal herbs (see the box on p. 224) and bleeding. Although the latter was practiced regularly, moderation was frequently recommended. Some advised carefulness as well: "Who dares to undertake a bleeding should see to it that his hand does not tremble."

Physicians were also available when people faced serious illnesses. Many were clerics, and monasteries trained their own. Monastic libraries kept medical manuscripts copied from ancient works and grew herbs to provide stocks of medicinal plants. Carolingian medical manuscripts contained scientific descriptions of illnesses, recipes for medical potions, and even gynecological advice, although monks in particular expended little effort on female medical needs. Some manuals even included instructions for operations, especially for soldiers injured in battle. Some sources clearly demonstrate that there were accurate techniques for amputating gangrenous limbs:

> If you must cut off an unhealthy limb from a healthy body, then do not cut to the limit of the healthy flesh, but cut further into the whole and quick flesh, so that a better and quicker cure may be obtained. When you set fire on the man [i.e., cauterize], take leaves of tender leek and grated salt, overlay the places so that the heat of the fire be more quickly drawn away.[8]

Although scholars are not sure whether anesthesia was used for such operations, medieval manuals recommended poppy, mandrake, and henbane for their narcotic properties.

Medical Practices in the Early Middle Ages

A number of medical manuscripts written in Old English have survived from Anglo-Saxon England. Although most of the medical texts date from the tenth to twelfth centuries, scholars believe that they include copies of earlier works and contain older influences as well. As the following selections from three of these treatises illustrate, herbs were the basic materials of the Anglo-Saxon physicians (or *leeches,* as they were called), and treatments consequently focused almost entirely on botanical remedies. The identity of many of the plants used remains unknown.

The Anglo-Saxon Herbal

Cress (Nasturtium)

1. In case a man's hair falls out, take juice of the plant which one names nasturtium and by another name cress, put it on the nose, the hair shall grow.
2. This plant is not sown but it is produced of itself in springs and in brooks; also it is written that in some lands it will grow against walls.
3. For a sore head, that is for scurf [dandruff] and for itch, take the seed of this same plant and goose grease, pound together, it draws from off the head the whiteness of the scurf.
4. For soreness of the body [indigestion], take this same plant nasturtium and pennyroyal, soak them in water and give to drink; the soreness and the evil departs.

The Leechbook of Bald

Here are wound salves for all wounds and drinks and cleansings of every sort, whether internally or externally. Waybroad beaten and mixed with old lard, the fresh is of no use. Again, a wound salve: take waybroad seed, crush it small, shed it on the wound and soon it will be better.

For a burn, if a man be burned with fire only, take woodruff and lily and brooklime; boil in butter and smear therewith. If a man be burned with a liquid, let him take elm rind and roots of the lily, boil them in milk, smear thereon three times a day. For sunburn, boil in butter tender ivy twigs and smear thereon.

The Peri-Didaxeon

For a Broken Head

For a broken or wounded head which is caused by the humors of the head. Take betony and pound it and lay it on the wound and it will relieve all the pain.

For Sleep

Thus must one do for the man who cannot sleep; take wormwood and rub it into wine or warm water and let the man drink it and soon it will be better with him.

For Sore Hands

This leechcraft is good for sore hands and for sore fingers which is called chilblains. Take white frankincense and silver cinders and brimstone and mingle together, then take oil and add it into this mixture, then warm the hands and smear them with the mixture thus made. Wrap up the hands in a linen cloth.

Q What were the basic medical remedies used by Anglo-Saxon physicians? How do these medical practices compare with those of the Romans? What notable similarities and differences do you find?

Physicians of the Early Middle Ages supplemented their medicines and natural practices with appeals for otherworldly help. Magical rites and influences were carried over from pagan times; the Germanic tribes had used magical medicine for centuries. Physicians recommended that patients wear amulets and charms around their bodies to ward off diseases:

> Procure a little bit of the dung of a wolf, preferably some which contains small bits of bone, and pack it in a tube which the patient may easily wear as an amulet.
>
> For epilepsy take a nail of a wrecked ship, make it into a bracelet and set therein the bone of a stag's heart taken from its body whilst alive; put it on the left arm; you will be astonished at the result.[9]

But as pagans were converted to Christianity, miraculous healing through the intervention of God, Jesus, or the saints soon replaced pagan practices. Medieval chronicles abound with accounts of people healed by touching a saint's body. The use of Christian prayers, written down and used as amulets, however, reminds us that for centuries Christian and pagan medical practices survived side by side.

Disintegration of the Carolingian Empire

Q **Focus Question:** What impact did the Vikings have on the history and culture of medieval Europe?

The Carolingian Empire began to disintegrate soon after Charlemagne's death. Charlemagne was succeeded by his son Louis the Pious. Though a decent man, Louis

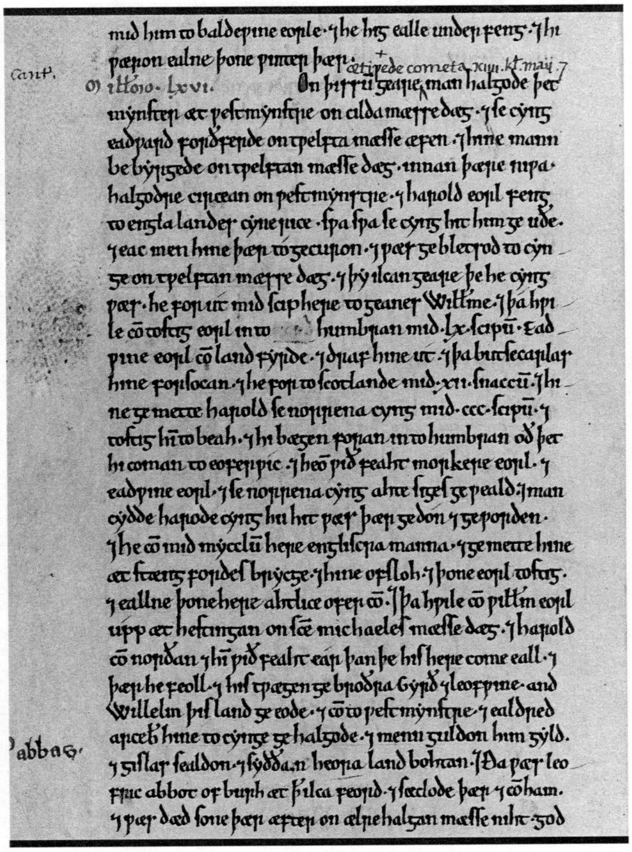

The First Bible of Charles the Bald. Charles the Bald, who took control of the western Frankish lands, is pictured here in an illustration from his first Bible, which dates from between 843 and 851. Illustrated Bibles were one of the finest achievements of Carolingian art. Also pictured is a page from a ninth-century chronicle, showing the use of the Carolingian minuscule style of writing.

was not a strong ruler and was unable to control either the Frankish aristocracy or his own four sons, who fought continually. In 843, after their father's death, the three surviving brothers signed the Treaty of Verdun. This agreement divided the Carolingian Empire among them into three major sections: Charles the Bald (843–877) obtained the western Frankish lands, which formed the core of the eventual kingdom of France; Louis the German (843–876) took the eastern lands, which became Germany; and Lothar (840–855) received the title of emperor and a "Middle Kingdom" extending from the North Sea to the Mediterranean, including the Netherlands, the Rhineland, and northern Italy. The territories of the Middle Kingdom became a source of incessant struggle between the other two Frankish rulers and their heirs. Indeed, France and Germany would fight over the territories of this Middle Kingdom for centuries.

Although this division of the Carolingian Empire was made for political and not nationalistic reasons (dividing a kingdom among the male heirs was a traditional Frankish custom), two different cultures began to emerge. By the ninth century, inhabitants of the western Frankish area were speaking a Romance language derived from Latin that became French. Eastern Franks spoke a Germanic dialect. The later kingdoms of France and Germany did not yet exist, however. In the ninth century, the frequent struggles among the numerous heirs of the sons of Louis the Pious led to further disintegration of the Carolingian Empire. In the meantime, while powerful aristocrats acquired even more power in their own local territories at the expense of the squabbling Carolingian rulers, the process of disintegration was abetted by external attacks on different parts of the old Carolingian world.

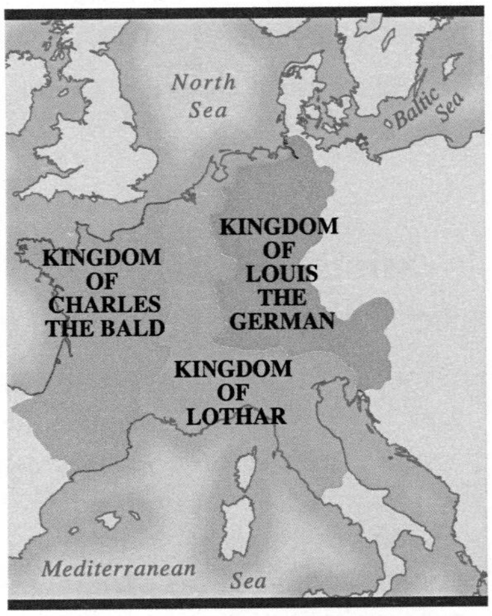

Division of the Carolingian Empire by the Treaty of Verdun, 843

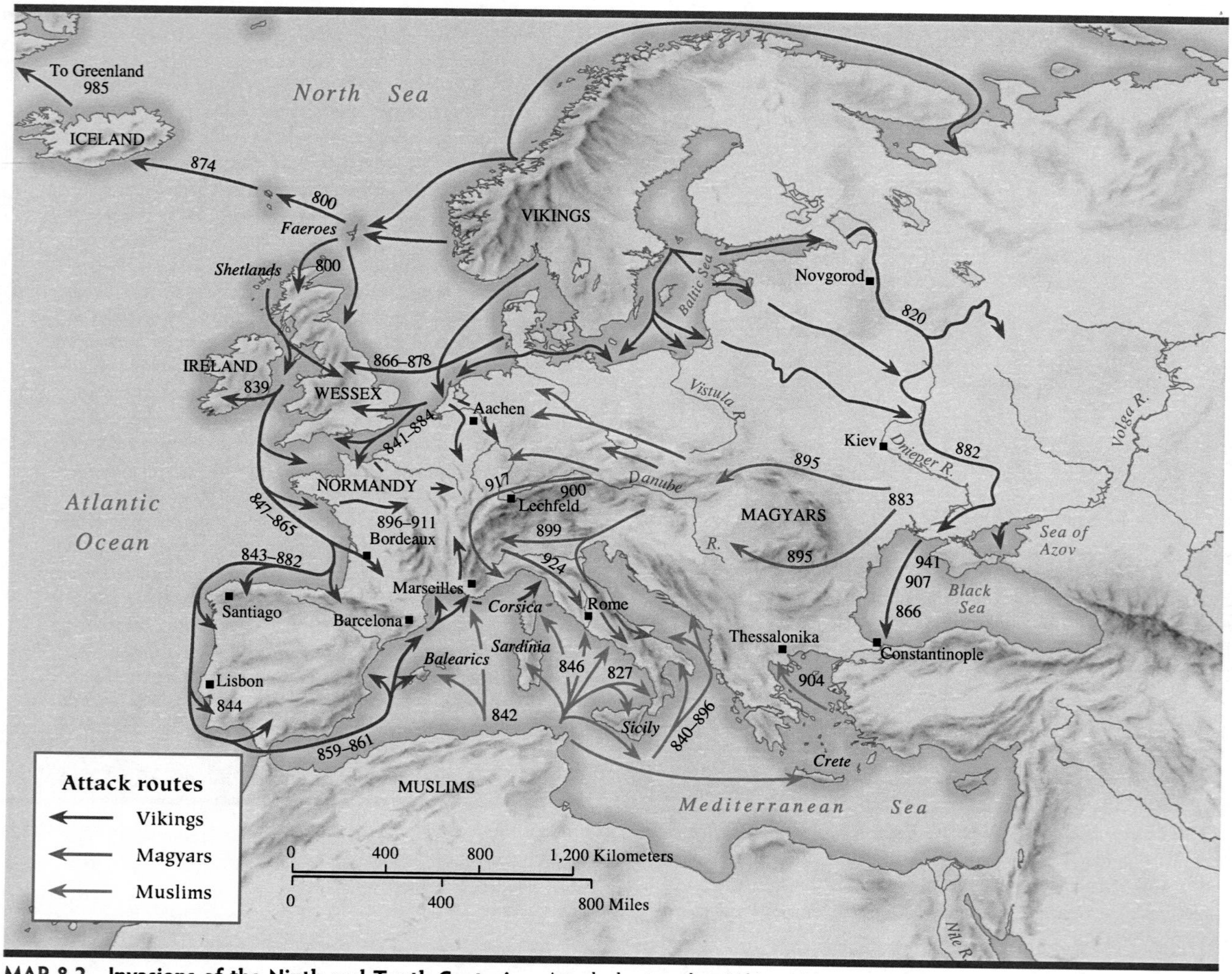

MAP 8.2 Invasions of the Ninth and Tenth Centuries. Attacks by invading Vikings, Magyars, and Muslims terrorized much of Europe in the ninth and tenth centuries, disrupting economic activity and spurring the development of fief-holding. The Vikings were the biggest problem, but they eventually formed settlements, converted to Christianity, and were assimilated.

Q ***Why was it important for the marauding Vikings to build sound boats and develop good seafaring skills?***

Invasions of the Ninth and Tenth Centuries

In the ninth and tenth centuries, western Europe was beset by a wave of invasions by several non-Christian peoples—one old enemy, the Muslims, and two new ones, the Magyars (MAG-yarz) and the Vikings (see Map 8.2). Although battered by these onslaughts, Christian Europe hung on and, with the exception of the Muslims, wound up assimilating its assailants into Christian European civilization.

MUSLIMS AND MAGYARS The first great wave of Muslim expansion had ended at the beginning of the eighth century (see Chapter 7). Gradually, the Muslims built up a series of sea bases in their occupied territories in North Africa, Spain, and southern Gaul and began a new series of attacks in the Mediterranean in the ninth century. They raided the southern coasts of Europe, especially Italy, and even threatened Rome in 843. Their invasion of Sicily in 827 eventually led to a successful occupation of the island. Muslim forces also destroyed the Carolingian defenses in northern Spain and conducted forays into southern France.

The Magyars were a people from western Asia. When the Byzantine emperors encouraged them to attack the troublesome Bulgars, the latter in turn encouraged a people known as the Pechenegs to attack the Magyars instead. Consequently, the Magyars, under severe Pecheneg pressure, had moved west into eastern and central Europe by the end of the ninth century. They established themselves on the plains of Hungary and from there made raids into western Europe. The Magyars were finally crushed at the Battle of Lechfeld in Germany in 955.

The Vikings Invade England

Near the end of the ninth century, a number of monks in England began to compile a series of chronicles, or yearly records of events. Although there are several chronicles, they have come to be known as the *Anglo- Saxon Chronicle*. Although much of the chronicle focuses on politics, there are also numerous accounts of events of immediate concern to the monks, such as the death of a bishop or inclement weather conditions. This selection from the *Anglo-Saxon Chronicle* focuses on the Danish Viking invasions of England. These selections, taken from the accounts for the years 994, 997, 998, 999, and 1003, show how regular and devastating the Viking invasions were.

Anglo-Saxon Chronicle

994. Olaf and Swein came to London, on the Nativity of St. Mary, with ninety-four ships, fighting constantly the city, and they meant, moreover, to set it on fire. But they there suffered more harm and evil than they ever believed any town-dwellers could have done them. In this God's holy mother showed her mercy to the town-dwellers and delivered them from their enemies; then they went from there, and wrought the most evil that any force had ever done, in burning, ravaging and killing, both along the seacoast, in Essex, and in Kent, Sussex and Hampshire; finally they seized horses for themselves, and rode as widely as they would, working unspeakable evil.

997. The Danes went around Devonshire into the mouth of the Severn, and there ravaged in Cornwall, Wales and Devon. Then they put in at Watchet and did much evil by burning and slaughtering. After that, they went around Land's End again on the south side, and went into the mouth of the Tamar, continuing up until they came to Lydford, burning or killing each thing they met—they burnt down Ordulf's monastery at Tavistock, and brought with them to their ships indescribable plunder.

998. The force went eastward again into the mouth of the Frome, and went inland as widely as they pleased into Dorset. Troops were often gathered against them, but as soon as they should have come together, always, in some way, flight was ordered, and they always had the victory in the end. Another time they settled themselves on the Isle of Wight, and fed themselves from Hampshire and Sussex.

999. The force came again into the Thames, and went up along Medway to Rochester; there the Kentish troops came against them, and they came together resolutely. But alas, they moved too quickly, and fled because they had not the help they should have had—then the Danes had the power of the battlefield, seized horses, and rode as widely as they pleased. They ravaged and destroyed nearly all West Kent.

1003. Exeter was ruined, because of the Frankish peasant Hugh, whom the lady had set up as her reeve [local official]; the Danish force destroyed the town completely, and took much booty. A very great army was gathered from Wiltshire and Hampshire, and went very resolutely against the force. The ealdorman [town official] Aelfric should have led the army, but he displayed his old wiles. As soon as they were close enough to look on one another, he feigned sickness, and began retching to vomit, and said that he was taken ill; so he betrayed the people he should have led, as it is said: "When the war-leader weakens, all the army is greatly hindered." When Swein saw that they were not resolute, and all scattering, he led his force into Wilton, ravaged and burnt the borough, went to Salisbury, and from there went back to the sea, where he knew his wave-coursers were.

Q What do you think were the tactics of the Viking invaders? How would you know from these accounts that the *Chronicle* was written by monks?

At the end of the tenth century, they were converted to Christianity and settled down to establish the kingdom of Hungary.

THE VIKINGS By far the most devastating and far-reaching attacks of the time came from the Northmen or Norsemen of Scandinavia, also known to us as the Vikings. The Vikings were a Germanic people based in Scandinavia and constitute, in a sense, the final wave of Germanic migration. Why they began to move is not very clear to historians. One common explanation focuses on overpopulation, although recent research indicates that this may have been true only in western Norway. Other reasons have included the Vikings' great love of adventure and their search for wealth and new avenues of trade.

Two features of Viking society help explain what the Vikings accomplished. First of all, they were warriors. Second, they were superb shipbuilders and sailors. Their ships were the best of the period. Long and narrow with beautifully carved arched prows, the Viking dragon ships carried about fifty men. They had banks of oars as well as a single great sail. Their shallow draft enabled them to sail up European rivers and attack places at some distance inland. Although Viking raids in the eighth century tended to be small-scale and sporadic, they became more regular and more devastating in the ninth (see the box above).

The Vikings Attack England. An illustration from an eleventh-century English manuscript depicts a group of armed Vikings invading England. Two ships have already reached the shore, and a few Vikings are shown walking down a long gangplank onto English soil. Also shown is a replica of a well-preserved Viking ship found at Oseberg, Norway. The Oseberg ship was one of the largest Viking ships in its day.

Vikings sacked villages and towns, destroyed churches, and easily defeated small local armies. Viking attacks frightened people and led many a clergyman to exhort his parishioners to change their behavior to appease God's anger, as in this sermon by an English archbishop in 1014:

> Things have not gone well now for a long time at home or abroad, but there has been devastation and persecution in every district again and again, and the English have been for a long time now completely defeated and too greatly disheartened through God's anger; and the pirates [Vikings] so strong with God's consent that often in battle one puts to flight ten, and sometimes less, sometimes more, all because of our sins. . . . We pay them continually and they humiliate us daily; they ravage and they burn, plunder, and rob and carry on board; and lo, what else is there in all these events except God's anger clear and visible over this people?[10]

Because there were different groups of Scandinavians, Viking expansion varied a great deal. Norwegian Vikings moved into Ireland and western England; Danes attacked eastern England, Frisia, and the Rhineland and navigated rivers to enter western Frankish lands. Swedish Vikings dominated the Baltic Sea and progressed into the Slavic areas to the east. Moving into northwestern Russia, they went down the rivers of Russia to Novgorod and Kiev and established fortified ports throughout these territories. There they made contact with the Byzantine Empire, either as traders or as invaders. They also made contact with Arab traders on the Volga River and the Sea of Azov.

Early Viking raids had been carried out largely in the summer; by the mid-ninth century, however, the Norsemen had begun to establish winter settlements in Europe from which they could make expeditions to conquer and settle new lands. By 850, groups of Norsemen had settled in Ireland, and the Danes occupied an area known as the Danelaw in northeastern England by 878. Agreeing to accept Christianity, the Danes were eventually assimilated into a larger Anglo-Saxon kingdom. Beginning in 911, the ruler of the western Frankish lands gave one band of Vikings land at the mouth of the Seine River, forming a section of France that ultimately came to be known as Normandy. This policy of settling the Vikings and converting them to Christianity was a deliberate one, since the new inhabitants served as protectors against additional Norseman attacks.

The Vikings were also daring explorers. After 860, they sailed westward in their long ships across the North Atlantic Ocean, reaching Iceland in 874. Erik the Red, a Viking exiled from Iceland, traveled even farther west and discovered Greenland in 985. The only known Viking site in North America was found in Newfoundland.

By the tenth century, Viking expansion was drawing to a close. Greater control by the monarchs of Denmark, Norway, and Sweden over their inhabitants and the increasing Christianization of both the Scandinavian kings and peoples tended to inhibit Viking expansion, but not before Viking settlements had been established throughout many parts of Europe. Like the Magyars, the Vikings were also assimilated into European civilization. Once again, Christianity proved a decisive civilizing force in Europe. Europe and Christianity were becoming virtually synonymous.

The Viking raids and settlements also had important political repercussions. The inability of royal authorities to protect their peoples against these incursions caused local populations to turn instead to the local aristocrats to provide security for them. In the process, the landed aristocrats not only increased their strength and prestige but also assumed even more of the functions of local government that had previously belonged to the kings; over time these developments led to a new political and military order.

Musée Condé, Chantilly//© Lauros/Giraudon/The Bridgeman Art Library

A Knight's Equipment Showing Saddle and Stirrups. In return for his fighting skills, a knight received a piece of land from his lord that provided for his economic support. Pictured here is a charging knight with his equipment. The introduction of the high saddle, stirrup, and larger horses allowed horsemen to wear heavier armor and to wield long lances, vastly improving the fighting ability of the cavalry.

The Emerging World of Lords and Vassals

Focus Question: What was fief-holding, and how was it related to manorialism?

The renewed invasions and the disintegration of the Carolingian Empire led to the emergence of a new type of relationship between free individuals. When governments ceased to be able to defend their subjects, it became important to find some powerful lord who could offer protection in exchange for service. The contract sworn between a lord and his subordinate is the basis of a form of social organization that later generations of historians called *feudalism.* But feudalism was never a system, and many historians today prefer to avoid using the term.

Vassalage

The practice of **vassalage** was derived from Germanic society, in which warriors swore an oath of loyalty to their leader. They fought for their chief, and he in turn took care of their needs. By the eighth century, an individual who served a lord in a military capacity was known as a *vassal.*

With the breakdown of governments, powerful nobles took control of large areas of land. They needed men to fight for them, so the practice arose of giving grants of land to vassals, who would in return fight for their lord. The Frankish army had originally consisted of foot soldiers, dressed in coats of mail and armed with swords. But in the eighth century, when larger horses and the stirrup were introduced, a military change began to occur. Earlier, horsemen had been throwers of spears. Now they wore armored coats of mail (the larger horse could carry the weight) and wielded long lances that enabled them to act as battering rams (the stirrups kept the riders on their horses). For almost five hundred years, warfare in Europe would be dominated by heavily armored cavalry, or *knights,* as they came to be called.

Of course, a horse, armor, and weapons were expensive to purchase and maintain, and learning to wield these instruments skillfully from horseback took much time and practice. Consequently, lords who wanted men to fight for them had to grant each vassal a piece of land that provided for the support of the vassal and his family. In return for the land, the vassal provided his lord with one major service, his fighting skills. Each needed the other. In the society of the Early Middle Ages, where there was little trade and wealth was based primarily on land ownership, land became the most important gift a lord could give to a vassal in return for military service.

The relationship between lord and vassal was made official by a public ceremony. To become a vassal, a man performed an act of homage to his lord, as described in this passage from a medieval treatise on law:

> The man should put his hands together as a sign of humility, and place them between the two hands of his lord as a token that he vows everything to him and promises faith to him; and the lord should receive him and promise to keep faith with him. Then the man should say: "Sir, I enter your homage and faith and become your man by mouth and hands [i.e., by taking the oath and placing his hands between those of the lord], and I swear and promise to keep faith and loyalty to you against all others, and to guard your rights with all my strength.[11]

As in the earlier Germanic band, loyalty to one's lord was the chief virtue (see the box on p. 231).

Fief-Holding

The land or some other type of income granted to a vassal in return for military service came to be known as a **fief.** In time, many vassals who held such grants of land came to exercise rights of jurisdiction or political and legal authority within their fiefs. As the Carolingian world disintegrated politically under the impact of dissension within and invasions from without, an increasing number of powerful lords arose. Instead of a single government, many people were now responsible for keeping order. In some areas of France, for example, some lords—called *castellans*—constructed castles and asserted their authority to collect taxes and dispense justice to the local population. Lack of effective central control led to ever-larger numbers of castles and castellans.

Fief-holding also became increasingly complicated as **subinfeudation** developed. The vassals of a king, who were themselves great lords, might also have vassals who would owe them military service in return for a grant of land from their estates. Those vassals, in turn, might likewise have vassals, who at such a level would be simple knights with barely enough land to provide their equipment. The lord-vassal relationship, then, bound together both greater and lesser landowners. Historians used to speak of a hierarchy with the king at the top, greater lords on the next level, lesser lords on the next, and simple knights at the bottom; this was only a model, however, and rarely reflected reality. Such a hierarchy implies a king at the top. The reality in the tenth-century west Frankish kingdom was that the Capetian kings (see "New Political Configurations in the Tenth Century" later in this chapter) actually controlled only the region around Paris. They possessed little real power over the great lords who held fiefs throughout France.

The lord-vassal relationship at all levels always constituted an honorable relationship between free men and did not imply any sense of servitude. Since kings could no longer provide security in the midst of the breakdown created by the invasions of the ninth century, subinfeudation became ever more widespread. With their rights of jurisdiction, fiefs gave lords virtual possession of the rights of government.

The new practice of lordship was basically a product of the Carolingian world, but it also spread to England, Germany, and central Europe, and in modified form to Italy. Fief-holding came to be characterized by a set of practices worked out in the course of the tenth century, although they became more prominent after 1000. These practices included a series of mutual obligations of lord toward vassal and vassal toward lord, but it is crucial to remember that such obligations varied considerably from place to place and even from fief to fief. As usual, practice almost always diverged from theory.

MUTUAL OBLIGATIONS Because the basic objective of fief-holding was to provide military support, it is no surprise to learn that the major obligation of a vassal to his lord was to perform military service. In addition to his own personal service, a great lord was also responsible for providing a group of knights for the king's army. Moreover, vassals had to furnish suit at court; this meant that a vassal was obliged to appear at his lord's court when summoned, either to give advice to the lord or to sit in judgment in a legal case, since the important vassals of a lord were peers, and only they could judge each other. Many vassals were also obliged to provide hospitality for their lord when he stayed at a vassal's castle. This obligation was especially important to medieval kings because they tended to be itinerant. Finally, vassals were responsible for aids, or financial payments, to the lord on a number of occasions, including the knighting of the lord's eldest son, the marriage of his eldest daughter, and the ransom of the lord's person if he was held captive.

In turn, a lord had responsibilities toward his vassals. His major obligation was to protect his vassal, either by defending him militarily or by taking his side in a court of law if necessary. The lord was also responsible for the maintenance of the vassal, usually by granting him a fief.

As this system of mutual obligations between lord and vassal evolved, certain practices became common. If a lord acted improperly toward his vassal, the bond between them could be dissolved. Likewise, if a vassal failed to fulfill his vow of loyalty, he was subject to forfeiture of his fief. Upon a vassal's death, his fief theoretically reverted to the lord, since it had been granted to the vassal for use, not as a possession. In practice, however, by the tenth century fiefs tended to be hereditary. Following the principle of primogeniture, the eldest son inherited the father's fief. If a man died without heirs, the lord could reclaim the fief.

New Political Configurations in the Tenth Century

In the tenth century, Europe began to recover from the invasions of the century before. The disintegration of the

Opposing VIEWPOINTS

Lords and Vassals in Europe and Japan

When we use the word *feudalism,* we usually think of European knights on horseback clad in armor and armed with sword and lance. Indeed, a social order based on lords and vassals arose in Europe between 800 and 900 and flourished for the next four hundred years. But Europe was not the only part of the world where a form of social organization based on lords and vassals emerged. In Japan, a social order much like that found in Europe developed between 800 and 1500. The first selection is the classic statement by Bishop Fulbert of Chartres in 1020 on the mutual obligations between lord and vassals. The second selection is taken from *Tale of the Heike,* a Japanese tale written in the first half of the thirteenth century about military struggles that took place at the end of the twelfth century.

Bishop Fulbert of Chartres

Asked to write something concerning the form of fealty, I have noted briefly for you, on the authority of the books, the things which follow. He who swears fealty to his lord ought always to have these six things in memory: what is harmless, safe, honorable, useful, easy, practicable. *Harmless,* that is to say, that he should not injure his lord in his body; *safe,* that he should not injure him by betraying his secrets or the defenses upon which he relies for safety; *honorable,* that he should not injure him in his justice or in other matters that pertain to his honor; *useful,* that he should not injure him in his possessions; *easy* and *practicable,* that that good which his lord is able to do easily he make not difficult, nor that which is practicable he make not impossible to him.

That the faithful vassal should avoid these injuries is certainly proper, but not for this alone does he deserve his holding; for it is not sufficient to abstain from evil, unless what is good is done also. It remains, therefore, that in the same six things mentioned above he should faithfully counsel and aid his lord, if he wishes to be looked upon as worthy of his benefice and to be safe concerning the fealty which he has sworn.

The lord also ought to act toward his faithful vassal reciprocally in all these things. And if he does not do this, he will be justly considered guilty of bad faith, just as the former, if he should be detected in avoiding or consenting to the avoidance of his duties, would be perfidious and perjured.

Tale of the Heike

Recognizing each other, master and retainer spurred their horses to join each other. Seizing Kanehira's hands, Yoshinaka said: "I would have fought to the death on the banks of the Kamo at Rokujō. Simply because of you, however, I have galloped here through the enemy swarms."

"It was very kind of you, my lord," replied Kanehira. "I too would have fought to the death at Seta. But in fear of your uncertain fate, I have come this way."

"We are still tied by karma," said Yoshinaka. "There must be more of my men around here, for I have seen them scattered among the hills. Unroll the banner and raise it high!"

As soon as Kanehira unfurled the banner, many men who had been in flight from the capital and Seta saw it and rallied. They soon numbered more than three hundred.

"Since we still have so many men, let us try one last fight!" shouted Yoshinaka jubilantly. . . .

Shouting, Yoshinaka dashed ahead. That day he wore armor laced with twilled silk cords over a red battle robe. His helmet was decorated with long golden horns. At his side hung a great sword studded with gold. He carried his quiver a little higher than usual on his back. Some eagle-feathered arrows still remained. Gripping his rattan-bound bow, he rode his famous horse, Oniashige.

Rising high in his stirrups, he roared at the enemy: "You have often heard of me. Now take a good look at the captain of the Imperial Stables of the Left and governor of Iyo Province—Rising-Sun General Minamoto no Yoshinaka, that is who I am! I know that among you is Kai no Ichijōjirō Tadayori. We are fit opponents for each other. Cut off my head and show it to Yoritomo!"

At this challenge, Tadayori shouted to his men: "Now, hear this! He is the commander of our enemy. Let him not escape! All men—to the attack!"

Q According to Bishop Fulbert, what were the mutual obligations of lords and vassals? Why were these important in the practice of fief-holding? The lord-vassal relationship was based on loyalty. What differences and similarities do you see in the loyalty between lord and vassals in Europe and Japan? How did the weapons used by a European knight and a Japanese warrior differ?

Carolingian Empire and the emergence of great and powerful lords soon produced new political configurations.

THE EASTERN FRANKS In the east Frankish kingdom, the last Carolingian king died in 911, whereupon local rulers, especially the powerful dukes (the title of *duke* is derived from the Latin word *dux,* meaning "leader") of the Saxons, Swabians, Bavarians, Thuringians, and Franconians, who exercised much power in their large dukedoms, elected one of their own number, Conrad of Franconia, to serve as king of Germany (as we think of it) or of the eastern Franks (as contemporaries thought of it). But Conrad did not last long, and after his death, the German dukes chose Henry the Fowler, duke of Saxony, as the new king of Germany (919–936). The first of the Saxon dynasty of German kings, Henry was not particularly successful in creating a unified eastern Frankish kingdom because he lacked the resources to impose effective rule over the entire area.

The best known of the Saxon kings of Germany was Henry's son, Otto I (936–973). He defeated the Magyars at the Battle of Lechfeld in 955 and encouraged an ongoing program of Christianization of both the Slavic and Scandinavian peoples. Even more than his father, he relied on bishops and abbots in governing his kingdom. This practice was in part a response to the tendency of the lay lords to build up their power at the expense of the king. Since the clergy were theoretically celibate, bishops and abbots could not make their offices hereditary, thus allowing the king to maintain more control over them.

Otto also intervened in Italian politics and for his efforts was crowned emperor of the Romans by the pope in 962, reviving a title that had fallen into disuse with the disintegration of Charlemagne's empire. Once again a pope had conferred the Roman imperial title on a king of the Franks, even though he was a Saxon king of the eastern Franks. Otto's creation of a new "Roman Empire" in the hands of the eastern Franks (or Germans) added a tremendous burden to the kingship of Germany. To the difficulties of governing Germany was appended the onerous task of ruling Italy as well. It proved a formidable and ultimately impossible task.

THE WESTERN FRANKS In the ninth and tenth centuries, the Carolingian kings had little success in controlling the great lords of the western Frankish kingdom. The counts, who were supposed to serve as the chief administrative officials, often paid little attention to the wishes of the Carolingian kings. In 987, when the Carolingian king died, the western Frankish nobles and chief prelates of the church chose Hugh Capet (YOO ka-PAY), count of Orléans and Paris, as the new king (987–996).

The nobles who elected Hugh Capet did not intend to establish a new royal dynasty. After all, although Hugh was officially king of the western Franks and overlord of the great nobles of the kingdom, his own family controlled only the Île-de-France, the region around Paris. Other French nobles possessed lands equal to or greater than those of the Capetians and assumed that the king would be content to live off the revenues of his personal lands and not impose any burdensome demands on the nobility. Hugh Capet did succeed in making his position hereditary, however. He asked the nobles, and they agreed, to choose his eldest son, Robert, as his anointed associate in case Hugh died on a campaign to Spain in 987. And although Hugh Capet could not know it then, the Capetian (kuh-PEE-shun) dynasty would rule the western Frankish kingdom, or France, as it eventually came to be known, for centuries. In the late tenth century, however, the territory that would become France was not a unified kingdom but a loose alliance of powerful lords who treated the king as an equal. They assisted him only when it was in their own interests to do so.

CHRONOLOGY New Political Configurations of the Tenth Century

Eastern Franks	
Conrad of Franconia	911–918
Saxon dynasty: Henry I	919–936
Otto I	936–973
Defeat of Magyars	955
Coronation as emperor	962
Western Franks	
Election of Hugh Capet as king	987
Anglo-Saxon England	
Alfred the Great, king of Wessex	871–899
Peace with the Danes	886
Reign of King Edgar	959–975

ANGLO-SAXON ENGLAND England's development in the ninth and tenth centuries took a course somewhat different from that of the Frankish kingdoms. The long struggle of the Anglo-Saxon kingdoms against the Viking invasions ultimately produced a unified kingdom. Alfred the Great, king of Wessex (871–899), played a crucial role. He defeated a Danish army in 879, according to an account by Asser, his adviser, who wrote a biography of the king:

> [Alfred] gained the victory through God's will. He destroyed the Vikings with great slaughter, and pursued those who fled as far as the stronghold, hacking them down; he seized everything which he found outside the stronghold—men (whom he killed immediately), horses and cattle—and boldly made camp in front of the gate of the Viking stronghold with all his army. When he had been there for fourteen days the Vikings, thoroughly terrified by hunger, cold and fear, and in the end by despair, sought peace.[12]

Alfred eventually made peace with the Danes after strengthening his army and creating a navy.

Alfred also believed in the power of education. He invited scholars to his court and encouraged the translation of the works of such church fathers as Augustine and Gregory the Great from Latin into Anglo-Saxon (Old English), the

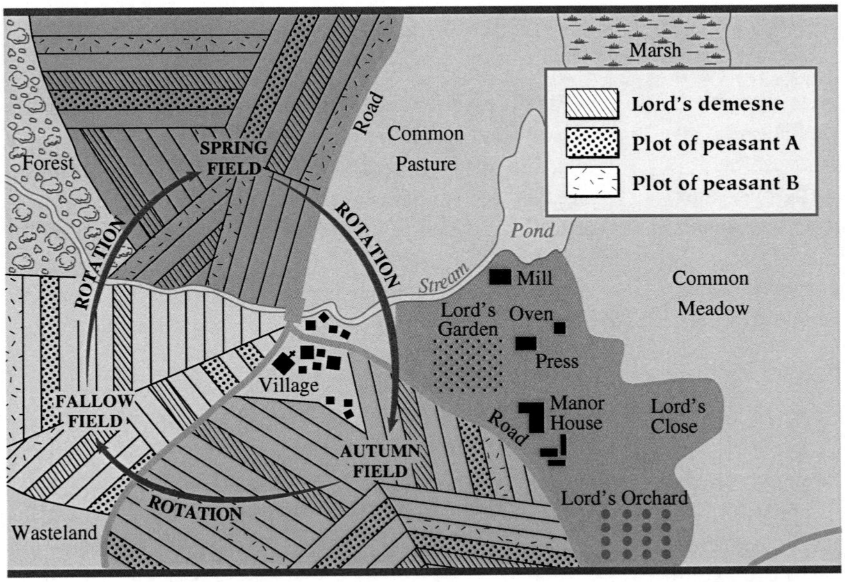

MAP 8.3 A Typical Manor. The manorial system created small, tightly knit communities in which peasants were economically and physically bound to their lord. Crops were rotated, with roughly one-third of the fields lying fallow at any one time, which helped replenish soil nutrients (see Chapter 9).

Q ***How does the area of the lord's manor house, other buildings, garden, and orchard compare with that of the peasant holdings in the village?***

vernacular, or the language spoken by the people. Old English was also soon used for official correspondence as well.

Alfred's successors reconquered the remaining areas occupied by the Danes and established a unified Anglo-Saxon monarchy. By the time of King Edgar (959–975), Anglo-Saxon England had a well-developed and strong monarchical government. Although the kingship was elective, only descendants of Alfred were chosen for the position. In the counties or *shires*, the administrative units into which England was divided, the king was assisted by an agent appointed and controlled by him, the shire-reeve or sheriff. An efficient chancery or writing office was responsible for issuing writs (or royal letters) conveying the king's orders to the sheriffs.

The Manorial System

The landholding class of nobles and knights comprised a military elite whose ability to function as warriors depended on having the leisure time to pursue the arts of war. Landed estates worked by a dependent peasant class provided the economic sustenance that made this way of life possible. A **manor** (see Map 8.3) was simply an agricultural estate operated by a lord and worked by peasants. Lords provided protection; peasants gave up their freedom, became tied to the lord's land, and provided labor services for him.

Manorialism grew out of the unsettled circumstances of the Early Middle Ages, when small farmers often needed protection or food in a time of bad harvests. Free peasants gave up their freedom to the lords of large landed estates in return for protection and use of the lord's land. Although a large class of free peasants continued to exist, increasing numbers of them became bound to the land as serfs. Unlike slaves, **serfs** could not be bought and sold, but they were subservient to their lords in a variety of ways. Serfs were required to provide labor services, pay rents, and be subject to the lord's jurisdiction. By the ninth century, probably 60 percent of the population of western Europe had become serfs.

A serf's labor services consisted of working the lord's **demesne,** the land retained by the lord, which might

Peasants in the Manorial System. In the manorial system, peasants were required to provide labor services for their lord. This thirteenth-century illustration shows a group of English peasants harvesting grain. Overseeing their work is a bailiff, or manager, who supervised the work of the peasants.

The Manorial Court

The way of life of the medieval lord was made possible by the labors of the serfs on his manor. In addition to his right to collect rents, labor services, and fees from his serfs, the lord also possessed political authority over them, including the right to hold a manorial court to try tenants for crimes and infractions of the manor's rules. This selection, taken from the records of an English manorial court, lists the cases heard, the decisions of the jurors, and the subsequent penalties.

Select Pleas in Manorial Courts

John Sperling complains that Richard of Newmere on the Sunday next before S. Bartholomew's day [August 24] last past with his cattle, horses, and pigs wrongfully destroyed the corn on his (John's) land to his damage to the extent of one thrave of wheat, and to his dishonor to the extent of two shillings; and of this he produces suit. And Richard comes and defends all of it. Therefore let him go to the law six handed [with three companions who will swear to his innocence]. His pledges, Simon Combe and Hugh Frith [like bail bondsmen, pledges stood surety for a person ordered to show up in court or pay a fine].

Hugh Free in mercy [fined] for his beast caught in the lord's garden. Pledges, Walter Hill and William Slipper, Fine 6d. [sixpence].

(The) twelve jurors say that Hugh Cross has right in the bank and hedge about which there was a dispute between him and William White. Therefore let him hold in peace and let William be distrained [forced to comply by seizing his property] for his many trespasses. (Afterwards he made fine for 12d.)

From the whole township of Little Ogbourne, except seven, for not coming to wash the lord's sheep, 6s. 8d. [six shillings, eight pence]....

It was presented that Robert Carter's son by night invaded the house of Peter Burgess and in felony threw stones at his door so that the said Peter raised the hue [alarm]. Therefore let the said Robert be committed to prison. Afterwards he made fine with 2s.

All the plowmen of Great Ogbourne are convicted by the oath of twelve men... because by reason of their default (the land) of the lord is damaged to the amount of 9s.... And Walter Reaper is in mercy for concealing (i.e., not giving information as to) the said bad plowing. Afterwards he made fine with the lord with 1 mark [thirteen shillings, four pence].

Q What do these legal decisions reveal about daily life on the manor, relations between the residents, and their sense of justice?

encompass one-third to one-half of the cultivated lands scattered throughout the manor (the rest would have been allotted to the serfs for their maintenance), as well as building barns and digging ditches. Although labor requirements varied from manor to manor and person to person, a common work obligation was three days a week.

The serfs paid rent by giving their lord a share of every product they raised. Serfs also paid the lord for the use of the manor's common pasturelands, streams, ponds, and surrounding woodlands. For example, if tenants fished in the pond or stream on a manor, they turned over part of the catch to their lord. For grazing a cow in the common pasture, a serf paid a rent in cheese produced from the cow's milk. Serfs were also obliged to pay a **tithe** (a tenth of their produce) to their local village church.

Lords also possessed a variety of legal rights over their serfs. Serfs were legally bound to the lord's land; they could not leave without his permission. Although free to marry, serfs could not marry anyone outside their manor without the lord's approval. Moreover, lords sometimes exercised public rights or political authority on their lands. This gave the lord the right to try serfs in his own court, although only for lesser crimes (called "low justice"). In fact, the lord's manorial court provided the only law that most serfs knew (see the box above). Finally, the lord's political authority enabled him to establish monopolies on certain services that provided additional revenues. Serfs could be required to bring their grain to the lord's mill and pay a fee to have it ground into flour. Thus, the rights a lord possessed on his manor gave him virtual control over both the lives and property of his serfs.

The administration of manors varied considerably. If the lord of a manor was a simple knight, he would probably live on the estate and supervise it in person. Great lords possessed many manors and relied on a steward or bailiff to run each estate. Note that manors were controlled not only by lay lords but also by monasteries and cathedral churches. Monasteries tended to be far more conscientious about keeping accurate records of their manorial estates than lay lords, and their surveys provide some of the best sources of information on medieval village life. The relationship between manors and villages was highly variable. A single village might constitute a manor, or a large manor might encompass several villages.

In the Early Middle Ages, the vast majority of men and women, free or unfree—possibly as many as 90 percent—worked the land. This period had witnessed a precipitous decline in trade. Coins and jewelry were often hoarded, and at the local level, goods were frequently bartered because so few coins were in circulation. But trade never entirely disappeared. Even in an agrarian society, surplus products could be exchanged at local markets. More significant, however, was that both aristocrats and wealthy clerics desired merchandise not produced locally, such as spices, silk cloth, wine, gold, and silver jewelry, and it took trade to obtain these items.

Much of the trade in luxury goods, especially beginning in the ninth century, was conducted with the Byzantine Empire, particularly the city of Constantinople, and the Islamic caliphs of Baghdad. Products from the west included iron, timber, furs, and slaves (many from eastern Europe, including captured Slavs, from whom the modern word *slave* is derived). Traders, often Jews, carried goods by boat on European rivers or on caravans with horses or mules. An Arab geographer of the ninth century left this account of Jewish traders from southern France:

> [They] speak Arabic, Persian, Greek, Frankish, Spanish, and Slavonic. They travel from west to east and from east to west, by land and by sea. From the west they bring eunuchs, slavegirls, boys, brocade, marten and other furs, and swords. They take ship from Frankland in the western Mediterranean sea and land at Farama, whence they take their merchandise on camel-back to Qulzum.... Then they sail on the eastern [Red] sea from Qulzum, and onward to India and China. From China they bring back musk, aloes, camphor, cinnamon, and other products of those parts, and return to Qulzum. Then they transport them to Farama and sail again on the western sea. Some sail with their goods to Constantinople and sell them to the Greeks, and some take them to the king of the Franks and sell them there.[13]

By 900, Italian merchants, especially the Venetians, were entering the trade picture. Overall, however, compared to the Byzantine Empire or Muslim caliphates, western Europe in the Early Middle Ages was an underdeveloped, predominantly agrarian society and could not begin to match the splendor of either of the other heirs of the Roman Empire.

The Zenith of Byzantine Civilization

Focus Question: What were the chief developments in the Byzantine Empire between 750 and 1000?

In the seventh and eighth centuries, the Byzantine Empire had lost much of its territory to Slavs, Bulgars, and Muslims. By 750, the empire consisted only of Asia Minor, some lands in the Balkans, and the southern coast of Italy. Although Byzantium was beset with internal dissension and invasions in the ninth century, it was able to deal with them and not only endured but even expanded, reaching its high point in the tenth century, which some historians have called the golden age of Byzantine civilization.

During the reign of Michael III (842–867), the Byzantine Empire began to experience a revival. Iconoclasm was finally abolished in 843, and reforms were made in education, church life, the military, and the peasant economy. There was a noticeable intellectual renewal. But the Byzantine Empire under Michael was still plagued by persistent problems. The Bulgars mounted new attacks, and the Arabs continued to harass the empire. Moreover, a new church problem with political repercussions erupted over differences between the pope as leader of the western Christian church and the patriarch of Constantinople as leader of the eastern (or Orthodox) Christian church. Patriarch Photius (FOH-shuss) condemned the pope as a heretic for accepting a revised form of the Nicene Creed stating that the Holy Spirit proceeded from the Father and the Son instead of "the Holy Spirit, who proceeds from the Father." A council of eastern bishops followed Photius's wishes and excommunicated the pope, creating the so-called Photian schism. Although the differences were later papered over, this controversy served to further the division between the eastern and western Christian churches.

The Macedonian Dynasty

The problems that arose during Michael's reign were effectively dealt with by a new dynasty of Byzantine emperors known as the Macedonians (867–1081), who managed to hold off the external enemies, go over to the offensive, and reestablish domestic order. Supported by the church, the emperors thought of the Byzantine Empire as a continuation of the Christian Roman Empire of late antiquity. Although for diplomatic reasons they occasionally recognized the imperial title of western emperors, such as Charlemagne and Otto I, they still regarded them as little more than barbarian parvenus.

The Macedonian emperors could boast of a remarkable number of achievements in the late ninth and tenth centuries. They worked to strengthen the position of the free farmers, who felt threatened by the attempts of landed aristocrats to expand their estates at the expense of the farmers. The emperors were well aware that the free farmers made up the rank and file of the Byzantine cavalry and provided the military strength of the empire. The Macedonian emperors also fostered a burst of economic prosperity by expanding trade relations with western Europe, especially by selling silks and metalwork. Thanks to this prosperity, the city of Constantinople flourished. Foreign visitors continued to be astounded by its size, wealth, and physical surroundings. To western Europeans, it was the stuff of legends and fables (see the box on p. 236).

In the midst of this prosperity, Byzantine cultural influence expanded due to the active missionary efforts of eastern Byzantine Christians. Eastern Orthodox Christianity was spread to eastern European peoples, such as the Bulgars and Serbs. Perhaps the greatest missionary success occurred when the prince of Kiev in Russia converted to Christianity in 987.

Under the Macedonian rulers, Byzantium enjoyed a strong civil service, talented emperors, and military

A Western View of the Byzantine Empire

Bishop Liudprand of Cremona undertook diplomatic missions to Constantinople on behalf of two western kings, Berengar of Italy and Otto I of Germany. This selection is taken from the bishop's description of his mission to the Byzantine emperor Constantine VII as an envoy for Berengar, king of Italy from 950 until his overthrow by Otto I of Germany in 964. Liudprand had mixed feelings about Byzantium: admiration, yet also envy and hostility because of its superior wealth.

Liudprand of Cremona, *Antapodosis*

Next to the imperial residence at Constantinople there is a palace of remarkable size and beauty which the Greeks call Magnavra . . . the name being equivalent to "fresh breeze." In order to receive some Spanish envoys, who had recently arrived, as well as myself . . . , Constantine gave orders that his palace should be got ready. . . .

Before the emperor's seat stood a tree, made of bronze gilded over, whose branches were filled with birds, also made of gilded bronze, which uttered different cries, each according to its varying species. The throne itself was so marvelously fashioned that at one moment it seemed a low structure, and at another it rose high into the air. It was of immense size and was guarded by lions, made either of bronze or of wood covered over with gold, who beat the ground with their tails and gave a dreadful roar with open mouth and quivering tongue. Leaning upon the shoulders of two eunuchs I was brought into the emperor's presence. At my approach the lions began to roar and the birds to cry out, each according to its kind; but I was neither terrified nor surprised, for I had previously made enquiry about all these things from people who were well acquainted with them. So after I had three times made obeisance to the emperor with my face upon the ground, I lifted my head, and behold! The man whom just before I had seen sitting on a moderately elevated seat had now changed his raiment and was sitting on the level of the ceiling. How it was done I could not imagine, unless perhaps he was lifted up by some such sort of device as we use for raising the timbers of a wine press. On that occasion he did not address me personally . . . but by the intermediary of a secretary he enquired about Berengar's doings and asked after his health. I made a fitting reply and then, at a nod from the interpreter, left his presence and retired to my lodging.

It would give me some pleasure also to record here what I did then for Berengar. . . . The Spanish envoys . . . had brought handsome gifts from their masters to the emperor Constantine. I for my part had brought nothing from Berengar except a letter and that was full of lies. I was very greatly disturbed and shamed at this and I began to consider anxiously what I had better do. In my doubt and perplexity it finally occurred to me that I might offer the gifts, which on my account I had brought for the emperor, as coming from Berengar, and trick out my humble present with fine words. I therefore presented him with nine excellent curaisses, seven excellent shields with gilded bosses, two silver gilt cauldrons, some swords, spears and spits, and what was more precious to the emperor than anything, four carzimasia; that being the Greek name for young eunuchs who have had both their testicles and their penis removed. This operation is performed by traders at Verdun, who take the boys into Spain and make a huge profit.

Q What impressions of the Byzantine court do you receive from Liudprand of Cremona's account? What is the modern meaning of the word *byzantine*? How does this account help explain the modern meaning of the word?

Emperor Leo VI. Under the Macedonian dynasty, the Byzantine Empire achieved economic prosperity through expanded trade and gained new territories through military victories. This mosaic over the western door of Hagia Sophia in Constantinople depicts the Macedonian emperor Leo VI prostrating himself before Jesus. This act of humility symbolized the emperor's role as an intermediary between God and the empire.

The Byzantine Empire in 1025

advances. The Byzantine civil service was staffed by well-educated, competent aristocrats from Constantinople who oversaw the collection of taxes, domestic administration, and foreign policy. At the same time, the Macedonian dynasty produced some truly outstanding emperors skilled in administration and law, including Leo VI (886–912) and Basil II (976–1025). In the tenth century, competent emperors combined with a number of talented generals to mobilize the empire's military resources and take the offensive. The Bulgars were defeated, and both the eastern and western parts of Bulgaria were annexed to the empire. The Byzantines went on to add the islands of Crete and Cyprus to the empire and defeat the Muslim forces in Syria, expanding the empire to the upper Euphrates. By the end of the reign of Basil II in 1025, the Byzantine Empire was the largest it had been since the beginning of the seventh century.

The Slavic Peoples of Central and Eastern Europe

Focus Question: What patterns of development occurred in central and eastern Europe as a result of the Slavic peoples?

North of Byzantium and east of the Carolingian Empire lay a spacious plain through which a number of Asiatic nomads, including the Huns, Bulgars, Avars, and Magyars, had pushed their way westward, terrorizing and plundering the settled peasant communities. Eastern Europe was ravaged by these successive waves of invaders, who found it relatively easy to create large empires that were in turn overthrown by the next invaders. Over a period of time, the invaders themselves were largely assimilated by the native Slavic peoples of the area.

The Slavic peoples were originally a single people in central Europe who through mass migrations and nomadic invasions were gradually divided into three major groups: the western, southern, and eastern Slavs (see Map 8.4).

Western Slavs

In the region east of the Germanic kingdom emerged the Polish and Bohemian kingdoms of the western Slavs. The Germans assumed responsibility for the conversion of these Slavic peoples because German emperors considered

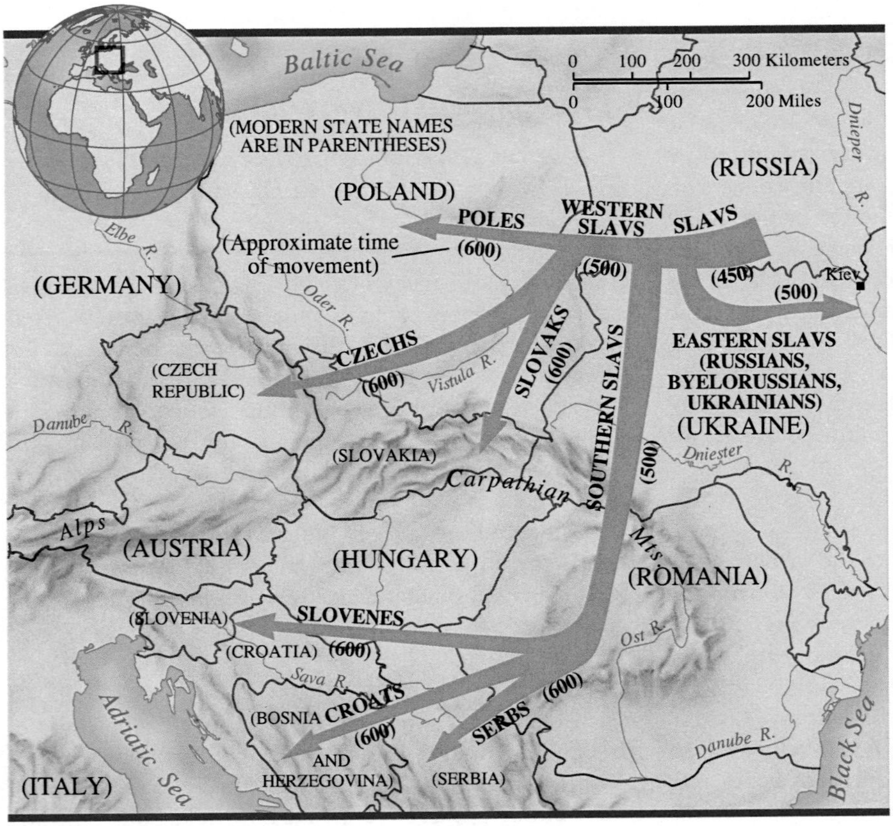

MAP 8.4 The Migrations of the Slavs. Originally from east-central Europe, the Slavic people broke into three groups. The western Slavs converted to Catholic Christianity, while the eastern Slavs and southern Slavs, under the influence of the Byzantine Empire, embraced the Eastern Orthodox faith.

What connections do these Slavic migrations have with what we today characterize as eastern Europe?

it their duty to spread Christianity to the "barbarians." Of course, it also gave them the opportunity to extend their political authority as well. German missionaries had converted the Czechs in Bohemia by the end of the ninth century, and a bishopric eventually occupied by a Czech bishop was established at Prague in the tenth century. The Slavs in Poland were not converted until the reign of Prince Mieszko (MYESH-koh) (c. 960–992). In 1000, an independent Polish archbishopric was set up at Gniezno by the pope. The non-Slavic kingdom of Hungary, which emerged after the Magyars settled down after their defeat at Lechfeld in 955, was also converted to Christianity by German missionaries. Saint Stephen, king of Hungary from 997 to 1038, facilitated the acceptance of Christianity by his people. The Poles, Czechs, and Hungarians all accepted Catholic or western Christianity and became closely tied to the Roman Catholic Church and its Latin culture.

Southern Slavs

The southern and eastern Slavic populations took a different path because of their proximity to the Byzantine Empire. The southern Slavic peoples were converted to the Eastern Orthodox Christianity of the Byzantine Empire by two Byzantine missionary brothers, Cyril and Methodius, who began their activities in 863. They created a Slavonic (Cyrillic) alphabet, translated the Bible into Slavonic, and developed Slavonic church services. Although the southern Slavic peoples accepted Christianity, a split eventually developed between the Croats, who accepted the Roman church, and the Serbs, who remained loyal to eastern Christianity.

Although the Bulgars were originally an Asiatic people who conquered much of the Balkan peninsula, they were eventually absorbed by the larger native southern Slavic population. Together, by the ninth century, they formed a largely Slavic Bulgarian kingdom. Although the conversion to Christianity of this state was complicated by the rivalry between the Roman Catholic and Eastern Orthodox churches, the Bulgarians eventually accepted the latter. By the end of the ninth century, they embraced the Slavonic church services earlier developed by Cyril and Methodius. The acceptance of Eastern Orthodoxy by the southern Slavic peoples, the Serbs and Bulgarians, meant that their cultural life was also linked to the Byzantine state.

Eastern Slavs

The eastern Slavic peoples, from whom the modern Russians, White Russians (Byelorussians), and Ukrainians are descended, had settled in the territory of present-day Ukraine and European Russia. There, beginning in the late eighth century, they began to contend with Viking invaders. Swedish Vikings, known to the eastern Slavs as Varangians, moved down the extensive network of rivers into the lands of the eastern Slavs in search of booty and new trade routes. After establishing trading links with the Byzantine state, the Varangians built trading settlements, became involved in the civil wars among the Slavic peoples, and eventually came to dominate the native peoples, just as their fellow Vikings were doing in parts of western Europe. According to the traditional version of the story, the semilegendary Rurik secured his ruling dynasty in the Slavic settlement of Novgorod in 862. Rurik (ROO-rik) and his fellow Vikings were called the Rus, from which the name that eventually became attached to the state they founded, Russia, is derived (see the box on p. 239). Although much about Rurik is unclear, it is certain that his follower Oleg (c. 873–913) took up residence in Kiev and created the Rus state, a union of eastern Slavic territories known as the principality of Kiev. Oleg's successors extended their control over the eastern Slavs and expanded the territory of Kiev until it encompassed the lands between the Baltic and Black seas and the Danube and Volga rivers. By marrying Slavic wives, the Viking ruling class was gradually assimilated into the Slavic population, a process confirmed by their assumption of Slavic names.

The growth of the principality of Kiev attracted religious missionaries, especially from the Byzantine Empire. One Rus ruler, Vladimir (c. 980–1015), married the Byzantine emperor's sister and officially accepted Christianity for himself and his people in 987. His primary motive was probably not spiritual. By all accounts, Vladimir was a cruel and vicious man who believed an established church would be helpful in developing an organized state. From the end of the tenth century on, Byzantine Christianity became the model for Russian religious life, just as Byzantine imperial ideals came to influence the outward forms of Russian political life.

The Expansion of Islam

Focus Question: What were the chief developments in the Islamic world between 750 and 1000?

The Umayyad dynasty of caliphs had established Damascus as the center of an Islamic empire created by Arab expansion in the seventh and eighth centuries. But Umayyad rule aroused resentment, and the Umayyads' corrupt behavior also helped bring about their end. One caliph, for example, supposedly swam in a pool of wine and drank enough of it to lower the wine level considerably. Finally, in 750, Abu al-Abbas (uh-BOOL-uh-BUSS), a descendant of the uncle of Muhammad, brought an end to the Umayyad dynasty and established the Abbasid (uh-BAH-sid *or* AB-uh-sid) dynasty, which lasted until 1258.

The Abbasid Dynasty

The Abbasid rulers brought much change to the world of Islam. They tried to break down the distinctions between Arab and non-Arab Muslims. All Muslims, regardless of their ethnic background, could now hold both civil and

A Muslim's Description of the Rus

Despite the difficulties that travel presented, early medieval civilization did witness some contact among the various cultures. This might occur through trade, diplomacy, or the conquest and migration of peoples. This document is a description of the Swedish Rus who eventually merged with the native Slavic peoples to form the principality of Kiev, commonly regarded as the first Russian state. This account was written by Ibn Fadlan, a Muslim diplomat sent from Baghdad in 921 to a settlement on the Volga River. His comments on the filthiness of the Rus reflect the Muslim emphasis on cleanliness.

Ibn Fadlan, *Description of the Rus*

I saw the Rus folk when they arrived on their trading-mission and settled at the river Atul (Volga). Never had I seen people of more perfect physique. They are tall as date-palms, and reddish in color. They wear neither coat nor kaftan, but each man carried a cape which covers one half of his body, leaving one hand free. No one is ever parted from his ax, sword, and knife. Their swords are Frankish in design, broad, flat, and fluted. Each man has a number of trees, figures, and the like from the fingernails to the neck. Each woman carried on her bosom a container made of iron, silver, copper or gold—its size and substance depending on her man's wealth. . . .

They [the Rus] are the filthiest of God's creatures. They do not wash after discharging their natural functions, neither do they wash their hands after meals. They are as lousy as donkeys. They arrive from their distant river, and there they build big houses on its shores. Ten or twenty of them may live together in one house, and each of them has a couch of his own where he sits and diverts himself with the pretty slave girls whom he had brought along for sale. He will make love with one of them while a comrade looks on; sometimes they indulge in a communal orgy, and, if a customer should turn up to buy a girl, the Rus man will not let her go till he has finished with her.

They wash their hands and faces every day in incredibly filthy water. Every morning the girl brings her master a large bowl of water in which he washes his hands and face and hair, then blows his nose into it and spits into it. When he has finished the girl takes the bowl to his neighbor—who repeats the performance. Thus, the bowl goes the rounds of the entire household. . . .

If one of the Rus folk falls sick they put him in a tent by himself and leave bread and water for him. They do not visit him, however, or speak to him, especially if he is a serf. Should he recover he rejoins the others; if he dies they burn him. But if he happens to be a serf they leave him for the dogs and vultures to devour. If they catch a robber they hang him to a tree until he is torn to shreds by wind and weather.

Q What was Ibn Fadlan's impression of the Rus? Why do you think he was so critical of their behavior?

military offices. This helped open Islamic life to the influences of the conquered civilizations. Many Arabs now began to intermarry with their conquered peoples.

In 762, the Abbasids built a new capital city, Baghdad, on the Tigris River far to the east of Damascus. The new capital was well placed. It took advantage of river traffic to the Persian Gulf and at the same time was located on the caravan route from the Mediterranean to Central Asia. The move eastward allowed Persian influence to come to the fore, encouraging a new cultural orientation. Under the Abbasids, judges, merchants, and government officials, rather than warriors, were viewed as the ideal citizens.

The new Abbasid dynasty experienced a period of splendid rule well into the ninth century. Best known of the caliphs of the time was Harun al-Rashid (huh-ROON al-rah-SHEED) (786–809), whose reign is often described as the golden age of the Abbasid caliphate. His son al-Ma'mun (al-muh-MOON) (813–833) was a great patron of learning. He founded an astronomical observatory and created a foundation for translating Classical Greek works. This was also a period of growing economic prosperity. The Arabs had conquered many of the richest provinces of the

Yakut, Baghdad under the Abbasids (c. 1000 C.E.)

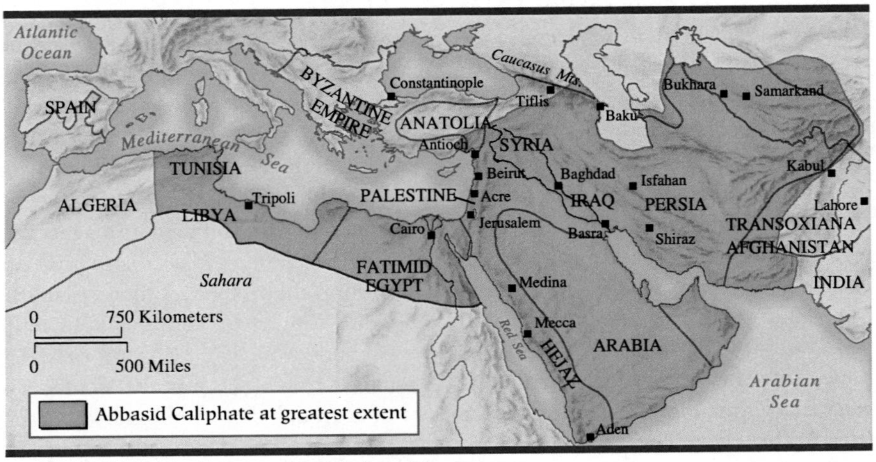

The Abbasid Caliphate at the Height of Its Power

CHRONOLOGY Byzantium, the Slavs, and the Islamic World

Byzantine Empire	
Michael III	842–867
Macedonian dynasty	867–1081
Leo VI	886–912
Basil II	976–1025
Slavic Peoples of Central and Eastern Europe	
Establishment of Novgorod	c. 862
Cyril and Methodius begin to convert Moravian Slavs	863
Oleg creates principality of Kiev	c. 873–913
Reign of Prince Mieszko; Slavs in Poland converted to Christianity	c. 960–992
Vladimir's conversion to Christianity	987
Saint Stephen, king of Hungary	997–1038
World of Islam	
Overthrow of Umayyad dynasty by Abbasids	750
Creation of emirate of al-Andalus	756
Harun al-Rashid	786–809
al-Ma'mun	813–833
Creation of caliphate of al-Andalus	929
Establishment of Fatimid caliphate in Egypt	973

old Roman Empire, and they now controlled the trade routes to the east. Baghdad became the center of an enormous trade empire that extended into Europe, Asia, and Africa, greatly adding to the wealth of the Islamic world.

Despite the prosperity, however, all was not quite well in the empire of the Abbasids. One problem was that there was much fighting over the succession to the caliphate. When Harun al-Rashid died, his two sons fought to succeed him in a struggle that almost destroyed the city of Baghdad. As the tenth-century Muslim historian al-Mas'udi wrote: "Mansions were destroyed, most remarkable monuments obliterated; prices soared.... Brother turned his sword against brother, son against father, as some fought for Amin, others for Ma'mun. Houses and palaces fueled the flames; property was put to the sack."[14]

Vast wealth also gave rise to financial corruption. By awarding important positions to court favorites, the Abbasid caliphs began to undermine the foundations of their own power and soon became figureheads. Provincial rulers broke away from the control of the caliphs and established their own independent dynasties. Even earlier, in the eighth century, a separate caliphate had already been established in Spain when Abd al-Rahman (ub-duh-rahkh-MAHN) of the Umayyad dynasty had fled there. In 756, he seized control of southern Spain and then expanded his power into the center of the peninsula. He took the title of *emir,* or commander, and set up the emirate of al-Andalus (the Arabic name for Spain) with its center at Córdoba (KOR-duh-buh). In 929, Abd al-Rahman III (912–961) proclaimed himself caliph. The rulers of al-Andalus developed a unique society in which all religions were tolerated. The court also supported writers and artists, creating a brilliant and flourishing culture.

The fragmentation of the Islamic empire accelerated in the tenth century. The Fatimid (FAT-i-mid) family established a caliphate in Egypt in 973, and an independent dynasty also operated in North Africa. Despite the political disunity of the Islamic world, however, there was an underlying Islamic civilization based on two common bonds, the Qur'an and the Arabic language.

Islamic Civilization

From the beginning of their empire, Muslim Arabs had demonstrated a willingness to absorb the culture of their conquered territories. The Arabs were truly heirs to the remaining Greco-Roman culture of the Roman Empire. Just as readily, they assimilated Byzantine and Persian culture. In the eighth and ninth centuries, numerous Greek, Syrian, and Persian scientific and philosophical works were translated into Arabic. As the chief language in the southern Mediterranean and the Near East and the required language of Muslims, Arabic became a truly international tongue.

The Muslims created a brilliant urban culture at a time when western Europe was predominantly a rural world of farming villages. This can be seen in such new cities as Baghdad and Cairo, but also in Córdoba, the capital of the Umayyad caliphate in Spain. With a population of possibly 100,000, Córdoba was Europe's largest city after Constantinople. It had seventy public libraries, and the number of manuscripts in the caliph's private library reached 400,000. One caliph, al-Hakem (961–976), collected books from different parts of the world and then had them translated into Arabic and Latin. These included works on geography that later proved valuable to Western sailors and merchants. Schools were also established, and the Great Mosque of Córdoba became a center for scholars from all over the Islamic world. Large numbers of women served as teachers and librarians in Córdoba.

Islamic cities had a distinctive physical appearance due to their common use of certain architectural features, such as the pointed arch and traceried windows, and specific kinds of buildings. The latter included palaces and public buildings with fountains and secluded courtyards, mosques for worship, public baths, and bazaars or marketplaces. Muslims embellished their buildings with a unique decorative art that avoided representation of living things because their religion prohibited the making of graven images. Other Islamic cities besides Córdoba were also distinguished by their numerous libraries. Baghdad had more than thirty libraries, and the library in Cairo contained 1.1 million manuscripts.

During the first few centuries of the Arab Empire, it was the Islamic world that saved and spread the scientific and philosophical works of ancient civilizations. At a time when the ancient Greek philosophers were largely unknown in Europe, key works by Plato and Aristotle were

© Glen Allison/Photodisc/Getty Images

Mosque at Córdoba. The first Great Mosque of Córdoba was built by Abd al-Rahman, founder of the Umayyad dynasty of Spain, in the eighth century. The mosque was later enlarged in the tenth century. Shown here is the interior of the sanctuary, with its two levels of arches. Although the Umayyad caliphs of Damascus were overthrown and replaced by the Abbasid dynasty in the eighth century, the independent Umayyad dynasty in Spain lasted until the eleventh century.

translated into Arabic. They were put in a library called the House of Wisdom in Baghdad, where they were read and studied by Muslim scholars. The library also contained texts on mathematics brought from India. The preservation of ancient texts was aided by the use of paper. The making of paper was introduced from China in the eighth century, and by the end of that century, paper factories had been established in Baghdad. Booksellers and libraries soon followed. European universities later benefited from this scholarship when these works were translated from Arabic into Latin.

Although Islamic scholars are rightly praised for preserving much of Classical knowledge for the West, they also made considerable advances of their own. Nowhere is this more evident than in their contributions to mathematics and the natural sciences. The list of achievements in mathematics and astronomy alone is impressive. The Muslims adopted and passed on the numerical system of India, including the use of the zero. In Europe, it became known as the Arabic system. Al-Khwarizmi (al-KHWAR-iz-mee), a ninth-century Persian mathematician, created the discipline of algebra. Muslim astronomers studied the positions of the stars from the observatory established by al-Ma'mun at Baghdad. They were aware that the earth was round and named many stars. They also perfected the astrolabe, an instrument used by sailors to determine their location by observing the positions of heavenly bodies. Later the astrolabe would make it possible for Europeans to sail to the Americas.

Muslim scholars also made many new discoveries in chemistry and developed medicine as a field of scientific study. Especially renowned was Ibn Sina (ib-un SEE-nuh) (980–1037), known as Avicenna (av-i-SENN-uh) in the West, who wrote a medical encyclopedia that, among other things, stressed the contagious nature of certain diseases and showed how they could be spread by contaminated water supplies. After its translation into Latin, Avicenna's work became a basic medical textbook for medieval European university students. Avicenna was but one of many Muslim scholars whose work was translated into Latin and contributed to the development of intellectual life in Europe in the twelfth and thirteenth centuries.

CHAPTER SUMMARY

At the end of the eighth century, a new kingdom—the Carolingian Empire—came to control much of western and central Europe, especially during the reign of Charlemagne. The coronation of Charlemagne, descendant of a Germanic tribe converted to Christianity, as Roman emperor in 800 symbolized the fusion of the three chief components of a new European civilization: the German tribes, the Classical tradition, and Christianity. In the long run, the creation of a western empire fostered the idea of a distinct European identity and marked a shift of power from the south to the north. Italy and the Mediterranean had been the center of the Roman Empire. The lands north of the Alps now became the political center of Europe, and increasingly, Europe emerged as the focus and center of Western civilization.

The Carolingian Empire was well governed but was held together primarily by personal loyalty to a strong king.

The economy of the eighth and ninth centuries was based almost entirely on farming, which proved inadequate to maintain a large monarchical system. As a result, a new political and military order, known as fief-holding, subsequently evolved to become an integral part of the political world of the Middle Ages. Fief-holding was characterized by a decentralization of political power, in which lords exercised legal, administrative, and military power. This transferred public power into many private hands and seemed to provide the security sorely lacking in a time of weak central government and invasions by Muslims, Magyars, and Vikings. In eastern Europe, the Slavic kingdoms of Poland and Bohemia were established. Their peoples were converted to Christianity by Catholic missionaries, while the eastern and southern Slavs adopted Orthodox Christianity.

While Europe struggled, the Byzantine and Islamic worlds continued to prosper and flourish. The tenth century was the golden age of Byzantine civilization. Under the Macedonian dynasty, trade flourished, the Bulgars were defeated, Muslim armies were repelled, and Byzantine territory was increased.

The Umayyad dynasty of caliphs had established Damascus as the center of an Islamic empire created by Arab expansion in the seventh and eighth centuries. In the eighth century, the new Abbasid dynasty moved the capital east to Baghdad, where Persian influence was more pronounced. Greek and Persian scientific and philosophical writings were translated into Arabic, and the Muslims created a brilliant urban culture.

The brilliance of the urban cultures of both the Byzantine Empire and the Islamic world stood in marked contrast to the underdeveloped rural world of Europe. By 1000, however, that rural world had not only recovered but was beginning to expand in ways undreamed of by previous generations. Europe stood poised for a giant leap.

CHAPTER TIMELINE

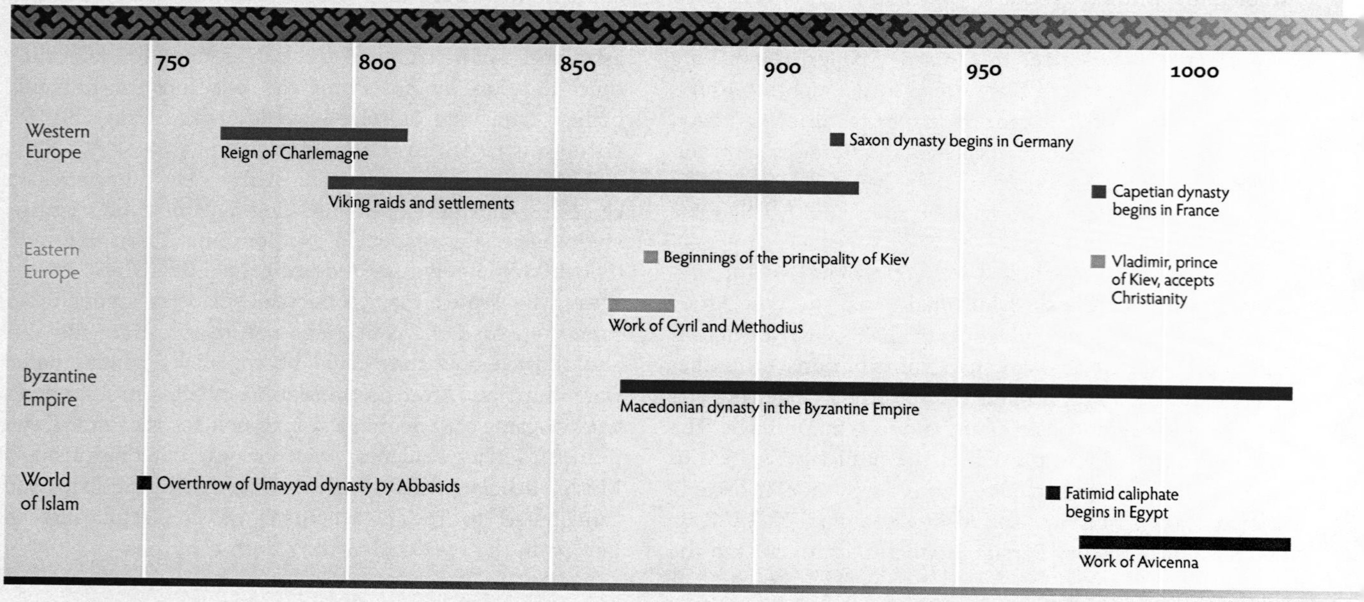

CHAPTER REVIEW

Upon Reflection

Q Of what significance was the Carolingian intellectual renaissance to western European civilization?

Q What role did the Vikings play in the history of medieval Europe?

Q Why does the author use the title "The Zenith of Byzantine Civilization" to describe Byzantine civilization in the ninth and tenth centuries?

Key Terms

scriptoria (p. 219)
monogamy (p. 220)
nuclear family (p. 221)
vassalage (p. 229)
fief (p. 230)
subinfeudation (p. 230)
manor (p. 233)
serfs (p. 233)
demesne (p. 233)
tithe (p. 234)

Suggestions for Further Reading

GENERAL HISTORIES OF THE MIDDLE AGES Good general histories of the entire medieval period can be found in **J. M. Riddle, *A History of the Middle Ages, 300–1500*** (Lanham, Md., 2008); **E. Peters, *Europe and the Middle Ages,*** 2nd ed. (Englewood Cliffs, N.J., 1989); and **D. Nicholas, *The Evolution of the Medieval World: Society, Government, and Thought in Europe, 312–1500*** (London, 1993). For a good general survey of the social history of the Middle Ages, see **C. B. Bouchard, *Life and Society in the West: Antiquity and the Middle Ages*** (San Diego, Calif., 1988). See also the brief works by **B. Rosenwein, *A Short History of the Middle Ages*** (Orchard Park, N.Y., 2002), and **C. W. Hollister** and **J. Bennett, *Medieval Europe: A Short History,*** 9th ed. (New York, 2001). For an excellent history of the period covered in this chapter, see **C. Wickham, *The Inheritance of Rome: A History of Europe from 400 to 1000*** (New York, 2009). See also **L. Olson, *The Early Middle Ages*** (New York, 2007). For a good collection of essays, see **R. McKitterick, ed., *The Early Middle Ages: Europe, 400–1000*** (Oxford, 2001).

CAROLINGIAN EUROPE Surveys of Carolingian Europe include **P. Riché, *The Carolingians: A Family Who Forged Europe*** (Philadelphia, 1993), and **R. McKitterick, *The Frankish Kingdoms Under the Carolingians, 751–987*** (London, 1983). On Charlemagne, see **A. Barbero, *Charlemagne: Father of a Continent,*** trans. **A. Cameron** (Berkeley, Calif., 2004). On Carolingian culture, see ***History and Memory in the Carolingian World*** (Cambridge, 2004) and ***Carolingian Culture: Emulation and Innovation*** (New York, 1994), both by **R. McKitterick.**

CAROLINGIAN SOCIAL LIFE Various aspects of social life in the Carolingian world are examined in **P. Riché, *Daily Life in the World of Charlemagne,*** trans. **J. A. McNamara** (Philadelphia, 1978); **C. B. Bouchard, *Life and Society in the West: Antiquity and the Middle Ages*** (San Diego, Calif., 1988), ch. 5; and **L. Bitel, *Women in Early Medieval Europe, 400–1100*** (Cambridge, 2002). On children, see **S. Shamar, *Childhood in the Middle Ages,*** trans. **C. Galai** (London, 1992).

THE VIKINGS The Vikings are examined in **M. Arnold, *The Vikings: Culture and Conquest*** (London, 2006); **R. Hall, *The World of the Vikings*** (New York, 2007); **G. Jones, *A History of the Vikings,*** rev. ed. (Oxford, 2001); and **P. Sawyer, ed., *The Oxford Illustrated History of the Vikings*** (New York, 1997).

FIEF-HOLDING For an important revisionist view, see **S. Reynolds, *Fiefs and Vassals*** (Oxford, 1994). Works on the new political configurations that emerged in the tenth century are cited in Chapter 9.

ECONOMIC HISTORY For the economic history of the Early Middle Ages, see **A. E. Verhulst, *The Carolingian Economy*** (Cambridge, 2002).

BYZANTINE EMPIRE AND SLAVIC PEOPLES Byzantine civilization in this period is examined in **R. Jenkins, *Byzantium: The Imperial Centuries, 610–1071*** (New York, 1969), and **W. Treadgold, *The Byzantine Revival, 780–842*** (Stanford, Calif., 1988). On the Slavic peoples of central and eastern Europe, see **Z. Vana, *The World of the Ancient Slavs*** (London, 1983), and **S. Franklin** and **J. Shepard, *The Emergence of Rus, 750–1200*** (New York, 1996).

WORLD OF ISLAM The world of Islam in this period is discussed in **H. Kennedy, *The Prophet and the Age of the Caliphates: The Islamic Near East from the Sixth to the Eleventh Century*** (London, 1986), and **J. Lassner, *The Shaping of Abbasid Rule*** (Princeton, N.J., 1980).

CourseMate

Visit the CourseMate website at www.cengagebrain.com for additional study tools and review materials for this chapter.

GLOSSARY

abbess the head of a convent or monastery for women.
abbot the head of a monastery.
absolutism a form of government in which the sovereign power or ultimate authority rested in the hands of a monarch who claimed to rule by divine right and was therefore responsible only to God.
Abstract Expressionism a post–World War II artistic movement that broke with all conventions of form and structure in favor of total abstraction.
abstract painting an artistic movement that developed early in the twentieth century in which artists focused on color to avoid any references to visual reality.
aediles Roman officials who supervised the public games and the grain supply of the city of Rome.
agricultural revolution the application of new agricultural techniques that allowed for a large increase in productivity in the eighteenth century.
Agricultural (Neolithic) Revolution *see* Neolithic Revolution.
anarchism a political theory that holds that all governments and existing social institutions are unnecessary and advocates a society based on voluntary cooperation.
anticlericalism opposition to the power of the clergy, especially in political affairs.
anti-Semitism hostility toward or discrimination against Jews.
apartheid the system of racial segregation practiced in the Republic of South Africa until the 1990s, which involved political, legal, and economic discrimination against nonwhites.
appeasement the policy, followed by the European nations in the 1930s, of accepting Hitler's annexation of Austria and Czechoslovakia in the belief that meeting his demands would assure peace and stability.
Arianism a Christian heresy that taught that Jesus was inferior to God. Though condemned by the Council of Nicaea in 325, Arianism was adopted by many of the Germanic peoples who entered the Roman Empire over the next centuries.
aristocracy a class of hereditary nobility in medieval Europe; a warrior class who shared a distinctive lifestyle based on the institution of knighthood, although there were social divisions within the group based on extremes of wealth.
audiencias advisory groups to viceroys in Spanish America.
Ausgleich the "Compromise" of 1867 that created the Dual Monarchy of Austria-Hungary. Austria and Hungary each had its own capital, constitution, and legislative assembly but were united under one monarch.
authoritarian state a state that has a dictatorial government and some other trappings of a totalitarian state but does not demand that the masses be actively involved in the regime's goals as totalitarian states do.
auxiliaries troops enlisted from the subject peoples of the Roman Empire to supplement the regular legions composed of Roman citizens.

balance of power a distribution of power among several states such that no single nation can dominate or interfere with the interests of another.
Baroque an artistic movement of the seventeenth century in Europe that used dramatic effects to arouse the emotions and reflected the search for power that was a large part of the seventeenth-century ethos.
benefice in the Christian church, a position, such as a bishopric, that consisted of both a sacred office and the right of the holder to the annual revenues from the position.
bicameral legislature a legislature with two houses.
Black Death the outbreak of plague (mostly bubonic) in the mid-fourteenth century that killed from 25 to 50 percent of Europe's population.
Blitzkrieg "lightning war." A war conducted with great speed and force, as in Germany's advance at the beginning of World War II.
Bolsheviks a small faction of the Russian Social Democratic Party who were led by Lenin and dedicated to violent revolution; they seized power in Russia in 1917 and were subsequently renamed the Communists.
bourgeoisie (burghers) inhabitants (merchants and artisans) of boroughs and burghs (towns).
boyars the Russian nobility.
Brezhnev Doctrine the doctrine, enunciated by Leonid Brezhnev, that the Soviet Union had a right to intervene if socialism was threatened in another socialist state; used to justify moving Soviet troops into Czechoslovakia in 1968.
Burschenschaften student societies in the German states dedicated to fostering the goal of a free, united Germany.

caliph the secular leader of the Islamic community.
capital material wealth used or available for use in the production of more wealth.
cartel a combination of independent commercial enterprises that work together to control prices and limit competition.
Cartesian dualism Descartes's principle of the separation of mind and matter (and mind and body) that enabled scientists to view matter as something separate from themselves that could be investigated by reason.
celibacy complete abstinence from sexual activity. Many early Christians viewed celibacy as the surest way to holiness.
centuriate assembly the chief popular assembly of the Roman Republic. It passed laws and elected the chief magistrates.
chansons de geste a form of vernacular literature in the High Middle Ages that consisted of heroic epics focusing on the deeds of warriors.
chivalry the ideal of civilized behavior that emerged among the nobility in the eleventh and twelfth centuries under the influence of the church; a code of ethics knights were expected to uphold.
cholera a serious and often deadly disease commonly spread by contaminated water; a major problem in nineteenth-century European cities before sewerage systems were installed.
Christian (northern) humanism an intellectual movement in northern Europe in the late fifteenth and early sixteenth centuries that combined the interest in the classics of the Italian Renaissance with an interest in the sources of early Christianity, including the New Testament and the writings of the church fathers.
civic humanism an intellectual movement of the Italian Renaissance that saw Cicero, who was both an intellectual and a statesman, as the ideal and held that humanists should be involved in government and use their rhetorical training in the service of the state.
civil disobedience a policy of peaceful protest against laws or government policies in order to achieve political change.

civilization a complex culture in which large numbers of humans share a variety of common elements, including cities; religious, political, military, and social structures; writing; and significant artistic and intellectual activity.

civil rights the basic rights of citizens, including equality before the law, freedom of speech and press, and freedom from arbitrary arrest.

Cold War the ideological conflict between the Soviet Union and the United States after World War II.

collective farms large farms created in the Soviet Union by Stalin by combining many small holdings into large farms worked by the peasants under government supervision.

coloni free tenant farmers who worked as sharecroppers on the large estates of the Roman Empire (singular: *colonus*).

Columbian Exchange the reciprocal importation and exportation of plants and animals between Europe and the Americas.

commercial capitalism beginning in the Middle Ages, an economic system in which people invested in trade and goods in order to make profits.

common law law common to the entire kingdom of England; imposed by the king's courts beginning in the twelfth century to replace the customary law used in county and feudal courts that varied from place to place.

commune in medieval Europe, an association of townspeople bound together by a sworn oath for the purpose of obtaining basic liberties from the lord of the territory in which the town was located; also, the self-governing town after receiving its liberties.

conciliarism a movement in fourteenth- and fifteenth-century Europe that held that final authority in spiritual matters resided with a general church council, not the pope; it emerged in response to the Avignon papacy and the Great Schism and was used to justify the summoning of the Council of Constance (1414–1418).

condottieri leaders of bands of mercenary soldiers in Renaissance Italy who sold their services to the highest bidder.

confession one of the seven sacraments of the Catholic Church; it provided for the forgiveness of one's sins.

conquistadors "conquerors." Leaders in the Spanish conquests in the Americas, especially Mexico and Peru, in the sixteenth century.

conscription a military draft.

conservatism an ideology based on tradition and social stability that favored the maintenance of established institutions, organized religion, and obedience to authority and resisted change, especially abrupt change.

consuls the chief executive officers of the Roman Republic. Two were chosen annually to administer the government and lead the army in battle.

consumer society Western society that emerged after World War II as the working classes adopted the consumption patterns of the middle class and payment plans, credit cards, and easy credit made consumer goods such as appliances and automobiles affordable.

containment a policy adopted by the United States in the Cold War. Its goal was to use whatever means, short of all-out war, to limit Soviet expansion.

Continental System Napoleon's effort to bar British goods from the Continent in the hope of weakening Britain's economy and destroying its capacity to wage war.

cosmopolitan the quality of being sophisticated and having wide international experience.

cottage industry a system of textile manufacturing in which spinners and weavers worked at home in their cottages using raw materials supplied to them by capitalist entrepreneurs.

council of the plebs a council only for plebeians. After 287 B.C.E., however, its resolutions were binding on all Romans.

Crusade in the Middle Ages, a military campaign in defense of Christendom.

Cubism an artistic style developed at the beginning of the twentieth century, especially by Pablo Picasso, that used geometric designs to re-create reality in the viewer's mind.

cultural relativism the belief that no culture is superior to another because culture is a matter of custom, not reason, and derives its meaning from the group holding it.

cuneiform "wedge-shaped." A system of writing developed by the Sumerians that consisted of wedge-shaped impressions made by a reed stylus on clay tablets.

curiales city councilors in Roman cities who played an important role in governing the vast Roman Empire.

Dadaism an artistic movement in the 1920s and 1930s begun by artists who were revolted by the senseless slaughter of World War I and used their "anti-art" to express contempt for the Western tradition.

de-Christianization a policy, adopted in the radical phase of the French Revolution, aimed at creating a secular society by eliminating Christian forms and institutions from French society.

decolonization the process of becoming free of colonial status and achieving statehood; it occurred in most of the world's colonies between 1947 and 1962.

deconstruction (poststructuralism) a system of thought, formulated by Jacques Derrida, that holds that culture is created in a variety of ways, according to the manner in which people create their own meaning. Hence, there is no fixed truth or universal meaning.

deism belief in God as the creator of the universe who, after setting it in motion, ceased to have any direct involvement in it and allowed it to run according to its own natural laws.

demesne the part of a manor retained under the direct control of the lord and worked by the serfs as part of their labor services.

denazification after World War II, the Allied policy of rooting out any traces of Nazism in German society by bringing prominent Nazis to trial for war crimes and purging any known Nazis from political office.

depression a very severe, protracted economic downturn with high levels of unemployment.

de-Stalinization the policy of denouncing and undoing the most repressive aspects of Stalin's regime; begun by Nikita Khrushchev in 1956.

détente the relaxation of tension between the Soviet Union and the United States that occurred in the 1970s.

developed nations a term used to refer to rich nations, primarily in the Northern Hemisphere, that have well-organized industrial and agricultural systems, advanced technologies, and effective educational systems.

developing nations a term used to refer to poor nations, mainly in the Southern Hemisphere, that are primarily farming nations with little technology and serious population problems.

dialectic logic, one of the seven liberal arts that made up the medieval curriculum. In Marxist thought, the process by which all change occurs through the clash of antagonistic elements.

Diaspora the scattering of Jews throughout the ancient world after the Babylonian captivity in the sixth century B.C.E.

dictator in the Roman Republic, an official granted unlimited power to run the state for a short period of time, usually six months, during an emergency.

diocese the area under the jurisdiction of a Christian bishop; based originally on Roman administrative districts.

divination the practice of seeking to foretell future events by interpreting divine signs, which could appear in various forms, such as in entrails of animals, in patterns in smoke, or in dreams.

divine-right monarchy a monarchy based on the belief that monarchs receive their power directly from God and are responsible to no one except God.

domino theory the belief that if the Communists succeeded in Vietnam, other countries in Southeast and East Asia would also fall (like dominoes) to communism; cited as a justification for the U.S. intervention in Vietnam.

Donatism a Christian heresy that argued that the sacraments of the church were not valid if administered by an immoral priest.

dualism the belief that the universe is dominated by two opposing forces, one good and the other evil.

dynastic state a state in which the maintenance and expansion of the interests of the ruling family is the primary consideration.

economic imperialism the process in which banks and corporations from developed nations invest in underdeveloped regions and establish a major presence there in the hope of making high profits; not necessarily the same as colonial expansion in that businesses invest where they can make a profit, which may not be in their own nation's colonies.

economic liberalism the idea that government should not interfere in the workings of the economy.

Einsatzgruppen in Nazi Germany, special strike forces in the SS that played an important role in rounding up and killing Jews.

empiricism the practice of relying on observation and experiment.

encomienda in Spanish America, a form of economic and social organization in which a Spaniard was given a royal grant that enabled the holder of the grant to collect tribute from the Indians and use them as laborers.

enlightened absolutism an absolute monarchy in which the ruler follows the principles of the Enlightenment by introducing reforms for the improvement of society, allowing freedom of speech and the press, permitting religious toleration, expanding education, and ruling in accordance with the laws.

Enlightenment an eighteenth-century intellectual movement, led by the philosophes, that stressed the application of reason and the scientific method to all aspects of life.

entrepreneur one who organizes, operates, and assumes the risk in a business venture in the expectation of making a profit.

Epicureanism a philosophy founded by Epicurus in the fourth century B.C.E. that taught that happiness (freedom from emotional turmoil) could be achieved through the pursuit of pleasure (intellectual rather than sensual pleasure).

equestrians a group of extremely wealthy men in the late Roman Republic who were effectively barred from high office but sought political power commensurate with their wealth; called equestrians because many had gotten their start as cavalry officers (*equites*).

estates (orders) the traditional tripartite division of European society based on heredity and quality rather than wealth or economic standing, first established in the Middle Ages and continuing into the eighteenth century; traditionally consisted of those who pray (the clergy), those who fight (the nobility), and those who work (all the rest).

ethnic cleansing the policy of killing or forcibly removing people of another ethnic group; used by the Serbs against Bosnian Muslims in the 1990s.

Eucharist a Christian sacrament in which consecrated bread and wine are consumed in celebration of Jesus's Last Supper; also called the Lord's Supper or communion.

Eurocommunism a form of communism that dropped its Marxist ideology. It was especially favored in Italy.

evolutionary socialism a socialist doctrine espoused by Eduard Bernstein who argued that socialists should stress cooperation and evolution to attain power by democratic means rather than by conflict and revolution.

exchequer the permanent royal treasury of England. It emerged during the reign of King Henry II in the twelfth century.

excommunication in the Catholic Church, a censure depriving a person of the right to receive the sacraments of the church.

existentialism a philosophical movement that arose after World War II that emphasized the meaninglessness of life, born of the desperation caused by two world wars.

family allowances one aspect of the welfare state whereby the state provides a minimum level of material assistance for children.

fascism an ideology or movement that exalts the nation above the individual and calls for a centralized government with a dictatorial leader, economic and social regimentation, and forcible suppression of opposition; in particular, the ideology of Mussolini's Fascist regime in Italy.

federates German troops enlisted in groups to fight as allies for the Romans.

feminism the belief in the social, political, and economic equality of the sexes; also, organized activity to advance women's rights.

fief a landed estate granted to a vassal in exchange for military services.

Final Solution the attempted physical extermination of the Jewish people by the Nazis during World War II.

Five Pillars of Islam the major tenets of the Muslim faith: belief in Allah and Muhammad as his Prophet; standard prayer five times a day and public prayer on Friday; observance of the holy month of Ramadan by fasting from dawn to sunset; making a pilgrimage (the *hajj*) to Mecca in one's lifetime if possible; and giving alms to the poor.

folk culture the traditional arts and crafts, literature, music, and other customs of the people; something that people make, as opposed to modern popular culture, which is something people buy.

free trade the unrestricted international exchange of goods with low or no tariffs.

Führerprinzip in Nazi Germany, a leadership principle based on the belief in a single-minded party (the Nazis) under one leader (Hitler).

functionalism the idea that the function of an object should determine its design and materials.

general strike a strike by all or most workers in an economy; espoused by Georges Sorel as the heroic action that could be used to inspire the workers to destroy capitalist society.

genocide the deliberate extermination of a people.

gentry well-to-do English landowners below the level of the nobility. They played an important role in the English Civil War of the seventeenth century.

geocentric conception the belief that the earth was at the center of the universe and that the sun and other celestial objects revolved around the earth.

Girondins a faction in the National Convention during the French Revolution that favored keeping the king alive; so-called because their leaders came from the Gironde in southwestern France.

glasnost "openness." Mikhail Gorbachev's policy of encouraging Soviet citizens to openly discuss the strengths and weaknesses of the Soviet Union.

global economy an interdependent economy in which the production, distribution, and sale of goods are accomplished on a worldwide scale.

globalization a term referring to the trend by which peoples and nations have become more interdependent; often used to refer to the development of a global economy and culture.

global warming the increase in the temperature of the earth's atmosphere caused by the greenhouse effect.

good emperors the five emperors who ruled from 96 to 180 (Nerva, Trajan, Hadrian, Antoninus Pius, and Marcus Aurelius), a period of peace and prosperity for the Roman Empire.

Gothic a term used to describe the art and especially architecture of Europe in the twelfth, thirteenth, and fourteenth centuries.

Gothic literature a form of literature used by Romantics to emphasize the bizarre and unusual, especially evident in horror stories.

Great Schism the crisis in the late medieval church when there were first two and then three popes; ended by the Council of Constance (1414–1418).

greenhouse effect the warming of the earth caused by the buildup of carbon dioxide in the atmosphere as a result of human activity.

guest workers foreign workers working temporarily in European countries.

guild an association of people with common interests and concerns, especially people working in the same craft. In medieval Europe, guilds came to control much of the production process and to restrict entry into various trades.

gymnasium in Classical Greece, a place for athletics; in the Hellenistic Age, a secondary school with a curriculum centered on music, physical exercise, and literature.

heliocentric conception the belief that the sun, not the earth, is at the center of the universe.

Hellenistic literally, "imitating the Greeks"; the era after the death of Alexander the Great when Greek culture spread into the Near East and blended with the culture of that region.

helots serfs in ancient Sparta who were permanently bound to the land that they worked for their Spartan masters.

heresy the holding of religious doctrines different from the official teachings of the church.

Hermeticism an intellectual movement beginning in the fifteenth century that taught that divinity is embodied in all aspects of nature; it included works on alchemy and magic as well as theology and philosophy. The tradition continued into the seventeenth century and influenced many of the leading figures of the Scientific Revolution.

hetairai highly sophisticated courtesans in ancient Athens who offered intellectual and musical entertainment as well as sex.

hieroglyphics a pictorial system of writing used in ancient Egypt.

high culture the literary and artistic culture of the educated and wealthy ruling classes.

Holocaust the mass slaughter of European Jews by the Nazis during World War II.

home rule in the United Kingdom, self-government by having a separate parliament but not complete independence.

hoplites heavily armed infantry soldiers in ancient Greece who entered battle in a phalanx formation.

Huguenots French Calvinists.

humanism an intellectual movement in Renaissance Italy based on the study of the Greek and Roman classics.

iconoclasm a movement against the use of icons (pictures of sacred figures) in the eighth-century Byzantine Empire

iconoclast a member of an eighth-century Byzantine movement against the use of icons, which was condemned as idolatry.

ideology a political philosophy such as conservatism or liberalism.

imperium in the Roman Republic, the right to command troops that belonged to the chief executive officers (consuls and praetors); a military commander was known as an *imperator.* In the Roman Empire, the title *imperator* (emperor) came to be used for the ruler.

Impressionism an artistic movement that originated in France in the 1870s. Impressionists sought to capture their impressions of the changing effects of light on objects in nature.

individualism emphasis on and interest in the unique traits of each person.

indulgence in Christian theology, the remission of part or all of the temporal punishment in purgatory due to sin; granted for charitable contributions and other good deeds. Indulgences became a regular practice of the Christian church in the High Middle Ages, and their abuse was instrumental in sparking Luther's reform movement in the sixteenth century.

infanticide the practice of killing infants.

inflation a sustained rise in the price level.

intendants royal officials in seventeenth-century France who were sent into the provinces to execute the orders of the central government.

interdict in the Catholic Church, a censure by which a region or country is deprived of receiving the sacraments.

intervention, principle of the idea, after the Congress of Vienna, that the great powers of Europe had the right to send armies into countries experiencing revolution to restore legitimate monarchs to their thrones.

isolationism a foreign policy in which a nation refrains from making alliances or engaging actively in international affairs.

Janissaries an elite core of eight thousand troops personally loyal to the sultan of the Ottoman Empire.

jihad "striving in the way of the Lord." In Islam, the attempt to achieve personal betterment, although it can also mean fair, defensive fighting to preserve one's life and one's faith.

joint-stock company a company or association that raises capital by selling shares to individuals who receive dividends on their investment while a board of directors runs the company.

joint-stock investment bank a bank created by selling shares of stock to investors. Such banks potentially have access to much more capital than private banks owned by one or a few individuals.

justification the primary doctrine of the Protestant Reformation, teaching that humans are saved not through good works but by the grace of God, bestowed freely through the sacrifice of Jesus.

Kulturkampf "culture conflict." The name given to Bismarck's attack on the Catholic Church in Germany, which has come to refer to conflict between church and state anywhere.

laissez-faire "let (them) do (as they please)." An economic doctrine that holds that an economy is best served when the government does not interfere but allows the economy to self-regulate according to the forces of supply and demand.

latifundia large landed estates in the Roman Empire (singular: *latifundium*).

lay investiture the practice in which someone other than a member of the clergy chose a bishop and invested him with the symbols of both his temporal office and his spiritual office; led to the Investiture Controversy, which was ended by compromise in the Concordat of Worms in 1122.

Lebensraum "living space." The doctrine, adopted by Hitler, that a nation's power depends on the amount of land it occupies; thus, a nation must expand to be strong.

legitimacy, principle of the idea that after the Napoleonic wars, peace could best be reestablished in Europe by restoring legitimate monarchs who would preserve traditional institutions; guided Metternich at the Congress of Vienna.

Leninism Lenin's revision of Marxism that held that Russia need not experience a bourgeois revolution before it could move toward socialism.

liberal arts the seven areas of study that formed the basis of education in medieval and early modern Europe. Following Boethius and other late Roman authors, they consisted of grammar, rhetoric, and dialectic or logic (the *trivium*) and arithmetic, geometry, astronomy, and music (the *quadrivium*).

liberalism an ideology based on the belief that people should be as free from restraint as possible. Economic liberalism is the idea that the government should not interfere in the workings of the economy. Political liberalism is the idea that there should be restraints on the exercise of power so that people can enjoy basic civil rights in a constitutional state with a representative assembly.

limited monarchy (constitutional monarchy) a system of government in which the monarch is limited by a representative assembly and by the duty to rule in accordance with the laws of the land.

major domus the chief officer of the king's household in the Frankish kingdom.

mandates a system established after World War I whereby a nation officially administered a territory (mandate) on behalf of the

League of Nations. Thus, France administered Lebanon and Syria as mandates, and Britain administered Iraq and Palestine.

Mannerism a sixteenth-century artistic movement in Europe that deliberately broke down the High Renaissance principles of balance, harmony, and moderation.

manor an agricultural estate operated by a lord and worked by peasants who performed labor services and paid various rents and fees to the lord in exchange for protection and sustenance.

Marshall Plan the European Recovery Program, under which the United States provided financial aid to European countries to help them rebuild after World War II.

Marxism the political, economic, and social theories of Karl Marx, which included the idea that history is the story of class struggle and that ultimately the proletariat will overthrow the bourgeoisie and establish a dictatorship en route to a classless society.

mass education a state-run educational system, usually free and compulsory, that aims to ensure that all children in society have at least a basic education.

mass leisure forms of leisure that appeal to large numbers of people in a society, including the working classes; emerged at the end of the nineteenth century to provide workers with amusements after work and on weekends; used during the twentieth century by totalitarian states to control their populations.

mass politics a political order characterized by mass political parties and universal male and (eventually) female suffrage.

mass society a society in which the concerns of the majority—the lower classes—play a prominent role; characterized by extension of voting rights, an improved standard of living for the lower classes, and mass education.

materialism the belief that everything mental, spiritual, or ideal is an outgrowth of physical forces and that truth is found in concrete material existence, not through feeling or intuition.

mercantilism an economic theory that held that a nation's prosperity depended on its supply of gold and silver and that the total volume of trade is unchangeable; its adherents therefore advocated that the government play an active role in the economy by encouraging exports and discouraging imports, especially through the use of tariffs.

Mesolithic Age the period from 10,000 to 7000 B.C.E., characterized by a gradual transition from a food-gathering and hunting economy to a food-producing economy.

Mesopotamia the valley between the Tigris and Euphrates rivers.

metics resident foreigners in ancient Athens who were not permitted full rights of citizenship but did receive the protection of the laws.

Middle Passage the journey of slaves from Africa to the Americas as the middle leg of the triangular trade.

militarism a policy of aggressive military preparedness; in particular, the large armies based on mass conscription and complex, inflexible plans for mobilization that most European nations had before World War I.

millenarianism the belief that the end of the world is at hand and the kingdom of God is about to be established on earth.

ministerial responsibility a tenet of nineteenth-century liberalism that held that ministers of the monarch should be responsible to the legislative assembly rather than to the monarch.

mir a peasant village commune in Russia.

mobilization the organization of troops and supplies for service in time of war.

Modern Devotion a movement founded by Gerard Groote in the fourteenth century, aimed at a practical mysticism based on leading lives serving the needs of fellow human beings.

Modernism the artistic and literary styles that emerged in the decades before 1914 as artists rebelled against traditional efforts to portray reality as accurately as possible (leading to Impressionism and Cubism) and writers explored new forms.

monasticism a movement that began in early Christianity whose purpose was to create communities of men and women who practiced a communal life dedicated to God as a moral example to the world around them.

monk a man who chooses to live a communal life divorced from the world in order to dedicate himself totally to the will of God.

monogamy the practice of being married to one person at a time.

monotheism the doctrine or belief that there is only one God.

Mountain a faction in the National Convention during the French Revolution that represented the interests of the city of Paris and favored the execution of the king.

multiculturalism a term referring to the connection of several cultural or ethnic groups within a society.

multinational corporation a company with divisions in more than two countries.

mutual deterrence the belief that nuclear war could best be prevented if both the United States and the Soviet Union had sufficient nuclear weapons so that even if one nation launched a preemptive first strike, the other could respond and devastate the attacker.

mystery religions religions that involve initiation into secret rites that promise intense emotional involvement with spiritual forces and a greater chance of individual immortality.

mysticism the immediate experience of oneness with God.

nationalism a sense of national consciousness based on awareness of being part of a community—a "nation"—that has common institutions, traditions, language, and customs and that becomes the focus of the individual's primary political loyalty.

nationalities problem the dilemma faced by the Austro-Hungarian Empire in trying to unite a wide variety of ethnic groups (Austrians, Hungarians, Poles, Croats, Czechs, Serbs, Slovaks, and Slovenes, among others) in an era when nationalism and calls for self-determination were coming to the fore.

nationalization the process of converting a business or industry from private ownership to government control and ownership.

nation in arms the people's army raised by universal mobilization to repel the foreign enemies of the French Revolution.

nation-state a form of political organization in which a relatively homogeneous people inhabits a sovereign state, as opposed to a state containing people of several nationalities.

NATO the North Atlantic Treaty Organization, a military alliance formed in 1949 in which the signatories (Belgium, Canada, Denmark, France, Great Britain, Iceland, Italy, Luxembourg, the Netherlands, Norway, Portugal, and the United States) agreed to provide mutual assistance if any one of them was attacked; later expanded to include other nations.

natural laws a body of laws or specific principles held to be derived from nature and binding on all human societies even in the absence of written laws governing such matters.

natural rights certain inalienable rights to which all people are entitled, including the right to life, liberty, and property; freedom of speech and religion; and equality before the law.

natural selection Darwin's idea that organisms that are most adaptable to their environment survive and pass on the variations that enabled them to survive, while less adaptable organisms become extinct; "survival of the fittest."

Nazi New Order the Nazis' plan for their conquered territories; it included the extermination of Jews and others considered inferior, ruthless exploitation of resources, German colonization in the east, and the use of Poles, Russians, and Ukrainians as slave labor.

Neoclassicism a late-eighteenth-century artistic movement that emerged in France. It sought to recapture the dignity and simplicity of the Classical style of ancient Greece and Rome.

Neolithic Revolution the shift from hunting animals and gathering plants for sustenance to producing food by sytematic agriculture that occurred gradually between 10,000 and 4000 B.C.E. (the Neolithic or "New Stone" Age).

Neoplatonism a revival of Platonic philosophy in the third century C.E., associated with Plotinus; a similar revival in the Italian

Renaissance, associated with Marsilio Ficino, who attempted to synthesize Christianity and Platonism.

nepotism the appointment of family members to important political positions; derived from the regular appointment of nephews (Latin, *nepos*) by Renaissance popes.

New Economic Policy a modified version of the old capitalist system introduced in the Soviet Union by Lenin in 1921 to revive the economy after the ravages of the civil war and war communism.

new imperialism the revival of imperialism after 1880 in which European nations established colonies throughout much of Asia and Africa.

new monarchies the governments of France, England, and Spain at the end of the fifteenth century, whose rulers succeeded in reestablishing or extending centralized royal authority, suppressing the nobility, controlling the church, and insisting on the loyalty of all peoples living in their territories.

nobiles "nobles." The small group of families from both patrician and plebeian origins who produced most of the men who were elected to office in the late Roman Republic.

nominalist a member of a school of thought in medieval Europe that, following Aristotle, held that only individual objects are real and that universals are only names created by humans.

nuclear family a family group consisting only of a father, a mother, and one or more children.

nuns women who withdrew from the world and joined a religious community; the female equivalent of monks.

old order (old regime) the political and social system of France in the eighteenth century before the Revolution.

oligarchy rule by a few.

optimates "best men." Aristocratic leaders in the late Roman Republic who generally came from senatorial families and wished to retain their oligarchical privileges.

orders *see* estates.

organic evolution Darwin's principle that all plants and animals have evolved over a long period of time from earlier and simpler forms of life.

Paleolithic Age the period of human history when humans used simple stone tools (c. 2,500,000–10,000 B.C.E.).

pantheism a doctrine that equates God with the universe and all that is in it.

panzer division in the German army under Hitler, a strike force of about three hundred tanks and accompanying forces and supplies.

papal curia the administrative staff of the Catholic Church, composed of cardinals who assist the pope in running the church.

parlements provincial law courts in France.

pasteurization a process developed by Louis Pasteur for heating a product to destroy the microorganisms that might cause spoilage.

paterfamilias the dominant male in a Roman family whose powers over his wife and children were theoretically unlimited, though they were sometimes circumvented in practice.

patriarchal family a family in which the husband dominates his wife and children.

patriarchy a society in which the father is supreme in the clan or family; more generally, a society dominated by men.

patricians great landowners who became the ruling class in the Roman Republic.

patronage the practice of awarding titles and making appointments to government and other positions to gain political support.

Pax Romana "Roman peace." A term used to refer to the stability and prosperity that Roman rule brought to the Mediterranean world and much of western Europe during the first and second centuries C.E.

Pentateuch the first five books of the Hebrew Bible (Genesis, Exodus, Leviticus, Numbers, and Deuteronomy).

perestroika "restructuring." A term applied to Mikhail Gorbachev's economic, political, and social reforms in the Soviet Union.

perioikoi in ancient Sparta, free inhabitants but not citizens who were required to pay taxes and perform military service.

permissive society a term applied to Western society after World War II to reflect the new sexual freedom and the emergence of a drug culture.

Petrine supremacy the doctrine that the bishop of Rome (the pope), as the successor of Saint Peter (traditionally considered the first bishop of Rome), should hold a preeminent position in the church.

phalanstery a self-sustaining cooperative community, as advocated by Charles Fourier in the early nineteenth century.

phalanx a rectangular formation of tightly massed infantry soldiers.

philosophes intellectuals of the eighteenth-century Enlightenment who believed in applying a spirit of rational criticism to all things, including religion and politics, and who focused on improving and enjoying this world, rather than on the afterlife.

Pietism a movement that arose in Germany in the seventeenth century whose goal was to foster a personal experience of God as the focus of true religious experience.

pig iron a type of iron produced by smelting iron ore with coke; of lower quality than wrought iron.

plebeians the class of Roman citizens that included nonpatrician landowners, craftspeople, merchants, and small farmers in the Roman Republic. Their struggle for equal rights with the patricians dominated much of the Republic's history.

plebiscita laws passed by the council of the plebs.

pluralism the practice of holding several church offices simultaneously; a problem of the late medieval church.

plutocrats members of the wealthy elite.

pogroms organized massacres of Jews.

polis an ancient Greek city-state encompassing both an urban area and its surrounding countryside; a small but autonomous political unit where all major political and social activities were carried out centrally.

political democracy a form of government characterized by universal suffrage and mass political parties.

politiques a group who emerged during the French Wars of Religion in the sixteenth century, placed politics above religion, and believed that no religious truth was worth the ravages of civil war.

polytheism belief in or worship of more than one god.

Pop Art an artistic movement of the 1950s and 1960s in which artists took images of popular culture and transformed them into works of fine art. Andy Warhol's painting of Campbell's soup cans is one example.

popular culture as opposed to high culture, the unofficial written and unwritten culture of the masses, much of which was traditionally passed down orally and centered on public and group activities such as festivals. In the modern age, the term refers to the entertainment, recreation, and pleasures that people purchase as part of the mass consumer society.

populares "favoring the people." Aristocratic leaders in the late Roman Republic who tended to use the people's assemblies in an effort to break the stranglehold of the *nobiles* on political offices.

popular sovereignty the doctrine that government is created by and subject to the will of the people, who are the source of all political power.

populism a political philosophy or movement that supports the rights and power of ordinary people in their struggle against the privileged elite.

portolani charts of landmasses and coastlines made by navigators and mathematicians in the thirteenth and fourteenth centuries.

Post-Impressionism an artistic movement that began in France in the 1880s. Post-Impressionists sought to use color and line to express inner feelings and produce a personal statement of reality.

Postmodernism a term used to cover a variety of artistic and intellectual styles and ways of thinking prominent since the 1970s.

praetor a Roman executive official responsible for the administration of the law.

praetorian guard the military unit that served as the personal bodyguard of the Roman emperors.

predestination the belief, associated with Calvinism, that God, as a consequence of his foreknowledge of all events, has predetermined those who will be saved (the elect) and those who will be damned.

prefect during the reign of Napoleon, an official appointed by the central government to oversee all aspects of a local government.

price revolution the dramatic rise in prices (inflation) that occurred throughout Europe in the sixteenth and early seventeenth centuries.

primogeniture an inheritance practice in which the eldest son receives all or the largest share of the parents' estate.

principate the form of government established by Augustus for the Roman Empire; it continued the constitutional forms of the Republic and consisted of the *princeps* ("first citizen") and the senate, although the *princeps* was clearly the dominant partner.

procurator the head of the Holy Synod, the chief decision-making body for the Russian Orthodox Church.

proletariat the industrial working class. In Marxism, the class that will ultimately overthrow the bourgeoisie.

propaganda a program of distorted information put out by an organization or government to spread its policy, cause, or doctrine.

psychoanalysis a method developed by Sigmund Freud to resolve a patient's psychic conflict.

purgatory defined by the Catholic Church as the place where souls went after death to be purged of punishment for sins committed in life.

Puritans English Protestants inspired by Calvinist theology who wished to remove all traces of Catholicism from the Church of England.

quadrivium arithmetic, geometry, astronomy, and music; four of the seven liberal arts (the others made up the *trivium*) that formed the basis of medieval and early modern education.

quaestors Roman officials responsible for the administration of financial affairs.

querelles des femmes "arguments about women." A centuries-old debate about the nature of women that continued during the Scientific Revolution as those who argued for the inferiority of women found additional support in the new anatomy and medicine.

rapprochement the rebuilding of harmonious relations between nations.

rationalism a system of thought based on the belief that human reason and experience are the chief sources of knowledge.

Realism a nineteenth-century school of painting that emphasized the everyday life of ordinary people, depicted with photographic accuracy.

realist a subscriber to the medieval European school of thought that held, following Plato, that the individual objects we perceive are not real but merely manifestations of universal ideas existing in the mind of God.

Realpolitik "politics of reality." Politics based on practical concerns rather than theory or ethics.

reason of state the principle that a nation should act on the basis of its long-term interests and not merely to further the dynastic interests of its ruling family.

Reconquista in Spain, the reconquest of Muslim lands by Christian rulers and their armies.

relativity theory Einstein's theory that, among other things, (1) space and time are not absolute but are relative to the observer and interwoven into a four-dimensional space-time continuum and (2) matter is a form of energy ($E = mc^2$).

relics the bones of Christian saints or objects intimately associated with saints that were considered worthy of veneration.

Renaissance the "rebirth" of Classical culture that occurred in Italy between c. 1350 and c. 1550; also, the earlier revivals of Classical culture that occurred under Charlemagne and in the twelfth century.

rentier a person who lives on income from property and is not personally involved in its operation.

reparations payments made by a defeated nation after a war to compensate another nation for damage sustained as a result of the war; required from Germany after World War I.

revisionism a socialist doctrine that rejected Marx's emphasis on class struggle and revolution and argued instead that workers should work through political parties to bring about gradual change.

revolution a fundamental change in the political and social organization of a state.

revolutionary socialism a socialist doctrine that violent action was the only way to achieve the goals of socialism.

rhetoric the art of persuasive speaking; in the Middle Ages, one of the seven liberal arts.

risorgimento a movement in Italy in the nineteenth century aimed at the creation of a united Italian republic.

Rococo an eighteenth-century artistic movement that emphasized grace, gentility, lightness, and charm.

Romanesque a term used to describe the art and especially architecture of Europe in the eleventh and twelfth centuries.

Romanization the process by which Roman culture and institutions were spread to the provinces; often accomplished through the Roman army as colonies of veterans were established wherever the legions were stationed throughout the empire.

Romanticism a nineteenth-century intellectual and artistic movement that rejected the emphasis on reason of the Enlightenment. Instead, Romantics stressed the importance of intuition, feeling, emotion, and imagination as sources of knowing.

sacraments rites considered imperative for a Christian's salvation. By the thirteenth century, these consisted of the Eucharist or Lord's Supper, baptism, marriage, penance, extreme unction, holy orders, and confirmation of children; Protestant reformers of the sixteenth century generally recognized only two—baptism and communion (the Lord's Supper).

salons gatherings of philosophes and other notables to discuss the ideas of the Enlightenment; so called from the elegant drawing rooms (salons) where they met.

sans-culottes "without breeches." The common people, who did not wear the fine clothes of the upper classes and played an important role in the radical phase of the French Revolution.

satrap a governor with both civil and military duties in the ancient Persian Empire, which was divided into satrapies, or provinces, each administered by a satrap.

scholasticism the philosophical and theological system of the medieval schools, which emphasized rigorous analysis of contradictory authorities; often used to try to reconcile faith and reason.

scientific method a method of seeking knowledge through inductive principles, using experiments and observations to develop generalizations.

Scientific Revolution the transition from the medieval worldview to a largely secular, rational, and materialistic perspective that began in the seventeenth century and was popularized in the eighteenth.

scriptoria writing rooms for the copying of manuscripts in medieval monasteries.

scutage in the fourteenth century, a money payment for military service that replaced the obligation of military service in the lord-vassal relationship.

secularism the process of becoming more concerned with material, worldly, temporal things and less with spiritual and religious things; a characteristic of the Italian Renaissance.

self-determination the doctrine that the people of a given territory or a particular nationality should have the right to determine their own government and political future.

senate the leading council of the Roman Republic; composed of about three hundred men (senators) who served for life and dominated much of the political life of the Republic.

separation of powers a doctrine enunciated by Montesquieu in the eighteenth century that separate executive, legislative, and judicial powers serve to limit and control each other.

serf a peasant who is bound to the land and obliged to provide labor services and pay various rents and fees to the lord; considered unfree but not a slave because serfs could not be bought and sold.

skepticism a doubtful or questioning attitude, especially about religion.

social Darwinism the application of Darwin's principle of organic evolution to the social order; led to the belief that progress comes from the struggle for survival as the fittest advance and the weak decline.

socialism an ideology that calls for collective or government ownership of the means of production and the distribution of goods.

socialized medicine health services for all citizens provided by government assistance.

social security government programs that provide social welfare measures such as old-age pensions and sickness, accident, and disability insurance.

Socratic method a form of teaching that uses a question-and-answer format to enable students to reach conclusions by using their own reasoning.

Sophists wandering scholars and professional teachers in ancient Greece who stressed the importance of rhetoric and tended toward skepticism and relativism.

soviets councils of workers' and soldiers' deputies formed throughout Russia in 1917 that played an important role in the Bolshevik Revolution.

sphere of influence a territory or region over which an outside nation exercises political or economic influence.

squadristi in Italy in the 1920s, bands of armed Fascists used to create disorder by attacking Socialist offices and newspapers.

stagflation a combination of high inflation and high unemployment that was prevalent in the United States and elsewhere from 1973 to the mid-1980s.

Stalinization the adoption by Eastern European Communist countries of features of the economic, political, and military policies implemented by Stalin in the Soviet Union.

Stoicism a philosophy founded by Zeno in the fourth century B.C.E. that taught that happiness could be obtained by accepting one's lot and living in harmony with the will of God, thereby achieving inner peace.

subinfeudation the practice whereby a lord's greatest vassals subdivided their fiefs and had vassals of their own, who in turn subdivided their fiefs, and so on down to simple knights, whose fiefs were too small to subdivide.

suffrage the right to vote.

suffragists advocates of extending the right to vote to women.

sultan "holder of power." A title taken by Turkish leaders who took command of the Abbasid Empire in 1055.

surplus value in Marxism, the difference between a product's real value and the wages of the worker who produced the product.

Surrealism an artistic movement that arose between World War I and World War II. Surrealists portrayed recognizable objects in unrecognizable relationships in order to reveal the world of the unconscious.

syncretism the combining of different forms of belief or practice, as, for example, when two gods are regarded as different forms of the same underlying divine force and are fused together.

tariffs duties (taxes) imposed on imported goods, usually to raise revenue and to discourage imports and protect domestic industries.

tetrarchy rule by four; the system of government established by Diocletian (284–305) in which the Roman Empire was divided into two parts, each ruled by an "Augustus" assisted by a "Caesar."

theocracy a government ruled by a divine authority.

Third Estate one of the traditional tripartite divisions (orders) of European society based on heredity and quality rather than wealth or economic standing, first established in the Middle Ages and continuing into the eighteenth century; consisted of all who were not members of the clergy or nobility (the first two estates).

three-field system in medieval agriculture, the practice of dividing the arable land into three fields so that one could lie fallow while the others were planted in winter grains and spring crops.

tithe a portion of one's harvest or income, paid by medieval peasants to the village church.

Torah the body of law in Hebrew Scripture, contained in the Pentateuch (the first five books of the Hebrew Bible).

totalitarian state a state characterized by government control over all aspects of economic, social, political, cultural, and intellectual life, the subordination of the individual to the state, and insistence that the masses be actively involved in the regime's goals.

total war warfare in which all of a nation's resources, including civilians at home as well as soldiers in the field, are mobilized for the war effort.

trade union an association of workers in the same trade, formed to help members secure better wages, benefits, and working conditions.

transformism the theory that societies evolve gradually.

transnational corporation another term for "a multinational corporation," or a company with divisions in more than two countries.

transubstantiation a doctrine of the Roman Catholic Church that during the Eucharist, the substance of the bread and wine is miraculously transformed into the body and blood of Jesus.

trench warfare warfare in which the opposing forces attack and counterattack from a relatively permanent system of trenches protected by barbed wire; a characteristic of World War I.

triangular trade a pattern of trade in early modern Europe that connected Europe, Africa, and the Americas in an Atlantic economy.

tribunes of the plebs beginning in 494 B.C.E., Roman officials who were given the power to protect plebeians against arrest by patrician magistrates.

trivium grammar, rhetoric, and dialectic or logic; three of the seven liberal arts (the others made up the *quadrivium*) that were the basis of medieval and early modern education.

Truman Doctrine the doctrine, enunciated by Harry Truman in 1947, that the United States would provide economic aid to countries that said they were threatened by Communist expansion.

tyrant in an ancient Greek *polis* (or an Italian city-state during the Renaissance), a ruler who came to power in an unconstitutional way and ruled without being subject to the law.

ultraroyalists in nineteenth-century France, a group of aristocrats who sought to return to a monarchical system dominated by a landed aristocracy and the Catholic Church.

uncertainty principle a principle in quantum mechanics, posited by Heisenberg, that holds that one cannot determine the path of an electron because the very act of observing the electron would affect its location.

unconditional surrender complete, unqualified surrender of a belligerent nation.

utopian socialists intellectuals and theorists in the early nineteenth century who favored equality in social and economic conditions and wished to replace private property and competition with collective ownership and cooperation.

vassalage the granting of a fief, or landed estate, in exchange for providing military services to the lord and fulfilling certain other obligations such as appearing at the lord's court when summoned and making a payment on the knighting of the lord's eldest son.

vernacular the everyday language of a region, as distinguished from a language used for special purposes. For example, in medieval Paris, French was the vernacular, but Latin was used for academic writing and for classes at the University of Paris.

viceroy the administrative head of the provinces of New Spain and Peru in the Americas.

***volkish* thought** the belief that German culture is superior and that the German people have a universal mission to save Western civilization from "inferior" races.

war communism Lenin's policy of nationalizing industrial and other facilities and requisitioning the peasants' produce during the civil war in Russia.

war guilt clause the clause in the Treaty of Versailles that declared that Germany (with Austria) was responsible for starting World War I and ordered Germany to pay reparations for the damage the Allies had suffered as a result of the war.

Warsaw Pact a military alliance, formed in 1955, in which Albania, Bulgaria, Czechoslovakia, East Germany, Hungary, Poland, Romania, and the Soviet Union agreed to provide mutual assistance.

welfare state a sociopolitical system in which the government assumes primary responsibility for the social welfare of its citizens by providing such things as social security, unemployment benefits, and health care.

wergeld "money for a man." In early Germanic law, a person's value in monetary terms, paid by a wrongdoer to the family of the person who had been injured or killed.

world-machine Newton's conception of the universe as one huge, regulated, and uniform machine that operated according to natural laws in absolute time, space, and motion.

wrought iron a high-quality iron first produced during the eighteenth century in Britain; manufactured by puddling, a process developed by Henry Cort that involved using coke to burn away the impurities in pig iron.

zemstvos local assemblies established in Russia in 1864 by Tsar Alexander II.

ziggurat a massive stepped tower on which a temple dedicated to the chief god or goddess of a Sumerian city was built.

Zionism an international movement that called for the establishment of a Jewish state or a refuge for Jews in Palestine.

Zollverein the customs union of all the German states except Austria, formed by Prussia in 1834.

Zoroastrianism a religion founded by the Persian Zoroaster in the seventh century B.C.E., characterized by worship of a supreme god, Ahuramazda, who represents the good against the evil spirit, identified as Ahriman.

CHAPTER NOTES

CHAPTER 1

1. Jean-Marie Chauvet et al., *Dawn of Art: The Chauvet Cave* (New York, 1996), pp. 49–50.
2. Quoted in Amélie Kuhrt, *The Ancient Near East, c. 3000–330 B.C.* (London, 1995), vol. 1, p. 68.
3. Quoted in Michael Wood, *Legacy: The Search for Ancient Cultures* (New York, 1995), p. 34.
4. Quoted in Marc van de Mieroop, *A History of the Ancient Near East, ca. 3000–323 B.C.* (Oxford, 2004), p. 69.
5. Quoted in ibid., p. 64.
6. Quoted in ibid., p. 106.
7. Quoted in Thorkild Jacobsen, "Mesopotamia," in Henri Frankfort et al., *Before Philosophy* (Baltimore, 1949), p. 139.
8. Quoted in Thorkild Jacobsen, *The Treasures of Darkness: A History of Mesopotamian Religion* (New Haven, Conn., 1976), p. 97.
9. *The Epic of Gilgamesh,* trans. N. K. Sandars (London, 1972), p. 62.
10. James B. Pritchard, *Ancient Near Eastern Texts,* 3rd ed. (Princeton, N.J., 1969), p. 372.
11. Quoted in Angela P. Thomas, *Egyptian Gods and Myths* (London, 1986), p. 25.
12. Pritchard, *Ancient Near Eastern Texts,* p. 445.
13. Quoted in B. G. Trigger, B. J. Kemp, D. O'Connor, and A. B. Lloyd, *Ancient Egypt: A Social History* (Cambridge, 1983), p. 74.
14. Pritchard, *Ancient Near Eastern Texts,* p. 34.
15. Ibid., p. 36.
16. Quoted in Rose-Marie Hagen and Rainer Hagen, *Egypt: People, Gods, Pharaohs* (Cologne, 2002), p. 148.
17. Pritchard, *Ancient Near Eastern Texts,* p. 413.
18. Quoted in John A. Wilson, *The Culture of Ancient Egypt* (Chicago, 1956), p. 264.
19. Pritchard, *Ancient Near Eastern Texts,* p. 412.
20. Ibid., p. 413.

CHAPTER 2

1. 2 Samuel 8:2.
2. Psalms 137:1, 4–6.
3. Psalms 145:8–9.
4. Psalms 121:2–3.
5. Exodus 20:13–15.
6. Isaiah 2:4.
7. Proverbs 31:10–20, 24–28.
8. Judges 5:24–27.
9. Quoted in Roland de Vaux, *Ancient Israel: Its Life and Institutions* (New York, 1961), p. 49.
10. Quoted in Marc van de Mieroop, *A History of the Ancient Near East* (Oxford, 2004), p. 242.
11. Quoted in H. W. F. Saggs, *The Might That Was Assyria* (London, 1984), pp. 261–262.
12. John C. Rolfe, trans., *Quintus Curtius I* (Cambridge, Mass., 1971), pp. 337–339.
13. Quoted in John M. Cook, *The Persian Empire* (New York, 1983), p. 32.
14. Herodotus, *The Persian Wars*, trans. George Rawlinson (New York, 1942), p. 257.
15. Isaiah 44:28, 45:1.
16. Quoted in Albert T. Olmstead, *History of the Persian Empire* (Chicago, 1948), p. 168.
17. Quoted in Cook, *The Persian Empire,* p. 76.
18. Yasna 44:3–4, 7, as quoted in A. C. Bouquet, *Sacred Books of the World* (Harmondsworth, England, 1954), pp. 111–112.

CHAPTER 3

1. H. D. F. Kitto, *The Greeks* (Harmondsworth, England, 1951), p. 64.
2. Homer, *Odyssey,* trans. E. V. Rieu (Harmondsworth, England, 1946), p. 337.
3. Xenophon, *Symposium,* trans. O. J. Todd (Cambridge, Mass., 1968), 3.5.
4. Homer, *Odyssey,* pp. 290–291.
5. Quoted in Thomas R. Martin, *Ancient Greece* (New Haven, Conn., 1996), p. 62.
6. Quoted in Victor David Hanson, *The Wars of the Ancient Greeks,* rev. ed. (London, 2006), p. 14.
7. These words from Plutarch are quoted in Elaine Fantham et al., *Women in the Classical World* (New York, 1994), p. 64.
8. Hesiod, *Works and Days,* trans. Dorothea Wender (Harmondsworth, England, 1973), pp. 77, 71, 68.
9. Theognis, *Elegies,* trans. Dorothea Wender (Harmondsworth, England, 1973), pp. 118, 100.
10. Aeschylus, *The Persians,* in *The Complete Greek Tragedies,* vol. 1, ed. David Grene and Richmond Lattimore (Chicago, 1959), p. 229.
11. Herodotus, *The Persian Wars,* trans. Robin Waterfield (New York, 1998), p. 3.
12. Thucydides, *History of the Peloponnesian War,* trans. Rex Warner (Harmondsworth, England, 1954), p. 24.
13. Ibid.
14. Ibid.
15. Sophocles, *Oedipus the King,* trans. David Grene (Chicago, 1959), pp. 68–69.
16. Sophocles, *Antigone,* trans. Don Taylor (London, 1986), p. 146.
17. Plato, *The Republic,* trans. F. M. Cornford (New York, 1945), pp. 178–179.
18. Quotations from Aristotle are from Sue Blundell, *Women in Ancient Greece* (London, 1995), pp. 106, 186.

CHAPTER 4

1. Quoted in Sarah B. Pomeroy et al., *Ancient Greece: A Political, Social, and Cultural History* (Oxford, 1999), p. 390.
2. Polybius, *The Histories,* trans. W. R. Paton (Cambridge, Mass., 1960), 18.37. 8–10.
3. Quoted in Graham Shipley, *The Greek World After Alexander, 323–30 B.C.* (London, 2000), p. 53.
4. Quoted in ibid., p. 304.
5. Maureen B. Fant and Mary R. Lefkowitz, *Women's Life in Greece and Rome: A Source Book in Translation* (Baltimore, 1992), no. 208.
6. Roger S. Bagnall and Peter Derow, *Greek Historical Documents: The Hellenistic Period* (Chico, Calif., 1981), p. 113.

7. Plutarch, *Life of Marcellus,* trans. John Dryden (New York, n.d.), p. 378.
8. Celsus, *De Medicina,* trans. W. G. Spencer (Cambridge, Mass., 1935), Prooemium 23–24.
9. *Epicurus: The Extant Remains,* trans. Cyril Bailey (Oxford, 1926), pp. 89–90, 115, 101.
10. Diogenes Laertius, *Life of Zeno,* vol. 2, trans. R. D. Hicks (London, 1925), p. 195.
11. Quoted in W. W. Tarn, *Hellenistic Civilization* (London, 1930), p. 324.

CHAPTER 5

1. Polybius. *The Histories,* trans. W. R. Paton (Cambridge, Mass., 1960), Book I, 37.7–37.10.
2. Quoted in Chester Starr, *Past and Future in Ancient History* (Lanham, Md., 1987), pp. 38–39.
3. Cicero, *Laws,* trans. C. W. Keyes (Cambridge, Mass., 1966), 2.12.31.
4. Cato the Censor, *On Farming,* trans. Ernest Brehaut (New York, 1933), 141.
5. Quoted in J. Wright Duff, *A Literary History of Rome* (London, 1960), pp. 136–137.
6. Terence, *The Comedies,* trans. Betty Radice (Harmondsworth, England, 1976), p. 339.
7. Pliny, *Natural History,* trans. W. H. S. Jones (Cambridge, Mass., 1963), 29.7.
8. Mary Beard and Michael Crawford, *Rome in the Late Republic* (London, 1985), p. 3.
9. Quoted in Adrian Goldsworthy, *Caesar: Life of a Colossus* (New Haven, Conn., 2006), p. 235.
10. Quoted in ibid., p. 358.
11. Appian, *Roman History: The Civil Wars,* trans. H. White (Cambridge, Mass., 1961), 4.2.149–151.
12. Florus, *Epitome of Roman History,* trans. E. S. Forster (Cambridge, Mass., 1960), 2.22.327.
13. *The Poems of Catullus,* trans. Charles Martin (Baltimore, 1990), p. 109.
14. Lucretius, *On the Nature of Things,* trans. Anthony M. Esolen (Baltimore, 1995), 2.115–123.
15. Quoted in Anthony Everitt, *Cicero* (New York, 2001), p. 181.
16. Julius Caesar, *The Gallic War and Other Writings,* trans. Moses Hadas (New York, 1957), 2.25.

CHAPTER 6

1. Livy, *The Early History of Rome,* trans. Aubrey de Sélincourt (Harmondsworth, England, 1960), p. 35.
2. Tacitus, *The Annals of Imperial Rome,* trans. Michael Grant (Harmondsworth, England, 1956), p. 30.
3. Velleius Paterculus, *Compendium of Roman History,* trans. Frederick Shipley (Cambridge, Mass., 1967), 2.117.
4. Tacitus, *Annals of Imperial Rome,* p. 37.
5. Virgil, *The Aeneid,* trans. C. Day Lewis (Garden City, N.Y., 1952), p. 154.
6. Horace, *Satires,* in *The Complete Works of Horace,* trans. Lord Dunsany and Michael Oakley (London, 1961), 1.1.
7. Ibid., 1.3.
8. Livy, *Early History of Rome,* p. 18.
9. Tacitus, *Annals of Imperial Rome,* p. 31.
10. Tacitus, *The Histories,* trans. Kenneth Wallesley (Harmondsworth, England, 1964), p. 23.
11. Quoted in Martin Goodman, *The Roman World, 44 B.C.–A.D. 180* (London, 1997), p. 67.
12. Quoted in ibid., p. 72.
13. Seneca, *Letters from a Stoic,* trans. Robin Campbell (Harmondsworth, England, 1969), let. 5.
14. Tacitus, *Annals of Imperial Rome,* p. 147.
15. Juvenal, *The Sixteen Satires,* trans. Peter Green (Harmondsworth, England, 1967), satire 7, p. 171.
16. Ibid., satire 10, p. 207.
17. Tacitus, *A Dialogue on Oratory,* in *The Complete Works of Tacitus,* trans. Alfred Church and William Brodribb (New York, 1942), 29, p. 758.
18. Ovid, *The Amores,* trans. Grant Showerman (Cambridge, Mass., 1963), 2.14. 26–27.
19. Matthew 5:17.
20. Matthew 7:12.
21. Mark 12:30–31.
22. John 18:36.
23. Matthew 26:26–28.
24. *Early Christian Writings* (Harmondsworth, England, 1968), pp. 76–77.
25. These lines and the one by Polycarp are quoted in Colin Wells, *The Roman Empire* (Stanford, Calif., 1984), pp. 263–264.
26. Quotations by Tertullian can be found in David Chidester, *Christianity: A Global History* (New York, 2000), pp. 74, 79, 82.
27. Tertullian, "The Prescriptions Against the Heretics," in *The Library of Christian Classics,* vol. 5, *Early Latin Theology,* ed. and trans. S. L. Greenslade (Philadelphia, 1956), p. 36.
28. Colossians 3:10–11.

CHAPTER 7

1. Naphtali Lewis and Meyers Reinhold, eds., *Roman Civilization,* vol. 2 (New York, 1955), p. 191.
2. "The Creed of Nicaea," in Henry Bettenson, ed., *Documents of the Christian Church* (London, 1963), p. 35.
3. Charles C. Mierow, trans., *The Gothic History of Jordanes* (Princeton, N.J., 1915), pp. 88–89.
4. Quoted in Averil Cameron, *The Mediterranean World in Late Antiquity* (London, 1993), p. 37.
5. Ernest F. Henderson, *Selected Historical Documents of the Middle Ages* (London, 1892), p. 182.
6. Ibid., p. 181.
7. Anne Fremantle, ed., *A Treasury of Early Christianity* (New York, 1953), p. 91.
8. Matthew 16:15–19.
9. R. C. Petry, ed., *A History of Christianity: Readings in the History of Early and Medieval Christianity* (Englewood Cliffs, N.J., 1962), p. 70.
10. Brian Pullan, ed., *Sources for the History of Medieval Europe* (Oxford, 1966), p. 46.
11. Quoted in Sidney Painter and Brian Tierney, *Western Europe in the Middle Ages, 300–1475* (New York, 1983), p. 106.
12. Mark 10:21.
13. Norman F. Cantor, ed., *The Medieval World, 300–1300* (New York, 1963), pp. 104, 101, 108, 103.
14. Bede, *A History of the English Church and People,* trans. Leo Sherley-Price (Harmondsworth, England, 1968), pp. 86–87.
15. Quoted in Peter Brown, *The Rise of Western Christendom: Triumph and Adversity, A.D. 200–1000* (Oxford, 1997), p. 98.
16. Procopius, *Secret History,* trans. Richard Atwater (Ann Arbor, Mich., 1963), p. 3.
17. H. B. Dewing, trans., *Procopius,* vol. 1 (Cambridge, Mass., 1914), p. 48.
18. Procopius, *Buildings of Justinian* (London, 1897), pp. 9, 6–7, 11.
19. Quoted in Jonathan Harris, *Constantinople: Capital of Byzantium* (New York, 2007), p. 40.

20. Quoted in ibid., p. 118.
21. Quoted in Arthur Goldschmidt Jr., *A Concise History of the Middle East,* 7th ed. (Boulder, Colo., 2001), p. 60.

CHAPTER 8

1. Einhard, *The Life of Charlemagne,* trans. Samuel Turner (Ann Arbor, Mich., 1960), p. 30.
2. Ibid., p. 57.
3. Alessandro Barbero, *Charlemagne: Father of a Continent,* trans. Allan Cameron (Berkeley, Calif., 2004), p. 4.
4. Quoted in Pierre Riché, *Daily Life in the World of Charlemagne,* trans. Jo Ann McNamara (Philadelphia, 1978), p. 56.
5. 1 Corinthians 7:1–2, 8–9.
6. Quoted in Derrick Bailey, *Homosexuality and the Western Christian Tradition* (London, 1955), p. 73.
7. Quoted in Paul Veyne, ed., *A History of Private Life,* vol. 1, *From Pagan Rome to Byzantium,* trans. Arthur Goldhammer (Cambridge, Mass., 1987), p. 440.
8. Stanley Rubin, *Medieval English Medicine* (New York, 1974), p. 136.
9. Quoted in Brian Inglis, *A History of Medicine* (New York, 1965), p. 51.
10. Quoted in Simon Keynes, "The Vikings in England, c. 790–1016," in Peter Sawyer, ed., *The Oxford Illustrated History of the Vikings* (Oxford, 1997), p. 81.
11. Quoted in Oliver Thatcher and Edgar McNeal, *A Source Book for Medieval History* (New York, 1905), p. 363.
12. Simon Keynes and Michael Lapidge, *Alfred the Great: Asser's "Life of King Alfred" and Other Contemporary Sources* (Harmondsworth, England, 1983), pp. 84–85.
13. Quoted in Bernard Lewis, *The Arabs in History* (London, 1958), p. 90.
14. al-Mas'udi, *The Meadows of Gold: The Abbasids,* ed. Paul Lunde and Caroline Stone (London, 1989), p. 151.

CHAPTER 9

1. Quoted in Joseph Gies and Frances Gies, *Life in a Medieval Castle* (New York, 1974), p. 175.
2. Quoted in Robert Delort, *Life in the Middle Ages,* trans. Robert Allen (New York, 1972), p. 218.
3. Quoted in Jean Gimpel, *The Medieval Machine* (Harmondsworth, England, 1976), p. 92.
4. Quoted in Charles H. Haskins, *The Rise of Universities* (Ithaca, N.Y., 1957), pp. 77–78.
5. Ibid., pp. 79–80.
6. Quoted in David Herlihy, *Medieval Culture and Society* (New York, 1968), p. 204.
7. Quoted in John H. Mundy, *Europe in the High Middle Ages, 1150–1309* (New York, 1973), pp. 474–475.
8. *The Goliard Poets,* trans. George Whicher (Cambridge, Mass., 1949), p. 111.
9. Helen Waddell, *The Wandering Scholars* (New York, 1961), p. 222.
10. Quoted in John W. Baldwin, *The Scholastic Culture of the Middle Ages, 1000–1300* (Lexington, Mass., 1971), p. 15.

CHAPTER 10

1. Quoted in John K. Fairbank, Edwin O. Reischauer, and Albert M. Craig, *East Asia: Tradition and Transformation* (Boston, 1973), p. 164.
2. Ernest F. Henderson, ed., *Selected Historical Documents of the Middle Ages* (London, 1892), p. 332.
3. Ibid., p. 365.
4. Oliver J. Thatcher and Edgar H. McNeal, eds., *A Source Book for Medieval History* (New York, 1905), p. 208.
5. Quoted in R. H. C. Davis, *A History of Medieval Europe from Constantine to Saint Louis,* 2nd ed. (New York, 1988), p. 252.
6. Luke 18:23–25.
7. Quoted in Rosalind Brooke and Christopher N. L. Brooke, *Popular Religion in the Middle Ages* (London, 1984), p. 19.
8. Henry T. Riley, ed., *Memorials of London and London Life in the Thirteenth, Fourteenth, and Fifteenth Centuries* (London, 1868), vol. 2, pp. 148–149.
9. Thatcher and McNeal, *Source Book for Medieval History,* p. 517.
10. Quoted in Thomas Asbridge, *The First Crusade: A New History* (Oxford, 2004), pp. 79–80.
11. Quoted in Hans E. Mayer, *The Crusades,* trans. John Gillingham (New York, 1972), pp. 99–100.

CHAPTER 11

1. Quoted in H. S. Lucas, "The Great European Famine of 1315, 1316, and 1317," *Speculum* 5 (1930): 359.
2. Quoted in Christos S. Bartsocas, "Two Fourteenth-Century Descriptions of the 'Black Death,'" *Journal of the History of Medicine* (October 1966): 395.
3. Quoted in David Herlihy, *The Black Death and the Transformation of the West,* ed. Samuel K. Cohn Jr. (Cambridge, Mass., 1997), p. 9.
4. Quoted in Rosemary Horrox, ed., *The Black Death* (Manchester, England, 1994), pp. 18–19.
5. Giovanni Boccaccio, *Decameron,* trans. Frances Winwar (New York, 1955), p. xxv.
6. Ibid., p. xxvi.
7. Jean Froissart, *Chronicles,* ed. and trans. Geoffrey Brereton (Harmondsworth, England, 1968), p. 111.
8. Quoted in James B. Ross and Mary M. McLaughlin, *The Portable Medieval Reader* (New York, 1949), pp. 218–219.
9. Quoted in Barbara W. Tuchman, *A Distant Mirror* (New York, 1978), p. 175.
10. Froissart, *Chronicles,* p. 212.
11. Ibid., p. 89.
12. Oliver J. Thatcher and Edgar H. McNeal, eds., *A Source Book for Medieval History* (New York, 1905), p. 288.
13. Quoted in D. S. Chambers, *The Imperial Age of Venice, 1380–1580* (London, 1970), p. 30.
14. Quoted in Robert Coogan, *Babylon on the Rhône: A Translation of Letters by Dante, Petrarch, and Catherine of Siena* (Washington, D.C., 1983), p. 115.
15. Quoted in Caroline Walker Bynum, *Holy Feast and Holy Fast: The Religious Significance of Food to Medieval Women* (Berkeley, Calif., 1987), p. 180.
16. Dante Alighieri, *Divine Comedy,* trans. Dorothy Sayers (New York, 1962), "Paradise," canto 33, line 145.
17. Petrarch, *Sonnets and Songs,* trans. Anna Maria Armi (New York, 1968), no. 74, p. 127.
18. Quoted in Millard Meiss, *Painting in Florence and Siena After the Black Death* (Princeton, N.J., 1951), p. 161.
19. Geoffrey Chaucer, *The Canterbury Tales,* in *The Portable Chaucer,* ed. Theodore Morrison (New York, 1949), p. 67.
20. Christine de Pizan, *The Book of the City of Ladies,* trans. E. Jeffrey Richards (New York, 1982), pp. 83–84.
21. Quoted in Susan Mosher Stuard, "The Dominion of Gender, or How Women Fared in the High Middle Ages," in Renate Bridenthal, Claudia Koonz, and Susan Stuard, eds., *Becoming Visible: Women in European History,* 3rd ed. (Boston, 1998), p. 147.

22. Quoted in David Herlihy, "Medieval Children," in Bede K. Lackner and Kenneth R. Philp, eds., *Essays on Medieval Civilization* (Austin, Tex., 1978), p. 121.
23. Quoted in Jean Gimpel, *The Medieval Machine* (New York, 1976), p. 168.

CHAPTER 12

1. Quoted in Jacob Burckhardt, *The Civilization of the Renaissance in Italy,* trans. S. G. C. Middlemore (London, 1960), p. 81.
2. Baldassare Castiglione, *The Book of the Courtier,* trans. Charles S. Singleton (Garden City, N.Y., 1959), pp. 288–289.
3. Quoted in De Lamar Jensen, *Renaissance Europe* (Lexington, Mass., 1981), p. 94.
4. Quoted in Iris Origo, "The Domestic Enemy: The Eastern Slaves in Tuscany in the Fourteenth and Fifteenth Centuries," *Speculum* 30 (1955): 333.
5. Quoted in Gene Brucker, ed., *Two Memoirs of Renaissance Florence* (New York, 1967), p. 132.
6. Quoted in Margaret L. King, *Women of the Renaissance* (Chicago, 1991), p. 3.
7. Quoted in Gene Brucker, ed., *The Society of Renaissance Florence* (New York, 1971), p. 190.
8. Quoted in Garrett Mattingly, *Renaissance Diplomacy* (Baltimore, 1964), p. 42.
9. Ibid., p. 95.
10. Niccolò Machiavelli, *The Prince,* trans. David Wootton (Indianapolis, 1995), p. 48.
11. Ibid., p. 55.
12. Ibid., p. 27.
13. Petrarch, "Epistle to Posterity," *Letters from Petrarch,* trans. Morris Bishop (Bloomington, Ind., 1966), pp. 6–7.
14. Quoted in Frances Yates, *Giordano Bruno and the Hermetic Tradition* (Chicago, 1964), p. 211.
15. Giovanni Pico della Mirandola, *Oration on the Dignity of Man,* in E. Cassirer, P. O. Kristeller, and J. H. Randall Jr., eds., *The Renaissance Philosophy of Man* (Chicago, 1948), p. 225.
16. Ibid., pp. 247, 249.
17. Quoted in W. H. Woodward, *Vittorino da Feltre and Other Humanist Educators* (Cambridge, 1897), p. 102.
18. Quoted in Iris Origo, *The Light of the Past* (New York, 1959), p. 136.
19. Quoted in Elizabeth G. Holt, ed., *A Documentary History of Art* (Garden City, N.Y., 1957), vol. 1, p. 286.
20. Quoted in Rosa M. Letts, *The Cambridge Introduction to Art: The Renaissance* (Cambridge, 1981), p. 86.
21. Quoted in Johan Huizinga, *The Waning of the Middle Ages* (Garden City, N.Y., 1956), p. 265.

CHAPTER 13

1. Desiderius Erasmus, *The Paraclesis,* in John Olin, ed., *Christian Humanism and the Reformation: Selected Writings of Erasmus,* 3rd ed. (New York, 1987), p. 101.
2. Thomas More, *Utopia,* trans. Paul Turner (Harmondsworth, England, 1965), p. 76.
3. Quoted in Alister E. McGrath, *Reformation Thought: An Introduction* (Oxford, 1988), p. 72.
4. Quoted in Gordon Rupp, *Luther's Progress to the Diet of Worms* (New York, 1964), p. 82.
5. Martin Luther, *On the Freedom of a Christian Man,* quoted in E. G. Rupp and Benjamin Drewery, eds., *Martin Luther* (New York, 1970), p. 50.
6. Quoted in Roland Bainton, *Here I Stand: A Life of Martin Luther* (New York, 1950), p. 144.
7. Quoted in De Lamar Jensen, *Reformation Europe* (Lexington, Mass., 1981), p. 83.
8. Quoted in Lee Palmer Wandel, *Voracious Idols and Violent Hands: Iconoclasm in Reformation Zürich, Strasbourg, and Basel* (New York, 1995), p. 81.
9. Quoted in A. G. Dickens and Dorothy Carr, eds., *The Reformation in England to the Accession of Elizabeth I* (New York, 1968), p. 72.
10. Quoted in Lewis W. Spitz, *The Renaissance and Reformation Movements* (Chicago, 1971), p. 414.
11. John Calvin, *Institutes of the Christian Religion,* trans. John Allen (Philadelphia, 1936), vol. 1, p. 220.
12. Ibid., vol. 1, p. 228; vol. 2, p. 181.
13. Quoted in Roland Bainton, *Women of the Reformation in Germany and Italy* (Minneapolis, 1971), p. 154.
14. Quoted in Bonnie S. Anderson and Judith P. Zinsser, *A History of Their Own: Women in Europe from Prehistory to the Present* (New York, 1988), vol. 1, p. 259.
15. Quoted in John A. Phillips, *Eve: The History of an Idea* (New York, 1984), p. 105.
16. Quoted in John O'Malley, *The First Jesuits* (Cambridge, Mass., 1993), p. 76.
17. Quoted in R. J. Knecht, *The French Wars of Religion, 1559–1598,* 2nd ed. (New York, 1996), p. 47.
18. Quoted in Mack P. Holt, *The French Wars of Religion, 1562–1629* (Cambridge, 1995), p. 86.
19. Quoted in Garrett Mattingly, *The Armada* (Boston, 1959), pp. 216–217.
20. Quoted in Theodore Schieder, *Handbuch der Europäischen Geschichte* (Stuttgart, 1979), vol. 3, p. 579.

CHAPTER 14

1. Quoted in J. R. Hale, *Renaissance Exploration* (New York, 1968), p. 32.
2. Quoted in J. H. Parry, *The Age of Reconnaissance: Discovery, Exploration, and Settlement, 1450 to 1650* (New York, 1963), p. 33.
3. Quoted in Richard B. Reed, "The Expansion of Europe," in Richard De Molen, ed., *The Meaning of the Renaissance and Reformation* (Boston, 1974), p. 308.
4. Quoted in K. N. Chaudhuri, *Trade and Civilization in the Indian Ocean: An Economic History from the Rise of Islam to 1750* (Cambridge, 1985), p. 65.
5. Quoted in Ian Cameron, *Explorers and Exploration* (New York, 1991), p. 42.
6. Bernal Díaz, *The Conquest of New Spain* (New York, 1963), pp. 405–406.
7. Quoted in J. H. Parry and Robert G. Keith, eds., *New Iberian World,* vol. 2 (New York, 1984), pp. 309–310.
8. Quoted in J. H. Elliott, *Empires of the Atlantic World* (New Haven, Conn., 2006), p. 125.
9. Quoted in A. Andrea and J. H. Overfield, *The Human Record: Sources of Global History,* 3rd ed. (Boston, 1998), p. 460.
10. Quoted in Basil Davidson, *Africa in History: Themes and Outlines,* rev. ed. (New York, 1991), p. 198.
11. Quoted in Cameron, *Explorers and Exploration,* p. 42.
12. Quoted in Louis J. Gallagher, ed. and trans., *China in the Sixteenth Century: The Journals of Matthew Ricci* (New York, 1953), p. 154.
13. Quoted in G. V. Scammell, *The First Imperial Age: European Overseas Expansion, c. 1400–1715* (London, 1989), p. 62.
14. Miguel Leon-Portilla, ed., *The Broken Spears: The Aztec Account of the Conquest of Mexico* (Boston, 1969), p. 51.

CHAPTER 15

1. Quoted in Joseph Klaits, *Servants of Satan: The Age of the Witch Hunts* (Bloomington, Ind., 1985), p. 68.
2. Quoted in Peter H. Wilson, *The Thirty Years War: Europe's Tragedy* (Cambridge, Mass., 2009), p. 783.
3. Quoted in John B. Wolf, *Louis XIV* (New York, 1968), p. 134.
4. Quoted in James B. Collins, *The State in Early Modern France* (Cambridge, 1995), p. 130.
5. Quoted in Wolf, *Louis XIV,* p. 618.
6. Quoted in D. H. Pennington, *Europe in the Seventeenth Century,* 2nd ed. (New York, 1989), p. 494.
7. Quoted in J. H. Elliot, *Imperial Spain, 1469–1716* (New York, 1963), p. 306.
8. Quoted in B. H. Sumner, *Peter the Great and the Emergence of Russia* (New York, 1962), p. 122.
9. Quoted in Simon Schama, *A History of Britain,* vol. 2, *The Wars of the British, 1603–1776* (New York, 2001), pp. 182, 185.

CHAPTER 16

1. Quoted in Alan G. R. Smith, *Science and Society in the Sixteenth and Seventeenth Centuries* (London, 1972), p. 59.
2. Edward MacCurdy, *The Notebooks of Leonardo da Vinci* (London, 1948), vol. 1, p. 634.
3. Ibid., p. 636.
4. Frances Yates, *Giordano Bruno and the Hermetic Tradition* (New York, 1964), p. 448.
5. Ibid., p. 450.
6. Quoted in Smith, *Science and Society,* p. 97.
7. Logan P. Smith, *Life and Letters of* Sir *Henry Wotton* (Oxford, 1907), vol. 1, pp. 486–487.
8. Quoted in John H. Randall, *The Making of the Modern Mind* (Boston, 1926), p. 234.
9. Quoted in Smith, *Science and Society,* p. 124.
10. Quoted in Betty J. Dobbs, *The Foundations of Newton's Alchemy* (Cambridge, 1975), pp. 13–14.
11. Jolande Jacobi, ed., *Paracelsus: Selected Writings* (New York, 1965), pp. 5–6.
12. Ibid., p. 21.
13. Quoted in Londa Schiebinger, *The Mind Has No Sex? Women in the Origins of Modern Science* (Cambridge, Mass., 1989), pp. 52–53.
14. Ibid., p. 85.
15. Quoted in Phyllis Stock, *Better than Rubies: A History of Women's Education* (New York, 1978), p. 16.
16. René Descartes, *Philosophical Writings,* ed. and trans. Norman K. Smith (New York, 1958), p. 95.
17. Ibid., pp. 118–119.
18. Francis Bacon, *The Great Instauration,* trans. Jerry Weinberger (Arlington Heights, Ill., 1989), pp. 2, 8, 16, 21.
19. Descartes, *Discourse on Method,* in *Philosophical Writings,* p. 75.
20. Margaret C. Jacob, *The Cultural Meaning of the Scientific Revolution* (New York, 1988), p. 73.
21. Stillman Drake, ed. and trans., *Discoveries and Opinions of Galileo* (New York, 1957), p. 182.
22. Benedict de Spinoza, *Ethics,* trans. R. H. M. Elwes (New York, 1955), pp. 75–76.
23. Ibid., p. 76.
24. Spinoza, *Letters,* quoted in Randall, *The Making of the Modern Mind,* p. 247.
25. Blaise Pascal, *Pensées,* trans. J. M. Cohen (Harmondsworth, England, 1961), p. 100.
26. Ibid., pp. 31, 52–53, 164, 165.

CHAPTER 17

1. Quoted in Paul Hazard, *The European Mind, 1680–1715* (New York, 1963), pp. 304–305.
2. Quoted in Dorinda Outram, *The Enlightenment* (Cambridge, 1995), p. 67.
3. Quoted in Hazard, *The European Mind,* p. 12.
4. John Locke, *An Essay Concerning Human Understanding* (New York, 1964), pp. 89–90.
5. Baron Paul d'Holbach, *Common Sense,* as quoted in Frank E. Manuel, ed., *The Enlightenment* (Englewood Cliffs, N.J., 1965), p. 62.
6. Jean-Jacques Rousseau, *A Discourse on Inequality,* trans. Maurice Cranston (Harmondsworth, England, 1984), p. 109.
7. Jean-Jacques Rousseau, *The Social Contract,* trans. Maurice Cranston (Harmondsworth, England, 1968), p. 141.
8. Mary Astell, *A Serious Proposal to the Ladies,* in Moira Ferguson, ed., *First Feminists: British Women Writers, 1578–1799* (Bloomington, Ind., 1985), p. 190.
9. Mary Astell, *Some Reflections upon Marriage,* in ibid., p. 193.
10. Kenneth Clark, *Civilization* (New York, 1969), p. 231.
11. Voltaire, *The Age of Louis XIV,* trans. Martyn P. Pollack (New York, 1961), p. 1.
12. Cesare Beccaria, *An Essay on Crimes and Punishments,* trans. E. D. Ingraham (Philadelphia, 1819), pp. 59–60.
13. Quoted in René Sand, *The Advance to Social Medicine* (London, 1952), pp. 86–87.
14. Quoted in Peter Burke, *Popular Culture in Early Modern Europe* (New York, 1978), p. 179.
15. Quoted in ibid., p. 186.
16. Quoted in C. A. Macartney, *The Habsburg and Hohenzollern Dynasties in the Seventeenth and Eighteenth Centuries* (New York, 1970), p. 157.

CHAPTER 18

1. Frederick II, *Forms of Government,* in Eugen Weber, *The Western Tradition* (Lexington, Mass., 1972), pp. 538, 544.
2. Quoted in Reinhold A. Dorwart, *The Administrative Reforms of Frederick William I of Prussia* (Cambridge, Mass., 1953), p. 36.
3. Quoted in Sidney B. Fay, *The Rise of Brandenburg-Prussia to 1786,* rev. Klaus Epstein (New York, 1964), p. 92.
4. Quoted in Hans Rosenberg, *Bureaucracy, Aristocracy, and Autocracy: The Prussian Experience, 1660–1815* (Cambridge, Mass., 1958), p. 40.
5. Quoted in Fernand Braudel, *Civilization and Capitalism* (London, 1981–1984), vol. 3, p. 378.
6. Quoted in ibid., p. 245.
7. Quoted in Witold Rybczynski, *Home: A Short History of an Idea* (New York, 1986), p. 105.
8. Quoted in Jonathan Dewald, *The European Nobility, 1400–1800* (Cambridge, 1996), pp. 91–92.
9. Quoted in Peter Gay, *Age of Enlightenment* (New York, 1966), p. 87.
10. Quoted in Paul Hazard, *The European Mind, 1680–1715* (Cleveland, Ohio, 1963), pp. 6–7.
11. Igor Vinogradoff, "Russian Missions to London, 1711–1789: Further Extracts from the Cottrell Papers," *Oxford Slavonic Papers,* New Series (1982), 15:76.
12. Quoted in Jeffrey Kaplow, *The Names of Kings: The Parisian Laboring Poor in the Eighteenth Century* (New York, 1972), p. 134.

CHAPTER 19

1. Quoted in R. R. Palmer, *The Age of the Democratic Revolutions* (Princeton, N.J., 1959), vol. 1, p. 239.
2. Quoted in ibid., p. 242.

3. Quoted in O. J. Hufton, "Toward an Understanding of the Poor of Eighteenth-Century France," in J. F. Bosher, ed., *French Government and Society, 1500–1850* (London, 1973), p. 152.
4. Arthur Young, *Travels in France During the Years 1787, 1788, and 1789* (Cambridge, 1929), p. 23.
5. Quoted in D. M. G. Sutherland, *France, 1789–1815: Revolution and Counter-Revolution* (New York, 1986), p. 74.
6. Quoted in William Doyle, *The Oxford History of the French Revolution* (Oxford, 1989), p. 156.
7. Quoted in ibid., p. 184.
8. Quoted in J. Hardman, ed., *French Revolution Documents* (Oxford, 1973), vol. 2, p. 23.
9. Quoted in W. Scott, *Terror and Repression in Revolutionary Marseilles* (London, 1973), p. 84.
10. Quoted in H. Morse Stephens, *The Principal Speeches of the Statesmen and Orators of the French Revolution* (Oxford, 1892), vol. 2, p. 189.
11. Quoted in Leo Gershoy, *The Era of the French Revolution* (Princeton, N.J., 1957), p. 157.
12. Quoted in J. M. Thompson, ed., *French Revolution Documents* (Oxford, 1933), pp. 258–259.
13. Quoted in Doyle, *Oxford History of the French Revolution,* p. 254.
14. Quoted in R. R. Palmer, *Twelve Who Ruled* (New York, 1965), p. 75.
15. Quoted in Darline Gay Levy, Harriet Branson Applewhite, and Mary Durham Johnson, eds., *Women in Revolutionary Paris, 1789–1795* (Urbana, Ill., 1979), p. 132.
16. Ibid., pp. 219–220.
17. Quoted in Elizabeth G. Sledziewski, "The French Revolution as the Turning Point," in Geneviève Fraisse and Michelle Perrot, eds., *A History of Women in the West* (Cambridge, 1993), vol. 4, p. 39.
18. Quoted in François Furet and Mona Ozouf, *A Critical Dictionary of the French Revolution,* trans. Arthur Goldhammer (Cambridge, Mass., 1989), p. 545.
19. Quoted in J. Christopher Herold, ed., *The Mind of Napoleon* (New York, 1955), p. 43.
20. Quoted in Felix Markham, *Napoleon* (New York, 1963), pp. 92–93.
21. Quoted in Doyle, *Oxford History of the French Revolution,* p. 381.
22. Quoted in Herold, ed., *The Mind of Napoleon,* pp. 74–75.
23. Quoted in Steven Englund, *Napoleon: A Political Life* (New York, 2004), p. 285.

CHAPTER 20

1. Quoted in W. Gordon Rimmer, *Marshall's of Leeds, Flax-Spinners, 1788–1886* (Cambridge, 1960), p. 40.
2. Daniel Defoe, *A Plan of the English Commerce* (Oxford, 1928), pp. 76–77.
3. Quoted in Albert Tucker, *A History of English Civilization* (New York, 1972), p. 583.
4. Quotations are from Lara Kriegel, *Grand Designs: Labor, Empire, and the Museum in Victorian Culture* (Durham, N.C., 2007), p. 120.
5. Quoted in E. Royston Pike, *Human Documents of the Industrial Revolution in Britain* (London, 1966), p. 320.
6. Ibid., p. 314.
7. Ibid., p. 343.
8. Ibid., p. 315.
9. Charles Dickens, *The Old Curiosity Shop* (New York, 2000), p. 340.
10. Quoted in A. J. Donajgrodzi, ed., *Social Control in Nineteenth-Century Britain* (London, 1977), p. 141.
11. Quoted in Pike, *Human Documents,* pp. 343–344.
12. Quoted in Eric J. Evans, *The Forging of the Modern State: Early Industrial Britain, 1783–1870* (London, 1983), p. 113.
13. Henry Mayhew, *London Labour and the London Poor* (London, 1851), vol.1, pp. 342–343.
14. Quoted in Pike, *Human Documents,* pp. 60–61.
15. Quoted in Evans, *Forging of the Modern State,* p. 124.

CHAPTER 21

1. Quoted in Charles Breunig, *The Age of Revolution and Reaction, 1789–1850* (New York, 1970), p. 119.
2. Quoted in M. S. Anderson, *The Ascendancy of Europe, 1815–1914,* 2nd ed. (London, 1985), p. 1.
3. Quotations from Burke can be found in Peter Viereck, *Conservatism* (Princeton, N.J., 1956), pp. 27, 114.
4. Quoted in René Albrecht-Carrié, *The Concert of Europe* (New York, 1968), p. 48.
5. Quoted in M. C. Eakin, *The History of Latin America: Collision of Cultures* (New York, 2007), p. 188.
6. Quoted in G. de Berthier de Sauvigny, *Metternich and His Times* (London, 1962), p. 105.
7. Quoted in S. Joan Moon, "Feminism and Socialism: The Utopian Synthesis of Flora Tristan," in Marilyn J. Boxer and Jean H. Quataert, eds., *Socialist Women* (New York, 1978), p. 38.
8. Quoted in Stanley Z. Pech, *The Czech Revolution of 1848* (Chapel Hill, N.C., 1969), p. 82.
9. Quoted in Clive Emsley, *Policing and Its Context, 1750–1870* (New York, 1984), p. 58.
10. Quoted in Clive Emsley, *Crime and Society in England, 1750–1900* (London, 1987), p. 173.
11. Quoted in Emsley, *Policing and Its Context,* p. 66.
12. Quoted in ibid., p. 102.
13. Quoted in Emsley, *Crime and Society in England,* p. 226.
14. William Wordsworth, "The Tables Turned," *Poems of Wordsworth,* ed. Matthew Arnold (London, 1963), p. 138.
15. William Wordsworth, *The Prelude* (Harmondsworth, England, 1971), p. 109.
16. Quoted in H. G. Schenk, *The Mind of the European Romantics* (Garden City, N.Y., 1969), p. 205.
17. Quoted in Siegbert Prawer, ed., *The Romantic Period in Germany* (London, 1970), p. 285.
18. Quoted in John B. Halsted, ed., *Romanticism* (New York, 1969), p. 156.

CHAPTER 22

1. Quoted in James F. McMillan, *Napoleon III* (New York, 1991), p. 37.
2. Quoted in Robert Gildea, *Barricades and Borders: Europe, 1800–1914,* 2nd ed. (Oxford, 1996), p. 170.
3. Quoted in Otto Pflanze, *Bismarck and the Development of Germany: The Period of Unification, 1815–1871* (Princeton, N.J., 1963), p. 60.
4. Louis L. Snyder, ed., *Documents of German History* (New Brunswick, N.J., 1958), p. 202.
5. Quoted in Pflanze, *Bismarck and the Development of Germany,* p. 327.
6. Quoted in György Szabad, *Hungarian Political Trends Between the Revolution and the Compromise, 1849–1867* (Budapest, 1977), p. 163.
7. Quoted in Rondo Cameron, "Crédit Mobilier and the Economic Development of Europe," *Journal of Political Economy* 61 (1953): 470.

8. Karl Marx and Friedrich Engels, *The Communist Manifesto* (Harmondsworth, England, 1967), p. 79.
9. Ibid., pp. 79, 81, 82.
10. Charles Darwin, *On the Origin of Species* (New York, 1872), vol. 1, pp. 77, 79.
11. Quoted in Albert Lyons and R. Joseph Petrucelli, *Medicine: An Illustrated History* (New York, 1978), p. 569.

CHAPTER 23

1. Quoted in David Landes, *The Unbound Prometheus: Technological Change and Industrial Development in Western Europe from 1750 to the Present* (Cambridge, 1969), p. 353.
2. Quoted in Barbara Franzoi, ". . . With the Wolf Always at the Door: Women's Work in Domestic Industry in Britain and Germany," in Marilyn J. Boxer and Jean H. Quataert, eds., *Connecting Spheres: Women in the Western World, 1500 to the Present* (New York, 1987), p. 151.
3. Quoted in W. L. Guttsman, *The German Social Democratic Party, 1875–1933* (London, 1981), p. 63.
4. Quoted in Leslie Derfler, *Socialism Since Marx: A Century of the European Left* (New York, 1973), p. 58.
5. Karl Marx and Friedrich Engels, *The Communist Manifesto* (Harmondsworth, England, 1967), p. 102.
6. Quoted in Paul Avrich, *The Russian Anarchists* (Princeton, N.J., 1971), p. 67.
7. Quoted in Nicholas Bullock and James Read, *The Movement for Housing Reform in Germany and France, 1840–1914* (Cambridge, 1985), p. 42.
8. Quoted in Gary Cross, *A Social History of Leisure Since 1600* (State College, Pa., 1990), pp. 116, 119.
9. Quoted in Sibylle Meyer, "The Tiresome Work of Conspicuous Leisure: On the Domestic Duties of the Wives of Civil Servants in the German Empire (1871–1918)," in Boxer and Quataert, *Connecting Spheres,* p. 161.
10. Quoted in Lenard R. Berlanstein, *The Working People of Paris, 1871–1914* (Baltimore, 1984), p. 141.
11. Quoted in Robert Gildea, *Barricades and Borders: Europe, 1800–1914,* 2nd ed. (Oxford, 1996), pp. 240–241.
12. Quoted in Cross, *Social History of Leisure,* p. 130.
13. Quoted in Shmuel Galai, *The Liberation Movement in Russia, 1900–1905* (Cambridge, 1973), p. 26.

CHAPTER 24

1. Quoted in Charles Rearick, *Pleasures of the Belle Époque: Entertainment and Festivity in Turn-of-the-Century France* (New Haven, Conn., 1985), p. 120.
2. Quoted in Arthur E. E. McKenzie, *The Major Achievements of Science* (New York, 1960), vol. 1, p. 310.
3. Friedrich Nietzsche, *Twilight of the Idols and the Anti-Christ,* trans. R. J. Hollingdale (New York, 1972), pp. 117–118.
4. Friedrich Nietzsche, *Thus Spake Zarathustra,* in *The Philosophy of Nietzsche* (New York, 1954), p. 6.
5. Herbert Spencer, *Social Statics* (New York, 1896), pp. 146, 150.
6. Friedrich von Bernhardi, *Germany and the Next War,* trans. Allen H. Powles (New York, 1914), pp. 18–19.
7. Quoted in Edward R. Tannenbaum, *1900: The Generation Before the Great War* (Garden City, N.Y., 1976), p. 337.
8. William Booth, *In Darkest England and the Way Out* (London, 1890), p. 45.
9. Quoted in John Rewald, *The History of Impressionism* (New York, 1961), pp. 456–458.
10. Quoted in Anne Higonnet, *Berthe Morisot's Images of Women* (Cambridge, Mass., 1992), p. 19.
11. Quoted in Craig Wright, *Listening to Music* (Saint Paul, Minn., 1992), p. 327.
12. Quoted in Catherine M. Prelinger, "Prelude to Consciousness: Amalie Sieveking and the Female Association for the Care of the Poor and the Sick," in John C. Fout, ed., *German Women in the Nineteenth Century: A Social History* (New York, 1984), p. 119.
13. Quoted in Bonnie G. Smith, *Changing Lives: Women in European History Since 1700* (Lexington, Mass., 1989), p. 379.
14. Quoted in Paul Massing, *Rehearsal for Destruction: A Study of Political Anti-Semitism in Imperial Germany* (New York, 1949), p. 147.
15. Quoted in Abba Eban, *Heritage: Civilization and the Jews* (New York, 1984), p. 249.
16. Quoted in John Merriman, *A History of Modern Europe* (New York, 1996), p. 953.
17. Quoted in ibid., p. 965.
18. Karl Pearson, *National Life from the Standpoint of Science* (London, 1905), p. 184.
19. Quoted in John Ellis, *The Social History of the Machine Gun* (New York, 1975), p. 80.
20. Quoted in ibid., p. 86.
21. Quoted in Louis L. Snyder, ed., *The Imperialism Reader* (Princeton, N.J., 1962), p. 220.
22. Quoted in K. M. Panikkar, *Asia and Western Dominance* (London, 1959), p. 116.

CHAPTER 25

1. Martin Gilbert, *The First World War: A Complete History* (New York, 1994), p. 259.
2. Quoted in ibid., p. 264.
3. Arnold Toynbee, *Surviving the Future* (New York, 1971), pp. 106–107.
4. Quoted in Joachim Remak, "1914—The Third Balkan War: Origins Reconsidered," *Journal of Modern History* 43 (1971): 364–365.
5. Quoted in Robert G. L. Waite, *Vanguard of Nazism* (New York, 1969), p. 22.
6. Quoted in J. M. Winter, *The Experience of World War I* (New York, 1989), p. 142.
7. Quoted in ibid., p. 137.
8. Quoted in Hew Strachan, *The First World War* (New York, 2004), pp. 94–95.
9. Quoted in ibid., p. 72.
10. Quoted in Gail Braybon, *Women Workers in the First World War: The British Experience* (London, 1981), p. 79.
11. Quoted in Catherine W. Reilly, ed., *Scars upon My Heart: Women's Poetry and Verse of the First World War* (London, 1981), p. 90.
12. Quoted in Robert Paxton, *Europe in the Twentieth Century,* 2nd ed. (New York, 1985), p. 110.
13. Quoted in William M. Mandel, *Soviet Women* (Garden City, N.Y., 1975), p. 43.
14. Quoted in Mark D. Steinberg, *Voices of Revolution, 1917* (New Haven, Conn., 2001), p. 55.

CHAPTER 26

1. Quoted in Stéphane Audoin-Rouzeau and Annette Becker, *14–18: Understanding the Great War,* trans. Catherine Temerson (New York, 2002), pp. 212–213.
2. Quoted in ibid., p. 41.
3. Quoted in Robert Paxton, *Europe in the Twentieth Century,* 2nd ed. (New York, 1985), p. 237.
4. Quoted in Denis Mack Smith, *Mussolini* (New York, 1982), p. 51.

5. Benito Mussolini, "The Doctrine of Fascism," in Adrian Lyttleton, ed., *Italian Fascisms from Pareto to Gentile* (London, 1973), p. 42.
6. Quoted in Alexander De Grand, "Women Under Italian Fascism," *Historical Journal* 19 (1976): 958–959.
7. Adolf Hitler, *Mein Kampf*, trans. Ralph Manheim (Boston, 1943), p. 22.
8. Ibid., p. 161.
9. Quoted in Joachim Fest, *Hitler*, trans. Richard Winston and Clara Winston (New York, 1974), p. 241.
10. Quoted in Jeremy Noakes and Geoffrey Pridham, eds., *Nazism, 1919–1945* (Exeter, England, 1983), vol. 1, pp. 50–51.
11. Quoted in Jackson J. Spielvogel and David Redles, *Hitler and Nazi Germany: A History*, 6th ed. (Upper Saddle River, N.J., 2010), p. 83.
12. Irving Howe, ed., *The Basic Writings of Trotsky* (London, 1963), p. 162.
13. Quoted in Sheila Fitzpatrick, *Everyday Stalinism. Ordinary Life in Extraordinary Times: Soviet Russia in the 1930s* (New York, 1999), p. 87.
14. Paul Valéry, *Variety*, trans. Malcolm Cowley (New York, 1927), pp. 27–28.
15. Quoted in Matthis Eberle, *World War I and the Weimar Artists: Dix, Grosz, Beckmann, Schlemmer* (New Haven, Conn., 1985), p. 54.
16. Norman H. Baynes, ed., *The Speeches of Adolf Hitler, 1922–1939* (Oxford, 1942), vol. 1, p. 591.

CHAPTER 27

1. Adolf Hitler, *Mein Kampf*, trans. Ralph Manheim (Boston, 1971), p. 654.
2. *Documents on German Foreign Policy* (London, 1956), ser. D, vol. 2, p. 358.
3. Ibid., vol. 7, p. 204.
4. Quoted in Norman Rich, *Hitler's War Aims* (New York, 1973), vol. 1, p. 129.
5. Quoted in Williamson Murray and Allan Millett, *A War to Be Won: Fighting the Second World War* (Cambridge, Mass., 2000), p. 66.
6. Quoted in ibid., p. 137.
7. Albert Speer, *Spandau*, trans. Richard Winston and Clara Winston (New York, 1976), p. 50.
8. *Nazi Conspiracy and Aggression* (Washington, D.C., 1946), vol. 6, p. 262.
9. International Military Tribunal, *Trial of the Major War Criminals* (Nuremberg, 1947–1949), vol. 22, p. 480.
10. Adolf Hitler, *My New Order*, ed. Raoul de Roussy de Sales (New York, 1941), pp. 21–22.
11. Quoted in Lucy Dawidowicz, *The War Against the Jews* (New York, 1975), p. 106.
12. *Nazi Conspiracy and Aggression*, vol. 5, pp. 341–342.
13. Quoted in Raul Hilberg, *The Destruction of the European Jews*, rev. ed. (New York, 1985), vol. 1, pp. 332–333.
14. *Nazi Conspiracy and Aggression*, vol. 6, p. 789.
15. Quoted in John Campbell, *The Experience of World War II* (New York, 1989), p. 170.
16. Quoted in Claudia Koonz, "Mothers in the Fatherland: Women in Nazi Germany," in Renate Bridenthal and Claudia Koonz, eds., *Becoming Visible: Women in European History* (Boston, 1977), p. 466.
17. Quoted in Campbell, *The Experience of World War II*, p. 143.
18. Quoted in ibid., p. 177.
19. Quoted in Robert E. Sherwood, *Roosevelt and Hopkins: An Intimate History* (New York, 1948), p. 870.
20. Quoted in Norman Graebner, *Cold War Diplomacy, 1945–1960* (Princeton, N.J., 1962), p. 117.
21. Quoted in ibid., p. 117.
22. Quoted in Wilfried Loth, *The Division of the World, 1941–1955* (New York, 1988), p. 81.

CHAPTER 28

1. Quoted in Joseph M. Jones, *The Fifteen Weeks (February 21–June 5, 1947)*, 2nd ed. (New York, 1964), pp. 140–141.
2. Quoted in Walter Laqueur, *Europe in Our Time* (New York, 1992), p. 111.
3. Quoted in Wilfried Loth, *The Division of the World, 1941–1955* (New York, 1988), pp. 160–161.
4. Quoted in William I. Hitchcock, *The Struggle for Europe: The Turbulent History of a Divided Continent, 1945–2002* (New York, 2003), p. 215.
5. Quoted in Peter Lane, *Europe Since 1945: An Introduction* (Totowa, N.J., 1985), p. 248.
6. Quoted in Robert F. Kennedy, *Thirteen Days: A Memoir of the Cuban Missile Crisis* (New York, 1969), pp. 89–90.
7. Quoted in Larry Collins and Dominique Lapierre, *Freedom at Midnight* (New York, 1975), p. 252.
8. R. Hilton, *Military Attaché in Moscow* (London, 1949), p. 41.
9. Nikita Khrushchev, *Khrushchev Remembers*, trans. Strobe Talbott (Boston, 1970), p. 77.
10. Quoted in Bonnie G. Smith, *Changing Lives: Women in European History Since 1700* (Lexington, Mass., 1989), p. 513.
11. Quoted in Hilda Scott, *Sweden's "Right to Be Human": Sex-Role Equality—The Goal and the Reality* (London, 1982), p. 125.
12. Simone de Beauvoir, *The Second Sex*, trans. H. M. Parshley (New York, 1961), p. xxviii.
13. Quoted in Henry Grosshans, *The Search for Modern Europe* (Boston, 1970), p. 421.
14. Richard Maltby, ed., *Passing Parade: A History of Popular Culture in the Twentieth Century* (Oxford, 1989), p. 8.
15. Quoted in ibid., p. 11.

CHAPTER 29

1. Quoted in Marsha Rowe et al., *Spare Rib Reader* (Harmondsworth, England, 1982), p. 574.
2. Betty Friedan, *The Feminine Mystique* (New York, 1963), p. 10.
3. Quoted in Tony Judt, *Postwar: A History of Europe Since 1945* (New York, 2005), p. 390.
4. "To Walk the Moon," *New York Times*, July 20, 1969.

CHAPTER 30

1. Quoted in Tony Judt, *Postwar: A History of Europe Since 1945* (New York, 2005), p. 585.
2. Mikhail Gorbachev, "Report to the 27th Party Congress," February 25, 1986, in *Current Soviet Policies* 9 (1986): 10.
3. Quoted in William I. Hitchcock, *The Struggle for Europe: The Turbulent History of a Divided Continent, 1945–2002* (New York, 2003), pp. 399–400.
4. Quoted in Renate Bridenthal, "Women in the New Europe," in Renate Bridenthal, Susan Mosher Stuard, and Merry E. Weisner, eds., *Becoming Visible: Women in European History*, 3rd ed. (Boston, 1998), pp. 564–565.
5. Quoted in Judt, *Postwar Europe*, p. 743.
6. Quoted in Joan W. Scott, *The Politics of the Veil* (Princeton, N.J., 2009), p. 1.
7. Elise Boulding, *Women in the Twentieth-Century World* (New York, 1977), pp. 186–187.

DOCUMENTS

Continued from page xix

CHAPTER 10

CHAPTER 11

CHAPTER 12

OPPOSING VIEWPOINTS: THE RENAISSANCE PRINCE: THE VIEWS OF MACHIAVELLI AND ERASMUS 353

Machiavelli, *The Prince* (1513). From *The Prince* by Machiavelli, translated by David Wootton, pp. 51–52. Copyright © 1995 by Hackett Publishing Company, Inc. Reprinted by permission of Hackett Publishing Company, Inc. All rights reserved.

Erasmas, *Education of a Christian Prince*. From *The Education of a Christian Prince*, by Erasmus, translated by L. K. Born. Copyright © 1936 by Columbia University Press. Reprinted with permission of the publisher.

PETRARCH: MOUNTAIN CLIMBING AND THE SEARCH FOR SPIRITUAL CONTENTMENT 354

From *The Renaissance Philosophy of Man* by Ernst Cassirer, Paul Kristeller, and John Randall, Jr. Copyright © 1948 by University of Chicago Press. Reprinted by permission of the publisher.

PICO DELLA MIRANDOLA AND THE DIGNITY OF MAN 356

From *The Renaissance Philosophy of Man* by Ernst Cassirer, Paul Kristeller, and John Randall, Jr. Copyright © 1948 by University of Chicago Press. Reprinted by permission of the publisher.

A WOMAN'S DEFENSE OF LEARNING 357

Laura Cereta, "Defense of the Liberal Instruction of Women," from *Her Immaculate Hand: Selected Works by and about the Women Humanists of Quattrocentro Italy*, ed. by Margaret King and Albert Rabil (Pegasus Press, Asheville, NC, 2000). Reprinted by permission.

THE GENIUS OF LEONARDO DA VINCI 364

From LIVES OF THE ARTISTS VOLUME I by Giorgio Vasari, translated by George Bull (Penguin Classics, 1965). Translation © George Bull, 1965. Reproduced by permission of Penguin Books, Ltd.

CHAPTER 13

ERASMUS: IN PRAISE OF FOLLY 379

"The Praise of Folly" from THE ESSENTIAL ERASMUS by Erasmus, translated by John P. Dolan, copyright © 1964 by John P. Dolan. Used by permission of Dutton Signet, a division of Penguin Group (USA) Inc.

LUTHER AND THE NINETY-FIVE THESES 382

From *Martin Luther: Documents of Modern History* by E. G. Rupp and Benjamin Drewery. Palgrave Macmillan, 1970. Reproduced with permission of Palgrave Macmillan.

LUTHER AND THE "ROBBING AND MURDERING HORDES OF PEASANTS" 385

From *Martin Luther: Documents of Modern History* by E. G. Rupp and Benjamin Drewery. Palgrave Macmillan, 1970. Reproduced with permission of Palgrave Macmillan.

OPPOSING VIEWPOINTS: A REFORMATION DEBATE: CONFLICT AT MARBURG 391

"The Marburg Colloquy," from GREAT DEBATES OF THE REFORMATION, edited by Donald Ziegler, copyright © 1969 by Donald Ziegler. Used by permission of Modern Library, a division of Random House, Inc.

THE ROLE OF DISCIPLINE IN THE "MOST PERFECT SCHOOL OF CHRIST ON EARTH" 396

From *The Reformation: A Narrative History Related by Contemporary Observers and Participants* by Hans J. Hillerbrand. Copyright © 1964 by Harper & Row, Publishers. Reprinted with permission of Hans J. Hillerbrand.

A PROTESTANT WOMAN 397

From *Not in God's Image: Women in History from the Greeks to Victorians* by Julia O'Faolain and Lauro Martines. Copyright © 1973 by Julia O'Faolain and Lauro Martines. Reprinted by permission of the authors.

LOYOLA AND OBEDIENCE TO "OUR HOLY MOTHER, THE HIERARCHICAL CHURCH" 400

Excerpt from *The Spiritual Exercises of St. Ignatius of Loyola* translated by Louis J. Puhl, S.J. (Newman Press 1951). Reprinted with permission of Loyola Press. To order copies of this book, call 1-800-621-1008 or visit www.loyolabooks.org.

QUEEN ELIZABETH ADDRESSES PARLIAMENT (1601) 408

From *Elizabeth I and Her Parliaments* by John E. Neale. London: Jonathan Cape, 1953.

CHAPTER 14

THE PORTUGUESE CONQUEST OF MALACCA 419

From *The World of Southeast Asia: Selected Historical Readings*, Harry J. Benda and John A. Larkin, eds. Copyright © 1967 by Harper & Row Publishers. Used with permission of John A. Larkin.

COLUMBUS LANDS IN THE NEW WORLD 421

From *Letters by Christopher Columbus*, translated and edited by R. H. Major (London: Hakluyt Society, 1843), pp. 35–43.

THE SPANISH CONQUISTADOR: CORTÉS AND THE CONQUEST OF MEXICO 423

From *The European Reconnaissance: Selected Documents* by John H. Parry. Copyright © 1968 by John H. Parry. Reprinted by permission Walker & Co.

LAS CASAS AND THE SPANISH TREATMENT OF THE AMERICAN NATIVES 425

From *The Tears of the Indians*, Bartolome de Las Casas. Copyright © 1970 by The John Lilburne Company Publishers.

THE ATLANTIC SLAVE TRADE 428

From *European Society in the Eighteenth Century*, ed. Robert and Elborg Forster. New York: Walker & Co., 1969. Reprinted by permission of Walker & Co.

OPPOSING VIEWPOINTS: WEST MEETS EAST: AN EXCHANGE OF ROYAL LETTERS 431

From *The World of Southeast Asia: Selected Historical Readings*, Harry J. Benda and John A. Larkin, eds. Copyright © 1967 by Harper & Row Publishers. Used with permission of John A. Larkin.

AN IMPERIAL EDICT TO THE KING OF ENGLAND 434

From *China's Response to the West: A Documentary Survey, 1839–1923* by Ssu-yu Teng and John K. Fairbank (Cambridge, Mass.: Harvard University Press, 1982).

THE MISSION 438

Excerpt from *Latin American Civilization* by Benjamin Keen, ed. (Boston: Houghton Mifflin, 1974), Vol. I, pp. 223–224. Reprinted by permission of the estate of Benjamin Keen.

CHAPTER 15

A WITCHCRAFT TRIAL IN FRANCE 448

From *Witchcraft in Europe, 1100–1700: A Documentary History* edited by Alan C. Kors and Edward Peters. Copyright © 1972 University of Pennsylvania Press. Reprinted with permission of the University of Pennsylvania Press.

THE FACE OF WAR IN THE SEVENTEENTH CENTURY 453
Excerpt from *The Adventures of Simplicius Simplissimus* by Hans Jacob Christoffel von Grimmelshausen, translated by George Schulz-Behrend, © 1993 Camden House/Boydell & Brewer, Rochester, New York. Reprinted with permission of Camden House Publishers.

TRAVELS WITH THE KING 459
From THE AGE OF MAGNIFICENCE by Sanche de Gramont, copyright © 1964, renewed 1991 by G. P. Putnam's Sons. Used by permission of G. P. Putnam's Sons, a division of Penguin Group (USA), Inc.

PETER THE GREAT DEALS WITH A REBELLION 465
From *Readings in European History,* vol. 2, by James Harvey Robinson (Lexington, Mass.: Ginn and Co., 1906).

OPPOSING VIEWPOINTS: OLIVER CROMWELL: THREE PERSPECTIVES 475
Oliver Cromwell on the Victory at Naseby. Oliver Cromwell on the Massacre at Drogheda. From Thomas Carlyle, ed., *The Letters and Speeches of Oliver Cromwell,* 3 vols. (New York: G. P. Putnam's Sons, 1904), Vol. 1, p. 204, Vol. 3, p. 15.
Edmund Ludlow, *Memoirs*. From C. H. Firth, *The Memoirs of Edmund Ludlow* (Oxford: Oxford University Press, 1894), Vol. 2, pp. 10–11.
Lord Clarendon, *The History of the Rebellion and Civil Wars in England.* From Lord Clarendon, *The History of the Rebellion and Civil Wars in England* (Oxford: Oxford University Press, 1839), Vol. 6, pp. 349–350.

THE BILL OF RIGHTS 478
From *The Statutes: Revised Edition* (London: Eyre and Spottiswoode, 1871), Vol. 2, pp. 10–12.

WILLIAM SHAKESPEARE: IN PRAISE OF ENGLAND 483
Excerpt from *Richard II* in *Shakespeare, The Complete Works,* edited by G. B. Harrison (New York: Harcourt Brace & World, 1952).

CHAPTER 16

***ON THE REVOLUTIONS OF THE HEAVENLY SPHERES* 492**
From *The Collected Works* by Copernicus, translated by Edward Rosen. Rev. ed. published 1978 by Palgrave Macmillan. Reproduced with permission of Palgrave Macmillan.

KEPLER AND THE EMERGING SCIENTIFIC COMMUNITY 494
From *Johannes Kepler, Life and Letters by* Carola Baumgardt, copyright 1951 by the Philosophical Library. Used by permission.

***THE STARRY MESSENGER* 495**
From DISCOVERIES AND OPINIONS OF GALILEO by Galileo Galilei, translated by Stillman Drake, copyright © 1957 by Stillman Drake. Used by permission of Doubleday, a division of Random House, Inc.

OPPOSING VIEWPOINTS: A NEW HEAVEN? FAITH VERSUS REASON 496
Galileo, Letter to the Grand Duchess Christina, 1614. From DISCOVERIES AND OPINIONS OF GALILEO by Galileo Galilei, translated by Stillman Drake, copyright © 1957 by Stillman Drake. Used by permission of Doubleday, a division of Random House, Inc.
Robert Bellarmine, Letter to Paolo Foscarini, 1615. From *Galileo, Science, and the Church* by Jerome J. Langford (New York: Desclee, 1966).

NEWTON'S RULES OF REASONING 498
From Isaac Newton, *The Mathematical Principles of Natural Philosophy,* 2 volumes (London, 1803), vol. 2: pp. 160–62.

THE "NATURAL" INFERIORITY OF WOMEN 503
From *A Political Treatise,* Benedict de Spinoza, copyright 1895 by George Routledge & Sons.

THE FATHER OF MODERN RATIONALISM 505
From *Descartes' Philosophical Writings,* translated by Norman Kemp Smith, copyright © 1958 by Macmillan Education. Reproduced with permission of Palgrave Macmillan.

PASCAL: "WHAT IS A MAN IN THE INFINITE?" 510
From PENSEES by Blaise Pascal, translated with an introduction by A. J. Krailsheimer (Penguin Classics, 1966). Copyright © A. J. Krailsheimer, 1966. Reproduced by permission of Penguin Books Ltd.

CHAPTER 17

THE SEPARATION OF POWERS 518
From *Les Philosophes* by Norman L. Torrey, copyright © 1961 by Norman L. Torrey, G. P. Putnam's Sons, a division of Penguin Putnam, Inc.

THE ATTACK ON RELIGIOUS INTOLERANCE 520
Voltaire, *The Ignorant Philosopher*. From CANDIDE OR OPTIMISM by Voltaire, translated by John Butt (Penguin Classics, 1947). This edition copyright © John Butt, 1947. Reproduced by permission of Penguin Books, Ltd.
Voltaire, *Candide.* From CANDIDE OR OPTIMISM by Voltaire, translated by John Butt (Penguin Classics, 1947). This edition copyright © John Butt, 1947. Reproduced by permission of Penguin Books, Ltd.

DIDEROT QUESTIONS CHRISTIAN SEXUAL STANDARDS 521
From *Rameau's Nephew and Other Works* by Denis Diderot. Copyright © 1956 by Jacques Barzun and Ralph Bowen. Used by permission of Jacques Barzun.

A SOCIAL CONTRACT 524
Extract from A SOCIAL CONTRACT by Jean-Jacques Rousseau translated by Maurice Cranston (translation copyright © Estate Maurice Cranston 1968) is reproduced by permission of PFD (www.pfd.co.uk.) on behalf of the Estate of Maurice Cranston.

OPPOSING VIEWPOINTS: WOMEN IN THE AGE OF THE ENLIGHTENMENT: ROUSSEAU AND WOLLSTONECRAFT 525
Rousseau, *Emile* (1762). Copyright ©1979 Jean-Jacques Rousseau, Michael Wu. Reprinted by permission of Basic Books, a member of the Perseus Books Group.
Mary Wollstonecraft, *Vindication of the Rights of Woman (1792).* From Mary Wollstonecraft, *A Vindication of the Rights of Woman* (1792).

THE PUNISHMENT OF CRIME 533
From *Les Nuits de Paris or Nocturnal Spectator: A Selection,* trans. L. Asher and E. Fertig, pp. 7–8. New York: Knopf, 1964.

THE CONVERSION EXPERIENCE IN WESLEY'S METHODISM 539
From *The Journal of the Reverend John Wesley AM,* vol. 2. J. M. Dent & Sons Ltd., 1920.

CHAPTER 18

THE FRENCH KING'S BEDTIME 545
From *Memoirs of the Comtesse de Boigne.* Ed. M. Charles Nicoullaud. New York: Heinemann, 1907.

FREDERICK THE GREAT AND HIS FATHER 550

From *Readings in European History,* vol. 2, by James Harvey Robinson (Lexington, Mass.: Ginn and Co., 1906).

OPPOSING VIEWPOINTS: ENLIGHTENED ABSOLUTISM: ENLIGHTENED OR ABSOLUTE? 551

Letter of Baron de Breteuil. From G. Vernadsky, *A Source Book for Russian History* (New Haven: Yale University Press, 1972), Vol. 2, p. 451.

Catherine II, Proposals for a New Law Code. From *Documents of Catherine the Great,* W. F. Reddaway © 1931 by Cambridge University Press. Reprinted with permission of Cambridge University Press.

Decree on Serfs. From G. Vernadsky, *A Source Book for Russian History* (New Haven: Yale University Press, 1972), Vol. 2, pp. 453–454.

BRITISH VICTORY IN INDIA 557

From *Readings in European History,* vol. 2, by James Harvey Robinson (Lexington, Mass.: Ginn and Co., 1906).

MARITAL ARRANGEMENTS 559

From *The Rivals* by Richard Sheridan (London, 1775).

PROPAGANDA FOR THE NEW AGRICULTURE 563

Arthur Young, *Travels during the Years, 1787, 1788, and 1789 ... in the Kingdom of France* (London: W. Richardson, 1794).

THE BEGINNINGS OF MECHANIZED INDUSTRY: THE ATTACK ON NEW MACHINES 565

Leeds Woolen Workers' Petition (Leeds, 1786).

POVERTY IN FRANCE 571

From *European Society in the Eighteenth Century* by Robert Forster and Elborg Forster. Copyright © 1969 by Robert and Elborg Forster. Reprinted by permission of Walker & Co.

CHAPTER 19

THE ARGUMENT FOR INDEPENDENCE 577

From *The Federal and State Constitutions,* S. N. Thorpe, compiler and editor, volume 1, pp. 3–4. Washington, D.C., 1909.

THE FALL OF THE BASTILLE 583

From *The Press in the French Revolution: a selection of documents taken from the press of the Revolution for the years 1789–1794.* J. Gilchrist and W. J. Murray, eds. (London: Ginn, 1971).

OPPOSING VIEWPOINTS: THE NATURAL RIGHTS OF THE FRENCH PEOPLE: TWO VIEWS 584

Declaration of the Rights of Man and the Citizen. From *The French Revolution* by Paul H. Beik. Copyright © 1970 by Paul H. Beik. Reprinted by permission of Walker & Co.

Declaration of the Rights of Woman and the Female Citizen. From *Women in Revolutionary Paris, 1789–1795: Selected Documents Translated with Notes and Commentary*. Translated with notes and commentary by Darline Gay Levy, Harriet Branson Applewhite, and Mary Durham Johnson. Copyright 1979 by the Board of Trustees of the University of Illinois. Used with permission of the editors and the University of Illinois Press.

JUSTICE IN THE REIGN OF TERROR 592

From J. M. Thompson, *English Witness of the French Revolution* (Oxford: Blackwell, 1938).

ROBESPIERRE AND REVOLUTIONARY GOVERNMENT 593

From *Robespierre,* edited by George Rudé. Copyright © 1967 by Prentice-Hall, Inc. Reprinted by permission of the Estate of George Rudé.

DE-CHRISTIANIZATION 594

From *The French Revolution* by Paul H. Beik. Copyright © 1970 by Paul H. Beik. Reprinted by permission of Walker & Co.

NAPOLEON AND PSYCHOLOGICAL WARFARE 598

From *A Documentary Survey of the French Revolution* by John Hall Stewart. Copyright © 1951 by Macmillan Publishing Company, renewed 1979 by John Hall Stewart.

CHAPTER 20

THE TRAITS OF THE BRITISH INDUSTRIAL ENTREPRENEUR 609

From *The History of the Cotton Manufacture in Great Britain* by Edward Baines (London: Fisher, Fisher, and Jackson, 1835), pp. 195–96.

DISCIPLINE IN THE NEW FACTORIES 614

From *Documents of European Economic History,* Vol. I by Sidney Pollard & Colin Holmes. Copyright © Sidney Pollard and Colin Holmes. Reproduced with permission of Palgrave Macmillan.

"S-T-E-A-M-BOAT A-COMING!" 620

From *Life on the Mississippi* by Mark Twain. New York, Harper and Brothers, 1911.

THE GREAT IRISH FAMINE 622

From *A History of Ireland under the Union* by P. S. O'Hegarty. Copyright © 1952 by Methuen & Co.

OPPOSING VIEWPOINTS: ATTITUDES OF THE INDUSTRIAL MIDDLE CLASS IN BRITAIN AND JAPAN 626

Samuel Smiles, *Self-Help,* London, 1859.

Shibuzawa Eiichi, *The Autobiography of Shibusawa Eiichi: From Peasant to Entrepreneur*, 1927 (Tokyo: University of Tokyo Press, 1994).

CHILD LABOR: DISCIPLINE IN THE TEXTILE MILLS 628

From *Human Documents of the Industrial Revolution in Britain* by E. Royston Pike. London: Unwin & Hyman, 1966.

CHILD LABOR: THE MINES 629

From *Human Documents of the Industrial Revolution in Britain* by E. Royston Pike. London: Unwin & Hyman, 1966.

CHAPTER 21

THE VOICE OF CONSERVATISM: METTERNICH OF AUSTRIA 639

Reprinted from Klemens von Metternich, *Memoirs,* Alexander Napler, trans. (London: Richard Bentley & Sons, 1881).

UNIVERSITY STUDENTS AND GERMAN UNITY 645

From *Metternich's Europe,* Mack Walker, ed., copyright © 1968 by Mack Walker. Reprinted by permission of Walker & Co.

THE VOICE OF LIBERALISM: JOHN STUART MILL ON LIBERTY 648

From *Utilitarianism, On Liberty, and Representative Government* by John Stuart Mill. Published by Viking Press, 1914.

OPPOSING VIEWPOINTS: RESPONSE TO REVOLUTION: TWO PERSPECTIVES 653

Thomas Babington Macaulay, Speech of March 2, 1831. From *Speeches, Parliamentary and Miscellaneous* by Thomas B. Macaulay (New York: Hurst Co., 1853), vol. 1, pp. 20–21, 25–26.

Carl Schurz, *Reminiscences.* From *The Reminiscences of Carl Schurz* by Carl Schurz (New York: The McClure Co., 1907), vol. I, pp. 112–13.

THE VOICE OF ITALIAN NATIONALISM: GIUSEPPE MAZZINI AND YOUNG ITALY 659

From *Joseph Mazzini: His Life, Writings, and Political Principles* (New York: Hurd & Houghton, 1872), pp. 62–69, 71–74.

THE NEW BRITISH POLICE: "WE ARE NOT TREATED AS MEN" 660
From Clive Emsley, *Policing and Its Context, 1750–1870* (London: Palgrave Macmillan, 1983).

GOTHIC LITERATURE: EDGAR ALLAN POE 663
From *Selected Prose and Poetry,* Edgar Allan Poe. New York: Holt, Rinehart, and Winston, 1950.

CHAPTER 22

OPPOSING VIEWPOINTS: THE PRACTICE OF *REALPOLITIK:* TWO APPROACHES 672
Louis Napoleon, *Proclamation to the People* (1851). From *The Constitutions and Other Select Documents Illustrative of the History of France 1789–1907*, by Frank Maloy Anderson (Minneapolis: H. W. Wilson, 1904).
Bismarck, *Speech to the Prussian Reichstag,* 1862. From Louis L. Snyder, *Documents of German History* (Rutgers University Press, 1958), p. 202.
Bismarck, *Speech to the German Reichstag,* 1888. From Brian Tierney and Joan Scott, eds., *Western Societies: A Documentary History,* Vol. 2 (Alfred Knopf, 1984), p. 366.

GARIBALDI AND ROMANTIC NATIONALISM 678
From the *Times* of London, June 13, 1860.

EMANCIPATION: SERFS AND SLAVES 686
Tsar Alexander II, Imperial Decree, March 3, 1861. From *Annual Register* (New York: Longmans, Green, 1861), p. 207.
President Abraham Lincoln, Emancipation Proclamation, January 1, 1863. From *U. S. Statutes at Large* (Washington, D.C., Government Printing Office, 1875), vol. 12, pp. 1268–69.

THE CLASSLESS SOCIETY 693
From *The Communist Manifesto* by Karl Marx and Frederick Engels, trans. Samuel Moore, 1888.

DARWIN AND THE DESCENT OF MAN 695
From *The Descent of Man* by Charles Darwin (New York: Appleton, 1876), pp. 606–607, 619.

ANESTHESIA AND MODERN SURGERY 697
From *The History of Medicine in the United States: A Collection of Facts and Figures* by Francis Randolph Packard (Philadelphia: Lippincott, 1901).

REALISM: CHARLES DICKENS AND AN IMAGE OF HELL ON EARTH 700
From Charles Dickens, *The Old Curiosity Shop* (London: Chapman & Hall, 1841).

CHAPTER 23

THE DEPARTMENT STORE AND THE BEGINNINGS OF MASS CONSUMERISM 707
From *Documents of European Economic History,* Vol. I by Sidney Pollard & Colin Holmes. Copyright © Sidney Pollard and Colin Holmes. Reproduced with permission of Palgrave Macmillan.

THE VOICE OF EVOLUTIONARY SOCIALISM: EDUARD BERNSTEIN 713
From Eduard Bernstein, *Evolutionary Socialism*, Edith C. Harney, trans. (New York: B. W. Huebsch, 1911), pp. x–xii, xiv.

THE HOUSING VENTURE OF OCTAVIA HILL 718
From Octavia Hill, *Homes of the London Poor* (New York: Macmillan, 1875), pp. 15–16, 17–18, 23.

OPPOSING VIEWPOINTS: ADVICE TO WOMEN: TWO VIEWS 721
Elizabeth Poole Sanford, *Woman in Her Social and Domestic Character.* From Elizabeth Poole Sanford, *Woman, in Her Social and Domestic Character* (Boston: Otis, Broaders & Co., 1842), pp. 5–7, 15–16.
Henrik Ibsen, *A Doll's House.* Excerpt as appeared in *Roots of Western Civilization* by Wesley D. Camp (Wiley, 1983).

THE FIGHT SONG: SPORTS IN THE ENGLISH PUBLIC SCHOOLS 728
From *Athleticism in the Victorian and Edwardian Public School* by J. A. Mangan (Cambridge University Press, 1981).

A LEADER OF THE PARIS COMMUNE 731
From Louise Michel, THE RED VIRGIN: MEMOIRS OF LOUISE MICHEL, pp. 64, 68, trans. by Bullitt Lowry and Elizabeth Ellington Gunter (University of Alabama Press, 1981). Reprinted by permission of University of Alabama Press.

BISMARCK AND THE WELFARE OF THE WORKERS 733
From *Bismarck,* edited by Frederick B. M. Hollyday, pp. 60, 63, 65. Copyright © 1970 by Prentice-Hall, Inc.

CHAPTER 24

FREUD AND THE CONCEPT OF REPRESSION 741
From *Five Lectures on Psycho-analysis* by Sigmund Freud, translated by James Strachey. Copyright © 1961 by James Strachey. Used by permission of W. W. Norton & Company, Inc. and Sigmund Freud Copyrights Ltd.

SYMBOLIST POETRY: ART FOR ART'S SAKE 744
"The Drunken Boat" by Arthur Rimbaud from *Realism, Naturalism, Symbolism: Modes of Thought and Expression in Europe* by Roland Stromberg. English translation copyright © 1968 by Roland Stromberg. Reprinted by permission of the Estate of Roland Stromberg.

THE STRUGGLE FOR THE RIGHT TO VOTE 750
From Emmeline Pankhurst, *My Own Story* (New York: Hearst International Library, 1914).

THE VOICE OF ZIONISM: THEODOR HERZL AND THE JEWISH STATE 754
From Theodor Herzl, *The Jewish State*. Trans. Sylvia d'Avigdor. 3rd edition (New York: Federation of American Zionists, 1917), pp. 7–8, 11, 12.

BLOODY SUNDAY 757
From George Gapon, *The Story of My Life* (New York: Dutton, 1906), pp. 182–85.

OPPOSING VIEWPOINTS: WHITE MAN'S BURDEN VERSUS BLACK MAN'S BURDEN 760
Rudyard Kipling, *The White Man's Burden.* From *Rudyard Kipling's Verse* (Garden City, N.Y.: Doubleday, 1919), pp. 371–72.
Edward Morel, *The Black Man's Burden.* From E. D. Morel, *The Black Man's Burden: The White Man in Africa from the Fifteenth Century to World War I* (London: National Labour Press, 1920).

THE EMPEROR'S BIG MOUTH 770
From *The Daily Telegraph,* London, October 28, 1908.

CHAPTER 25

"YOU HAVE TO BEAR THE RESPONSIBILITY FOR WAR OR PEACE" 779

From *Diplomatic Documents Relating to the Outbreak of the European War*. Ed. James Brown Scott (New York: Oxford University Press, 1916).

THE EXCITEMENT OF WAR 781

Stefan Zweig, *The World of Yesterday*. From THE WORLD OF YESTERDAY by Stefan Zweig, translated by Helmut Ripperger, copyright 1943 by the Viking Press, Inc. Used by permission of Viking Penguin, a division of Penguin Group (USA) Inc. and by permission of Williams Verlag AG.

Robert Graves, *Goodbye to All That*. From Robert Graves, *Good-Bye to All That* (London: Jonathan Cape, 1929).

Walter Limmer, Letter to His Parents. From Jon E. Lewis, ed., *The Mammoth Book of Eyewitness: World War I* (New York: Caroll and Graf Publishers, an imprint of Avalon Publishing Group, 2003), p. 24.

THE REALITY OF WAR: TRENCH WARFARE 786

Reproduced by permission of the Estate of the Late Paulette Goddard Remarque.

THE SONGS OF WORLD WAR I 789

"Die Wacht am Rhein (The Watch on the Rhine)," Max Schneckenburger, 1840; "The Old Barbed Wire," lyrics anonymous; "Over There," George M. Cohan, 1917.

WOMEN IN THE FACTORIES 795

From "Munition Work" by Naomi Loughnan, in *Women War Workers,* edited by Gilbert Stone (London: George Harrap and Company, 1917), pp. 25, 35–38.

WAR AND THE FAMILY 796

Personal Letters of Reginald B. Mott family.

SOLDIER AND PEASANT VOICES 801

From *Voices of Revolution,* 1917 by Mark D. Steinberg. Copyright © 2001 Yale University Press. Reprinted by permission.

OPPOSING VIEWPOINTS: THREE VOICES OF PEACEMAKING 806

Georges Clemenceau, *Grandeur and Misery of Victory*. From Georges Clemenceau, *Grandeur and Misery of Victory* (New York: Harcourt, 1930), pp. 105, 107, 280.

Pan-African Congress. Excerpts from Resolution from the Pan-African Congress, Paris, 1919.

CHAPTER 26

THE GREAT DEPRESSION: UNEMPLOYED AND HOMELESS IN GERMANY 817

From *Living Age*, Vol. 344, no. 4398 (March 1933), pp. 27–31, 34–38.

THE STRUGGLES OF A DEMOCRACY: UNEMPLOYMENT AND SLUMS IN GREAT BRITAIN 818

Men Without Work: A Report to the Pilgrim Trust, 1938. From *Men without Work: A Report Made to the Pilgrim Trust* (Cambridge: Cambridge University Press, 1938).

George Orwell, "A Woman in the Slums." From George Orwell, The Road to Wigan Pier (London: Victor Gollancz, 1937).

THE VOICE OF ITALIAN FASCISM 825

Reprinted by permission of the publisher from *International Conciliation,* No. 306 (Washington, D.C., Carnegie Endowment for International Peace, 1935), pp. 5–17. www.carnegieendowment.org.

ADOLF HITLER'S HATRED OF THE JEWS 827

From MEIN KAMPF by Adolf Hitler, translated by Ralph Manheim. Copyright © 1943, renewed 1971 by Houghton Mifflin Company. Reprinted by permission of Houghton Mifflin Harcourt Company. All rights reserved.

PROPAGANDA AND MASS MEETINGS IN NAZI GERMANY 830

Adolf Hitler, Speech at the Nuremberg Party Rally, 1936.

A Teacher's Impression of a Hitler Rally, 1932. From Louise Solmitz, "Diary," trans. and quoted in Jeremy Noakes and Geoffrey Pridham, *Documents on Nazism, 1919–45* (New York: Viking, 1974), p. 161. Reprinted by permission of Peters Fraser and Dunlop on behalf of Jeremy Noakes and Geoffrey Pridham.

THE FORMATION OF COLLECTIVE FARMS 835

From Fedor Belov, *The History of a Soviet Collective Farm* (New York: Frederick A. Praeger, Inc., 1955). Reproduced with permission of Greenwood Publishing Group, Inc., Westport, CT.

OPPOSING VIEWPOINTS: SPAIN DIVIDED: THE POEMS OF TWO BROTHERS 837

Reprinted by permission of the publisher from ANTONIO MACHADO: SELECTED POEMS, translated by Alan S. Trueblood, pp. 263, 265, Cambridge, Mass.: Harvard University Press, Copyright © 1982 by the President and Fellows of Harvard College.

HESSE AND THE UNCONSCIOUS 846

From *Demian* by Hermann Hesse (New York: Bantam Books, 1966), p. 30.

CHAPTER 27

HITLER'S FOREIGN POLICY GOALS 851

Excerpts from *Hitler's Secret Book* by Adolf Hitler, copyright © 1961 by Grove Press, copyright renewed © 1989 by Grove Press, Inc. Used with permission of Grove/Atlantic Inc.

OPPOSING VIEWPOINTS: THE MUNICH CONFERENCE: TWO VIEWS 855

Winston Churchill, Speech to the House of Commons, October 5, 1938. From *Parliamentary Debates, House of Commons* (London: His Majesty's Stationery Office, 1938), vol. 339, pp. 361–369.

Neville Chamberlain, Speech to the House of Commons, October 6, 1938. From Neville Chamberlain, *In Search of Peace* (New York: Putnam, 1939), pp. 213–215, 217.

A GERMAN SOLDIER AT STALINGRAD 863

From Vaili Chuikov, *The Battle for Stalingrad* (Grafton Books / HarperCollins UK), 1964.

HITLER'S PLANS FOR A NEW ORDER IN THE EAST 866

From *Hitler's Secret Conversations 1941–1944* by Hugh Trevor-Roper (New York: Farrar, Straus & Young, 1953).

THE HOLOCAUST: THE CAMP COMMANDANT AND THE CAMP VICTIMS 872

From *Nazism 1919–1945: A Documentary Reader, Vol. 3: Foreign Policy, War and Racial Extermination.* Edited by J. Noakes and G. Pridham, new edition, 2001 pp. 590–592. Reprinted by permission of University of Exeter Press.

THE BOMBING OF CIVILIANS 876

From John Campbell, ed. *The Experience of World War II* (New York: Oxford University Press, 1989), p. 180.

EMERGENCE OF THE COLD WAR: CHURCHILL AND STALIN 882

From the Congressional Record, 79th Congress, 2nd Session, A (Washington, D.C.: U.S. Government Printing Office), pp. 1145–1147.

CHAPTER 28

OPPOSING VIEWPOINTS: WHO STARTED THE COLD WAR? AMERICAN AND SOVIET PERSPECTIVES 887

Origins of the Cold War: The Novikov, Kennan, and Roberts 'Long' Telegrams of 1946. (Kenneth M. Jensen, editor) Washington, DC: Endowment of the United States Institute of Peace, 1993. pp. 20–21, 28–31, 8, 16. Reprinted with permission.

THE TRUMAN DOCTRINE 888

Reprinted from the Congressional Record, 80th Congress, 1st Session (Washington, D.C.: U.S. Government Printing Office), Vol. 93, p. 1981.

THE CUBAN MISSILE CRISIS FROM KHRUSHCHEV'S PERSPECTIVE 894

From Strobe Talbot, ed., *Khrushchev Remembers,* copyright © Andrew Numberg Associates. Reprinted by permission.

FRANTZ FANON AND THE WRETCHED OF THE EARTH 897

"Colonial War and Mental Disorders, Series B" from *The Wretched of the Earth* by Frantz Fanon, copyright © 1993 by Presence Africaine. Translation copyright © 2004 by Richard Philcox. Used by permission of Grove/Atlantic, Inc.

KHRUSHCHEV DENOUNCES STALIN 901

Reprinted from the Congressional Record, 84th Congress, 2nd Session (Washington, D.C.: U.S. Government Printing Office), Vol. 102, Part 7, pp. 9389–9402.

SOVIET REPRESSION IN EASTERN EUROPE: HUNGARY, 1956 904

From the Department of State *Bulletin,* Nov. 12, 1956, pp. 746–47.

THE VOICE OF THE WOMEN'S LIBERATION MOVEMENT 913

From THE SECOND SEX by Simone de Beauvior, translated by Constance Borde and Sheila Malovany-Chevallier, translation copyright © 2009 by Constance Borde and Sheila Malovany-Chevallier. Introduction copyright © 2010 by Judith Thurman. Used by permission of Alfred A. Knopf, a division of Random House, Inc.

CHAPTER 29

"THE TIMES THEY ARE A-CHANGIN'": THE MUSIC OF YOUTHFUL PROTEST 923

Copyright © 1963; renewed 1991 by Special Rider Music. All rights reserved. International copyright secured. Reprinted by permission.

1968: THE YEAR OF STUDENT REVOLTS 924

Reprinted from *Student Protest* by Gerald F. McGuigan. Copyright © 1968 by Methuen & Co., Publishers.

OPPOSING VIEWPOINTS: CZECHOSLOVAKIA, 1968: TWO FACES OF COMMUNISM 928

Two Thousand Words Manifesto. Used with permission of Central European Press, from THE PRAGUE SPRING 1968, Jaromir Navratil, 1998; permission conveyed through Copyright Clearance Center, Inc.

A Letter to Czechoslovakia. From "A Letter to Czechoslovakia," *Moscow News,* Supplement to N. 30917 (1968), pp. 3–6.

MARGARET THATCHER: ENTERING A MAN'S WORLD 930

Pages 62–65 from THE PATH TO POWER by Margaret Thatcher. Copyright © 1995 by Margaret Thatcher. Reprinted by permission of HarperCollins Publishers and HarperCollins Publishers Ltd.

THE FURY OF THE RED GUARDS 936

From *Life and Death in Shanghai* by Nien Cheng. Copyright © 1986 by Nien Cheng. Reprinted by permission of Grove/Atlantic, Inc.

THE LIMITS OF MODERN TECHNOLOGY 939

Reuse of excerpt from SMALL IS BEAUTIFUL: ECONOMICS AS IF PEOPLE MATTERED by E.F. SCHUMACHER. Copyright © 1973 by E.F. Schumacher. Reprinted by permission of HarperCollins Publishers.

GRANDMASTER FLASH AND THE FURIOUS FIVE: "THE MESSAGE" 943

"The Message" by Clifton Chase, Edward Fletcher, Melvin Glover, and Sylvia Robinson. Performed by Grandmaster Flash and the Furious Five. Copyright © 1982 E/A Music, Inc. and Grandmaster Flash Publishing Inc. Print rights administered by Sugar Hill Music Publishing, Ltd.

CHAPTER 30

GORBACHEV AND *PERESTROIKA* 950

Pages 140–141, 253–254 from PERESTROIKA by MIKHAIL GORBACHEV. Copyright © 1987 by Mikhail Gorbachev. Reprinted by permission of HarperCollins Publishers.

VACLAV HAVEL: THE CALL FOR A NEW POLITICS 953

From *The Washington Post,* February 22, 1990, p. 28d.

A CHILD'S ACCOUNT OF THE SHELLING OF SARAJEVO 956

From *Zlata's Diary* by Zlata Filipovic, copyright © 1994 by Fixot et editions Robert Laffont. Used by permission of Viking Penguin, a division of Penguin Putnam, Inc.

OPPOSING VIEWPOINTS: ISLAM AND THE WEST: SECULARISM IN FRANCE 969

French President Jacques Chirac on Secularism in French Society. From "France's President Lays Out His Views on the Principle of Secularism in the French State—In Schools and the Public Sector," from http://news.bbc.co.uk/go/em/fr/-2/hi/europe/3330679.stm.

North African Women in France Respond to the Headscarf Affair. Caitlin Killian, GENDER AND SOCIETY, Vol. 17, No. 4, pp. 567–590, copyright © 2003 by SAGE Publications. Reprinted by Permission of SAGE Publications.

POPE JOHN PAUL II: AN APPEAL FOR PEACE 971

From *John Paul II and the Laity,* edited by Leonard Doohan (The Jesuit Educational Center for Human Development; published by Le Jacq Publishing, Inc., 1984), pp. 48–50. Reprinted by permission of Human Development.

A WARNING TO HUMANITY 977

World Scientists' Warning to Humanity, 1992. Union of Concerned Scientists. 1992. World Scientists Warning to Humanity. Excerpt. Cambridge, MA: UCS. Online at www.ucsusa.org

Findings of the IPCC Fourth Assessment Report, 2007. Reprinted with permission from Union of Concerned Scientists. 1992. World Scientists Warning to Humanity. Excerpt. Cambridge, MA: UCS. Online at www.ucsusa.org.

INDEX

Italicized page numbers show the locations of illustrations and maps.

Engineering: Inca, 424; in Rome, 134, 162
England (Britain), 931; agriculture in, 561–562, *562*; Allied war conferences and, 879–880; American colonies of, 436, 545; American Revolution and, 575, *576*; Anglo-Saxons in, 190, 232–233; appeasement policy of, 852; Black Death in, 308; Canada and, 689–690; China and, 433; cities in, 622–623; civil wars in, 275, 367–369, 473–476; conservatism in, 643–644; Crimean War and, 674–675; decolonization and, 895, 896, 898, 899; economy in, 685, 818, 906–907, 930; exploration by, 414; factory acts in, 630–631; Falklands War and, 930; financing in, 562–563; foreign policy of, 408–409; in 14th century, 312; France and, 315, 601–602; French American possessions to, 461; Glorious Revolution in, 477; government of, 233, 608–609; Great Depression in, 818–819; Greece and, 643; in High Middle Ages, 274–278; holdings of (1154–1337), *279*; Huguenots in, 457; Hundred Years' War and, 315–319; immigrants in, 967; imperialism of, 429, 762, 763, 764, *764, 765,* 768; imports of, 443; India and, 432, 441, 763, 764, 768, 820–821, 898; Industrial Revolution in, 564, 608–616, *612*; Ireland and, 474, 475, 729–730, 754–755; Irish missionaries in, 197–198; Jews in, 295, 297; Latin America and, 642, 643; law in, 275; liberalism in, 753–755; Lollardy in, 370; magazines in, 532; megaliths in, *28,* 28–30; Middle East and, 785; military alliances of, 892; monarchy in, 477, 544–546; Monroe Doctrine and, 643; Napoleon and, 598, 601–602; in NATO, 890; navy of, 461, 601–602, 643; since 1980s, 959; Norman conquest of, 274–275, *275*; at Paris Peace Conference, 805; Peasants' Revolt (1381) in, 313–314; police in, 659–661, *662*; population of, 558, 621; Protestant revivalism in, 538–539; Quadruple Alliance and, 637, 640; reform in, 652–654, 729–730; religion in, 392–394, 407–408; restoration in, 476–477; Rome and, 156; sciences in, 497; in Second Industrial Revolution, 708; in Seven Years' War, 555–557; in South Africa, 762; Southeast Asia trade and, 429; Spanish Armada and, 409–410; Suez crisis and, 897–898; suffragists in, 749–750, *751*; textile industry in, 690; Thirty Years' War and, 450; trade unions in, 631, 713; transportation in, 611–612; Triple Entente and, 770; in United Kingdom, 544; universities in, 262; Victorian Age in, 685–688; Viking attacks on, 227–228, *228*; after War of the Spanish Succession, 461; welfare state in, 906; women in, 793–794, 912; World War I and, 792, 808, 817–818; World War II and, 873. *See also* Stuart dynasty; Tudor dynasty; World War I; World War II; specific rulers
English Football Association, 727, *728*
English language, 232–233, 275
English Royal Society. *See* Royal Society (England)
Enki (god), 13
Enkidu, 14
Enlightened absolutism, 543, 551, 554
Enlightenment, 441, 513–514, *517,* 647; American Revolution and, 578; arts in, 526–531; culture and society in, 526–536; families and, 559–560; Jews and Muslims in, 538; later period in, 522; philosophes in, 513, 516–524; politics and, 542–543; revolutions and, 578; science in, 514–515, *515*; social status and, 565–566; travel literature in, 515–516; women in, 523–524. *See also* Scientific Revolution
Enlil (god), 13
Entertainment: in amusement parks, 704; in Egypt, 27–28; in Middle Ages, 336, *336*; in 1920s, 839–840
Entrepreneurs, 260, 343, 705; industrial, 608, 609, 625–627
Enuma elish (Babylonian creation epic), 12
Environment, 215, 938–939, 962; Enlightenment view of, 516; globalization and crisis in, 976, 977–978; of medieval cities, 258, 260. *See also* Climate; Pollution
Environmental Protection Agency, 941
Epaminondas (Thebes), 76
Ephesus, 157
Epic literature: of Homer, 58, 59
Epic of Gilgamesh, The, 13, 14, 17
Epicureanism, 107, 109, 144
Epicurus, 107, *108,* 143
Epicycles: of planetary bodies, 489–490
Epidaurus, miraculous cures at, 108
Epidemics, 621, 717. *See also* Disease
Epirus, 120
Epistle to the Colossians (Paul), 176
Equality: in France, 595, 600, 644; in Soviet Union, 835; of women, 524, 651, 924
Equal rights amendment (U.S.), 924
Equestrians (Rome), 135, 138, 151
Equites (equestrians) (Rome). *See* Equestrians
Erasistratus, 106
Erasmus, Desiderius, 353, 377–378, *378,* 379, 380
Eratosthenes, 105
Erechtheum (Greek temple), 79
Eretria, 68
Erhard, Ludwig, 906
Eridu, 7
Erik the Red, 229
Eroica symphony (Beethoven), 666
Esarhaddon (Assyria), 41
Essay Concerning Human Understanding (Locke), 516
Essay on the Principles of Population (Malthus), 647
Essenes, 171
Estates (land): in Rome, 129–130
Estates (political): in Denmark, 467
Estates (social orders), 312, 344; in France, 578–580, *579*; in Renaissance, 344–345
Estates-General: in France, 279, 321–323, 366, 581
Este family (Ferrara), 349; Isabella d', 349, 350
Estonia, 466, 807, 949, 954, 960
Ethelbert (England), 198
Ether, in surgery, 697
Ethics Demonstrated in the Geometrical Manner (Spinoza), 509
Ethiopia, 762, 763, 768, 852
Ethnic cleansing, by Serbs, 955
Ethnic groups. *See* Ethnic cleansing; Minorities; Nationalities; specific groups and locations
Etruria, 114, 116, 123, 159
Etruscans, 113, 114–116, *115,* 120
EU. *See* European Union (EU)
Eucharist, 173, 292, 329
Euclid, 105, 263
Eumenides (Aeschylus), 77
Euphrates River region, 6, 7
Eurasia, Mongols and, 306, 307–308
Euripides, 77–78, 355, 484
Euro, 960, 976
Eurocommunism, 931
Europa, Europa (movie), 869
Europe: in 15th century, *367*; in 1763, *547*; in 1871, *683*; in 1914, *777*; in 1919, *808*; alliances in (1950s–1960s), *891*; American empires of, 435–436; American Revolution and, 578; in Asia, 429–435, *430*; Black Death in, 308–312; changes in central (1936–1939), *854*; coalition against French Revolution, 589; after Congress of Vienna (1815), *638*; Continental industrialization in, 616–618, *617*; economic zones in, 708; English industrialization in, 608–616; environment in, 215; industry and, 563–565, *709*; kingdoms in, 274–286; lords and vassals in, 229–235; New Europe (1980s), *949*; population in 17th century, 447; religious populations in 18th century, *537*; Renaissance monarchies in, 366–370; in Seven Years' War, 555–556, 557; southeastern, *371*; state system and, 543; trade within, 564; unification of, 960–961, *961*; after World War II, 885–886, 909–913. *See also* specific countries and regions
European Atomic Energy Community (EURATOM), 907
European Central Bank, 960
European Coal and Steel Community (ECSC), 907
European Community (EC), 931, 959. *See also* European Union (EU)
European Economic Community (EEC, Common Market), 907, *907,* 931
European Parliament, 960
European Recovery Program. *See* Marshall Plan
European Union (EU), 954, *961*; bailout of Greece, 959, 960; eastern European states in, 960–961; identity and, 960; Muslims in, 968
Evangelicalism, 661, 743; of Lutheranism, 384; of Zwingli, 384
Evans, Arthur, 55
Evolution, Darwin on, 694–695, 968
Evolutionary socialism, 712, 713
Evolutionary Socialism (Bernstein), 712, 713
Exchange Bank of Amsterdam, 471
Exchange between Pliny and Trajan, An, 174
Exchequer (England), 275
Excommunication, 288
Executions: in 18th century, 533; in Middle Ages, 259, *259*
Existentialism, 913, 915, 939
Exodus, 36, 37
Expansion, 414–415; of Amsterdam, 471; of Carolingian Empire, 215–217; economy and, 440–441, 442–443; during French Revolution, *591*; Hitler and, 850; impact of European, 437–441; of Islam, 208–211, *210,* 238–241; of Rome, 120–121, 156; by Russia, 466, *467,* 552; by Venice, 325. *See also* Colonies and colonization; Exploration; Imperialism; New Imperialism
Exploration: in 15th and 16th centuries, *417*; of New World, 419–425; Portuguese, 416–419; of space, 937, *938*; Spanish, 419–425. *See also* Colonies and colonization
Exports, 443; of grain, 100; from Latin America, 643
Expressionism: German, 842
Extended family: Carolingian, 221
Extermination camps. *See* Death camps

Fabian Socialists, 753
Fabius, Quintus Maximus, 123
Facebook, 972

Long Parliament, 473
Long Telegram, The (Kennan), 887
Looms, 564
Lope de Vega, Félix, 484
Lorca, Federico García, 837
Lord Protector (England), 474
Lords, 229–235, 231, 247, 566. *See also* Nobility
Lord's Supper, 173, 386, 392, 395. *See also* Eucharist
Lorraine, 460, 681, 807. *See also* Alsace-Lorraine
"Lost generation," 804, 813
Lothar, 225
Loughnan, Naomi, 795
Louis VII (France), 302
Louis IX (Saint Louis, France), 278, *278*, 302
Louis XI ("Spider" king, France), 366
Louis XIII (France), 451, 454, *455*
Louis XIV (France), 446, *446*, 459, 542, 544; absolutism of, 454, 455–461; letters to king of Tonkin, 431; parlements and, 580; religious minorities and, 536; Royal Academy of Sciences and, 508; Versailles court of, 455, 458–459, 567; wars of, 459–461, *460*
Louis XVI (France), 544, 545; execution of, 588, *588*; French Revolution and, 574, 587; National Assembly and, 582
Louis XVIII (France), 604, 637, 644
Louisbourg, 555, 556
Louis Napoleon. *See* Napoleon III (France)
Louis of Hungary, 388
Louis-Philippe (France), *651*, 652, 655
Louis the German, 225, *225*
Louis the Pious, 220, 224–225
Louvois, marquis de (François-Michel Le Tellier), 460, 466
"Love-in," *922*
Low Countries, 308, 369, 616. *See also* Belgium; Netherlands
Lower Austria, 463
Lower classes, 151, 454, 559, 661, 720, 910. *See also* Classes
Lower Egypt, 19
Loyalists: in American Revolution, 575
Loyola, Ignatius of (Saint), 400, *401*
LSD, 921
Lübeck, *343*, 451
Lucretia, rape of, 116
Lucretius, 143–144
Luddites, 632
Ludendorff, Erich, 783, 791–792, *792*, 803
Ludlow, Edmund, 475
Lueger, Karl, 752
Luftwaffe, 852, 858, 876
Luke: Gospel of, 198
Lusitania (ship), 790
Lussault, Françoise, 403
Luther (movie), 383
Luther, Martin, *376*, 376–377, 380–383, 646; on education, 398; marriage of, 396; Peasants' War and, 385–386; Zwingli and, 390, 391
Lutheranism, 383–386; in 18th century, 536; in Netherlands, 405; in Scandinavia, 389; spread of, 384–386
Luther Versus the Pope, 384
Lützen, Battle of, 451
Luxembourg, 369, 406, 858, 890, 907
Luxemburg, Rosa, 804
Luxor, temple center at, 23
Luxury goods, 235, 458, 631
Lycurgus (Greece), 63, 64, 85
Lydia, 48, 49, 82
Lyons, 589, 590
Lysistrata (Aristophanes), 78
Maastricht Treaty, 960
Ma'at (Egyptian principle), 18, *20*
MacArthur, Douglas, 864, 892
Macartney (Lord), China trade and, 433, 434
Macaulay, Thomas Babington, 653
Maccabaeus, Judas, 110
MacDonald, Ramsay, 818
Macedonia, 55, 90, 771, 954, 957; Alexander the Great and, 26, 89, 91–96; Antigonid kingdom in, 96, 97; Celts and, 98; Persia and, 68; Philip II of, 55, 76, 89; Rome and, 124
Macedonian dynasty, as Byzantine emperors, 235–237, 297
Machado, Antonio, 837
Machado, Manuel, 837
Machiavelli, Niccolò, *351*, 351–352, 353
Machine gun, 763, 784, *784*, *785*, 791
Machinery, 616, 618, 708
Madagascar Plan, 868
Madame Bovary (Flaubert), 698
Madison, James, 518, 658
Madras (Chennai), 432, 555
Madrid: terrorism in, 965
Madrigals, 365–366
Mafia, 931
Magazines, 532, 727, 785
Magellan, Ferdinand, *413*, 413–414, 420, 429
Magenta, battle at, 677
Maghreb, 969
Magi, 355
Magic, 224, 489, 491
Magic Flute, The (Mozart), 529
"Magic realism," 941
Maginot Line, 858
Magistrates (Rome), 116, 117, 118, 126, 127, 135
Magna Carta, 276–277
Magyar language (Hungary), 733
Magyars, 226–227, 232, 284, 682, 733, 756
Maimonides, Moses, *38*, 263–264
Maine, France, 276, 278, 366
Mainz: Jews of, 295
Maistre, Joseph de, 639–640
Maize. *See* Corn
Major, John, 959
Major domus (mayor of the palace), 189
Malacca, 401, 418–419, 429
Malaya, 856, 857
Malay States, 764
Malay world, 429, 430
Malcolm X, 908–909
Mallarmé, Stéphane, 748
Mallians, 95
Malnutrition, 307
Malta, 29, 960
Malthus, Thomas, 647, 694
Al-Ma'mun, 239, 241
Man and Woman Gazing at the Moon (Friedrich), 664, *664*
Manchester, demonstration in (1819), 644
Manchu dynasty (China), 433, 764, 766
Manchukuo, 856
Manchuria, 433, 764, 813, 856, 879
Mandates, 808, 820, 896
Mandela, Nelson, 895–896
Manetho (Egypt), 17
Manhattan Project, 874
Mannerism, 479–480
Mantua, 349, 355, 356, 463
Manufacturing: on Continent, 618; in France, 458; industrialization and, 563; in medieval cities, 258–260; trade and, 159; in World War II, 873. *See also* Industry; specific countries
Manuscripts, Carolingian, *219*, 219–220
Many Happy Returns of the Day (Frith), *724*
Manzikert, battle at, 297
Mao Zedong, 892, 899–900, 935, 936
Mapplethorpe, Robert, 971
Maps, 415, *416*, 441, *441*
Marathon, Battle of, 48, 68, 70, *70*
Marburg Colloquy, 390, 391
Marcel, Étienne, 323
Marcella (Rome), 200
March on Washington, 908
March Revolution (Russia), 797–799
Marconi, Guglielmo, 705, 839
Marcus Aurelius (Rome), 155, 167, 169
Marcuse, Herbert, 923
Marduk (god), 45
Mariana Islands, 856
Maria Theresa (Austria), 549, *549*, 555
Marie Antoinette (France), 544, *549*, 589
Marie Antoinette (movie), 546
Marijuana, 921
Marius (Rome), 126, 136–137
Mark: Gospel of, 195
Markets: for British products, 609–610; in Champagne, 253–254; in 18th century, *570*; industrial production and, 706–708; transportation and, 611
Marlborough, duke of (Charles Spencer-Churchill), 720
Marlborough, duke of (John Churchill), 461
Marne: First Battle of, 782; Second Battle of, 803
Marriage, 292; age at, 249–250, 561; in aristocracy, 252, *252*, 719–720; Aristotle on, 80; arranged, 559; Carolingian, 220–221; clerical, 393; in Egypt, 26–27; in 18th century, 560–561; Frankish, 190–192; Habsburg dynastic, 369; Hammurabi's Code and, 11; Hebrew, 39; in Islam, 208; in late 1800s, 720–722; Luther on, 382, 386; in Middle Ages, 334; Protestantism and, 396–397; in Renaissance Italy, 345, 346; in Rome, 118, 130
Marriage of Figaro, The (Mozart), 529
Married Love (Stopes), 842
Mars (god), 127, 170
"Marseillaise," 587
Marseilles, 589, 590
Marshall, George C., 888
Marshall, John, 608, 658
Marshall Islands, 856
Marshall Plan, 888, 904, 907
Marsiglio of Padua, 328
Martin V (Pope), 328
Martinique, 435
Martyrdom of Saint Sebastian, The (Pollaiuolo), 358–359
Martyrs: Christian, 175
Marx, Karl, and Marxism, 650, *691*, 691–692, 693, 711, 712, 799
Marxist Social Democratic Labor Party (Russia), 712
Mary. *See* Virgin Mary
Mary, queen of Scots, 407–408, 472
Mary (Burgundy), marriage of, 369
Mary I (England), 393–394, 407
Mary II (England), 477, 478
Masaccio, 358, *359*
Masaryk, Thomas, 836
Masons, 526
Mass (Catholic Church), 916
Massachusetts, 436, 619
Massagetae, 47
Mass consumerism, 707, 910
Mass culture, expansion of, 838–842, 845
Mass education, 725–727, 738
Massive retaliation policy, 892
Mass leisure, 704, 727–729, 840–842, 910

Missile gap, 893
Missiles, 893
Mission, The (movie), 439
Missions and missionaries, 173; in Asia, 430; Byzantine, 235; in colonies, 437–439; English, 198–199; imperialism and, 761; Irish monks and, 196–198; in Japan, 435; Jesuit, 401; learning revived by, 219; Methodist, 667. *See also* specific orders
Mitanni kingdom (Hurrians), 30, 41
Mitchel, John, 622
Mithraism, 171
Mithridates (Pontus), 137
Mitterrand, François, 931, 959
Moabites, 35
Mobility (social): in United States, 619
Mobilization, 777; in World War I, 778–780, 791–792; in World War II, 872–877
Moctezuma (Aztecs), 422
Model T Ford, 706
Modern Devotion, 329
Modernism (arts), 743, 744–749; Postmodernism and, 940, 941
Modernism (religious movement), 743
Mohács, Battle of, 388
Mohenjo-Daro, 6, *6*
Moldavia, 643, 674, 675, 949
Molière, Jean-Baptiste, 484
Molotov, Vyacheslav, 881, 887
Moluccas (Spice Islands), 401, 413, 418, 419, 429, 442
Monarchists, in France, 656, 730
Monarchs and monarchies: Anglo-Saxon, 190; Austrian, 464; Carolingian, 218–219, 225, *225*; divine right and, 454; in Dutch Republic, 471; in eastern Europe, 284, 369; in Egypt, 17–20; in England, 190, 274–278, *315*, 367–368, 471–479, 544–546; in 14th century, 319–321; in France, 278–279, 315, *315*, 323, 349, 366, 544, 580–581, 588, 604; Frankish, 189–190; Germanic, *187*, 187–192; in Germany, 281–283, 323–324; Greeks on, 98–99; Hellenistic, 96–100; Holy Roman Empire and, 281–283, 369; in Israel, 34–36; in Italy, 281–283; limited, 470; Maistre on, 640; in northern Europe, 283–284; in Ostrogothic Italy, 187–189; Persian, 49–50; in Poland, 470; in Renaissance, 366–370; in Rome, 116; in 17th century, 446–447; in Spain, 279–281, 349, 368–369; in Sparta, 64; in Sumeria, 8; in Sweden, 467–468; in Visigothic Spain, *187*, 189. *See also* Absolutism; Limited monarchies; specific rulers and locations
Monasticism. *See* Monks and monasteries
Monet, Claude, 745, *745*
Monetary system, in Rome, 170
Money: medieval trade and, 252. *See also* Currency; Inflation
Money payments, as scutage, 319
Mongol Empire, *285*
Mongolia, 284, 432
Mongols, 284–285, 306, 307–308, 319, 369
Monism. *See* Pantheism
Monks and monasteries, 195–200, 286–287, 293, *293*; Carolingian Renaissance and, *219*, 219–220; social services and, 292; travel, hospitality, and, 222. *See also* specific orders and monasteries
Monogamy, 26, 220
Monopolies: in England, 408
Monotheism, 36, 50–51
Monroe, James, 642
Monroe Doctrine, 642–643
"Monroe Doctrine for Asia," 856
Montcalm, Louis-Joseph, 557
Montecino, Antón, 424
Montefeltro family (Urbino), 349
Montenegro, 769, 771, 957
Montesquieu, baron de (Charles de Secondat), 517–518, 524, 526
Montessori, Maria, 752
Montgelas, Maximilian von, *637*
Montpellier, 335
Mont Sainte-Victoire (Cézanne), 745, *746*
Moon, U.S. landing on, *938*
Moore, Charles, 941, *941*
Morality: in Egypt, 21; in Jewish tradition, 37
Moravia, 392
More, Hannah, 536
More, Thomas, 378–379, 393
Morel, Edward, 760–761
Morisot, Berthe, 745, *746*
Moro, Aldo, 931
Morocco, 762, 895
Mortality. *See* Death rates
Mortgages: subprime, 975, 976
Moscow, 285, 464, 603, 859
Moses, 36, 207
Moses ben Maimon. *See* Maimonides, Moses
Mosques: in Córdoba, 240; Hagia Sophia as, *205*
Mother, The (de Hooch), 472, *472*
Mothers, 346, 723, 725. *See also* Families; Women
Motion, 490, 492, 495–497, 499
Mott, John, World War I letters from, 796
Mountain, the (France), 588
Mountains. *See* specific mountains
Mount Olympus, 82
Mount Vesuvius, eruption of, *134*, 166
Movable type, 358
Movies, 738, 839, 840, 916–917, 973. *See also* specific films
Mozambique, 762, 896
Mozart family: Leopold, Nannerl, and, *530*; Wolfgang Amadeus, 529, *530*, 531, 666
Mrs. Dalloway (Woolf), 845
Muawiya, as caliph, 209–210
Mudejares, 280
Mughal Empire, 430–432, *432*
Muhammad, *21*, 207–208
Mühlberg, Battle of, 388, *388*
Mulattoes, 437
Mule, in cotton industry, 610
Mulroney, Brian, 932, 962
Multiculturalism, 973, 974, *974*
Multinational (transnational) corporation, 975
Multinational states: Austria as, 646, 682; nationalism and, 649–650
Multiracial society, in Latin America, 437
Mumbai (Bombay), 417
Mummification, in Egypt, 22
Munich: Hitler in, 814, 827; terrorism at Olympic Games in, 943, 964
Munich Conference (1938), 853
Munitions factories: women in, 794, *794*, 795
"Munitions Work" (Loughnan), 795
Münster, Anabaptists in, 392
Müntzer, Thomas, 385
Murad (Ottoman Turks), 370
Murder: punishment of, 257
Museums: in Alexandria, 104; of Modern Art, 914
Music: American influence on, 917; atonal, 845, 942; current, 942, 943, 971–972; digital technology for, 973; in Enlightenment, 528–529; of Hildegard of Bingen, 290; Impressionist, 748; jazz, 839; Modernism in, 747–749; in Renaissance, 365–366; Romanticism in, 665–667, 700–701; World War I songs, 785, 789; youth protest, 923. *See also* specific composers; specific types
Music video, 942
Muslim Bosnians, 956
Muslim-Croat federation: in former Yugoslavia, 956, 957
Muslim League, 898
Muslims, 207, 643; Byzantine Empire and, 210; Crusades and, 301–302; in 18th century, *537*; Enlightenment and, 538; in EU nations, 968; in France, 959; in India, 430, 898–899; invasions by, 226–227; medieval thought and, 263; in North Africa, 762; Palestine, Israel, and, 897; in Spain, 279–281, 368–369; terrorism and, 965–966; trade and, 307. *See also* Crusades; Islam
Mussolini, Benito, 823–826, 852, 858, 859, 864, 865
Mutsuhito (Japan), 767–768
Mutual deterrence, 890
Myanmar. *See* Burma (Myanmar)
Mycenae and Mycenaean Greeks, 30, 55, *56*, 56–57, *57*, 58
My Own Story (Emmeline Pankhurst), 750
Mystery religions, 83, 109–110, 170–171, 176
Mysticism, 329

Nabonidus (Chaldean), 45
Nabopolassar (Chaldeans), 45
Nagasaki, *434*, 435, 865, 877, 878
Nagy, Imry, 903, 904
Names (personal): in Rome, 118
Nanjing, Japanese seizure of, 856, 872
Nanterre, University of, 920
Nantes, in French Revolution, 582
Naples, 114, 461, 640, 644, 677; Austria and, 463; kingdom of, 324, 348, 350, 553; market square in, *570*; population of, 258; revolt in, 454
Napoleon I Bonaparte (France), 575, 596, 597–603, *598*, 641, *671*, 671–675; Civil Code of, 600, 644; Congress of Vienna and, 638; defeat of, 603–605; Grand Empire of, 601–603, *602*
Napoleon II (France), 671
Napoleon III (France), 656, 676–677, 681, 718, 730
Napoleonic wars, 636, 637–639, 646, 762
Naram-Sin (Akkad), 9, 10
Narva, Battle of, 466
Naseby, battle at, 475
Nasser, Gamal Abdel, 897, 898
National Assembly (France), 581–582, 586, 587, 656, 671, 730, 931, 959
National Bloc (France), 819
National Convention (France), 588–589, 590, 593, 594
National debt, 562
National Endowment for the Arts (NEA), 971
National Front (France), 967
National Government (England), 818
National Guard (France), 582, 587
National Insurance Act (1911), 753
Nationalism, 602, 636–637, 644, *649*, 649–650, 670; in Africa, 767; in Austria, 646, 657; in former Yugoslavia, 956, *957*, 978; German, 602–603, 645–646, 678, 756; in Greece, 643; of Hitler, 826; in India, 768; in Italy, 644, 677; liberalism and, 650; Napoleon and, 602–603; in Prussia, 603; revolutions of 1830 and, 652; in Soviet Union, 949; Spanish, 602; terrorism and, 964; in United States, 658–659, 766; World War I and, 776–777, 780

Second Empire (France), 671–675, 730
Second Estate: in European society, 344; in France, 579, 581
Second German Empire, 682
Second Industrial Revolution, 704, 705–711, 725
Second International, 712
Second Punic War, 122–123
Second Republic (France), 656
Second Vietnam War, 899, 900, 921, 931, 932–935, *934*; protests against, 908, 923, 924
Second World War. *See* World War II
Secret Book (Hitler), 851
Secret police: in East Germany, 927, 958–959; in Italy, 824; in Nazi Germany, 867; in Romania, 927; in Russia, 646, 734, 802; in Soviet Union, 902, 926
Secret societies: in Enlightenment, 526; in Italy, 644; in Russia, 646
Sectionalism, in Italy, 731
Secular humanism, 968
Secularism, 352, 446, 487, 694, 820, 968; France and, 968, 969–970
Sedan, battle at, 681
Seed drills, 561, *562*
Segregation: in colonies, 767; in United States, 908
Ségur Law, 579
Seibertz, Engelbert, *637*
Sejm (Polish diet), 369, 470
Select Society of Edinburgh, Scotland, 526
Seleucid dynasty, 96, 97, 124; Jews and, 110, 171
Seleucus, 97, 99
Self-determination, 649; for eastern Europe, 886; World War I and, 805, 807, 808, 809; after World War II, 895
Self-government, in towns, 256
Self-Help (Smiles), 626
Self-interest: as economic principle, 522
Self-Portrait (Basquiat), *972*
Seljuk Turks, 297, 298, *298*, 370
Semitic languages, 9; of Hebrews, 34; of Hyksos, 23; of Phoenicians, 40
Senate: in Rome, 117, 135, 157, 180; in Venice, 325
Senate (France), 730
Senatorial order, in Rome, 151
Seneca, 154, 161
Sennacherib (Assyria), *35*, 44
Separation of church and state, 392, 647
Separation of powers, Montesquieu on, 518
Separatist movement(s): in Quebec, 962; in Yugoslavia, 954
Sephardic Jews, 537–538
Sepoys, 763
September 11, 2001, terrorist attacks, 948, 959, 962, 964, *965*, 968
Septimius Severus (Rome), 169, *169*
Serbia, 370, 769, 771, 772, 776, 957; World War I and, 778, 783, 807
Serbs, 235, 657, 954, 955, 956
Serfs and serfdom: in Austria, 682; in eastern Europe, 566; in Egypt, 20; in manorial system, 233–234; as peasants, 247; in Prussia, 548, 645; in Russia, 552, 683–685, 686; in 16th century, 442–443. *See also* Peasants
Serialism, in music, 942
Serious Proposal to the Ladies, A (Astell), 524
Sermon on the Mount, 171, 172
Serrano, Andres, 971
Servants, 720, 723; as urban workers, 627; women as, 630
Servius Tullius (Rome), 116
Seth (god), 21
Settlements: Neolithic, 4; Viking, 228–229. *See also* Colonies and colonization; specific empires and countries
Sevastopol, 675
Seventh Idyll, The (Theocritus), 105
Seven Wonders of the ancient world, 45
Seven Years' War, 545, *555*, 555–557, *576*; French Canada and, 436; India and, 432; Prussia in, 548
Sewage and sewer systems, 570, 715, 717
Sex and sexuality: in Carolingian Empire, 220; Christianity and, 221–222; Diderot on, 521; Freud on, 740; Hammurabi's Code on, 12; in marriage, 396; in Mesopotamia, 12; prostitution in 19th century, 711; in Renaissance Italy, 346–347; VD and, 711; after World War I, 842; after World War II, 921. *See also* Gender
Sexual revolution, 921
Seymour, Jane, 393
Seyss-Inquart, Arthur, *853*
Sforza family (Milan), 347–348; Battista, 349; Ludovico, 350
Shakespeare, William, 483
Shalmaneser III (Assyria), *35*, 41, 42
Shamash (god), *10*, 11
Shang dynasty (China), 6
Sharecroppers: in Rome, 159
Shari'a, 208
Shelley, Mary, 664
Shelley, Percy Bysshe, 664
Shelter: of Paleolithic peoples, 3. *See also* Housing
Sheridan, Richard, 559
Sherman, Roger, *577*
Shibuzawa Eiichi, 626
Shi'ite Muslims, 297, 965
Shikoku, 439
Ship money (English tax), 473
Ships and shipping, 442; Dutch *fluyt*, 471; in 18th century, 558; exploration and, 415; Napoleon and, 601–602; Phoenician, 40; Portuguese, 419; slave trade and, 426–427; trade and, 564, 690; Vikings and, 227, *228*; warships and, 99; in World War II, 862. *See also* Navy; Steamboats; Triremes
Shires (England), 233
Shogun (Japan), 433, 767
Shonibare, Yinka, 973, *974*
Shrines: pilgrimages to, 294, *294*
Siam. *See* Thailand (Siam)
Siberia, 763, 834, 902
Sic et Non (Abelard), 264–265
Sicily, 114, 348, 644, 677, 864; Aragon rulers in, 324; Athenian defeat in, 75; Belissarius in, 201; Bourbons in, 553; Carthage and, 122; Kingdom of, *281*, 282; Phoenicians in, 40; revolts in, 454, 657; as Roman province, 124
Sidon, 40
Siege warfare: by Alexander the Great, 92; Assyrian, 43; in 18th century, 558; by Visigoths, 185
Sieveking, Amalie, 749
Sieyès, Abbé, 581
Sigismund (Holy Roman Empire), 328, 371
Sigismund III (Sweden and Poland), 470
Signing of the Declaration, The (Trumbull), *577*
Signoria (Florence), 325
Signorini, Giovanni, *535*
Silesia, 285, *462*, 555, 556
Silesia: Prussia and, 548
Silicon chip, 938
Silk and silk industry, 207
Silk Road, 159, *159*, 307, 308
Silt, 16
Silver: Spanish, 404, 405; for trade, 254, 443
"Silver age," of Latin literature, 160–162
Simeon the Stylite (Saint), 195–196
Simons, Menno, 392
Simplicius Simplicissimus (Grimmelshausen), 453
Sin (god), 45
Sinai peninsula, 156, 898
Single Europe Act (1986), 960
Sisters of Charity, 571
Sisters of the Common Life, 329
Sistine Chapel, Michelangelo and, *340*, 340–341, 362–363
Six Day War (1967), 898
Sixtus IV (Pope), 372
Skepticism, 514–515, 543
Skilled workers: mass education for, 725–726; in World War I, 795
Skyscrapers, 844
Slater, Samuel, 618
Slave labor: of Japanese, 872; of Nazi Germany, 866, 871; in Rome, 129–130
Slavery: African, 345, 416, 426–429; in Athens, 83; in French Revolution, 595; in Haiti, 435–436; in Hellenistic world, 102–103; origins of term, 235; in Renaissance, 345; Rome and, 129–130, 167, 168; Sumerian, 9; in United States, 429, 686, 688–689, *690*
Slave trade, 426–429, *427*, 437, 564; in Latin America, 436
Slavic peoples, 237–238, 683, 771; Charlemagne and, 217; eastern, *237*, 238; in eastern Europe, *284*, 369; Germany and, 284; migrations of, *237*; Nazis and, 850, 866, 871; southern, *237*, 238; trade and, 235; western, *237*, 237–238; World War I and, 778
Slavonic alphabet. *See* Cyrillic (Slavonic) alphabet
"Slop work," 710
Slovakia, 853, 953, 960
Slovenes, 657, 954
Slovenia, 463, 954, 955, 957, 960
Slums, in England, *624*, 818
Small Is Beautiful (Schumacher), 938, 939
Smallpox: Aztecs and, 422; Inca and, 424; vaccinations for, 715
Smiles, Samuel, 626
Smith, Adam, 521, 522
Smith, Kiki, 973
Smithson, Robert, *940*, 941
Snefru (Egypt), 22
Soccer. *See* Football (soccer)
Social classes. *See* Classes
Social contract: Rousseau on, 522–523
Social Contract, The (Rousseau), 523, 524
Social Darwinism, 741–742, 827; imperialism and, 759
Social Democrats: in Austria, 756; Communist parties and, 903; in Germany, 711–712, 732, 755, 780, 804, 826, 829, 905, 906, 929; in Russia, 756–757, 798; in Scandinavia, 819
Socialism, 650–651; Bismarck and, 732; in France, 712, 819; Marx and, 691–692; Marxist, 743, 819, 822; revolutionary, 712, 713, 740; in Russia, 756–757; in western Europe, 903; World War I and, 777, 780, 792–793
Socialist Party, 711–712; in France, 931, 959; in Italy, 823
Socialist realism, in Soviet Union, 845
Socialist Revolutionaries (Russia), 800
Socialized medicine, in Great Britain, 906
Social justice, 39
Social networking, 972